REVELATION COMES FROM ELSEWHERE

Cultural Memory in the *Present*

Hent de Vries, Editor

REVELATION COMES FROM ELSEWHERE

A Contribution to a Critical History and a Phenomenal Concept of Revelation

Jean-Luc Marion

Translated by
Stephen E. Lewis and
Stephanie Rumpza

STANFORD UNIVERSITY PRESS
Stanford, California

Stanford University Press
Stanford, California

English translation and introduction ©2024 by the Board of Trustees of the Leland Stanford Junior University. All rights reserved.

Revelation Comes from Elsewhere was originally published in French in 2020 under the title *D'ailleurs, la Révélation* © Éditions Grasset & Fasquelle, 2020.

 This book has been published with the support of the Centre national du livre.

Printed in the United States of America on acid-free, archival-quality paper

Library of Congress Cataloging-in-Publication Data

Names: Marion, Jean-Luc, 1946- author. | Lewis, Stephen E. (Stephen Evarts), translator. | Rumpza, Stephanie, 1986- translator.
Title: Revelation comes from elsewhere : a contribution to a critical history and a phenomenal concept of revelation / Jean-Luc Marion ; translated by Stephen E. Lewis and Stephanie Rumpza.
Other titles: D'ailleurs, la révélation. English | Cultural memory in the present.
Description: Stanford, California : Stanford University Press, 2024. | Series: Cultural memory in the present | "Originally published in French in 2020 under the title D'ailleurs, la révélation." | Includes bibliographical references and index.
Identifiers: LCCN 2023055998 (print) | LCCN 2023055999 (ebook) | ISBN 9781503633377 (cloth) | ISBN 9781503639348 (paperback) | ISBN 9781503639355 (ebook)
Subjects: LCSH: Revelation—Christianity. | Phenomenological theology.
Classification: LCC BT127.3 .M36613 2024 (print) | LCC BT127.3 (ebook) | DDC 231.7/4—dc23/eng/20231229
LC record available at https://lccn.loc.gov/2023055998
LC ebook record available at https://lccn.loc.gov/2023055999

Cover design: Aufuldish & Warinner
Typeset by Newgen in Garamond Premier Pro 11/13.5

Is God unknown?
Is he manifest (*offenbar*) as the sky?
This I tend to believe.
Such is man's measure.

—HÖLDERLIN*

---

* "Ist unbekannt Gott? Ist er offenbar wie der Himmel? dieses glaub' ich eher. Des Menschen Maaß ist's." Friedrich Hölderlin, "In lieblicher Bläue," in *Sämtliche Werke*, ed. F. Beißner, Bd. II/1 (Stuttgart: Kohlhammer, 1951), 372; English translation: *Hymns and Fragments*, translated and introduced by Richard Sieburth (Princeton, NJ: Princeton University Press, 1984), 249, 248.

Contents

Translators' Note	xi
Introduction by Stephanie Rumpza	xiii
Foreword	xxxiii

PART I
ENVOY

1	The Privilege of a Question	3
2	The Privilege of a Notion: Revelation	17

PART II
THE CONSTITUTION OF THE APORIA

3	Thomas Aquinas and the Epistemological Interpretation	37
4	Suárez and the Sufficiency of the Proposition	49
5	The Magisterium's Reserve	63
6	The Metaphysical Origin of the Common Concept of Revelation	74

PART III
THE RESTITUTION OF A THEOLOGICAL CONCEPT

7 The Possibilities and the Aporias of a Theological
   Concept of Revelation — 93

8 Unconcealment or Uncovering — 109

9 "Ista revelatio, ipsa est attractio" — 124

10 The Other Logic and Its Determinations — 137

PART IV
CHRIST AS PHENOMENON

11 Nobody's Manifestation — 165

12 What the "Mystery" Uncovers (Paul) — 181

13 Parable and Confession (the Synoptics) — 204

14 The "Mystery"—of Whom? (John) — 227

PART V
THE ICON OF THE INVISIBLE

15 Monotheism and Trinity: An Ontic Model — 257

16 Immanence and Economy: A Historical Model — 273

17 The Trinity as Icon: A Phenomenal Model — 296

18 The Trinity as the Phenomenality of the Gift — 316

PART VI
THE OPENING

19 Being, Uncovered from Elsewhere — 337

20 Time, Uncovered from Elsewhere — 357

Notes — 379

Index — 487

Translators' Note

The footnotes make use of a number of standard scholarly abbreviations: *Ak. A.* for the *Gesammelte Schriften of Immanuel Kant,* reprinted with Walter de Gruyer; AT for *Œuvres de Descartes*, edited by Charles Adam and Paul Tannery and reprinted by Vrin; CSM or CSMK for the English translation of Descartes by John Cottingham, Robert Stoothoff, and Dugald Murdoch (and Anthony Kenny on the third volume) in Cambridge's *Philosophical Writings of Descartes*; BA for the *Bibliothèque Augustinienne*, a project of the Institut d'Études Augustiniennes, which publishes Augustine's texts in the original Latin alongside the French (originally printed by Desclée de Brouwer and now Brepols); GA for the *Gesamtausgabe* of Martin Heidegger, published by Vittorio Klostermann; Hua for Edmund Husserl's Husserliana series, published first by Martinus Nijhoff and now Kluwer Academic Publishers; PG and PL for Jacques-Paul Migne's nineteenth-century *Patrologiae cursus completus*, in the *Series Graeca* and *Series Latina*, respectively; and SC for the *Sources chrétiennes* series published by Les Éditions du Cerf, which print Patristic texts in their original language alongside a French translation. We have opted to keep the Hebrew and Greek in their original alphabets, judging that experts will find this easier to read, while nonexperts will benefit from the more thorough linguistic support available online, including not only transliterations, but also interlinear translations, lexicons, concordances, and parallel translations. A quick web search will reveal the most current resources; for this project we have made use of a number of online reference tools, especially Sefaria Library and BibleHub for biblical texts and the Perseus Digital Library for classical texts.

INTRODUCTION

Stephanie Rumpza

It is no great secret that Jean-Luc Marion is a philosopher with a passion for paradox. Instead of shying away from an apparent contradiction he leans into it to rustle up an unexpected turn, a twist ending, a reversal of our ordinary assumptions, always challenging us with something more to think. And nowhere do we see this more clearly than the present book, which stands as a milestone in contemporary phenomenology and signals the accomplishment of a project that Jean-Luc Marion has been developing from the very beginning. For since his earliest work, he has been deeply concerned with what is perhaps the greatest paradox of all: the possibility of finding, from our finite human horizons, a meeting point with the unconditioned, infinite God. The implications of such an investigation extend beyond theology, of course, but its reverberations will be felt far beyond it; here is a question that concerns the scope of human reason and the very nature of truth.

Early Work: Idols and Icons

In some of his earliest works, *L'Idole et la distance* (1977) and *Dieu sans l'être* (1982), Marion explored two approaches to God, framing them around the conceptual poles of "idol" and "icon." Philosophy has often attempted to understand God as a maximization along the lines of its highest questioning, leading to what Marion calls an "idol." Since the historical development of metaphysics, some of the most significant idolatries have taken the form of "onto-theo-logy," placing God as the Supreme Being ("*ens supremum*"), ultimate cause ("*causa sui*"), or ground that guarantees a rational grasp of being; although in Marion's eyes we might just as well add to this list of idols Kant's "God of morality" or Heidegger's thinking of the "being of beings."[1] Every idol is an expression of the maximum we can grasp of the divine, the greatest extent to which God becomes visible to us. But anything that can be comprehended by our finite concepts will necessarily fall short of the infinite and unconditioned God. As Marion explains, the idol "is characterized solely by the subjection of the divine to the human conditions for experience of the divine."[2] Or again: "the measure of the concept comes not from God but from the aim of the gaze."[3] As long as our investigation is tethered to the ego's possibilities, we will never be able to get beyond idols. We remain bound to the realm of the visible, the finite horizon of our comprehension.

Where the idol seeks the maximum visibility we can grasp, the "icon" seeks "to render visible the invisible as such."[4] To do this, we must change the stakes. It is no longer a question of how far I can see (or fail to see), but of the fact that *I am seen*. Thus the motivation behind the choice of terms: as the painted eyes of a Byzantine icon remind us, God is not a substance to be grasped, but one who always sees us first. This "inversion of intentionality" is the key to the paradigm shift. Where the idol's "center of gravity" lies "in a human gaze,"[5] bound to the conditions of human knowing, the icon "unbalances human sight in order to engulf it in infinite depth," that is, "the advance of God" to us.[6] Where the idol is anchored around my aim which reaches toward God (and falls short), an icon is anchored around God's aim which reaches me (and succeeds), even though its invisibility never translates into something fully visible for me.[7] Only love can bear this "distance," or paradoxical simultaneity of visible and invisible. For in contrast to the idol which reabsorbs, appropriates, or secures possession of this experience within human terms, love is precisely the disappropriation or dispossession of one's own conditions, giving without holding back.[8]

The differentiation of the idol and the icon thus leads us to this central question: Could we reach heaven by an ever-greater tower of our best concepts, our best ideas? Or, would God appear, but on his own terms and his own initiative, from outside any horizon we make, from *elsewhere* than the conditions of understanding? Marion clearly argues for the latter, the approach of the icon, where the living God stoops down to us.

Middle Work: Non-Metaphysical Phenomenology

In reaching these conclusions, Marion made use of theological resources, which he separated from his philosophical investigation in *God Without Being* in a literal way, grouping them under the title "*Hors-Texte*," "outside the text." As he later commented, "The critical portion of this essay was accomplished within the field of philosophy, but I could not, at that time, glimpse its constructive side (access to charity) except through recourse to theology." The reason for this was the absence of "a non-metaphysical method of philosophy," which means, building on his historical work, a "phenomenology thoroughly rescued" from the influence of metaphysical rationality.[9] The word *metaphysics* can of course be used in many ways, but Marion's work in the history of thought has given it a very precise definition, linked to a very specific and influential era in philosophy.[10] To distill it to its central movement: metaphysics is a method of thinking that limits what can be known to the conditions of rationality as determined by the knower: an idolatry by definition, in Marion's technical sense.

Over the next twenty years Marion worked to find an alternative to this impasse. With its rallying cry, "back to the things themselves (*Zu den Sachen selbst*)," phenomenology already seemed to have promise as just such a philosophy. To take these words seriously, Marion suggested, one would have to push past *all* prior conditions, all limiting presumptions or theories, in order to let what comes to appear for us do so first and foremost on its own authority, by an act of "clearing away… obstacles to manifestation" that phenomenology calls "reduction."[11] However, Marion argued, the founding phenomenologists retreated from these professed aspirations by imposing their own conditions on phenomena: Husserl, in his reduction, led us only as far as objects, while Heidegger's reduction halted us at the horizon of being. Might it not be possible to advance a step further, to end up with no conditions other than the phenomena themselves, to lead to nothing other than "the given"? Marion's bold claim was precisely this: that *givenness* is the sole grounding authority of phenomenology, that if we let ourselves carry out the reduction to its fullest extent, we will be led past objects and past being to givenness as such. This can be formulated in a new principle of phenomenology: "So much reduction, so much givenness."[12] If *Réduction et donation* (1989) first sketched out the possibility of a third reduction, *Étant donné* (1997) elaborated it in systematic detail. The major breakthrough of the latter text was Marion's claim that the phenomenological discussion of *Gegebenheit* or "givenness" was not a simple fluke of German (playing on the phrase *es gibt*, "there is"), but fundamentally related to the idea of the "gift," then under discussion in works of anthropology and sociology.

The advance of this conjunction was not, as some critics feared, an attempt to sneak in God the Giver and relapse into metaphysical methodology, leaping outside of the thicket of experience to secure a bird's-eye view of what "really" is. Such a move would be profoundly antithetical to phenomenology, where there is no exit from experience, the event of a given vividly rising up to me without clearly indicating the mysterious depths from which it arises. To be true to phenomenology, I must renounce any metaphysical temptation to claim mastery over the domain of knowledge ruled by the economy of sufficient reasons. I must instead be open to receive the experience that precedes and exceeds me. And recognizing this will bring us precisely to Marion's real advance, the claim that we can elaborate a new non-metaphysical phenomenology according to the logical structure of the gift. In its essence, the gift marks a total break in any self-contained, self-sustaining system of exchange, for as soon as I try to absorb it as my possession or an object under my control, it ceases to be a gift. In order to preserve the gift *as* a gift, I must preserve my openness to its asymmetry, recognizing that it arrives before me from a depth that cannot be exhausted by my grasp. This is more difficult than it sounds, for it means I must renounce any claim of self-sufficiency or autonomy, my sense that "I don't owe anything to anyone." In the gift, then, I receive not only something given, but I receive myself in a new way. A phenomenology that shares the structure of the gift will be marked by this same asymmetry altering our relation to the world and ourselves.

This insight also clears the way for the development of one of Marion's most important philosophical discoveries: the saturated phenomenon. When the conditions of appearing are strictly defined by the conditions of my rationality, there are only two possibilities: what is given in experience is adequate to perfectly fulfill my concept, signification, or intention of it (as in "poor phenomena," like math problems, which require little or no experience to confirm their truth); or, what is given in intuition falls short, only partially fulfilling my intention (as in everyday "common phenomena," like material objects I can see only from one side at a time).¹³ In the latter case my concepts and significations then compensate for this shortage of intuition. But if, as Marion suggests, I am free to drop my standards as the critical measuring rod of appearance, if the authority can be ceded to what gives itself, then a new possibility opens up: what is given in my experience so exceeds my intention or significations that I am unable to clearly grasp what nevertheless appears to me. *I* am the one who falls short of what is offered. This is what Marion calls a "saturated phenomenon." In this asymmetrical experience of saturation, I am always "late" to what shows up, always catching up, and unable to get a full grip on the experience that I nevertheless see. In *Being Given*, Marion sketches four structural possibilities for this experience: the event, the idol, flesh, and the icon.¹⁴ In later work, Marion even proposes that saturation is not so much an exception to everyday life, but perhaps its truest form: any banal and ordinary phenomenon, in principle, may be capable of being experienced as saturated, although in practice we are only rarely in a position to receive anything at this fullest level of givenness.¹⁵

Most critical for our purposes is the culmination of the discussion of the saturated phenomena in *Being Given* in §24: "The Last Possibility—the Phenomenon of Revelation."¹⁶ Marion begins on the defensive: after pointing out that some phenomena seem to be more saturated than others, he challenges any reader who would resist the question about a "maximum" phenomenality simply out of fear it may open the question of God. Yet, the few pages dedicated to the question of maximum phenomenality remain sparse and somewhat undecided. On the one hand, Marion terms this maximum saturation "revelation" and uses Christ as his primary example. On the other hand, "revelation" is defined almost mathematically, in the purely formal terms of saturation to the second degree: that is, one intense experience simultaneously involving all four types of saturation. References to the Gospels are used, not as an appeal to divine authority, but simply to illustrate how Christ as discussed by the Scriptures would meet these structural conditions. Marion then critically distinguishes this general structural possibility of a *revelation* from the intensified *Revelation* of God from himself, which would follow its own maximally paradoxical logic. But Marion is also clear that the *possibility* of revelation discussed by phenomenology must be distinguished from Revelation as the *actual* experience of God, which is the domain of theology, or "*theo*-logical" investigation. And this would exceed the scope of any human science, including phenomenology: "Only a theology, and on condition of constructing itself on the basis of this fact alone ... could reach it."[17]

If this status of "actual" and "possible" Revelation remains contested, the overall result of this phenomenological breakthrough is clear. In the late 1970s, Marion found no philosophy that could address the questions of God, since all philosophy, even phenomenology, restricted truth to the conditions of human rationality (leading to idolatry). In the late 1990s, *Being Given* opened up a path of non-metaphysical phenomenology whose authority comes from the given, not from the conditions of the one who receives it. Could this "phenomenology thoroughly rescued" from metaphysical idolatry finally be linked back to Marion's original questions about God? As he commented in his 2001 preface to the English edition of *Being Given*, this work "completes in the particular case of the phenomenon of Revelation, a sketch of what *God Without Being* bluntly intended through direct recourse to theology." He then promised, "I hope thus to shed some light on the relations, at once essential for the future and poorly illuminated in the past, between phenomenology and theology."[18] But if it took Marion twenty years to work out the phenomenological dimensions of this breakthrough, it would take even longer before he succeeded in bringing these two major questions together.

The Present Work: Unfolding Revelation

Now, at last, we see the full force of Marion joining his early questions of God together with his phenomenology of givenness in a rigorous conceptual interrogation of an idea underlying them both. From its etymology alone, *revelatio* ("un-veiling") or *apokalypsis* ("un-covering") seems to suggest a fully phenomenological register of truth. Yet, as Marion observes, throughout most of history, the word has been taken to mean an extra source of information that we can know through God's special intervention (through the Scriptures, the prophets, through the Incarnation, and so on) in contrast to what we can know from our own rationality. This sense of the word remains so "obvious" to us we have not yet begun to reckon with the implications of redefining it. This can be seen in the wonderful irony of the fact that the first sketch of this book was presented as the 2014 Gifford Lectures, a series of conferences historically devoted to the development of "natural theology." In his opening comments, Marion was tactful, acknowledging that he "would not take for granted" the "concept of natural knowledge of God," as neatly distinct from revealed or "supernatural" theology.[19] Modest words, as the ensuing lectures would demolish this very distinction as built on a history of deeply flawed presuppositions. In the full and definitive version of this text that we present here, the arguments from 2014 have been expanded at every stage, deepening the engagement with the Scriptures and Trinitarian theology, incorporating a more explicit phenomenological conception of revelation and its relation to our ordinary experience, and amplifying everything by tracing its development within the history of thought.

The scope of Marion's questioning dazzles by its breadth and rigor. This marks perhaps the most basic and pragmatic challenge of this book: the vast audience it concerns will likely identify with one of the five poles of the account, or perhaps two; very few of us can speak with mastery on all five. This is not the first time Marion has accomplished careful readings of the history of philosophy that work against the "obvious" interpretations and revive the contemporary import of older texts. This is clear in his work on modern philosophy (from *Descartes' Metaphysical Prism* to *Questions cartésiennes III*) as well as in his study of phenomenology (such as *Reduction and Givenness*). Of course, we have also seen Marion systematically pursue conceptual problematics (as in *Being Given* or *The Erotic Phenomenon*) to make original advances to contemporary thought. One of the truly remarkable ambitions of this book is to do both at the same time, and without betraying either. It is hard to imagine any other contemporary figure capable of achieving such a monumental task. Yet despite the demand it makes on the reader, there is no question that Marion has done the lion's share of the work, distilling major thinkers across the history of thought to their central questions and tensions in a few masterfully precise pages, while simultaneously braiding them into his central investigation. The resulting weave may feel a little less tight-knit than readers are accustomed to expect from Marion's pen: a number of thematic strands wind in and out of the central narrative, and these threads may feel at time distinct or disparate, especially since they are not all tied up in a neat bow. Yet it is critical, in keeping with the scholarly seriousness of this work, that Marion refuses to force a harmony. With a hermeneutic finesse that respects the heterogeneity of his sources, he has unfolded for us a living polyphony of thinkers and methodologies,

xx   *Introduction*

rallied around the central question of Revelation, which they address each in their own voices, each allowing this great paradox to be uncovered for us in its own particular way. In this tapestry, Marion presents a real challenge to his readers, or even a vote of confidence: to understand what is said here requires us to penetrate beyond the surface level of each of these perspectives to recognize their profound resonation.

To better orient the reader through this rich text, it will be helpful to present a brief overview.

Overview of Revelation Comes from Elsewhere

Before we talk of divine *R*evelation, we must first understand how our lives are already marked by moments of *r*evelation. And so Part I, "Envoy," begins by tracing how such events rise up within everyday experience and call for a new logic of understanding: events that reveal themselves from outside my expectations, that reveal me to myself in a new way, that reveal a new place for me in the world, and that reveal in a new way my relation to others, even or especially because something unseen remains at the heart of its manifestation (chapter 1). This becomes a starting place to understanding the Revelation of God (chapter 2), tracking its formal characteristics as a saturated phenomenon through three key terms that will be refined further in Part III: it involves a *witness* who sees without fully comprehending, it provokes *resistance* by the ordeal of truth, and it is necessarily structured as a *paradox*. If Revelation thus offers its own rules of appearing, it is not an exception from phenomenality, but an exceptional case of it. This means in turn that phenomenology offers "the privileged point of view" to consider it. Marion will go so far as to claim that not only is Revelation an exceptional case of phenomenality; it *is its preeminent form,* a phenomenality par excellence. For, Revelation accomplishes the fullest development of the phenomenological principle: it shows itself to the most radical extent, for it gives itself without holding back. Ultimately, this Revelation, we are told, is Trinitarian, a claim that will be developed as the book progresses.

With this Marion has laid out his bid, setting out the central leitmotifs that will run through his analyses. But Marion is also a serious historian of philosophy. And so before he can take up this line of questioning in a constructive way, he must reckon with the long and charged history of this word that would build up a very different idea of what "Revelation" might be. Part II, "Constitution of the Aporia," thus takes up a historical reconstitution of this term "Revelation." Dating from the thirteenth century, the "epistemological interpretation" of Revelation was first set in motion when Aquinas suggested that *"sacra doctrina,"* or the knowledge that considers divine matters based on the Scriptures (what we might today call theology), might be treated as a sort of quasi-science (chapter 3). While Aquinas set it in the place of honor as the queen of the pyramid of knowing, this cracked open the door that less subtle or less restrained thinkers would fling wide open and rush through head first. Subsequent arguments sought to promote Revelation's superiority, developing a more rigorous understanding of its status as the highest of "sciences" in the strict sense, dropping Aquinas's cautious prefix *quasi* (chapter 4). Revelation is then submitted to the common criteria of human knowing, to the authority of human reason, which, in effect, enacts a complete reversal of the lines of authority set up by Aquinas. As this notion of science was sharpened into the certain and evident knowledge of objects, revealed theology's potential to operate by these criteria was recognized as demonstrably lacking. Theology was first degraded to a parallel to the truths of human reason, a "weaker" shortcut for the ordinary believer, and eventually eroded to the point where it was shut out by reason as a form of non-knowledge or fideism, until the Enlightenment ultimately judged that no knowledge of God could be produced from the rational conditions that were said to govern it (chapter 6). And by Marion's reading, they are absolutely right. The massive failure of this "epistemological interpretation" of Revelation does not mean we must abandon this word, but it does suggest we must develop it from an entirely different track. And it is not impossible to do so: however entrenched this notion of Revelation has become in our history and methodologies, the Magisterium of the Catholic Church has not only avoided explicitly confirming it, but *Dei Verbum* (1965) has offered an alternative interpretation of Revelation as the very self-manifestation of God (chapter 5). And if this is the case, Marion argues, we must not begin from the human conditions of knowledge, but God's conditions of showing himself: a *theo*logical approach, not a theo*logical* one. But how can Revelation be unfolded for us on God's own terms, if this contradicts the conditions of human experience?

Part III, "The Restitution of a Theological Concept," thus raises the question: Is it possible to find a *theo*-logical concept of God's self-Revelation, not bound by the limitations of human reason, but beginning from the conditions of God alone? To defend the possibility of an answer, Marion takes a route that is the most complex of the five parts, interweaving three different approaches. It begins with an overview of twentieth-century theologians who attempted to understand Revelation as God's self-Revelation (chapter 7), which in turn opens onto an alternate historical tradition that supports this possibility (chapters 8–9). Building on these key insights, Marion finally investigates how these insights can be articulated in phenomenology (chapter 10), picking up on the framework he had already begun to sketch in chapters 1–2. While each approach follows a different route, they all work to develop the central idea that there are two possible logics: the logic defined by human rationality, and the logic defined by the invisible, unconditioned infinite that exceeds us. We might think that the second logic would be simply an unbridgeable contradiction. But in the case of God, as we see in chapter 7, there is no contradiction precisely because of how this meeting point is revealed: in the form of love. For love is absolutely unconditioned, pouring itself out without reserve, without limits. Chapters 8–9 thus begin to flesh out the logic of love in a structure that is already recognized to be Trinitarian: we are attracted from *elsewhere* than our human limits, to see Jesus as the only Son of the Father, through the work of the Spirit, who, if we accept this cooperation of conversion, transforms the limitations of our ego into a possibility of seeing. Meanwhile, chapter 10 transposes the discussion to a phenomenological plane with a distinction between two modes of truth: *alētheia* and *apokalypsis*. The former, *alētheia*, includes both the metaphysical definition of truth and its phenomenological expansion; its defining feature is whatever is centrally fixed according to the conditions of the ego.[20] The latter, *apokalypsis*, remains oriented toward what comes from *elsewhere*, a center that cannot be defined or absorbed into the horizon organized by my ego. This upsets the stability of the transcendental ego proper to *alētheia*, turning the *I* into a witness, and provoking resistance before the ordeal of facing a paradox that cannot be resolved into my own terms. But I can accept for it to change me, and take on a point of view that is not my own. In this path directed by "anamorphosis," which takes its lead from the directions of the phenomenon, I will not know from the outset where I will be directed or what will be demanded of me. All I know is that I must let myself be guided step by step by the phenomenon that is given.

After recovering an alternate *theo*-logical path to the epistemological interpretation of Revelation, supported by an alternate tradition in the history of thought and elaborated in its phenomenological structures, Marion will turn to ask how this operates in the central event of Revelation: the coming of Christ. Part IV, "Christ as Phenomenon," is the longest of the five and arguably the very heart of the work. Its task is to consider how this conceptual distinction can help us understand the way that God appears, without violating the biblical principle that no one can see God and live. An initial chapter contrasts how the Greek gods apparently manifest themselves openly to our sight, but in fact only ever under masks that do not reveal their true selves; whereas the God of Israel is never seen openly, but reveals himself in his very invisibility through the Name and the exchange of words (chapter 11). This opens the way for the following three chapters to discuss the ultimate intensification of this encounter in the Revelation of Christ in the Pauline epistles (chapter 12), the Synoptic Gospels (chapter 13), and the Gospel of John (chapter 14), which Marion persuasively lays out as ripe with conceptual rigor. Attentive to the context and language of the source material, Marion's original retranslations break any overfamiliarity with the text and unveil critical insights that tend to be passed over. Building upon the themes raised in each source, these chapters progress from the natural wisdom of the Greeks to the uncovering of Jesus in his Trinitarian identity, and precisely in a Trinitarian way. For no one can confess Christ as the Son of the Father unless the Father grants it, through the Spirit of Truth; this Revelation or uncovering is necessarily Trinitarian.

All three of these explorations center on whether or not we will be open to the anamorphosis demanded to see Christ, but in different ways. The chapter on the epistles of Paul focuses on the conflict of *logoi*, and the break in rationality from a worldly horizon of being; the chapter on the Synoptics focuses on the parable, and how our way of hearing it calls *us* into light; the Gospel of John focuses on the paradox, and how it cannot be understood without a logic come from *elsewhere*. In each of these cases, what is uncovered provokes resistance, not simply as a rejection of the content of what would be revealed, but by the *way* it is revealed, and more specifically, what it would demand of us in order for us to see: a breaking open of the ego as self-grounding, self-possessed, self-sufficient. To put it differently, the challenge is: Do we accept our native understanding in its philosophical, social, religious, or historical dimensions, confirming the comfortable horizon where we already find ourselves? Or do we allow ourselves to be moved by something we do not yet understand? Do we hold ourselves open to receive a "signification" or "concept" that would come to us from *elsewhere*, to tune ourselves to the logic of givenness that is accomplished to its perfection in the uncovering of Christ, who is poured out in an excess of charity without reserve? To choose this second path requires a fundamental shift in our stance, that we be moved or transformed by the work of the Spirit, who will place us within the Trinitarian unveiling of Christ as the Son of the Father.

And so Part V, "The Icon of the Invisible," considers the meaning of the Trinitarian dimensions in Revelation, critically retrieving the doctrine of the Trinity from the shadow of its metaphysically-slanted interpretations, and drawing on phenomenology to propose a new way of recognizing the Trinity as the central way to God's self-manifestation. A first common attempt to understand God's Trinity is through terminology built on an "ontic" model of identity (chapter 15). But this leads to a tension between God's unity of substance (accessible to natural reason) and God's plurality of persons (inaccessible to reason and thus available only as revealed), which in turn leads to Kant's estimation that the Trinity is irrelevant to reason, a precedent that other philosophers followed. A second strategy (chapter 16) attempts to unfold God's unity in his community through his action in history, which leads to a tension between the economic Trinity (as revealed to us within worldly time) and the immanent Trinity (the Trinity as it is in itself). The greatest temptation has been to prioritize the former, as did Hegel and Schelling, which risks flattening God into human terms; prioritizing the latter, however, is no solution, for it risks suggesting God's action in history does not really reveal *himself*, an equally serious problem.

The alternative Marion proposes to these dead-end paths is to recover a phenomenological model of the Trinity that preserves the pivot point from *elsewhere* than our human logic, and which seeks to understand God's Revelation in history as isomorphic with God's Trinitarian identity. He first unfolds these relations under the structure of the "icon" (chapter 17) through the work of Saint Basil of Caesarea. For no one can see the invisible Father, except through the visible face of Christ, who can be recognized as his icon;

to see this would require a viewpoint "from *elsewhere*" than our human frame, an anamorphic transposition to God's point of view that can only be enabled by God himself, in the person of the Holy Spirit. Building on this model, Marion turns to Saint Augustine to further elaborate the Trinitarian communion according to the model of the gift (chapter 18), which allows us to understand the Trinity as a communion of perfect abandonment to the gift of love. Key to both of these chapters is that it is not *despite* God's Trinitarian character, but precisely *because of it* that this Revelation is possible: Trinitarian communion is not an extra doctrine of God's Revelation we must come to understand, but the very way that we come to understand God's Revelation. The *way* Revelation is uncovered to us is essential to *what* is revealed in it; and it is also simultaneously the shape of the *way we must* receive it.

Finally, Part VI, "The Opening," considers the transformations that this Trinitarian anamorphosis will demand on our experience: nothing less than a rethinking of all phenomenology, resituating the most basic *a priori* structures of being (chapter 19) and time (chapter 20) by grounding them in the *a priori* of what is given from *elsewhere*. Following in each case the model of what has been accomplished in Christ, these chapters critically draw out the deeper phenomenological dimensions of being, if received as gift, elevating the daily experience described in the first chapter to an existence oriented toward a decision of a divine "now" that transpierces every instant and opens within the temporal flux of our lives (chapter 1) to bring us before the highest eschatological possibilities "for good."

Concluding Questions

It would be unproductive to offer a definitive interpretation on a book that has only begun to stir up discussion. I will instead close this introduction by highlighting some of the major areas of questions that arise from this text, especially in light of Marion's past work.

First, we can note how clearly Marion has reconfigured the way the lines are often drawn. If his early work seems to trace a sharp distinction between God and the world, his middle work seems more expansive, setting human experiences of saturated phenomena alongside revelation in opposition to objective worldly experience. The present book preserves both of these distinctions at the same time, and still shows their deeper continuity.

In other words, while Marion wants to indicate a fissure within experience, the continuity of the r/Revelation means that the experience of God is already on the side of all of the interesting, transformative, and meaningful events that make me who I am. The divide is not about the *things*, in other words, but the *way we access them*: Is their mode of disclosure fundamentally centered on the limited horizon of the ego? In this text, Marion calls this mode *alētheia*; we can also recognize it as a development of what his early work called "idol." Or do we approach things through an uncovering of a horizon not centered around my grasp, which implicates me and demands a personal transformation? Marion names this *apokalypsis* here, but we can also see this as a fuller articulation of what he first termed the "icon." In laying out these two logics, he draws out more deeply themes that have been stated in various degrees in prior works, notably the way that the truth can make demands on me, that I may need to change to be able to receive it. This is not only the case before the question of God, as Marion argues, but in any revelation of the world where the self is brought into question. Can theology recognize itself in this newly refined phenomenology of givenness? And, more importantly, what should philosophy make of this expanded understanding of truth?

Of course, we cannot raise this point without acknowledging that Marion has once again inspired new reflection on the relation of phenomenology and theology. Against the argument enforced most famously by Dominique Janicaud that phenomenology must remain "methodologically atheist,"[21] Marion has already for many years set forth a challenge that phenomenology is strengthened, not weakened, by entering terrain that might be considered "theological." But to this point, he has done so with some caution. In *The Idol and Distance* and *God Without Being*, he turns to theology as an outside source to resolve what philosophy cannot. In *Being Given*, having expanded the power and scope of phenomenology, he offers a sketch of Revelation only as a structural possibility for philosophy. Some readers have objected that Marion was disingenuous for claiming that his phenomenology of givenness was not a move toward theology. But the account of "Revelation" found in those few pages pales in comparison to the depth of what Marion finally offers here, moving far beyond the mere structural possibility of a "saturation of saturation" and into a genuinely *theo*logical discussion of a Revelation manifest in its origins from *elsewhere*, drawn out into its full Trinitarian dimensions and reaching to transform the fundamental structures of our experience. Gone is any defensive stance to justify his approach. Phenomenology, Marion insists, has the goal to make visible those things that are unseen, and if Revelation is God's self-showing, it has intrinsic phenomenological relevance. Marion is doing phenomenology here, this is indisputable. He is also doing theology, he admits it. Can one do both at the same time? Evidently so: this book stands as a rare example of an intellectual history that freely enters the heart of philosophical territory and crosses to the deeps of theology without reservation, in a scope that yields wide-reaching results. What does this book, in its approach as well as its themes, intend to communicate about the possibility of thinking about God?

From the distance of some years, we can see that the choice to stop at the threshold of theological terrain in *Being Given* served a critical purpose: it encouraged readers to consider Marion's phenomenological insights on their own terms, as a discussion of phenomenological givenness does not as such require any theological positing of the Giver. But now Marion has finally entertained the question of what it would mean to allow his inquiry to advance to this level: What are the implications if we *did* trace the givenness back to its Giver, if we really did consider Christ as the apex of phenomenality? By his careful reading of Scriptures as a source of conceptually substantial claims, Marion's formulation of the first principle of phenomenology, "the more reduction, the more givenness," expands to its maximum aperture: "the more *mystērion*, the more *apokalypsis*." Here Christ becomes more than a "saturated phenomenon par excellence"; he is the phenomenon of phenomena, the only phenomenon who has ever completed the full project of phenomenology, and the one who constantly models and performs for us a new way of being. For if we follow the standard phenomenological rule that the phenomenon "shows itself in itself and by itself only to the extent that it gives itself in and by itself," then Christ alone shows himself fully, because he alone gives himself to the point of total abandon in his Incarnation and death, and from the depths of an invisible that no eye has ever seen. Revelation therefore perfectly accomplishes the essence of phenomenality, in its maximum dimensions; all that is needed to achieve its phenomenalization is our reception of what is offered. This is an astonishing claim. How can it be understood? What major restructuring of our thinking would follow if it were true?

While Christ's preeminence places him at the center of Revelation, we can also note the attention paid to the role of the Holy Spirit, who rarely comes to the foreground in Marion's earliest work. But after reading these pages, we also understand why: the Holy Spirit, above all, is not given to be seen, but given as the very way that we *can* see, working in us through the subterranean push and pull of attraction and opening the anamorphic point that could grant us access to the Father's point of view. This offers us not only a clearer view of God through the person of the Son, but a clearer view of the world, ourselves, and everything else, modifying the very framework of our existence as we give ourselves over to what is offered. We see these principles already at work in the scriptural exegesis throughout the book, especially Part IV, which centers on the drama of the possibility of recognizing Christ as the Son of the Father, as well as the possible choice of rejection. Together with the focused exploration of the Trinity in Part V, this book examines questions that are ordinarily reserved for systematic theologians from a powerful new trajectory. Notably, Marion's command of the history of philosophy in its metaphysical deformations clears a new path through some of the thorniest doctrinal difficulties regarding the Triune God. While this deconstructive work alone offers critical insights for theology, it is then followed by an extensive rereading of the Trinity in phenomenological terms, as illustrated by the Church Fathers, reaffirming the audacious claim that emerges in Marion's extensive reading of the Scriptures: that in order to see Christ, human beings are placed at the point of view of the Father. The implications of this work go far beyond what Marion has explicitly developed, as we begin to see in his brief sketches of baptism and confession. What perspectives might this open for traditional doctrines of the Trinity, salvation, or deification of the human person?

Further, it is clear that for Marion the Trinity is not some optional embellishment of Revelation that Christians happen to believe; it is the very way God manifests himself. But if the Trinity is the nonnegotiable form of Revelation, what kind of genuine discourse about God could be held outside of Christianity? Marion's position here is inconvenient, to say the least, for attempts to compare and contrast faith traditions through a "neutral" or "methodologically atheist" lens. Of course, Marion would critique as an idolatry the presumption that reason could or should have universal access to something that remains so far beyond our limits. An apocalyptic approach to God need not for this reason shut down discussion of other religious traditions, but it is clear that it would demand another way of negotiating these claims. What would this approach look like? Would it be a threat or an enrichment to genuine interreligious dialogue?

These are only a few of the rich provocations to thought offered by this book, which is saturated with challenging insights, pressed down, running over, as it unfolds in crystalline clarity a question Marion has been asking since the beginning. Under what conditions could a finite human knower reach knowledge of the unconditioned infinite God? On the one hand, we could appeal to the authority of divine Revelation to the point of banishing the weakness of human reason, leading to irrationalism, fideism, fantasy. It is not likely that this strategy will appeal to a readership with the intellectual drive to wrestle with this question. On the other hand, we can define the conditions of possibility of Revelation by the limits of the human knower. This is the route taken by the epistemological interpretation. But the more Revelation is forced into this frame, the more it is found wanting, poorly conforming to the limits we draw, and thus ultimately degraded and eliminated. We can also enlarge these conditions from metaphysical rationality to the horizon of texts, or history, or being, but if the tactic is ultimately the same, what is to make us think that the outcomes would be any different? As long as God is limited to the conditions defined by human finitude, we have not left the path of idolatry. But, as Marion asks, what if we refuse both moves? What if we refuse to resolve the contradiction and let the tension stand? This is Marion's central claim: the only faithful articulation of Revelation is the one that preserves this paradox of God's infinite and unconditioned Revelation meeting a finite, conditioned human being. Marion wants to confront us with this irresolvable paradox as paradox, illuminating what is at issue while refusing to dissolve the necessity of its incomprehensibility. He traces this problem across the history of thought, articulates it in an expanded phenomenology, and finds it again and again in the Scriptures, but we must not pass over what is perhaps its simplest articulation: that God is love, and given to us as love to be received by love. This isomorphism of love is simultaneously one of the greatest rewards and the greatest risks of Revelation. Not only is it difficult to understand what this deceptively simple phrase means, but it demands everything of us, it puts us on trial while making itself vulnerable to the risk of our choice. For if Revelation is given freely from its depths, could any finite human being bear to receive it, in its depths, and thus render it manifest? The apokalyptic logic of Revelation conflicts with the central stance of autonomy that we wish to claim for ourselves, grasping our knowledge within the horizon of our possession, our well-earned right. It demands instead that we be willing to pass to a new horizon that is not in control of the ego. And herein lies perhaps the most serious challenge offered here: Might our ability to recognize what is at stake in these pages in fact be a matter of the aperture of the heart? A matter of conversion, even? In his preface, Marion boldly suggests as much, even if it in no way diminishes the need for philosophical and theological acumen. What is certain is that the challenge of this book will richly reward any reader who takes it on.

1. Jean-Luc Marion, *Dieu sans l'être* (Paris: Fayard, 1982), translated by Thomas A. Carlson as *God Without Being* (Chicago: University of Chicago Press, 1991), §§3–4. For more background on "onto-theo-logy," see Marion's work on Descartes, notably, *Sur la théologie blanche de Descartes. Analogie, création des vérités éternelles, fondement* (Paris: PUF, 1981) and *Sur le prisme métaphysique de Descartes (1986)*, translated by Christina M. Gschwandtner as *On Descartes' Metaphysical Prism: The Constitution and the Limits of Onto-theo-logy in Cartesian Thought* (Chicago: University of Chicago Press, 1999).

2. Marion, *L'Idole et la distance* (Paris: Grasset, 1977), translated by Thomas A. Carlson as *The Idol and Distance: Five Studies* (New York: Fordham University Press, 2001), 6.

3. Marion, *God Without Being*, 16. Note that Marion's use of optic terminology is not limited to the visual plane, but stands in for any way that God could "show up" in human experience.

4. Ibid., 17.

5. Ibid., 24.

6. Ibid., 24.

7. Marion, *The Idol and Distance*, 7.

8. Marion, *God Without Being*, 47–48; see also *The Idol and Distance*, §16.

9. While not printed in the original French, this text is found on p. xiv in the 2001 "Preface" to the English version of Jean-Luc Marion's *Étant donné. Essai d'une phénoménologie de la donation* (Paris: Presses Universitaires de France, 1997), translated by Jeffrey L. Kosky as *Being Given: Toward a Phenomenology of Givenness*, 2nd ed. (Stanford, CA: Stanford University Press, 2012).

10. As an overview and culmination of Marion's work in this area, see his *La Métaphysique, et après* (Paris: Grasset, 2023).

11. Marion, *Being Given*, 10.

12. Jean-Luc Marion, *Réduction et donation: Recherches sur Husserl, Heidegger et la phénoménologie* (Paris: PUF, 1989), translated by Thomas A. Carlson as *Reduction and Givenness: Investigations of Husserl, Heidegger and Phenomenology* (Evanston, IL: Northwestern University Press, 1998), 203. Michel Henry first pointed to this as a "Fourth Principle of phenomenology" in "Les Quatres principes de la phénoménologie," *Revue de Métaphysique et de Morale* 1 (1991): 3, 26.

13. *Being Given*, 222–223.

14. Ibid., 228–33; this is further developed in Jean-Luc Marion, *De surcroît. Études sur les phénomènes saturés* (Paris: PUF, 2001), translated by Robyn Horner and Vincent Berraud as *In Excess: Studies of Saturated Phenomena* (New York: Fordham University Press, 2002).

15. Jean-Luc Marion, "The Banality of Saturation," from *Le Visible et le révélé* (Paris: Cerf, 2005), 154–56, translated by Christina M. Gschwandtner in *The Visible and the Revealed*, 135–36.

16. Marion, *Being Given*, 234–41.

17. Marion, *Being Given*, 367 n90.

18. Marion, in the 2001 English "Preface" to *Being Given*, xiv.

19. The earliest sketch of the present work was thus first available in English, in the publication of the Gifford Lectures: Jean-Luc Marion, *Givenness and Revelation*, trans. Stephen E. Lewis (Oxford: Oxford University Press, 2016). A further draft was published two years later in German, *Das Erscheinen des Unsichtbaren: Fragen zur Phänomenalität der Offenbarung*, trans. Alwin Letzkus (Freiburg im Breisgau: Herder, 2018).

20. Note carefully: Marion does *not* use the term *alētheia* as a way of collapsing metaphysics and phenomenology. Of the four distinctions Marion draws between *alētheia* and *apokalypsis*, the former two concern *alētheia* in the limited metaphysical sense, while the latter two concern the broader character of *alētheia* in phenomenology.

21. Dominique Janicaud, *Phenomenology and the "Theological Turn": The French Debate*, trans. Bernard G. Prusak (New York: Fordham University Press, 2000), picking up on a strain in Heidegger and Husserl.

Foreword

Almost forty years ago I dared to claim "that theology, of all writing, certainly causes the greatest pleasure."[1] I still hold to that claim, with one reservation: there is neither anything as difficult, nor indeed as painful as theology, where one must embark directly onto the high seas, unfathomable and without end—*duc in altum* (Luke 5:4). In his early days Barth was already warning anyone who would dare to take this path: "Every human work is a draft, a preliminary labor, and this is especially the case for a theological book!"[2] All the books that I have produced I have completed like a cyclist making the climbs in a mountain stage, with training and method, strength and endurance, cunning and will; but none has cost me so much, nor held me back as long as this book, precisely because there has never been an ascension that was so hard, or so beautiful.

In fact, before the delivery of this version in French, which I hope is the final one, I first had to publish two initial sketches in foreign languages, contrary to custom. When the University of Glasgow honored me with the invitation to give the Gifford Lectures in 2014, I began a first series of studies that resulted, in 2016, in a first publication, *Givenness and Revelation*.[3] Then the invitation from the University of Regensburg to occupy the *Papst Benedikt XVI–Gastprofessur* chair, in the spring of 2018, led me to return to the whole enterprise in a version published that same year under the title *Das Erscheinen des Unsichtbaren. Fragen zur Phänomenalität der Offenbarung*.[4] In fact, ever since my book *The Visible and the Revealed*, which already collected some older sketches and attested to an obsessive theme, I had begun to confront the question of Revelation. Or rather, of the phenomenality of revelation in general, and thus of biblical Revelation in particular—unless it was the reverse: Revelation as such opening the case of the phenomenon of revelation within common phenomenality. I plunged into this long-distance odyssey, starting from a seminar for the "Chaire Dominique Dubarle" at the Institut Catholique de Paris (2011–16), continuing throughout my teaching at the Divinity School of the University of Chicago (especially the seminars from 2013 to 2019), and culminating during a trimester when I was invited by the Autonomous Theology Faculty at the Université de Genève (2018).

For as long as one avoids venturing into the theological domain, there is nothing easier than to denounce the deficiencies of theologians (too often I gave in to this puerile ritual). But as soon as one takes a first step in theology; as soon as one stops hovering around theology as if it were a reservation of primitives, strange and open, defenseless (like all the kindly atheists do, fearing neither God nor man, frolicking in the theological domain in order to plunder a few treasures from which to draw some small change); as soon as one goes to theology in a serious way, that is, in realizing that one must hear a question there, and respond to it in person—only then does one measure its real difficulty—a difficulty of knowledge, first of all. While in philosophy it is enough (unless one sets up ignorance as a methodological principle, as is often done in the analytic tradition) to know the Greek, Latin, French, English, and German texts (and Italian, as well), in theology it is necessary to enter into the biblical text in all its languages and, in order to do this, explore at least a little the Christian "Talmud" (as Levinas put it), the Fathers, both Latin and Greek. Thus one must follow the history of dogma, the authors of the Middle Ages (high and low), the metaphysical turn of modern theology (the easiest for a historian of philosophy), and, finally, the spiderweb of the theology of the last two centuries, subtle, full of traps, and indispensable.

But the real difficulty lies elsewhere, literally in the *elsewhere*. A novelist or a poet knows what he is talking about and can hope that his readers know it as well, even if he must set it out for them in his own words. A philosopher, if he truly talks about something and not merely about another text (which is not so often), can appeal to an experiential verification of his thesis; of course, he must reconstruct this experience in order to make it accessible to a competent reader; but the experience can, in principle, become the field for a discussion in common, or even a shared conviction. The theologian does not have this recourse. Not that he cannot invoke an experiential verification of what he is arguing; on the contrary, he knows perfectly well where to find it: in liturgical practice, the sacraments, communal and personal prayer, in short in the life of the Church in the widest sense. But he cannot know if he himself is correctly and fully attaining this experience, nor if his readers can do so better than he. To write a line of authentic theology exposes one to a tremendous interrogation and a radical doubt. Not about that of which one speaks, but about the one of whom one speaks. A good theologian does not doubt the existence of God (which in fact makes no sense), but his own existence (which is more than uncertain); he does not doubt the mystery that he is aiming at, but the rise of his aim, his own loftiness of view. He knows what he is aiming at, if only because he is drawn there and follows its rising and descending slope. But he also knows that he is still aiming too low, with an impetus that falls short and, as the cyclists say, that he is going to "hit the wall" or "blow up."[5] And if dogma remains a formulation subjected to eschatological rectification, all the more so for the theological statement. There is no theology without development because no theology can totally accomplish the hermeneutic of the infinite. The theologian avoids sinking into bad philosophy (unknown to itself) or ideology (which wants to remain ignorant of everything outside itself) solely on the condition of becoming convinced of this. The theologian knows that he still cannot say very well what he sees, nor see very well what he aims at, but that he must at least aim at it the best he can. His holiness measures his accuracy. But he knows that this situation not only is in no way abnormal, but that it alone preserves him.

My own aim is summed up here quite simply in a few questions. (Pt. I) Why did the first centuries of the (best) Christian (and moreover Jewish) theology never use anything that falls under the modern concept of "Revelation"? (Pt. II) Why was this modern concept (in its essentials) constructed only polemically by metaphysicians and in contrast to what they understood by "reason"? (Pt. III) Why not instead privilege a concept of Revelation that would start from the phenomenality of that which unveils itself or rather uncovers itself, from that which reveals itself among phenomena? (Pt. IV) Could it be that the principle of the synoptic gospels, "nothing is veiled (κεκαλυμμένον) that will not be uncovered (ὃ οὐκ ἀποκαλυφθήσεται, *revelabitur*), or hidden (κρυπτὸν) that will not be known (ὃ οὐ γνωσθήσεται)," already puts into operation a privileged mode of phenomenality? (Pt. V) Is this uncovering summed up by the commonly held meaning of "monotheism," or does it imply its reinterpretation, beginning from the trinitarian communion? (Pt. VI) I have pushed the attempt as far as I can, and thus I knows its limits. They are those that Nicholas of Cusa pointed out perfectly: "Trusting in your infinite goodness, I have ventured to surrender myself to rapture in order to see you, who are invisible, and the unrevealable vision revealed (*ut viderem te invisibilem et visionem revelatam irrevelabilem*)."[6]

I want to express my gratitude to the institutions that enabled me to conduct this work—the University of Chicago, the Institut Catholique de Paris, the University of Glasgow, the University of Regensburg, the University of Geneva—and to the students and listeners who supported me with their patience and their questions, and the longtime companions, who will recognize themselves in the pages that follow. I bear responsibility for the errors and insufficiencies; the rest, which does not belong to me, will take care of itself.

J.-L. M.
May 2020

I

Envoy

Immensum est autem quod exigitur,
incomprehensibile est quod audetur;
ut ultra praefinitionem Dei, sermo de Deo sit.

—Hilary of Poitiers, *De Trinitate* II, 5*

---

* Hilary of Poitiers, *De Trinitate* II.5, PL 10, 54b; English translation: "I must undertake something that cannot be limited and venture upon something that cannot be comprehended, so that I may speak about God who cannot be accurately defined." *The Trinity*, trans. Stephen McKenna, C. SS. R. (Washington, DC: Catholic University of America, 2002), 39.

ONE

The Privilege of a Question

The world does not open up at first like a space; it advances, emerges, and unwinds like a flow. In this river, I do not bathe where I please, I do not go where I want, because it endlessly happens to me, rises up over me, and practically drags me into the torrent of what appears to me. A flow of consciousness is not the issue, because this flow does not belong to my consciousness, does not run within it; rather, my consciousness belongs to it, and runs with and pours into it. An immobile world, of a totality of beings fixed in present existence, is not the issue, but instead the totality of the possibles that befall me like things, and observe me "with familiar looks"[1]; for my senses are constantly receiving, like a possible that never repeats itself, not colors, sounds and tastes, odors, or resistant surfaces that are smooth or rough, but things, directly, that happen to me in person: a house that is white and blue, a hard and sour apple, a badly paved path that slips under my foot. The issue is not appearances but apparitions, which spring out of an unseen mouth of shadow, and immediately, or almost immediately, gather together, are fixed, and form into things, the things of the world, that world that determines my life and allows me to live in it. I cannot say whether such a continual current grasps me or instead flows across me, if it slips over me or rather invades and submerges me. "Everything rises up against me, besieges me, tempts me."[2] That is, unless the flow is not everywhere all at once, and I conquer my identity simply by trying, without ever definitively succeeding, to distinguish it in order to resist the flow.

Forgetting, and What Remains with Me

An inevitable question, then, arises: Among all these apparitions, which truly concern me, which ones remain with me and *tell* me something? "Into eternal darkness swept away, / Are we never to anchor on time's sea / Even for one sole day?" (Lamartine).[3] Or again: To what degree do these apparitions give themselves to me sufficiently so that they give me access to a reality instead of dissipating, swallowed up by those that follow? Or again: Which of these apparitions truly matter to me and concern me, because they organize a real world around me? All these apparitions, in their indefinite number, are not equivalent, and not all of them deliver up things: illusions, fantasies, or simple appearances are not mixed up (at least I can hope so) with forms, presentations, and observations that either deliver objects to me or make me gain access to things. I can reasonably accept that most of the time I perceive objects that are momentarily stable and not mere appearances of objects, things truly given and not representations of absent things; I name this operation knowledge, or more exactly the distinction of degrees of certainty; and this spontaneous distinction is enough for me to get my rough bearings in daily experience. But daily experience in its reassuring (if not well assured) banality in the end explains nothing to me, because its sole function is to allow me to manage my surrounding environment, the confines of my daily subsistence. Daily experience limits itself to sorting through what happens to me, distinguishing the useful from the useless, the harmful from the favorable, and the convenient from the inconvenient. In order to lead me through it in greater safety, it allows me (and even enjoins me) to *forget* in the flow of possibles those that do not immediately concern me at the moment. Most of the time, each of my days ends with the reassuring observation that "today nothing happened," by which I do not mean that nothing occurred, but that nothing notable happened, nothing out of the routine; in other words, everything that happened turned out to be old hat, there's nothing new or remarkable, nor anything that could add a new bit of knowledge to my experience of the world and of myself. In this way the supposedly normal course of experience allows me to *forget* most of it—and happily so. As a result, from what appears, I know almost nothing that defines me most intimately—and indeed, I don't *want* to know any such thing. So goes the course of what appears, wherein the major part of possible experience fades without leaving traces, and where what happens passes away. And perhaps it is best this way.

And yet, in the current of the world that never ceases to surround me and where everything that appears assails me, the utility of the moment does not make me forget everything without exception, and indeed it must not. There always remains, more or less detected, more or less accessible to consciousness, *a something that I will never forget*, even if I force myself to censure it when I do not want to see it, or see it again. In the case of this something that is resistant to forgetting, it is no longer a simple image of a thing, or the distant representation of an object or even a blurry fantasy of the imagination; nor is it a stock of information available to the gaze, set aside in a visual take and of which I could remain the detached, or even completely disinterested, spectator. In this case, when *what I will never forget* happens, what appears no longer bears on anything other than me; particular apparitions arise that affect me, directly and in person, apparitions whose impact I cannot avoid and whose wound in my memory will never heal. This traumatic shock fixes a criteria for discerning the apparitions that are going to *stay with me* from those that pass: this shock no longer comes only from the quantity of reality of the thing appearing, but from *the one* who receives it; it first depends on the force of impact that an apparition (it matters little whether authentic or perhaps illusory) exerts on me (on my consciousness, whether clear or not, it matters little), and the degree of intensity with which the effort of such an apparition affects me, and of the effect that the thing has on me. What is significant is the power, the effect, and the affect of the impression that a phenomenon exerts on me; first, the impression is such that it will never pass into oblivion; next, and above all, it won't allow me to persist in the state in which I found myself before it exerted itself and tested me. This type of phenomenon manifests itself by first exerting its phenomenality on the one who receives it and sees it; it is not summed up, then, in the neutral representation of another, of a third (the thing or the object); indeed, it is sometimes exempt from such things—like the lightning flash that manifests itself by dazzling me without, however, showing me any substance, any substratum, or any thing, thus affecting me through nothing (*res* in the Old French oblique case: *rien*). Therefore this type of phenomenon is not distinguished so much by *what* it makes manifest (or by the truth that it sometimes evokes) as by *the one to whom* it is addressed, whom it affects and transforms. So the flow takes form, time no longer passes, but it takes me, or rather I am taken with it. "May it come, may it come, / The time we are taken with" (Rimbaud).[4] In the moment of a provisional sketch, let us call that which *is taken with me* a *revelation*.

The Athletic Movement

A revelation is defined, then, as a phenomenon that cannot be forgotten, like a presence that will not go away because it affects and transforms the one who sees it, perceives it, and receives it. Such revelations are actually not so rare, and each of us can face them in sensual or aesthetic experience, in theoretical or ethical experience, in intellectual, moral, or religious experience, and so on.

Let us describe a case that at first glance seems trivial, without anything exceptional or rare about it: the athletic movement. From among thousands, let us choose the example of skiing, or more precisely, learning to turn by lifting the ski, shifting one's weight, skidding, etc. The beginner knows how to explain these movements with clarity; she sees them detailed in the images in the skier's manual and executed by her certified French School of Skiing instructor; and yet, as soon as she tries to accomplish them herself she persists most of the time in not doing what she should; indeed, she keeps tensing her upper leg, digging in with the ski edges, and refusing to square with the slope; when she finally gets going she loses all control of her speed, precisely because she remains on the edges; and so she falls, sometimes even on purpose, out of fear of falling further on and at greater speed. This performance-related failure can repeat itself many times, despite a litany of advice and demonstrations ("Watch closely how I do it!", "It's so easy!"); it can even be prolonged to the point of becoming a habit, a lasting state of affairs, and sometimes even discourage the beginner from ever skiing again. But sometimes, suddenly, without being able to explain it, and without having anticipated it or even truly willed it, this de facto impossibility can disperse like a cloud; all at once, without knowing why or how, I accomplish, or rather I feel accomplishing itself in me the movement that had remained inaccessible and prohibited; I shift my weight, I turn, I skid, and I've banked and stopped! And I didn't fall! I control my trajectory and the slope becomes my ally; in short, for the first time and going forward, I am skiing. This previously unfeasible and secret movement suddenly opens up to me and unfolds within me. Whence its first effect: it *reveals itself*, accessible, simple, evident, manifest.

But the event—that the athletic movement reveals *itself*—has additional consequences. In a second instance, it opens a new field of exercise for me by making accessible the space that is now skiable, or more precisely the mountain as skiable space; that is, it transforms for me a site that up to now was inaccessible, or at least closed to walking (because snowy, slippery, icy, marked by crevasses), into an open run, feasible, and even inviting movement across it in every direction, metamorphosing a hostile and unknown field into an open and possible space, or rather into a spatial possibility. Thus the movements of skiing, by revealing themselves to me, reveal to me their space, or rather, reveal to me as henceforth potentially mine a new possible, one that up to that point was prohibited and that excluded me. In revealing itself, the athletic movement *reveals to me a different world*. And as this new world becomes for me a new environment, it in fact also opens me up to myself, for it extends my horizon as far as the ski runs I will be able to cover, and, should I choose to venture there, even beyond the runs. Finally, henceforward *revealed* and *revealing a world to me*, the athletic movement *reveals me to myself*. The one I am becoming—no longer a limited walker, but a wide-ranging skier in a broadened space—I owe not to myself but to this movement that, by revealing itself as feasible and performable, revealed me to myself, because it gave me access to another me that I did not know. The one I have become thus does not first come to me from myself, but from the movement's revelation, of which I remain in some way the spectator (engaged, of course), the collaborator (almost involuntary), and the beneficiary (incredulous and surprised). Going forward, the one who I am, more me than myself, no longer results from me: he was revealed to me by the revelation of the pioneering movement. I owe myself to that which revealed itself to me and which as a consequence revealed me to myself. And this revelation of the movement that reveals me to myself also reveals me to others. For the revelation of the movement that, in this example, made me ski, not only made me become a skier but brought me into the community of skiers, which is to say into the community of those for whom natural space is extended beyond the terra firma of towns, plains, and valleys, to the mountain (or at least a part of the mountain, for the same transformation would be accomplished again, beyond the skiable domain, if I gained access to the movements of rock climbing). Not only do I change feasible space, then, but I gain access to another community, to another way of living and dwelling (the chalet, the resort, the mountain hut). I suddenly appear in another community where others take account of me as one of their new active members. And who welcome me, sometimes even with a song: "He is one of us. *He is an Englishman!*" In a word, *I reveal myself to other* partners in a new social setting.[5]

The Erotic Deed

These three moments of revelation are found, under almost the same forms, in many other situations: the actor and the artist, the teacher and the one who prays, among others, know intimately this sequence of openings and perfectly recognize themselves in it. In all these occurrences, what is revealed never remains closed in on itself, nor on its beneficiary, but of itself is spread—*phaenomenon diffusivum sui*.

The most obvious case, however, remains the deed of the erotic phenomenon. Between, on the one hand, an erotically neutral consciousness, a consciousness that is not affected by another (whoever he may be), and on the other hand one that discovers itself erotically engaged, or put differently, between a neutral ego and a lover, the erotic reduction carries out at least a triple revelation. First, the erotic reduction *reveals itself* by establishing an absolutely new time. New, for it no longer depends on the present, or more precisely, on the present such as *my* temporal consciousness apprehends it, the present defined by the instant during which *my* consciousness maintains (through protention and retention) a presence as an atom of duration, which only lasts on condition of its not lasting but inevitably dissolving. Going forward, in the situation of the reduction, the erotic present is defined as it happens—no longer on the basis of the flow and the presence of my consciousness, but starting from the presence of an *other* consciousness, the beloved consciousness, and it alone. Consequently, nothing has presence unless it is in relation to what the beloved consciousness contains, that is, expects and retains in *its* present. In this way, if the lover spends a day without knowing anything of the consciousness that he loves, which is to say without knowing what was present *to it*, or in other words without "this strange and penetrating dream / Of an unknown woman, whom I love and who loves me,"[6] he can declare with a perfect exactitude that, during this lapse of time, *for him*, "nothing happened," "nothing came about." Not that the world around the lover ceased to turn, people stopped moving about, relatives stopped gossiping, or things stopped happening; but all of this only continues to happen in the lover's presence; this lover, and he alone, contrary to all that surrounds him, does not live in his own present, but in the sole presence of the present happening to the beloved consciousness and accomplishing itself in it. Inversely, everything that the lover learns to have been present to the beloved consciousness (the lover himself, the little incidents in the life of the beloved other, even the whole of the entire world seen starting from the presence of the beloved, who from now on is the center of time and the sole constitutive authority of presence), all that, in so far as it is present to the beloved consciousness and uniquely so, is gathered and saved by the sole erotic presence possible, that of the other, and absolutely not that of the ego. The erotic reduction *reveals to the lover another present*, more present than his own, because it comes from the beloved consciousness and *remains there*. And *this time does not pass*, at least as long as the erotic reduction is carried out.

Next, the erotic reduction *reveals to me a space that is other*. This space is other because it is centered otherwise, since as lover my ego no longer constitutes the center, which is henceforward instead fixed by the beloved ego. If I move away from it, I am no longer *here*, but *over there*; of course even *over there* I still remain localized in a *here*, the one where, after a trip or a separation, I find myself empirically situated in the geographical space defined by Cartesian coordinates. But this *here of mine* nevertheless no longer constitutes the center of my apprehension of the world; my true world (my *Umwelt*, if you like) remains governed by the *here* that I have just left, or even abandoned; in this *here* that is henceforward *over there*, there remains the only center of the true world that, as lover, I still recognize, the *here* of this other that I love (whether the beloved loves me or not). With the performance of the erotic reduction the center of the constitution of the world is overturned, reversed, and displaced: the center of the world of objects, which my theoretical consciousness (my cogitating ego, the zero point, the *Nullpunkt* of the transcendental ego, the nonlover) continues to constitute, no longer coincides with the center of the erotic world that this other consciousness that is always *elsewhere* structures and rules, and which made me its *lover*. We must go further: in the encounter of two eroticized fleshes, the objectifiable space (that of geometry and Cartesian reference points) becomes inoperative, because the lover with her other is situated elsewhere, no longer recognizing any "high" or "low," any "right" or "left" side once they take with them their *here*, around which they turn. They recognize only the unique site that they occupy erotically, the one that they are for themselves, at the crossed point where their ever-displaced fleshes interpenetrate. And this *a-topical* site only leaves its new space open for as long as the erotic reduction is performed.

Lastly, the erotic reduction *reveals me to myself,* in at least two ways. First because the flesh of the other's climactic enjoyment gives me access to my own flesh by eroticizing it (each of our fleshes giving to the other's what it does not have and cannot give to itself, namely its own eroticization). Thus I become other than what I was: this enjoyment, probably the most extreme (and at the same time the least definable), this saturated-*erased* phenomenon, makes me become another man—a man inaccessible to myself without the other of my enjoyment, and a man also who reaches at last a radical possibility: that another human flesh, the child, may spring forth.[7] Next, and above all, the erotic reduction reveals me to myself by refuting probably definitively every attempt to define my proper ipseity on the basis of self-consciousness alone. The issue is not so much the two-part debate, probably too badly posed to constitute a veritable interest, about (1) knowing whether or not my consciousness (in fact, my consciousness of the things of the world and of objects) can turn back on itself (which, however, is neither an object nor a thing); and then (2) about knowing if, in this return, my consciousness can take the full measure and mastery of that which defines it deep down (the unconscious, as the reigning nihilism strangely designates consciousness). No, instead what is at issue is the fact that under the erotic reduction my ego can no longer stay at the center of the self, nor must it: my ego's place is by definition outside of it, and its *here* becomes for it an *over there*, through reference to the only *here* henceforth in operation, that of the beloved other. Not only do I *not think* (it thinks there where I am not), but I *am not* without the other who loves me (or not). Like a migrant magnetized by a distant shore, the lover knows herself outside of herself, staggered by a site that is decidedly other, this other more inward to her than herself, higher in her than her highest grasp—literally, *interior intimo suo, superior summo suo*. The erotic reduction forbids all access to the self that does not pass through another other than me. It closes every place of the self that would reside only in me, the ego. The ego is another, and if ever it comes to itself, it will always be *from elsewhere*.[8]

The Unforgettable and The Elsewhere

The most humble of revelations (the athletic movement) and the most accomplished (the erotic deed) both involve the same, necessarily related moments: the revelation of the phenomenon by itself, the revelation of myself to myself (and of my world, of my space), and, finally, the revelation to others of the one that I have become from elsewhere. This triple dimension of revelation (as if *to reveal oneself* and *to reveal oneself to the other* constituted the two ricochets of a first launch and a first rebound, *to be revealed [se révéler]*) allows us to comprehend that its mode of phenomenality makes of revelation an *unforgettable* phenomenon: because it comes to me from *elsewhere*, from the *self* of that which reveals itself, and because it therefore appears on its own initiative (or at least not on mine), it cannot be identically repeated, or reproduced, or above all produced as one produces an object. Arising once, or once at a time, or even once and for all, the phenomenon of revelation alone retains the initiative of its manifestation. And this is why it imposes itself on me more radically than any noema, since even the core of the noema still depends on my intentional aim (even if only because it fills and secures that aim). This preserved initiative allows the phenomenon of revelation to be reserved (in the sense that someone not very expansive keeps to himself in society, or does not wholly commit himself). The phenomenon of revelation always remains *reserved*. Not only does it not repeat itself endlessly, nor happen regularly, since it only manifests itself when and for as long as it decides; but above all, at the unexpected and unforeseeable moment when it starts it maintains a reserve of the *unseen* at the heart of what it manifests of itself. It's not that this reserve and my incomprehension render it opaque or negligeable to me; rather, it is precisely *because* I will never be able to make it totally intelligible, nor reduce it to its primary components according to the final conditions, nor master it and thus reproduce it, that I also will not be able to forget it. The phenomenon of revelation does not pass, because it passes *of itself* starting from itself. Such a past that does not pass, a past that is not forgotten, offers the sole lasting present—that which lasts because it unfolds its reserves of the unseen at each instant of its consequent moments. What Péguy called "the singular happening, the event, the arising of the future over the past through the ministry of the present"[9] arises from the unseen that remains in it and allows it not only to happen, but to make history, to hold and maintain presence. Here, the future does not prolong the past by taking the present hostage, or rather by extending an imperialist present into the past (which it prolongs) and through the future (which prolongs it); instead the future snatches up the past and transforms it because its innovation erupts into the present, which acts as a happening which *events* (to take up Péguy's word).[10] I do not forget what reveals itself, precisely because I do not understand it, from the beginning of its manifestation to now, nor from where, or how, or why, or up to what point it arises. And my real life, that which defines me most intimately, that which fits me like a glove and from which I never detach myself, not even a whit, is summed up in the final instance by the collection—only disparate in appearance—of the successive revelations that I did not understand, but which comprehend me. Everything else passes and has already disappeared; they have not.

What distinguishes the phenomenality of revelation from other forms of phenomenality thus lies in this reserve of the unseen, which is not poured out entirely into the appearing that is initially representable, but always exceeds it in some way. Each revelation in this way withdraws from its availability to the gaze of the one who receives it. This excess and this unavailability show that the revelation does not depend on my gaze (which nevertheless suspects nothing), because it comes from *elsewhere*. Of course, every perception and every intuition assume an external origin; but in these simple cases, this provenance exerts itself temporarily, most of the time without leaving a memorable trace; sooner or later, it fades away and the unseen ends up disappearing without remainder into the final visible, to the point that an objectification can eliminate it entirely (even and above all in the noematic fulfillment). On the contrary, a phenomenon can lay claim to the status of revelation only if the knowledge that one gains from it confirms (or even reinforces) the *elsewhere* from which it comes, instead of eliminating it in the end. Thus it will be necessary constantly to consider even the possibility of further questioning the origin of such a phenomenon of revelation, by following an often complex hermeneutic that is never complete. While every common law phenomenon demands (according to Kant) to enter into relation with at least one other to become intelligible, the phenomenon of revelation on the contrary imposes its isolation and its irreducibility on every relation or placement in series with another phenomenon—it always appears without a genealogy, as if at odds with its origin, as if self-initiating (a kind of self-made show), like an unheralded new beginning that will never be summed up or repeated. This uncommon character probably cannot avoid an objection: Does what arises under the aspect of a revelation truly merit this status, and might not a more thorough investigation reduce it to the common order of phenomena that are always relative to one another? Probably so, indeed, and why not? But at least it will first be necessary to lead this hermeneutical investigation as far as possible, so as to measure where the supposed *elsewhere* extends to, and, if by chance it should disperse into the known, to understand why it had resisted doing so for so long.

Figure

One can measure from whence the *elsewhere* comes and how far it extends most of all because it can arise anywhere and at any moment, even in an unremarkable way. As we saw already with the athletic movement and the erotic deed, each known to all, the *elsewhere* imposes itself on everyone without exception, precisely because it requires no exceptional circumstance in order to arise. It comes about woven into the regular thread of works and days, surprising and disrupting precisely because it appears there where I was not expecting it. "It has been found again. / What has?—Eternity. / It is the sea gone off / With the sun."[11] This eternity (what preeminently is not forgotten, because in it nothing passes) is merely banal, since *here* it has only to do with water and light. But that they meet together (and how?): that is the *elsewhere*. This female figure passes and disappears (Baudelaire), an apparition of that woman arises (Flaubert), this madeleine dipped in tea reawakens the taste of long ago (Proust), that call come out of nowhere resounds (Samuel): all these facts seem insignificant, and indeed they are for a noncommittal spectator. But they strike the one for whom they are intended with an absolutely determinant flash, the one who, therefore, perceives them as intended *for him;* for him this tenuous banality sounds like a stroke of destiny that reveals him to himself as poet, lover, narrator, or prophet. A different plot can begin, precisely because a beginning is introduced *from elsewhere*: the fact no longer passes (*"rien ne va plus,"* "no more bets") but remains and is frozen definitively in the unforgettable, having rent the banal cloth of that which passes. The apparition *from elsewhere* shines all the more against the background of banality, and that which is not forgotten stands out in contrast to all that is forgotten.

Thus the apparition from *elsewhere* must distinguish itself by its mode of phenomenality; its visibility must dwell and remain, instead of passing and dissolving, like the other phenomena of the flux. What dwelling, and what rest? Hölderlin can enlighten us here with the first lines of a poem that is exemplary in many ways: "In Lovely Blueness."

In lovely blueness with its metal roof the steeple blossoms.
Around it the crying of swallows hovers, most moving blueness surrounds it. The sun hangs high above it and colours the sheets of tin, but up above in the wind silently crows the weathercock. If now someone comes down beneath the bell, comes down those steps, a still life it is [*ein stilles Leben*], because, when the figure is so detached [*abgesondert so sehr die Gestalt ist*], the man's sculpted form (*Bildsamkeit*) is brought out. The windows from which the bells are ringing are like gates in beauty. That is, because gates still conform to nature, these have a likeness to trees of the wood. But purity too is beauty.

The calm banality of a steeple that stands out against the deep blue of an August sky, surrounded by the flight and the cries of the birds, under the creaking of the weathercock. And now against the sunlight, through the frame of a window of the belfry, a form of a man descends, and suddenly the form stands out, is fixed, distinct, in the bright lines of a figure. From that point this figure is no longer inscribed in the whole of the visible, among the birds, the building, and the sky; it arises from there and adds itself to it, because it emerges out of the visible and literally *detaches* itself (*abgesondert*); at issue is a figure that rises, establishes itself, and stands by itself (*Gestalt*).[12] More than a form (*Bild*), at issue is its being put into form, its formation, the possibility for a form to accomplish its visibility (*Bildsamkeit*). The man who descends the stairs in the belfry in fact climbs toward his form by taking on a figure. He imposes his figure by making it attain by itself to its visibility: not only was it necessary, in order to see the figure, that it come to be inscribed in the frame of the belfry window, but it was also necessary that the figure be willing to do so and that in this way it outclass the common visible, which surrounds the figure but does not channel it into itself: the figure's evidence (*enargeia*) comes from its accomplishment (*energeia*). This figure that puts itself in form by itself can thus only barely describe itself, because it imposes itself so authoritatively. "These images are so simple, so very holy are these, that really often one is afraid to describe them." The figure establishes itself as an event not made by human hands (*acheiropoiētos*), for it arises *from elsewhere*. As the figure comes from the possibility of its being put into form, no spectator can define it or measure it; on the contrary, it is this possibility of being put into form that "is man's measure." If the measure of this figure does not come from the one who sees it, but from itself alone, one can recognize there the proper name of the *elsewhere*: divinity. "But the darkness of night with all the stars is not purer, if I could put it like that, than man, who is said to be a form of the divinity (*der heißet ein Bild der Gottheit*)."[13]

From the simple opening of the poem, Hölderlin in this way marks the singularity of the phenomenon of revelation that appears by coming from elsewhere; not as a rare exception to the conditions of visibility but as a calm and serene irruption in its banality, which it transpierces and overdetermines. The possibility of the form institutes a figure, normalized by itself, without any other limit than its very own.

To Show Itself, to Give Itself

In order to conceive that such an unforgettable phenomenon can be accomplished in itself, can remain, and not pass, we need to conceive that this type of phenomenon can not only render visible the unseen and make itself visible on the basis of the unseen (like every other phenomenon that always adds to the already seen visible a new visible, up to that point unseen), but also render visible an unseen that appears *as invisible* and remains that way— as the *elsewhere* from which this revelation comes, and of which it guards the provenance. May we admit the possibility of such a privilege? Probably, if we do not consider such a phenomenon (certainly exceptional) as an exception to common phenomenality (assumed to be normal and normative), but rather as the confirmation of the original definition of *every* phenomenon as such. Now, the degrees of manifestation are measured by the scale of the degrees of givenness; thus, concerning phenomena, we must not say merely that the more the reduction is practiced, the more giving is accomplished, but also that the more giving is accomplished, the more manifestation is unfolded.

The first of these principles results from the intersecting of two decisive observations. First that of Husserl, supposing "*that every originarily giving intuition* [originär gebende Anschauung] *is a legitimizing source of cognition, that whatever presents itself* to us *in 'Intuition' in an originary way . . . is to be taken simply as what it gives of itself* [als was es sich gibt], but also *only within the limit in which it gives itself.*"[14] In other words, what shows itself shows itself uniquely as it gives itself, and is thus reduced to the given in it. Next, the observation of Heidegger, stating, "Hence phenomenology means: ἀποφαίνεσθαι τὰ φαινόμενα—to let what shows itself be seen from itself, just as it shows itself from itself."[15] In other words, what shows itself must show itself from itself and therefore in itself. In this way, the modes and the degrees of such a manifestation depend directly on the modes and degrees of the givenness within it. For the intuition that the thing gives, or more exactly the intuition through which the thing *gives itself* and *shows itself*, responds to no other measure than its own, and is constrained by no other limit (*Schranken*). This implies that the intuition is not limited (*begrenzt*) to what our concepts and our significations could anticipate and foresee each time; it may and in fact it must happen that sometimes certain phenomena spill over and thwart, at least at first, what we expect to receive from them. Whence a second principle: if (according to Kant) the conditions of possibility of experience are also and at the same time the conditions of possibility of the objects of experience,[16] this coincidence concerns only objects and even defines them as such: as phenomena alienated from themselves, leased out to the ego, like things *not in themselves*. Thus, when we are concerned with things giving and showing themselves in themselves, their conditions of possibility *never coincide* on principle with the conditions of possibility of *our* experience. This is true of all phenomena (even negatively for objects) and it allows us to inventory them as well as to arrange them hierarchically.

In this way essential distinctions emerge among all phenomena that show themselves in as much as they give themselves and are led back to their given. First is the fundamental distinction between objects and events,[17] or between poor phenomena, common law phenomena, and saturated phenomena. And let us add, among the saturated phenomena, the hypothesis of phenomena that combine in themselves several or all the different types of saturation, that we have been able to name phenomena of revelation.[18] If then we aim to conceive, if only in outline, a phenomenality of the type called revelation, along the lines that we have already seen (it reveals itself from elsewhere, preserving the unseen in its very manifestation; it reveals me to myself in a new world; it reveals me to others), we will have to succeed in ascertaining it strictly within phenomenology, and in all its powerful banality.

TWO

The Privilege of a Notion: Revelation

In the course of the flow and according to custom, then, many events and manifestations, among those that are not forgotten, can be called phenomena of revelations. We have just outlined a few examples: the athletic movement, the erotic deed, the figure in which the possibility of a form is fulfilled. And indeed, there are others, following the dimensions of the unseen, in saturated phenomena. For, just as a lover can experience and make another experience an erotic emotion or sensation that is absolutely new, and which, without her, would have remained *untouched*, a musician can experience and make others experience the sensation and the emotion of what is *unheard* (a pure sound or a melody) that, without his performance, would have remained inaudible; and the painter or the sculptor can render sensible and visible something *unseen* that she is the first and still the only one to experience, an unseen that, through her mediation, comes to be added to the sum of the visible that up to that point was invisible. And the same goes for the invention of tastes and odors never previously experienced, but revealed by chefs, vintners, and perfumists. The rich banality of these phenomena revealing *themselves*, and which reveal *us* to ourselves, nevertheless gives way in an even more banal manner to a particular and dominant usage of the term: its religious meaning.

This term, Revelation, especially when endowed with a capital *R*, is almost taken over by that which, for lack of anything better, it is often and by dubious convention conflated with under the heading "religions": according to the most current meaning, there is Revelation especially when there is religion, and there is religion especially when there is Revelation. Perhaps no other term designates as clearly the rather strange claim—for it consists in this very strangeness—of having received *from elsewhere* a communication of what God in person (or however one likes to call him) has (or would have) wanted to make known of his name among human beings. For everyone knows God, *at least by name*, including those who *believe* they don't know him. Revelation becomes then so distinguishing a feature that it constitutes the premier criterion for discerning between religions: those that claim a Revelation, partially or totally consigned in a text, establish themselves as religions in the strict sense, in opposition to those that do not claim a Revelation, and which, consequently, are customarily taken to be related to the "wisdom traditions." This distinction, summary though it is, nevertheless marks an essential division or gap that determines the origin and therefore the ambition of said religions: either they result from effort and an impetus, so to speak, come from *below*, from their devotees, or they come, so to speak, from *above*, from the divinity in person, itself ordaining its manifestation toward its addressees, who are thus established as witnesses, by definition privileged and set apart from the rest of humankind. This division distinguishes between those who believe in heaven and those who do not, because it opens precisely the question of what one means by "heaven"—the preeminent open that allows for every phenomenal apparition, much more than the world does (even the world understood phenomenologically as the whole set of possibles to come). Revelation, whether real or not, authentic or not, opens through its possibility alone the whole field of the possible. Now, among all the concepts that arise from this division, we must take note of the three most decisive: the *witness*, *resistance*, and the *paradox*.

The Witness

The religions known as revealed offer a strange characteristic: contrary to what is often repeated (when denouncing the supposed "fanaticism" of believers), they do *not* presume that their members already and from the outset accept the concerns of their (supposed) Revelation. The proper and authentic character of Revelation implies on the contrary that what is at issue (the revealed) exceeds all efforts to receive it, or even the magnitude of any desire to adhere to it. To be sure, a Revelation always aims in the last instance to fill the gap between what is revealed and those to whom it is revealed in a final vision; but its first intention and effect is to register and even to *deepen* this gap. Precisely because it manifests what exceeds common knowledge, Revelation implies that no can ever perceive it adequately or receive it according to *its* measure. And in any case, if it could be received adequately and without remainder, it would no longer have to do with a revelation (and *a fortiori* a Revelation), but the mere pedagogical transmission of a knowledge accessible as such, about which it would only offer a provisional teaching. A Revelation is worthy of this title only as long as it remains incommensurable with those who accept it—for if they accepted it according to their measure and even wholeheartedly, they would not be able to receive it according to *its* measure; if they accept it *as such*, they therefore can, on principle, at least at first, only miss it, and also refuse it, or indeed even deny it, well before the cock crows three times.

From this there follows the first concept: the *witness*. In the daily routine of what happens as a banal event and not as an object, a witness is defined by the gap within himself between, on the one hand, what he saw, heard, or in short experienced of the incident that he can, with all the veracity of sincerity, transmit *to others* as verifiable information; and, on the other hand, what he can *himself* understand or explain about the incident, which often remains for him limited, if not unclear, because he is not in the theoretical position required to reconstitute the context, the plot, and therefore the signification of what unfolded. The witness encounters the event that is revealing itself without, however, wholly understanding it; indeed, he has encountered it all the more indisputably when he does not understand it completely; the honest witness should always begin by saying, "I heard, but I did not understand" (Daniel 12:8, LXX). And this is why it sometimes happens that the witness leads another to suspect or understand more, sometimes even much more, than he himself understands. More precisely, he reports to another the very things that escaped him in what he nevertheless really and truly experienced, leaving this other to attempt to understand it more than he himself succeeds in doing.[1] In the case of a Revelation, then, the witness discovers himself all the more lost in this gap when it is ultimately a question of the irruption of God or of the divine, or in short of what "no one has ever seen (οὐδεὶς ἑώρακεν πώποτε)" (John 1:18, taking up Exodus 33:20–23).

What is more, deep down, no one is more aware than the witness that he does not understand what he has nevertheless seen (maybe without seeing, in the usual sense of a vision that possesses what it perceived); he is all the more aware of it if he thinks that it is a matter of nothing less than "the icon of the invisible God" (Colossians 1:15) and "the brightness of his glory" (Hebrews 1:3). What qualifies the witness, then, as authentic and credible lies strangely in his knowing better than anyone else that he really has seen and heard what he cannot and often *must* not truly understand.

An episode from the Gospel of John perfectly illustrates this hermeneutic situation. When a man born blind recovers his sight after Christ smeared his eyes with mud and saliva, and then sent him to wash in the pool of Siloam, and he is first asked if he is indeed the man born blind, who was healed, he naturally doesn't doubt it for an instant: "I am he" (John 9:9); and again, when someone asks him who healed him, he confirms that it was "the man called Jesus" who healed him (John 9:11, and see 9:15), for he can witness to this fact. But to the question whether he knows "where he [Jesus] is" (in fact, "where he comes from," 9:29), he, as witness, cannot know. He thus answers very precisely: "I don't know (οὐκ οἶδα)" (9:12),[2] though he knows very well that he has been healed: "One thing I do know (ἓν οἶδα) is that I was blind and now I see" (9:25); he does not know, nor does he claim to know, how or by whom he was so indisputably healed. Here again, the witness knows what he knows, without being able to explain adequately that which nevertheless he has no doubts about and can stand by even at the cost of possible retaliation. Now, it is precisely by exposing himself for what he does not understand that he testifies in an epistemologically correct manner to the invisible *as such*, and thus to the inconceivable *as such* by which he finds himself confronted, without having sought it out. In a sense, then, the witness always witnesses in spite of his incomprehension; or rather, by testifying *despite himself*, he testifies correctly through his very incomprehension.

Of course, in a second moment, the man born blind, who now sees, will cross over the threshold where his parents have stopped short: "to recognize (ὁμολογεῖν) him [Jesus] [as] the Christ" (9:22). But not yet in front of the Pharisees: "If he is a sinner, I do not know (οὐκ οἶδα). One thing I know (ἓν οἶδα) is that I was blind and now I see" (9:25): here, he continues to hold the strict posture of the witness, riveted to the facts, without claiming to understand them. It is the Pharisees who, without wanting to, push him by their accusation to become not only a witness, but a believer: "You are that man's disciple" (9:28); but in doing this they indicate the division or gap between the witness and the disciple, because they themselves claim to have crossed it; they affirm indeed that they understand clearly the signification of the sign, namely that of Christ: "You are that man's disciple; we are disciples of Moses! We know (οἴδαμεν) that God spoke to Moses, but we do not know where this one is from (οὐκ οἴδαμεν πόθεν ἐστίν)" (9:29). Their claim is false, for in fact they "do not know" what they imagine that they understand clearly, as the man born blind, still a witness, points out to them, knowing that they do not know: "This is what is so astonishing (θαυμαστόν), that you do not know (οἴδατε) where he is from, yet he opened my eyes. We know (οἴδαμεν) that God does not listen to sinners" (9:30–31). His last reply perfectly defines the posture of the witness: it is a fact that "It is unheard of that anyone ever opened the eyes of a person born blind!"; but the interpretation of the believer is already showing, which allows him to understand correctly the signification of the sign: "If this man were not from God, he would not be able to do anything" (9:32–33). It is only once he is "thrown out" (9:34) by the Pharisees, and thus liberated from the false understanding of the fact, that the witness can rise, as believer, to the correct signification. Or rather, he receives it from *elsewhere*, from Jesus who calls him and, for once, identifies himself: "'You have seen him and the one speaking with you is he.' He said, 'I do believe, Lord'" (9:37–38). In order to see truly, the witness must not only testify that he saw, but believe in the one who made him see. To see is not enough to understand; one must love in order to know: "I have called you friends [whom I love and who love me, φίλοι], because everything I have heard from my Father I have made known to you (ἐγνώρισα ὑμῖν)" (John 15:15). Now the vision returns: to see, it is not enough to see as a reliable witness (the man born blind) or a challenger (the Pharisees), for the witness does not understand everything he sees; to see, one must believe: "I came into this world for judgment, so that those who do not see might see, and those who do see might become blind" (John 9:39). The witness does not claim on his own to understand what he sees; rather, he awaits precisely that which gives itself to be seen.[3]

A first characteristic of every Revelation thus stands out: it shows itself not through a comprehensive knowledge, but through the recognition of an incomprehensibility; neither at first nor ever, perhaps, does it let itself be led back to a full intelligibility according to our rationality and following a finite hermeneutics; it is exposed *thanks to* the nevertheless certain non-knowing of the witness who accepts to understand from *elsewhere*.

Resistance

There is more. The same episode of the man born blind restored to sight suggests another dimension of Revelation: aside from the certain incomprehension of the witness, a Revelation always involves his *resistance*,[†] which here in this case is the refusal—by the scribes and the Pharisees, those wise and learned men who know, who know that they know and wish to know nothing else—to understand what they see. In this specific case, not only do they not admit that Jesus is the Messiah, but first and logically, they cannot accept the clear gap that every testimony involves, where someone reports with certainty what he nevertheless cannot wholly comprehend, or as it happens here, what no one, not even the learned, can comprehend on the basis of and in continuity with what one has always known by certain science. Because they first challenge this *elsewhere*, the learned then challenge the certain testimony of the incomprehensible, in order to maintain what they understand, even if this understanding contradicts what a witness saw with certainty; they thus hold literally to the tradition of men: "We are disciples of Moses! We know (οἴδαμεν) that God spoke to Moses" (John 9:28–29). In saying this they foreshadow the "philosophers and learned men" to come, who likewise understand what God is all about, and are both fooled and confirmed by "philosophy and the vain deceit of the tradition of men" (Colossians 2:8). God, they think, always thinks like them; for example, God geometrizes when he creates the world, for in all things he calculates the same way we do; likewise, God scrupulously respects the demands of our logic (in fact, of metaphysics), namely the principles of identity and of sufficient reason; and further, God conforms himself without reserve to his function as moral legislator required by our world. For the "philosophers and learned men," the wise and the scribes know enough about it to understand what we must think of God; thus, when a witness maintains with certainty the incomprehensibility of God, they always know enough about it to be able to know nothing about it: in every case they throw the witness out (John 9:34).

We add, then, to the intrinsic division within the witness (her certain knowledge without comprehension) a refusal that is not at all subjective, optional, or anecdotal, but rather which results from the incommensurability proper to every Revelation—*resistance*. Resistance comes from the fact that no one ever finds herself immediately prepared for, favorable to, or in agreement with a Revelation, but instead each one is opposed to it, at least at first, because it redefines the entire field of possibility. A feature of Revelation is to appear *as such* intolerable and unacceptable precisely because it gives itself as absolute and thus seems, *to our eyes*, intolerant according to our conception, and therefore intolerable. Consequently the revealed character of a religion, to the exact extent that the Revelation (like every revelation) comes from *elsewhere*, confers on the Revelation a very ambiguous privilege that can sometimes become a mark of infamy: certainly the Revelation can claim an authority that is exterior and seemingly superior to the human condition, but this exteriority and this superiority themselves elicit resistance, commensurate with what the eventual receivers of its announcement are able to accept.[5] Therefore such a trial of the *elsewhere* must be balanced by the increased number of witnesses, since none among them can furnish the exact and exclusive comprehension of what she testifies to, nor claim to abolish testimony's intrinsic gap within itself. If Revelation there must be, it can never come from one person alone. Even in the person of Christ who testifies in the name of the Father ("I testify on my behalf and so does the Father who sent me," John 8:18),[6] the testimony stands on its recognition of the will of the Father and on its paschal confirmation by the Father. The gap in testimony therefore remains, but validated ever since, *within* the Trinity itself. *A fortiori* for all the other witnesses, human each one, the gap never disappears. Whence the phenomenal necessity of a plurality of testimonies. The First Testament establishes and underlines it again and again, and the New Testament rests on the "apparent discrepancies between the Gospels" (Pascal).[7] Only the effect of depth, deepened by the nonalignment of the witnesses, maintains the gap and allows above all for the preservation of the *elsewhere* from which comes the signification of the signs, literally the Revelation. It could be, then, that the claim to restrict testimony to *only one* (like that of the prophet in the Quran), far from consecrating Revelation, closes it. For, according to the principle established by Dionysius the Mystic, "the darkness remains even after the manifestation, or, if I may speak in a more divine fashion, the darkness remains even amid the manifestation itself. . . . What is said remains quelled, and what is conceived, unknown."[8]

This resistance, as we know at least since Hume (see *infra* chapter 6), is concentrated around the discussion of the proofs and the criteria of authenticity for any "miracle," and in fact for any Revelation. But, as experience has abundantly shown, the possible authenticity of a Revelation does not attenuate the resistance that it elicits. Instead, it increases it: the more resistance there is to a Revelation the more it can appear credible and trustworthy, to the point that seriously resisting it will lead to resisting even and above all the evidence. A rather strange situation results. If in the case of a supposed Revelation we have in the end only a fraud, what is at stake in the conflict disappears immediately, and with it the resistance: everything reverts to the order of a happy and closed immanence. But if, on the contrary, the Revelation surmounts the suspicion about its origin and ends up proving its authenticity, then the resistance to its reception augments all the more: nothing elicits more resistance to Revelation than its potential authenticity. And the witness knows this by experience. Resistance and Revelation go together: of course, a resistance to the revealed character of a religion is not enough to authenticate it, but its reception without resistance would be enough to disqualify it as revealed. Resistance indicates subjectively the degree of the unseen and the depth of the *elsewhere* of a Revelation. Henceforward identified as its intrinsic character, resistance explains that every Revelation may, and in a sense must, stir up a conflict. And this conflict moreover increases: first there arises the conflict between the Revelation and its witness, who is surprised, subverted, and divided between his certainty and his incomprehension; then there comes a second conflict between the witnesses who receive the Revelation and the learned who challenge it; to which is added a third conflict between the direct witnesses and the other adepts of the same Revelation who must defer to the first witnesses, to their writings and their traditions ("Because you have seen you have believed; blessed are those who believe without having seen [μὴ ἰδόντες]," John 20:29); finally there comes the conflict between the witnesses of different supposedly revealed religions, who imagine themselves to be in competition, or between competing interpretations of a same Revelation. In short, without these conflicts and the *resistance* out of which they all arise, and which they lay out in multiple senses, there could not be even the possibility of a Revelation. We must admit, then, that no Revelation can manifest itself without *danger*: "Do not think that I have come to bring peace on earth; I have not come to bring peace, but a sword" (Matthew 10:34). Perhaps salvation grows there where danger lies, but salvation itself puts us in danger, because it completely modifies our conception of things. We are only left with making good use of a good danger—of what cannot be avoided, and whose ordeal sets free the truth.

Resistance defined in this way is best illustrated in the conflict that opposes the legislation of metaphysics to the legitimacy of a revealed religion, whatever religion it may be. Here is the question: What common intelligibility, or rather what rationality (by definition universal) will one be able to maintain in religion (and morality) if one assigns them two sources as heterogeneous as metaphysics and Revelation? The histories of philosophy and of theology show that two tactics have been attempted to pierce this aporia. Either one admits as a fact the consequence that the heterogeneity of the two sources imposes, and then disqualifies one of the two terms, resulting in either knowledge without revelation, or knowledge by revelation of the divinity, the former falling under the accusation of impiety, idolatry, atheism, etc., and the latter under the accusation of illusion, irrationality, fanaticism, etc. Or one reestablishes a minimal but forced continuity between the two authorities: Revelation would indeed come from *elsewhere*, but it would only have formulated without a concept what reason itself ends up saying with a concept (or inversely, Revelation will repeat without a concept what reason already said with a concept); Revelation would then limit itself to making accessible by other means what reason already knows, or soon will know. But then it has become merely a matter of pedagogically more efficient shortcuts that leave the reason for effects unknown. Thus at one time there were efforts to make *reasonable* a Christianity that, through Revelation, most likely would have said nothing other than what the human consciousness already knew, if only confusedly, through pure reason.[9]

It is hardly surprising that these two tactics always fail. But the essential lies in the single motive behind their double failure: if a thought of Revelation lays claim to a meaning and therefore to producing concepts, it must accept its distance from the common rationality that it has subverted or completed. In other words, it should *demonstrate a rationality* that is both *compatible with rationality without revelation* and *resolutely distinct from it*. No concept of Revelation can be imposed without remaining, in a certain problematic but also necessary way, like a Revelation *in* the concept that nevertheless cannot be dissolved into the common logic *of* the concept. That is, a correct concept of Revelation must remain a concept, even and above all if it contradicts what, of itself and following common logic (in other words, following metaphysics), the concept can conceive. Schelling, at the moment when he was attempting to move beyond "negative philosophy" with a "positive philosophy," clearly defined what it is that makes of Revelation a useless hypothesis and an empty concept when one claims to remain within metaphysics (the only one, that of the Enlightenment): "If revelation contained nothing more than what is in reason, then it would have absolutely no interest; its sole interest can only consist in the fact that it contains something that exceeds (*hinausgeht*) reason, something that is more than what reason contains.... In practice, it would not be worth the trouble to concern oneself with revelation if it were not something special, if it contained nothing more than what one already had without it."[10] It remains that this *exceeding* itself only has conceptual meaning if Revelation still *knows*, even when it steps over the supposed limits of rationality. But then what other reason, come from what *elsewhere*, can decide that one should step over the limits of rationality? And once these limits are crossed, by what reason could we be assured that we are still thinking rationally? And in this case, does this other reason maintain a certain univocity with the rationality that it supposedly surpasses? Descartes demonstrated that the thought of finitude depends on a concept of the infinite, as strangely rational as it seems. It may be that reciprocally the thought of a Revelation that surpasses reason once again requires a rationality of this surpassing. It would be necessary to have a *concept* of Revelation that contradicts neither the concept nor Revelation. Can it be thought?

The Paradox

This question of limits, nevertheless, does not allow itself to be led back to a question of borders. Such questions about borders (*Grenzfragen*) effectively concern less the borders of rationality (by definition variable) than they do rational questions that nevertheless still (or ever) remain without an answer, because their answer would be situated on the other side of the border; in this case, beyond the border defining possible experience, that of the objects given by intuition, whether sensible (Kant) or categorial (Husserl). The response to the border question is, at best, an ideal of reason, the object of an idea that will never be given in sensible experience; this ideal problem maintains a legitimate role as a need of reason that it aims at without accomplishing or incarnating it; but this ideal adds nothing to the actual field of rational knowledge. Opposed to such a border question, which though known and endowed with meaning has no corresponding answer that is rationally verifiable, there is the *paradox*, which completes a passage to the limit of the concept. This passage to the limit was defined by Mallarmé as "pushing an idea as far as it will go, even if it bursts in the manner of a paradox."[11] In other words, as such, the "inconceivable paradox (*unausdenkbares Paradox*)"[12] unceasingly pushes logic to its limit. Thus the paradox is not to be confused with contradiction and non-sense, which are defined by a fault or an absence of logic; nor with what is commonly called a paradox in philosophy (the Cretan affirming that all Cretans lie), which concerns an undecidability resulting from the self-reference of the one who says what he says; there once again we find a fault in logic (the logic of classes). Instead, the "para-dox is what is opposed to the pre-established conception, to the *doxa* and the expectation that result from it. In contrast, the contradiction is what contradicts *itself*."[13] The paradox, then, shows something and, in this sense, it accomplishes a rational and intelligible operation; but what it shows is not understood, or not yet, because it is opposed to what the *doxa* (what *everyone knows* very well in advance) allows one to understand. Thus it puts into question the horizon of rationality held to that point as defined and definitive.

To approach the originality of the paradox, we can proceed in two stages. First, by observing that, far from formulating an irrationally constructed question to which no noticeable object responds, the paradox puts into crisis the limits and the conditions of rationality, which is supposed to know and thus claims to understand. Here we should be inspired by the example of the true philosophers who, in order to remain faithful to the concept and to the thing itself, never hesitate to overturn common logic with radical paradoxes. For example: in order to be, it is necessary to think, and not the reverse, as it went without saying before Descartes; and this is so because the act of thinking in truth precedes the act of being, and offers to thinking the first case of the ego's point of view, a point of view that is henceforth originating. Or, time and space depend on the mind as forms of its intuition, and not the reverse, as it went without saying before Kant; and this is so because experience models itself on the *I think*, the finitude of which henceforward becomes originating. Or, being is defined according to the meanings of time, and not the reverse, as it went without saying before Heidegger; and this is so because the modes of temporality alone allow us to distinguish the manners of being of the different realms of beings, by following the features of *Dasein*, henceforth the exceptional being. It is by following these examples that it makes sense to reread the famous paradoxes of Tertullian, almost always the objects of misreading: "*Crucifixus est Dei filius; non pudet, quia pudendum est*—the Son of God is crucified: you must not be ashamed, since it is by definition shameful. *Et mortuus Dei filius: credibile est quia ineptum est*—and the son of God is dead: this is believable because it is not fitting. *Et sepultus resurrexit: certum est quia impossibile*. And he rose from the tomb: this is certain, because it is impossible."14 This triple argument puts into operation a simple hermeneutic principle, well known by exegetes: a lying witness would never report a fact that is absurd and thus unbelievable; in order to get someone to believe his false testimony he will on the contrary choose to remain within the bounds of the plausible; if therefore a witness testifies to excessive, implausible, or even apparently impossible facts, it must be assumed that he testifies in a sense against his own interest, that is to say in a *disinterested* manner, close to what he has seen or believes he saw. The shame of a crucifixion, then, so contradicts our image of divinity that, if some witnesses affirm it (or even, like Paul or Ignatius, glory in it), that signifies that one must no longer blush at it (*pudendum*). The putting to death of the son of God so little suits (*ineptum*) our image of divinity that one must believe witnesses that had no other choice than to report it as a fact. That a dead man returns to life seems, according to our representation of the possible, in principle impossible (*impossibile*); we must then conclude first of all that the witnesses had to resign themselves to vouch for the impossible despite the almost certain impossibility of convincing anyone, and second that on the contrary they wanted thus to manifest another rationality, according to which the impossible for man is possible for God and God alone: "Nothing is impossible for God."15 By rights the three paradoxes rest on the final argument: the facts to which the Christians testify merit a double consideration, first because they lay out the hermeneutic logic of testimony, and next and above all because, in order to become perfectly intelligible, they make an appeal to a change of paradigm, radical of course, but rational, concerning the possible. That is, possibility defined according to our finitude is inscribed and inverted in a possibility according to the infinity of God, which, from *our* point of view, signifies: to be overturned in the impossible. The paradox thus plays logically within the intrinsic gap in testimony.

Next, and this time moving to theology, one can say that the paradox, by changing the paradigm of rationality (from the possible to the impossible), states a response that is *very* intelligible, *perfectly* rational, and saturated with multiple meanings, in answer to a question that has until now remained unformulated, never yet explicitly posed, whose rationality has not yet been conceived. More exactly, the paradox brings to thinking the *trace* of an eschatological response, in advance of every question that would have prepared or anticipated it—a response without a question, a clearly perceived response to a question not yet glimpsed. In a paradox it is not the answer that is missing but the sense of the question. Among others, we find confirmation in Gilbert of Poitiers: "In each faculty, but above all in theology, few are the secrets of wisdom that are known. But, as the glory of their dignity arouses the admiration of the philosophers, even the greatest, they have called them 'paradoxes.'"[16] This definition also points out what is truly at stake in the paradox, which corresponds to a requirement proper to theology, according to a rule formulated by William of Saint-Thierry: "Therefore, when words are used to treat of God, the reasons must be fitted to the realities, and not Him [God] to the reasons."[17] In general, and in theology, the paradox is born from the anteriority of the answer to the question—the statement answers a question that the witness cannot yet conceive. As soon as theologians seriously approach Revelation, they radicalize, or should radicalize, this gesture: even common logic must be revised according to the requirements of God's manifestation of himself. Then this manifestation will become *all the more rational*, since a question suited to its height and its measure will succeed in welcoming it, at least partially, as straightaway definitive.

The paradox, in this case that of Revelation, seeks to bring about the discovery of the question to which it already expresses the answer, adding to the apparent logical conflict a second, more essential step. In this way, following its own, certainly strange, mode, it accomplishes *appearing*: in effect, a para-*dox* always and initially designates an apparition that separates from itself (or at least *seems* to separate from itself), or rather, that separates from what *we* expected to see or hear; and it is only if this separation surpasses what *we* can consider that it avoids degrading into a mere appearance. In order to see this better, let us read the text that offers the only occurrence of *paradoxos* in the entire New Testament: "Then astonishment seized them all (ἔκστασις ἔλαβεν ἅπαντας) and they glorified (ἐδόξαζον) God, and, struck with awe (φόβου), they said, 'We have seen paradoxes (παράδοξα) today'" (Luke 5:26).[18] What paradoxes are the concern here? At the same time both statements that are incomprehensible for us and actions that are outside of what is possible for us.

Clearly, they all stem from the healing of a paralytic. But this healing is merely a sign, the sign of an answer given to this invalid who absolutely wanted to appeal to Jesus (to the point of getting his bed lowered by ropes through a hole opened in the roof). Now Jesus's answer to this question at first precisely does not consist in his healing, but in the remission of his sins: "And when he saw their faith he said, 'Man, your sins are forgiven you'" (Luke 5:20). Jesus thus substitutes for the explicit question of the paralytic (the request for healing) another question (the request for forgiveness of sins), which he had not asked. The "scribes and Pharisees" are not fooled by this substitution of one question for another: before any physical miracle (a visible fact for a testimony), they are immediately scandalized because they see the other, spiritual question that Jesus poses (and already responds to); they thus immediately contest his right not only to respond to it, but even to pose it: "'Who is this that speaks blasphemies? Who can forgive sins but God only?'" (5:21) But they identify the spiritual question precisely in order not to listen to it; they do not believe but instead cling to their "reasonings (διαλογισμούς, διαλογίζεσθε)" (5:22), so as to limit themselves to their reasons, and thus to their common definition of rationality. And because for them, despite their protestations of spirituality, the remission of sins remains "easier" (5:23) than the healing (when instead the opposite is true from Christ's point of view), Jesus heals: "'I say to you, rise, take up your bed and go home'" (5:24). What reveals the "power" of Christ is therefore not found in the visible sign that a witness would report (the healing) in order to recognize him, but in the silent question that Christ opposed to the explicit request of the paralytic (the forgiveness of sins). There is a paradox because, through the evidence of the first question (the request for healing) there appears at the end the second question (the power of forgiving sins, which Christ shares with God). In fact, the entire intrigue aims, starting from a sickness and a healing, to reveal the divinity of Jesus.

Even if sometimes the issue is only perhaps an appearance of apparition, the paradox always plays out in the margins of phenomenality, not in the contradiction of formalism. It is detected in the extreme regions of phenomenality, working on the manifestation of that which can only let itself be seen or said by contradicting what *we* held as the (objective) conditions of experience—what irrupts into our experience as an event, as the premier event. Revelation cannot unfold itself in *our* world, or at least in what we conceive as such, as ours: "*How* the world is, is completely indifferent for what is higher. God does not reveal himself (*offenbart sich*) *in* the world."[19] For if what shows itself in no way surprises us, it is not worthy of any attention; and reciprocally, what is worthy of attention is what surprises, and therefore what contradicts our expectation, our forecasts, and our common regimen of rationality: "Certain days one must not fear naming the things impossible to describe."[20] We draw the conclusion that no revelation can be received without a paradox accepted as such. This requirement confirms the previous remark: no revelation can do without the resistance of the witnesses that it summons and who can in one way or another challenge it; it must be able to explain the possibility of this refusal, not as a contingent incident and a collateral loss, but as one of the possibilities that its very *rationality* implies. It belongs to a true revelation intrinsically, and not accidentally, that someone can challenge it, because it imposes such novelty.

This rule *of method* holds for all revelation, in the sciences, the arts, history, the erotic phenomenon, and so on, and consequently first and foremost in a religious happening. In this context, the question of a Revelation becomes much more intelligible and significant. Much *more intelligible* first: revelation is inscribed in the phenomenality of the given as a case that is certainly exceptional, but perfectly coherent with all the others, the case of a phenomenon that would carry to its excess additional intuition over every concept (or every set of concepts) supposed to regulate and constitute it; it would be a, or even *the* saturated phenomenon par excellence, unconstitutable and giving itself from itself to the point of showing itself absolutely in itself and by itself. It probably consists of an exception, compared with the other phenomena, but an exception that confirms the general definition of every phenomenon as that which only shows itself to the degree that it gives itself. Next, and much *more significant*: the privilege of the phenomenon of revelation, which allows it to *show itself* in itself and by itself in an unmatched way, would arise from its other privileged feature: *giving itself* in an unmatched way. In fact, the biblical revelation puts into operation the privilege of a giving that surpasses all expectation, all forecasting, and, finally, all reception.

A Question of Phenomenality

But an intelligibility as significant as that of Revelation presupposes that we approach it (and receive it) from a point of view that may at first seem strange—that of *phenomenality*.[21] Nevertheless, like every revelation, Revelation (Jewish and Christian) obviously plays out in terms of phenomenality. For it is precisely because "No one has ever seen God (θεὸν οὐδεὶς ἑώρακεν πώποτε)" (John 1:18) that he remains "invisible, the only God (ἀοράτῳ μόνῳ θεῷ)" (1 Timothy 1:17), and that he dwells "in unapproachable light, whom no man has ever seen or can see (ὃν εἶδεν οὐδεὶς ἀνθρώπων οὐδὲ ἰδεῖν δύναται)" (1 Timothy 6:16), and that it was necessary that "the only Son, who is turned toward the bosom of the Father, has made the exegesis (ἐκεῖνος ἐξηγήσατο)" (John 1:18), under the premier paradoxical title of "icon of the invisible God (εἰκὼν τοῦ θεοῦ τοῦ ἀοράτου)" (Colossians 1:15; see 2 Corinthians 4:4). To be sure, Christ makes this "exegesis" through a linguistic interpretation of the Scriptures (διερμήνευσεν, Luke 24:27), but he nevertheless accomplishes it in the end through a phenomenal paradox, that of manifesting himself by a sacramental gesture (breaking bread), where presence coincides with absence: "And their eyes were opened and they recognized him; and he became invisible to them (ἄφαντος)" (Luke 24:31).[22] In fact, Christ accomplishes this "exegesis" of the invisible God by making himself seen among men and women, a phenomenon among phenomena, by phenomenalizing himself without reserve—by making himself a phenomenon in our phenomenality, by making himself man. He makes himself the visible commentary on the Revelation of the invisible God, through a visibility multiplied according to the modes of every possible gaze: "the mystery of piety, which manifested itself (ἐφανερώθη) in the flesh, was vindicated in the Spirit, showed itself (ὤφθη) to the angels, was announced to the nations, was believed in the world, was taken up in glory" (1 Timothy 3:16). Through a radically phenomenal performance, "the grace of the saving God has appeared (ἐπεφάνη) to all men" (Titus 2:11), and "we have contemplated (ἐθεασάμεθα) his glory" (John 1:14). We have contemplated this phenomenon, we have certainly seen it well, not because we constituted it, much less induced it, but because he decided and wanted to manifest *himself*, starting from himself: "That which was from the beginning, which we have heard, which we have seen (ἑωράκαμεν) with our eyes, which we have contemplated (ἐθεασάμεθα), what our hands have touched of the *logos* of life—and the life manifested itself (ἐφανερώθη), and we have seen it (ἑωράκαμεν), we bring you testimony and proclaim to you the eternal life which was with the Father and which manifested itself (ἐφανερώθη) to us—that which we have seen (ἑωράκαμεν) and heard we proclaim also to you" (1 John 1:1–3).[23] Revelation, as its name indicates, plays out in phenomenality, which thus offers the privileged point of view for describing and receiving it. If it can ever be conceived, it will be by following the guiding thread of the question of phenomenality, much more than in accordance with the question of beings and their being (existence), and infinitely more than according to the question of a knowledge of objects (demonstration). Coming onto this terrain still remains, to a large extent, a future work for theology.[24]

Of course, the point is not for the theologian to apply uniformly to the biblical texts the (supposedly fixed) rules for the description of the phenomena. The phenomena of Revelation (like all the phenomena of revelation) modify the rules of phenomenality according to their proper exigencies, against all reductionism, even that of phenomenology. Hölderlin's warning should be enough here: "*wo aber / Ein Gott noch auch erscheint, / Da ist doch andere Klarheit*— but where / A God as well appears, / A different clarity shines."[25] This binding consequence follows: in the end all the manifestations of God in Jesus Christ, all the biblical "theophanies" (if we provisionally admit this too imprecise term here) can constitute only a single paradox, which exposes the apparition, arisen among the phenomena that our world untiringly makes bloom, of a phenomenon coming from *elsewhere* than from the world, the apparition of the inapparent par excellence, the visibility of the invisible *as such, and which remains invisible in its very visibility*. No serious theology of Revelation can develop without confronting this phenomenological paradox. What do we see, what can we ever see of the invisible? Such is the question.

Revelation in its phenomenality nevertheless has at its disposal a privilege that makes it particularly appropriate for a phenomenological approach. We have insisted (chapter 1) on the principle according to which that which shows itself shows itself uniquely to the extent that it gives itself and is thus reduced to the given within it. Now, in a sense both strictly identical and marked by a radicality without common measure, Revelation follows the same principle: *"At vero dando Spiritum per quem revelat, etiam ipsum revelat: dando revelat et revelando dat*—It is by giving the Spirit, through whom he [Christ] reveals, that he shows us himself; in giving he reveals, and in revealing he gives."[26] Gift and giving [*donation*] offer, in every case, a perfectly univocal concept: givenness [*donation*] in phenomenology (the excess of intuition and the advent of significations that are unthinkable to men and women) finds itself and is radicalized in "every perfect gift that comes from on high" (James 1:17). Paradoxically and therefore also logically, Revelation would accomplish, by virtue of the giving that it alone performs perfectly, the essence of phenomenality.

II

The Constitution of the Aporia

THREE

Thomas Aquinas and the Epistemological Interpretation

We have outlined, on the basis of the phenomenal privilege of the concept of revelation (chapter 1), the formal characteristics of a possible concept of Revelation (chapter 2)—namely, a saturated phenomenon that manifests itself in coming from *elsewhere*. It now remains to gauge whether and to what extent the historical tradition of theology responds to it, or not. For it does not go without saying that this tradition has always recognized Revelation on the basis of the phenomenality that is in it, or thought about Revelation on the basis of the givenness that secures it and unfolds it. Other imperatives have weighed on the concept's history, namely the decision to conceive of it within the metaphysical horizon of being and, through a binding consequence, the attempt to raise it to the status of a science—in short, to interpret Revelation first of all as the communication of a propositional knowledge. We must begin our research, therefore, with the reconstitution of this interpretation, so as to deconstruct it (Part II, chapters 3–6), in order to recover the true ground that alone will allow for its *theo*-logical comprehension (Part III, chapters 7–10).

The Blind Spot

The modern (but when does this "modernity" begin?) and current usage of the term, even when confined to common revelation as we experience it in daily life (chapter 1), tends most often and immediately to interpret it as a mode of communication of knowledge. To reveal signifies on the one hand an eventual acquiring of information for oneself (to reveal a secret, a code, the result of an exam or a lottery, to reveal the answer to a riddle, etc.); thus Malebranche often has recourse to this term in order to designate a sensible and unclear knowledge that nevertheless dispels uncertainty through an incontestable albeit unintelligible fact: "that sensation of pain we have is a kind of revelation."[1] Or, on the other hand, to reveal signifies to have communicated long hidden information through another, by strength of persuasion or under duress; Montaigne understands it as what an admission extracted through torture can make known, or what the obstinacy not to confess holds back: "Epicharis glutted and wearied the cruelty of Nero's satellites and endured their fire, their beatings, and their instruments one whole day without a word to reveal her conspiracy [*sans aucune voix de révélation de sa conjuration*]."[2] To reveal, then, would mean, in the first instance, to know or make known. One ought, therefore, to be able to begin from knowledge by sensory revelation in order to pass, possibly, by *natural* derivation to a knowledge of Revelation that is properly theological. Malebranche practices this back-and-forth movement often: "Thus, I am assured that bodies exist, not only by the natural revelation of the sensations of them which God gives me, but even more by the supernatural revelation of faith."[3] Since the strictly philosophical (in fact Cartesian) demonstration does not allow us to conclude the existence of bodies (that is, of material things), we must, in order to know them with certainty, rely on biblical faith, which secures such certainty for us through Revelation. The two uses of R/revelation are superimposed and cross over, because they share the same presupposition: in both cases the concern is to acquire a knowledge. In this situation, therefore, one will not be surprised that Montesquieu (one example among others) claims to justify the "revelation" of the "Christian religion" through "natural religion": "Have I not always heard that we were all imbued with a natural religion? Have I not heard that Christianity was the perfection of natural religion? Have I not heard that natural religion was used to prove revelation against the deists? And that the same natural religion was used to prove the existence of God against atheists?"[4] On the other hand, one will be much more surprised to find out that Nicolas-Sylvestre Bergier, one of the best opponents of the "*philosophes*," nevertheless assimilates the natural knowledge of God to a Revelation. What is more, he recognizes this as the first, fundamental, and "general" meaning of every revelation: "*To reveal* a thing to someone is to *make it known* to him; *in its general sense*, God reveals to us what we discover by the natural lights of reason, since he is the one who gave us this faculty and who preserves it in us. But it is established *by usage* that *to reveal* means *to make known* truths to men by other means than by the exercise they can make of their intelligence."[5] To reveal would thus consist in making known, first and in the full sense through natural light (God intervening indirectly as creator of our "intelligence"), and then later and maybe by "other means" than the natural light (God intervening directly as Revelator of a religion). This hierarchy that subordinates Revelation to the revelation of the "natural lights" rests on the feature common to both: to reveal amounts to "making known." This is what we will therefore call the *epistemological* interpretation of Revelation. Everything proceeds as if it went without saying that to reveal consisted only in making known, and even in making known, in a univocal manner, truths that nevertheless in principle are incommensurable. The imprecision and the indecision in these formulations provides a first hint of the problematic character of the theological concept of Revelation.

But there is another: the *lateness* of the very term *revelation* in imposing itself as a major concept in dogmatic theology, a point on which the best historians of dogma agree. Thus, regarding its mention by Vatican Council I, Heinrich Fries notes that this expression arises "on principle view at a relatively later date." Avery Dulles confirms the point: "Since revelation did not emerge as a major theological theme until after the Enlightenment, . . . in most early theologians, as in the Bible itself, there is no systematic doctrine of revelation." And likewise for Bernard Sesboüé: "Revelation was not the object of special consideration in the patristic period, either. The idea went without saying: God had spoken to men through the prophets, and then in His Son Jesus Christ. The term itself (*apokalypsis*) referred instead to a particular literature: apocalyptic literature. Scholastic theology spoke of revelation relatively little in its doctrinal statements, but more often in scriptural commentaries and in reflection on prophecy."[6] One might then be surprised, and rightly so, that such a late-arriving concept, for so long on the sidelines during the first twelve or thirteen centuries, took on an ever-growing importance in a very recent era (in the seventeenth century and above all the nineteenth century), to the point of appearing to be almost a synonym for "theology."[7]

Jean-Yves Lacoste soberly notes this time lag and marks this inconsistency: "A central reality of Christian experience, and yet a long-marginal concept, revelation undoubtably figures as an organizing notion in contemporary theology."[8] But can we or should we content ourselves with these contradictory determinations—belatedness, and then dominant usage? For it is not enough to juxtapose these two features to overcome their at least apparent incoherence: "Everything depends on divine revelation, everything refers to it, nothing is explained except in its light, and this is perhaps the reason why it remains *paradoxically* as one of these great truths that are so radiant and so certain that they do not need to be explained."[9] But couldn't we also honestly ask ourselves if the issue here is an authentic paradox, or a dangerous failure? Especially as a third indicator of the fragility of the current concept of Revelation is added here: a certain reticence, sometimes, in the Scriptures. For instance, the Book of Revelation itself uses the term only a single time, in its title. And Paul warns against the excess of the charism of prophecy: "If something is revealed (ἀποκαλυφθῇ) to another sitting by, let the first be silent" (1 Corinthians 14:30). The concern here is with the consequences of a massive fact: the term *apocalypse* (ἀποκάλυψις) does not match the recent and global concept of Revelation, but ends up by designating only the "apocalyptic" literary genre, in its scattered bursts and its occasional excesses. For this is not the least of the surprises: the biblical texts do not seem to offer a term or a network of terms allowing us to construct, incontestably and right away, a coherent concept of Revelation.

"*Theologia sive scientia*"

Where then do we find a starting point? As so often in Christian theology when one does not know where to stand, it is necessary to go back to Saint Thomas Aquinas to set our feet on solid ground. Indeed, it may be that the difficulties that we have just encountered find their origin with him who was one of the first, if not the first, to develop a precise concept of Revelation. Let us begin with the opening of the *Summa Theologiae* which, in its first question, asks whether the knowledge of God can come from philosophy alone, or if it requires another, higher authority. The first article of this first question concludes that one necessarily must admit, alongside philosophical approaches to God simply through reason, another doctrine, *sacra doctrina*, which proceeds from revelation: "*Necessarium igitur fuit, praeter philosophicas disciplinas, quae per rationem investigantur, sacram doctrinam per revelationem haberi.*"[10] By right, and in fact, the *theologia* developed by the "philosophical disciplines" (according to Aristotle in *Metaphysica* E) does not exhaust our knowledge of divine matters; there remains another possible theology, of another genus, that puts into operation the *sacra doctrina*: "*theologia, quae ad sacram doctrinam pertinet, differt secundum genus ab illa theologia, quae pars philosophiae ponitur*—theology included in sacred doctrine differs in genus from that theology which is part of philosophy."[11]

What is the generic difference involved here? That which Thomas Aquinas had already clearly established in his previous commentary on the *De Trinitate* of Boethius: theology is in effect split, for "*theologia sive scientia est duplex*—theology, or divine science, is twofold."[12] And only theology in the sense of *sacra doctrina* can claim to know divine things in themselves, since it alone receives them according to their proper genus of manifestation, namely "*secundum quod ipsae se ipsas manifestant*—according as they themselves manifest of themselves"; for manifesting itself by and on the basis of itself characterizes the divine things, "*secundum quod requirit rerum divinarum manifestatio*—because the manifestation of divine things requires this."[13] *Sacra doctrina* alone can approach these "divine things" as the direct subject of its knowing, because it alone receives them as such through the Scriptures: "*ipsas res divinas considerat propter se ipsas ut subiectum scientiae, et haec est theologia, quae in sacra scriptura traditur*—of another sort is that theology which considers divine things on their own account as the very subject matter of its science, and this is called Sacred Scripture."[14] In contrast, philosophical theology, also called metaphysics ("*quam philosophi prosequuntur, quae alio nomine metaphysica dicitur*"[15]), can reach the divine things only indirectly, through their effects ("*secundum quod per effectus manifestantur*"[16]); in other words, metaphysics reaches them only inasmuch as they come under, in their effects but not in themselves, its only legitimate subject, the entity as being: "*res divinae non tractantur a philosophis, nisi prout sunt rerum omnium principia. Et ideo pertractantur in illa doctrina, in qua ponuntur ea quae sunt communia omnibus entibus, quae habet subiectum ens in quantum est ens*—divine things are not dealt with by philosophers except in so far as they are the principles of all things; and hence they are considered in that science in which things common to all beings are studied, which has being as its subject, inasmuch as it is being."[17] The science of the being or entity as such can deal with "divine things" only in a derived measure, where they enter in as the principle of their ontic effects; and, as only their effects (and not they themselves) are articulated according to beingness (*ens in quantum ens, Seiendheit*), it is necessary to conclude that the divine things as such *do not* lie directly within metaphysical theology, but only enter it indirectly, as the principles of these things, but not as these things as such: "*omnium rerum principia*," "*non tamquam subiectum scientiae, sed tamquam principia subiecti*—not so much as the substratum of the science but as the principle of this substratum."[18] In short, the "divine things" do not enter into the substratum (*subiectum*) that philosophical theology treats, precisely because they are its principle. On the other hand, these "divine things" do become substrata in *theologia sacrae Scripturae*, which alone makes them directly accessible, while *theologia philosophica* limits itself to indirectly noting their effects in the *ens in quantum ens*, without approaching them immediately, but mediately as the principle of these effects.[19] From this first distinction there follows a first conclusion: the duality of the theologies is defined through the limiting of philosophical theology to the *ens in quantum ens*, which, by contrast, clears a field for a theology of *sacra Scriptura* or *sacra doctrina*. And yet this conclusion raises a difficulty, since this unquestionable *possibility* remains undetermined: the fact that revelation according to Scripture is opposed to, completes, and surpasses the philosophical science of God is not enough to assure it the status of a science *as well*, despite its function of *going beyond* philosophical science. Thus, the insufficiency of nonrevealed knowledge is not enough to establish right away the merely postulated concept of a revealed *knowledge*.

And yet this possibility is enough for Thomas Aquinas to unfold an *epistemological* interpretation of revelation, however essentially indeterminate it may remain. The body of the response in the *Summa Theologiae*, Ia, q.1, a.1 poses, develops, and in effect privileges the epistemological function of *sacra doctrina* (or *theologiae sacrae Scripturae*) by two arguments. First, through an implicit syllogism: God constitutes the final end of man's desire (a nonhypothetical thesis, for Thomas Aquinas accepts no *duplex beatitudo*); nevertheless, man can neither desire nor love anything that he does not first know (according to the principle that one may love only what one knows[20]); therefore, since God, as we have just seen, remains unknown to the merely natural light of *theologia philosophica* or "*metaphysica, quae circa divina versatur*—metaphysics, which deals with divine things,"[21] it is necessary that another source of knowledge enter in so as to allow the natural desire for God to know what it already loves of necessity: this will be the function of knowledge by revelation, which comes from God and therefore exceeds human reason ("*per revelationem divinam, quae rationem humanam excedit*"). This first argument rests on a strong point, the essential paradox made evident by Henri de Lubac: that man as a rational creature, *capax Dei*, enjoys the *privilege* of naturally desiring a supernatural end, which he cannot attain without the (supernatural) aid of a divine revelation; the epistemological insufficiency (the inability to know by the means of his nature, nor therefore to attain his naturally supernatural end) constitutes, nevertheless, from the point of view of beatitude and the final destiny of man, an infinite gift; in other words, "*Creatura ergo rationalis in hoc praeeminet omni creaturae, quod capax est summi boni per divinam visionem et fruitionem, licet ad hoc consequendum naturae propriae principia non sufficiant, sed ad hoc indigeat auxilio divinae gratiae*—Therefore, the rational creature then excels every other creature in this: that he is capable of [receiving] the highest good in virtue of having as his ultimate end the vision and enjoyment of God, although the principles of his own nature are not sufficient to attain this but he needs the help of divine grace."[22] Against all the seemingly neo-Thomist but in fact, ultimately Suárezian deviations of a theology of double beatitude, Thomas Aquinas holds firmly to the paradox of human nature's supernatural end, thus taking his place within a patristic tradition that is uncontestable and absolutely sure. Yet the interpretation that he makes of it relies on a point that is less sure and more debatable: because he conceives the privilege of the supernatural destiny of man as a deficit of *knowledge*, he interprets the help of grace necessary to divinize man, in this case the help of a Revelation from the Scriptures, as a (different) source of *knowledge*; in victorious competition, certainly, with human reason, Revelation becomes in that very way comparable and commensurable to it, since it shares its function. The help of grace thus comes at the price of a strictly and initially epistemological interpretation of Revelation itself.

This *epistemological* interpretation of Revelation is immediately confirmed in a second argument, itself negative, for it disqualifies the natural knowledge of God by mere reason (as exercised by the *theologia* of philosophy) because of its epistemological insufficiency. The argument proceeds in this way: supposing that God could (make himself) be known by human reason pure and simple, Revelation would be no less necessary ("*ad ea etiam quae de Deo ratione humana investigari possunt, necessarium fuit hominem instrui revelatione divina*"); for, if the knowledge of God amounted to what human reason left to its own light could attain, it would suffer from a triple limitation: only certain people (*pauci*: the experts, the learned, the philosophers) would know God, after a long search (*per longum tempus*) and not without many errors (*admixtione multorum errorum*).[23] In other words, if philosophical theology held exclusive ownership of the knowledge of God, the great majority of men would have very little of it and very poor access to it. It would be convenient, then, if Revelation entered in precisely at the level of what mere reason *ought* to know, for an imperative pastoral reason: the ignorant (the *rudes*) also have the right to salvation. The superiority of Revelation over human reason thus proves itself to be double, but always for epistemological motives: first of all because it alone allows us to know God (directly) as *subiectum scientiae* (directly as *theologia* of *sacra doctrina*) and not only as *principium subiecti* (indirectly, as the *theologia* of philosophy); and next it also allows everyone to know God, and with certainty, by substituting itself for philosophy and completing the deficient contributions of the natural light of human reason.

Subalternation

The answers to the objections confirm, in the same article from the first question, that Revelation must first and foremost be understood as a communication of different kinds of knowledge, without explicit consideration of the possible equivocity of a knowledge thus dispensed by the two sources, nor especially of the other functions of this Revelation (foremost among these the grace of the sanctification of its witnesses). In this way, the answer to the first argument emphasizes that the truths revealed must not be examined by reason ("*non . . . per rationem inquirenda*"[24]), thus already setting up an opposition between the truths known by Revelation and those known by pure reason. The answer to the second argument goes even further: it attempts to join epistemologically these two competing modes of knowledge into two sciences, according to the principle that "*diversa ratio cognoscibilis diversitatem scientiarum inducit*—sciences are diversified according to the diverse nature of their knowable objects." At issue, in fact, is the Aristotelian principle of the subordination of the sciences: for instance, the roundness of the earth can be demonstrated mathematically, leaving matter aside, but it can also be demonstrated physically, through consideration of matter; it follows then that astronomy is subordinate to geometry just as music is to arithmetic and, in general, physics to mathematics. Consequently, concludes Thomas Aquinas, "there is nothing to prevent that on the same things, *nihil prohibet de eisdem rebus*," in this case the "divine things," the two ways of knowing be brought together at the same time, the one subordinated to the other, the natural light of reason (the reason of the philosophers) subordinated to the light of divine Revelation (*sacra doctrina*).[25] So the supremacy of *theologia sacrae doctrinae* over *theologia philosophiae* is reinforced, but at the (high) price of an even starker assimilation of the former to the epistemological function of the latter: Revelation would make us know better and know more than the natural light, because it would first and foremost make us *know*—without any specification as to what "to know" means *here*, or whether it remains univocal or is exposed to an irreducible equivocity.

This imprecision becomes patent when one considers another difficulty. For the objection cannot be avoided that this principle of the subordination (or rather, of the subalternation) of the sciences remains for Aristotle purely philosophical, since he joins two equally human and philosophical sciences (mathematics, and mathematics applied to physics); it therefore cannot be carried out, as Thomas Aquinas attempts to do, on two perfectly heterogeneous forms of knowledge, one that is human, come from our experience of this world, and the other come from *elsewhere*, from a direct Revelation of God granted by God. The incommensurable relation between a human knowledge of God and a divine knowledge of God cannot be conceived using a device appropriated from the human sciences with the same status, even though they are hierarchically distinguished. Perhaps sensing the audacious incoherence of this assimilation, Thomas Aquinas seems cautious enough to attenuate it by suggesting that the "*habitus fidei est* quasi *habitus principiorum*—the habit of faith... is *comparable* to the habit of principles," or that "those truths that we hold in the first place by faith are for us *quasi*-first principles—*ipsa, quae fide tenemus, sint nobis* quasi *principia*."[26] In short, at best (or at worst) it is only a matter of a *quasi*-subordination. And yet, the ambiguity of the primarily epistemological interpretation of Revelation here takes a further step and its ambiguity grows along with it: henceforth, Revelation as a science joins itself to the *philosophical* science of God and conforms itself to what will become the system of the sciences, as the constitution of the system of *metaphysica* develops. To be sure, the successors of Thomas Aquinas will attempt this system while claiming to govern it; but this claim will only secure them a primacy as provisional as it is in principle fragile.[27]

The patent indecision, not to say the imprecision, of this interpretation of Revelation becomes manifest in the Thomistic doctrine of "the revealable" (*revelabile*). A doctrine that is Thomist rather than held by Thomas, moreover, since it has to do simply with a *hapax* in the body of the work,[28] upon which the tradition of the commentators, from Cajetan to Gilson, conferred an inordinate importance, but one that signals a deep ambiguity. At issue is the maintenance of a rational commerce between the two ways of knowing God, the assumption being that Revelation also and before anything else constitutes a(nother) *knowledge*; thus it is said that, "because Sacred Scripture . . . considers certain things under the formality of being divinely revealed, all things whatever they may be insofar as they are revealable by God, have in common the formal reason of the object of this science."[29] Put another way, all that is, whatever it may be, thus all things insofar as they are beings, the entire domain of the *theologia* of the philosophers, can fall under the authority of *sacra doctrina* (*theologia revelata*) inasmuch as they are already related implicitly to the same formal object *of knowledge*, in this case God. Reciprocally, therefore, every natural knowledge becomes *ipso facto* potentially subject to Revelation, as a revealed thing that does not know itself as such, in short as an *anonymous revelation* [un *révélé anonyme*]. Certainly, one can understand this *revelabile* as a "virtual revelation," as a "human learning, taken up by theology for its own ends,"[30] or indeed a properly theological requirement, if one accepts that "philosophy claims many things as its proper object which secretly cross over into the realm of theology."[31] Nevertheless the concern here is still a knowledge, through theological if not strictly philosophical interpretation. Between the *demonstrabilia* and the *revelata*, the *revelabile* would assure a continuity, or even an *epistemological* univocity.

The Gap

So, once again, we cannot avoid asking what *scientia* means here, insofar as it is assumed to be common to these two domains and applied to revealed theology on the model of philosophical theology. The difficulty emerges clearly in a number of texts, for example in the opening of Book IV of the *Summa contra Gentiles*. Here Thomas Aquinas distinguishes no longer two, but three sciences or, more prudently, three possible ways of knowing God. (a) First there is the knowledge by *lumen rationis*, which remains weak (*debilis*) because it depends on the always confused sensations and can only *climb* from creatures toward God ("*naturalis ratio per creaturas in Dei cognitionem ascendit*"), partially and obscurely; we recognize here the *theologia philosophica*. (b) Then comes revealed knowledge, which proceeds from hearing ("*fides ex auditu*," Romans 10:17) and elicits faith: it *descends* from God ("*fidei vero cognitio a Deo in nos e converso divina revelatione descendit*"), but it remains unintelligible ("*revelantur et tamen non intelligantur*") to philosophical reason in the strict sense and therefore rests only on the accepted authority of the Scriptures ("*auctoritate sacrae Scripturae, non autem ratione naturali*"). (c) Finally, and above all, there is knowledge through the vision (*intuitus*) of the blessed ("*non sicut credita, sed sicut visa*"), which prevails over the first two.[32] It is possible that the juxtaposition of these three attitudes, so heterogeneous in principle, holds together only through their forced assimilation to one and the same epistemological model: in all cases, the question would be simply that of knowing, certainly to various degrees, as if, even in the final beatitude, our relation to God played out *first of all* in the more or less exact, more or less evident, more or less clear and distinct knowledge that we would, or would not, have of him.

And Thomas Aquinas himself recognizes that such an equivocity of the modes of knowledge of God cannot, without other precautions, result in the univocity of the divine science.[33] If it is necessary to allow at least *two* definitions of science ("*duplex est scientiarum genus*"), and if the first must be valid for all sciences whose subject is accessible to us, and therefore not for God as such ("*Omnis enim scientia procedit ex principiis per se notis. Sed sacra doctrina procedit ex articulis fidei*"), one can apply the *quasi* subalternation of *theologia philosophiae* to *theologia sacrae doctrinae* only to the second meaning of the term science: that of a *sacra doctrina* itself subordinated to the science of the blessed ("*ex principiis superioris scientiae, quae Dei et beatorum propria est, derivata*"). Thus there would be not just one, but in fact two subalternations among the sciences about God: the subalternation of *theologia philosophiae* to *theologia sacrae doctrinae*, and then and above all the subalternation of the knowledge of faith (Revelation by the Scriptures, *theologia sacrae Scripturae*, which believes without understanding) to *scientia Dei et beatorum*. The science of the blessed, and it alone, sees (*intuitus*) in God the first principles that make of it, at last, an authentic *scientia Dei* ("*quae scilicet est scientia Dei et beatorum*—namely, the science of God and the blessed"). This modification does not signal any failure of Thomas Aquinas's initial argument, but confirms the difficulty of the thing itself, which Saint Thomas detects with his typical rigor, and which here must be firmly taken into account: what makes revealed theology possibly a science consists in the final analysis not only in its overdetermining the natural knowledge (philosophical, through human reason) of God, but above all in its subordinating itself to *scientia beatorum*.[34] From this there arises an inevitable interrogation: when we, *in via*, here and now, try to develop the *theologia sacrae doctrinae* that God reveals to us in his Word, we precisely do *not* have access to the "science of the blessed," which is by definition still to come, eschatologically; *our* revealed theology, then, cannot have access to the principles that alone would make it a science. Thus it does not have the status of a rigorous science.

Once again, this conclusion does not disqualify the Thomistic argumentation; rather, it perfectly displays what is at stake in it. This stake can be formulated, at this point, in the following question: Can, and *must*, Revelation, understood according to its unquestionable features—proceeding, mediately or immediately, from the Word of God, particularly as transmitted by the Scriptures (*sacra doctrina, sacra Scriptura*)—lay claim to the status of a science? Thomas Aquinas claims it de jure, but on one condition (subordination to the *scientia Dei et beatorum*) that is de facto impossible to satisfy here and now, *in via*. Perhaps we should instead consider that Thomas Aquinas does not decide the question of theology as science because he understands it, in the final instance and as is appropriate, starting from the *scientia beatorum*, and thus eschatologically. But, even with this prudent reserve, he only succeeds in bringing the difficulty fully to light. In this case, he leads us to choose between two possible answers to the one difficulty: that of validating the *epistemological* interpretation of Revelation, or that of challenging it. We will begin by challenging it (chapters 4–6). Afterward, there will remain the charge of assigning to Revelation a more fitting understanding—that is, one that is more powerful, because *non-epistemological* (chapters 8–10).

FOUR

Suárez and the Sufficiency of the Proposition

The innovations and the hesitations, or even the ambiguities of the doctrine of Saint Thomas on Revelation, testified at the very least to a clear consciousness of the difficulty of defining the concept. In his case, where genius is allied with holiness, even audacious decisions that are sometimes in outright rupture with the entire previous tradition (on the divine names, for example) do not compromise the balance of the theological edifice. But "unfortunately, St. Thomas did not then command the attention he has as a doctor of Catholic theology in modern times; apart from his own school, . . . his following was negligeable."[1] Rather than debating, much less challenging, the epistemological interpretation of Revelation, the evolution of theology has, for a time at least, validated and radicalized it by pushing it to its ultimate consequence, under the figure of a propositional theory of revealed truths, where the "object of *sacra doctrina* risks becoming no longer essentially religious things, but the more or less rational propositions."[2] This path could be imposed as self-evident only because it appeared from the outset as the most rational, or at least the most coherent. But Christian theology only reaches and proves its rationality by facing paradoxes that at the same time make it more difficult and more powerful; in contrast, logic that is too direct and evidence that is too clear often lead to the ruin of faith and the absurdity of doctrine. Experience proves this: heresies are only ever born from very logical, almost obvious solutions supplied for the inevitable paradoxes of Revelation, conciliations that are diplomatic, or

49

even piously pastoral, between what God gives to be thought and what the ideologies and cultures of a time allow (or rather forbid) to conceive of them. This is how the epistemological interpretation of Revelation leads to its assimilation to a science, and this assimilation identifies it with a knowledge that is fundamentally and first of all theoretical. Among a thousand examples, we can recall one, Hermann Dieckmann, who without embarrassment argued that "truths are the object [of Revelation], that is to say, it concerns the order of intellectual knowledge; but its finality is religious."[3] One sees, however, the patent difficulty in this statement: How can a purely theoretical object have a religious finality, how can the transition from one domain to the other be accomplished? If one responds that "this manifestation of the divine mind is by its very nature *intellectual* and conceptual, having truths for its object, and man can perceive it only through his understanding,"[4] the difficulty increases: Is the *mens divina* defined *truly* by an intellectual and even conceptual nature? Does it consist *first* in truths, and truths such that the finite understanding of man can perceive them? Should we not reverse the terms and say, since the *mens divina* proposes and pronounces truths that *do not* come under (or not only, and not at first) an intellectual or conceptual nature, these truths therefore cannot be perceived simply by a finite understanding, appropriate to the truths of objects? If one truly holds to defining Revelation as beginning from God conceived as an "efficient cause" (which is debated), is it necessary that man as "receiver" (also debated) receive it as a spoken word (*locutio*), a knowledge (*cognitio*) that is understood (*intellectio*), or is Revelation instead about an event of another order, and a manifestation of an entirely different scope? While Saint Thomas distinguished two forms of *scientia divina* (*scientia quam Philosophi prosequuntur* and *theologia sacrae Scripturae*), or even three (adding *scientia beatorum* through direct vision), thus maintaining the epistemological interpretation in a strict equivocity, the modern drift, seemingly Thomistic but in fact anti-Thomas, confines itself to a unique meaning of knowledge, not only purely "intellectual, *intellectualis*" and "theoretical, *theoretica*," but "scientific, *scientifica*" in the sense understood by the "*subjectum recipiens*"[5] of *the* science of the moderns. This univocal flattening of the modes of *scientia divina* radicalizes the epistemological interpretation to the point of reducing Revelation to a set of propositional statements.

A Science without Faith

This late and properly speaking senseless result nevertheless could present itself as obvious only because it concluded an already long-standing and well-established drift. If the epistemological interpretation of Revelation understood it as a knowledge worthy of the title of science, it still had to be determined how to understand this title, for the claim was to apply it to nothing less than Revelation. Suárez responded to this question in an exemplary and apparently obvious manner: "If someone begins by asking what we understand by the name of 'Revelation,' I respond in one word: every *sufficient proposition of faith*, whether it be made only inwardly or by exterior preaching. In order to make this better understood, I note that two things are necessary to the knowledge of faith: one is the apprehension (*apprehensio*) of the things to believe in as much as they are proposed to man as statements said by God and, therefore, credible following the divine testimony; the other is the assent (*assentio*) given to the things thus proposed, assent in which faith properly consists."[6] This distinction can certainly be conceived: if Revelation has the rank of science, it is indeed necessary that it apprehend statements, propositions on "things," if they are to be believed. But it must also surprise us: For if faith properly termed is located in assent alone, must we infer that it does not concern the apprehension itself of the "things to believe"? And in this case, would the sufficient proposition dubbed *of faith* not be accomplished precisely as an apprehended proposition *without faith*?

Before deciding this point, let us elucidate the thesis under discussion. In the situation where there is Revelation, a man could refuse consent to the revealed truth and therefore not know it, while indeed apprehending it, exactly like one who, "hearing it said, in astronomy, that the stars are all alike without consenting (*non assentit*), and without judging whether or not they are so, and thus without understanding, apprehends only (*tantum apprehendit*), and hears what is affirmed and said."[7] Once again, the situation of Revelation is explained by assimilation to the epistemological situation of the sciences, such that philosophical rationality defines them: in astronomy (one of the applied mathematics of Aristotle), one can apprehend (a statement obtained by hearsay and thus truly understood) without giving one's assent. But does what holds here and in all the other sciences of natural reason also hold for a proposition of *faith*, even one that is sufficient? Supposing that it has the rank of science, does Revelation come under the same and univocal definition of knowledge as all the other sciences? Do faith and its assent add themselves, as if from the outside, to apprehension, or, on the contrary, does apprehension *already* imply, straightaway and by itself, an assent? Does the faith of assent come after apprehension (in order to confirm or invalidate it), or instead does it come *with* apprehension, in order to make it possible? In short, is it necessary to see in order to believe, or believe in order to see?

Suárez's decision leaves no doubt: there can always be an *apprehensio* of the revealed proposition without any *assentio* of faith. To support this rather strange thesis (a purely intellectual and *in via* grasp of the revealed, but without faith) he draws on the most extreme *opposite* case, that of the intuitive science of the blessed (*beati*): "a first preacher of the faith can be taught by God an infused and blessed science (*per scientiam infusam vel beatam*), yet it is not necessary that the proper object of faith, as such, be proposed to anyone immediately by God, other than as an *object of science and vision* (*objectum scientiae vel visionis*)."[8] To be sure, it can't be contested that the blessed no longer have to believe in order to know the revealed (if only on the authority of 1 Corinthians 13:12); but how can their situation (a direct vision of God) shed light on ours, when we remain *in via*? Without lingering over this incoherence, Suárez proceeds to his conclusion: "the name of Revelation signifies, however (*interdum*), the only sufficient proposition of the revealed object (*solam objecti revelati sufficientem propositionem*), whether he to whom such a revelation was made believes it, or not (*sive credatur ab eo, cui fit talis revelatio, sive non*)."[9] In order for the sufficient proposition to finally include assent it will be necessary to add to it a supernatural grace from God (faith); nevertheless, in itself, the *propositio sufficiens* comes to suffice.[10] So, then, the apprehension of the revealed, which is possible without faith, enters under natural reason, while assent comes under grace because it presupposes faith.

Moreover, one can arrive at the same result with other arguments. For instance, one can distinguish the "conclusion of faith"—which starts from a statement of faith in order to draw a conclusion (all the baptized are justified, therefore this baptized child is justified)—from the theological conclusion, which starts from a statement of reason in order to draw a conclusion (all men laugh, therefore Christ laughed).[11] In this case, "I assure that every theological assent, self-grounded in a discursive reasoning as the proper reason of assent, is not only distinct from faith, but natural in substance, and that consequently its certitude does not exceed the natural certitude of the principle upon which it depends"; and therefore that "its assent is of a different species from the assent of faith."[12] Not only does theological assent not require faith, but one can even go so far as to conclude that, when it remains mediate (by passing through a teaching), Revelation does not yet attain the assent of faith, but only theological assent: "The merely virtual and mediate revelation does not suffice for the formal object of faith, and consequently the assent founded on it by the help of some principle of natural evidence does not suffice either for the proper assent of faith, but only for theological assent (*sed tantum ad theologicum*)."[13] Literally, what reveals itself (mediately, to be sure, but what revelation is not mediated?) is summed up in a proposition evident to reason, a statement of "science,"[14] and, more radically, it does not come under faith, but theology—what reveals itself *comes under theology, precisely as it does not require faith* in order to be received, and does not reach faith either.

But, one might ask, what authority supports the claim to a "theological assent" if it is distinguished from and dispenses with faith? What validity should we grant to the "theological" proposition if it precedes and conditions the act of faith, since the very object of faith "in itself is not seen"?[15] In fact, in "theological" teaching, where theology as science is reduced to a set of ("sufficient") propositions, faith becomes optional for the teacher as well as for the student. For the teacher a permanent *habitus* of faith is not required; all that is required is that, at a given and actual (*actualiter*) moment, he transmit the proposition as coming from God.[16] As for the student, he is not yet held to believe, but he can expect that the proposition will appear credible to him, and thus that it will be communicated to him without and before any revelation or assent of faith. "Wherefore I say that the evidence of credibility comes not from the light of faith, as from a *habitus* eliciting this evident judgment.... This credibility is not revealed by God, but is drawn from signs known through experience; nor is it dark but bright; therefore it does not come from the formal object of faith."[17] Surprising reversals: here credibility precedes faith and Revelation leaves faith in the darkness, while the credibility of the proposition is already clear. In short, Revelation obscures for faith what credibility illuminates without faith in the propositional statement. And Suárez does not hesitate to draw the ultimate consequences from this reasoning: "The general answer is, therefore, that the evidence of credibility is sufficient, which can be found in both the external proposition and the purely internal one."[18] In this way credibility requires and allows belief in the proposition of faith *before* the faith that God gives plays a role, because the object of the "theological" proposition (that is, without faith) must and can be conceived rationally, like every other object of human science, or even better. By assuring credibility, the sufficient proposition becomes the *quasi*-sufficient reason of faith: "while we cannot always give proper reasons for the things that we believe, we can nevertheless give a sufficient reason why we believe—*posse nihilominus sufficientem rationem reddere cur credamus.*"[19]

Why does Suárez risk so openly contradicting the principle that Saint Augustine had read in Isaiah, "If you do not believe, you will not understand (*nisi credideritis, non intelligetis*)"? An irenic interpretation will say that what is involved is a widening of the *ex opere operato* beyond the pastoral domain of the sacraments to the domain of theory: just as a sacrament remains valid even when distributed by an unworthy minister, so a theological teaching can remain correct despite the unbelief of the professor. This analogy, however, does not hold, precisely because the sacrament has as its function the transmission of a grace that the minister cannot compromise since he does not control it in any way, while the unbelieving teacher is supposed to transmit the *propositio sufficiens* precisely without (the) grace (of faith) by dispensing himself of any sanctifying intention. We must then move on to the strict interpretation: the doctrine of the *propositio sufficiens* aims only at making the content of Revelation independent enough from the assent of faith so that it may be assimilated to a statement of *scientia*. To make the content of Revelation an objective proposition means first to make of Revelation a knowable content, a statement endowed with meaning, and then to reduce it to a proposition stating an object available for knowledge. In this way the epistemological interpretation of Revelation is accomplished through the reduction of Revelation to a set of sufficient propositions. But sufficient for what? Sufficient to satisfy the criteria of *scientia*, sufficient for the sufficiency of the knowledge of objects. Through a stupefying reversal of the Thomist position (but demonstrating that this position *could* lead to such a result, clearly against the intention of Thomas Aquinas himself), Suárez tends to render the revealed independent of the *scientia beatorum*, precisely in order to assure it a status as a *sufficient* proposition in a science. Establishing *scientific sufficiency* in theology effectively imposes the decoupling of Revelation from faith (as confirmed by the scholarly division between the treatise *de revelatione* and the treatise *de fide*). Going forward, one can say, quite literally, that revelation is summed up, so to speak, as a piece of information—"*Revelatio autem est quasi informatio.*"[20] Thus everything is in place for Revelation to make information known about God without this "science" owing anything to the science of the blessed, which is to say, to the vision of God in God.

A Theology without Faith

But Suárez does not end up at this result alone, or separately; on the contrary he concludes an evolution among the majority of scholastic thinkers after Saint Thomas Aquinas. Without entering into a detailed history of this drift, let it be enough to give an example, significant but rather banal, from Ockham. In the opening of his *Commentary on the Sentences*, he establishes the scientific features of *theologia* (for, despite Saint Bernard, usage has henceforth established this innovation of Abelard's) by breaking with the subalternation of *sacra doctrina* to *scientia beatorum*: "It is childish to say that I know the conclusions of theology, because God knows the principles in which I believe, because he reveals them to me."[21] Thus, not only is the beatific vision no longer required to make of *theologia* a science, but, no sooner has this first bond been loosed than a second is undone: faith is not required, either. "Aside from this *habitus* [namely, acquired faith], it is a fact that, for the majority, the one who studies in theology, whether he is a believer or a heretic, or even an unbeliever (*sive sit fidelis, sive haereticus, sive infidelis*), acquires all the scientific dispositions (*habitus*) that can be acquired in other sciences.... With regard to them all... any student in theology can acquire the *habitus* of apprehension."[22] Teaching, preaching, strengthening others in the faith, and so on—all of these can be gained by virtue of exercise without requiring faith, and without the least *habitus* of adhesion, but instead through a simple *habitus* of acquisition, for example through a "*habitus* [of declaration], which makes the understanding imagine something much better without requiring any attachment."[23] Faith makes no difference in the practice of theological teaching (revealed *sacra doctrina*), since "every *habitus* acquired naturally that a believer could have, an unbeliever could have as well."[24] Ockham even emphasizes that, if such were not the case—if it were truly necessary to believe in order to teach theology, if it were not enough to be well "trained in theology, *exercitatus in theologia*"—then "the theologian [that is, of the university, by profession] would not have a better *habitus* than that of a little old lady [that is, an ignorant old woman] (*vetula*)," which, he adds with as much naïveté as clericalism, "would not seem fitting, *videtur inconveniens*."²⁵ Theology, in wanting to constitute itself as a science among the sciences, depends from that point forward no longer on *sacra doctrina*, nor *scientia beatorum*, but on itself, in this case on chairs of university theology. We know where that has led modern theology. And monastic wisdom had denounced this drift in advance: "Many people of this sort know many things about God, or study in order to know them; whether they know them simply because curiosity pushes them, or they imagine themselves knowing, or they know, it is their own glory that they seek, and not God's."²⁶ As if the professor, unbeliever in theology or unbeliever plain and simple, were not also (and above all) seeking his own scholarly glory!

The grip of this interpretation of Revelation as *science* leads not only to abstracting from Revelation a revealed *statement*, understood as a *propositio sufficiens*, and therefore independent of the *habitus* of attachment, or in short, faith; it also leads above all to bringing this now informational Revelation closer to natural knowledge through mere reason, precisely through their common trait of "science," so that the dependance between them is reversed, or at least could be. Following the same reasoning that strives to enforce the concept of *propositio sufficiens*, Suárez suggests that the natural knowledge of God, far from remaining weak and insufficient (according to the explicit position of Thomas Aquinas), could on the contrary ground supernatural knowledge (termed revealed), and therefore find itself, if not revealed, to be at least an integral part of Revelation as its condition of possibility: "From which it follows that, while these things may be known naturally about God, nevertheless, because they are *like the ground* for those that are known supernaturally (*veluti fundamenta eorum quae supernaturaliter cognoscuntur*), it was thus necessary that *they also* were known and revealed in a supernatural manner (*illa etiam supernaturali modo cognosci et revelari*), because supernatural faith cannot ground itself according to the judgment and the certitude of natural knowledge."²⁷ The argument seems completely made up: it continues, of course, the role Thomas Aquinas assigned to Revelation, that of confirming natural knowledge of God; but this time, it is on a pretext contrary to Thomas Aquinas, that the natural forms of knowledge would serve as *ground* to the supernatural forms of knowledge. The intention is clear: if both the natural and supernatural forms of knowledge overlap, this is not (or at least not initially) because revealed knowledge would reinforce and secure natural knowledge, which is always incomplete and mixed with error, but rather the reverse: because, first of all, natural knowledge serves as a ground (*fundamenta, fundari*) for revealed knowledge, and next because revealed knowledge itself remains incapable of justifying itself according to the criteria of natural science (certitude and judgment); so much so that its epistemological deficiency must be compensated for by the epistemological sufficiency of natural science. This stupefying reversal of the traditional position (or at least that of Thomas himself), which establishes natural knowledge as ground for supernatural knowledge, nevertheless should not be surprising: it simply and logically results from the interpretation of Revelation as a science, and thus as propositional, an interpretation that must subject it to the characteristics and criteria of the only science that is accessible and definable for us: the science of natural reason.

The logical and almost inevitable development of this situation will be traced by John Locke (see below, chapter 6). If knowledge through natural reason and knowledge through Revelation can sometimes, or even often, speak "about the same things, *de eisdem rebus*," should not the relation of subalternation between them be reversed? Evidently, everything depends on the identity of these "same things." Thomas Aquinas (and his successors, even the unfaithful ones) understood by the "same things" statements concerning at least indirect knowledge of God (*revelabilia*). Locke understands them in a completely opposed way, as rational truths that God would have rendered accessible by Revelation; therefore, the subalternation is turned into subordination, to the benefit of knowledge by pure reason:

So GOD might, by Revelation, discover the Truth of any Proposition in *Euclid*; as well as Men, by the natural use of their Faculties, come to make the discovery themselves. In all Things of this Kind, there is little need or use of *Revelation*, GOD having furnished us with natural, and surer means to arrive at the Knowledge of them. For whatsoever Truth we come to the clear discovery of, from the Knowledge and Contemplation of our own *Ideas*, will always be certainer to us, than those which are conveyed to us by *Traditional Revelation*. For the Knowledge, we have, that this *Revelation* came at first from God, can never be so sure, as the Knowledge we have from the clear and distinct Perception of the Agreement, or Disagreement of our own *Ideas*, *v.g.* If it were revealed some Ages since, That the three Angles of a Triangle were equal to two right ones, I might assent to the Truth of that Proposition, upon the Credit of the Tradition, that it was revealed: But that would never amount to so great a Certainty, as the Knowledge of it, upon the comparing and measuring my own *Ideas* of two right Angles, and the three Angles of a Triangle.[28]

As strange as the hypothesis appears that Revelation might serve for the learning of Euclid's *Elements* (in a way the extreme opposite of the path followed by the young Pascal), and however absurd the result (God would be a bad professor, teaching the theorems without explaining the demonstrations), the consequence is nonetheless flawless: if Revelation undergoes an epistemological interpretation, it will be subjected to epistemological criteria (certitude, verification, etc.), and it will lose its supposed priority among the sciences.

Overturning Subalternation into Subordination

But in fact Suárez himself had already advanced far in this direction, when he overturned the whole relation between theology and philosophy, which he understood from that point forward very much explicitly as a *metaphysica* (a term nearly unknown to Thomas Aquinas).[29] On this subject, the rather solemn prologue to the *Disputationes Metaphysicae* leaves no doubts about the radicality of his thesis. Suárez sets it out in three stages. (a) First, the "divine and supernatural theology, while it relies (*nitatur*) on principles revealed by God and in the divine light, because it is perfected through human discursivity and reasoning, also receives the aid (*etiam . . . juvatur*) of truths known by the natural light and, in order successfully to carry out its reasonings and shed light on the divine truths, it makes use of them (*utitur*) as its means and, so to speak, as its instruments"; in other words, theology depends as much on natural knowledge as it does on supernatural knowledge, on reason as much as on Revelation. Nevertheless, one cannot understand this thesis as the banal observation that the theologian, even when working on the basis of Revelation, reasons, argues, and thus follows the rules of logic and of common philosophy. This is because, second, (b): going forward, natural science determines directly, under the name of *metaphysics*, the theological discussion: "in the discussion of the divine mysteries there arise these *metaphysical dogmas*, without the knowledge and intelligence of which it is *hardly, or not at all, possible* (*vix, aut ne vix quidem*) to treat these higher mysteries in a suitable manner." The mixture (*admiscere*) of theology and metaphysics therefore cannot, indeed must not be avoided; and it is no longer logic, grammar, or rhetoric that is at issue, but *metaphysical dogmas*, whose canonical formulas (univocal concept of being, principle of identity, principle of causality, division of being into finite and infinite, doctrine of the analogy of being, etc.) will be established by the *Disputationes Metaphysicae* in great style and for at least two centuries. Third (c), it becomes therefore imperative that we then suppose this "mixture" as a cohesion, already in the form of what will soon be called a system: "In this way, these metaphysical principles and truths (*haec principia et veritates metaphysicae*) form a whole so coherent (*cohaerent*) with the theological conclusions and demonstrations that to do away with the science and the perfect knowledge of the former necessarily also involves the complete ruin of the science of the latter."[30] The conclusion, then, stands out clearly: without metaphysics, *revealed* theology would lose its grounds and its principles. In fact and in principle, *metaphysica* imposes its epistemological demands on theology, which owes to Revelation nothing more than some of its informative content (some *propositiones sufficientes*), and not its procedures or its proper logic.

Thus ensue consequences whose importance should not be underestimated, even though they have become so evident that we hardly notice them and, far from being scandalized, accept them almost as if they went without saying. To be sure, the knowledge of God implies the knowledge of his reality and begins with it, for how could I encounter, experience, and love another, *a fortiori* God, without presuming that he indeed belongs to that which seems real to me, and therefore without assuring myself of this reality? But it is not self-evident that this assurance must pass through the gauntlet of a demonstration of the existence of God. And this is so for at least two uncontestable reasons. First: because existence is only a recent concept, obtained through the division (itself highly problematic) of *ousia* into essence and existence; Descartes was able to claim this division as "known to all, *omnibus nota*,"[31] but this is not the case, and it probably comes to him only from Suárez. But there is more: this existence, derived from *ousia* and thus the beingness of the being, presupposes a concept of being; *metaphysica* understands this *conceptus entis* as the primary concept, universal and univocal; it owes this character as ground to the fact of accepting no determination and remaining entirely abstract and undefined; whence an inevitable question: Can such a concept be applied, even provisionally and in the initial stages, to God? Did not Thomas Aquinas, with perfect lucidity, exclude God from the *ens commune* and explain that one can qualify God with the title of *ipsum esse* only by recognizing that this *actus essendi* remains for us, as such, "utterly unknown, *penitus ignotum*"?[32] Before wanting to assign to God being and above all the existence proper to beings, it is necessary to be sure that they concern him: Do being, beings, and existence have the requisite dignity to concern God? Do they offer enough divinity to be fitting to God? Everything and almost anything (the living and cadavers, concepts and images, stars and stones, gods and demons, and above all, today, garbage) falls under the determination of being or of potential for being, and thus of being a being; but does this determination extend so evidently to God, and above all to God as Christians and others consider him, as creator of all things (of every being) *ex nihilo*? Might it not be that God surpasses what beings, the being of beings, and being pure and simple can conceive and qualify? Neither Saint Augustine, nor Denys the Areopagite, nor John Scotus Eriugena, nor Saint Bonaventure considered being as a primary divine name. Who will contest philosophy's right, above all in its metaphysical figure, to do as even Hegel did, and begin with being and beings? But that Revelation must likewise pass through this prerequisite and make of it one of its *præambula fidei*—who will accept such a requirement without debate?

"*Ratio metaphysica revelationis*"[33]

From this there arises a second set of questions. We hope and think that the knowledge of God through Revelation, in whatever manner one intends it (and we cannot, at this stage, say any more than this), can and must give us an assurance of God and of ourselves; but this does not mean that we can prove it by necessary reasons. And this is so for two indisputable reasons. First, every demonstration that we could make of this knowledge would in every case presume the necessities of our logic; these necessities follow from the finitude of our understanding, a finitude that permits only this logic of ours to state rules, to exercise constraints, and thus to demonstrate propositions from time to time; in order to do precisely that, it must admit at least two intangible limits. First, we do not know how to demonstrate an existence, we can only observe it, like a position outside of logical thought itself (Kant established this); this holds for the possible existence of God, which is as undemonstrable through reasoning as is the existence of whatever may *be*, but *not more undemonstrable*. Second: if it is indeed God at issue when we say or think "God," his concept comprehends that we cannot comprehend him; God remains incomprehensible by definition, for, if I who am finite comprehended him, what I comprehend would not be him, who is by definition outside of all definition and infinitely incomprehensible.[34] Furthermore, if, for example, in order to demonstrate his existence I wanted to proceed *a priori*, by pure concepts (without taking account of the Kantian prohibition), I should submit the concept of God (infinite, incomprehensible) to the rules, the operations, and the principles of my logic (finite, comprehensible), which would result in an absurdity. It is probably not by chance that, before the constitution of *metaphysica*, neither the *argumentum* of Saint Anselm nor the *viae* of Saint Thomas were presented as logically binding proofs of the existence of God. And it is not by chance either if Descartes, probably the first to have undertaken the demonstration by pure reason of the existence of God (applying in Suárezian terms what seemed to him to be the program for "Christian philosophers" fixed by the Lateran Council),[35] was not able to succeed by a single proof, but rather three different ones, which do not overlap or agree with one another, but which define in advance all the drifts and impasses that subsequent metaphysics will explore in its effort to integrate God into the constitution of its system.[36] Once again, we ask: Who will contest the right of philosophy, above all its metaphysical figure, to be able, from its point of view, to attempt to integrate even God into its logic? But that Revelation must likewise pass through this prerequisite logic and make it one of its *præambula fidei*—who will accept such a requirement without examination?[37]

There remains a second temptation, even more fearsome because it seems to be a response to the first. It consists in transferring the weight and the authority of the *propositio sufficiens* of natural knowledge onto supernatural knowledge, of philosophy and its *scientia* onto *sacra doctrina*, understood as *Sacra Scriptura*.[38] If we must have a *propositio sufficiens*, it would be best if it came to us from the Scriptures, the original form of Revelation. Such was the choice of the Reformation at its beginnings, if not in its results; the supposedly absolute primacy of *sola Scriptura*, as untenable as it very quickly became, consisted in reversing the ground from *metaphysica* (in fact, from the *scolastico more* philosophy) to the biblical text, but in the process the text itself inevitably became in its letter, a store of propositions. The scriptural fundamentalism that immediately followed (and which continues to reappear in our days) constitutes only an inversion or a displacement of the epistemological interpretation of Revelation, passing from the *propositio sufficiens* (in the *scientia* of natural reason) to the sufficiency of Scripture (in literalism or biblicism).[39] But to move beyond the temptation of a *propositio sufficiens* it is not enough to pass from one term (natural knowledge) to another (supernatural knowledge). In the end, we must surpass the decision made in favor of an epistemological interpretation of Revelation.

FIVE

The Magisterium's Reserve

Faced with this orientation, or rather this fundamental drift of the entirety of Christian theology (for here the Reformers, especially the Calvinists, did not remain behind the Catholic evolution for long, participating in a common propositional practice of polemics), the resistance or at least the prudent reticence of the Roman magisterium stands out all the more.

An Absence

We can notice to begin with that the term *revelatio* itself remains absent from the texts of the Council of Trent: the session of 1546, when it treats of the relation between tradition(s) and Scripture(s), refers only to the "purity of the gospels, *puritas ipsa Evangelii*," without resorting to the term "Revelation."[1] One notes above all that it is only in 1870, during the First Vatican Council, that this very question about the sources of faith is taken up again under the chapter title—used for the first time—*De revelatione*, in the dogmatic constitution *Dei Filius*.[2] Such a very late introduction therefore ought to be justified, which was indeed done, with an ostentatious fidelity to the thematic of Thomas Aquinas: appealing to the *Summa Theologiae* Ia, q.1, a.1, the council distinguished two modes of knowledge: one, which invokes Romans 1:20 ("*invisibilia conspiciuntur intellecta a creatura mundi per ea quae facta sunt*"), allows that "God, the beginning and end of all things, can be known with certainty from the things that were created through the natural light of human reason (*naturali humanae rationis lumine*)"; the other, relying on Hebrews 1:1–2 ("In many and various ways God spoke of old to our fathers by the prophets; but in these last days he has spoken to us by his Son"), assures that God "reveal[s] (*revelare*) himself (*se ipsum*) and the eternal decrees of his will in another and a supernatural way (*supernaturali via*)."³

Despite its simple and incontestable appearance, this dichotomy calls for several explanations. (a) To be sure, in keeping with the doctrine of Thomas Aquinas, the knowledge by *revelatio* is seen to have a double validity, with regard to the very mystery of God, but also with regard to all "things divine that of themselves are not beyond human reason (*humanae rationi per se impervia non sunt*)."⁴ And yet, at no moment is reference made to the subordination of the sciences (the subalternation of *theologia philosophica* to *sacra doctrina*), nor to the identification of natural knowledge with *philosophia* (much less with *metaphysica*), nor to the third way of the *revelabile*, nor especially to the epistemological interpretation of these two ways of knowing: to my knowledge, never is the revealed *cognitio* assimilated to a *scientia* of any sort whatsoever, much less to a *demonstratio* of any sort (one is confined to the formula "*certo cognosci posse*"). (b) Next, the *supernaturalis revelatio* appears only in order to evoke the question of the sources of faith and the relation between tradition(s) and Scripture(s), in explicit reference to the "universal belief of the Church, declared by the sacred Council of Trent."⁵ (c) Finally and above all, the sole authority admitted for this knowledge (of course never qualified as scientific) of these "true revealed things, *vera . . . revelata*" comes not from "the intrinsic truth of things . . . recognized by the natural light of reason (*intrinsecam rerum veritatem naturali rationis lumine perspectam*)," but exclusively from "the authority of God himself revelator (*ipsius Dei revelantis*)."⁶ There is no better way than through this re-centering on the biblical texts to show that Suárez's propositional drift and even the epistemological interpretation of Revelation are, if not rejected outright, at the least held to the margins. The silence here weighs heavily, and what is not said is not said. The First Vatican Council remains ostensibly withdrawn from the coming evolution of university-based neo-Thomism toward a growing propositional (and thus metaphysical) treatment of Revelation.

The Breakthrough

As we know, it is up to the Second Vatican Council to explicitly and extensively confront the doctrine of Revelation in its constitution *Dei Verbum* in 1965. We must not underestimate the authority of this text, which offers without any doubt an inarguable dogmatic contribution among others that are assumed to be more pastoral; all the more so because it commanded the attention of the Fathers throughout the whole of the Council, since its first draft, rejected in 1962, was only definitively replaced at the closure of work in 1965.[7] Now, *Dei Verbum* does not depart from the characteristic reserve of the councils of Trent and Vatican I. Nevertheless, it radically distinguishes itself from them by reversing the order of presentation of the ways of knowing God: instead of proceeding from "natural" knowledge to "supernatural" knowledge like Vatican I, it begins directly with the Revelation of God himself in person. Consequently, when it takes up (and probably closes) the debate stemming from the Reformation on the relation between Revelation by tradition (written and non-written) and the Scriptures, it radically redefines the entire concept of Revelation. Under the undeniable, albeit implicit, influence of Barth (and several others[8]), Revelation is no longer supposed to communicate above all a knowledge (much less a *scientia*), but to manifest God himself by himself: "*Placuit Deo . . . Seipsum revelare et notum facere sacramentum voluntatis suae*—God chose to reveal Himself and to make known to us the hidden purpose of his will." Or further, "*Semetipsum manifestavit*—He manifested himself" in effect through an "*oeconomia . . . gestis verbisque intrinsece inter se connexis*—plan of . . . deeds and words having an inner unity."[9] When God "appeared (ἐφανερώθη)" (Colossians 1:26, 1 Timothy 3:16), he first and exclusively manifested Himself and "the mystery of his will" (Ephesians 1:9); for Revelation's goal is not to grant us the knowledge of something other than God himself, nor simply to increase our *scientia* about God, and even less to augment our science in general. God in manifesting himself has a radically different plan: He "Himself wanted to communicate Himself to us, *Ipse nobiscum communicare voluerit*."[10] The singular, evidently non-epistemological, intention of Revelation consists in manifesting God in person. Or rather, God, in revealing himself, wants not only to make himself known, but above all to make himself *re*-cognized *as such.* Making himself known is not yet sufficient for accomplishing the "mystery" that consists in establishing, or more exactly in reestablishing in Christ a communion with men and all of his creation; making himself known does strictly speaking fulfill a condition of this plan, but it is not sufficient (chapter 12). To be sure, the manifestation allows a communication, but the communication must allow, beyond itself and the knowledge that it delivers, a communion of men with God. The communication is only accomplished in the communion. The communion implies that, as with Moses, God can "speak face to face, like a man speaks to his friend" (Exodus 33:11; see chapter 11); and thus with all men, whom, moreover, Christ henceforth "calls his friends" (John 15:15).

One might assume that the term "communication" used here by *Dei Verbum* echoes another especially precise formulation of Paul VI, found in his contemporaneous encyclical *Ecclesiam suam*: "Revelation . . . can be looked upon as a kind of colloquium (*quasi quoddam colloqium*), through which in the Incarnation and in the Gospel God's Word speaks . . . . [It is t]hat fatherly, sacred colloquium between God and man, . . . like a conversation of Christ with men (*quasi sermocinatione*)," following a verse from Baruch 3:38. Of course, the epistemological function (or propositional, if one prefers) of Revelation does not disappear, but it remains entirely subordinate to the final intention that one could call liturgical or mystagogical: establishing communion with the One who transforms us in Him: "And we all who, with unveiled face (ἀνακεκαλυμμένῳ), reflect as in a mirror the glory of the Lord, we are transformed into this same icon (κατοπριζόμενοι τὴν αὐτὴν εἰκόνα μεταμορφούμεθα), passing from glory to glory, as it is fitting to the action of the Spirit, the Lord" (2 Corinthians 3:18). It is certainly a matter of seeing what is manifested, but precisely in order to find oneself transformed, literally transfigured; and the communication of a knowledge would have no meaning or even any importance if it were not accomplished in a communion in the glory of the Spirit. Which is what Paul VI clearly pointed out: "At the same time He tells us how (*qualis*) He wishes to make himself recognized (*agnosci*): as Love pure and simple (*uti Amor plane*)."[11] For in a situation involving Revelation, knowledge always aims at recognition, and thus science is subordinated and ordered to communion.

Visible Things and the "Wrath" of God

But, one will probably object, in 1870 *Dei Filius* still maintained an order of doubled knowledge ("*duplex ordo cognitonis*")[12], and thus the distinction between a natural and a supernatural knowledge of God. In fact, these two adjectives precisely do not appear, even if, of course, the text of Romans 1:19–20 is cited: "what can be known about God is manifest to them [men], because God has made himself manifest to them. For the invisible things of God are seen, understood as they are since the creation of the world through the things made (τὰ γὰρ ἀόρατα αὐτοῦ ἀπὸ κτίσεως κόσμου τοῖς ποιήμασιν νοούμενα καθορᾶται)."[13] But—and this point changes everything—*Dei Verbum* places this text, which certainly validates the knowledge of God in his creation by "the natural light of human reason," within the Revelation (elsewhere called "supernatural") of God by himself, by first citing the canonical texts of Saint Paul on the *mystērion* of God manifested in Jesus Christ.[14] And in fact, this famous verse, deemed to establish first and paradigmatically the possibility of the *natural* knowledge of God on the basis of creation, fulfills this role well (one can neither contest this fact, nor the constant role of the verse in the theological tradition); nevertheless, it only accomplishes this by including this knowledge termed *natural* within the economy of the Revelation (*apokalypsis*) of God by himself ("supernaturally," if you will). Indeed, how can one avoid noticing that Romans 1:19–20, which we have just read, follows immediately on a double mention of the act of "revealing" (if one accepts this translation of ἀποκαλύπτειν)? "For I do not blush at the gospel. For the power of God is for the salvation of every one who has faith, to the Jew first and also to the Greek. For the justice of God *is revealed* in him (ἐν αὐτῷ ἀποκαλύπτεται) from faith toward faith, as it is written, 'The righteous shall live by faith' (Habakkuk 2:4). Indeed, the wrath of God is revealed (ἀποκαλύπτεται) from heaven against all ungodliness and injustice of men who hold the truth [prisoner] in injustice" (Romans 1:16–18). By introducing the knowledge of God through human reason (verses 19–20) only *after* and thus *within* divine Revelation (verses 16–18), *Dei Verbum* understands precisely what the evidence from the Pauline text imposes on our understanding, and what the scholastic reading missed or masked: knowledge of God on the basis of creation, even if it is exercised through the "natural light of human reason" alone, *does not precede* Revelation (thus called "supernatural"), but finds itself *already* comprised in it, as it determines and renders possible all knowledge.

It is only under this condition that the Pauline argument becomes intelligible: God reveals himself on the basis of faith (Romans 1:17); but men, who "naturally" had knowledge of this truth (verses 19–20), prove to be "without excuse" for "holding [prisoner] in injustice" (v. 18) a "truth" (v. 18) that has *already* "manifested" itself (v. 19) to them. Consequently, "the wrath of God is revealed" (v. 18) because men "knowing God did not glorify God or give thanks to him as such a God" (v. 21). In short, "the wrath of God" is revealed because the knowledge of God *already* revealed and manifested itself and is *already* refused; it is *already* refused and condemnable, precisely because it turns out to be *already* revealed. Once again, the question does not bear on the knowledge of God (which Paul takes to be established, since God "manifests himself" ever since the vision of visible nature), but on the *recognition* that befits what men know already. And the accusation against men bears on their refusal to *recognize* the one whom they know perfectly well, their refusal to glorify and to give thanks to God *as such* (θεὸν ὡς θεὸν δοξάζειν καὶ εὐχαριστεῖν). God thus reveals himself *before* knowledge in faith, and *after* knowledge in wrath, in the hypothesis—real for the pagans—that misrecognition leads to nonrecognition of this knowledge. "Natural" knowledge does not constitute the preamble to Revelation, but rather what Revelation produces, and in relation to which it unfolds its economy ("faith," "wrath"). Revelation encompasses all "natural" knowledge and, in every sense, comprehends it.[15]

The conciliar texts on the definition of Revelation thus remain as rare (in fact they appear only on two occasions, in one single century) as they are cautious (lagging far behind the theoretical discussions of university theology). We must appreciate this reserve as one case among others, if certainly remarkable, of the will of the magisterium not to transpose into the ordinary teaching of the Church the debates and quarrels of the schools. It was already like this, in the modern period, with regard to the explanation of the eucharistic sacrament (the Council of Trent did not take up Thomas's lexicon on transubstantiation), as well as and above all for the conciliation between grace and free will (the quarrel *de auxiliis*), which remains even today undecided, the very terms of the question showing their inadequacy to what was fundamentally at stake. The same is probably true today of the polemics that for a long time were burning issues and now find themselves on the way to exhaustion (like those surrounding the political engagement of Christians, the theology, or rather theologies, of liberation, or even the "traditional" character, or not, of the *ordo missae*, etc.). The real fulfillment of the mystery of Christ by the faithful is not always reflected in the discussions of the professors, and has no need of them; the life of the Church in the Spirit does not depend on what the learned can conceive of or claim to explain about it, and indeed it must not. This prudential reserve is verified in the case of the concept (if indeed one must be found) of Revelation.

Creation

Creation is known only if one succeeds in recognizing it as a Revelation. This Pauline paradox, found in Vatican II in *Dei Verbum*, will not surprise us if we think of the thesis of Étienne Gilson, who argued that the philosophical knowledge of the world has not yet succeeded in interpreting it as a creation: "No one can possibly attain to the idea of creation, or to the real distinction of essence and existence in all that is not God, as long as he admits forty-nine 'beings as being.' What Plato and Aristotle both lacked was the *Ego sum qui sum*."[16] However, the difficulty perhaps lies not so much in the conception of the divine *esse* as pure act, as in the admission of a world arising radically from God and not from itself, from its intrinsic division from itself, which allows it to manifest more than itself. And the question of this division and its origin from *elsewhere* does not initially come under the *esse*, nor under beings, nor under the question of being (in whatever way one understands it), but instead from *recognition* itself. Thomas Aquinas was not wrong when he justified creation directly through faith, thus anticipating the thesis that Gilson borrows from him: "That the world began we hold by faith alone (*sola fide tenetur*). This cannot be demonstrated by reason, but to believe it is supremely advantageous (*sed id credere maxime expedit*)."[17] How do we conceive it? The world, when it manifests itself as such (supposing one can know it strictly philosophically, or even consider it in its totality, which does not go without saying), still reveals nothing other than its own fact. Even if we suppose, following the principle of causality (or sufficient reason), that it refers back to an efficient cause (or reason) of which it would constitute the effect, it would still never reveal what plucks it out of nothing; the certain finding of the contingency and therefore dependence of all things of the world still reveals nothing, not even that the world may have the status of a creature. For the efficient cause draws its preeminence from the ambiguous privilege of being exempt from any likeness to its effect, so that the world can indeed make the greatest effect on us, without opening for us the least access to its cause, that is, without coming from *elsewhere*, nor leading us there. The world cannot reveal anything unless it appears to us as coming from elsewhere, according to the formal definition of every revelation conceived according to its phenomenality.[18] Thus the world can reveal nothing of God as long as it is not first taken into view as coming from Him, that is to say, as a revelation (*supra*, chapter 2)—only in this way does the world take on the status of creation. The world reveals itself as a creation only to the extent that it straightaway appears revealed and revealing, in the light of Revelation. The world appears as a phenomenon of creation when it happens in the brightness of Revelation. It would make sense to think here also of Rosenzweig's more radically theological paradox, that "creation" is "a becoming-manifest on the part of God," and it follows that "creation itself is *already* the first revelation." But such a first Revelation by the world assumes that the world is from the outset *already* seen as a revealing phenomenon, and thus has come from *elsewhere*, which can only be if in this world itself someone can hear the voice that reveals and saves: "He who has not yet been reached by the voice of revelation has no right to accept the idea of creation as if it were a scientific hypothesis."[19] For lack of hearing, or rather of *seeing* "the *voices* of the thunder and of the lightnings,"[20] one cannot see what is revealed, nor the Revelation of the One who reveals himself there.

Such a reticence regarding the manifestation of the world as creation must not be understood solely as caution in theorizing, resisting (despite the charms of Chateaubriand's *Le Génie du christianisme*) the disorderly pastoral zeal that would invoke the beauties of nature in order to lead us to the goodness of the creator. In the case of Revelation, this restraint must be understood above all as a principled reserve, sustained by a positive theoretical stringency. At issue is an exemplary hermeneutic circle: Revelation, even that which unfolds in the phenomenon of the revelation of the world (understood as a preeminent saturated phenomenon), reveals, as Paul pointed out, the world as a creation only because this world is *directly* received in and as a

Revelation. Here as always, the difficulty with the hermeneutic circle consists not in getting out of it (this circle is not vicious), but in entering it correctly. One gains access to Revelation only by accepting it—first by accepting that it has to do with a phenomenon of revelation that, as such, happens from *elsewhere*; and next by admitting that, as a fact from *elsewhere*, it is a Revelation that comes from God. Every attempt to approach Revelation from a univocal and thus uncritical epistemological viewpoint, that is, through reference to a science, or at minimum a knowledge whose rationality would not make at least *some* exception to the common rules of our rationality, can only be exposed to a double failure.

What Is Worthy of a Revelation?

We might begin by asking if the entire enterprise of defining Revelation as knowledge or as the source of a potential science does not amount to judging it on the basis of an interest different than its own. Would this not be to cut down Revelation to the role of a mere complement to common knowledge, awaited but lacking, to downgrade it to the undignified role of substitute for certain knowledge, to reduce it to a shortcut (or even a short circuit) to gaining fraudulent access to conclusions for demonstrations and principles we do not know, in short, to construct a machine for producing inadequate ideas (Spinoza)? Conversely, assuming that Revelation conceived in this way achieved some success, how can we avoid diagnosing it as anything other than an indiscreet curiosity regarding God, a sacrilegious intrusion? And, in the more probable case of failure, would it not disqualify itself as an illusion, or worse, an imposture, a "fanaticism" (Kant)? The Fathers critiqued this first temptation as firmly as the "philosophers," just as they fought against the second among the Gnostics. We can formulate the objection even more radically: Does God reveal himself in order to make himself known and take up a position in our rationality, gaining admittance there by claiming, at best, to merely compensate for its weaknesses? Or would he have a different intention in revealing himself? Would God have unfolded within our history the whole economy of salvation, the coming of Christ, his death and Resurrection, in order to make us know, for example, that he always thinks like a geometer, or to assure us that he respects the "laws of nature" and that he encourages the progress of morality and civilization, or merely to demonstrate to us that he too includes himself within what we understand (or believe we understand) by *existence*, etc.—or was it instead to teach us to love him and to love one another? Conceiving Revelation correctly requires we consider its motivation—and from God's own point of view. What sufficiently divine motive can justify (if this word still has meaning in such a case) God revealing himself in person? Without posing this question first and last, any inquiry on the concept of Revelation will be without sense or legitimacy.

From this follows a second point of resistance. If the definition of a possible Revelation forbids its being limited to furnishing a science or an additional knowledge without reason (or worse, *with* a sufficient reason), if Revelation must have another motive than simply making something known in general, what then is the sense in seeking to define it by concept? For the concept, whatever it may be, has precisely as its function to make us know what we can understand, possess, and produce through it. The concept forbids and is forbidden from coming to us from *elsewhere* (chapters 1–2); its entire function consists in exempting us from resorting to or even admitting the least *elsewhere*. Consequently, following a very clear logic, it would belong to the function of the quasi-concept of Revelation to be excluded from any concept. Formally speaking, the concept of Revelation is that it has none. What makes it compatible with the only notion of God that we can accept (whether we say we are believers or unbelievers makes no difference) is its irreducibility to the concept as understood by metaphysics. This *quasi*-concept of God consists in the impossibility of a concept (one that is adequate, as every concept by definition must be) for God—according to the grammatical rule that, if I understood it, it would not be him (Saint Augustine). Or again, according to this other rule, that incomprehensibility belongs to the formal definition of the infinite (Descartes). At issue here is not a contradiction but a rational requirement. Nor is it a matter of agnosticism or ineffability, since we can think about and say this paradox. But such is not yet the question here—perhaps it will come up again later. Discussing the bearing of Revelation's resistance to every concept that would claim to make it comprehensible is not yet at issue here either. First, and more modestly, we must understand how it was possible and necessary for the question of Revelation to be confronted with the authority of the concept.

On this point, we can appreciate all the more the magisterium's reserve, and even the balance of that reserve. The constitution *Dei Verbum* places the two ways of knowing God, the one previously called "natural" as well as the one consequently called "supernatural," back under the aegis of a single Revelation that encompasses both of them. In this way the opposition is disqualified between the so-called "natural" knowledge of God, on the one hand, supposedly obtained without Revelation (by pure reason and through philosophy alone), and the "supernatural" knowledge, on the other, which alone is revealed (and reserved to theology, even if sometimes without faith). This consolidation becomes possible only from the clear awareness that Revelation encompasses everything we know of God, because it consists neither solely nor initially in a supererogatory knowledge, but in the manifestation of God in himself and from himself. Only the attribution of the *elsewhere* to God reestablishes the possibility of a properly *theo*-logical understanding of Revelation. This in turn implies the destruction of the theo-*logical*, or in fact *logical*, concept that metaphysics (that is, metaphysics in the strict sense) had imposed little by little on Christian theology during modernity.

SIX

The Metaphysical Origin of the Common Concept of Revelation

The distinction between the question of Revelation and that of faith, clearly assumed in modern theology through the distinction between the two treatises *de revelatione* and *de fide*, had ensured multiple advantages for theology (or at least for the faculty of theology, under Kant's correction): claiming to set forth rational theses, intelligible in themselves (even without faith), to establish itself as a science, to be counted among the "superior faculties," to the point of claiming to reign over all the other sciences by virtue of the operation borrowed from Aristotle, the subordination (or subalternation) of the sciences. But this advantage came with a price which in the end had to be paid: the scientific character claimed by theology remained imprecise and above all dubious in its validity, since in this life the *scientia Dei et beatorum* (which alone could serve as its foundation) remained inaccessible. By consequence, the epistemological privilege of Revelation had to be assured by other means—precisely those allowed and even required by its propositional interpretation (according to the *propositio sufficiens*), that is, its foundation by the principles of *metaphysica*.

Conditions

This sets off the reversal of the situation that culminated in the properly *philosophical* formulation of the concept of Revelation. When Descartes distinguished "Revelation, which I call Theology in the strict sense," from what "is on the other hand a metaphysical question which is to be examined by human reason,"[1] he still admits that "the revealed truths . . . are beyond our understanding" because "to undertake an examination of them and succeed, I would need to have some extraordinary aid from heaven and to be more than a mere man."[2] However, this declared superiority of Revelation will soon provoke not only its marginality, but its de facto dependence on metaphysics. Thus Leibniz repeats the position of Suárez when he claims to found Revelation not on itself, but on what philosophy (in this case *metaphysica*) can secure for it by logical principles: "Christian theology . . . is founded on Revelation, which corresponds to experience; but to make it into a completed system we have also to bring in natural theology, which is derived from the axioms of eternal Reason."[3] Thus, to earn its status as a science, theology must henceforth align itself with the norms and conditions of rationality prescribed for it by philosophy, which has no doubt that it thinks "according to axioms of eternal reason."

One of the first to fix such conditions on the validity of Revelation was Herbert of Cherbury, who in 1624 dared to do so explicitly. If we admit that the ground of a revealed truth derives from the authority of the one who revealed it ("*veritatis revelatae fundamentum e revelantis auctoritate*"), he argued, then false revelations become at least possible, and we must arbitrate with great care ("*summa cautela*") between them; a task that can only be carried out on certain *conditions* that must be clearly indicated ("*Istae tamen* conditiones, *si adsint, fidem revelationi adhibere consulimus*"). These conditions require (a) that we do not prevent providence by wishes and prayers; (b) that revelation opens itself directly and from itself ("*tibi ipsi patefiat*"), without intermediary or relation to another; (c) that it teach a true and eminent good ("*bonum aliquod eximium et verum doceatur*"); and finally, (d) that the divine breath is felt ("*afflatum divini numinis sentias*"). Only once these *conditions* are met, and provided too that the given in question surpasses the reach of the human mind ("*superat captum*"), does it become licit to accept this Revelation ("*propitium numen venerare!*").[4] It goes without saying that it is nearly always impossible to satisfy all of these conditions, if only because we lack criteria for deciding for example when the "divine breath" or immediate opening occurs or not. And above all we may already suspect that such a Revelation, as submitted to the criteria of the human mind, thus regulated from the outside and in particular by the one who is supposed to receive it, is no longer a Revelation to begin with. The very imposition of conditions is already enough to compromise its logical possibility: coming from *elsewhere*.[5]

Passing to the following step was then almost inevitable: denying that some of these conditions could be met, for example the immediate opening and the sense of the "divine breath." This is what Hobbes does: "God's sensible word hath come but to few; neither hath God spoken to men by Revelation except particularly to some, and to diverse diversely; neither have any Lawes of his Kingdome beene publisht on this manner unto any people."[6] As a result, "when we believe that the Scriptures are the word of God, having no immediate revelation from God himself, our belief, faith and trust is only in the church, whose word we take, and acquiesce therein."[7] In this new system, where the condition of immediacy imposed by Cherbury disappears, Revelation is thus reduced to its strict propositional interpretation. All the more so since, of the three "ways" which can be used by the word of God (based on how it makes itself known as *rationale*, *sensibile*, or *propheticum*), two are no longer acceptable: prophecy (the only Revelation properly speaking, the *sensus supernaturalis*), because it concerns only the solitary individual and thus does not offer any collective doctrine; and faith (*fides ex auditu*), in this case the faith of the Church, because it believes without understanding and therefore remains without rational authority. Only the "voice" of pure reason (*recta ratio*) remains, which is certainly universal, but which cannot be universally imposed, because its proposition does not admit univocal content.[8] All Revelation, taken in the broad sense, is thus compromised.

Miracle and Possibility

Faced with the breakdown of the idea of Revelation as such, there remains only one path, following Locke's example: to secure it upon what is now defined under the title of *reason*—in a word, Christianity cannot hope for anything better than to be recognized for its *reasonableness*, to be admitted as rational by the self-proclaimed tribunal of *reason*. "It still belongs to *Reason* to judge of the truth of its being a Revelation."[9] The argument remains apparently respectful and theologically acceptable:

Whatever God hath revealed is certainly true: no doubt can be made of it. This is the proper object of *faith*: but whether it be a divine revelation or no, *Reason* [alone] must judge; which can never permit the mind to reject a greater evidence to embrace what is less evident, nor allow it to entertain probability in opposition to knowledge and certainty. There can be no evidence that any traditional revelation is of divine original, in the words we receive it, and in the sense we understand it, so clear and so certain as that of the principles of Reason: and therefore *nothing that is contrary to, and inconsistent with, the clear and self-evident dictates of Reason, has a right to be urged or assented to as a matter of faith, wherein Reason hath nothing to do.*[10]

Revelation therefore has no other validity (be it only propositional) than within the limits of reason and under its guarantee.

Yet several questions immediately arise. Is it so self-evident that we could ever ensure the content, even propositional, of Revelation? And what roles should we assign to hermeneutics and therefore to exegesis and ultimately to the history of philological traditions, etc.? Besides, is it self-evident that Revelation is limited to a propositional content which could be judged by "reason"—or is there more, something else which surpasses its scope? And above all, what does it mean to speak of "reason" and its "principles," what are their qualifications and limits? Such are the three blind spots—biblical science, hermeneutics, and the limits of pure reason—that condition and compromise the argument of Locke. These objections, still implicit, will appear again and again, up through Kant and Fichte, and they weigh on every modern theology.

We owe it to Hume to have tried to ground this still very vague argument by plainly asking if, once we grant that reason holds the exclusive right to judge any claim to the rank of Revelation as acceptable or not, we can fix a fundamental criterion for deciding it in all cases. We can indeed attempt a response: no claim to Revelation should include miracles, because this would be defined as "a violation of the laws of nature."[11] On principle, it would be necessary to exclude miracles and every testimony in their favor: "we may establish it as a maxim, that no human testimony can have such force as to prove a miracle, and make it a just foundation for any such system of religion."[12] If, in order to claim itself as revealed, a religion tries to make us believe in miracles, in every case it will turn out to be a sham; either because there are no miracles, in fact and literally; or because there is at least the ironic miracle that certain people believe in these alleged miracles, for in this case, to admit one miracle will require another: "whoever is moved by *Faith* to assent to it, is conscious of a continued miracle in his own person, which subverts all the principles of his understanding, and gives him a determination to believe what is most contrary to custom and experience."[13] Not only can reason judge the claim to Revelation (Locke), but it now has a criteria for excluding this claim—the impossibility of miracles (Hume). In other words, no religion can claim to be revealed, except by invoking the possibility of a miracle; but the miracle remains by principle impossible; therefore, any revealed religion proves to be impossible. The condemnation is redoubled, because it no longer relates only to the (propositional) content, but to the status and origin of Revelation.

It is easy to see the consequences of this problematic. First, the reversal of the hierarchy between supernatural knowledge (theology) and natural knowledge (philosophy) of God does not result in granting Revelation a metaphysical foundation (as Suárez and Malebranche still aimed to do); instead, it does the exact opposite, establishing its impossibility on principle (Locke and Hume). Second, theology sought to become a science by reducing Revelation to a propositional form, but this concession led to a double defeat: not only did theology fail to win the character of a science, but the epistemological interpretation of Revelation has compromised that very possibility in the face of the strict sciences. Third, the very concept of "Revelation" becomes from then on problematic, since it is primarily constructed by philosophers even more than by theologians, and by philosophers who contest, limit, or refuse on principle the slightest *elsewhere* being revealed;[14] to the point that the very term "Revelation" no longer seems more than a contradictory *artifact,* an *ad hoc* foil, raised as a specter for a phony fight. And it is astounding that serious and sincere theologians could have taken up such a devalued term as it stands in order to claim it as their prerogative.

But there is more, for the weakness of the critique reinforces the imprecision of the concept of Revelation. Indeed, Hume's argument not only failed to remedy the blind spots that hinder Locke's argument, but aggravated them; for the dogmatic definition of miracle by its impossibility presupposes what it would be necessary to establish. Indeed, it would be necessary to first know all the "laws of nature," at the very least to know universally that there are some and that they do not admit any exceptions; this claim, which only dates from Malebranche, remains at best a prolepsis that anticipates a state of the positive sciences still to come; in fact, to establish such "laws" seems, to us today, at least as random as a religion's pretension to the rank of Revelation seemed to Hume. Further, the exclusion of miracles by virtue of their impossibility in principle supposes a strong determination of impossibility, and therefore of possibility; yet, clearly, the impossible contradicts the very thing that possibility supposes—namely, that nothing can be thought (and exist) if it contradicts itself; but what is noncontradiction a law for, if not a *finite* understanding? It follows that a miracle (both its immediate relation and belief in it) only contradicts a possibility for *us*; or, what amounts to the same thing, only contradicts the "laws of nature" such as *we* know some of them and *we* imagine most of the others, which *we* do not know. We imagine the "laws of nature" more than we know them and, not knowing them all absolutely, we imagine them based on our probability. They resemble us and come from us, more than they govern us.[15]

Far from disqualifying its concept, it would be necessary to ask if this impossible *for us* does not constitute precisely the very field and the formal definition of every thinkable and *possible* Revelation. Does not the very notion of Revelation suppose this very thing—that is, it gives to thought that which, without Revelation, we could neither think nor even imagine ever being able to think? Conversely, would it still be a Revelation if it did not claim to open for us, in some way or other, that which would remain impossible to think without it? To ask it another way, is is not the case that what seems impossible *for* "reason," that is *for us* mortals, defines precisely what is designated—whether it is possible or effective is not the question here—by the concept of Revelation (see chapters 1–2)?[16] The question of Revelation is not a matter of its impossibility, because this impossibility does not disqualify its concept, but instead is precisely its very definition; it is a matter of the possibility that this impossibility *for us* remains possible *in itself*. The supposed refutation thus does not close the question of Revelation but, without even realizing it, poses it clearly. And perhaps for the first time so openly: for to define the possibility of the thinkable constitutes the initial claim of metaphysics, as the first characteristic of what its *ontologia* names, by fact of its being, the pure and empty *cogitabile*.[17] Thus, opposing Revelation to its impossibility comes down to recognizing the conflict, which is doubtless unsurmountable, between Revelation (which concerns the impossible, or does not count) and metaphysics (which only aims to fix the limits of the possible).

Kant knew it well, and took the simple precaution of specifying the rational criterion authorizing the limitation of possibility; the limits that "simple reason" imposes on biblical texts are justified because they result from the limits that pure reason imposes on itself in its theoretical exercise: one can claim to know by concepts (*a priori*) what intuition (in its forms of space and time) can give and thus validate; the limits reason applies to the epistemological (and propositional) interpretation of Revelation are only the limits it imposes on its own epistemological function. Yet this argument is immediately overturned: For if reason only legislates according to its essential finitude, and, respecting this finitude, restricts itself to knowing only *objects*, by what right can it claim to impose its limits, by rights the simple norms of its finitude, on that which, by principle, aims to transgress finitude by the intervention of the infinite and which could never be reduced to the rank of an *object*? The *Aufklärung* raised this debate to the level of the concept when J. G. Fichte formulated his critique of every Revelation (*Versuch einer Kritik aller Offenbarung*, 1793), anticipating by one year the limitation of religion (*Religion innerhalb der Grenzen der bloßen Vernunft*), which Kant was to draw out of his own critique of pure reason. It prevailed, since the most conservative adherents of Revelation themselves came to invoke reason as a "natural revelation." And it prevailed in a number of ways that it is appropriate to reconstitute, if only briefly, as many variations of the same critique (in Kant's sense), deployed under different faculties or modes of the *res cogitans* (in Descartes's sense) in which reason, taken in its metaphysical sense, recognized itself: intuition (*sensus*), imagination, will, and understanding (concept). We will thus see more clearly how these modes of thought, each in its own way, makes it possible to censure, close off, and finally forbid any *theological* understanding of something like Revelation. In other words, we will see what Revelation becomes when it is defined starting from the *cogitatio* without an *elsewhere*.

According to Intuition

The first approach finds its paradigm in Schleiermacher, as he tries to measure Revelation starting from intuition, that is, from *sensus*, from sentiment or feeling. His starting point is identified without any ambiguity: it is "[t]o be gripped by awe and faith in the invisible," whatever it may be.[18] Or again, "Everything that exists is necessary for religion, and everything that can be is for it a true indispensable image of the infinite (*ein wahres unentbehrliches Bild des Unendlichen*)."[19] For "religion's essence is neither thinking nor acting, but intuition (*Anschauung*) and feeling. It wishes to intuit (*anschauen*) the universe."[20] Whatever the content or goal (the infinite in the

The Metaphysical Origin of the Common Concept of Revelation 81

finite, totality, freedom, the realism of the world, etc.), it is always attained or at least aimed at by intuition. "Intuiting (*anschauen*) the universe . . . this is the hinge of my whole speech; it is the highest and most universal formula of religion."[21] Of course, the prevalence of intuition can be balanced by the role of feeling: "Intuition without feeling is nothing . . . feeling without intuition is also nothing"[22]; but, aside from the fact that feeling is hardly opposed to intuition, whose primacy is not called into question, it in no way prohibits the very concept of Revelation as a whole from being led back to intuition alone. "What is revelation (*Offenbarung*)? Every original and new intuition of the universe is one."[23] In other words, Revelation comes down to intuition, and not the other way around. It is not simply a difference of words, because the two concepts do not rest on the same center: intuition, as a faculty, refers to man, while Revelation (or religion understood *stricto sensu*, see chapter 2) comes from God. This is in fact a radical reversal: Revelation, understood as intuition, becomes more an effect of man than a manifestation of God. And so, quite logically, Schleiermacher *veils* God by *veiling* him through man. He nevertheless sees the danger of this thesis: "most" of his readers could anticipate Feuerbach by already concluding that "God is obviously (*offenbar*) nothing more than the genius of humanity. Men are the prototype of their God (*Urbild ihres Gottes*)."[24] To escape this idolatrous drift, he specifies that the intuition of religion such as he defines it neither aims at "the single example of a particular type" nor "an individual intuition," nor even "a spirit of the universe who rules it with freedom and understanding" but, once again, "to have religion means to intuit the universe (*das Universum anschauen*)."[25] But to escape the idolatrous drift in this way, intuition only frees itself from every image (*Bild*) by rejecting God even in religion, by excluding him at the very least from the center of gravity and attraction of religion: "God is not everything in religion, but one, and the universe is more." In effect, the very idea of God has no decisive importance, because "one religion without God can be better than another with God."[26] Intuition (of whatever we want to call it, and in a myriad of equivalent and indifferent ways) reveals human feeling, man's "taste for the infinite," but nothing about God.

To be sure, Revelation proves to be not only possible, but still effective—but this no longer matters, since what it reveals is not and must not be named God.[27] To save religion by bringing Revelation back to intuition alone, it must not be God who reveals himself, or at least not at first.

According to Imagination

The second approach was initiated by Spinoza when he tried to determine Revelation starting from *imaginatio*, the fourth Cartesian mode of the *cogitatio*. Let's take as a starting point something that seems perfectly traditional: "Prophecy or revelation is certain knowledge about something (*rei alicujus certa cognitio*) revealed to men by God."[28] We can nevertheless observe several decisions, implicit and therefore all the stronger; first, the *revelatio* here is from the outset treated as a form of knowledge, thus ratifying the propositional definition of Revelation and assuming in advance its aporias; then, this knowledge adopts the Cartesian paradigm of certitude, which implies the constitution of objects and their mode of verification by clear and distinct ideas, or in other words, for Spinoza, by an adequate idea; and added to this is the ambiguity of the domain of this knowledge by *revelatio* already seen in Thomas: it indeed concerns what exceeds the limits of understanding ("*multa extra intellectus limites*," "much beyond the limits of the intellect") as well as what does not, but the *revelatio* repeats this in its own way.[29] And yet, even if the domains can be superimposed, the difference of modes of knowledge remains clear; *the very certain* knowledge of the prophets, thus *revelatio*, rests on the imagination: "they perceived things revealed by God only by way of their imagination (*non nisi ope imaginationis*)."[30] Yet this certainty by imagination only provides a moral certainty, not a demonstrative (or, for Spinoza, a geometric) one.[31] It follows that even if they are certain, the propositional statements obtained by *revelatio* (by simple imagination) cannot assure a theoretical certitude, nor demonstrate in reason. They can therefore only claim a practical obedience, on the sole condition that they do not contradict what reason defines as good.[32] There follows an inevitable consequence for the interpretation of Scriptures: the prophetic texts cannot claim to come from rational knowledge, since they result from revelations made by imagination alone; it is of course necessary to interpret prophecies, but without necessarily assuming the meaning that the prophets give them.[33] They must be therefore interpreted "at the level of reason" without trying to reconcile them with the imaginative meaning that presided over their writing.[34] The two levels of certainty remain absolutely heterogeneous and if, by any chance, we want to maintain a theoretical validity for prophetic revelation, it must be limited to reconstituting a political constitution, the very one that Moses conceived of for the Jewish people.

The reason for this downgrading of prophetic revelation surely comes from its radically propositional interpretation, but above all from its assignment to the imagination alone. Yet, as a matter of principle for Spinoza, the imagination does not allow knowledge by causes. The *Tractatus* already teaches this explicitly. "We are now compelled to ask what could be the source of the prophets' assuredness or certainty about things which they perceived only by the imagination and not from certain principles of thought (*certitudo eorum, quae tantum per imaginationem, et non ex certis mentis principiis percipiebant*). But whatever can be ascertained about this must also be derived from Scripture, since we do not have true knowledge of the matter . . . that is, we cannot explain it by its own causes (*hujus rei . . . veram scientiam non habemus sive eam per primas suas causas explicare non possumus*)."[35] But it is up to the *Ethics* to provide the canonical explanation: the ideas of the exterior body that we obtain by imagination sometimes represent them to us without their perception (following the Aristotelian definition of imagination as representing the very thing that is absent), but above all without ever giving us access to their causes; and so my imagination of another person (visible in his body) teaches me more about the state of my own body than that of the body of this other, who himself remains an effect without cause in me (and in my imagination),[36] "like consequences without premises."[37]

Subjected in this way to the epistemology exclusive to the imagination, Revelation, in this case biblical Revelation, remains possible, but downgraded to an inferior level: it can qualify political and moral practices, but does not allow any experience of God. The path thus closed off, metaphysics *ordine geometrico* is left with the crushing and impossible task of gaining adequate knowledge of the essence of God.[38] For it is up to the reason of understanding to attain with certainty what it denounces as an illusion of knowledge by imagination, and thus of Revelation. But claiming to have succeeded is not enough to have actually accomplished it.

According to the Will

It was Kant who privileged the *will*, the third mode of *cogitatio* according to Descartes, to take measure of Revelation. This decision results first of all from the critique of pure reason: since now the imagination must not be separated from the understanding (nor from intuition) in knowledge of phenomena (reduced to objects), its downgrading, still partial for Spinoza, affects the whole of pure reason for Kant, which is henceforth characterized by its essential finitude. Thus follows the impossibility in principle of a Revelation that would transgress these limits: "God has revealed nothing to us, nor can he reveal anything, for we would not *understand* it (*nicht verstehen würden*)."[39] This very decision is prolonged in extracting the question of God from the realm of theory into that of practice. Or, more precisely, from reason insofar as it determines the exercise of our will, because it formally, categorically, and imperatively establishes the moral law. And it is by contrast to the universal and unconditional categorical imperative that it seems clear that no Revelation, especially a biblical one consigned to texts that are culturally and historically determined, retains authority in moral matters. Kant thus echoes the starting point of Spinoza: "Their [the holy books'] historical element (*das Historische*), which contributes nothing to this end [i.e., morality], is something in itself quite indifferent, and one can do with it what one wills. (Historical faith is 'in itself dead'...)."[40] This principle of radical ahistoricality leads to the disqualification of every claim of historically conditioned religious faith to establish norms that are not only theoretical, but even moral. If therefore religion, "to have universality, must always be based on reason alone,"[41] all that remains for it is to conform, at any cost and by every means, to the moral law, which alone can impose itself legitimately on the will. In order to regain moral legitimacy, the biblical text must let itself be radically reinterpreted, again, according to Spinoza's rule: "For the theoretical element of ecclesiastical faith (*Kirchenglauben*) cannot be of moral interest to us, if it does not work toward the fulfillment of all human duties as divine commands (which constitutes the essential of every religion). This interpretation may often appear to us as forced, in view of the text (of the Revelation) and be often forced in fact; yet, if the text can at all bear it, it must be preferred to a literal interpretation that either contains absolutely nothing for morality, or even works counter to its incentives."[42] With the essential difference that the spiritual sense opens the biblical text to Revelation, while the moral sense according to Kant closes it. In other words, "It is in this way, according to the principle of morality (*Sittlichkeit*) which Revelation has in view, that we must interpret the Scriptures insofar as they have to do with religion (i.e. as opposed to the faith of the Church); otherwise our interpretations are either empty of practical (*praktisch*) content or are even obstacles to the good."⁴³ Resisting this command, warns Kant, would be a price so high for Church theologians—the absolute exclusion of scriptural and historical Revelation from the field of rationality—that they could not reasonably want to pay it: "If biblical theologians will stop using reason for their purposes, philosophical theologians will stop using the Bible to confirm their propositions."⁴⁴ The resolution of conflict, because it supposes the diktat of one of the two competitors, thus stands under the threat of a conflict-ridden divorce.

One additional step is thus taken in the closure of Revelation: "for since we cannot understand anyone unless he speaks to us *through our own understanding and our own reason*, it is only by concepts of *our reason (durch nichts, als durch Begriffe unserer Vernunft)*, insofar as they are pure moral concepts and hence infallible, that we can recognize the divinity of a teaching promulgated to us."⁴⁵ This conclusion immediately calls for two remarks and objections. First, the claim that a Revelation could only be manifested *through* the intermediary of our concepts and our reason could be understood in two very different ways; either it is obviously true (what other means would be at the disposal of God and us, if not reason and human concepts?), or it begs the question: for our concepts may not be ours alone, *a priori* according to the conditions of experience of worldly objects (and Kant knows it), just as our reason can think according to the infinite and unconditioned (and Kant knows that too). And so the real question lies elsewhere: must our concepts and our reason be governed by the experience of objects (pure theoretical reason) or only by universal and formal morality (practical reason)? Wouldn't another form of reason and therefore of concepts (or, if you like, of ideas) then be possible, precisely because it would be required—by Revelation, which would then be possible and thinkable? If not, we must of course concede that Revelation is not possible according to theoretical reason, nor even indispensable according to practical reason. But why concede this "if not"?

According to the Concept

It is Fichte who will accomplish the final step, by measuring Revelation according to the *intellectus*, the second mode of *cogitatio* according to Descartes. For his *Attempt at a Critique of All Revelation* (1788) draws the theological conclusions of the *Critique of Practical Reason* (1788) before Kant himself does, and very rigorously. The primary reason for disqualifying every Revelation (especially biblical Revelation) remains, as for Kant, its historical contingency, and thus its sensible origin, which forbids it from reaching any other concept of God than the "concept of an effect produced by God in the *sensuous* world by means of supernatural causality."[46] We must therefore refute it by resolutely passing to the only strictly intelligible and rational concept of God, that of a "moral God," crowning the finitude of man by "the acknowledgment of God as moral lawgiver."[47] From this comes the decisive step: the moral law, which remains in the field of *practical* reason for Kant, not only enables man's moral action, but gives him a *theoretical* access to the "concept of God as a moral lawgiver (*Begriff Gottes, als moralischen Gesetzgeber*)."[48]

The critique of every Revelation is no longer played out only on the practical terrain, because practical reason now allows us to define a *concept* or an *idea* of God: "The *idea of God*, as lawgiver through the moral law *in us*, is thus based on an externalization of ourselves (*Entäußerung des unsrigen*), on translating something subjective (*Übertragung eines Subjektiven*) into an essence (*Wesen*) *outside us*; and this externalization (*Entäußerung*) is the real principle of religion, insofar as it is to be used for determining the will."[49] The God of the moral law not only applies for us, but, in theory, defines God for himself. And forbids all the more any recourse to the slightest Revelation, which is now not only useless or even harmful, but simply false.

This transformation and amplification of the critique nevertheless raises a formidable difficulty: we could detect in it, at the very heart of the refutation of a first-level anthropomorphism (thinking God by sensible representation), a second-level anthropomorphism (thinking God by conceptual representation), which, while believing it had broken free from the former, makes use of an unexamined and all the more insistent reference to the concept—under the sole pretext of its morality *for us*. Of course, we understand well that "the sensuous objectification of the concept of God may contradict God's moral attributes and all morality with them."[50] But according to Fichte, this can be understood in two ways. Either we attribute to God too-human passions (anger, vengeance, hate, etc.) that would undermine his role as moral lawgiver: this would be anthropomorphism of the first level; or we attribute to him a receptivity to affect and a sensitivity to prayer, homage, sacrifices, etc., thus giving men other ways to honor him besides morality, and conferring an objective validity on what should remain a simple subjective approximation. In short, "If we are really able to determine God by our sensations, to move him to sympathy, pity, or joy, then he is not the Unchangeable, the Only sufficient, the Only Holy One (*der Unveränderliche, der Alleingenugsame, der Alleinselige*)."³¹ But how can we fail to notice an anthropomorphism at a second level here, as patent as the first? For, according to Fichte, it seems to go without saying that immutability, self-sufficiency (i.e., the *causa sui*), and self-referential beatitude, i.e., the most classical definitions of God in metaphysics, are sufficient, without any other precaution or reexamination, to characterize the God, the very "moral legislator," that he believes he is thus placing beyond doubt and dispute. But doesn't the moral definition of God in its concept, which supposes a positive and unexamined definition of God, reinforce a specifically conceptual idolatry? It is thus no surprise that in the course of the "atheism dispute" Fichte was compelled to respond to his opponents by accusing *them* of idolatry, since he could seem to be succumbing to it first himself, having only substituted a conceptual idolatry for their sensible idolatry. For Fichte could accuse his theologians—"*They* are the true atheists. They are completely godless and have created for themselves a terrible idol (*heillosen Götzen*)"—only by assuming and asserting in turn a closed and finite, and therefore also idolatrous, definition of God: "What *they* call God is an idol *to me*. To me, God is an essence (*Wesen*) completely liberated from all sensibility and every sensible addendum. . . . To me, God is merely and solely (*bloß und lediglich*) the regent of the supersensible world."³²

This opens the space where Nietzsche's breakthrough becomes not only possible, but irrefutable: the "moral God" can himself be formulated as merely an idol, certainly the last and the highest, but all the more necessary to destroy: "So one understands that an antithesis to pantheism is attempted here: for 'everything perfect, divine, eternal' *also compels a faith in the 'eternal recurrence.'* Question: does morality make impossible this pantheistic affirmation of all things, too? Fundamentally, it is only the moral god that has been overcome (*Im Grunde ist ja nur der moralische Gott überwunden*)."³³ By resulting in an identification of God with the concept of the "moral God," as unrestricted by practical reason, Fichte puts forth an idol, this time a conceptual one. Nietzsche draws from this the inevitable conclusion: the twilight of the metaphysical idols of God, in this case of the knowledge of God starting from the ego and the modes of its *cogitatio* alone, does not so much shut down the question of God as open onto another question—can God become accessible in any other way than by arriving from *elsewhere*? In other words, by revelation, or even Revelation.

Manifestation or Revelation

At the very least, we have achieved one result: the uncovering, unveiling, and bringing to light that the truly *theo*-logical Revelation claims to bring about can no longer be included, even as a crowning achievement and ultimate variation, within the same mechanism that interprets this as a knowledge that is simultaneously propositional and yet devoid of universality and deprived of the *a priori,* which characterizes "reason" in its metaphysical sense. Without admitting it, the concept of "Revelation" can be simplified into an *artifact,* conjured up with the sole purpose of being disqualified at will by "reason."[34] In order not to destroy the possibility of a *theological* concept of Revelation, we must therefore do nothing less than free it from its *philosophical* constitution as metaphysics has historically built it, and in the same move, destroyed it.

Doubtless, this means that we must remove an ambiguity, hidden in *almost* the same concept: *revealed* knowledge (*geoffenbarte*) is not always the same as *manifest* (*offenbare*) knowledge. Yet Hegel, on the contrary, does not cease making use of this ambiguity and draws on it for his logical (dialectical) recovery of the biblical event. We see this, in an exemplary way, in the solemn opening of the exposition of "religion consummate": "For this reason, the Christian religion is the religion / α) of *Revelation* (*der Offenbarung*); in it is manifest (*offenbar*) what God *is*, and the fact that he is *known as he is,* not merely in historical or in some similar fashion, as in the other religions, Revelation [*Offenbarung*], manifestation [*Manifestation*] is to the contrary its *determination* and its very content. That is to say that *revelation*, manifestation (*die Offenbarung, Manifestation*) [is] the *being-for* the consciousness and for consciousness is the fact that God is himself spirit FOR [spirit], i.e. by consequence consciousness and *for* consciousness."[35] Here the ambivalence between *Offenbarung* (which could remain *theo*-logical) and *Manifestation* (resolutely theo-*logical*, metaphysics) is clearly admitted by Hegel himself. This ambivalence could not be avoided, since it comes from the still more original ambiguity of the Hegelian understanding of *Offenbaren, to reveal,* which can (and must) be divided between the purely and simply manifest (*offenbar*) and the properly *revealed* (*geoffenbart*), an ambiguity that arises often from Hegel's very text: "this religion is the *revelatory* (offenbare) religion. God reveals himself (*offenbart sich*). As we have seen, 'revealing' (*Offenbaren*) refers to the primal judgment of infinite subjectivity or infinite form; it means to determine oneself, to be for an other. This revealing or self-manifesting (*dieses Offenbaren, sich Manifestieren*) belongs to the essence of spirit itself. *A spirit that is not manifest* (offenbar) *is not a spirit.*"[56] Is what is manifest to us, even in absolute consciousness, the same as what reveals itself as coming from itself, and which therefore is from *elsewhere* for us? If God gives himself in order to make himself known, does it follow that we, by concept, know him as such? Does God give himself to be known (for he certainly gives himself to be known if he really reveals himself) as that which can become manifest to the concept?

In the end, everything depends on the power of the concept—of the concept of the concept. Can the concept, the ultimate outcome of the *cogitatio*, now set free from the finitude of the ego, abolish the gap between the manifest (of itself to itself by the spirit reconciled with itself) and the revealed (given from *elsewhere*)? "In this religion, the divine essence (*Wesen*) is for that reason revealed (*geoffenbart*). Its being revealed (*Offenbarsein*) manifestly (*offenbar*) consists in this, that what it is, is known. However, it is known precisely because it is known as spirit, or as essence (*Wesen*) that is essentially self-consciousness.... This—to be what is revealed (*das Offenbare zu sein*) according to its *concept*, is therefore the true shape of spirit."[57] Here the reduction of Revelation (*geoffenbart*, therefore *Offenbarung*) to the manifest (*offenbar, Offenbarsein*) becomes obvious, since it leads us to take them up equally in the concept, understood as the accomplishment of the mind. But perhaps Fichte was saying something else, saying much more, when, perhaps without measuring the whole scope of his warning, he proclaimed, "Yes, just say this to them directly—this theology [i.e., the doctrine of God's essence of God in and for himself] should be entirely annihilated for being a phantasm of the brain that surpasses every finite power of comprehension."[58] For, indeed, *this* theology does not so much belong to Revelation as to metaphysics.

III

The Restitution of a Theological Concept

SEVEN

The Possibilities and the Aporias of a Theological Concept of Revelation

Our inquiry into a potential concept of Revelation has ended up in a surprising and aporetic conclusion. The surprise lies in the lateness in its use, which can be summed up by a sober observation of Paul Tillich: "As an idea, Revelation is as old as religion.... Revelation as a concept is much more recent."[1] As to the aporia, it arises from the origin of this supposed concept, which is less *theo*-logical than it is philosophical (theo-*logical*, metaphysical). The two aspects of the conclusion mutually reinforce one another: the concept of Revelation only appeared late because the first era of theological thought (patristic and monastic) could do without it, for as long as the norms of philosophy, and then the principles of the system of *metaphysica*, were not being imposed on *sacra doctrina*. Yet it remains the case that over two centuries ago modern usage in university theology sanctioned the term "Revelation." Thus one cannot avoid an investigation, even if only in outline, that measures the strength and legitimacy of this usage. In a word, one must ask about the value of the concept or concepts of "Revelation" in force today, and the extent to which they respond to the formal exigencies of a *theo*-logical thinking.

An Inappropriate Concept

Indeed, one notices first of all that the thinkers of the first (twelve?) centuries of what is generally referred to as Christian theology, in fact its most decisive period even for us today, did not feel the need to thematize a univocal concept of Revelation; the all-too-common explanation that this notion seemed too obvious to need explanation to them does not so much answer the question as formulate the difficulty.[2] And the question therefore remains to know why Thomas Aquinas found himself led or authorized to elaborate his doctrine of the two ways of knowing God. Second, the later development of this doctrine led to the privileging of the propositional, or epistemological, interpretation of such a Revelation, with the ambiguities and contradictions that we have seen. To the point that the claim to establish the *sacra doctrina* first as a science, and then as a dominant science subjecting to itself (by subalternation) the human sciences, required the application of the univocal and modern concept of science—a certain and evident knowledge—that by definition could only bear upon objects; thus contradicting the conditions for the knowledge of God, who, also by definition, cannot be constituted as an object, even an infinite one (infinite object: an oxymoron). Third, the concept of science that (modern) metaphysics *had to* develop could not avoid seeming inapplicable to the theology of *sacra doctrina*; the concept thus ends up by simply disqualifying theology as science. And so it is that the *Aufklärung legitimately* disqualified theology's claim to set itself up as such a "science," by conferring upon it a non-epistemological status, even if it *illegitimately* continues to call theology "Revelation." In fact, this strictly metaphysical concept had only a polemical intention, that of disqualifying Christian theology by imposing on it a resolutely discriminatory title. Put otherwise, under the term "Revelation," the *Aufklärung* labelled *sacra doctrina* as a non-knowledge, but from a point of view that is radically *non*-theological (chapter 6). Fourth, one can only be astonished, or even scandalized, that despite the very inspired prudence of the Roman magisterium, so many theologians and professors of theology threw themselves into taking up and appropriating such a concept as "Revelation/*Offenbarung*." As if the final and, literally, overturning recuperation of this critical, polemical, and discriminatory concept by German idealism would (despite the patent ambiguities of Hegel, the confused corrections of Schelling, and the heroic resistance of Kierkegaard) offer a stable ground for the Christian thinking of *sacra doctrina* and assure it a sound theological origin.

It is easy to understand how the rampant development of *a particular* concept of Revelation, combined with its absence in the early stages, eventually became problematic in contemporary theology. Far from being qualified by the widespread circulation of its "small change,"[3] it could appear as the proof of an "inflation,"[4] or even a carcinogenic growth.[5] This indetermination explains only too well the fact that some have felt tempted to reject this fragile concept, or even renounce the thing itself.[6] However, the historical delay of a concept does not eliminate its importance, provided that its possibility remains incontestable. We have already sketched this possibility (chapters 1–2), just as we have in contrast noted its role by retracing the aporias that provoke its misunderstanding (chapters 4–6). And, in fact, redefining a truly *theo*-logical concept of Revelation has constituted the challenge and the great debate of Christian reflection in the twentieth century. This project could not unfold without confronting or at least opening two questions that the epistemological interpretation of Revelation had missed or masked. First: if to be revealed, in the case of God, means not simply or even primarily to make (himself) known through propositions (and predicative statements), but instead to manifest himself, we must ask *how* this manifestation is accomplished, and according to what phenomenality. Then, if this phenomenality must be able to manifest God, and God *as God*, by what sign, by what criteria, and according to what identity would a finite mind be able to recognize him *as such*? These two questions can be summed up in one: in order to attain to Revelation as the manifestation of God, it is also necessary that that which attests to him as true God also manifest itself, that there be manifested "the knowledge of the *agape* . . . that surpasses all knowledge" (Ephesians 3:19). It is by starting from this question that one can, if only schematically, define the requirements of a possible response.

The Word as Revelation

Clearly, Karl Barth offers the unquestionable starting point (which the constitution *Dei Verbum* did not forget at Vatican II, see above chapter 4) by posing as principle a statement that is, for him, a quasi-tautology: "*God reveals Himself. He reveals Himself through Himself. He reveals Himself.*"[7] Revelation comes only from itself. God makes himself the content and thus also the sole means, the unique mediation and the exclusive process. If God had not *manifested* himself by his own mode, he would not have properly manifested *himself*—as such. It is precisely this coincidence that is lacking in the epistemological interpretation of Revelation, where the one who seemingly reveals himself must manifest himself according to propositions formally homogeneous with those of the human sciences, henceforth translated and betrayed, so to speak, into our words and our predications of something on something—whereas of God one can predicate nothing. This is so first of all because one can predicate everything of God, but above all because God *is not* some substratum of which one might predicate whatever may *be*. How then do we conceive the coincidence of that which manifests itself with its mode of manifestation? By conceiving it as the Word [*Parole*], itself heard as the Word [*Verbe*] "that is with God and that is God" (John 1:2).[8] The Word [*Verbe*] offers that which, or rather *the one who* manifests himself, and that through which, or rather through *whom* it manifests itself, indissolubly. Therefore the word [*parole*] (theo-*logical*) must be thought on the basis of the Word [*Parole*] (*theo*-logical), that is to say, conceiving the Word [*Parole*] on the basis of the Word [*Verbe*] and receiving the Word [*Verbe*] from God, thus seeing God as Father through the Son. These transitions define a path that is *almost* impassible, but without traveling it, Revelation loses its meaning and its legitimacy. For those who want to advance *in via*, the first step consists at least in refusing to cut the Word down to the level of our use of the words of the tribe, to the propositional usage of biblical words, reduced into objectifiable predications or fixed within sufficient propositions. No one was as well-informed as Barth about this division and the difficulty of the mode of the Word of God: "the question 'What is the Word of God?' can be answered only by indicating the How of God's Word. . . . We thus ask: 'How is the Word of God (*wie ist das Wort Gottes*)?' and the answer is: It is on our lips and in our hearts as the mystery of the Spirit who is the Lord."[9] And Barth draws at least three characteristics from this Word.

First, it is a statement (*Rede*), but one that, from the outset, is not limited to the stating of a proposition, because, if it is stated rationally, even so it is not limited to the rationality of objects. In place of stating something about something, this statement is addressed *to* someone, by opening to her at least the possibility of realizing *who is speaking to her*. The statement is accomplished as an *address* addressed to the one to whom it calls out and takes aback; the one thus singled-out [*l'interloqué*] hears or can hear in it not only what a third person would also hear (according to the obvious sense of the statement), but

The Possibilities and the Aporias of a Theological Concept of Revelation 97

first and above all what she alone discerns in it—an absolutely singular call addressed to me alone and that no neutral hermeneutic could generalize. This is the third characteristic effect of every revelation: the revelation of oneself to oneself, but which comes to one from *elsewhere*, from the *elsewhere* itself (chapter 1). This is exactly what Saint Augustine understood upon suddenly reading the verse from Paul in the garden at Cassiciacum; he did not merely understand the obvious sense of a general warning, but a call particularly addressed to him that he took for himself and upon himself: "Not in rioting and drunkenness, not in chambering and wantonness, not in fighting and envy, but wrap yourself in the Lord Jesus Christ and do not become a purveyor of the flesh in concupiscence."[10] The issue was hearing and comprehending the urgency of the conversion, or more precisely, of *his* own conversion; he, who was perfectly able to ignore it, thus took upon *himself*, *hic et nunc*, the warning that was available to any other reader. From this first moment, the Word, as statement and address, exceeds its propositional interpretation.

Next, the Word accomplishes (itself) (as) an act; but a multiplied act, for the address does not end with the interpellation of the first witness (the prophet); it is repeated in the Scripture, then in the preaching of the Church, so that the listener each time can find himself taken aback by the ever-contemporary action of the Word [*Verbe*]. And so the Word [*Parole*] is only received (through listening or reading) by exerting a power that puts the hearer in a new situation, in a situation to become new and other than who he was before. The address of the Word thus provokes a decision, or at least offers the possibility for a decision. At the very least, the Word demands a choice for or against it, because the refusal, even the simple refusal to choose, already constitutes a choice. One does not compromise with the act that the Word accomplishes, when it demands of the one it has singled out the act of a decision in return: the decision in any case will be made, whether positive, negative, or even undecided. Indecision, above all, if it turns me away from the question, by contrast makes the question stand out that much more, alone, in itself. Just as an abandoned gift remains a fully accomplished gift, so an address that is left without a response remains an appeal that resounds.

Finally, the Word keeps a secret. It remains a secret how much of the Word was actually received by the faith of the one singled out, and likewise what was truly addressed to her in the word that was spoken. The gap between the Word and what the witness heard or believed she understood increases the gap between what the Word asked of her and what her response decided (or not) to make actual within her. Consequently the one singled out always remains, by virtue of her faith and not by her failure, in at least partial ignorance of what has been accomplished within herself and the world by the action of the Word. Veiling and unveiling coincide, precisely because the spoken word preceeds and surpasses our listening and our decision. Thus the spoken word always remains eschatological for us (like every dogmatic formulation that we nevertheless can and must produce from it). The secret of the Word comes from the Spirit.[11] What the Word wants to tell me and the response that it awaits from me are known only by the Spirit, not by me. This quasi-superego does not belong to my self, precisely because it redefines my *I*. While truly on our lips, like an address read and received, while truly in our hearts like a decision to make, even so the Revelation by the Word remains ever in the secret of the Spirit.

In this sense, Barth's reflection opens the dimensions of the question more than it sheds light on its difficulty: Revelation imposes and elicits a structure of call and response between the Word and its witness. But how is this structure deployed, according to what logic is it decided, and following what phenomenality does it manifest itself? Is it a matter of a pure dramatics between the one speaking and the one singled out, or does a correlation link them together? And then according to what analogy?—for it is perhaps not enough to challenge (and doubtless rightly so) the *analogia entis* for the *analogia fidei* to unfold in all its dimensions.

Revelation through Mere Address

The difficulty going forward becomes clear: at issue is thinking the Word itself as Revelation, or put another way, conceiving how and to what extent the Word of God can reveal him, which is to say make manifest the mystery. What does the Word *show*—God? One can try to respond to the question by examining and delimiting the *content* of Revelation. Along this path, one must follow Bultmann, for he radicalizes *one* of the possible developments of the theses of Barth, from whom he takes up the critique of Revelation as "communication of propositions (*Wissensmitteilung*)" about God, instead favoring its reception as an event (*Geschehen*) having to do with "an understanding of *Dasein*."¹² Indeed, Revelation always concerns the finitude of my *Dasein*: "Therefore to know about revelation means to know about our own authenticity (*Eigentlichkeit*)—and, at the same time, thereby to know of our limitation."¹³ These limits, or rather this unique limit consists in our death, which we carry with us in each instant of our life and for as long as it lasts. The Word of Revelation concerns us deep down only because it is addressed to us in this situation; it therefore only matters to us to the extent that it can "be understood as . . . a *personal address* (*Anrede*)."¹⁴ For the Word reveals that in Christ, life overcomes our death: "revelation can only be the gift (*Geschenk*) of life through which death is overcome."¹⁵ Still following Barth, it remains that the Revelation of this life through death is a "hidden Revelation,"¹⁶ a life that is still hidden, to which we cannot assign any content. As a consequence, the suppression of its worldly and discursive content (otherwise called demythologization, this time against Barth) would change nothing fundamentally in the Revelation that, in faith without content, "consists in nothing other than the fact of Jesus Christ (*in dem Faktum Jesus Christus*)."¹⁷ The Barthian interpretation of the Word as address thus reaches its zenith: "the preaching [of the Word] is itself revelation (*die Predigt ist selbst Offenbarung*)."¹⁸ But right away this zenith becomes a nadir, for preaching accomplishes only a naked and abstract fact: "what does he [Christ] reveal? *The fact that* [*Daß*] he is sent as the revealer [*als Offenbarer*]."¹⁹ Reduced to its pure, hard impact on mortal *Dasein*, this brute fact, by virtue of the demythologization (itself neither questioned nor critiqued), thus reveals *nothing*: "What, then, has been revealed? *Nothing* at all, so far as the question concerning revelation asks for doctrines."²⁰ Revelation is accomplished in the address, but the response to this address provides no manifestation whatsoever. Or rather, the concept of Revelation in the New Testament is summed up by the demand alone that it accomplishes through its pure and simple address. However, what is ignored or annulled here is the phenomenological principle according to which, if the question provokes and precedes the response, the meaning and the truth of the question is understood only in the response. An address without a response that makes it resonate disappears as an address and, in the case of a Revelation, as Word of God. If the response says nothing, the address not only will never say anything, but it will never have been addressed to anyone—it is a mute Word.

Revelation by Correlation

Even so, the final (or initial) aporia of Bultmann is still instructive: it shows that approaching Revelation as Word and approaching the Word as an address (*Anrede*) can be dissolved into the abstraction of a mere fact (*Faktum, daß*) that in the end is empty if this revelatory Word is not opened to the depth of the revealed, to its *elsewhere*. The *fact* of Christ has meaning only if it has to do with the fact *of Christ*—arising according to the "mystery" of its source. A Word that is limited to happening (*geschehen*) cannot provoke the least event (*Geschehnis*), nor leave a mark in any history (*Geschichte*), because it doesn't allow for any advent (*Ereignis*). The Word of Christ of course calls, but never in his own name, always in the name of another, the Father (see chapter 14). Without this point of reference, the simple fact of his Word reveals nothing.

In this context, we can better understand why other theologians had followed an opposing path: they never separated the fact of Revelation (the event of Jesus manifesting himself as the Word of God) from the right that legitimates this Revelation. For if, taking up Barth's rather basic metaphor, the announcement of the Revelation (the kerygma) pierces through human experience like a rock falling into water—with a plunge that disturbs the entire surface and plumbs the entire depth—there must already be water, even if polluted and stagnant, to allow the shock wave to be diffused. Only such a receptivity (*capacitas*), even minimal and conflicting, opens up the depth where the *elsewhere* of Revelation can, partially but clearly, manifest itself. It is in this sense that we must hear the distinction made by Karl Rahner between Revelation as "categorical" and (the same) Revelation as "transcendental," which manages in advance the site of that which is said and exposed to faith in the Church: it is truly necessary "to recognize that the history of revelation and what is usually called revelation as such, is the historical self-unfolding in predicamental [categorical] terms, or, even more simply and correctly, the history of that transcendental relation between man and God."[21] It is also in this sense that we must envisage the principle stated by Paul Tillich that "[s]ystematic theology uses the method of correlation."[22] While maintaining without ambiguity that what is revealed remains "the unconditional strangeness (*das Unbedingt-Fremde*)" of an "unconditioned revealed (*das Unbedingt-Offenbare*),"²³ and that "even once revealed ... the revelation does not dissolve the mystery into knowledge,"²⁴ the method of correlation continues to suppose that "God answers man's questions, and under the impact of God's answers man asks them."²⁵ Doubtless this is so, yet this thesis is exposed to an objection that was already made, at the first definition of the paradox (chapters 2 and 4): Revelation from *elsewhere* responds neither first nor always to questions that man has already posed, but most often and primarily to questions that he *cannot* or *does not wish* to pose. And so we understand the resistance that it inevitably provokes among those who receive it (or not). In revealing himself, God poses *his* questions to them, which coincide only very rarely with the questions that naturally and spontaneously occupy us; and the displacement of the questions also implies the displacement of answers—for God answers man by responding to the questions that man must or ought to pose, if he took God's point of view on himself. This is how the first motive of the necessary *metanoia* appears: in order to receive God's answers, it is first necessary to conform oneself to the strangeness of his questions—for his ways are not our ways, nor his thoughts our thoughts (Isaiah 55:9), even with regard to ourselves and our questions.

This objection is further reinforced when the method of correlation becomes clearer by identifying what Revelation reveals with "what concerns us ultimately";²⁶ and, further, albeit just as vaguely, by assimilating it to "the manifestation of the depth of reason and the ground of *being*."²⁷ For in this context, God would in the end allow himself to be assimilated to the transcendental of being: "The religious word for what is called the ground of *being* is God."²⁸ Thus we find repeated, almost literally, Rahner's thesis: "The intrinsic intelligibility and the ontological justification for understanding the notion of self-communication this way is found in the transcendental experience of the orientation of every finite existent *to the absolute being and mystery of God*. In transcendence as such, *absolute being* is the innermost constitutive element by which this transcendental movement is borne towards *itself* [God]."²⁹ The initial stake still remains: Revelation cannot be accomplished without the depth of its *elsewhere* being manifested and persisting up to the very moment of its impact (in the kerygma). But a question is not posed: must this depth be identified as something other than itself, for example as Being or as the "ground of Being"? And can it be thus identified without repeating the metaphysical idolatries of the "moral God" or "God the moral lawgiver"?

History as Indirect Revelation

This aporia found its clearest illustration in the offensive led in the grand style by Wolfhart Pannenberg against Barth (and Rahner as well), starting with the manifesto *Revelation as History*, which he initiated and contributed to in 1961. The clear objective of the polemic is the Barthian thesis (and its radicalization by Bultmann) of a self-Revelation of God through the kerygmatic impact of the Word alone, especially expressed in the Scriptures: "What has the reflection revealed so far? We have shown that neither the Old nor New Testaments know of any terminological expression for the 'self-Revelation of God' (*Selbstoffenbarung Gottes*)."[30] Indeed, neither the Name of Yahweh nor the name of Jesus expresses or accomplishes such a direct and in-person Revelation of the biblical God. And this is not the result of a failure of revelatory intention on God's part, but because "the self-Revelation of God in the biblical witnesses is not of a direct type in the sense of a theophany, but is indirect and brought about by means of the historical acts of God."[31] Indeed, far from weakening the impact, the substitution of an indirect Revelation for a direct Revelation augments it in at least two senses. First, it requalifies the revelatory function of all the biblical writings taken as a whole, and above all allows that "Revelation is not comprehended completely in the beginning, but at the end of the revealing history." Second, it recognizes that historical Revelation has a universal validity (against the contingency to which the *Aufklärung* restricted it), traversing and englobing *all* of history instead of being lost in a contingent particularity: "in distinction from special manifestations of the deity, the historical revelation is open to anyone who has eyes to see. It has a universal character." Henceforth, Revelation becomes an affair of truth; it is patent, noticeable, accessible in the stubborn facts of history, according to an almost positivistic interpretation (which has nothing "supernatural") of 2 Corinthians 4:2: "by manifestation of the truth (τῇ φανερώσει τῆς ἀληθείας), we would commend ourselves to every man's conscience (πᾶσαν συνείδησιν ἀνθρώπων) in the sight of God."[32] The truth of that which is thus revealed universally cannot, by coherent sequence, be limited to the history of Israel, even if that history remains revealing of the acts of

The Possibilities and the Aporias of a Theological Concept of Revelation 103

God; the truth is also developed in the "Gentile Christian churches," to the point of "the universality of the eschatological self-demonstration of God in the fate (*Geschick*) of Jesus."³³ The "indirect" Revelation thus no longer unfolds in historical contingency, but, with the accomplishment of Jesus, in an eschatological universality. The strength of such an approach to the concept of Revelation cannot be contested, and its contributions are evident as positive gains. In particular the central point: if self-manifestation of God there must be—and every doctrine of Revelation implies it (Barth and *Dei Verbum* require it)—nevertheless a theology of the Word (and of the kerygma) is not enough to conceive it.

But this result only serves to underscore two other difficulties. First: the choice of history as the ultimate horizon of Revelation, even if it has its credentials (from Bloch and Rahner to Metz and Moltmann), also has its limits: the universality it lays claim to remains ambiguous. For exactly what *totality* is at issue? Even if human history became the theater of divine Revelation, which thus no longer limits itself to a "theology of the church," this history does not make up a totality; and, if only the whole of history still to come, namely eschatological history, accomplishes the Revelation, how would we avoid reducing the manifestation of Jesus Christ (about which there is agreement, of course) to the status of one moment (among others) of "indirect" Revelation? How do we maintain, on the contrary, that the accomplishment of Jesus ("πάντα τετέλεσται," John 19:28) "recapitulates all things in Christ" (Ephesians 1:10)? In short, how do we properly account for "his love perfectly accomplished in us (ἀγάπη τετελειωμένη ἐν ἡμῖν)" (1 John 4:12)? Resorting to eschatology does not exempt us from knowing if it completes history by prolonging it (and if so, how and through what addition?), or if through it history is absorbed in the *eschaton*, in an *omega* who right away constitutes an *alpha*, and who is "before Abraham came to be" (John 8:58, and Revelation 1:8). At stake is not only consideration of the *eschaton*, but seeing that it also turns out to be a beginning: "I am Alpha and Omega, the beginning and the accomplishment (τέλος)" (Revelation 21:6), "the first and the last, the beginning and the accomplishment" (Revelation 22:13). The second does not complete the first, because they are one and the same, "once for all" (Hebrews 7:27, 9:12, and 10:10). If it is not thought through, the unsettled connection between history and eschatology renders problematic even the distinction between "direct" and "indirect" Revelation, which otherwise seems correct. And then another question surfaces: Can one legitimately set up history as the final horizon of Revelation?[34] Is this not once again an effect of the Hegelian aporia? And more radically, that of a new institution of a general horizon of Revelation, after so many others (the horizon of being, the horizon of metaphysics, the horizon of the Word alone, and so on), whose inadequacies were already established? This amounts to asking—finally—if it is not fitting, once and for all, to refuse to assign another horizon to Revelation than itself and another *a priori* than it alone. Because it is defined as arising from *elsewhere*, Revelation has no other horizon than itself. Or better, it only allows as horizon this *elsewhere*, which is defined by the absence of limits known to us, since nothing of ours limits it (ὁρίζειν). For God alone fixes limits by "definite plan, ὡρισμένῃ βουλῇ" (Acts 2:23), by "determining appointed events, ὁρίσας προστεταγμένους καιρούς" (Acts 17:26), in "the Son of God established (ὁρισθέντος)" by him (Romans 1:4).

A second unsettled decision confirms the first. If history, this "language of facts," renders even "indirect" Revelation "fully revealed, *ganz offenbar*," and if it is enough to have eyes to see it, how do we account for the quite common refusal to see the visible?[35] To understand this refusal, it is necessary to resort to a *certain* hermeneutic, where the factuality of things is not sufficient to make manifest the evidence of Revelation. In this manifestation, the issue is not solely the historical incompleteness of a merely "indirect" communication, as it is with voluntary blindness or the refusal to see; here, eschatology no longer consists exclusively nor above all in completing and universalizing the manifestation; it provokes a *judgment* from each of the believers about his or her evidence and about him- or herself, for it reveals that each witness always remains in part an unbeliever. Here again, it is a question of knowing (or seeing) how Revelation regulates itself by itself, in its unconditionality (against every transcendental *a priori*, including those of being or history) as much as in the logic of its acceptance or rejection (against every epistemological interpretation, whether direct or indirect). Responding to Friedrich Gogarten, who assumed, "There is no understanding of man without understanding of God, but . . . again I cannot understand this God without already understanding man,"[36] Barth had defined Revelation negatively but definitively as "something which has no basis (*Grund*) or possibility (*Möglichkeit*) outside itself, which can in no sense be explained in terms of man and man's situation, but only as knowledge of God from God, as free and unmerited grace."[37] Let us hold to this lesson: without furnishing a sufficient answer, it at least allows us to formulate correctly the difficulty.

There remains another way of understanding Barth, that of Hans Urs von Balthasar, which concerns the *conditions* of possibility, or rather the unconditionality, of Revelation. Take the aporia we have just sketched: a Revelation, understood radically, can admit no *a priori* that would fix its conditions of possibility (Barth, and on the contrary, chapter 6); but, it will be objected, without the determination of the conditions of its reception (limits of the *modus recipientis*), this Revelation becomes empty (Bultmann), whence the inevitable reestablishment of certain conditions (Tillich, Rahner, Pannenberg, etc., chapter 7). And yet, we have already glimpsed the presupposition that underlies this aporia: humanity poses only those questions to which it can respond. Now, in principle and in fact, Revelation (chapter 2), like perhaps every revelation (chapter 1), does not respond to questions that man already poses to himself, but imposes on him questions that, by himself, he *does not* ask himself—at least, not yet, nor spontaneously or explicitly. Hence the difficulty of receiving and understanding Revelation, more than responding to it: first off and most of the time, its call remains unintelligible, and thus takes the form of a paradox, which asks for a response to questions that are still incomprehensible, and thus never formulated in advance. And yet this paradox does not exclude Revelation from respecting conditions, nor from defining its own possibility. It only asks that these conditions of possibility (of reception, of understanding) not be imposed on Revelation by the limits of its addressee and of its respondent, but that the limits arise from what Revelation reveals and makes manifest. The horizon of Revelation never arises from our side, in the land of *our* possibilities, under *our* conceivable horizons of manifestation (neither "history," nor "being," nor the "Word," much less the text), but instead from *its* side, in "the self-interpreting revelation-form of love itself (*die sich selbst auslegende Offenbarungs-Gestalt der Liebe selber*)."[38] With this breakthrough, everything is changed and much is clarified. From this moment, at least three decisions stand out. First, Revelation comes from *elsewhere*, for nothing seems stranger to us than the perfection of love (God loves and he alone loves all the way). Second, this *elsewhere* admits no condition of possibility, because love is accomplished without any condition—a gift given up [*un don abandonné*] can remain a perfect gift (which is called the Cross). Finally, this *elsewhere* can manifest itself, because it enters into visibility by taking a human figure (the Incarnation as entry into our visibility, that of the flesh).

Love and the Figure

There's nothing illogical in these decisions, for the issue remains a logic—not ours, of course, but the "logic of absolute love."³⁹ At issue is even a sort of "transcendentality" (to speak like Rahner, after Kant), because that is what is necessary in order to determine that a phenomenon is showing itself; but this transcendentality reflects what is possible *for God*, which is to say what is impossible *for us*; at this point this transcendentality turns out to be governed by the true transcendent that the impossible freely and in itself manifests itself, yet without having to be alienated under another figure than its own.⁴⁰ We have already identified this unconditioned possible (an oxymoron *for us*), through which what appears manifests itself in itself, as the possibility for the phenomenon to *give itself*. If then every phenomenon shows itself to the extent that it gives itself, then the Revelation of God as charity, and of a God who consists only in his charity, will manifest itself absolutely, without reserve or compromise, to the extent, itself absolute, unconditioned, and infinite, that God gives himself: "*Dando se revelat, revelando se dat.*"⁴¹ God thus reveals himself according to the laws of phenomenality, except this phenomenality does not unfold according to the rules of our mode and our phenomena, but according to the proper exigencies of that which *gives itself*. Revelation is phenomenalized, but its phenomenality has no other law than the (erotic) logic of the gift, of *agapē*. This transcendentality come to give itself from itself alone approaches us radically from *elsewhere*, and yet is accomplished "among us" (John 1:14)—in the figure of Christ, the norm and unique condition of Revelation which does not arise *from* us precisely because it comes *to* us. This transcendentality is revealed through and in Christ as "truly figure," showing "itself to be *of itself*," patent and with an "evidential power . . . [that] lies in the phenomenon itself."⁴²

At stake, indeed, is a phenomenon par excellence, and not a phenomenon that we would constitute as an object, through the intuitive fulfillment of a signification, according to a noetico-noematic correlation governed by our intentionality. It is not even a saturated phenomenon that we are dealing with, where the intuition surpasses the limits of the concept (or of the concepts mobilized to retain it); nor is it even a simple phenomenon of revelation that is at issue, which combines in one single appearance several of the possible figures of saturation. What is at stake is *the* phenomenon of *Revelation*, which constitutes itself absolutely by itself, because it gives itself absolutely by itself. What we can dare to call "the phenomenon of Christ"[43] accomplishes an infinite phenomenalization, because it brings about, in charity, an infinite gift. A gift with the status of *ultima forma*, according to von Balthasar, and "fundamental form (*Urbild*),"[44] which crosses the finite and the infinite without any compromise or contradiction. This figure contains in itself its own horizon of manifestation, the charity according to which it gives itself without any other measure than itself. In this sense, as it gives itself infinitely and therefore passes toward the point of being annihilated (kenosis), it remains all the more manifestly infinite. But as it only manifests itself insofar as it gives itself and in order to give itself, this figure goes to the point of revealing itself as in-finite within finitude itself: love manifests itself all the more as it gives itself to the point of self-abandonment in this figure; thus without question this figure inhabits the finite. The flesh that God takes on reveals "Christ's form of love (*Liebesform Christi*)";[45] infinite love manifests itself in the finite (body) of the flesh of Jesus. This phenomenon overflows itself starting from itself, just as love *diffusivum sui* by definition exceeds itself.

In this way the aporia of Revelation and its conditions of possibility, or rather the condition of its essential *impossibility*, is resolved in the original paradox of the figure of Christ—in this visibility, where nothing less than the invisible is given to be seen as the "icon of the invisible God, εἰκὼν τοῦ θεοῦ τοῦ ἀοράτου" (Colossians 1:15) and "the radiance of his glory, the imprint of the person [of God]" (Hebrews 1:3). But this "figure of revelation remains unintelligible unless it is interpreted in light of God's love," for "either one sees it or one does not."[46] This figure thus implies that no gaze captures it, and even that it escapes the rules of a common vision. Consequently it culminates in the "appearance of an infinitely determined super-form, *eine unendlich bestimmten Über-Gestalt*."[47] The form of the phenomenon is found in the figure that Christ's body of flesh accomplishes.[48] But this assumes that we admit that Revelation, the phenomenon of Christ, be interpreted only beginning from the place and site where the Father unfolds himself in the Son in the communion of the Spirit—in a Trinitarian manner, that is. For the more a phenomenon reveals itself as saturated, the more it requires an endless hermeneutic. "Though it remains a light inaccessible to the understanding, God's triunity is the sole hypothesis capable of clarifying the phenomenon of Christ (*das Phänomen Christi*) . . . in a phenomenologically adequate manner, without doing violence to the facts."[49] Revelation through becoming-man (*Menschwerdung*) no longer means only nor above all that God enters into our finite humanity, but that we see him there in *his* infinite horizon—"being like the manifestation of himself through himself (ἔκφανσιν ὄντα ἑαυτοῦ δι' ἑαυτοῦ)"[30]—where *we* also enter. By contradicting us through paradoxes, by deforming and reforming us, this phenomenon conforms to his glory. The task now is to clarify, as far as possible, this decisive result.

EIGHT

Unconcealment or Uncovering

The breakthrough of Hans Urs von Balthasar thus results in the introduction of the notion of *figure* (*Gestalt*). The enshrinement of this term would not be decisive if it were merely a new notion added to all of those already privileged by theology for thinking Revelation (an addition to the list of theological "sites" or yet another concept imported from a dominant philosophy). It concerns a yet more radical turn: a successful effort to think Revelation starting from itself. This means we must not only avoid thinking it from a prior horizon that predetermines it, but we must receive it as it gives itself from itself. If Revelation can reveal itself from itself, it is because it gives itself from itself, following the adage *dando revelat et revelando dat*, which here plays out in full. It reveals itself from itself, that is to say, for us, from *elsewhere* in the exact measure that it gives itself. To give itself—this means to manifest the *elsewhere*, for the one who receives it. To manifest itself—this means to give itself from itself because it arrives from *elsewhere* to the one who receives it. This common play of givenness from *elsewhere* and manifestation *of itself by itself* can only be seen by approaching Revelation no longer from a formal concept, but directly following its mode of *phenomenality*.

A Question of Logic

The phenomenality of Revelation (or at least of its possibility) raises questions of logic. In particular, that the figure claims to unite in itself the two poles whose tension essentially defines Revelation: the unconditioned infinite and the finitude of our minds. Or, if we transpose these terms into those of theology, the figure claims to articulate the appearing "among us," in our phenomenal field, of something that "no one has ever seen" (John 1:14 and 18). Before this "apparent formlessness,"[1] which metaphysics can only claim to reduce with brute conceptual force that ultimately fails to have any effect, the thought of Revelation succeeds in surpassing the aporia with one stroke and in a radical way, by recognizing a figure in the unfigurable itself—that of charity, "as the form which fulfills all the prior forms."[2] But in what sense can we understand that the "form of Christian love, as it appears in the sign of Christ, is absolutely indivisible (*absolut unteilbar*)"?[3] We must understand it precisely in this sense, that it is a question of the "form of love"; for love indeed takes form; or rather it in-forms itself, it gives (itself) a form in giving itself. As it makes itself seen in a gift, a gift by definition without return or reserve, it manages to make itself seen even at the point of abandonment, to the point of manifesting itself where no one expects it, where "the world did not recognize him" (John 1:10), in the finitude which cannot "receive" him (John 1:12), and finally in death, "and death on the cross" (Philippians 2:8). If infinite love can take figure in the finite, it is because it not only does not fear "the figure of the poverty and humility of love (*Armut- und Demutsgestalt der Liebe*),"[4] but in a way because it requires it. That is, finitude up to death, as long as it is understood on the basis of the love that gives itself (and there is no other kind), perfectly constitutes the privileged, even inevitable setting for manifesting the infinity proper to the gift without reserve. A love that abandons itself in the finite does not contradict the infinity of the gift in it, but, to the contrary, it manifests it. This dissolves the contradiction and (philosophical and metaphysical) impossibility of a manifestation of the infinite in the finite, the unconditioned in the conditioned, the invisible in the visible; for, in the figure of the (infinite) gift to the point of (finite) abandon, at least as Christ (and he alone) accomplishes it by his human death, the logic of God is perfectly manifest, without restriction or condition, in the *fixed* figure of love that "blows where it will" (John 3:8). And this is exactly what is lacking in every metaphysical interpretation of kenosis (see chapter 19).

Then and only then unfolds a Revelation received in conformity with the logic of love, where even the world unfolds in a new light: "when we view creation with the eyes of love, then we will understand it despite all the evidence that seems to point us to the absence of love in the world. We will understand the ultimate purpose (*Worum-willen*) of creation: not only the purpose of its essence . . . , but also the purpose of its existence [in general], for which no philosophy can otherwise find a sufficient reason (*zureichender Grund*). Why love something rather than nothing (*Warum in der Tat lieber etwas als nichts*)?"⁵ Clearly, Hans Urs von Balthasar is modifying the terms of Leibniz here, and rightly so, for from now on, it is no longer a matter of responding to the question, "Why is there something rather than nothing?" by assigning it a cause, a reason, or a foundation according to metaphysical logic; nor even by bringing it back from "the essence of truth and metaphysics up to the truth of Being" (Heidegger);⁶ rather, it has to do with understanding the properly *erotic* question, which requires us to conceive what reveals itself from the point of view of love's own logic: "Why love something rather than nothing?"⁷

Deconstructing the epistemological (and thus metaphysical) interpretation of Revelation, or even overcoming it in order to reestablish a *theo*-logical concept, thus supposes nothing less than passing from one logic to another: from the logic of the concept to that of the manifestation where love is phenomenalized. For this other logic must come exclusively from that which Revelation reveals—love. We have seen that the rationality deployed by metaphysics imposes no limits on the pretensions of theological "science" except those it imposes on its own epistemological function (chapter 6 above); and that this argument is immediately overturned as soon as we ask reason, which as a rule only legislates under its finitude and is consequently limited to knowing only *objects*, by what right it could impose its limits (the norms of its finitude) on that which, by definition, must and cannot do otherwise than transgress finitude in virtue of the infinite. There is no need to resort to Hegel to oppose the authority of the infinite to "critique": it is enough to listen to Schleiermacher: "Everything that exists is necessary for religion, and everything that can be is for it a true indispensable image of the infinite."⁸ What is left is to formulate this "image of the infinite." It is absolutely necessary to ask if what appears impossible for "reason," that is, *for us* mortals, is still impossible *for the gods* (or their proxies, if there are any), for whom, everyone agrees, nothing is impossible (above, chapters 2, 6–7). Yet it is not enough to evoke the rights of the impossible to make an "image" of it. It is still necessary to attain the *figure* (*Gestalt*), where the infinite and the finite meet as the impossible transpierces the possible; that is, it is necessary to enter into the logic of love, which alone explains and reveals such a figure, and its standing. But can this passage from one logic to the other be accomplished? Can we exempt ourselves from the common grammar of our spontaneous metaphysics? Ought we not, at least, keep silence before what we can neither say nor think?

Or, rather, should we perceive a conflict between logics, an incompatibility of the supposedly unique rationality accessible *to us* with that which ultimately concerns the figure of love? In other words, should we uphold the hypothesis of Wittgenstein: "If Christianity is the truth, then all the philosophy about it is false—*Wenn das Christentum die Wahrheit ist, dann ist alle Philosophie darüber falsch*"?[9] Unless it is appropriate to reverse the relation between terms: instead of judging Revelation from what philosophy authorizes for it in terms of rationality, we must instead gauge a philosophy by the degree that it allows (or at least does not forbid) us to think about Revelation. Schelling, at the moment he turns negative philosophy into positive philosophy in order to at least allow a philosophy of Revelation, asked precisely this: "But also, in the case of Christianity, we should not ask ourselves how we should think, in order to bring it into agreement with any philosophy; but conversely, what kind must philosophy be in order that it could also take on Christianity and understand it by concept (*in sich aufnehmen und begreifen*)."[10]

What the Concept Understands

Here the question that had remained implicit since the beginning of this research now fully comes to light: What is the meaning of what would have to be surpassed in order to think Revelation according to its own phenomenality? What does it mean "to comprehend (*comprendre*) by a concept"? What does the logic of the concept allow us to think and what does it forbid? In fact, the expression is redundant, because its two terms are literally one and the same: com*prendre* implies grasping (*prendre, greifen, capere*) and results in the *grasp* (*prise*) of what is thus conceived and kept (*Begriff, conceptus*). Of course, thinking does not always lead to a concept, because not every thought strives for a stranglehold (*emprise*) on the thing that is grasped (*comprise*); but in the conception of the concept, comprehension snatches up (*s'empare*) what it thinks, and only thinking by concept comprehends by stranglehold (*emprise*). This stranglehold is accomplished in two moments that are distinct but inseparable.

First of all, the concept proceeds by eliminating the unthinkable, itself understood in the narrow sense as the uncertain. Yet this assimilation of truth to knowledge and of knowledge to certainty is far from banal. For, if knowing implies thinking what we already know, it also consists in considering what we do not know yet, but what we sense still belongs to what we know already; in short, it consists in also confronting what we should know and what precisely we do not. For ancient thought, it followed that any knowledge that includes *hylē*, material matter, cannot result in a certain, immutable, and definitive science, for it does not cease to be changed, to pass from one form to another (to be transformed), in short, to "play" (as with time, air, and water, wood moves beyond the frame imposed on it by the carpenter). Hence the essential imprecision, for the Greeks (and the Latins), of the knowledge of the nature of the world: there cannot, *naturally*, be a concept of the natural world. Unless—and this is the epistemological revolution of (Cartesian) modernity—one attempts the *dematerialization* of things. That is, to admit as known only what the knowing mind can possess of it in unchangeable certainty, which means to *take* and *retain* from a thing only that which has no "play" in it; thus to eliminate from it all uncontrollable variations, in short, to abstract as much of its matter as possible—to dematerialize it. The concept thus reduces the thing to the sum of its calculable forms, which are precise and delimited, permanent and predictable, repeatable and reproducible. What is loosely named the mathematization of the world is only one of the tactics of this abstraction; others could be found that are not directly mathematical, which Descartes groups together under the title of *Mathesis universalis*. The contemporary dematerialization of data by network technology provides the most recent example. Of course, we do not suppress all material support (we still have the screen, the keyboard, the ports, the data storage centers, etc.), but it is precisely no longer primarily a matter of supports, which are interconnected, interchangeable, indifferent, and none of which are fixed as the privileged and durable form of the material. Nothing in-forms the material, because the form passes, indifferent and undifferentiated by them, from support to support. The form is dispensed with by "pure information" (endlessly coded, decoded, recoded), without ever being identified or phenomenalized in a material, without ever in-forming a thing. Dematerialized in this way, it becomes more and more a pure object of thought. In general, the concept dematerializes the thing to maintain only what thought can use from it and keep at its disposition; hence the possibility of being able to produce it at any moment and *almost* in its entirety, that is, to reproduce it, without the resistance of matter. The object, understood in this way, reproduces the thing and produces it *almost* as such (*an sich*).[11]

In a second step, it follows that the concept authorizes, or rather aims at, an appropriation: when I think an object of any kind, what it ends up being (precisely a thing restricted to the certitude *grasped* in it) is determined through and through more by the way I grasp it (my way of conceiving it) than by its own essence, which is in fact reduced and bracketed. For, following Descartes, "we must consider singular things according to the order they have for our knowledge of them in a different way than if we were speaking of these same things as they exist in reality (*aliter spectandas esse res singulas in ordine ad cognitionem nostram, quam si de iisdem loquamur prout revera existunt*)."[12] The object, because it only is as reduced by and to thought, is therefore radically defined according to this thought, as a thinkable of the *cogitatio*. As strange as it is logical, the ontology of metaphysics will not define being as a substance, nor as a something (*aliquid, tode ti*), but as a pure and simple thinkable—*ens ut intelligibile, ut cogitabile*.[13] Not only is my *cogitatio* able to reach nothing but objects, but every object is reduced to what my *cogitatio* produces, in such a way that it appropriates it. In other words, thought about myself ("I think") already "accompanies" (Kant)[14] every other thought, that is to say, every *cogitabile*, every possible object. We could thus approve the formula (which, however, is not Cartesian) that Heidegger constructs to expose the *ego cogito* of Descartes: *cogito me cogitare rem*—provided that we do not understand it to mean the reflection or redoubling of thought by itself (which Descartes always rejected), but the fact that the thinkable is always thought on the (transcendental and *a priori*) condition that my thought produces and permits it. We can qualify this as *appropriation*. In this concept, the consciousness of knowing is certainly founded on the consciousness of self, but a consciousness of self understood as the certain consciousness where the self governs the object (and consequently is itself certain). I cannot understand anything by concept unless *I* already find *myself* in it, grasping and comprehending. By concept, I recover everything, but only insofar as I retain what is certain for me in the thing; I lose nothing by reducing it to its object, because this object alone concentrates its certainty. By concept, I distill the thing into its spirit, the object; and, as I find all possible certainty (for me) in it, I lose nothing by losing the thing. Thus, I *find myself* there by finding my part in it. In other words, with the concept, I *always find my way—I know what I mean*.

The knowledge of the object, such as metaphysics establishes it and by which it is accomplished, can only reach poor and common law phenomena, not saturated phenomena, and still less phenomena of revelation (chapter 2). Proceeding by dematerialization and appropriation, it prohibits and indeed abstains from everything that could happen in and by itself, from *elsewhere*. And that means first and foremost what can be sensed under the still ambiguous term of Revelation.

Unconcealing or Uncovering

Thus, it is by dematerialization of the thing and appropriation of the object that the modern definition of truth is determined—the domain where nothing still remains in withdrawal, where everything is put forward and made available, where the *I* is served: *cogito me cogitare rem*. Whatever the shifts that lead to this ultimately nihilist figure, such a definition of truth is still founded on the *adaequatio rei et intellectus*, now understood as setting into order and at our disposition, organizing and bringing to reason. This definition is identified with the constitution of the metaphysical system, where the conditions of possibility of bringing something to certain evidence are formulated by Leibniz: in the principle of contradiction and the principle of sufficient reason.[15] They open and close, like gates of bronze, the only access to the true proposition, now object of a certain, and at least possible, possession. It is not surprising if I omit here a confrontation with the different states of the truth understood as *adaequatio* according to the example of Heidegger, who is still the only one, or nearly so, to consider what preceded *adaequatio* in the Greeks and what completed it in the moderns.[16] Retracing this genealogy not only surpasses what I myself could merely sketch, but it is also not required *here*. For I am pursuing another question, and to ask it, it is enough (it's already plenty) to interrogate the contemporary state of metaphysics in its terminal nihilism: If metaphysics accomplishes its mode of truth according to an un-concealment (*alētheia*) without withdrawal, which confirms the being that is brought to light for it as an object, might not Judeo-Christian *theo*-logy adopt another way of shedding light, comparable yet different, as an un-covering (*apokalypsis*)?

Following here a remark of Saint Jerome, who noticed that "this very word, ἀποκαλύψεος *(apokalypseōs)*, 'of revelation,' is peculiar to the Scriptures and was employed by none of the wise men of the age among the Greeks,"[17] I will provisionally choose to define such an un-covering by contrast with un-concealing, in order to perhaps succeed, little by little, in sketching out *theo*logically what Nicholas of Cusa called the "unrevealable vision revealed, *visio revalata irrevelabilis.*"[18] Yet again, let us specify that un-covering, which we seek in order to take up the concept of Revelation, *does not* correspond (chapters 5–7 above) to what was imposed, restricted, and ignored by metaphysics under the title of "revelation." Rather, we are asking if and how the un-covering, the bringing to light accomplished by Revelation, can *any longer* be included (even as the crowning achievement and ultimate variation) within the same mechanism as the "reason" of metaphysics (even taken up by speculative dialectics), which brings to evidence and takes up possession of a statement unveiled without remainder by concept. We ask: How *must* what Revelation un-covers (whatever it is) overflow the field where reason un-conceals its truth? Or yet again: When reason *unconceals* the truth (*alētheia*), does it proceed according to the same operations as Revelation (*apokalypsis*) when it *uncovers* what it gives to know? Clearly, this question could not be formulated as long as the epistemological interpretation of Revelation seemed self-evident (chapters 3–4, above). This questionable decision masked the originality and the difficulty of the *uncovering* that Revelation carries out, because it was assimilated without critical precaution to what (philosophical) truth carries out when it unconceals; the screen of its epistemological interpretation and of the *propositio sufficiens* obscures the character proper to Revelation as *apokalypsis*, which is missed, or masked, by the evidence of the truth as *alētheia*. Indeed, since the vulgar (and indeterminate) concept of "revelation" stems from a recent polemic between theologians and metaphysicians, the result is that the "revelation" that the former was reconstructed against was still defined in terms of the latter; the complicit antagonism of "revelation" and "reason" has closed all access to the determination proper to *apokalypsis*, or, at best, has left it radically undetermined, prisoner of a frantic polemic. The only thing that remained for this lost "revelation" was to try, rather poorly, to justify itself by establishing itself as a belief based on reason and thus by setting forth its own proven propositions in conformity with the metaphysical definition of truth. Only in this way did theology believe it could elicit the assent of the understanding and receive approval from the will, following Descartes's formulation: "From a great light in the intellect followed a great inclination in the will—*Ex magna luce in intellectu magna consequuta est propensio in voluntate.*"[19]

However, against the logic of unconcealment (according to *alētheia* and its metaphysical destiny), there is another logic just as thinkable, which can rigorously conceive the un-covering of Revelation as *apokalypsis*; not only does this other logic differ from that of un-concealment, but it exactly reverses its terms. Even though marginal in appearance, this tradition nevertheless regularly crops up with a perfect coherence in a number of texts; in William of Saint-Thierry we even find the two terms used by Descartes, but in reverse order: "*non tam ratio voluntatem, quam voluntas trahere videtur rationem ad fidem*—for it is not so much the reason that draws the will [toward the evidence], as the will that draws the reason toward faith."[20]

Pascal's Reversal

Let us first confirm that this logic of knowledge, where the will (understood here as love) determines the understanding, is indeed opposed to the common logic of knowledge (understood here in its Cartesian sense). Pascal, a shrewd reader of Descartes and at least indirectly familiar with the Fathers, perfectly thematized their antagonism: "Hence, instead of speaking about human things that have to be known before they can be loved, which has become a proverb, the saints, speaking of divine things, say that you have to love them in order to know them, and that you enter into truth only by charity, which they have made into one of their most useful pronouncements."[21] In fact, Pascal (and probably William of Saint-Thierry) comments here on a remarkable formula of Saint Augustine, which one must read in its context: "*Probamus etiam ipsum* [i.e., *Spiritum Sanctum*] *inducere in omnem veritatem, quia non intratur in veritatem, nisi per charitatem: 'Charitas autem Dei diffusa est,' ait Apostolus, 'in cordibus nostris per Spiritum Sanctum qui datus est nobis'* (Rom 5:5)."[22] In other words: as revealed truth is only discovered in fact and by right because the Holy Spirit, poured out in our hearts (according to Saint Paul) leads us to it, so the condition of possibility of *un-covering* is no longer ensured by the ego following the conditions of possibility of the experience of *finite* objects (namely, "critique," the principles of metaphysics, clear and distinct ideas, evidence that is certain); but this possibility comes to it from *elsewhere* according to charity, which henceforth plays the role of a first (and new) condition to know what, for finite reason, remains still as inaccessible and *impossible* (or unthinkable), unless it is admitted *as impossible*. In both cases, it is a question of knowing "things" (human or divine), but the conditions of knowledge diverge. Either the finite ego redefines the thing to its measure (according to its conditions) in order to constitute it as an object and thus the inaugural light in the understanding (the proposition) is then found validated (or not) by the will; or, conversely, the ego, whose understanding remains finite but, for all that, inscribed in the horizon of the infinite[23] (as proven by the will which nothing limits),[24] begins by willing (or not), by loving (or not), what could eventually surpass its understanding. Then in the light of the infinite will, the ego conceives (or not) what it cannot even try to constitute as an object, because the "thing" appears to it from *elsewhere*.

Two logics and two determinations of knowledge thus come into conflict here: either knowing according to the measure of the ego, thus according to the finite understanding which redefines the thing as an object; or knowing according to the measure of the thing that gives itself, regardless of the finitude of the understanding, and which is therefore manifest as a saturated phenomenon. The antagonism of these two logics is neatly defined according to where the center of gravity lies in the act of knowing. Thus, it is not a contradiction, offering no other way out than absurdity or the wager (as is most often concluded, by a stubborn misinterpretation that conversely attests the rigor of the antagonism between both logics). Rather, it is a rational distinction between two uses of reason, based on the intended goal (the certainty of the object or else the phenomenality of *elsewhere*) and according to the hierarchy of modes of thought (primacy of understanding or primacy of the will, and therefore of love). Pascal thematized this critical scheme by the doctrine of the three orders, bodies, mind, and charity. Just as the world of bodies obeys the logic of the sensible visible and the world, and mind (e.g., the scholars, the philosophers, in this case Descartes) founds mathematical evidence and worldly beings on the *ego cogito* (and not the inverse, as the evidence of the first order stubbornly imagines it), so the saints, who live and see all things according to the logic of charity, overturn the hierarchy of the first two orders by ordering all things according to what they make appear in the spectral light of love. The distinction of the orders does not abolish logic; it complicates it by multiplying it.

The Pronouncement of the Saints

Without advancing further into the theoretical elaboration of this confrontation between, on the one hand, "a proverb" (knowing in order to love), and on the other, the "most useful pronouncements" (loving in order to know) (see below, chapter 10), let us try to confirm the historical consistency Pascal claims this confrontation has. Indeed, testimonies confirming a well-established opposition abound.

Keeping to the Latin tradition, we can go back at least as far as Saint Augustine: "*Alia sunt enim quae nisi intelligamus, non credimus; et alia sunt quae nisi credamus, non intelligimus*—For there are some things we do not believe if we do not understand them; and other things that we do not understand if we do not [first] believe."[25] This dichotomy can be precisely given in a triple specification:

Credibilium tria sunt genera. Alia sunt quae semper creduntur et nunquam intelliguntur: sicut est omnis historia. . . . Alia quae mox, ut creduntur, intelliguntur, sicut sunt omnes rationes humanae. . . . Tertium, quae primo creduntur et postea intelliguntur, qualia sunt ea, quae de divinis rebus non possunt intelligi, nisi ab his qui mundo sunt corde—What can be believed is of three kinds. First, there are those things which always are believed, but never understood, such as any historical report. . . . Second, there are things which are understood as soon as they are believed, such as all human reasons. . . . Third, everything that is first believed and afterwards understood, as that which, concerning divine things, cannot be understood except by those who are pure in heart.[26]

This complication has the merit of indicating without ambiguity that it is not a matter of opposing ignorant belief to pure and simple knowledge (as for Plato, Aristotle, or Spinoza, along with the majority of philosophers), but of surpassing this aporia by a third way: enlightening and opening understanding by the decision of the will, in short, *believing in order to understand*, believing in order to see. This line also passes through Gilbert of Poitiers, who clearly marks this reversal: "In other faculties, we always accommodate the generality and necessity of the habitual rule, it is not reason that follows faith, but faith that follows reason. . . . In the theological domains, however, where the necessity of true and absolute denomination reigns, it is not reason that precedes faith but faith that precedes reason. For here we do not believe by knowing, we know by believing. Indeed, faith conceives without principles of reasons not only of things that human reasons are not sufficient to comprehend, but also those for which these very things can serve as principles."[27] Faith is no longer in the situation of having to choose between rejecting to the point of absurdity arguments of simple reason, or submitting to them automatically; no, faith can also at times provoke arguments, triggering and inciting them, by first admitting new data of experience or new principles of reason. It is not only a question of inverting the common philosophical scheme: "*Doctrina Aristotelis est de his de quibus ratio facit fidem, sed Christi doctrina de his quorum fides facit rationem*—The doctrine of Aristotle concerns the things wherein it is reason that produces faith, but the doctrine of Christ concerns those wherein faith produces reason"[28]—but of understanding that rationality and intelligence increase in direct proportion to voluntary decision and faith: "*Inquantum* [sc. *Deus*] *creditur, in tantum cognoscitur*—the more one believes in God, the more one knows him." Or again, "*Fides enim qua creditur est lumen animarum, quo quanto quis magis illustratur, tanto magis est perspicax ad inveniendas rationes, quibus probentur credenda*—For the faith by which one believes is however that of souls, such that the more one is illuminated, the more perceptive it is in finding reasons that prove what must be believed."[29] The compensation of ignorance by belief (which philosophy describes) is indeed inverted in the provocation of understanding by faith (which opens to theology).

Knowing Love by Loving

However, the best exposé of this other logic is found first in William of Saint-Thierry, who formulated it in Augustinian terms, pushing them to their final consequences: "Indeed, in human things, human reason [first] prepares itself to have faith; but in divine things faith advances first, then it forms itself a rationality appropriate to its own kind. For taking faith according to what the thing is [in itself] and thus having to adjust the form of faith to its expression, this is the most rational way of proceeding—*In rebus enim humanis humana ratio parat sibi fidem; in divinis vero præcedit fides, deinde ipsa sui generis format sibi rationem. Sicut enim res est, sic de ea fidem captare, et locutionis formam fidei coaptandam esse, rectissima ratio est.*"[30] Here the inversion of the order between faith (thus the will) and reason (thus the understanding) is deepened as reason conforms to what it aims at, which only becomes accessible to it through faith. Faith is not substituted for reason, but reforms and reformulates it. For in fact, the intervention anticipated by faith is not accomplished by a simple methodological preamble as, for example, in Descartes, where leading back from what is given in experience to what is formalized in the *ordo et mensura* serves to prepare the thing as a potentially certain object, which the *mathesis universalis* can then include in its system. To the contrary, faith, by believing, believes in (divine) love, and in order to believe in it, it must already love it. Faith begins to love at once and hence at once experiences love, precisely because love is not known except by being practiced, by loving in return. The act of faith consists therefore and without delay in immediately "understanding by loving, and loving by understanding—*amando intelligere et intelligendo amare.*"[31] Or more explicitly,

Conforming his life and morals not only to believe what is believed, but also to hope for it and love it, [the faithful] also understands by loving and by understanding he loves. Thus, having had faith in God, this spirit merits the Holy Spirit, grace merits grace, faith merits understanding, the affect of piety and the understanding of love, "which takes every understanding captive to make it obedient to Christ" (2 Cor. 10:5) such that, according to what is written, "if you do not believe, you will not understand" (Is. 7:9), the one who believes in loving, that one merits understanding what he believes—Vitam etiam moresque coaptans, ut quod creditur non solum credatur, sed et speretur et diligatur, et diligendo intelligatur et intelligendo diligatur. Sic enim creditus cum Deo, spiritus meretur Spiritum Sanctum, gratia gratiam, fides intellectum et affectum pietatis et intellectum amoris, "in captivitatem redigentem omnem intellectum in obsequium Christi," ut secundum quod scriptum est, "nisi credideritis, non intelligetis," qui credit amando, intelligere mereatur quod credit.[32]

Thus rationality is not abolished in love, nor does it vanish before it; but, under the figure of faith, which puts it into practice, it is conformed to love by envisaging it in person and even in accepting it: "love is fortified by reason, but reason is enlightened by love. . . . Reason effects love, while love affects reason—*amor ratione munitur, ratio vero ab amore illuminatur. . . . Ratio efficit amorem, amor autem afficit rationem.*"³³ The essential point is in this: as long as it accepts what faith proposes, reason instantly experiences what faith accomplishes from the outset—it loves. From then on it has access to a domain of investigation and contemplation that is radically new but open to intelligence (precisely what we call the understanding *of faith*)—love. In this way we can not only reconcile and entangle these two terms, but can even equate them: "For love of God itself is *itself* understanding of him; he who is only understood by being loved, and loved by being understood; and, absolutely speaking, he is only understood insofar as he is loved, and he is only loved insofar as he is understood—*Amor quippe Dei ipse intellectus est, qui non nisi amatus intelligitur, nec nisi intellectus amatur; et utique tantum intelligitur, quantum amatur, tantum amatur quantum intelligitur.*"³⁴ In the final instance, not only do reason and faith coincide tangentially as the intellect and love,³⁵ but, according to a profoundly Augustinian thematic, thinking is the same as loving: "Who thinks and does not love? Surely, God is, he is that very thing, because thinking and loving are this, the same—*Quis cogitat et non amat? Nimirum Deus est, idipsum est, quod cogitare et amare idipsum est.*"³⁶

We can note this first result: before the logic of *unconcealment*, performed in philosophy by truth as *alētheia*, another logic can be detected, that of *uncovering*, implemented by Revelation as *apokalypsis*. They radically differ, beginning with the way they order the will and understanding: in the one case, to admit a truth, it is always necessary to understand its proposition; in the other, to understand what it is about (love or charity), it is necessary to will it first, to will it *well*, and therefore ultimately to love it. To go any further, we must pass from a purely theoretical rationality to a rationality that is *also pragmatic*: Revelation uncovers and is uncovered because it must do so and it cannot be known except by being practiced. It is not only a question here of the pragmatic use that philosophy has learned to recognize as one of the possibilities of language, but of a requirement of that which Revelation uncovers: it uncovers love, and therefore the practice of love, which can only be seen and conceived if I do it myself. For love does not allow itself to be known except by the one who practices it, puts it into action, or in short, who makes love. So it is with Revelation above all else, if at least it is finally approached as an un-covering of love. In the case of love, it is necessary to believe it in order to see.

Believing here thus takes on a precise function: to indicate, or rather to accomplish what faith knows by putting it into *practice*; such that it is no longer only a matter of propositional and predicative knowledge without certainty, nor that of a foundation, but of a knowledge tested in action—the knowledge of love verified by the act of loving. Such an act of loving, an essential precondition that precedes knowledge of love and which makes it possible, alone justifies the reversal of the principle "seeing in order to believe" into the paradox "believing in order to see." Indeed, it puts into action the character that has allowed us from the beginning to identify revelation as a phenomenon that comes from *elsewhere* (chapters 1–2). The one who agrees to believe *first* opens the possibility that what she will see may come to her from *elsewhere*. And by exposing herself to the *elsewhere*, she reverses its intentionality by an anamorphosis; from a self-centered ego, she becomes a witness of what she sees without being ever able to reduce it to her concept. From now on it is a question of describing more precisely how this *elsewhere* invests and replaces the one who believes in order to see.

NINE

"Ista revelatio, ipsa est attractio"

We have confirmed, if only in a summary fashion, the historical consistency of this other logic, according to which the will determines the understanding and one must believe in order to see. Now the task is to identify the conceptual origin of this reversal of terms. This origin could come only from a phenomenality that is properly *theo*-logical, which cannot not appear impracticable, at least at first: "So we must begin again with this in mind. To think God is difficult, to tell of him is impossible, as a theologian among the Greeks [Plato] has taught.... But even to tell of him is impossible, while to think him, so my argument runs, is very impossible (νοῆσαι δὲ ἀδυνατώτερον)."¹ Nevertheless, this impossibility must not discourage us, since it registers within the mode of knowledge (epistemologically, we might say) the phenomenal dimension of the *elsewhere* that we are seeking to penetrate. In order to travel the anamorphosis that leads from one logic to the other, it is necessary to cross it through the experience of a serious and effective *elsewhere*—it is necessary that this passage *elsewhere* indeed come to us from *elsewhere*.

Not by Will

At first one might try to avoid such an anamorphosis. In order to approach this other logic, one could simply repeat the priority of the will over the understanding in the practical use of reason, taking up Kant's approach of defining the will in general as the faculty that can produce not only representations but even the object of these representations. "The power of desire is a being's *power to be by means of its representations the cause of the reality of the objects of these representations*."² In other words, instead of adjusting its representations to already-known objects, reason adjusts objects according to its own representations, in such a way that it could also render them real through its own causality—that is, through its will. With this usage, once again we have an application of theoretical reason within the practical, since the will either makes real the objects that it already represents to itself, or normalizes its actions according to a (moral) law that it already thinks. In this way the distinction between the faculties remains, but their hierarchy is inverted, and the will can determine the understanding. Remaining strictly within the philosophical realm, we would thus find an analogy with the Pascalian reversal, where one must love "divine things" in order to know them.

And yet this is not the case, and it is instructive to see the differences that remain between the two doctrines. The first difference goes without saying: the simple fact that the will (the power of desiring) is applied directly to the reality of the objects is not sufficient to substitute practical reason for theoretical reason. Practical reason (the will) knows nothing other than what theoretical reason knows, even if it puts it into operation; a particular maxim becomes neither true nor even more precise by the mere fact that an individual will tries to accomplish it. The moral law itself is perfection known without the will (through *factum rationis*) and its always imperfect realization by the will adds nothing to it. The mere inversion of the order of the faculties for the benefit of the will does not allow knowledge to grow. To this we can add a second difference: clearly, at stake here is precisely not the inverting of the uses of pure reason, nor of assigning to the will a power to *know*; reason recognizes in the will a pragmatic function, but this pragmatic function allows only for *acting* according to reason, and not for extending the field of the understanding. But the third difference is even more important. For immediately after the critique of theoretical (pure) reason, knowledge always proceeds from the knowing mind, taken as the absolute pole (through consideration of the *a priori*, of transcendental apperception, of the anticipations of experience, of the postulates of empirical thought in general, etc.); such that nothing comes to the ego from *elsewhere*, apart from "the manifold of intuition," which precisely is not yet phenomenalized of itself. When practical reason and the primacy of the will are at issue, and thus the ego as cause of the objects of its representations, the exclusion of the *elsewhere* is all the more enforced; in this case, the ego can even claim a complete autonomy, since nothing empirical determines it any longer from *elsewhere*.[3] In this way the overturning of the hierarchy of the faculties and the primacy of the will in the practical usage of reason not only do not reestablish the opening to *elsewhere*, but intensify the closure. Another path must be followed, then, in order to conceive the "pronouncement of the Fathers." With "divine things" not only does the will (the power of believing or of loving) allow and elicit a new knowledge (in the understanding), but, according to William of Saint-Thierry, "to ponder him and to love him is the same—*cogitare et amare idipsum est*."[4] In other words, when knowing love is the question, only love thinks correctly. The distinction between theoretical reason and practical reason collapses.

An interaction of the faculties is not conceived by combining them, even in a novel way, and simply redistributing them in another organization than that of common theory. It is conceived only by bringing them back to the new *elsewhere* that calls them all together. This new *elsewhere* is located in Revelation, because only there does Revelation open itself.

Attraction

Although he did not have frequent recourse to the concept of *revelatio*,[5] we owe it to Saint Augustine to have reformulated the question and noted so starkly that the *elsewhere* cannot arise in us except from a radical *elsewhere*; in other words, it must not arise from us, but from another, from the one who by definition precedes us because we proceed from him—the Father. The beginning of a response could come from a more attentive reading of one of his rare formulations that echoes the paradox that we seek under the title of Revelation: "*Ista revelatio, ipsa est attractio*—That which uncovers is precisely what draws."[6] These words are grasped only as the result of a rather detailed commentary on John 6:44: "No one can come to me unless the Father who sent me has drawn him—ἑλκύσῃ αὐτόν, *traxerit eum*." Yet this formula raises an evident and sensible objection: if, according to the Beatitudes, those who "hunger and thirst for righteousness . . . shall be filled" (Matthew 5:6), then a desire, a hunger, a prior will must be supposed, if only that God might fill it; but, in this case, how can one believe passively, through drawing and attraction (*"Nemo venit nisi tractus"*)? Indeed, we all experience that we believe only if we will it (*"credere non potest nisi volens"*)[7]; and that when we do not will it we in fact do not believe; and inversely that "to confess is to say what you have in your heart—*Hoc est enim confiteri dicere quod habes in corde.*"[8] However, there remains the declaration of John 6:44, which can be confirmed by the common experience, that "the soul is drawn also by love—*trahitur animus et amore.*"[9]

But this aporia opens the way to its surpassing: for I am in fact less drawn through my will than, above all, the desire for my own pleasure (*"Parum est voluntate, etiam voluptate traheris"*). Everyone learns this as soon as he finds himself loving with passion (*"Da amantem, et sentit quod dico*—Give me a man that loves, and he understands what I say").[10] To confirm it, one could even invoke Virgil's authority (*"Trahit sua quemque voluptas*—His own pleasure draws each man"),[11] as well as that of the Scriptures: "Take pleasure in the Lord (*delectare in Domino*), and he will grant you your heart's desires" (Psalms 36:4); or "They will be inebriated by the richness of your house; and you will give them to drink of the torrent of your pleasure (*et torrente voluptatis tuae potabis eos*). For with you is the fountain of life" (Psalms 35:8–10). We have not only the right (*licet*) but also the duty (*debemus*) to admit that we are "drawn," swept away, pulled by the desire for the pleasure of what we love, when we love truly, and thus when we love God.[12] In the experience of being drawn, we experience nothing less than the fundamental logic of love: *"Amando trahitur*—By loving, one is drawn."[13] And yet, this attraction remains free, for without it we absolutely could not love at all. What is more, the spreading of this attraction into hearts (through the Holy Spirit) properly characterizes the God who loves and makes others love: "*trahere Dei est.*"[14] For Christ would not let anyone come to him if he did not render manifest in himself the Father; that is to say, if he did not uncover (reveal) him: *"non trahit revelatus Christus a Patre?*—does not Christ uncovered by the Father draw?" (here the ablative bears on the two verbs).[15] Or again: "*Trahit Pater ad Filium eos qui propterea credunt in Filium, quia eum cogitant Patrem habere Deum*—The Father draws to the Son those who believe in the Son for the reason that they think that he has God as his Father."[16] To see Jesus with the eyes of flesh as the Christ, and thus also as the Son, presupposes ("naturally," if you like) that one believes him to be such, that is, that one believes in the Father, something that only the Father ("supernaturally," if you like) can give.

From this there follow the two essential features of a theological understanding of Revelation. First: Revelation consists precisely in our attraction by the Father toward the Son, so that we see the Father in him: "*Ista revelatio, ipsa est attractio*" (see below, chapters 16–17).[17] Whether this attraction is felt as gentle or violent[18] (or both at once) changes nothing: Revelation simultaneously exerts these two effects, simply because it brings itself fully to bear. We believe in God when we will it, clearly; but we will it only when we love that which we desire; and in the case of God, we receive this desire (a desire for pleasure) first of all from *elsewhere*, from God alone: "A person is drawn to Christ who is given the gift to believe in Christ.... Unless this power is given by God, it cannot arise from free choice, because it will not be free for what is good if the deliverer has not set it free."[19] Revelation assumes a plot, in which the attraction acts first on the will, which then makes the reason choose to see what it would otherwise not will to see. Seeing is the result of the decision to see, but this decision, made by me, nevertheless comes to me from *elsewhere*. I must make the decision to make a decision, will to be willing in order to arrive at seeing. Revelation comes to me, when I will it, from an attraction from *elsewhere*.

Yet the attraction holds as Revelation only because it allows us to see Jesus as the Christ, that is to say, as the Son of the Father, as the visibility of the invisible. There is nothing to add: "*Nisi ergo revelet ille qui intus est, quid dico aut quid loquor?*—Unless he who is within should uncover, what do I say, or what do I speak?"[20] We understand better why vision (uncovering) depends on a will (decision): I see the Father only if I interpret (in "the Holy Spirit poured out in our hearts") Jesus as the Son of the Father—if I *am willing* to interpret him in this way, and thus if I love him. Here we can no longer allow for any *propositio sufficiens objecti revelati* known even without being believed (*etsi non credatur*), for without a hermeneutic decision, there is nothing to see, nothing to believe, and therefore nothing that is uncovered. When it comes to Revelation, the one who wants to see without having to believe sees nothing. Clement of Alexandria conceived of genuine *gnōsis* in this way: "There is no knowledge without faith, nor faith without knowledge, nor is the Father without the Son—οὔτε ἡ γνῶσις ἄνευ πίστεως οὔθ' ἡ πίστις ἄνευ γνώσεως, οὐ μὴν οὐδὲ ὁ πατὴρ ἄνευ υἱοῦ."[21] Revelation happens to me through hermeneutics, which is to say, through the *conversion* from one intentionality into another.²² This reversal of the ego's intentionality to that which appears to it (and not only the reversal of the hierarchy between the will and the understanding) is phenomenologically defined as anamorphosis. Here the anamorphosis imposes on the ego a counter-intentionality arising from Christ, in order to aim at the Father, through Christ as the Son of the Father. Because such an anamorphosis inscribes itself within a radically *theo*logical field, only the Holy Spirit can accomplish it in the ego that accepts such a conversion. The phenomenal practice of the *elsewhere* in me depends therefore on the "spirit of sonship" that, "poured out in our hearts," allows us to "cry *Abba*, Father" (Romans 5:5 and 8:15; see also Galatians 4:6). In this sense, Revelation uncovers itself to me only through an other than me within me, more me than me. I am an other, but that other remains *for that very reason* me within me, *interior intimo meo*.

Sensus Mentis

In a direct line from Saint Augustine, William of Saint-Thierry reinforces this *theo*logical understanding of Revelation. Taking up the Augustinian adage freely drawn from Isaiah 7:9 in the Septuagint, "Unless you believe, you will not understand,"²³ he contests, in terms that are already like those of Pascal, the notion that one could know the "divine things" without having first believed: "*In eis vero quae sunt ad Deum, sensus mentis amor est*—In those things which pertain to God, the sense that allows the mind to attain them is love."²⁴ Here, "this science consists only in a mode or disposition of the mind for receiving [and taking up] those things which derive properly from faith";²⁵ consequently, it is first necessary to believe, and therefore first to love, for the same operation is at play in both acts (*idipsum*): "Who knows without loving? Surely God is one and the same (*idipsum*)! To ponder him and to love him is the same (*idipsum*)! I say ponder *him* and not ponder *about* him. Many persons [only] ponder *about* him, because they do not love him. But no one ponders *him* without loving him."²⁶ Thus to claim to know a *propositio sufficiens* without believing it would be equivalent to agreeing to be cared for and healed without trusting or loving one's doctor.²⁷ This first conclusion follows: *no one can see that which is uncovered (apokalypsis) unless he believes it.*

Next, taking up the Augustinian commentary on John 6:44 on revelation as attraction (*"nisi Pater traxerit eum"*), William of Saint-Thierry repeats its logic: "If you do not will to believe, you do not believe. Yet you believe if you will it; but you do not will it unless you are first helped by grace. For 'no one comes to the Son unless the Father draws him.' . . . But you do not will to [believe] unless you are drawn by the Father; and if you will it, you will it because you are drawn by the Father."[28] From this paradox he draws the second significant consequence: willing consists in loving, and signifies nothing else. The will only wills if it finds and experiences an attraction that puts it into operation. Now, this attraction, always coming from *elsewhere* (generally, from the thing willed), comes, in the case of God, from that which gives itself all the more to be loved as he himself, God, loves; when the subject is love, which consists only in love, knowing it amounts to loving it. From this point I can only will by loving, by a universal rule, but all the more so because what is loved *here* identifies itself with love: "*Voluntas enim haec aliquatenus jam amor Christi est*—This will is in a certain sense already the love of Christ."[29] This maxim, above all, must not be understood as a medieval anticipation of the implicit faith of the "anonymous Christian," as if every will were unconsciously oriented toward Christ; rather, precisely the opposite: as the recognition of the fact that no will comes to will except in proportion to what attracts it, and thus to what it loves. We understand, then, that it wills more the more it loves Christ, who is God revealing himself as loving. In this way William of Saint-Thierry is able to take up, and even deepen, the Augustinian definition of love: "*Voluntas enim initium amoris est. Amor siquidem vehemens voluntas est*—The will is the beginning of love. Love then is a vehement will."[30] Or: "*Nichil enim aliud est amor, quam vehemens et bene ordinata voluntas . . . bonae voluntatis vehementia amor in nobis dicitur*—Love is nothing other than a will that is vehement and well-ordered . . . we call love the vehemence of a good will."[31] A second conclusion follows here: no one can see that which is uncovered (*apokalypsis*) unless he believes it; but no one can believe if he does not will it, and *no one can will unless he loves what he believes and wills to will*.

This leads to a third and decisive conclusion. If indeed no one can see that which is uncovered (*apokalypsis*) unless he believes it; if, in addition, no one can believe if he does not will to do so, and no one can will if he does not love, then no one can see unless he loves—and thus, in the end, *in a situation of Revelation (apokalypsis, uncovering), seeing is the same as loving*, which is the contrary of the situation of truth (*alētheia*, *unconcealment*), where knowing means seeing and knowing directly: "*Ratio docet amorem, et amor illuminat rationem*—reason teaches love and love enlightens reason."³² Or further: "*amor ex fide spe mediante per cognitionem oriatur; et fides itidem in amore per cognitionem solidetur*—love arises from faith through the knowledge that hope mediates; and faith too is reinforced in love through knowledge."³³ Love knows and makes itself known, but on *one* condition: that its freedom to set the conditions of *its* knowledge be recognized; that is, that it be free to begin with the will, insofar as it can first be converted and convert the mind to love from *elsewhere*. This condition defines what going forward we shall call *un-covering*, or in other words *apokalypsis*. Such an uncovering of love by itself puts into operation a rule known by the Church Fathers: "to learn *about* God *from* God, παρὰ θεοῦ περὶ θεοῦ . . . μαθεῖν." Or put another way: "The Lord taught us that no one can know God unless God himself is the Teacher; that is to say, without God, God is not to be known—*Edocuit autem Dominus quoniam Deum scire nemo potest nisi Deo docente, hoc est sine Deo non cognosci Deum.*"³⁴ If God unfolds himself as love, the Revelation of his love can be fulfilled and received only through loving. The mode of Revelation is determined by the mode of its reception, by what is uncovered there: "Let us at least agree to speak mystically of mystical things and in a holy manner of holy things—μυστικῶς τὰ μυστικὰ φθέγγεσθαι, καὶ ἁγίως τὰ ἅγια."³⁵

Thus Revelation puts itself into operation when I come to will from *elsewhere* than myself, or in other words, from *elsewhere* than from what my understanding immediately represents to me; so that I only know by being willing and after having willed it; I will without the precondition of knowing it, but in willing it I know that I accomplish it, and thus, all of a sudden, I know it, period. This perfect coincidence between the will and knowledge (which invert not only their order of operation, but merge in their *idipsum*) is completed eminently and above all when I will to love, for love is conceived only in its act; love is only proven when it *is made*; and it is made only when I consent to making it. I know my love—what I love truly and what it is deep down to love—only in making the decision to will to love. Revelation, therefore, happens to me from *elsewhere*, finally uncovering me to myself. This is enough to distinguish Revelation from imposition: it is not a question of undergoing an external imposition that, against my free will, would force me to do what I do not want; here I do from *elsewhere* what I did not believe I spontaneously wanted to do, because before doing it voluntarily I did not yet have the least idea or knowledge of it. And this is what distinguishes Revelation from ideology: it is not an empty or dominated will that would will what it neither can nor wants to comprehend, or what it exempts itself from even conceiving, because it bracketed the work of its understanding in order to rely on the rationalized delusion that dispenses it from thinking by persuading it to know without having sought; instead, here I understand from *elsewhere* what I do by willing it, because, to my great amazement, when I accomplish it, it uncovers itself to me.

Knowing the Gift

A situation of Revelation gives rise to what I did not yet know, by letting my desiring will finally accomplish what it truly wills; and here I truly will what I truly will *because* (and not *although*) what I didn't myself know (that I was able) to will comes to me from *elsewhere*. Henceforth I must learn to know what my will *truly* wills. For the truth about my will comes to me from much further away than my mere understanding can imagine knowing. I will much more than what I think, not because I simply could not know what I will (out of weakness or hesitation), but because my desire escapes me, surpasses me, and comes to me from *elsewhere*. To be sure, my understanding is always outstripped by my will (as Descartes says), but my will itself lags behind my desire (as Saint Augustine says). For my desire happens to me without my knowing it or measuring it or awaiting it—without my even expecting it. What I will I must therefore believe, because, spontaneously and as things are, it is something I do not know. Like Perceval, I fancy I am seeing a lance pass by without knowing that it is the precise and glorious object of my desire and of my deepest will—the Grail. What is given exceeds what can be shown, because it overflows what my gaze can *actualize*. The objective is never limited to an object because desire has no object, even if it always aims at an objective.

Paradoxical as the conceptual formulation may appear, this logic nevertheless puts itself into operation constantly in the banality of everyday life. Or rather, the banality of everyday life can often demonstrate a simplicity that is paradoxical—and sometimes essentially *theo*logical. Take for example the account of the encounter between a Samaritan woman and Christ, which sets the paradigm of the unknown objective and the unknown gift in a dialogue with several moments that fit together with precision (John 4:3–42).[36] First, this was an encounter that should not have taken place, for

"*Ista revelatio, ipsa est attractio*" 133

several reasons: in public a woman must not initiate a conversation with a man; and a Jew never speaks to a Samaritan, much less a woman of Samaria ("How is it that you, a Jew, ask a drink of me, a woman of Samaria? For Jews have no dealings with Samaritans," verse 9); all the more so because this woman, as Jesus knows, lives in an irregular situation (a "sinner," verse 17). And the disciples, for their part, "marveled, ἐθαύμαζον" at this encounter (verse 27), even if they dared not say anything. Jesus therefore had to take the initiative in opening a dialogue that was in principle forbidden to men, and once spoken, this speech immediately accomplished what remains impossible for man. But there is more: this speech speaks of (and begins from) what for man remains most difficult, or even almost inaccessible, but which belongs properly to God: the gift. Man does not spontaneously practice the gift, preferring appropriation. At best, he conceives the gift as a ruse for appropriating that which he believes he lacks. In asking her for a gift ("Give me a drink," verse 7), Jesus thus provokes the Samaritan woman, not only by speaking to her, not only by asking her for help and in that way inverting the inequality of their respective conditions (man/woman, Jew/Samaritan), but, more radically, by asking of a human precisely what he or she accomplishes the least often, and the most badly: a *gift*. Jesus thus undertakes to open a forbidden dialogue in order to ask his dumbfounded interlocutor for an act that remains impossible for her.

It is unsurprising, then, when the discussion, refused at first, immediately turns into a misunderstanding. I say a discussion that is at first refused because the Samaritan woman reminds Jesus with insolence of his duties as a Jew: precisely, not to speak to her (verse 9). And a discussion that next turns into a misunderstanding because, faced with the rebuff of his request for physical water to drink, Jesus repeats his request, but this time by reversing the direction of the gift and playing on the equivocation about the water, now called "living water": "If you knew the gift of God, and who it is that is saying to you, 'Give me a drink,' you would have asked him, and he would have given you living water" (verse 10).[37] The Samaritan woman's refusal and the equivocation in her response come together into two heterogeneous but perfectly rational arguments. The first is a material argument: How could Jesus give water when he has no container with which to draw it from the well (verse 11)? The next is a religious argument: to find water without drawing it (the only other possibility left after the first argument) it would be necessary to do without this well (not depend on it, find another, etc.), and thus to claim to be superior to "our father Jacob," who made the gift of it to "us" (verse 12). Jesus, this time without irony, answers these two arguments (verses 13–14): he doesn't need anything in order to give the water, neither a pitcher nor a well, because in fact he does not need to draw it, since it comes from himself (thus at his death, from his side "there came out blood and water," John 19:34). The Samaritan woman, for the first time, accepts this response: "Sir [Lord, Κύριε], give me this water, that I may not thirst, nor come here to draw" (verse 15); but she only accepts it to the extent that she understands it. For her, they are still talking about natural water, simply endowed with better physio-chemical properties because it flows from a higher source; she does not yet understand that it has to do with Christ himself. The question is thus indeed reversed, and the direction of the gift as well, but the signification of what is at stake, the "water" and the "life," remain masked in the materiality of the thing drunk and seen.

What is still needed to succeed in recognizing the gift? In the midst of the "true worshippers" (verse 23) the whole "truth" (verse 18) must be brought out, the whole truth in its double meaning: for the truth of Christ and his gift (the truth that sheds light, *veritas lucens*) can be uncovered only if the one to whom it is proposed accepts it, even if it manifests by contrast her faults and failings (the accusatory truth, *veritas redarguens*, which turns against the one who receives it and outlines her faults).[38] As it happens, Jesus provokes the Samaritan woman into this trial (recognizing who she truly is) by asking her to call her husband to join her. This is where the *metanoia* begins: instead of hiding her personal situation, she admits it; or, at least, she *almost* admits it. For her avowal ("I have no husband—οὐκ ἔχω ἄνδρα," verse 17) remains ambiguous, a lie by omission. Jesus therefore must make it explicit ("you have had five husbands, and he whom you now have is not your husband") and credit it to her so that the half-truth becomes a full truth ("this you said truly," verse 18). Having done this, he nevertheless validates the essential act of the Samaritan woman: in order that the truth she is about to see may be uncovered, she has accepted (she *willed*) that this light that shines would lay her bare as well. She *loved* recognizing her sin, so as to know the truth, more than closing herself off from truth's uncovering, so as to possess her sin; she *willed to love* the truth more than she *loved* her habitual sin that took the place of the truth for her. She realizes that in order to believe, to see that which is being revealed, one must *love* the truth more than what it stigmatizes in me, and maybe against me. Far from humiliating her, her avowal frees her, and the Samaritan woman can make it public as a proof of the Revelation: "Come, see this man, who told me all the things I did, is he not the Christ?" (verse 29)

Now the discussion can finally reach its profoundest point: understanding how to "worship in spirit and truth" (verse 24). This will be neither on Mount Gerizim, nor in the temple in Jerusalem, but in "he who is called Christ" (verse 25), whom the Samaritan woman henceforward calls "Lord— Κύριε" (verses 11, 15, 19) and who, only now, uncovers himself as such: "Jesus said to her, 'I who speak to you am he'" (verse 26). Now it becomes possible not only to "see" (θεωρῶ) (verse 19), but to "know" (οἴδαμεν) (verse 42). The gift is finally received, once two conditions have been fulfilled: first, the recognition that it is necessary to love the truth (believe) in order to see it uncovered, and then the admission that the gift comes not from us, but that we receive it from *elsewhere*, and it surpasses what our desire of itself fancies it desires.[39] And from that point, in the final moment of this Revelation, we find the uncovering that opens up to "many" (verse 39), because they had heard it for "themselves" (verse 42).

Pragmatism

The accurate reading of John 4 allows us an unexpected return to an objection to Christian theology, as seductive as it is trivial, made by William James (among others). This is the founding principle of pragmatism: "If there were any part of a thought that made no difference in the thought's practical consequences, then that part would be no proper element of the thought's significance."[40] These are the criteria that follow from it: the "cash-value" of the notions, their productive return.[41] Taking up an objection already made by Kant and Schleiermacher on the practical uselessness of, for example, the dogma of the Trinity (see below, chapter 15), James bravely concludes: "We must therefore, I think, bid a definitive good-by [*sic*] to dogmatic theology."[42] And yet, the real question begins exactly here. For this conclusion can and must be understood in two ways. On the one hand, if one holds (as James clearly does) to a strictly propositional interpretation of what metaphysics has constructed under the title of "Revelation," the task is to disqualify the practical neutrality of the *propositio sufficiens*, which one can understand without believing, precisely because understanding it requires nothing and implies no serious consequence for the one who says she understands it; and this disqualification can or even *must* be imposed if on the contrary one thinks starting from Revelation understood as uncovering. On the other hand (as James also sees it), "*If theological ideas prove to have a value for concrete life, they will be true for pragmatism, in the sense of being good for so much*";[43] it is then necessary to decide if these "ideas" prove themselves in fact valid in terms of effectiveness in any way whatsoever. Now that seems precisely to be the case as soon as "God is real since he produces real effects."[44] Thus, the entire question amounts to identifying the pragmatic effects of God.

And James, sincerely yet perhaps without measuring the scope of his terms, conceives of several hypotheses: "*God is not known, he is not understood; he is used* [namely, we are familiar with him, we frequent him]—sometimes as meat-purveyor, sometimes as moral support, sometimes as friend, sometimes as an object [namely, objective] of love."[45] In these effects we recognize several different possible figures of divinity; first, divinity as nutritive (Mother Earth), and next as moral legislator (metaphysical); then as the community of one's choosing (the civic religion); and finally as communion. But in this last case, are we not in fact back to the Christian definition of Revelation? So it is for William of Saint-Thierry: "For what is your salvation, O Lord, whose 'salvation and blessings are upon your people' (Psalms 3:9), if not that which we receive from you, namely that we love you or that we are loved by you? . . . 'Justice according to men' (Psalms 102:17) is like this: love me, because I love you. Rare, on the contrary, is he who can say: I love you, so that you may end up loving me. This is what you did . . . , you who loved us in advance. And this is how it is, entirely how it is, that you loved us first so that we may love you."[46] In fact, because Revelation can be conceived only if its manifestation *is accomplished*, not only in its evidence but also in the will that gladly accepts it, the pragmatic interpretation of theology does not disqualify it, but instead qualifies it. "Therefore your truth or your life, toward which and through which we go, describes for us the pure, the true, and the simple form of divine and true philosophy (*formam divinae et verae philosophiae*), saying to the disciples, 'As the Father has loved me, so I have loved you' (John 15:9)."[47]

It now remains for us to define as precisely as possible the laws of this *divina et vera philosophia*.

TEN

The Other Logic and Its Determinations

How can we attain what William of Saint-Thierry called the *divina et vera philosophia* and Gregory of Nyssa "the philosophy of the Song of Songs"?[1] Strict application of the rule of thought instituted by the Fathers is probably necessary here: one must "learn about God from God, παρὰ θεοῦ περὶ θεοῦ ... μαθεῖν." In other words: "*Edocuit autem Dominus quoniam Deum nemo potest scire nisi Deo docente, hoc est sine Dei non cognosci Deum*—For the Lord taught us that no one can know anything about God, unless he be taught of God; that is, that God cannot be known without God."[2]

But how can one follow this command, which seems to open the way only to close it again? How can one claim to take (in fact, usurp) the viewpoint that God has of God, except by falling into what the Enlightenment would have reason to consider as extravagance and fanaticism (*Schwärmerei*)? Invoking the "metaphysics of the blessed" is not enough: for, supposing that the *theologia mystica* introduced by modern categorization (in contrast to the *theologia scholastica* and *theologia positiva*) could outline a thinkable point of access to a knowledge of God starting from himself, this could only be done in any case by renouncing the logic of *metaphysica*, or by going beyond it; which leaves the difficulty intact. On the other hand, any attempt to establish a connection (other than that of subalternation) between a properly revealed knowledge of God and a so-called "natural" knowledge of him, as we have seen, risks not only subjecting the latter to the former, but the former itself to the universal logic of the latter. How then can we make good use of the dichotomy of Pascal, opposing the knowledge of "human things" to that of "divine things"? Even though it is already symptomatic of metaphysical modernity, this dichotomy could still indicate a direction, as it already identifies two terms. However, if, as our inquiry has proven to us, there is nothing to be gained for either one in attempting to reconcile and unify them, it is still possible to think their opposition. Thus, at the conceptual level, we will contrast the first way, which follows a philosophical (and even metaphysical) logic and proceeds according to unconcealment (*alētheia*), with the second way (*apokalypsis*), which proceeds by *theo*logical uncovering. Their very opposition allows us to characterize their relevance and their respective domains, term for term.

Both Logics

For uncovering (*apokalypsis*) does not simply reject unconcealment (*alētheia*) or claim to annul it, but intensifies it, thus limiting the field of logic in order to clear the way for that of faith which, although it is not formulated by the common use of the concept nor by its reason, is lacking in neither. For in this division, it is again a question of *two logics*, both of which must fall under a *logos*; and indeed the *logos tou staurou* ("the logos of the cross," 1 Corinthians 1:18) also constitutes a *logos*, to the point of unfolding God himself under the title *Logos* (John 1:1). Moreover, the "wisdom of this world" would not be able to enter into contradiction with the "wisdom of God" (1 Corinthians 1:20–21) and neither could both mutually disqualify each other as "foolishness" (1 Corinthians 1:18, 20, 24) if they did not clash with each other by each claiming a superior logic. In fact, "foolishness" only arises because common logic (that of the "philosophy of the world and the hollow deception following the tradition of men and elemental forces of the world," Colossians 2:8) does not succeed in conceiving and receiving the logic and the *logos* of the *Logos*.[3] And this common logic does not succeed because "the world," that is, us, we who boast of remaining Greek in *our* understanding of logic, "search for wisdom" (1 Corinthians 1:22) just as Aristotle did, in being as beings; and especially because we never *seriously* ask ourselves why this "science that is always sought after" always remains "aporetic" for us (ἀεὶ ζητούμενον καὶ ἀεὶ ἀπορούμενον)";[4] and, finally, because we do not *seriously* question the obviousness of our conception of wisdom, however long ago devalued into a science of beings, and today into a production of objects, according to a limited, but still supposedly obvious logic. The *apokalypsis* of uncovering, by contrast, does not lack logic, but opposes the unconcealment of *alētheia* with another logic, which it claims is more powerful and comprehensive, because it is even more rigorous. The question of the relation between uncovering and unconcealment, *apokalypsis* and *alētheia*, plays out within a *certain* logic, or rather, in two modes of *logos*. For, in the end, it is a matter of knowing if *our* conception of logic could govern every *logos*, and even the *logos* of the *Logos*—in short, if it can and must allow itself to be reformed by the logic of the *Logos*.

The weight of the question reformulated in this way falls first of all on philosophy (*alētheia*): how can philosophical logic reform itself so that it is no longer so unsettled before the *Logos*? For, at least as the biblical event claims, the *Logos* uncovers and phenomenalizes itself of its own right, while what philosophy (or rather the logic elaborated by the system of metaphysics) understands by phenomenon does not allow us to conceive this as possible. This difficulty does not only arise from philosophy, however, but above all from the *Logos* itself and the condition of its manifestation. For, when the Logos manifests itself, "coming in human likeness and found *as* human in appearance, σχήματι εὑρεθεὶς ὡς ἄνθρωπος" (Philippians 2:7), it manifests itself precisely as a man, and not as an object or an objectifiable utterance; yet metaphysics ultimately thinks the phenomenon as an object that appears and that lets itself be said according to the condition of experience: "The *a priori* conditions of a possible experience in general are at the same time (*zugleich*) conditions of the possibility of the *objects* of experience."[3] The fact that a phenomenon does not reduce itself to an object or its utterance means that it does not appear starting from the gaze that anticipates it (in the pure forms of intuition), thinks it in advance (according to the *a priori* concepts of the understanding) and synthesizes it (according to its active apperception), but instead that it appears or *can* appear on its own basis. It must therefore be the case that some phenomena not only appear in the opening of the visible, but appear there by imposing themselves from themselves, rising up from *elsewhere* than the visible that we know in advance; for what there is to be seen does not always allow itself to be *fore*-seen, but instead offers with its appearing the opening of its visibility and rises up by bringing the very space of its apparition which, before its rising up, remained closed: "what is there to see does not come from [already] visible phenomena (μὴ ἐκ φαινομένων τὸ βλεπόμενον γεγονέναι)" (Hebrews 11:3). Christ, as resurrected, and thus as prime phenomenon because extraordinary, also *shows himself* in an exceptional way as he *gives himself* in an exceptional mode. Without his givenness, which opens the place of his manifestation, he would not appear. Thus, in the pivotal phenomenon of biblical uncovering we find the character of the phenomenon in its properly phenomenological (and not metaphysical) definition as *event* (and not as object), and an event that reveals itself to the extent that it *gives itself.* "Dando revelat et revelando dat,"[6] but this time in person: "In Jesus alone the truth of God has appeared—*In solo Jesu veritas Dei apparuit.*"[7] For, as always, the mode and the degree of givenness decide what shows itself.

We must now attempt to sketch how uncovering (*apokalypsis*) is distinguished from unconcealment (*alētheia*) according to its ways of giving itself to be seen. And therefore, at the same time, according to its ways of *not* letting itself be seen, because they are also a result of its modes of givenness. They can be distinguished by four moments of divergence. We will see that the first two relate more precisely to the philosophical, and thus metaphysical, definition of truth (*alētheia*) as adequation, while the last two relate to truth (*alētheia*) and its phenomenological meaning as what unconceals itself in itself and through itself.

Homogeneity, Heterogeneity

The first divergence falls under epistemology. It opens up between the homogeneity or heterogeneity of the known and its knowing, in other words, between the adequation or inadequation of what shows itself to the one who sees it. Thus, it directly concerns the canonical definition of the truth as "adequation of the thing and its understanding, *adaequatio rei et intellectus.*"[8] Indeed, in unconcealment (*alētheia*), what gives itself to be seen remains at the level of the one who sees it; in French, it can be said literally: what is seen is *seen to [a à voir]* by the one who sees it. We can say, in true knowledge, intuition fills the concept *on equal terms*; or, more phenomenologically, that the intuitive fulfillment *equals* the aim of the signification, the noema *equals* the noesis. This equality of principle alone ensures or at least allows, if only as a regulating idea, an adequation between the two terms, the thing and the mind, the visible and the gaze. Because I know what I ought to see, because I know in advance that I will only see an object, the particularity of what presents itself to be known is not taken into account: indeed, the majority of the time I am expecting what arises, since it is an object that arises according to my *a priori*, or at least according to *a priori* conditions of verification. Thus, I can reasonably hope for an adequation between what gives itself and what is known, for reason consists precisely in the accomplishment of this *adaequatio*.[9] In short, I know because I recognize, and I recognize because I can identify (by concept) what I see (by intuition). The singular identity of the one who perceives does not enter into account, because perception can always and in principle be universalized by the common constitution of inter-objectivity (for what we understand as intersubjectivity, following Husserl, consists only in the common constitution of a common object). It follows, then, that the neutrality of the given (grasped as an object in its adequate concept) allows and even requires the neutralization of the receiver and the situations of its reception. Adequation leads to the epistemological homogeneity of the object (also called the common law phenomenon).

By contrast, in uncovering (*apokalypsis*), that which gives itself cannot and even ought not remain at the level of the one who receives it. This holds in the case where incomprehensibility positively defines what shows itself, according to the rule fixed by Descartes: "*ipsa incomprehensibilitas in ratione formali infiniti continetur*."[10] But it also holds more broadly for every saturated phenomenon, where the intuition that gives (itself) overflows, and sometimes abundantly, what can be received and thus conceived by the concept or the signification aimed at in advance by intentionality; the excess of what gives itself over what one expected to find results in an inverted inequality: no longer by lack of verifying intuition (as in the case of error or incertitude before a common phenomenon or object), but by excess of this intuition over the signification or significations that are *fore*-seen. This inequality of principle therefore forbids the adequation between the two terms, the thing and the mind. Sometimes definitively (as in the case of the infinite). More often for a time, when, not knowing at first what I see, a finite given takes me by surprise; then, taken aback [*interloqué*] by the encounter, I never expect what happens to me; deprived of foresight, I do not understand what nevertheless can perfectly well observe. In short, caught on my heels by what I receive, I cannot get a hold of it, but I find myself held by it ("*Non tam capere quad capi*").[11] What gives itself can only manifest itself beyond the measure and despite the capacity of the one who receives it (or not), who catches sight of it (if barely). For, let us repeat, *if what shows itself gives itself, not everything that gives itself shows itself.* The inadequation between the terms ensures that an irreducible inadequation rises up between what gives itself and the one who receives it: the latter (and not the *former*) is from now on stripped of the rank of the transcendental *I* and, under the figure of *witness*, shows his epistemological heterogeneity before the *saturated phenomenon*.

Internal Withdrawal, External Withdrawal

But this difference between the two modes of reception arises from a prior difference between the two modes of withdrawal of what gives itself over what shows itself. The withdrawal of what gives itself without the witness being able to see it adequately can in fact be understood either as an internal withdrawal (in phenomenal immanence), or as an external withdrawal (by phenomenal transcendence); in other words, either as an *ad intra* withdrawal of the manifestation of the phenomenon itself, or as an *ad extra* withdrawal added on to this manifestation. In unconcealment (*alētheia*), which depends only on what is uncovered there, I remain neutral, a distant spectator, disengaged, in withdrawal; I understand the phenomenon all the more as I do not find myself implicated in it, interfere with it, or modify it. It remains objective and available to me, independent (*vorhanden*), and I make a scrupulous effort not to appropriate it for my use (*zuhanden*). Further still, truth requires that, while constituting this phenomenon according to the *a priori* conditions of experience, I take the same scrupulous care to uphold universality, so that what appears to me can also appear to anyone (to any rational mind), without the interference of my individuality or disruption from my idiosyncrasies. Thus, if the manifestation is imperfect and the uncovering partial, the covering up that partially covers over the thing once again stems from what should have or would have been able to manifest itself. Withdrawal (error, obscurity, contradictory concept, lack of meaning, materially false idea, etc.) always belongs to the phenomenological immanence of the uncovering. I may have allowed this withdrawal by unintelligence or negligence; I did not want it, it is not my affair.[12]

In the opposite case, that of uncovering (*apokalypsis*), if manifestation can remain in withdrawal for a time from its full deployment, or even *must* definitively remain so, this does not depend on its own withdrawal, on its holding back a reserve that still remains to be given, or on its phenomenal stinginess. Rather, it is a matter of the limits of the capacity of the one who receives it (the *modus recipientis*), her drawing back before what she perceives as the threat of an arrival, her fear of the great displacement demanded by what gives itself. In short, it depends on her *resistance*. The incompleteness of manifestation is no longer the result of the withdrawal of what would not give itself from its depths, but the withdrawal of the one who does not want to surrender from her depths, even in order successfully to receive what gives itself from the depths. For here, before a saturated phenomenon, which does not show itself except to the extent that it gives itself, and thus to the extent that it can make itself be received, what gives itself cannot show itself without being received by the only one who can see it. The extent of the uncovering depends on the capacity of receiving, thus on risking oneself with what gives itself. It can also happen that the evidence is obscured, even rejected, precisely because it gives itself without measure.[13] The one who receives is directly and essentially involved, although *ad extra*, in the manifestation of what nevertheless gives itself from *elsewhere*. Withdrawal (confusion, deliberate or spontaneous blindness, refusal, etc.) belongs to the phenomenological transcendence of the uncovering.

Folding Up and Unfolding the Fold

Now that we have clarified how unconcealment and uncovering differ, we can attempt to define the contrasting reasons for their withdrawal. This third opposition between the two logics can only be understood, however, if we move beyond the simple (metaphysical) definition of truth as adequation and grant its more properly phenomenological determination. The difference here becomes even more clear as, in both cases, the withdrawal results from the very phenomenality of what *gives itself* to show itself. Indeed, it is a question of the gift. The gift is always given along a fold, and the fold of the gift always gives by unfolding itself; and it can unfold itself in two ways, provoking withdrawal according to two distinct, or even inverse modes.

For unconcealment (*alētheia*), the withdrawal arises from the *folding back up of the fold* of givenness. We owe it to Heidegger to have been one of the best, if not the only one, to see and describe the paradox of the gift.[14] In order to understand the withdrawal of being that inevitably provokes *alētheia*, he successfully carried out the first serious analysis of "it gives, *es gibt*." He knew not to disfigure it by spatializing it (in an "*il y a, there* is"), or by closing it off in an auxiliary verb (to have, "*il y a*," "*hay*," or to be, "there *is*," "c'est") as we usually translate it;[15] indeed, "it gives" involves no space, no having, nor even any being; literally it involves a gift that *gives* (itself) without being identified with something other than the gift, which remains anonymous, of an unknown origin (*es*, *cela*, it). It is necessary to approach it as such, without a screen. But precisely how should this "it gives" be understood? Or rather, what does the "it gives" give—in the sense that a painter, after working on his painting, takes one or two steps back, looks at it, and reflects on what he sees, in order to see and know "what it gives" in this gift (in this given, this *rendering*)? It gives a gift, of course; but we must still understand the logic followed by this gift. Clearly, "it gives" the final gift—here, for example, the finished painting—but in general "it gives" a being henceforth unconcealed, manifest and present. And "it gives" the given being, extensively, continuously, and clearly, because the rise and advance of the still unseen toward this ultimately visible being is accomplished (through being and time, no doubt). The given being in this way is only rediscovered as given because it accomplishes the givenness that provoked, produced, and proposed it. The being given (the gift), in giving *itself*, gives *also* a glimpse of the givenness from which it arises. Hence, the fold of the gift, which unfolds the gift given and *also* the givenness according to which it gives itself.

With regard to the question of the ontological difference, we can thus say that the given being (*Gabe*) only gives itself through and according to the givenness (*Gebung*) of being; the arrival (*Ankunft*) of the one implies the arising or coming about (*Überkomnis*) of the other. However, the final arrival of the given being does *not* directly or evidently manifest what it implies, the arising of being; or rather, the arrival of a being *implicates* (in the old sense of *implicare*)[16] the arising of being, that is, replaces and covers it over again. In other words, the being confiscates the presence of being, overshadowing it, because it alone occupies the entire phenomenal stage. Hence the paradox that, the more a being is given and manifest (by being), the less the being [*l'être*] that gives it appears. With respect to the general question of the gift as such, the same paradox states that the more the gift manifests itself, the less givenness appears; in short, that it is a function of the gift to hold back and conceal the givenness in it. It is necessary to see that this withdrawal of givenness has nothing accidental about it, but that it obeys the very logic of the gift. For, if the givenness remained clearly visible, it would remain so by the visibility of the giver still looming over or behind the gift given; thus the gift would not find itself really given as such, but would remain lent on mortgage. To the contrary, the gift does not appear as definitively given unless the givenness (and the giver) *abandons* it, and thus disappears from the phenomenal scene. And so, for unconcealment (*alētheia*), the being and being, and therefore ultimately the gift and givenness, appear in inverse proportion, and out of an essential necessity: if the one is manifest, the other must withdraw, and vice versa. In unconcealment, it is an essential function of the fold of the gift (givenness/gift) to fold itself back up. As a consequence, this mode of withdrawal never implies the least refusal of what is manifested by a third party (transcendent to phenomenality) because it results exclusively from conditions of the *folding back up of the fold* of the gift, that is of the gift itself.

On the other hand, in the situation of uncovering (*apokalypsis*), the withdrawal results directly in the *unfolding of the fold* of givenness itself. Here the gift does not overshadow givenness any more than givenness holds back the gift; for *here* givenness gives to the point of abandon, in such a way that the gift does not accomplish itself any longer by being fixed as a possession (simply passing from one owner to another), but in the emerging of givenness "to the end, εἰς τέλος" (John 13:1). Thus, "the one whom God sent speaks God's words. And he does not give the Spirit by measure, οὐ γὰρ ἐκ μέτρου" (John 3:34). Here gift and givenness do not mutually overshadow one another, but expand together in direct proportion. That is, they are no longer defined by possession, even of presence, but by communion, where each term ceaselessly gives itself to the other and receives itself from it: the Father glorifies the Son and "at once, εὐθὺς" (John 13.32) the Son glorifies the Father. Coming from the Father to the Son, the gift returns from the Son to the Father, without ever coming to a standstill as an exclusive possession. Given and received without ceasing, it in no way masks this fact but manifests itself *to the same extent as* the givenness in it. As a result, since there is no longer any contradiction between gift and givenness, the uncovering (*apokalypsis*) unfolds itself according to its only measure, that of God, who has none.

But then, how can we explain that a positive situation (gift and givenness increasing in direct proportion) leads to a new difficulty, which could not be encountered before: that is, if everything that shows itself gives itself, and if everything shows itself to the measure that it gives itself, why does the uncovering (*apokalypsis*), which has the privilege of giving itself without measure, not also uncover itself without measure? Why doesn't that which gives itself "to the end" already appear "in abundance, περισσὸν" (John 10:10) "according to the measure of the givenness of Christ, κατὰ τὸ μέτρον τῆς δωρεᾶς τοῦ χριστοῦ" (Ephesians 4:7)? Because of a reason already evoked under the name of the phenomenological transcendence of uncovering: because that which gives itself and shows itself cannot manifest itself without the one who receives it, thus, to the measure of his capacity, which in our case is limited. Only Christ can receive without measure the Father who gives himself without measure, and no one besides him is able to receive without measure in this moment (*in via*) what the Father gives: this "hyperbole of charity" (Ephesians 3:19), no man "can yet bear it, βαστάζειν ἄρτι" (John 16:12). Here the principle of "finding oneself measured by the measure with which one will measure" (Matthew 7:2, par.) plays out phenomenologically. Not only does the finite measure of reception limit the manifestation of what nevertheless gives itself without measure, but it is exactly this measure of givenness that reveals the restricted measure of reception. The enormity of the givenness thus *judges* the finitude of reception. In this way, the very finitude of reception becomes an integral part of the manifestation of what gives itself infinitely but can show itself only by bursting upon the finite screen of the one who receives it, as a gift, but also as a shock. There is always place for refusal, because this place coincides with the very place of its welcome. *Unfolding the fold* of the gift involves the call and the response; but the call is only heard to the extent that the response gives the echo of its initial voice; thus the unfolding of the fold always includes the possibility of refusal. It can always happen that "looking, you look and do not see (καὶ βλέποντες βλέψετε καὶ οὐ μὴ ἴδητε)" (Matthew 13:14, citing Isaiah 6:10). The gift is abandoned to the point that it leaves the accomplishment of its full manifestation to the mercy of an authority that remains phenomenally heterogeneous and exterior to it: the uncovering, which comes from *elsewhere*, allowing its truth to depend on its reception *by elsewhere*. Because giving and manifesting itself can increase in inverse proportion, *unfolding the fold* allows and eventually provokes its folding back up.

Verification and Falsehood

From this comes a final contrast, concerning the modes of verification of the gift in its givenness. For unconcealment (*alētheia*), verification is measured directly: the truth is unconcealed all the more as evidence unfolds itself, and whoever has eyes to see, sees it. Evidence, of course, should not be confused with intuition, and sometimes can even do without it; but even the strictest formalism aims at it by other means, which are supposedly more secure. Evidence, of course, can be rare, only attained at the end of a long process, or it may even remain simply an ideal of reason. However, evidence alone decides everything and can settle any question. And no one can refuse to accept it, except by remaining blind, placing oneself outside rationality (*demens*, or rather, *amens*).

It is entirely different for uncovering (*apokalypsis*), which is only verified *indirectly*. For, when the truth uncovers itself, it does not appear as much as it gives itself (without measure, to the end), but as much as one is able and willing to receive it (*ad modum recipientis*). So that when what gives itself by definition exceeds the one that receives it, it cannot, and thus it *ought* not, show itself as it gives itself, as such. In the eminent case of God—"No one has seen God" (John 1:18)—an invisibility of principle *positively* forbids any adequate manifestation, even any possible manifestation according to the common conditions of visibility. Instead of glossing this as *Deus absconditus*, it is better to consider the real difficulty and unsurpassable aporia: if God can be seen, one of two things must be the case. Either it would not in fact be God (according to the principle that if we comprehend it, it is not him)[17]; or if it were him, his glory would burn up and obliterate every eye exposed to it. However, this unsurpassable paradox does not concretely forbid conceiving God in any way, since the same text adds in the same sentence that "God the only Son, who is in the bosom of the Father, has provided us with an exegesis of him (ἐκεῖνος ἐξηγήσατο)." How to unite these two claims?

By recognizing that, even without direct verification, *apokalypsis* allows an *indirect* verification that validates its accomplishment and its reception.

The invisibility of God will never be eliminated, but it is transposed to the only visibility that our eyes could support: "in this we know that we know him, when we keep his commandments" (1 John 2:3). Jewish thought translates this transference by the principle "better the Torah than God": to which we must add that respecting the Torah in fact offers the only non-idolatrous visibility of divine invisibility; for to see God does not consist in making an image of him, but in seeing how he sees and acting how he acts—thus in following his commandments. My knowledge (without comprehension) and my vision (without immediate visibility) of God is verified on the stage that opens in and on the face of my neighbor, whom I incontestably see, and who, for that very same fact, becomes an ordeal for my gaze, an ordeal that measures what it can bear to see. Incidentally, when someone asks Jesus what is the first commandment, he responds by identifying two commandments as one: "And Jesus said to him: 'Love the Lord your God with all your heart, with all your soul, and all your thought,' which is the great and first commandment. The second is like it (ὁμοία αὐτῇ): 'Love your neighbor as yourself.' All the Law and the prophets depend on these two commandments" (Matthew 22:37–40). Following the commandments of God results in truly seeing a face, but the face of a man (beginning with that of Jesus)[18] that is *indirectly* and *mediately* superposable on that of God. This transposition and superposition finds its explicit formulation as a hermeneutic principle in the first epistle of John: "If someone says he loves God and hates (μισῇ) his brother, he is a *liar*. For he who does not love the brother *he sees* (ὃν ἑώρακεν) does not love God, *whom he does not see* (ὃν οὐχ ἑώρακεν). And we have received from him this [one] commandment: that the lover of God love his brother *also* (καὶ)" (1 John 4:20–21). In this way, the commandment (and thereby the entire Torah) begins a phenomenal situation in conformity with uncovering (*apokalypysis*) and determines the criteria of its phenomenality: in the arena of manifestation, visibility transfers from the invisible face of God to the visible face of my brother, so that in loving the one who is here, I am certain in return that I love the one who is there, precisely because that one, God, "first" loves this one, my brother (1 John 4:19). And thus the visible face of my brother also receives the anointing of the invisibility of God, appearing as an invisible face—which the saturated phenomenon of the icon type confirms in everyday ethical experience. This can also be said of faith, which is likewise invisible, but which manifests in its works: "And so it goes without saying that faith, if it does not have acts (ἔργα), it is itself dead.... Show me (δεῖξόν μοι) faith without acts, and I from my acts will show you faith" (James 2:17–18). The visible act of charity toward brothers manifests invisible faith toward God, thus uncovering indirectly the gift of God, for "every good giving and every fulfilled gift is from above (πᾶσα δόσις ἀγαθὴ καὶ πᾶν δώρημα τέλειον ἄνωθέν ἐστιν), coming down from the Father of Light" (James 1.17).

We can understand what is done (or rather not done) by the one who is qualified here as "liar": he dissociates the two faces, the visible and the invisible, and refuses the transference of their common manifestation; while he clearly does not *say* any false statement, he does not *do* what the commandment asks, the transference of visibility; to the contrary, what he does (dissociating the two faces) is precisely what forbids him from seeing the true face of God—that of my brother insofar as he finds himself loved by me according to the very mode of God. The "liar" (ψεύστης) does not say anything false, but forbids the practical performance of manifestation; he blocks and holds back the uncovering (*apokalypsis*); he holds on to the neutrality of unconcealment (*alētheia*), which separates the two faces as two distinct phenomena, or even as two objects, and thus rejects Revelation. Not loving his brother (not loving his brother as himself) amounts to denying him his face, but, at the same time and above all, to denying *God's* face in the one whom God chose and entrusted to me. Here again the analysis of Saint Augustine is confirmed: to see what the *veritas lumens* manifests (the light which illuminates and unconceals) depends on what love can receive of the *veritas redarguens* (the light that accuses the topography of my interior landscape and thus which accuses me)[19]. Because the former arrives upon me from *elsewhere*, the latter in return depends on *somewhere else* than itself—on me, according to my capacity of reception of (and resistance to) this *elsewhere*. Because the phenomenon manifests itself from its depths and gives itself in itself from its depths, it precisely *cannot* impose itself on me without me; it can only propose itself to me, as I *have the capacity to not receive its arising*, and thus to decide to not see it. The phenomenon that uncovers itself *can* be refused, rejected. This, paradoxically, confirms its greatest power.

Saturation and Transfiguration

We have thus determined more closely the phenomenality proper to Revelation: now distinguished from its metaphysical *artifact* as well as from unconcealment (*alētheia*), it unfolds as the uncovering (*apokalypsis*) that is differentiated by four characteristics: the epistemological heterogeneity of the thing and one's view of it, the phenomenological transcendence *ad extra* of the one taken aback by the call [*l'interloqué*], the direct possibility of refusal (starting from the unfolding of the fold), and the indirect verification by transfer of visibility. Having determined Revelation as uncovering in this way allows us now to take up the three concepts (witness, resistance, and paradox) that we could only sketch (chapter 1) abstractly (chapter 2) in the introduction. They take on their full significance once related to the saturated phenomenon par excellence, Revelation.

A saturated phenomenon, as we have seen,[20] is defined by excess of its intuition over the concept (or signification), in contrast to the common law phenomenon (and still more the poor phenomenon), which, following metaphysical phenomenality, only allows two different relations between its terms: either a deficiency of intuition in relation to signification that it only validates in part (but sufficiently for its use, or even for knowledge of the technical object); or the rarer case of equality between the two (in the case of evidence, the ideal where the intuition of truth fulfills the entire signification). However a third relation is still possible: the intuition is no longer included under the concept, or resolved by it, but overflows every definite signification of it; hence, in the case of an event (without foreseeable antecedent), an idol (the maximum of the visible a gaze can support), my own flesh (relative to nothing other than itself, immanent to itself), or finally the icon (the face of the other, which my gaze does not modalize). Henceforth, the one who sees such a phenomenon must accept that he will never be able to foresee it (by an already known concept), explain it (by a relation, causal or otherwise), replicate it (by fabrication and reproduction), or condition it (by the postulates of experimentation). He can and should only observe, from incontestable empirical evidence, what is conceived without, however, allowing itself to be understood. Thus, the event leaves us with neither a say nor a way, because it deprives us of every meaning that would make it adequately comprehensible, that is to say possible (in the metaphysical sense); it imposes on us, however, an effectiveness that, having never been possible or thinkable in advance, earns by that fact the title of impossible. Take the collapsing of Manhattan's towers, or Notre-Dame in flames. "It isn't possible!": this spontaneous cry before what imposes itself on us all the same is precisely what characterizes the emergence of a saturated phenomenon: it leaves us literally without the exact words to speak of it, or adequate concepts to comprehend it. We can certainly speak of it all the more, up to the point of chatter and endless media coverage, but always in hindsight, in order to find, or rather retrieve, its hypothetical explanations, approximate causes, and ideological claims, which are all induced from the effects that are alone indisputable, wholly inadequate, or even inept. In short, we will speak along the lines of a hermeneutics always to be corrected or completed, only to say nothing. Or, more exactly, without arriving at exhaustive significations that would be adequate to the excess of the given over what we can understand of it—to the excess of the given over what we are able to frame of it in an obvious visible. Yet this situation of excess of the given *in itself* over what can be shown as visible *for us*, already banal in common experience, is verified impeccably and preeminently before the phenomenon of the manifestation of Christ.[21]

Thus, during the Transfiguration, the disciples chosen to see an anticipation of the glory of the Resurrection have absolutely no doubt about what they see—that his "face became different" (Luke 9:29) "like the sun" and his garments "like light" (Matthew 17:2) "with a whiteness so excessive (λίαν) as no fuller on earth could whiten them" (Mark 9:3). Far from any lack in intuition, the difficulty in seeing resides in its excess: the disciples fall face down on the ground, unable to support the intensity of this vision, and they "were very (σφόδρα) afraid" (Matthew 17:6).[22] It follows that the real ordeal before this saturated phenomenon comes from "lack of divine names" (Hölderlin), or at least of words appropriate to this manifestation. When Peter tries to say something (about the three tents that would be "good" to set up for Christ and the two figures assumed to be Moses and Elijah), he reacts well, borrowing one of the concepts already available from the Scriptures (no doubt the φιλοξενία of Abraham, Genesis 18:1–15), and yet it is empty chatter, for the text explains that "he did not know what he was saying, μὴ εἰδὼς ὃ λέγει" (Mark 9:6, Luke 9:33). The signification appropriate to the saturated phenomenon will thus not come from those who see the phenomenon, but from the phenomenon itself: it is "a voice coming from the cloud" that delivers the adequate signification to this excess of intuition; but the signification itself is excessive and, literally, incomprehensible: "This is my beloved Son, listen to him." In fact, this signification was already delivered during the Baptism, but it remained misunderstood by the crowd. It will also be repeated in the last public manifestation in the Temple, before the Passion, but once again be poorly understood or squarely refused (John 12:27–28). The quasi-impossibility of naming Jesus, of giving him a name, his Name, results, at least on the level of phenomenological analysis, from a deficit of the concept at the very moment of superabundance of intuition, and *not the inverse*.[23]

Examples of staging such a saturated phenomenon are not lacking, and all obey the same logic. Herod, who, at the report of "all that happened with him [i.e., Jesus]" immediately stated his ignorance: "Who is he?" (Luke 9:7–9). Pilate, when he later heard Jesus accused of "making himself God," "was even more afraid" (John 19:8). The blind man healed at the pool of Siloam, who was astonished that the priests of the Temple, where he had his healing verified in accordance with the Law, blame him without, however, being able (in fact, without wanting) to identify his healer: "In all this, the astonishing thing is that you do not know where this man comes from (οὐκ οἴδατε πόθεν ἐστὶν)" (John 9:30). Even, or rather *especially* after the Resurrection, the hermeneutic situation remains the same; for the disciples on the road to Emmaus were not lacking in intuition ("approaching, Jesus in person walked with them")[24]; but they were clearly lacking in adequate significations (precisely the ones that Jesus would give them by commenting on the Scriptures to relate them to him); because they do not understand anything (ἀνόητοι), they do not see anything ("slow of heart to believe, βραδεῖς . . . τοῦ πιστεύειν", Luke 24:25); it is only with one final signification, the sign of the eucharistic bread, that they understand and "recognize, ἐγνώσθη" (Luke 24:25) him; the un-covering thus only operates if a signification coming from *elsewhere* allows the already given intuition to show a realized phenomenon. The same for Mary Magdalene, who certainly "sees (θεωρεῖ)" Jesus, but without recognizing him, at least before the adequate signification arises for her, the living voice of Jesus in person, who names her, and thus makes himself recognized: "Mary!"[25]

Finally, in the last chapter of John, the case of the disciples becoming again fishers of fish displays explicitly the perfect phenomenalization of the Resurrected (ἐφανέρωσεν, twice in John 21:1, then in 21:14), and accomplishes the principle of manifestation we find in the Synoptics.[26] The disciples return

The Other Logic and Its Determinations 153

to the lake, their boats, and their nets; as before, when "Simon Peter said to them 'I am going fishing,' they said, 'We will go with you'" (21:3). This return to their business is the exact reversal of their first call by Jesus: "He said to them, 'Come with me, and I will make you fishers of men'" (Matthew 4:19). They no longer believe and thus no longer see anything; subsequently, they do not even see the schools of fish and do not catch anything. But "as morning was breaking," like the morning at the tomb, Jesus "stood on the beach"; he sees them, but they "did not know, οὐκ ᾔδεισαν," that it was Jesus (21:4). Then he speaks to them, giving (or rather, suggesting) the signification adequate to an intuition still not identified; first with a familiar word, "boys, guys, παιδία!" (21:5, corresponding to the call, "Mary!"); then with the advice to cast the net "to the right" (the "right hand of God"?); finally, by the sign of the net filled (literally, *saturated*: ἀπὸ τοῦ πλήθους τῶν ἰχθύων) with fish, and yet intact (21:6). One of them, the disciple whom Jesus loved, perceives the signification immediately ("It is the Lord," 21:7), and thus sees the saturated phenomenon. Another does not yet perceive, but plunges into the water to go see; he thus receives the sign—the brazier (21:9),[27] the fish and the bread—and above all will receive the gift of the signification, that is the gift itself: "Come, eat" (21:12), which takes up the Eucharistic gift: "He took the bread, blessed it, broke it and gave it to them, ἔδωκεν αὐτοῖς" (Luke 22:19; see Matthew 26:26: δοὺς τοῖς μαθηταῖς; Mark 14:22). Jesus gives them, with the sacramental sign, the correct signification that was missing: "Jesus came, took the bread and gave it to them, δίδωσιν αὐτοῖς, and so with the fish" (John 21:13). From that point, the disciples no longer ask anything, because they know and see: "None of the disciples dared to question him: 'Who are you?' knowing full well (εἰδότες) that it was the Lord" (21:12). At last, the phenomenalization is accomplished.

In each case, as a saturated phenomenon par excellence because it arises radically from *elsewhere*, the uncovering of Christ at first imposes an excess of intuition that results in the deficiency of all our significations; it next proposes, as the only adequate signification, his very name, which becomes either an index of the absurdity of this phenomenon, or the signification itself, come from *elsewhere*, at first inconceivable although it is still heard. ("This is my Son, listen to him!" "This is my Son, my beloved, in whom I am well pleased.") This name can be received either as the incomprehensible, or as the Name itself. Consequently this signification is defined literally as a sign that contradicts what *we* consider as *our logic*, the "sign of contradiction, σημεῖον ἀντιλεγόμενον" (Luke 2:34), a *logos* that, in the name of the *Logos*, goes against our *logos*. A metalogic against metaphysics.

In the Place of the Self, the Witness

Determining the manifestation of Christ as the preeminent saturated phenomenon will allow us to consider its second characteristic: the *I* takes the status of witness.[28]

In the regime of *alētheia* or unconcealment the *I* always anticipates the phenomenon, whether by apperception (Kant) or by intentionality (Husserl); by definition, the phenomenon will be known by the *I*, since it organizes every possible intuition of it according to the measure of the concept or signification that will be assigned to it *in advance*. The *I* knows what it speaks about, since in a radical sense it speaks about what it has itself made visible (if not already produced within visibility) from its aim alone. Moreover, the concept or intentional signification could not turn out to be empty at times, unless they were deployed in advance of the phenomenon possibly given to be seen (or not). The *I* always knows more about its intentional object than it sees, because it has no need to really see something (in full intuition) to already understand it, at least in its signification or its concept. The *I* knows (or can know) its phenomenon without it appearing fully, or at all, because it always finds itself in it.

But, in front of a saturated phenomenon, this posture becomes untenable. The excess of intuition over the significations or available concepts prevents us not only from knowing without having to see (everything), but especially from knowing adequately, precisely because we foresee it too well. Here, the *I* must be substituted for the witness, who sees and sees indisputably, but without being able to register the superabundant intuition in the synthesis of the concept (by recognition) or the (noematic) constitution of the signification. The witness knows what he says, quite certainly and quite surely, because he speaks about what he has received by intuition (sight, hearing, etc.); but he does not *understand* what he says, because he cannot unify it in a complete concept, nor identify it in a sufficient signification (*propositio sufficiens*). Karl Barth has explained this situation quite well: "Why and in what respect does the biblical witness have authority? Because and in the fact that he claims no authority for himself, that his witness amounts to letting that other itself be its own authority."[29] The witness has authority precisely by not claiming it for himself, but in allowing it to come *from elsewhere*. He allows what he himself does not understand to be said in him. When a police officer or a judge examines a witness, what he is asked to report (and what the witness knows full well, even without understanding it) allows them to understand something *other* than what the witness is reporting, something they alone suspect and therefore are looking for: the concept, the signification, the final word of the affair. The investigator tries to redefine the saturated phenomenon, which has reduced the *I* to the rank of witness, as an objectifiable, common law phenomenon, where a concept could make the whole of the event comprehensible.[30] To the contrary, the witness, for example the blind man at Siloam, observes and makes visible the intuitive fact of his healing (that he, someone blind from birth, now sees), but without knowing the origin or the signification of it, and without ever pretending to: "And they asked him: 'Where is he?' He said to them, 'I do not know, Οὐκ οἶδα'" (John 9:12). At the same time, all the interlocutors of the first witness, the healed blind man, go on repeating that they "do not know, οὐκ οἴδαμεν" (John 9:21–22, 30). It is the normal and inevitable phenomenological posture that every *I* must take before a saturated phenomenon, especially before the saturated phenomenon of the type of the event, indeed, before the eventhood of every saturated phenomenon.

The posture of the witness proves to be so essential to uncovering that it marks the difference between on the one hand the devil, "a murderer from the beginning," who, "when he speaks falsehood, speaks from his own depths, because he is a liar" (John 8:44), and, on the other, Christ, who does not speak from himself: "the words which I say to you, I do not say them from myself" (John 14:10). Certainly, the witness can *also* end up stating the true signification, but then it does not come from him. Rather, it causes the saturated phenomenon to appear from *elsewhere*, not from an intentional *I* but from the phenomenon itself. To make itself known, this phenomenon must make itself recognized starting from itself; and to make itself recognized from itself, it is necessary for it to speak from itself. In short, the truth must uncover itself *in person*. Thus the blind man of Siloam ends up saying, "I believe, Lord," because to his question, "Who is the Son of God, that I may believe in him?" Christ responded in the first person: "And Jesus said to him: 'But you have seen him and he is the one who is speaking to you'" (John 9:36–37). Similarly, the centurion at the foot of the cross ends up recognizing that "This man was innocent" (Luke 23:47), and even that "Truly, this man was the Son of God" (Matthew 27:54; Mark 15:39), because he "sees" "the events that happened, τὰ γινόμενα" (Matthew 27:54, Luke 23:48) from themselves, as an event rising up from itself in itself.[31] The witness never says *I* in his own name, but speaks in the name of an *I* that comes to him from *elsewhere*. Hence John the Baptist takes the rank of witness par excellence ("The one who will come after me is mightier than I," Matthew 3:11; Mark 1:7; Luke 3:16), because he will reverse the order of priorities: "Behind me comes a man who has passed in front of me, because he was before me (πρῶτός μου ἦν)" (John 1:30). In a way, the fact that "the first shall be last, and the last, the first" (Matthew 19:30 and par.) can be seen as the very definition of the witness, the one who discovers she is not able to speak in her own name, nor say *I* without lying, the one who inhabits neither an (empirical) *me*, nor a transcendental *I*, but in a transcended *I*, a borrowed *I*, an *I* received as given.

And as the preeminent witness, Jesus does not speak except exclusively in the name of the Father, thus perfectly confirming himself as the Son. This is even (or especially) so when he says *I am*, because he only says it *in the name of* the Father. "*I am* the bread of life . . . I have come down from heaven, not to do my own will, but the will of him who sent me" (John 6:35, 38). There is no contradiction between the fact that he says "Ἐγώ εἰμι, I am" and the fact that he only draws his legitimacy from his submission to the will of the Father, for the Son is defined precisely by abandoning accomplishment to the Father. Also, when he responds to the question of Caiaphas asking him if he is indeed "The Christ, the Son of the Blessed," Jesus affirms in the same sentence "I am, ἐγώ εἰμι," and cites "the Son of Man who sits at the right hand of the power of God"[32]: in other words, he returns his ego to the one from whom it comes, he claims it as received, as the *name of the Father*, that is to say *received* from the Father. The Son, like every son—but he the most perfectly—receives his ego (εἰμί) par excellence from *elsewhere*. And it would certainly not be illegitimate to translate "ἐγὼ ἐκ τῶν ἄνω εἰμί" not by "I am from above," but literally, "my *I* comes to me from above, from *elsewhere*"; which also allows the converse: "ἐγὼ οὐκ εἰμὶ ἐκ τοῦ κόσμου τούτου, and my *I* does not come to me from this world" (John 8:23–24).

The Paradox and the Hyperbole of Charity

From this point there follows the third determination of the manifestation of Christ as a saturated phenomenon: the *paradox* that results in counter-experience.

One must not be too quick to pass over the paradox. Kierkegaard, upon making use of it, sang its praises: "This seems to be a paradox. But one must not think ill of the paradox, for the paradox is the passion of thought, and the thinker without the paradox is like the lover without passion: a mediocre fellow. . . . This, then, is the ultimate paradox of thought: to want to discover something that thought itself cannot think."[33] Consider the classical definition: "Things which, because they are astonishing and go against appearances, are also called paradoxes. *Quae, quia sunt admirabilia contraque opinionem omnium, ab ipsis etiam paradoxa appellantur*" (Cicero).[34] This gives rise to several points. First, it is a question of appearance, thus ultimately of phenomenality. Next, this phenomenality is directly linked to the possibility of its logical formulation (*doxa* can be translated by both terms, opinion and appearance), which means that the paradox calls into question the possibility of articulating that which appears (or not) in a proposition. Finally, in this first approach, nothing determines the validity (truth) of what contradicts opinion and appearance. One can thus approach it equally well from the opinion it states as from the appearance that it offers.

Consider first the paradox from the point of view of the utterance, of the logic formulated by philosophy, that is, the paradox as it calls into question this very philosophy. In this first case, the paradox constitutes a logical obstacle to the correct utterance of a state of affairs. Take the statement "All Cretans are liars": as it stands, it can receive a confirmation or empirical refutation; it is thus correctly formulated, as it is true or false. But if it is included in another utterance, ". . . says a Cretan," it becomes formally undecidable: if the Cretan is telling the truth, then he is also lying and his utterance is false. If he is lying, his utterance is false, so the contrary is true, and Cretans do not all lie, thus his utterance can be true, etc. In fact, the solution of the paradox is found in its dissolution: it is not correct to apply an operation (here a comparison) to another operation; an operation can only be applied to objects, not to other operations; here the truth/lies difference cannot itself be applied to the difference between truth/lies.[35] The paradox is not the equivalent of a logical contradiction of the proposition (or non-sense), nor an (empirical) impossibility of knowledge, nor an obscurity (confusion) in phenomenality; it is an error in the use of the logical laws: "Clearly the laws of logic cannot in their turn be subject to laws of logic."[36] Have we thus resolved the paradox in its logical sense? No, for it opens another question: its formulation supposes a dichotomy between two terms or concepts that are (apparently) contradictory and which therefore rest on the principle of the excluded third. But the opposition of terms that operate in *such a case* can be debated. None of these terms is appropriate to the statement uttered, but are these terms of opposition really self-evident? Are they even appropriate for the matter at hand? Do they exhaust the possibilities? Is there no way of finding other terms that would be more suitable to this particular case?

Or take this example: if I say that "the face of the other remains invisible," it sounds like a paradox, as it seems self-evident that the face is the most visible aspect of the other. But to maintain this obvious commonsense position, it is necessary that I already take for granted the opposition of the visible/invisible, and that I assume that every face is visible. Yet, one could argue (I have done so) that the opposite of the visible and the seen [*vu*] is not found only in the invisible or what is yet unseen [*invu*], but also (and even primarily, if we are speaking about the other) in the sight *that sees*, in the *seer*. In this case, the face of the other is characterized *more* by the fact that he sees me than by his supposedly seen visibility (for he can conceal himself, mask himself, disguise himself, withdraw from visibility, and he does so very often). The paradox was therefore only apparent, not because it had nothing to say, but because it naively assumed (against every phenomenality) that every face shows itself as visible according to the common conditions of visibility of things in the world. Yet, the face, starting from what the other *sees*, belongs neither first nor fundamentally to the visible that is *seen*, but belongs to the *invisible who sees*.[37] When understood and corrected in this way, the first paradox dissolves into a second. In this sense, every paradox requires us to question the relevance of the terms that lead it to a logical contradiction; or to be more exact, the phenomenal validity of its logical contradiction. We must not rule out too quickly that "this paradox (which indeed has the form of a truism) can also be expressed in this way: one can *think* what is not the case."³⁸ What does it mean to think what is not the case?

Now consider the paradox from the appearance that it presents or seems to present. For this is the point: it is not self-evident that a paradox shows nothing when it says nothing. As Henri de Lubac remarked, one must distinguish "paradoxes of mere expression: one exaggerates in order to emphasize" from "real paradoxes." The latter involve a resistant antinomy: a real paradox does not result from the logical difficulty of stating a proposition, but is the only way of logically describing the particularity of certain phenomena: "Paradoxes: the word specifies, above all, then, the things themselves, not the way of saying them."³⁹ It tries to describe, among the phenomena that I unquestionably experience, those that happen (like true events, for example) only by *contra*-dicting the conditions of my experience, which impose themselves only by confronting me with a *counter*-experience. Transposed into terms of phenomenality, this caveat suggests that a paradox could offer the correct *logical* form to formulate saturated phenomena, for in fact none of *our* significations or concepts are able to constitute them as an object. Or perhaps: the paradox could offer the correct logical form for describing (saturated) phenomena that appear in experience by *contra*-dicting the (finite) conditions of possibility of experience. Far from reducing the paradox, it is necessary to save it, so that it can introduce us to a nonstandard but unavoidable logic. For it does not cancel out an experience, but makes it bearable and describable, even when a proven and experienced phenomenality nevertheless refuses to take the status of an object, of a common law phenomena (where the intuition lets itself be understood in the concept and the signification). The paradox, therefore, far from excluding experience or excluding itself from it, extends it; it extends it by allowing it to describe a nonobjectifiable experience that is all the more manifest as it originates from phenomena that manifest themselves in themselves, because they give themselves starting from themselves. This experience can be called a counter-experience.

This logical figure of phenomenality is the experience that contradicts the conditions of experience in the field of philosophy and, in particular, phenomenology—this we know. But it could also be the case that it is exercised preeminently and first of all in the territory of Jewish and Christian theology which is *open* to infinity (chapter 2, above). Of course, we think about the radical description of Revelation imposed by Barth: God's self-manifestation by himself intervenes in the experience of man as a radical counter-experience, as a stone that suddenly falls and pierces through everything under its impact. However, this precise brutality does not say too much (as the common critique goes), but still too little. And for two reasons.

First of all, because it goes without saying that Revelation, in the sense of the irruption of God into what is finite, limited, and without holiness, cannot by definition be received there, nor conceived, nor adequately seen. It cannot and *must not ever* find in this unclean world a dwelling place, an opening, or a temple suited to its holiness. There is no greater misunderstanding of the Revelation of God than that of Heidegger (here a paradigm of the *Auflkärung*, and more Hegelian than he seems), who wanted to submit the Revelation of God to the prior manifestation of gods, and this to the dwelling of the divine, which in turn is submitted to the opening of the holy, and this to the intact opening of being.[40] It is not that there is Revelation *because* the paths would be effectively straightened, the valleys filled, the hills laid low, and all that was crooked set straight (Luke 3:4–5, citing Isaiah 40:3–5), as so many preconditions to be fulfilled before God *could* manifest himself. There is Revelation, to be sure, but precisely *despite* the fact that these paths remain crooked—or *in order* to show even more clearly that they are. If God is manifest as God, who can stand, who can understand it, who can see him without dying? And if we were able to understand it, to see without dying and to stand before him, would it still be God or already an idolatry? Not only are the conditions of the possibility of Revelation not satisfied, and never will be, but they *must* not be, at least right away, if this revelation should merit the title of the Revelation of God by himself: "It does not stand, therefore, under any condition—one can say this only of our knowledge of revelation—but is itself the condition"; indeed, "[a]bove this act there is nothing other or higher on which it might be based or from which it might be derived. . . . It is the condition which conditions all things without itself being conditioned. This is what we are saying when we call it revelation."[41] The question in theology thus does not consist in knowing whether Revelation contradicts the conditions of finite experience—indeed, this contradiction characterizes it analytically and by definition—but in conceiving *how* it contradicts them and *how* it nevertheless succeeds, indeed, succeeds all the *more,* in manifesting itself perfectly and definitively. It is possible that so-called dialectical theology, with all its instantiations, has not seen or has scarcely glimpsed this question.

Hence the second reason: this new question remains unknown for a reason that is clear enough: it belongs first of all to the study of phenomena in general and is only required in a phenomenological approach of Revelation as phenomenon—an exceptional phenomenon, but which formally remains a case of saturated phenomena, or more exactly of a phenomenon of revelation, combining in it the four types of phenomenological saturation (event, idol, flesh, and icon).[42] How does Revelation make itself manifest by contradicting, as it *should*, the *a priori* conditions of experience? By what paradoxes is this counter-experience accomplished? These theological questions cannot be confronted without mastering the possibility of a phenomenality of saturated phenomena. And we must not claim to resolve them too quickly, by mobilizing, under the cover of theological categories, concepts and formulas derived directly from philosophy in its metaphysical state.[43]

We must then attempt to describe the counter-experience of Revelation as a saturated phenomenon par excellence. And to do so respecting two already established certainties. First, we must never leave the position and the status that the saturated phenomenon imposes on the *I*—that of the witness. This requires we always keep in mind the warning of Christ, that "I still have many things to say to you, but you cannot bear them now (οὐ δύνασθε βαστάζειν ἄρτι)" (John 16:12). Not only the "many other things" (John 20:30 and 21:25) that were not written in the biblical texts, but especially, among those already recorded, those cases where we are prevented from bearing the excess of evidence due to our lack of concepts and ignorance of the significations that come from God (ἀνόητοι, Luke 24:25). Thus it is absolutely essential that "the Spirit of truth open the way for us into the whole truth (τὸ πνεῦμα τῆς ἀληθείας, ὁδηγήσει ὑμᾶς εἰς τὴν ἀλήθειαν πᾶσαν)" (John 16:13). But to show the way is the definition of "*method*": the Holy Spirit thus determines the method of interpretation of the saturation of the phenomenon of Revelation. Hence the second certitude: we must always consider that what reveals itself in the saturated phenomenon of Revelation, as its *alpha* and its *omega*, concerns one and only one excess, that of charity. It is only a matter of "grasping with all the saints what is the width and breadth and length and height, [in other words] to know the hyperbolical love of Christ, which surpasses knowledge (γνῶναί τε τὴν ὑπερβάλλουσαν τῆς γνώσεως), so that you may be saturated with God up to the point of total saturation (πληρωθῆτε εἰς πᾶν τὸ πλήρωμα τοῦ θεοῦ)." But to arrive at this, to *bear* this saturation and this hyperbole, we must first let ourselves be "rooted and established on the foundations of charity" (Ephesians 3:17–19). Christ determines the element with which the phenomenon of Revelation is saturated and saturating: charity.

Provided that we respect these two certainties of method, it becomes possible not only to liberate the concept of theology from every metaphysical grasp and every epistemological interpretation, but also, using these resources, to succeed at times in correcting them, to contemplate Revelation as a phenomenon through the details of the biblical texts. We begin by this *hapax* of the New Testament: "An ecstasy (ἔκστασις) seized them all, they gave glory (ἐδόξαζον) to God and, filled with fear (φόβου), they said 'We have seen paradoxes (παράδοξα) today'" (Luke 5:26).

IV

Christ as Phenomenon

ELEVEN

Nobody's Manifestation

Seeing and conceiving of paradoxes: we can probably conceive of such things in our experience of the world in general, but what about when it comes to the divine, the gods, and God? As Homer warns, at the very least, "for in no way do the gods make themselves manifest to everyone; οὐ γὰρ πως πάντεσσι θεοὶ φαίνονται ἐναργεῖς."[1] Or rather, we should never see them, since "God then said: 'You cannot see my face, for man cannot see me and remain living'" (Exodus 33:20). The question of fact cannot be separated here from a question of principle: Is the manifestation of the divine, the gods, and God not above all a matter of what should, in principle, remain silent? (The word *mystery* comes from *muō*, "to be silent, to not speak.") Is not the limit of the phenomenal, that is, what can be phenomenalized *for us*, fixed here by principle? Since the domain of the divine is distinguished from our own by the two privileges of immortality and invisibility, it cannot and must not appear to us. The argument of banal atheism, according to which "God does not exist" because no one has seen him, would thus have its validity, provided that we take it more seriously than it takes itself: the realm of manifestation (like that of immortality) only holds *for us* and closes up as soon as it no longer concerns us, but instead the divine, the gods, and above all God.

The Gods on View

Nevertheless, if we consider paganism in its Greek variety, in fact if we follow Homer, it goes without saying that the gods appear; indeed, they never cease appearing.

For example, during the battle where Diomedes wins renown (in Book V of the *Iliad*), when Ares comes to support the Trojans, he does it "in the likeness of the lord of the Thracians, swift-footed Akamas (εἰδόμενος Ἀκάμαντι)" (v. 462); and even Diomedes admits that he cannot pursue Hector, when he sees him (and him alone) protected by Ares "in the likeness of a man mortal (βροτῷ ἀνδρὶ ἐοικώς)" (v. 604).[2] During the final battle, Apollo incites Aeneas to combat, and thus to a probable death, by taking the voice and features of Lycaon.[3] And when Aeneas complains to Apollo about not having such support himself (v. 97–98, p. 406), the god retorts, "Hero, then make your prayer, you also, to the everlasting gods" (v. 104, p. 407); in other words, find your own help from a god intervening in the guise of a man. But the assistance that in Hector's case does not last arrives again and again for Odysseus thanks to Athena, and sometimes even against Zeus.[4] If she "poured down marvelous grace (θεσπεσίην χάριν) over him, on his head and his shoulders / made him seem (ἰδέσθαι) taller than he had been, more mighty to look at / so he would become dear (φίλος), inspire fear (δεινός), and seem noble (αἰδοῖός) to all the Phaiákan people," and above all to Alkínoös, such that he "seemed like the gods (ἀθανάτοισιν ὁμοῖος),"[5] it is because she herself first guides him through the city in disguise, "making herself to resemble sagacious Alkínoös' herald (εἰδομένη κήρυκι),"[6] or because she herself intervenes, "making herself like a man (ἀνδρὶ δέμας εἰκυῖα)"[7] to judge Odysseus's victory over his local rivals at the discus throw. In short, she makes him appear beautiful like a god, because she herself appears as a human.

This apparition of Athena is never accomplished more clearly than in the return to Ithaca and the massacre of the suitors, and always with two characteristics. First, the goddess takes action among men to support Odysseus (she deflects the opposing arrows, she deploys the shield) and ultimately to reestablish peace among the inhabitants of Ithaca.[8] Second, even if Odysseus recognizes her, she only ever appears with features other than her own: "Then came up and approached them Athena the daughter of

Great Zeus / making herself like Mentor in speaking as well as in appearance (Μέντορι εἰδομένη ἠμὲν δέμας ἠδὲ καὶ αὐδήν). / As he beheld (ἰδὼν) her, Odysseus rejoiced."⁹ These two characteristics are confirmed when, together, they are reversed: Athena intervenes in the combat, but does not exempt Odysseus from having to wage the battle and win it; also, in the same instant, she both withdraws from the fray and withdraws from the human likeness that she had worn: she disappears behind the features of a "swallow."¹⁰ Like all the gods, she appears only for a time and never in person, but remains withdrawn from her appearance.

No One to See

What can we conclude from this? We can of course hold to the naively optimistic opinion of Alkinoös, assured that "Always before have the gods been clearly manifest (θεοὶ φαίνονται ἐναργεῖς) / to us (ἡμῖν) here, when glorious hecatombs ever we offer; / seated beside us, right where we are, they have taken their dinner. / Nor from a traveler who was alone, if he met with immortals / never themselves would they hide (οὐ κατακρύπτουσιν), since we in fact are a race / as near to them (σφισιν ἐγγύθεν) as the Cyklōpes or ravening tribes of the giants."¹¹ Longinus understands this proximity by affirming that Homer had "made, in terms of power, gods of his men and men of his gods."¹² In a sense, the whole interpretation of Walter Otto, still so decisive today, privileges this proximity and sets it up as his fundamental thesis: "The thing that distinguishes the Greek is the ever lively awareness of the nearness of the divine.... The meaningful combination of the natural and the miraculous, which leaves the rights of each unimpaired, has found classic expression in the famous stories of the gods who appear upon the earthly scene in *human form*."¹³ This would be the particularity of polytheism, or even its superiority over what we imagine as biblical "monotheism."

Nevertheless, we must question this supposed nearness, if only because Homer himself contests it. First, we can observe that Odysseus immediately rejects Alkinoös's conclusion that his beautiful appearance shared true resemblance with the gods: "Otherwise trouble your mind, Alkínoös, since I am surely / not like any immortal (οὐ γὰρ ἐγώ γε / ἀθανάτοισιν ἔοικα) of those who hold the broad heaven, / either in form or in stature, but like mere men who are mortal."¹⁴ The nearness of appearance between gods and mortals does not extend to the real encounter, nor does it imply any fundamental resemblance, still less a communion of destiny: the men at war before Troy, and Odysseus above all, have learned this from long experience. Second, we have seen that while certain gods manifest themselves to certain men (above all to heroes and to half-gods), not everyone is able to recognize them, according to the other Homeric principle that "It is most difficult, goddess (i.e., Athena), for even the cleverest mortal, / when he meets you, to know you; for anything (παντὶ ἐΐσκεις) you may resemble;"[15] so that the supposed familiarity of gods with men remains haphazard, provisional, and revocable. Is it even necessary to choose between the two hypotheses, between familiarity and estrangement of gods and mortals? It could be that the opposition of these two theses remains itself an illusion: in fact, the gods can more freely take human form, intervene in the affairs of mortals, and play a decisive role there, precisely because they never show themselves *as such*, nor do they ever dare it *in person*; in short, they never manifest themselves under their own features, *face uncovered*. They intervene all the more often as they always proceed intermittently, disappearing just as they came into view—under a borrowed likeness, masked by a strange face.[16] They manifest themselves all the more freely as this manifestation commits them to nothing, exposes them to nothing, and ultimately reveals nothing about them.

This indeed points to the real question. Ovid, who completed what Homer had started, understood perfectly: the gods only take a form so easily and so often because they can leave it at will. Thus at no point does the face that they present really show themselves, since they make themselves seen only by proxy, or rather by usurping the appearance of a man or an animal, which actually have faces (or good looks, an analogue of a face): thus Zeus presents himself "*in specie mortali*" to visit Philemon and Baucis, as Diana to approach Callisto, or as a bull to abduct Europa;[17] similarly, Apollo presents himself "*in serpente Deus*" to pass from Delphi to the Tiber.[18] In this context, what would it mean, anyway, that a god would regain his original godly form when he leaves his temporary mask, just as Apollo, having become a serpent, finally "*specie cælesta resumpta*,"[19] becomes himself again? In fact, this *specis cælesta* has no meaning: either the god disappears from mortal view, or he takes up another form of another mortal, for as a celestial being he has no face that would show him in person. This is why the whole of the *Metamorphoses* is concluded by the apotheosis of a real man, and therefore a real face, that of the visible Caesar, taken up to the heavens by a goddess that "no one sees (*alma Venus, nulli cerenda*)."[20] The gods thus only appear masked, and, as such, never reach the visibility of a face-to-face encounter in person—they cannot do it or, perhaps, they do not *dare*. They take an appearance only in order *not* to have to appear.

When a philosopher later said that he came forward masked ("*larvatus prodeo*"[21]), overly subtle critics suggested that he also masked himself before God ("*Larvatus pro Deo*"). It could be that here it is the gods themselves who can only come forward masked before men; and that it would be only under these masks that they play their role as gods, that they perform their function as gods, in short that they take place as gods: "*Larvati pro diis*." If these gods, *simple placeholders (lieu-tenants) of themselves*, have, like the Great Pan, ended up dying, it would be first of all because they never really manifested themselves *as such*, never dared to commit themselves to a face that would be seriously their own, truly out in the open, where they could be exposed in their nudity because they gave themselves fully. They had to disappear, by definition and from the outset, since they had neither decided nor managed to appear in person, and therefore to appear for good, for *real*. Not that they were simply concealed gods (hidden, inaccessible, *absconditi*), but because they only offered masks of gods, as perfectly visible as they were perfectly empty. As gods without true faces, how could they manifest a real divinity? The Greek gods of course "gave signs" (as Heraclitus said of the oracle of Delphi) that they are here, but they signal as well that they are never here to stay, nor are they present for good among mortals. They come only to show us that they do not share our fate, even and above all if they sometimes play on our side, and often against it.

The supposed familiarity with these gods does not lead to any nearness with mortals, but attests to its absence. We find confirmation of this by the opposite hypothesis: What would happen if a god was manifested *as such*, but without a face? Ovid, once again, answers this question: no mortal would survive, as is clear from his story of the vengeance of Hera (in this case Juno): Semele, daughter of Cadmos the Theban, had conceived Dionysius from her union with Zeus. Hera, as was her jealous wont, sought revenge. Taking the appearance and voice "of an old woman (*simulavit anum*)," she pretends to advise Semele. She is concerned that this lover is not actually Zeus, rightly reminding her that, quite often, "Many, pretending to be gods, have found entrance into modest chambers"; she therefore suggests that Semele demand the supposed god "prove his love, if it is really him," and more precisely, that he "give himself to [her] such as [he] offers himself to the embraces of the daughter of Saturn when [they] are united by the bonds of Venus," in short, that he show himself nakedly, as such. This is to suppose that Zeus takes a real body of flesh and makes love in person. But this he cannot do, because he has no body, no flesh, no face of his own; if he must show himself as such, it would be without these bodily features, immediately, without human form, or rather without form, by his thunder, pure power of blind and invisible destruction, which kills: "Her mortal body (*corpus mortale*) bore not the onrush of heavenly power, and by that gift of wedlock she was consumed [by flames] (*donisque jugalibus arsit*)."[22] The god *as such* has no more a body and flesh than a face to offer; if he wants to give himself, he can only give death; and so he cannot manifest himself in person, because he cannot give himself in the flesh. And for this very reason, the development that will result in the mystery cults tends toward no longer naming the gods directly, and most often, toward designating them by ambiguous or even threatening euphemisms (they call the Furies or Erinyes "the Eumenides," "the Kindly Ones").[23] The most perfect body of the gods, which does not die, whose blood is not shed, which eats without need of nourishment, which flies through the air without any effort, in short, what we might wish to call a "super-body," is, in fact, not a body at all—it offers the temporary support for an appearing, itself a simple appearance, the sign of a name, which in fact gives access to no flesh, the substitute for a face that flees the face-to-face encounter.[24]

Nobody's Idol

And so the image and the figure taken by the divine do not manifest him. Either the Great Pan dies by not manifesting himself *as such*, or Zeus brings death by manifesting himself as no one, or more exactly as the absence of a face, from whom mortals are protected only by a mask. The image, the figure, and the form do not manifest anything of the gods, nor of the divine. Their apparitions remain only apparent because they appear each time under figures and masks (*persona*), or in short, as characters who certainly indicate them, but never identify them *as such*. If we still wish to speak of theophanies here, they must be conceived as anonymous manifestations: "[the gods] almost always appear incognito,"[25] or else as visions that annihilate those who would see them. The gods are not invisible, but rather cannot be aimed at (*invisable*), since they have no body, and therefore no face.

The apparitions of gods retain the appearances of apparitions because their images (forms, figures, *personæ*) do not really take on a body definitively, since they are not incarnated and do not deliver in person either the face or the name of the god.[26] The apparition does not give the god, because it does not possess him any more than the god appropriates it; he borrows it, occupies it, in short *leases* it for a time, in order to be able to vacate it, desert it as soon as he pleases. If therefore this apparent apparition does not open onto the face of the god, by its visibility, it can only refer back to the face of the one who sees it. In fact it no longer refers to anyone but the one who sees it, because one does not see in it the face of any divine *other*, but only the reflection of himself. It is thus the question of an *idol*: that which is seen, in a permanent and ritualized way, without giving the presence of the god in person; and therefore that which measures, by interposed visibility, the maximum visible that the human gaze can bear, thereby fixing under the appearance of a god the invisible mirror of one's aim.[27] The exact illustration of this aporia—the idol that manifests nothing but the gaze of the one who aims—is found in the marvelous version of the Narcissus myth offered by Ovid. Narcissus's error is not that he loved himself too much, but that he imagined he loved a body of flesh while he only loved an image reflected in the water, his own, of course, but without a body: "while he drinks he is smitten by the sight of the beautiful form he sees (*visæ correptus imagine formæ*). He loves an unsubstantial hope (*sine corpore*), and thinks that substance which is only shadow. He looks in speechless wonder at himself." The image has no body, and therefore it does not open onto any alterity; from this incorporeality of the image there follows the adoration of himself, idolatry in its common meaning: "and he admires everything by which he is admired; without caution, he desires himself, and the one whom he experiences and approves is himself experiencing himself and approving himself (*qui probat ipse probatur*)." The egocentricity does not provoke the incorporeality of the image that shows no one; to the contrary, it results from it. The image shows nothing, and so there is nothing left but the one who sees it: "What you seek is nowhere (*nusquam*). What you love, if you turn away, you will lose. This shadow is that of your image turned back to you. It has no substance of its own (*Nil habet ista sui*)." The emptiness of the image, which no longer manifests anything in itself or of itself, thus returns it to the one who aims at it;

he discovers himself to be the origin: "That one is me, I feel it! (*Iste ego sum, sensi!*) The image does not deceive me." But then it no longer leads me to the least original, for, if it is I who produce it, I always destroy it, whether I turn away, muddle it, or kiss it: "a novel kind of lover, I would that what we love would withdraw (*vellem quod amamus abesset*)!"[28] For an image to take body, then, must it distance itself from me? Must it distinguish itself from me to come to me? Must it take on a body to open me to a face-to-face? But then, would an image still even be the concern—would it instead be an advent that would come in person, and therefore from *elsewhere*? Manifestation is not first of all determined by an apparition (or an appearance of an apparition), but by the advent of the visible from the *elsewhere*, or from an *elsewhere* which takes on a body, to remain there.

Making Invisibility Appear

An understanding of these questions, and their response, can be clearly found in the inversion of terms proposed by the Old Testament, or, to be more exact, the sacred Scriptures of the Jews (to take up a phrase of Joseph Ratzinger). Here arises a crucial paradox, since it is up to Israel, in contrast to the Greeks and probably most of the religions of the surrounding peoples, *to make appear the radical invisibility* of God: "The veto on images in the Old Testament is by no means a general religious truth, but the most abrupt affront to this conception of deity [i.e., the deity as present in the image]."[29] For here, when the divine manifests itself in person (which implies passing from undetermined *gods* to a *determined God*), it does so without direct visibility and even attests in every visibility its own character as invisible. Henceforth, the prohibition of direct vision, certainly sometimes already observed by the "nations," can no longer mean merely the observation of an impossibility of fact: namely, that no mortal gaze can bear divine glory—"if God spoke to us, we would die" (Exodus 20:19).[30] It can also and above all be understood as the revelation of a possibility *a contrario*: there is glory *in God* precisely because it exceeds the measure and span of our gaze, and therefore appears in its very invisibility *for us*. Countless texts confirm this.

When God proclaims his manifestation at Sinai, he explains (for the first time, it seems), the prohibition: "And Yahweh said to Moses: 'Go down and warn the people, lest they come look at the Lord and many of them perish'"

(Exodus 19:21, repeating 19:12), but this prohibition also sets the condition that makes the *quasi*-theophany bearable. "And Yahweh said to Moses: 'See, here (הנה), it is I who come to you in a thick cloud, that the people may listen (ישמע) when I speak (בדברי) with you, and that they may always trust you'" (19:9). Not seeing because of the cloud is precisely what allows God to speak to Moses (and Moses to "respond") and the people to "tremble" (19:16) upon hearing the sound of a trumpet: the text goes so far as to say that "the people *saw* (ראים) the thunder and the flashes of lighting, and saw (ירא) the sound of the trumpet" (20:18).³¹

Moreover, Moses had already proposed the Covenant to the people by setting before their eyes, *so to speak,* only *words,* but words uttered and set before them by God: "he placed before their faces (וישם לפניהם) all the words (הדברים) that the Lord had commanded him" (19:7). Seeing here is equivalent to seeing what one hears, for there is nothing to see other than the word, which God takes, gives, and holds (the three go together).³² As a direct consequence, the account of Exodus 19 (which is both Elohist and Yahwist) is abruptly interrupted ("So Moses went down to the people and told them," 19:25) to leave a place for the (Priestly) account of the proclamation of the Decalogue (first mentioned in Exodus 20:1–17, which will be taken up again by Exodus 34:10–28): the manifestation is in fact accomplished in the word of the Ten Words, which itself is inscribed in the exchange of words, since "Moses spoke (ידבר), and God answered him in the sound (בקול) [of thunder]" (Exodus 19:19).

The manifestation is thus shifted from vision to hearing, or more exactly the face-to-face encounter is accomplished by an exchange of words, which allows the unfolding of the whole figure of the call and response. This is how we can understand the significance of the second covenant (after the episode of the golden calf, Exodus 32), where, once again, "Yahweh would speak (דבר) with Moses" (33:9), and even "used to speak with Moses face to face (פנים אל פנים) as a man speaks to his friend (ידבר איש אל רעהו)" (33:11). And yet Moses, in this encounter, formulates once again an inadmissible request: "Now show me your glory" (33:18), a request which, once again, is denied him, according to the principle that "You cannot see my face, for man shall not see me and live" (33:20). But couldn't we nevertheless suppose that the "face-to-face, פנים אל פנים" (granted in 33:11) implies the uncovering of the "face, פנים" (refused in 33:20)?

In other words, how can Moses see *in some way* face-to-face without fearing death before the face, or crying out as Isaiah does: "And I said: 'Woe is me! For I am lost; for I am a man of unclean lips, and I dwell in the midst of a people of unclean lips; for my eyes have seen the King, the Lord of hosts!'" (Isaiah 6:5)? A first answer is found explicitly in the conclusion of the story: Moses sees the face, but without seeing it face-on: the glory of Yahweh, veiled by his hand, passes by Moses, who is hidden in the cleft of a rock, and Moses sees the face, but only "from the back"; when Yahweh removes his hand, he sees the trace and the reflection of the glory, but not face-to-face, for "my face shall not be seen (ופני לא יראו) . . ." (Exodus 33:23).

But then in what sense can we nevertheless say that Moses saw God face-to-face, if he could not see the face of his glory, but only the trace of his face—from the back?

We must therefore seek out a second explanation. It can be surmised, if we reread Moses's request for Yahweh to attest his mission, that Yahweh himself lead the people by accompanying them and marching in front of them; in other words, to come in person to the head of the people. And it is indeed in person, literally with "my own face (פני)" (33:14), that Yahweh responds positively to the call of Moses, asking him to come in person, literally with "his own face (פניך)" (33:15).

The "face" here thus no longer means a visible phenomenon in the world, among the other spectacles that are accessible and available to the mastery of the gaze; rather, it reveals presence in person, involvement in our presence by the one who comes there because he consents to it, who comes by arriving there from *elsewhere*.[33] While the pagan gods only manifest themselves by making themselves seen as phenomena of the world, by presenting themselves in a worldly form, thus always under another face than their own (for properly speaking they have none), so that they only take it on for a time and do not remain with us mortals, Yahweh here takes on *his own* face, not in order to give himself in a spectacle, nor to make himself seen as a phenomenon of the world, but to manifest that he is committed to us, his people; and to do this, he becomes word, remains in his word, holds it and is held by it. The face gives itself in person not by showing itself as a thing of the world, but in giving his word, as a promise that comes from and is kept from *elsewhere*. The pagan gods overtly show themselves under their borrowed faces, because they do not ever give themselves in person;

Yahweh never manifests his glory as a phenomenon of the world, because he only gives his face in person (פני) as his person, in the word he speaks, holds, and gives. He gives himself in person (in his face) by giving his word. But to shift the in-person presence of manifest visibility to the invisibility of a given word should not surprise us; it could even be that we are confirming a phenomenological rule set by Levinas: a face only reveals the other if it remains invisible, yet speaks. For the other is not phenomenalized in his face if this face shows itself directly like another phenomena, enclosed in the visible world of objects; of course, he *also* bears the visibility of a worldly phenomenon, among others; but this visibility can *also* be masked or lying, in short, concealed under a borrowed form. In fact, the other does not phenomenalize himself by showing himself, but insofar as he *speaks to me* (silently as well as with words), makes a claim on me and addresses me; only then does his face concern me, then only does this face open up, and it gazes at me. Since it gazes at me, his face, now invisible as a thing of the world, truly concerns me.

Facing the Name

But then, how better to understand that a "face" whose "glory" (33:19) cannot and must not be seen nevertheless allows for God to gaze at Moses, and that Moses concerns God, and God concerns Moses? What do Moses and Yahweh thus exchange in this faceless "face-to-face"? The text does not hide it, but even declares it openly: Yahweh knows Moses by his name: "And Moses said to Yahweh . . . 'Yet you have said "I know you by your name and you enjoy my favor (חן)"'" (33:12 and 17).

This is what the Greeks understand by *eudokia*: the charm recognized in someone which makes him attractive and makes others wish to engage with him as a friend or a spouse; in fact, it is the reflection of the very glory of God on a man who is preferred in this way. The glory of Yahweh now becomes accessible because it distinguishes Moses and radiates from him: entering into "this glory which assumed the appearance of a devouring fire in the sight of the people of Israel" (25:17), "the skin of Moses's face was shining (קרן עור פני משה)" (34:35).

His face reflected the glory of the invisible face of Yahweh to the point that he, too, had to veil his own visible face. This favor results from the fact that God was glad to know and to name Moses, whom he made a "friend"; thus they could spend "forty days and forty nights" (34:28) together.³⁴ But then we might expect that it must be the case that Moses, too, should have access to the Name of God. Otherwise, how could this faceless face-to-face have taken place in the mode of a name-to-Name?

The story of the calling of Moses has already answered this question and already accomplished the transition from seeing to hearing, from vision to the Name. In fact, everything begins with a manifestation: an angel "made himself seen (וירא)" and Moses then goes to be able to "see" (Exodus 3:2); he even rushes with impatient curiosity: "I will go see this strange sight (אסרה נא ואראה את המראה)" (3:3). But at the moment he stepped forward "to see (לראות)" God "called out (ויקרא)" to him (3:4) from the middle of a bush that burned without being consumed: "Do not come any closer; take the sandals off your feet, for the place where you are standing is holy ground" (4:5). From this point, the barrier of holiness³⁵ requires that sight give way to the call and vision to listening. The word responds to words ("Moses, Moses!—Here I am (הנני)" (3:4) and words to the Name. For Yahweh presents himself and gives himself in his presence by taking up the ancient name: "It is I, I (אנכי), the God of your father, the God of Abraham, the God of Isaac, and the God of Jacob" (3:6). Not only is this name not identified by a neutral knowledge, but it does not reveal him at all; rather, it recalls a previous covenant (Genesis 17:19–21), such that the new word marks that God is here keeping a promise made in the past. The Name, "I am who I will be (אהיה אשר אהיה)" signifies—as a sign and pledge—that Yahweh is committed in person to his people, or rather for those who will become a people by finding themselves called "my people" by him: "This is what you will say to the children of Israel: 'I am (אהיה)' has sent me to you" (3:14). Clearly, this name does not categorically tell the essence of God, any more than it states only negatively that God remains God by the name of God, nor even that God is what he will be, in his secret. It says that God speaks himself, and speaks himself to promise salvation to his people. God uncovers himself and proclaims himself in his Name as the one who comes in person to save.³⁶

Where, then, lies the privilege recognized to Moses, by Yahweh himself? "I will raise up for them from among their brothers a prophet like you" (Deuteronomy 18:18, see 18:15). Certainly not in having seen the invisible, but rather in having seen it *as invisible,* thus in having *heard* the invisible, the Name. Of course, "he sees the form (תמנת) of Yahweh," but this consists in the fact that "Yahweh speaks with him (אדבר בו)" (Numbers 12:8).

And Moses is not set apart primarily because he spoke with God or saw him, but because God spoke to him and crowned him with his glory. Moreover, if the Pentateuch concludes by declaring that "there has not arisen since in Israel a prophet like Moses, whom Yahweh knew (ידעו יהוה) face to face" (Deuteronomy 34:10), it is not so much because no one else knew God face-to-face, but because no one else *was known* to that extent in person by God. In this sense, the situation of Moses does not contradict that of the people, to whom he repeats that, before Horeb, "You heard the sound of words, but saw no form (ותמונה); only the call of a voice (קול)" (Deuteronomy 4:12).[37] Revelation is not uncovered by the phenomenon of a spectacle, nor the vision of a form, but by the opening of the word and the unfolding of a Name. The word and the Name come to me from *elsewhere*; they do not come from me, nor fall under my gaze. Moses did not see Yahweh, but he heard the Name when he went to see the Bush. And so the Name called him and was manifested to him. Thus the prophet in a sense says nothing about God and transmits nothing in his name. For he immediately cedes the word to the Word while he himself remains silent. He does not take up his speech to say: "I say that he says, etc.," but he gives up his speech; from the outset he gives speech back to the Word, which he lets speak for itself: "Thus saith the Lord": "I say, *says the Lord.* . . ."[38] Revelation does not say that "god is . . ." nor even that "god is God, for God's sake [*nom de dieu*]!" but "God speaks and says his Name, and so I listen."

The Call of the "I"

Manifestation, because it culminates in listening to the Name, thus begins by hearing the call. Like at Sinai, on Moriyya, the "mountain of seeing,"[39] one must first listen to the call of the Name. The figure of Abraham (like that of Jacob at Yabboq) confirms what is at stake: the order of phenomenalization only ends up in a manifestation by starting from a call, and thus first of all a listening. But this listening makes one see. And so before Moses and in order to make him possible, one needs Abraham.

Abraham begins by a call. Or rather, before Abram was himself, before he became "the father of a multitude of peoples" (Genesis 17:5), already a call summoned him, or more precisely called him away. Abram was *called away* by being placed in exile, by a call that made him enter headlong what men want more than anything to return from, as Odysseus did—exile. "Leave your country, your kindred, and your father's house" (12:1). It is only after the call to exile is heeded and accepted that God "made himself seen (הנראה, ὤφθη)" (12:7).

And Abram sets out for a space without a place, in radical destitution, because he leaves "childless" (15:2). But because he listens and leaves, he receives a "vision" (מחזה), even though this vision does not make anything seen; it remains precisely that of "a word" (15:1) (דבר), a promise of descendants. The same logic orders the episode of the encounter at Mamre: of course, Yahweh "makes himself seen (וירא, ὤφθη)" (18:1), but perhaps only indirectly, by the "three men," who enter the scene almost like a manifestation of Greek gods. And if it is "by raising his eyes (וישא עיניו, ἰδού)" (18:2) that he sees them, then before raising his eyes Abraham has, strictly speaking, not yet caught any glimpse of this supposed apparition. What decides everything comes from the fact that Abraham experiences that the "Lord," of whom he acknowledges himself the "servant," places "favor (חן)" (18:3) in him, as he did later in Moses. What follows (the promise of a son made to Sarah, the judgment of Sodom, the birth of Isaac) is the result of Abraham's heeding the word of Yahweh and his fidelity to it, which constitutes the single, solid reality of a manifestation stripped of apparition in the strict sense. The manifestation does not consist in Abraham's knowledge of the Name of God—which he still only knows under the title "I am el-Shaddai" (Genesis 17:1, the same as Jacob, Genesis 28:13); the manifestation consists in the fact that Sarai receives her name Sarah (17:15) as Abram receives his own, Abraham, from Yahweh; and that Isaac is born as Yahweh "had said" (21:2). What validates the presence of God does not consist in a theophany, but in the sign and the promise of the birth of Isaac (18:9). The attestation of the uncovering of the invisible by listening, without visible manifestation, in short, by faith, as Paul identifies it—"Abraham believed in God and God counted it to him as righteousness" (Genesis 15:6 = Romans 4:3)—of course culminates in the nonsacrifice of Isaac. Here everything is played out in terms of the call (word) and response (word): "God put Abraham to the test and said to him, 'Abraham! Abraham!' 'Here I am,' he replied" (22:1). What is astonishing of course is the demand to sacrifice Isaac; but it could also be argued that all God is doing here is simply reclaiming his gift (he miraculously gave this son to this father) and his due (the firstborn of the people are destined for the Temple). What is the most astonishing is above all the silence of Abraham, who does not demand any explanation from God (while he gives one to his son), or attempt any haggling (as he dared to do in Genesis 18:22–32), while Yahweh not only does not manifest himself, but is even silent (during the whole sequence: 22:3–10). And, just as a call and a response opened the test, the same call and response close it: "The angel of the LORD called to him from heaven and said, 'Abraham, Abraham!' 'Here I am, he replied'" (22:11 = 21:1). Thus follows God's "second" call (which confirms that the first two were one and the same), definitively sealing that "through your offspring all nations on earth will be blessed, because you have listened to my call (אשר שמעת בקלי)"(22:18). We cannot deny that there was Revelation—the choosing of the people of God and of all humanity in Israel. But this Revelation takes the form of a covenant, where the one who is shown shows himself in making himself heard ("seeing the voice"), without making himself seen in the least form. What shows itself gives itself, but it gives itself by saying itself. Nothing visible is uncovered, if not the very manifestation of the invisible.

Seeing the invisible means hearing the Name of the invisible as such. And this name says nothing other than itself: "I am Yahweh, your God (אנכי יהוה אלהיך)" (Exodus 20:2 and 5). We should be on guard against understanding "I, Yahweh, I am your God" as thus implying that we already know what "god" means, as if Yahweh were only claiming exclusivity in title; in which case the promise would only consist in recognizing as an ally a god identified as a certain Yahweh. To the contrary, we must stress that the one who manifestly declares himself as the God of the people remains without equal or rival, because he is not inscribed in any already identified role, because he keeps his name covered over and unknown.[40] The Name, because it says and gives everything, shows nothing in a worldly manifestation. In this way the "I" is merged with what is by right the only possible "I": "I—Yahweh" (Exodus 3:6, 16). It is not so much a claim to exclusivity, as if Yahweh were jealous of possible rivals in divinity (even though some of the first Hebrews may have understood it this way, as Nietzsche did much later), but as the affirmation that no one, without lying, can say "God" except the one who speaks himself in person because he gives himself in person. "I and no others [namely, I]."[41] In this sense, it is necessary to follow Rosenzweig: "God's 'I' remains the keyword, traversing revelation like a single sustained organ note."[42] When Yahweh reveals himself, there is nothing to see, if not the invisible as such, the word, where the Name gives itself.

TWELVE

What the "Mystery" Uncovers (Paul)

The Presupposition of the Mystery

"I," in other words, "I am"—the one who says he is truly "with us," uncovers himself in this way within our visibility without letting himself be directly seen. The accomplishment of this uncovering is explicitly claimed by Jesus, and as its only actor. He claims it first of all in the Synoptics, for example in the episode of the storm, where he walks on the waters toward the disciples: "Take heart, it is I (namely, I am, ἐγώ εἰμι), do not be afraid" (Matthew 14:27; Mark 6:50). But this claim is immediately exposed to a difficulty: How can we distinguish this *egō eimi* from the pretense of the false Messiahs, who also will say "in [his] name: I am the Christ" (Matthew 24:5, see Mark 13:6 and Luke 21:8)? Clearly by intensifying the present of the words through the presence of a body offered in person, even in a glorified flesh, to the point of allowing his resurrected body to be touched: "See my hands and my feet, for it is I myself that I am (ὅτι ἐγώ εἰμι αὐτός); handle me and see, for a spirit does not have flesh and bones, as you see that I have" (Luke 24:39). Nevertheless, this argument turns in another direction, for how can we hold and *touch* the resurrected flesh which must remain at a distance: "Do not hold me (back), *ne me (re-)tiens-pas!*" (John 20:17)? How can we stand before

181

the glory that bursts forth when "I am" is said—"He said, 'I am, ἐγώ εἰμι,' and they drew back and fell to the ground" (John 18:6)? In principle, if Christ can declare "I am," there is only one alternative: either he becomes unbearable to us, as Yahweh was since the time of Moses, or he blasphemes, as the high priest senses: "'Are you the Christ, the Son of the Blessed?' Jesus said, 'I am [he] (ἐγώ εἰμι), and you will see "the Son of man sitting at the right hand of the Power and coming with the clouds of heaven"' (Deuteronomy 7:3 and Psalms 110:1). Then the high priest tore his robes and said, 'What further witnesses do we need?'" (Mark 14:61–63) The claim "I am" by Jesus thus does not overcome the tension that structures the uncovering of the Name for Abraham and Moses, it radicalizes it: Jesus was condemned to death precisely because he claimed the Name, which never would have happened had they perceived and received him as a moralizing and liberal sage (such remains the hermeneutic error of readings in the style of Strauss or Renan). He was condemned because in him everyone recognizes, as clear as day, the at least possible irruption of the absolute and inconceivable presence of Yahweh. If Christ fulfills everything that the Jewish scriptures awaited and sketched out, he fulfills nothing other and nothing less than what they declared; thus he could only concentrate in himself all the apparently conflicting requirements that wrought their proclamations. Jesus does not modify the terms of the uncovering of God, as implemented by the Jewish scriptures; he claims to fulfill them only by bringing to them no other novelty than this fulfillment itself: he innovates because he "fulfills the Law" (Matthew 5:17) to the letter, without adding, subtracting, or modifying anything, precisely because in his person he performs it exactly. His unique innovation comes from the fact that he is the first to perform it: "And he began to say to them: 'Today this [word of the] Scripture is fulfilled (πεπλήρωται) to your ears'" (Luke 4:21). And he can claim to perform it, because first of all he also claims that "all" the Scriptures pertain "to him (περὶ ἑαυτοῦ)" (Luke 24:27).[1] The newness of Jesus does not consist in an addition to the Scriptures that prepare for him, and to which he continually refers; his newness consists in his coming in his newness, in himself, which alone succeeds in performing the Scriptures, putting them in action, fulfilling them. "What new thing then did the Lord bring to us by his coming? Know therefore that he brought every newness (*omnem novitatem attulit*) in offering himself (*seipsum afferens*)."[2] The difficulties, or even the aporias, of the uncovering of the Name and of the "I am" are thus neither weakened nor displaced in the newness that Jesus incarnates, but incorporated in him and concentrated in a perfect figure (*Gestalt*) that radicalizes them to the extreme. The same dark cloud from which Yahweh is uncovered when he speaks the Name always and necessarily shrouds Jesus when he appears as the Christ. During the transfiguration, on the mountain of a definitive Sinai, here and *especially* here, "a cloud came and overshadowed them. . . . And from this cloud came a voice saying, 'This is my Son whom I have chosen. Listen to him'" (Luke 9:34–35; see Mark 9:7 and Matthew 17:5). And like at Sinai, vision is darkened by the excess of light, and therefore turns to listening, which calls for believing. The question brought about by Moses, when he came down from Sinai carrying the tables of the Law in his arms and the glory of Yahweh on his face, was to know if and how the people would receive them; the same is true to a greater extent when Jesus, as the Christ, bears in himself the "Kingdom of God." The law of un-covering indicated that "in divine things," the manifestation of the phenomenon entails not only its own unfolding, but its acceptance by the witness who is meant to see it; for this phenomenon lets itself be seen only to the extent that we will to receive it (without being able to predict it) (chapter 10 above): attention preeminently governs the un-covering of Christ.

The Gift of the Mystery

The tension that comes to light here arises directly from the principle according to which no one can see God without dying (taken up from Exodus 33:20 by John 1:18) and is marked in the Synoptics by the use of the term *mystērion*—a use all the more remarkable since for each of them it remains a hapax, which only applies to the "Kingdom of God" (Matthew 13:11, Mark 4:11, Luke 8:10), and which at the same time coincides with the first occasion of Jesus's teaching in parables (see chapter 13 below). Everything indicates, then, that the "Kingdom of God" constitutes the *mystērion par excellence* and suffices to unfold its signification (without relying again on its polysemy, as in the Paulinian corpus). How should we understand this? It is not a matter of taking up "hidden mysteries (κρύφια μυστήρια)" (Wisdom 14:23), that stigmatized idols, nor of "mystery religions," which did not really develop until after the Gospels were written. It is necessary to go back to *raz* (רז), a term of Persian origin designating first of all the secret great council, where the king made his decrees with his ministers, then the secret of the king, and finally the mystery of premonitory dreams (Deuteronomy 2:19).³ But these secrets are evoked only because the prophet of Yahweh alone, in this case Daniel, was able to interpret them and make them understood. It becomes clear that higher than the secret of the king lies another secret, the mystery of God, which can also unveil the secret of the king because in a sense, God uncovers himself— as the king confesses explicitly: "And the king said to Daniel: 'In truth your god is the God of gods, the only revealer of the secret mysteries (ὁ ἐκφαίνων μυστήρια κρυπτὰ μόνος)'" (Deuteronomy 2:47). The *mystērion* lays bare [*met à découvert*] all things by un-covering itself. It indicates, beyond what was still conceived as even a (human) secret, what was absolutely not conceived, the inconceivable by definition. The coming of God even as invisible, his presence in person even as inaccessible, the gift of his Name even as unpronounceable, in short, the *mystēria theou* (Wisdom 2:22)—is laid bare. Not only does it uncover itself, but it "gives itself (δέδοται)" (Mark 4:11) and even "gives itself to be known (δέδοται γνῶναι)" (Matthew 13:11 and Luke 8:10). But how can we conceive that something not seen can give itself to be known?

Here the paradox of the *mystērion* of the "Kingdom of God" becomes manifest: however secret it is and remains, it is given, laid bare by itself, in person. This confirms what we have already seen: the instance of un-covering (*apokalypsis*) encompasses and precedes every knowledge of God, however "natural" and however based on "pure reason" it is claimed to be. But this does not imply that the *mystērion* is uncovered in immediate evidence, open to all and exposed to every gaze. Moreover, there would not be any place nor any need to un-cover, if there were nothing covered over or concealed. Something has thus been *silenced*: *mystērion* (the term comes from the verb *muō, to close one's mouth) indicates that what cannot or rather *must* not be said, that which must remain *silent* and *unseen*, known only by the initiates of a brotherhood (for example, that of the *mystēria* of Eleusis); thus, exactly the opposite of the witness who speaks without knowing everything (chapter 2), the initiated (*mustēs*) knows, but must therefore be silent; he must say nothing of what he experiences. Yet the Synoptics do not mention the least code of silence that would hush or hide the *mystērion;* for if not everyone knows it, this does not result from a withholding of the proclamation, but from the refusal to recognize it and hear it as it gives itself. The *mystērion* does not keep any secret, but it happens that certain hearers conceal it—because they conceal themselves from it.

If God remains master of un-covering himself to whomever he wills, so that this *mystērion* as such can "make itself known to all peoples" (Romans 16:26), he can nevertheless only un-cover himself to the one who can (and wills to) receive him. Hence the inevitable paradox, that his infinite power of un-covering cannot and *must* not liberate itself from the finite powerlessness of reception, since the reception is an integral part of the conditions of un-covering. Hence a question proper to Christian *apokalypsis*: How *must* the *mystērion* in principle be uncovered to everyone, and why is everyone nevertheless *able* to not recognize it?[4] For this resistance increases the more the *mystērion* becomes pressing, insistent, and seeks to "give" itself in principle to everyone; the "Kingdom" puts itself to work, into movement; "it has come near" (Mark 1:15; Luke 10:9), "it is very near" (Luke 21:31); the *mystērion* comes toward us, comes *upon* us, *comes over* us like the advent of an event; precisely because it approaches everyone without our anticipating or knowing it, it may be that all do not see it, do not expect it, and above all do not want it. This unexpected arrival, whose reception is unanticipated and thus potentially unwelcome, exactly confirms its status as a phenomenon, or more precisely as that of an event—in other words, an unforeseeable, unrepeatable phenomenon, held to be impossible up to the last minute and which, once actual, still remains impossible, at least in the sense that we do not succeed in understanding it entirely as an object. The un-covering of the *mystērion* can (and must) remain at the same time forever thinkable, but never complete, at once both possible and impossible, because the event of the "Kingdom of God" arrives as an advent. And the first advent of this event is signaled already in the ambiguous and unsettling fact that the *mystērion* unveils *that* it arrives among us, before we understand *what* it means; it comes as fact while still incomprehensible—too quickly accomplished, already given, not yet understood, in the strict sense known as unknown. "Calm block here fallen from obscure glory," it forever shows a sign of contradiction for our blasphemies and even for our blessings in the future.

The *mystērion* of the "Kingdom of God" thus demands its un-covering; it implies its proclamation (*kerygma*), calls for its reception (thus its hermeneutics), each responding to the other without end; and it is especially fitting that the one should ceaselessly delay the other. Since the coming of the "Kingdom of God," the withdrawal of the "mystery" is intensified by a delay in the receiving of the un-covering, or indeed, even in admitting it. Paul observes this as he addresses the Romans. On the one hand, the very thing which has been silenced is nevertheless published and proclaimed openly to all: "For I do not want you to be ignorant of this *mystērion*, brothers, so that you do not remain in your own wisdom (ἐν ἑαυτοῖς φρόνιμοι)" (Romans 11:25): henceforth not only the Jews, who have refused the first manifestation of God—"what is known of God is manifest (φανερόν) to them, for God has manifested himself to them (αὐτοῖς ἐφανέρωσεν)" (Romans 1:19)—but also the pagans, receiving the grace (and the difficult task) of un-covering what remained invisible and silent "in accordance with the good news that I announce and to the proclamation of Jesus Christ (κατὰ τὸ εὐαγγέλιόν μου καὶ τὸ κήρυγμα Ἰησοῦ Χριστοῦ), in accordance with the un-covering of a *mystērion* kept in silence for endless ages (κατὰ ἀποκάλυψιν μυστηρίου. . . σεσιγημένου), but today manifested (φανερωθέντος δὲ νῦν) and brought to the knowledge of all peoples (εἰς πάντα τὰ ἔθνη γνωρισθέντος) by the Scriptures which prophesied it according to the command of the eternal God in order that they obey by believing it" (Romans 16:25–26). In other words, the "Gospel," the happy proclamation that an emperor might make to his people at the moment of his rising to power, for example, becomes universal, like a spiritual Edict of Caracalla, granting citizenship to all in the "Kingdom of God." But, on the other hand, the knowledge of this news has been blocked and obfuscated by a lack of recognition: the manifestation of God through the glory of the created world, though already evident, was not enough to make him recognized by men; indeed, "knowing God, they had given him neither glory nor thanks as God (διότι γνόντες τὸν Θεὸν οὐχ ὡς Θεὸν ἐδόξασαν ἢ ηὐχαρίστησαν), but they became stupid (ἐματαιώθησαν) in their reasoning and their foolish hearts were darkened; calling themselves wise, they made themselves stupid (ἐμωράνθησαν)" (Romans 1:21–22). The *mystērion* was thus rejected *because* it uncovered itself.

It is therefore necessary, and this is Paul's initial point, to invert the order of operations of phenomenalization: since the manifestation cannot be known without prior recognition, it will be necessary for the recognition to precede the knowledge, to provoke it and restore it after the fact; and for that, manifestation (*phanerōsis*) must be radicalized in uncovering itself (*apokalypsis*) from the totality of the *mystērion*, abiding up to that point in endless silence. What is at stake here is a radical change of modes of phenomenality: truth (*alētheia*, un-veiling) gives way to the un-covering (*apokalypsis*) of the phenomenon when we are dealing with the phenomenon of God (chapters 8–10). *The un-covering of the mystery overdetermines the opening of the truth.* With the phenomenological horizon thus identified—a phenomenon uncovering itself on the basis of the *mystērion*—three questions emerge, still indistinct and awaiting confirmation. The first question asks: *What* does the *mystērion* allow to be phenomenalized? From the depths of what unseen arises what comes to show itself from itself and as itself (chapter 12)? The second question asks: *How* is that which gives itself uncovered? By what operation does the invisible make itself recognized *as* visible (chapter 13)? The third question asks: *What* un-covers itself to the extent that it gives itself: *who* shows himself inasmuch as he gives himself, without remainder, without reserve (chapter 14)?

The Mystery of Wisdom

Let us take up the first question: *What* does the *mystērion* allow to be phenomenalized? From the depths of what unseen arises what comes to show itself from itself and as itself? A prime response to this question is found in the Pauline corpus.[5] And in three stages.

The first moment, accomplished by 1 Corinthians, identifies the unseen *from which* the phenomenon arises as the *mystērion* of wisdom, "wisdom in a state of *mystērion*, wisdom remaining secret (σοφία ἐν μυστηρίῳ, τὴν ἀποκεκρυμμένη)" (1 Corinthians 2:7), defined at first only negatively, by contrast with the "wisdom of this age (σοφίαν τοῦ αἰῶνος τούτου)" (2:6), which the masters (the "ἀρχόντες") of the world put into operation. Indeed, the wisdom of God remains secret as long as we do not know that it is un-covered in itself by the very Spirit of God. "That which eye has not seen, what ear has not heard, what has not risen to the heart of man, what God" has prepared "for those who love him (ἀγαπῶσιν),"[6] can only come from God: "God has un-covered (ἀπεκάλυψεν) it for us by his Spirit, for the Spirit searches all things, and even the depths of God" (2:9–10, citing Isaiah 64:3). Only God un-covers God, and it is from God that we can learn what concerns God (παρὰ θεοῦ περὶ θεοῦ)[7]. The "depths of God"[8] correspond here to what Christ un-covers to his disciples in parables: "To you has been given the *mystērion* of the Kingdom of God" (Mark 4:11).[9] Thus, it is not our knowledge, "not the blood or the will of men" (John 1:13), "neither flesh, nor blood," but the recognition given by no one but "my Father who is in heaven who un-covers" (Matthew 16:17) the *mystērion*. The recognition, which alone makes possible the knowledge, comes from the "Father who is in heaven"; or more precisely what the Father *gives*, namely the Spirit, "the Spirit of his Son sent into our hearts, crying 'Abba! Father!' " (Galatians 4:6), in keeping with the fact that "God's charity has been poured into our hearts through the Holy Spirit which has been *given* to us" (Romans 5:5).[10] In order to see the un-covered *mystērion*, it is thus necessary to pass from our spirit to the Spirit of God, to *change places* from one to the other, so as to see it as God gives it to be seen. This is nothing less than an overturning of intentionality: taking the intentional gaze of God on God, instead of continuing to cling to our intentionality when the intuition of the *mystērion* arises. In other texts I have identified this overturning or displacement of intentionality as an *anamorphosis*: finding *the* point of view on a phenomenon such as it gives itself that does not immediately overlap with, or that even contradicts the view we would have in holding the neutral position of a transcendental spectator, constituting it as its object. This gaze is shifted toward the point of view, at first undecided and then assessed by feeling our way forward through successive approximations, from which, according to the demands of *this* phenomenon, what gives itself would succeed in showing itself, all at once and in its very own radiance.[11] In the case where what is trying to phenomenalize itself comes from God, accomplishing anamorphosis assumes a shift of the intentional gaze so radical that it provokes nothing less than a *conversion* of the *I* that bears this gaze. In the case of the *mystērion* of God, the conversion of the mind to the Spirit defines the anamorphosis. That is, for the *mystērion* of God, no vision, no interpretation, no constitution remains possible, unless through God's intentionality and by a constitution from God's point of view on his own phenomenon, because it can only be seen and received as it is given. In this sense, literally, the Spirit decides and "judges all things (ἀνακρίνει πάντα)" (1 Corinthians 2:15). Consequently, by his power to bring to light the *mystērion* of God, he also lays bare what is hidden in the hearts of the witnesses: "He will illuminate (φωτίσει τὰ κρυπτὰ) the things hidden in darkness and will manifest the desires of hearts (φανερώσει τὰς βουλὰς τῶν καρδιῶν)" (1 Corinthians 4:5).

The divide between the intentional gazes, between the transcendental point of view and anamorphosis, thus opens the field of an inevitable conflict of interpretations. Paul defines it as the conflict between the "wisdom of this world" and the "wisdom of God" (1 Corinthians 2:6–7 and 1:21). Here, the wisdom of this world must be understood very precisely as that of the Greeks: "Greeks seek wisdom" (1 Corinthians 1:22). Wisdom, for them, as for all philosophers and in every natural attitude, consists in searching for something yet unknown in order to seize it for oneself, to deliver it from unknown to known in our field of knowledge. Such a "wisdom" is identified by another term, decisive here because it is borrowed from Aristotle, in his famous definition of what philosophical thought seeks in its global and normative point of view: "What has been sought (τὸ ζητούμενον) for a long time and is still being sought today, and which has always been lacking [namely the answer to the question], 'what is *on*?' or in other words, what is *ousia*?"[12] Moreover Paul, during his discussion in Athens with certain "Epicurean and Stoic philosophers," defines them, in an ambiguous homage, with this same term: "they seek God (ζητεῖν τὸν θεὸν)" (Acts 17:18, 27); this suggests probably that they seek him as a being, like philosophers who know in advance what they want to find, according to the intentionality of their masterly gaze, which they never put into question. It may be that the angels who announce the Resurrection of Christ make the same reproach implicitly to the women at the tomb: "Why do you seek (ζητεῖτε) the living one among the dead?" (Luke 24:5, and see Mark 16:6); for they too knew in advance what they were looking for (a corpse to embalm) and within what horizon (that of death, which always wins in the end) without having yet converted their gaze through the anamorphosis that God's point of view would have them take: for God, the one for whom "nothing is impossible" (Luke 1:37), it had to do with Jesus as the one who defined himself as "the resurrection and the life" (John 11:25).

A symptom of the failure of anamorphosis, "seeking" also receives countless negative mentions: Herod "searches for the child" in order to kill him (Matthew 2:13), or "seeks to see" Jesus (Luke 9:9); exactly like the Jews who "seek to kill him" (John 5:18; 7:1, 19, 25, and 30). For it is a matter of possessing things that are still unknown in order to possess oneself: man loses his soul because he "seeks to preserve his life" (Luke 17:33), while love "does not seek its own interests" (1 Corinthians 13:5), patterning itself after Christ who "does not seek his own will" (John 5:30), nor his "own glory" (John 7:18). It may be that this "search" is enough to condemn "philosophy", because it follows "human tradition according to the elemental powers of the world," following its never-questioned intentional point of view (Colossians 2:8), challenging or quite simply not seeing that the "recognition of the *mystērion* of God" is found in Christ, "in whom are hidden (ἀπόκρυφοι) all the treasures of wisdom and knowledge" (Colossians 2:3). Let us also note that the primacy of the "seeking," thus the refusal of anamorphosis, does not only characterize the "wisdom" of the Greeks: Jews likewise "seek," even when, in place of the wisdom of the Greeks, they "ask for signs" (Mark 8:11; Luke 11:16 and 29; John 6:26). And these signs they seek remain under their power, in the horizon of their aim, against every intentional shift and against every anamorphosis, since they feel themselves to be authorized to disqualify these same signs when it is convenient. In this way, a resurrection will not lead them to convert, since they already do not listen to Moses or the prophets. "Scandals will inevitably occur" (Luke 17:1). Their refusal of the signs repeats the refusal of God's wisdom by the Greeks: they all refuse the anamorphosis of their intentionalities, or indeed the conversion of their gazes.

From One Logos, *the Other*

Such a conflict of interpretations results in a radical opposition, because it has to do not only with a divergence of opinions, or even with rival theses based on arguments, but with a rupture in the mode of rationality itself, which shatters the common space of communication, even of a simply divergent communication. Certainly, it has to do with opposing a *logos*, that "of the cross" on which the *Logos* dies and from which he is resurrected (1 Corinthians 1:18), to the "sublimity of the *logos* or the wisdom" (2:1) of the world: reason against reason, ostensibly, one rationality against another. But this is not the case: what makes the difference between each of these *logoi* finally lies not in the power (δύναμις, 1:18) of the *logos* that is opposed to ours, opposed to the "convincing *logoi* of wisdom" (1 Corinthians 2:5) and "empty *logoi*" (Ephesians 5:6). Rather, it lies in the *logos* endowed with *dynamis* (1 Corinthians 4:19–20), with "good news (εὐαγγέλιον) . . . not only in *logos*, but also in *dynamis* and in the Holy Spirit" (1 Thessalonians 1:5). Where does this actual power come from, that makes only one *logos* credible? It arises from the fact that, according to the anamorphosis of intentionality, and thus the conversion of heart, suddenly, in this *logos*, the gaze *sees* the *mystērion* un-cover itself. This view (let's not be too hasty and needlessly call it a *vision*, which could lead us astray from a rigorous phenomenological approach) is something we will specify later (chapters 17–18).

Let it suffice for the moment to make note of what this view provokes, by contrast—*mōria*: "For the *logos* of the cross is folly to those who are perishing, but to us who are being saved it is the power, *dynamis*, of God. . . . Has not God made foolish (driven mad, ἐμώρανεν) the wisdom of the world?" (1 Corinthians 1:18, 20) Here it is important not to confuse inspired delirium (*mania*) with *mōria*, which instead designates slowness of mind, intellectual laziness, in short, the stupidity that stands with leaden immobility in front of evidence, rational clarity, and the truth itself. This stupidity sees the evidence, the clarity, and the truth perfectly well, but it cares not a whit for them—it does not change its point of view for so little. It keeps to its uncertain certainties with an impassive immobility.[13] There is no lack of examples. For instance, the wise and educated philosophers of Athens: "Now when they heard [Paul] speaking of the resurrection of the dead, some mocked; but others said, 'We will hear you again about this.'" It is, however, not for lack of understanding that they turned a deaf ear, because Paul had argued rationally, at least enough, so that some, including Dionysius, came to "believe" (Acts 17:32–34); it was therefore a matter of "stupidity," stubborn disinterest lacking reason. Or the ridiculous dialogue of Paul with Festus and King Agrippa: "'Paul, you are mad (μαίνῃ); your great knowledge of the Scriptures is turning you mad (εἰς μανίαν),'" says Festus, at the end of arguments; and Paul responds: "I am not mad (οὐ μαίνομαι)." To confirm that he remains rational, he argues justly in suggesting another point of view than that of "stupidity," namely that of the prophets: "King Agrippa, do you believe the prophets? I know that you believe." And Agrippa responds to Paul by clinging to the "stupidity" of the one who does not *want* to understand what he knows and nevertheless sees: "A little while longer and you [by your reasons] will persuade me to make myself a Christian!'" (Acts 26:24–5, 27–8) And above all, in an exceptional moment of involuntary depth, there is the response of Pilate to Christ, whom he condemns while knowing he is innocent: "'What is truth?'" (John 18:38) opposes him to the one who says "I am the way and the truth" (14:16). But in order to recognize him as the truth, it would have been necessary to admit that he was the way; the refusal of the truth in person results from the refusal, obstinate and without argument, to accept the way. Everyone *knew* that Paul and Jesus were not mad, but instead spoke the *logos*; and yet, they did not want, nor were they able, to change their point of view and pass from a masterly intentionality to one of anamorphosis. Paul's warning is understandable: "Let no one deceive himself. If anyone among you thinks that he is wise in this age, let him become a fool (μωρὸς) that he may become wise" (1 Corinthians 3:18). How should we understand that "the foolishness of God is wiser than men" (1 Corinthians 1:25)? This means that before those who deny the evidence and do not take into account the truth that they nevertheless see, it is necessary, as Aristotle advises, to avoid arguing: against the one who denies the very principles of rational argument, one can only point out his contradictions, or remain firmly within the evidence of the truth, by accepting and enduring the fact that the foolishness of the world treats as folly the "wisdom coming from God (σοφία ἀπὸ Θεοῦ)" (1 Corinthians 1:30). The chiasmus of wisdoms and follies is only played out in the gap between the masterly intentionality and the shift of anamorphosis.

What Is Not

Between the intentionality of the world and the intentionality that the Holy Spirit teaches to the anamorphic gaze lies an infinite divide. It marks out a radical opposition between two visions, which can at times be concerned with the same phenomena. For the wisdom of the world, that of the Greeks, for example, who "seek" the answer to the question "what is being-a-being (τὶ τὸ ὄν)?" it goes without saying that everything that shows itself is manifested within the horizon of being; and thus it follows that, if the wisdom of God had not wished to become foolish, it would have made sense for it to unfold itself within this one and only horizon. God, in order to make himself understood and respected, ought to respect and follow the terms of phenomenality imposed by the horizon of being—namely, by assuming the distinction between beings and non-beings, between that which is and that which is not. "What is necessary is this: to say and to think the being being (ἐὸν ἔμμεναι); it is indeed being, but nothing is not (ἔστι γὰρ εἶναι, μηδὲν δ' οὐκ ἔστιν)."[14] But Paul—and we must emphasize that his epistles have no ambition to supply even the meanest outline of an ontological treatise—insists, several times, on God's right to overstep the distinction between being and non-being, and to annul and disqualify it by virtue of his "power (δύναμις)." This is seen first of all in the "election" of the believers: "but what is foolish (μωρά) in the world, this is what God has chosen (ἐξελέξατο) to shame the wise; what is weak in the world, this is what he has chosen to shame the strong; what is not well born and what is despised, this is what God has chosen, the non-beings to confound the beings (τὰ μὴ ὄντα, ἵνα τὰ ὄντα καταργήσῃ)" (1 Corinthians 1:27–28). In other words, God made visible his phenomenon from a point of view absolutely different from that of the world: *his* point of view. According to this *radical* anamorphosis, the same phenomena appear *sub contrario*: wisdom as folly (and vice versa), strength as weakness (and vice versa), the noble as plebeian (and vice versa); and then, finally and in order to overturn everything, non-beings as beings and beings as non-beings. There is more: according to another text, the ontic indifference of God (equivalency between beings and non-beings) even becomes, so to speak, an ontological indifference (equivalency between being and beings/non-beings), once we understand that "God brings the dead to life and calls non-beings *as* beings (καλοῦντος τὰ μὴ ὄντα ὡς ὄντα)" (Romans 4:17). For, if God makes the dead live, he in this way repeats in the Resurrection what he accomplished in creation—*making* a non-being be as a being—as master and Lord of all things, *including that which is not*. The difference between beings and non-beings is canceled out because God excludes himself from being, and thus from the difference between being and beings.

Here, a rather strange sentence takes on its full significance: "Every soul is subjected to powers that stand above it (ἐξουσίαις ὑπερεχούσαις). But there is no power (ἐξουσία) except from God, and those that are (οὖσαι) are ordered to God (ὑπὸ Θεοῦ τεταγμέναι εἰσίν)" (Romans 13:1). Perhaps this must not be understood only in a political sense, but also in an ontic one (besides, doesn't the political directly derive from the ontic?). Here the powers (*exousiai*), insofar as they are *beings* (*ousai*, *quæ sunt,* according to the Vulgate), no longer depend in the final instance on their own grounds nor on themselves alone, but, through their *ousia*, on the *exousia* of God. Every *ousia* comes from the *exousia*, and not the inverse. In this sense, as philosophically correct as Aristotle's thesis remains,[15] it must be said that, seen from the point of view of the *mystērion*'s anamorphosis, the *ousia* remains relative to the *exousia* according to the wisdom of God.[16] Seen from God's point of view, absolutely nothing *is* absolutely an *ousia*, that is, in itself and said by itself. Or rather, everything that *is* is by itself and is said by itself, but this does not define it in *the final instance*, for this something still happens to it from *elsewhere*. The warning made to the man who is too sure of himself must be universally extended to every being and every *ousia*: "For if anyone thinks himself to be something (εἶναί τι), when he is nothing (μηδὲν ὤν), he deludes himself" (Galatians 6:3). Not that there is nothing, nor that what is is nothing, but because everything that is only is by receiving it from God: "What do you have that you did not receive (τί δὲ ἔχεις ὃ οὐκ ἔλαβες)?" (1 Corinthians 4:7). A being does not receive being from itself, or from being, but from the gift of God—even and above all if the being does *not know* God's gift. Thus anamorphosis extends to the point that it de-figures and re-figures even beings in their being. As paradoxical as this result may seem (or precisely for that very reason) it is nothing but inevitable: What right does anything whatsoever of the world have to not depend on the "mystery of the wisdom," and what right does being have to exclude itself when beings are included in it (see chapter 20)?

The Mystery of Charity

If even beings in their being and even the being of beings are included in the "mystery of wisdom," this follows from the fact that wisdom itself implements *agapē*, and that "of all [the virtues] *agapē* is the greatest" (1 Corinthians 13:13).

The second moment is accomplished in the letter to the Ephesians. It identifies the unseen *from which* the phenomenon arises not only as the *mystērion* of wisdom, but also as charity, by an election "before the constitution of the world" (1 Corinthians 1:4). No longer are we concerned with the conflict-causing irruption of the *mystērion* received and refused (as in the opening of the first letter to the Corinthians), but rather with that of the *mystērion* henceforth received, if not conceived as such, "in Christ," "in him" (1:3, 4). The "mystery" does not come to us from outside, but reveals itself as what we are, in its *elsewhere* where we "are" (Acts 17:28), even before entering into being as beings. Charity encompasses us on the basis "of God's purpose (μυστήριον τοῦ θελήματος αὐτοῦ)" (Ephesians 1:9), according to "the plan of the mystery hidden (οἰκονομία τοῦ μυστηρίου τοῦ ἀποκεκρυμμένου) for ages in God" (Ephesians 3:9). Just as it was manifested first to Paul: "made known to me by the un-covering (κατὰ ἀποκάλυψιν ἐγνωρίσθη μοι τὸ μυστήριον)"

(Ephesians 3:3; see Galatians 1:11), it is "now un-covered to his holy apostles and prophets (νῦν ἀπεκαλύφθη τοῖς ἁγίοις ἀποστόλοις αὐτοῦ καὶ προφήταις)" (3:5), and finally "made manifest to all his saints (ἐφανερώθη τοῖς ἁγίοις αὐτοῦ)" (Colossians 1:26). The difficulty shifts: it is necessary to recognize as such that which in this way has made itself known as an originary, immemorial, and definitive fact. It is necessary to recognize that this "mystery, I mean that of Christ and the Church, is a great one (μυστήριον τοῦτο μέγα ἐστίν)" (Ephesians 5:32); great because it is about the assumption of the Church in Christ, to the point that "being all sons of God by faith in Christ Jesus" we are "neither Jew nor Greek, neither slave nor free, neither male nor female, but all one in Christ Jesus" (Galatians 3:26–28); intrinsically, radically, and massively great, because it unfolds "the unsearchable riches of Christ (ἀνεξιχνίαστον πλοῦτος τοῦ Χριστοῦ)" (Ephesians 3:8).

What meaning should be given to this immeasurable, immense richness? Here the radical substitution of one horizon for another enters in; but can we still speak of a horizon (*horizon*) where precisely every limit (*horos*) is effaced? Nothing less is necessary than leaving the essentially *finite* horizon of being and beings, which we saw in the first letter to the Corinthians as null and void, and which could not harbor the unseen of God, much less un-cover it. It would be necessary to enter into, or rather to allow oneself to be submerged by, the paradoxically unlimited horizon of charity, a charity by definition hyperbolic and excessive. And in fact, Paul asks for, recommends, and even demands one thing alone: to recognize "the hyperbolic riches of his grace (τὸ ὑπερβάλλον πλοῦτος τῆς χάριτος αὐτοῦ)" (Ephesians 2:7). There is only one prayer to address to the Father: that he give us the "Spirit of wisdom and of un-covering in order to know Christ (σοφίας καὶ ἀποκαλύψεως ἐν ἐπιγνώσει αὐτοῦ), the eyes of your hearts being enlightened, in order that you may know (εἰδέναι) what is the hope of his call, what is the richness of his glorious inheritance in the saints, and what is the hyperbolic greatness of his power (τὸ ὑπερβάλλον μέγεθος τῆς δυνάμεως αὐτοῦ) in us who believe, according to the energy of his great might which he accomplished in Christ, whom he has raised from the dead" (Ephesians 1:17–20). To the question, "what is the being in its being (τὶ τὸ ὄν)?", which is the question posed by the "wisdom of the world" and whose answer Aristotle "seeks," there is substituted another, which is posed in terms of itself, and which comes to seek us: "What is the hyperbole of his greatness (τὸ ὑπερβάλλον μέγεθος)?" (Ephesians 1:19) The hyperbole of the greatness "of his power" must not be understood according to the horizon of beings (the *dynamis* of an *energeia*), but instead according to the horizon of charity, which alone is hyperbolic in its unconditioned and indescribable power, "so that you may have power to comprehend (καταλαβέσθαι) with all the saints what is the breadth and length and height and depth (τί τὸ πλάτος καὶ μῆκος καὶ ὕψος καὶ βάθος), to know the hyperbolic charity of Christ which surpasses knowledge (γνῶναί τε τὴν ὑπερβάλλουσαν τῆς γνώσεως ἀγάπην τοῦ Χριστοῦ), that you may be saturated with all the *saturation* of God (ἵνα πληρωθῆτε εἰς πᾶν τὸ πλήρωμα τοῦ Θεοῦ)" (Ephesians 3:18–19). In the horizon of charity, knowing consists not in identifying that which shows itself to such-and-such object or being, which we would be able to constitute and determine according to our intentionality, but in recognizing an excess that saturates the gaze and submerges it in its immeasurable hyperbole.

In fact, this new "knowledge of charity that surpasses knowledge" presents a strange characteristic: hyperbolic charity is described according to four dimensions (breadth and length and height and depth), while the wisdom of philosophy has never mobilized more than three dimensions (breadth, length, and depth) to describe space. Does the Pauline addition (or rather, the division of height into height *and depth*), then, simply amount to a blatant error, or a bit of poetic license? On the contrary, such a question (hardly ever asked by the exegetes) receives a precise and clear answer: charity must not be conceived like a worldly space, because it does not belong to the world; but it can be conceived as a "divine milieu," in the strict sense. Indeed, it can be conceived as a milieu—an environment of sorts, or surroundings—because, once I consider it as a hyperbolic horizon, I absolutely can no longer describe it as a space that would spread out in front of me, in the external sense (Kant), where I constitute and store the objects of my masterful gaze; but I must allow myself to be situated *in the midst [au milieu]* of charity, to be encompassed by it to the point of losing myself in it and finding myself there. But then I will have to describe this inclusion in terms of four dimensions, no longer three: amidst the breadth and the length, between the height and the depth, according to the azimuth where I will turn my gaze, without the reference point of an object, but encompassed within what saturates it. Tri-dimensional space only allows us to see that which shows itself as an object, whereas the four-dimensional milieu imposes on us an experience of saturation—in this case, the saturation of charity—which fills me by encompassing me, the one who sees, without ever being able to phenomenalize that which gives itself in any way other than as precisely that which gives itself beyond all that shows itself to a finite gaze.[17] The hyperbole of "grace that overabounds, (ὑπερεπερίσσευσεν)" (Romans 5:20) remains ever irreducible to all that shows itself as phenomena for me. It certifies the "many-colored wisdom of God, πολυποίκιλος σοφία τοῦ Θεοῦ" (Ephesians 3:10), which is multiplied, for example, in "the multiple occasions and different ways, πολυμερῶς καὶ πολυτρόπως" (Hebrews 1:1) of his utterances, or in the "variety of his charisms," which nevertheless remain a single word and "manifestation of the Spirit" (1 Corinthians 12:4, 7).

But if my gaze, encompassed and saturated, cannot phenomenalize the overabundance of what is given, and if, in the milieu of charity there remains for me no central point of observation from which to receive and see the fullness of that which shows itself, then how can the *mystērion* genuinely (*nyn*) manifest itself? *Where* does the hyperbole of charity that gives itself uncover and show itself, if it saturates every phenomenalization carried out by a *finite* human gaze? The answer, audacious yet inevitable and exceptionally logical, is unavoidable: in the only human gaze that is not merely finite, that of Christ, the ultimate and unique instance in which, once and for all, all that is given shows itself, yet in an endless innovation: "Behold, I make all things new" (Revelation 21:5). For, in order to "make known to us the *mystērion* of his will," and so as to "manage the *saturation* of events (εἰς οἰκονομίαν τοῦ πληρώματος τῶν καιρῶν)," God "recapitulated all things, things in heaven and things on earth, under a single head, in Christ (ἀνακεφαλαιώσασθαι τὰ πάντα ἐν τῷ Χριστῷ)" (Ephesians 1:9–10). A head for the Church, but because he recapitulates in (and as) his body all that which is given, "*saturated with the saturation* of all in all (πλήρωμα τοῦ τὰ πάντα ἐν πᾶσιν πληρουμένου)" (Ephesians 1:23). The only gaze and the only point of view that can make the infinitely hyperbolical charity that gives itself show itself is found in Christ: the only phenomenological gaze that is infinite, yet in our flesh.

The Mystery of Christ

In order to respond fully to the first question (*what* does the *mystērion* allow to be phenomenalized?), we still need to understand, in a third moment, in what way Christ can accomplish the function of a phenomenological gaze adequate to the hyperbole of charity, so that all that gives itself to that gaze can, in principle and in fact, also show itself in it. For the *mystērion* of charity actually operates only in the gaze of Christ, and it thus appears in the end as the "μυστηρίῳ τοῦ Χριστοῦ, mystery of Christ" (Ephesians 3:4). The letter to the Colossians will take up and radicalize this phrase ("the mystery of Christ," Colossians 4:3) through the assimilation of Christ to God (the Father) in terms of the possibility of "knowing" charity, whose hyperbole surpasses knowledge: "for the knowledge of the *mystērion* of God, the Christ" (Colossians 2:2). It would perhaps be the case of a variant here, instead of a simple coordination ("*mystērion* of God *and* of Christ"), if there were not another identification of *mystērion* with the very person of Christ: "God indeed wanted to make known to the nations how great is the richness of the glory of this mystery, which is Christ in you (τί τὸ πλοῦτος τῆς δόξης τοῦ μυστηρίου τούτου ἐν τοῖς ἔθνεσιν, ὅς ἐστιν Χριστὸς ἐν ὑμῖν, ἡ ἐλπὶς τῆς δόξης)" (Colossians 1:27).[18] The mystery of charity is thus not only uncovered by Christ; it is uncovered in and as Christ.

What content should be assigned to this *mystērion*? We have already seen that according to Ephesians 1:10, it consists in opening the way to God for all, Jews and Greeks, by the hyperbole of charity so as to "recapitulate (ἀνακεφαλαιώσασθαι) all things in Christ." We must next explain how Christ is established as the head of all things: in fact, Christ recapitulates because he reconciles, he unifies because he makes peace: "He [Christ] is himself peace (αὐτὸς γάρ ἐστιν ἡ εἰρήνη), he who has made both [Jews and pagans] one [people], breaking down the dividing wall, abolishing hatred in his flesh (τὴν ἔχθραν, ἐν τῇ σαρκὶ αὐτοῦ ... καταργήσας), the law of commandments with its ordinances" (Ephesians 2:14–15). Making peace means that he "has killed hatred in himself (ἀποκτείνας τὴν ἔχθραν ἐν αὐτῷ)" (Ephesians 2:16). For Christ has perfectly accomplished the Law (in the double meaning of the word) by subverting it and fulfilling it at the same time; through the hyperbole of his charity, which satisfied the Law without consecrating it, he opens this hyperbolic fullness to all: even in his flesh, which was the same as ours, but which he, unlike us, assumed "without sin, (χωρὶς ἁμαρτίας)"[19] he canceled out the reason for sin, the Law, and brought together those that the Law was separating from one another, and that sin was separating from God. Christ "recapitulates" all things because he carries out the "service of reconciliation (διακονίαν τῆς καταλλαγῆς)" (2 Corinthians 5:18). In other words, "he has now really reconciled (νυνὶ δὲ ἀποκατήλλαξεν) [us] in his body of flesh" (Colossians 1:22). Reconciliation, pacification, and recapitulation that are sealed and manifested in his Resurrection, which uncovers Christ as the "firstborn from the dead" (Colossians 1:18), and thus also as the "firstborn of all creation, for in him all things were created" (Colossians 1:16). This "new creation in Christ" (2 Corinthians 5:17) confirms the recapitulation of all things under the head of Christ, but also flows from it, because he accomplishes it by "making peace" (Colossians 1:20) in himself. Thus, "this *mystērion* hidden for ages and generations—it is now (*nyn*) that it has been made manifest to his saints, to whom God chose to make known among the nations what is the richness of the glory of this mystery, which is nothing other than Christ in person among you, τί τὸ πλοῦτος τῆς δόξης τοῦ μυστηρίου τούτου . . . ὅς ἐστιν Χριστὸς ἐν ὑμῖν" (Colossians 1:26–27). Thus Christ, made man, dead, and resurrected, entirely visible, manifests for the first time, and once and for all (Romans 6:10), the *mystērion* of peace that he recapitulates. He appears as himself, as such, that is to say, as the unique phenomenalization of the Father, as the unique gaze in which is shown everything that gives itself, the phenomenal center of the glory of all things as given.

Consequently, all visibility comes back to him (recapitulation), exactly as all givenness comes from him (creation). Indeed, Christ does not reveal the mystery of charity only because he manifests it, but because he sees it; and he sees it because he makes it, he puts it into work in person, corporeally. His phenomenal gaze sees and makes visible, from the act of the cross, all the possible phenomenality of the invisibility of God. Christ is established as "the icon of the invisible God (εἰκὼν τοῦ Θεοῦ τοῦ ἀοράτου)" (Colossians 1:15), or, in another way, as the "splendor of his glory (ἀπαύγασμα τῆς δόξης), and effigy of his persistence" (Hebrews 1:2). In a word, he appears constituted in this way by the Father, who raises him from the dead, as the icon of his own invisibility, *as the hyperbolic phenomenon of charity*. But he appears instituted in this way in the Father's gaze, because on the cross his own gaze took the Father's point of view on all things, because he "gave up (παρέδωκεν) his spirit" to the Father (John 19:30). Transposed into a more phenomenological language, this comes down to saying: he accomplished the perfect anamorphosis of his gaze, which is transferred from the point of view of a man, Jesus, to the point of view of the Father, and which becomes at once that of the Son of the Father, the first gaze to see the glory of God, because it is the first to see it from God's point of view. The formula that states the "un-covering of the Lord Jesus, ἀποκαλύψει τοῦ Κυρίου Ἰησοῦ" (2 Thessalonians 1:7)[20] must be understood in a twofold but unique sense: the un-covering of the *mystērion* which constitutes Christ, as well as the un-covering of the same *mystērion* by the gaze of Christ (objective and subjective genitive). The communion of wills of the Father and of Christ on the cross amounts to their coinciding gazes, an anamorphosis which, in one stroke, tears the veil (Matthew 27:51; Mark 15:38) and bursts forth in a flash the singular mystery of charity.

Accomplishing Anamorphosis

This coinciding of gazes by the anamorphosis that shifts the human aim toward the point of view aimed at by God himself, is described, announced, and demanded as clearly as possible by Paul. Accomplishing the anamorphosis becomes possible only if our spirit is invested, replaced, and empowered by the Spirit: "you have received the spirit of sonship, in which we cry 'Abba, Father.' For it is the Spirit who bears witness in our spirits that we are sons of God" (Romans 8:15–16). This spirit, given by God, is also given by the Son, who put it into action himself as Jesus Christ, on the cross: "Since you are sons of God, God has sent the Spirit of his Son to cry in your hearts, 'Abba, Father'" (Galatians 4:6). And so it is not I who cries out to the Father, but the Spirit of God in me. It is not I who un-covers the mystery, but the Spirit, who alone allows my gaze to traverse the anamorphosis, in order to see according to and from the point of view of the Spirit. The phenomenal conversion of the gaze is accomplished only by the conversion of my spirit according to the Spirit: the phenomenological rule is fulfilled (if it ever is) only following the theological rule. The identity of gazes implies a transfer of idioms, a divinization of the human aim by the divine aim. That is, in the words of Paul, "it is not *I* who live (οὐκέτι ἐγώ), the one who lives in me (ἐν ἐμοί) is Christ" (Galatians 2:20). Or, "For me ('Ἐμοὶ) to live is Christ." The *I* is itself fulfilled as the correct point of view of the aim only if it becomes other than itself: and the *I* is not able to become other except *by* another than itself. This requirement, that Paul experiences on his own account, holds as well for all those who want to become sons. Indeed, the life of the *I* is not decided by itself, but according to its relation to God: "For no one of us lives for or through himself (ἑαυτῷ), as no one dies for or through himself. For if we live, we live for and through the Lord, if we die, we die by and for the Lord. So whether we live or die, it is by and for the Lord" (Romans 14:7–9). As a result, "You are not in the flesh, but in the spirit, since the spirit of God lives in you" (Romans 8:9). Therefore, we understand, or at least we sense that if the mystery is also un-covered for our gaze, now in anamorphosis, we will only see because it is also un-covered in us and by us. The mystery un-covers itself through the Spirit come into us, and, to the same extent, it covers us and shelters us in the Spirit. "Our life is hidden (κέκρυπται) with Christ in God. When Christ, our life, will be manifested (φανερωθῇ), then you also will be manifested (φανερωθήσεσθε) in glory with him" (Colossians 3:3–4). "Beloved, we are truly now (νῦν) sons of God, but what we are has not yet been manifested (οὔπω ἐφανερώθη). But we know that, during this manifestation, we will be like him, for we shall see him as he is" (1 John 3:1–2). As I do not see charity by facing it like an object, but by living in its midst, so I do not un-cover the mystery by facing it, but by sinking into it and exposing myself to it.

The prohibition of a vision of the invisible here attains its real meaning; it does not so much state an impossibility (God cannot be seen), as another possibility excluded by what prohibits it: we cannot see God, but God can put us in his place, where we enter into the mystery—he sees us. The ancient prohibition is thus overturned: if the invisible takes hold of our aim, and if, by anamorphosis, the Spirit conforms that aim to the very gaze of God, then we will not die from having seen the *mystērion*, but will rise to life by it: "Behold, I tell you a mystery: we will not die, but we will all be transformed. In an instant, in the blink of an eye, at the last sound of the trumpet—for the trumpet will sound—the dead will rise imperishable and we will be changed" (1 Corinthians 15:51–52).

The un-covering of the *mystērion* thus depends entirely on the path taken, or not, by the anamorphosis of the gaze. Consequently, despite the many hesitations we feel surrounding it, we too can attempt a reading of Paul's discourse at the Areopagus, beginning from its internal architecture, which is in fact quite clear.[21] We will begin with the end, whose interpretation raises the least difficulty: "Behold, God, no longer considering the times of ignorance, now proclaims (ἀπαγγέλλει) to everyone and everywhere that they must be converted (μετανοεῖν), for he has set a day for 'judging the universe with justice' (Psalms 9:8, 96:13, and 98:9) and by a man who he has destined for it, making him credible (πίστιν παρασχὼν) to everyone by raising him from the dead" (Acts 17:30–31). These lines indicate two points. First, it is clearly a question of leaving behind the "ignorance" of the mystery[22] through a universal proclamation for everyone and everywhere (following Matthew 28:18–29 or Hebrews 1:12?) on the necessity of being "converted"; in other words, to pass from one point of view to another by an anamorphosis; thus of turning (μετανοεῖν) the gaze (of the mind, νοῦς), of converting it to arrive at a new angle of vision, according to which what we did not know, the mystery, will be able to become manifest from itself. Second, these lines allow us to identify without any trouble the point of final aim that God makes personally "credible, πίστιν παρασχὼν" by resurrecting Christ: it is the resurrection of the dead; and it is clearly this resurrection that the majority of hearers reject: "Hearing 'resurrection of the dead,' some laughed, others said to him, 'We will hear you about this some other time'" (Acts 17:32). In doing so, most of them reject "Jesus and the Resurrection" (Acts 17:18),[23] as did "the philosophers, Epicureans and Stoics" before them.

Why does the single word "resurrection" lead the Athenians and philosophers, up until then fairly sympathetic because of their curiosity about "the new doctrine (διδαχή)" of Paul (Acts 17:19–22), to suddenly turn away from it? Responding to this question would allow us to identify the initial point of view that the philosophers want to maintain, and on behalf of which they decide to refuse anamorphosis. Here again, the response appears quite clear, as long as we do not cling to the hypothesis of a simple *captatio benevolentiae* when Paul invokes their recognition of an "unknown God" to praise the piety of the Athenians (legendary at the time); for, in fact, it is no mere commonplace. First, this is evident because Paul/Luke transforms the inscription which probably referred "to the other unknown gods" in a negative sense, as a statement of ignorance, into the singular, assuming an individual determination of this unknown, positively identified as such.[24] Next, by evoking this unknowing, he categorically builds on the unknowability of gods among the pagans and on the invisibility of Yahweh for the Jews (see chapter 11). In this way, thanks to this supposed point of agreement with his listeners, he could try a second time to make his "announcement (καταγγέλλω)" (17:23; see 17:18). But this proclamation, intended to state what Greek philosophers could conceive (the god or gods have no need for us to build them temples or statues), also states above all what they could not conceive: God created heaven and earth, he governs the time and space of men, he gives them life and breath. The pagan gods, as we have seen, even if they do not live with us (Epicurus), live in the world, even in our spirit (Aristotle, the Stoics): *"Prope est a te deus, tecum est, intus est."*[25] If they do not live in the temple, as the people thought, they dwell in our spirit, as the philosophers supposed. But God, such as the apostle proclaims him, or rather such as he announces himself (17:30), is found neither in a temple nor in the world, nor in our spirit as such, because to the contrary "we live in him, in him we have our movement and our being" (17:28a).[26]

From this follows an alternative: Does God remain in us so that we share with him the world and being? Or, rather, do we remain in him, where through creation we receive as gifts our living, moving, and being?[27] In the first case, the single world that men and gods inhabit only allows one aim, that of the world according to being; and it does not require any anamorphosis, because it does not even allow us to imagine that "we shall be changed" (1 Corinthians 15:52–53) by the innovation of a resurrection. This world is, it is enough for it to be, and it only aspires to continue being; yet what is proper to being lies in its persistence; being is unfolded in beings—and thus it never comes from *elsewhere*.[28] The second case remains, where the world in which we live and move, and therefore also the domain of being where we are beings, "lives neither for nor by itself (ἑαυτῷ)" but "for and by the Lord" (Romans 14:7–8); in other words, the case wherein God has indeed "made the world and everything in it" (Acts 17:24), as the Resurrection of Christ should convince us. In this case, anamorphosis no longer appears as merely possible, but as required. And the *mystērion* can be un-covered, as the manifestation of charity which surpasses all knowledge. The *mystērion* thus does not close, but *opens* access to the *elsewhere*.

THIRTEEN

Parable and Confession (the Synoptics)

The Principle of Phenomenality

Hence it becomes possible to pass to the second question, which asks *how* what gives itself is un-covered. In other words, by what invisible operation is it recognized in the visible, in what visible is it manifest *as* visible? Indeed, the phenomenality of *apokalypsis* cannot be accomplished unless it ends up manifesting the *mystērion*, by manifesting exactly what must remain closed and hidden as such. As surprising as it may at first seem, *apokalypsis* is only accomplished because the *mystērion* always ends up by manifesting itself in it; moreover, the secret of the *mystērion* can only be conceived by showing itself, by always already letting itself be glimpsed, if only *as* hidden and encrypted. The *mystērion*, at the same time hidden and already shown as something that can and must be unconcealed, does not therefore serve as the opposite of the *apokalypsis*, nor as the obstacle that would resist it, but as its background, the depths from which it arises; the *mystērion* designates and deposits the reserve of the unseen, which is recognized after the fact and in contrast to what illuminates it and consecrates it without canceling it—the *apokalypsis* itself. Thus, the *mystērion* offers less the crossed out point of departure of the *apokalypsis* than the depth of the field it presupposes. This un-covering is itself only manifested by attesting to the *mystērion*, of which it becomes the very principle. It is, so to speak, a principle of phenomenalization—so much *mystērion*, so much *apokalypsis*—that echoes, in biblical theology, this other principle established in phenomenology: so much reduction, so much givenness.

One could argue that this principle of phenomenalization is formulated, or almost even formalized, three times in the Synoptic Gospels. Since, according to the common (if in fact inaccurate) opinion, the Synoptics employ fewer concepts than Paul or John, this triple formulation, attested almost in the same terms by all three, reaches an authenticity that is all the more impressive as it could be traced back to a common unique source (even to the *ipsissima verba*). Let us cite this triple sequence.[1] Thus, Matthew 10:26: "Nothing, indeed, is veiled (κεκαλυμμένον) that will not be uncovered (ὃ οὐκ ἀποκαλυφθήσεται, *revelabitur*), nor hidden (κρυπτὸν) that will not become known (ὃ οὐ γνωσθήσεται)"; here it is explicitly a question of *apokalypsis*. Then, Mark 4:22: "Nothing, indeed, is hidden (κρυπτὸν) if not to be manifested (ἐὰν μὴ ἵνα φανερωθῇ), nothing secret (ἀπόκρυφον) that will not come to light (ἔλθῃ εἰς φανερόν)"; here it explicitly concerns the Kingdom of God (4:11). Finally, Luke 8:17: "There is nothing hidden (κρυπτὸν) that will not become manifest (φανερὸν), nor anything secret (ἀπόκρυφον) that will not become known and come to light (εἰς φανερὸν ἔλθῃ)"; and this is clearly a question of "listening" (8:18).[2] In spite of a major difference (only Matthew explicitly links this principle of phenomenality to *apokalypsis* itself), or rather under its guarantee, there remains one point in common: it is always a principle of the phenomenality of God, according to which not only does the manifest always end up overtaking the hidden, but the hidden is also always ultimately destined to manifestation. The event (and advent) of the *gesta Dei per Christum Iesum* makes one experience the manifestation of what would otherwise remain hidden, and uncovers the *mystērion* as such—the hidden *as* revealed.

What does it mean to claim that the *mystērion* as hidden is revealed without remainder? First, as we have just said, it means that the hidden, the *mystērion*, is destined from the outset by the will of God for this manifestation; it does not serve as the contradiction or prohibition, but the reserve and the depth of the unseen, the condition of possibility and the background of manifestation. But above all, it means that the entry of the *mystērion* into the *apokalypsis*, of the hidden into the manifest, seems to strangely yet indisputably point towards the program that anchors all contemporary phenomenology: to reach the point where that which is phenomenalized does not repeat or divide the *in-itself* in or from the thing itself, but makes the thing *as such* manifest *in its entirety*. Whether, in the terms of Husserl, "whatever presents itself to us in 'intuition' in an originary way . . . *is to be received simply as what it gives of itself,* but also *only within the limit in which it gives itself.*"³ Or, in the words of Heidegger, "Hence phenomenology means: ἀποφαίνεσθαι τὰ φαινόμενα—to let what shows itself be seen from itself, just as it shows itself from itself (*das was sich zeigt, so wie es sich von ihm selbst her zeigt, von ihm selbst her sehen lassen*)."⁴ However, the chronological succession of these two determinations of the phenomenon must, according to the necessity of the thing itself, be reversed and be read backward. For Husserl here goes farther than Heidegger, at least in intent if not in its realization. In the first step, the phenomenon is defined (against Kant and the Marburg tradition) as that which *shows itself* starting from itself, thus *in itself,* as the thing itself, without doubling or phenomenal re-presentation. In a second step (Husserl), the phenomenon thus shows itself *as and to the extent that it gives itself.* Hence it follows that the principle formulated in full states (or should state) that the phenomenon shows itself in itself and by itself only to the extent that it gives itself in and by itself (see chapter 2 above).

From this point another question may arise: *What phenomenon* has ever accomplished the phenomenological program without remainder or reserve, *what phenomenon* has actually and indisputably accomplished it "to the end, εἰς τέλος"? The claim of Christian theology here takes on the whole of its enormous presumption: only the one who "has loved his own to the end, εἰς τέλος" (John 13:1), to the point of saying in truth that in him "everything comes to its end, τετέλεσται" (John 19:30), has manifested and un-covered *the phenomenon in itself and starting from itself.* This phenomenon *shows itself absolutely* because it, and it alone, *gives itself absolutely*. In fact, Christ offers himself not only to be seen as one phenomenon among others, accomplishing the common program of phenomenology; he accomplishes it in act for the first and only time in his actions, and becomes the phenomenon of all phenomena. He, the total and saturated agent of the bringing to light of the absolute unseen, the *mystērion* of God hidden since the beginning of time, he who "was made manifest in the flesh, ἐφανερώθη ἐν σαρκί" (1 Timothy 3:16), has at the same time shed light everywhere around him. He has thus led all things to become manifest: "I have always taught (πάντοτε ἐδίδαξα) in the synagogue and the temple, where all the Jews come together. I have said nothing in secret, ἐν κρυπτῷ ἐλάλησα οὐδέν" (John 18:20).[5] This does not mean that Christ causes manifestation at every instant and when it pleases him;[6] for this final manifestation depends on the time, and the time depends on the Father. But this means that the word of Christ speaks in the name of the Father, as the Word of the Father. It has been observed that, while the formula "yes, *amen*," was in common usage to approve a speech at its conclusion, Jesus has inaugurated a use "without analogy" of the double amen, particularly in the Gospel of John: "truly, truly, *amen, amen*, I say to you..."[7] The *mystērion* thus does not make its *apokalypsis* depend on the will of God: for, in the *amen, amen* of Jesus Christ, God does not cease to give himself "once for all" (Hebrews 1:10); paradoxically, the uncovering ultimately depends on men, depending on whether *or not* they decide to allow themselves to be manifest (and therefore judged in their works and their heart) in the presence of the *apokalypsis* of Christ by himself. Christ, in a sense, does not do anything. He has no need to do anything, except to await the decision of men. He, "in whom all the promises of God find their *yes*" (2 Corinthians 1:20), awaits the *yes* or the *no* of men: "Let your '*yes*' mean '*yes*,' and your '*no*' '*no*'" (Matthew 5:37). Faced with this "great *Amen*" (to speak like Nietzsche, who hopes it without ever having been able to say it), the question, for us, concerns our capacity to also say "yes": "He [Jesus] asked them: 'Have you understood all these things?' They [the disciples, and therefore us] responded to him: Yes, ναί" (Matthew 13:15). But what does our "yes" want, and what is it worth? Everything depends on the way we respond to the question, and thus on the manner in which the question is presented to us—the parable.

The Parable

The first three chapters of Mark announce "the beginning of the good news about Jesus Christ" by mentioning that "he taught" (1:21–22, 27, 39); yet, these chapters do not record what he taught, but only insist on the effects of this teaching (wonder, fear, enthusiasm, or opposition, etc.). The good news is made known first and almost exclusively by the report of the acts of Jesus, by the *gesta Christi*: the miracles of physical healing (of the mother-in-law of Simon in 1:29–31; of a leper in 1:40–44; of a man with a withered hand in 3:1–5) or spiritual healing (the man possessed by an impure spirit, 1:23–27, 34), or both (the paralytic physically healed after his sins had been forgiven, 2:1–12). When Jesus chooses his disciples (1:16–20; 3:13–19), the text once again does not record any teaching. Even when the text mentioned that "he spoke the Word to them" (2:2), it does not report the words he said. By way of teaching, Jesus only announces one fact and only asks a decision in return: "The time is fulfilled and the kingdom of God has come near: repent and believe in the Gospel" (1:15; see 45). If he ends up speaking, it is not to set forth a doctrine, but only to claim, against those who deny them, the sovereign authority and the originary power (*exousia*) of his actions (2:6–12) and his way of speaking (1:21 and 27; 2:12). What is said and what is done coincide in one unique דבר, *dabar*, a unique inaugural event. This explains why no discursive speech, no predicative statement, no signification already classified could suffice to say, nor make understood what comes to the world. Mark sanctions this inevitable deficit of words to say what this teaching is about by explaining that "he taught them many things in parables" (4:2; see 3:23). To the point that the parables become the only mode of articulating the Word [*Parole*]: "And with many similar parables, he spoke the Word (*logos*) to them, as much as they could understand, he did not say anything to them without a parable" (4:33–34). On reflection, the rule is almost self-evident, since the parable makes of speech and teaching an act—a speech act. It does not transfer information or tell stories; it does not even give an address, nor open up a discussion *pro et contra*, since it acts on its listener, forcing her to understand it, and to understand it by including herself in it. Even more than a speech act, the word of the parable demands another act in response, an act of comprehension that puts into play the one who understands it and who understands herself in it. The parable does not open a conversation, but provokes a kind of conversion. It inaugurates and implements the original function of speech: and it is not by chance that the word for speech in French, *parole*, derives from *parabole*, and not the other way around.

In order to enter further into the parable's exceptional function, it is important to identify three characteristics which any further explanation of the parable must take into account. First of all, the parable defines the particular style of Jesus's teaching, his "real preference . . . for an antithetical parallelism," that is, for bringing together two contrasting elements that derive from the same story. For, as Joachim Jeremias has shown, "his parables

... are unique and without analogy,"[8] to the point that they constitute a literary form practically invented by Jesus and which remains particular to him: "We find nothing to be compared with the parables of Jesus, whether in the entire intertestamental literature of Judaism, the Essene writings, in Paul, or in Rabbinic literature."[9] Not only does the French term for speech, *parole*, come from the term *parable*, as mentioned above, but, if we recognize that the parable comes from the very *logos* of Jesus, we must infer from this that it constitutes *par excellence* the way of *speaking* [le mode *parlant*] of the *Logos*-made man. And that the way of teaching coincides exactly with what is to be taught.

Second, the parable directly performs the uncovering of the *mystērion*, in this case the uncovering of the "kingdom of God," which "has come near, ἤγγικεν" (Mark 1:15) and is now among us: "When he was alone, those who were around him with the Twelve asked him about the parables. And he said to them, 'To you has been given the mystery of the kingdom of God, Ὑμῖν τὸ μυστήριον δέδοται τῆς βασιλείας τοῦ θεοῦ'" (4:10–11). Thus it is no coincidence that the first parable, that of the sower (4:3–20), is explained, after the example of the lamp displayed on the lampstand which immediately follows it (4:21–23), by what we have identified as the principle of uncovering: "For nothing is hidden (κρυπτὸν) but to be manifested (ἐὰν μὴ ἵνα φανερωθῇ), nothing secret (ἀπόκρυφον) that will not come to light (ἔλθῃ εἰς φανερόν)" (4:22); by uncovering itself, the Kingdom of God also makes all things manifest. Nor is it a coincidence that this parable of the sower is found in the two other Synoptics (Matthew 13:4–9 and Luke 8:4–8), where it similarly inaugurates the teaching in parables: it does not offer so much one parable among others as the frame of all the teaching through parables: the arrival of the kingdom introduces a state of emergency among men, which compels them to make manifest what their "heart" desires and what their "heart" is worth. Nor is it a coincidence that the Synoptics conclude this teaching with the parable of the vineyard and the murderous tenants (Matthew 21:33–46; Mark 12:1–12, Luke 20:9–19); it describes the vicissitudes of introducing the seed no longer in terms of the sower and according to the modes of its reception but, conversely, in terms of the refusal of the recipients and the modes of this refusal.[10] We thus understand that the last parable common to the Synoptics, that of the blossoming fig tree (Matthew 24:32–36; Luke 21:29–33; Mark 13:28–32), again teaches that "The Kingdom of God is near, ἐγγύς"

(Luke 21:31), unavoidably close, despite the refusal of men that will end with the cross;[11] unavoidably, because "it is by its own movement (αὐτομάτη) that the earth bears fruit" (Mark 4:28). Thus, the parable not only announces the coming of the Kingdom of God, it accomplishes it already in all its states and in all its consequences.

Third, the parable leads to a rift among its hearers, who are separated because of it. And in several ways. First of all, the "teaching in parables" (Mark 4:2) ends with a recommendation that, in and of itself, announces or even already produces a division: "Whoever has ears to hear, let them hear" (4:9). Not hearing, or rather not understanding what one hears, is nothing surprising, but for Jesus, it is one of the inevitable alternatives that every hearer must face. He speaks in parables *in order that* those who hear may or *may not* understand. This first inevitable division defines the possible, yet opposite, effects of the parable. Then another break intervenes, not only possible but effective, when Jesus finds himself "alone," between "those who were around him" (4:10) and those who remained "outside" (4:11): "But for those on the outside (ἔξω), everything is said in parables, so that 'looking, they look and do not see, and hearing, they hear and do not understand, so that/lest they turn and their sins be forgiven them'" (Isaiah 6:10; Mark 4:10–12). The translation of *mēpote* offers here a crux to the translators, as they hesitate between "so that" and "lest."[12] Yet it is not certain that this difficulty changes anything essential: this parable, as every parable, is not understood by simply listening, but in understanding what one hears. Yet, each person only understands according to his measure, as he can and as he wills or accepts to will. It belongs to the parable that each person can understand it *as he wills,* because no one can understand it without wanting it, *well or badly.* Because understanding supposes the will to understand, the parable admits by definition the possibility that one *does not want* to understand. Finally, once we admit this fact that certain people understand and others do not, we must consider the demarcation that separates them. Does it coincide with the distinction between his "own disciples, ἰδίοις μαθηταῖς" (4:34) who surround him (4:10) and those "outside, ἔξω" (4:11)? Certainly not, for the very good reason that it is never said that the disciples understand the parables; otherwise, why would it be necessary to explain them? Rather, the explanations offered by Jesus seem instead to escalate their perplexity and eventually provoke their various misunderstandings; for, even if the disciples sometimes claim to have understood the parables (elsewhere in Matthew 13:51), more often than not, events prove that this is not the case: like the "outsiders," they, too, are afraid, astonished, scandalized, in doubt. Why then do they find themselves favored by a special teaching about the Kingdom of God? Because it was "given" (4:11) to them, because they were chosen and called by Jesus (1:16–20; 3:14–19), because Jesus himself "called to him those he willed" (3:13). Their privilege comes from the choice of Jesus, as a gift, but this privilege does not imply that they have themselves already fully accepted this gift, nor that they fully understand what they hear, nor that they will remain "around him" (4:10). Here the unwritten word of Jesus applies: "He who is near me is near the fire; and he who is far from me is far from the Kingdom."[13] Mark, on the other hand, stands out by his insistence on all the failings and betrayals of the disciples in general and of Peter in particular. We can simply say that the privilege of the disciples consists in experiencing, *more* than the other hearers from outside, the daunting requirement of parables: no one understands them, except to the measure that he wills it. And the measure fixes the only limit. Thus, the word speaking in parables perfectly implements the work of the *logos* "of contradiction" such that it provokes "the fall and the rise of many in Israel" and that in it "the thoughts of many hearts may be uncovered" (Luke 2:34–35).

Saying, Not Saying, Uncovering

Consequently, we see that every attempt to define the parables must meet three criteria: first, the mode of teaching must coincide with what is taught; next, the Kingdom of God must not only be described, but accomplished in all its states and all its effects; and finally, no one must be able to grasp [*comprendre*] it, except to the extent that he is willing to respond to it, that is to say, include himself in it [*s'y comprend lui-même*].

Let us begin from an obvious point of departure: the parable that Jesus practices does not correspond to that which Aristotle describes under the title *parabolē*, which he places under the category of similitude (and of the *eikōn*). Aristotle explains that when Socrates wants to demonstrate that magistrates should not be chosen by drawing lots, he argues by comparison with other possible cases of drawing lots (of athletes for the Olympic or Isthmian games, of a captain and his crew to outfit a ship); since a random selection would obviously be absurd in these two comparable cases, the former appears absurd as well.[14] It is always a question of comparing similar cases, but when it is impossible to appeal to a comparison, as with the example of a historical event (which, as it would not be identically repeated, would not allow for an exact approximation), or when it is undesirable to rely on a too-arbitrary folk tale (such as an animal fable), the only recourse is to resort to the parable. In this sense, it is a matter of comparing two similar cases, to make the second understood by the first, and thus establish their common intelligibility: the one always ends up being translated into the other, and vice versa. The best example of this is the allegory, which evokes a term that is already known and manifests it through other characteristics that are diverted from their common usage (like describing Achilles as an "eagle"), or explains a commonplace that has been previously concealed by an invented story (the three ages of men indicated by their three gaits). The parable here makes provisionally unknown evidence understandable by comparison with a provisionally enigmatic image. But in the end, the two terms of the comparison become equally comprehensible.[15]

The parable, as Jesus makes use of it, differs from comparison and allegory on two essential points. First, it does not refer to a fictive or invented *ad hoc* comparison, but to a common, everyday, and realistic, if not true, situation (the appeal to the agricultural world of Palestine or to the social facts and practices of Jerusalem is not arbitrary, and the study of the *Sitz im Leben* is quite legitimate),[16] such that everyone sees quite clearly what the parable means. For it "is always assigned to a project which aims at the obvious, the establishment of a truth, whether it is a matter of argumentation and proof, or the clarity of style. The term never designates, at least not deliberately, an illustration employed in order to hide something or make it less intelligible (no connection with mystery, no link with enigma)."[17] If we insist on maintaining a link to the rhetorical use of the parable in its Greek usage, it would more fittingly correspond to arguments by confrontation or counter-confrontation (*ek parabolēs* or *ex antiparabolēs*): setting one argument against another with the impact of a deck-to-deck encounter.[18] Through his parables, Jesus launches an obvious and common truth at his hearers, like boarding a ship, so that by the impact of a confrontation, he in turn causes (or *inspires*) them to sense a *mystērion* that remains inconceivable to them, at least in the terms they would expect to hear.

Parable and Confession (the Synoptics) 213

Next, from this well-known reference ("the sower went out to sow") the parable inversely refers to a term (the kingdom of God) that is incomprehensible to its hearers and *remains so*. For it does not try to express or describe what remains inaccessible, at least temporarily, to its listener; or rather, because it tries to make him catch sight of a signification ("the Kingdom of God") that he precisely cannot yet understand, the parable must first and foremost make him perceive (even touch with his finger) this very inconceivability. Likewise, the parable does not try to explicitly express a hidden signification (the *mystērion*), which can only remain unintelligible, since it contradicts the significations that the hearer takes for granted; but it does indeed give him the signification, and the responsibility to approach as much as he can the paradox which is uncovered, and to bear it. In the case of Mark, the situation that requires a parable can be described without difficulty. "From Judea and from Jerusalem, from Idumaea, and from beyond the Jordan, and around Tyre and Sidon, a great multitude (πολὺ πλῆθος), learning all that he did, came to him (ἦλθον πρὸς αὐτόν)" (Mark 3:7–8). Indeed, almost the whole world in those days expected the Kingdom of God, especially since many saw (and rightly so) the miracles accomplished by Jesus as signs of its coming. However, they (wrongly) understood this coming as the moment for Jesus to "restore the kingdom to Israel" (Acts 1:6), and it is quite natural that "they wanted to take him by force to make him king" (John 6:15). The proclamation of the "Kingdom of God," precisely by virtue of its authenticity, also inevitably provokes a misunderstanding about the new signification: the listeners understand this kingdom as a political kingship (at least in its effects, if not in its origin), while Jesus proclaimed another signification, even an opposing one, that of a Messiah "who must suffer many things" (Mark 8:31). Between these two significations, a triumphant king and a suffering Messiah, there is as much incompatibility (*schisma*) as between an old piece of cloth and a new one, or between a shriveled leather wineskin and new wine (2:21–22). And all the more as the conflict does not oppose two significations that are clearly and distinctly understood, but, on the one hand, significations that are supposedly well known and understandable, and on the other, a missing signification, as yet inconceivable and unimaginable.[19] Like standing before a saturated phenomenon (and indeed it is a preeminent one), where one must search for a missing signification to the measure of intuition that, as excessive, overflows all of the significations that are already available, the parable tries to evoke, incite, and indirectly suggest the missing signification. The parable does not explicitly express the new and excessive signification, precisely because its excess makes it inconceivable at first, but it opens the field where this newness can be understood and experienced.

From this follows the operations accomplished by the parable. First of all, the parable opens a field for the *possibility* of a listening [*écoute*] that grasps [*comprenne*], literally, an understanding [*entente*][20] of the inconceivable signification.[21] In the parable, it becomes possible to understand in a new way what is proclaimed through old names, with the chance as well as the risk of having to understand and suppose what one nevertheless cannot yet grasp. It opens, in a word, the space of confrontation with the saturated phenomenon *par excellence*, in its moment of crisis, where the excess intuition (*exousia* of a word of *Logos*, *exousia* of its miraculous power) surpasses and disqualifies the significations available in the tradition.[22] Each parable thus provokes a crisis, and becomes, according to Dodd's formula, a "parable of crisis," which inevitably provokes a judgment of its hearer, positive or negative, but always approximate. And yet, this judgment is not insignificant, because it significantly un-covers, in turn, what is in the heart. The parable functions exactly like a contradicting word ("*antilegomenos*") that "un-covers the thoughts of many hearts" (Luke 2:35). The parable thus does not teach the signification of the "Kingdom of God"; it enacts its coming in each hearer by imposing on him the choice to accept—*or not*—the event that is accomplished in the person of Jesus who addresses him. The parable does what it says and does not say anything other than what it does. But only the one who incarnates this proclamation (who *is* the "Kingdom of God") can do what he says. Jesus is precisely this, so in saying it, he does it.

The parable thus imposes, as the very condition of its opening, the possibility of *misunderstanding*, or in other words, of having ears *to not* understand. Not that the parable intends to obscure and hide (like the enigma, the prophetic dream, the fantastical image, which demand an allegorical exegesis), but because what it announces and advances, the *mystērion* thinkable by God alone, thought by God alone, can only be suggested as such, that is, as first of all unthinkable by us. It cannot and must not impose a master-signification that would be immediately understood, thus lowered to the level of our spontaneous expectation, our habitual understanding, in a simple slogan of propaganda, an idol of our world. The parable must offer the *mystērion* as such, and thus as a signification that is as yet inconceivable; and so it must entail the possibility of submitting not only to the hazy comprehension of certain hearers, but also the decided refusal among others to admit the least signification coming *from elsewhere*. The denial of the *mystērion*'s uncovering is an intrinsic part of the essence of un-covering, just as misunderstanding also belongs to the proclamation. Thus Jesus had to "send away the crowd himself" (Mark 6:45), as well as impose silence on those who were miraculously healed (1:44), on demons (3:12), and even on his "own." In fact, the ἔξω (*exō*) are confronted with exactly the same test as the ἴδιοι (*idioi*): they all must change, or at least *imagine* changing, their baseline concepts. They all rightly deserve the admonition made to Peter, "Get behind me, Satan! For your thoughts are not those of God, but of men" (8:33).[23] A clear and distinct parable would not reveal anything of the *mystērion*, but it provokes a radical "astonishment": "What is this new teaching, διδαχὴ καινή?" (Mark 1:27) that "makes all things new" (Revelation 21.5).

In this way, as a necessarily indirect speech,[24] the parable *speaks without saying anything*, without stating any object, any being, but by addressing the hearer and provoking him to another possibility than that which he held as possible. It says what cannot be said, the *impossible*. In this way, it leaves the hearer free to speak and to be spoken in what he says. It allows him to respond, forces him to a response. It provokes judgment.[25] For the paradox of the *mysteriōn* can only be said through a parable, and the parable only uncovers a single paradox: the Messiah must suffer and die in order to be raised on the third day. In this consists his Messiahship and his kingdom. The paradox thus constitutes the *ratio vivendi* of the parable, the parable offers the *ratio cognoscendi* of the paradox.[26]

It is clear that it arises in the horizon of a paradigmatic text of Isaiah (6:9–10): "They have indeed seen, they do not perceive; they have indeed heard, they do not understand." Hence, the warning of Christ intensifies this admonition: "Who has ears to hear, hear!" (4.9 = 4.23). The parable therefore marks the *mystērion*, which (without Christ) no one can properly understand, because no one can make the story manifest to himself if he cannot first become manifest to himself. Left to their doubled darkness (to themselves and to the manifest discourse), the listeners are found also "outside, ἔξω" and everything arrives for them in parables, everything remains unintelligible to them. For the disciples, on the other hand, "the *mystērion* of the Kingdom of God has been given, μυστήριον δέδοται" (4:11; see 4:34). Why to them and not the others? Because they have, half-consciously but already, in fact, taken the risk and made the choice to respond to the call of becoming disciples. An epistemological break has already taken place, where understanding is decided (and where disagreement will thus appear). The un-covering breaks through—if still only faintly—against the background of the covering over and the blanketing of the secret, of the *mystērion* experienced as such, unveiled *as* not yet un-covered. Hence this rule formulated by Eberhard Jüngel: the proclamation of the coming of the Kingdom is not announced as a thesis taught by Jesus, but arrives as a speech act that, as a parable, awaits and provokes a response: "*The* basileia *arrives in language in parable* as *parable. The parables of Jesus carry the kingdom of God to language* as *a parable.*"[27] The first effect of this proclamation in act consists in a pervasive feeling of fear. "Thus they were afraid with a great fear (ἐφοβήθησαν φόβον μέγαν)" (4:41). It is a question of fear before what cannot be understood, except by satisfying a condition as yet unattainable—by taking the point of view of the one who speaks it and above all of what he says. Fear designates here the state of the one who feels the *mystērion*, without yet being able to hear or grasp it, who experiences it as a *mysterium tremendum*, the same one that will overwhelm the women at the empty tomb (16:8), the same one that Paul can only speak about to the Corinthians "with fear and trembling, ἐν φόβῳ καὶ ἐν τρόμῳ" (1 Corinthians 2:3).

To Hear Seeing, to See Listening

Luke takes up the question where Mark left off: for him, too, the focus is the first parables (of the sower and of the lamp, Luke 8:5–19 = Mark 4:3–23), and the principle of uncovering that manifests what remains hidden (Luke 8:17 = Mark 4:22), the reminder that "to you it is given to know the *mystēria* of the Kingdom of God" (Luke 8:10 = Mark 4:11), and finally the citation of Isaiah 6:9ff: "looking, they do not look, hearing they do not understand," naturally followed by the same warning: "Whoever has ears to hear, hear!" (Luke 8:8 = Mark 4:9). This common framework reaches an identical admonition—at least, *almost* identical: where one writes, "Look *what* you hear (βλέπετε τί ἀκούετε)" (Mark 4:24), the other corrects it to "Look *how* you hear (βλέπετε πῶς ἀκούετε)" (Luke 8:18).[28] The common thread of the two exhortations offers no ambiguity: it is necessary to consider (see well, see face-to-face) what one hears, especially when what one hears (and sees) cannot be conceived. And here we cannot fail to recall the strange crossing of sight and hearing that occurred when Moses received the Law: "the people *saw* the thunder, the flames, the sound of the horn" (Exodus 20:18).[29] It is precisely when one can no longer see what one ought to see or conceive what one nevertheless sees that it becomes a question of seeing and taking into view (of having to take into consideration) what one has at least heard. Or rather—and the difference between the two formulas arises here—it is not only necessary to see *what* (τί, Mark) one has heard, but especially *how* (πῶς, Luke) one has heard. For all have heard what was said as clear as day, since experience proves that "the seed springs up and flourishes, even if he [namely, man] does not know how (ὡς οὐκ οἶδεν αὐτός)" (Mark 4:27); but everyone has not heard it in the same way. The difference is less due to a static division between those who are "of it" and those who remain "outside (ἔξω)" (Mark 4:11) than the rift between modes of hearing, a rift that cuts across every heart. This relocation of the rift between Mark and Luke is confirmed by another variant. In place of the obscure and unnerving oxymoron that "the one who has, to him it will be given, and the one who has not, what he has will be taken away from him" (Mark 4:25), a logical explanation (and not a rhetorical softening) is provided: "For, the one who has, to him will be given, and the one who has not, even *what he thinks he has* (ὃ δοκεῖ ἔχειν) will be taken away from him" (Luke 8:18). What will be taken from the one who has not, obviously, is not what he does not have, only what he *supposes he has*. What does he believe he has in this case? He believes he has a signification adequate to what he has heard: he believes he knows, thanks to what he knows of the Law and the tradition of men ("We have a father, Abraham") (Luke 3:8), what the parable of the sower, the Kingdom of God, and the identity of Jesus ("Isn't he the son of Joseph?"; Luke 4:22) mean for him and in themselves. It is precisely this signification, held and possessed (ἔχειν), that closes him in on himself, like one possessed by a demon, shut to the possibility of another signification, that which points in the undecided opening of the parable, that which would come from *elsewhere*. The one who does not see, deep down, does not see that he wants to possess what he hears within the signification that he possesses. He does not see that he does not want to receive a new signification (the good news that inaugurates a new realm), which by definition he cannot possess from his own store, but must receive from *elsewhere*. Paul too says it clearly. "What sets you apart (διακρίνει)? What do you have (ἔχεις) that you have not received (ὃ οὐκ ἔλαβες)? And if you have received it, why do you boast of it as if you had not received it (ὡς μὴ λαβών)?" (1 Corinthians 4:7). Everything is in the way (ὡς, πῶς) of not possessing one's own signification, in the art of receiving another signification from elsewhere, without measure, alone adequate to the opening made *possible* by the parable of the Kingdom of God: "To the one who has, it will be given, and it will overabound (περισσευθήσεται)" (Matthew 13:12). In other words, he will be saturated by what is uncovered to him yet remains out of his grasp.

The whole difficulty of the question lies not in the response, but first in the question itself, in hearing it. For, before responding to it, one must first hear it and understand [*entendre*] it, enter into agreement [*entente*] with it, which is played out in my way (πῶς) of posing it, whether in rejecting it or in accepting it. Listening to the fact of *not* knowing, admitting to *not* having any available signification: "What is this word (τίς ὁ λόγος) with authority (ἐξουσίᾳ) and power (δυνάμει)?" (Luke 4:36); or, as the disciples of John the Baptist know to ask: "Are you the one who must come?" (7:19). Admitting they "have seen paradoxes today (εἴδαμεν παράδοξα σήμερον)" (5:26) without refusing to see them, that is, without being scandalized by them: "Blessed is the one who will not be scandalized by me" (7:23), in other words, without refusing to see the "sign to be spoken-against (*contre-dit*, ἀντιλεγόμενον)" (2:34), to hear the "hard *logos*" which "scandalizes" (John 6:60, 62). Recognizing such a phenomenon, so uncovered on every side, so superabundant in possibilities and so powerful in intuitions, requires first of all not being afraid of being afraid, accepting one's fear (φόβος) of the miracles of healing (Luke 7:16, the son of the widow of Nain), the domination of nature (8:25, the storm that is quieted), and spiritual authority (8:25, the expulsion of demons).[30] But it requires as well knowing how to confront the fear of the very holiness of Jesus, and therefore to withstand the way one's own sin is brought to light by contrast (by *veritas redarguens*); as did Simon Peter, who "fell at Jesus' knees, saying 'Depart from me, for I am a sinful man, Lord.' For fear (θάμβος) had indeed seized him" (5:8–9), an attitude that is found in a number of vetero-testamentary episodes (Moses, Isaiah, etc.).

Toward a Practice of Un-covering

Since none of the common significations fit, the phenomenon of Jesus announcing the Kingdom of God appears as an "aporia"; as Herod "listened (ἤκουσεν) . . . to everything that had happened and was in aporia (διηπόρει)" (9:7). More precisely, being very well informed, he experiences more than anyone the plurality of the available significations applied to Jesus and, at the same time, their patent inadequacy: Should we recognize in him Elijah (9:8, Mark 8:28), John the Baptist (9:9; see 3:15 and Mark 8:28), or even Beelzebul (11:15–19, Mark 3:22)? This confusion offers the symptom of the anonymity (and thus the polyonymy) of the saturated phenomenon *par excellence*: when Jesus reads Isaiah 61 in the synagogue of Nazareth and proclaims that he "accomplishes (πεπλήρωται) in this day" (Luke 4:21) what he has read, he arouses almost in the same stroke the benevolent "wonder (ἐθαύμαζον)" (4:22) and murderous "fury (ἐπλήσθησαν πάντες θυμοῦ)" of everyone (4:28); for it sends into crisis the same hearers who admire the de facto accomplishment of the *saturated* phenomenon and who are enraged to see it now offered beyond the limits of Israel. The same ambivalence of the uncovering of the Kingdom of God erupts when "the multitude of the country of the Gerasenes asked Jesus to depart from them (ἀπελθεῖν ἀπ' αὐτῶν)" (8:37 and Mark 5:17), precisely because he was able to heal a possessed man of his demons. Those closest to him were able to react even more brutally: "His own [family] went out to seize him, for, they said, he is outside himself (ὅτι ἐξέστη)" (Mark 3:21). To reach the point of imagining that Jesus has "lost his head" manifests above all that one has oneself lost the slightest conception of "all that has happened"; like "the scribes and Pharisees," who, watching the healing of a man with a withered hand on the Sabbath, "were filled with madness (*démence*, ἀνοίας)" (Luke 6:11). This "manifest . . . madness (ἄνοια . . . ἔκδηλος)" (2 Timothy 3:9) also attests the inability to receive a signification from *elsewhere*, and by consequence, the stubborn determination to cobble together old significations in order to think, or rather in order *not* to think, the paradoxical phenomenon of Christ. This emptiness of mind (ἄνοια) leads the disciples themselves to not grasp (thus to not grasp *themselves*, or even to not let themselves be grasped by) the proclamation of the Passion; Jesus asks them however to "put in their ears" the unique signification of the "Son of Man"—that is, that "he will be delivered into the hands of men"; but they are not able to: "they did not understand this saying, and it remained as not un-covered (παρακεκαλυμμένον)" (Luke 9:44–45). This "madness" is extended even to the travelers from Emmaus, "senseless (ἀνόητοι) [because] slow to believe" (24:25) what the Scriptures nevertheless offer a clear signification for, *ex eventu*. The wisdom of God reduces the wisdom of the world not only to folly (μωρία), but *here* as well to madness (ἀνοία).[31]

Hence the paradox of interpretation: the miracles of Jesus are so manifest in their effectiveness, which no one contests (neither the crowds nor the Pharisees, nor the deacons), and yet they convince hardly anyone. Or rather, those who submit to Jesus must first be converted, that is they must believe. They must believe in order to see. Thus Jesus's admiration for the centurion: "Not even in Israel have I found such faith" (Luke 7:9; see also 5:20). Faith, the act of faith, becomes the criteria and the *practical* criteria of un-covering, the *response* to the proclamation. Jesus limits himself, if we can speak in this way, either to observing that "your faith has saved you" (7:50 and 8:48), or worrying about its slowness: "Where is your faith?" (8:25 and 19:5–6; Mark 6:5–6). For the crux of the un-covering (*apokalypsis*) is not found in intuition, here patent and saturating (by signs or miracles), but in the acceptance of a signification coming from elsewhere, in a clean break with those that the world provides for us in a wholly unified, regular, familiar way. Now, to accomplish the anamorphosis of the look, to change the interpretation, to pass to the point of view fixed by the *mystērion*, in short, to enter into the paradox that supports the parable in order *to conceive what one sees*, such a theoretical operation ultimately takes up a theoretical practice. It is a question of doing (ποεῖν) in practice: "Why do you call me 'Lord, Lord!' and do not do (οὐ ποιεῖτε) what I say? Whoever comes to me and hears my words *and acts on them* (καὶ ποιῶν), I will show you what he is like" (6:46–47)—a man who builds his house on rock. As long as faith is not the ground of understanding, even the correct significations, like the effective miracles, remain in suspense: that is why they must be kept silent (Matthew 17:9).

Of course, before the anamorphosis is accomplished *in practice*, Jesus appears already and from the outset as the Christ: but as the Christ *rejected*, as the logos *refuted*, as the *un-covering of the very covering over* of the uncovering, "the sign of contradiction (σημεῖον ἀντιλεγόμενον) . . . in whom the thoughts (διαλογισμοί) that many hearts bear within them will be uncovered (ἀποκαλυφθῶσιν)" (2:34–35).

The Confession as Un-covering

It is Matthew who finally breaks through the aporia described by Luke. He pushes the logic of anamorphosis to the limit by unfolding the confession of Peter in all its dimensions. For this sequence is distinguished by several remarkable characteristics.

First, it refers explicitly to *apokalypsis*; for when Jesus receives the confession of Peter, he consecrates it as an uncovering, and even as an exceptional un-covering: "Jesus, responding to him, said: 'Blessed are you, Simon son of John, because it is not flesh or blood who has uncovered (ἀπεκάλυψέν) this for you, but my Father, who is in heaven'" (Matthew 16:17). This exceptional character comes from the fact that the uncovering made to Peter takes up and indisputably accomplishes the Matthean formulation of the principle of uncovering: "Nothing, indeed, is veiled (κεκαλυμμένον) that will not be uncovered (ὃ οὐκ ἀποκαλυφθήσεται, *revelabitur*), nor hidden (κρυπτὸν) that will not become known (ὃ οὐ γνωσθήσεται)" (10:26); it must be emphasized all the more, as Matthew is the only one of the Synoptics to use the register of *apokalypsis* for this principle.[32] It is even possible to see in Peter's confession the height of a sequence (Matthew 10–17:9) devoted to the description and then implementation of *apokalypsis*: beginning with the calling and the sending of the Twelve (10:1–41), the principle of un-covering (10:16) leads to the warning about listening ("He who has ears to hear, let him hear!") (11:15) and the condemnation of Chorazin, Bethsaida, and Capernaum (11:20–24), and is then carried out with the parable of the sower (13:12–23) and others; it provokes the confession of Peter and is completed by the first proclamation of the Passion, which is answered by the Transfiguration (17:1–9). This long sequence unquestionably establishes that *apokalypsis* or un-covering offers the scene of every proclamation (as well as rejection) of the Kingdom of God in Galilee, and in the end allows the "ultimate game [*jeu suprême*]"[33] of its accomplishment in Jerusalem. Indeed, the principle of un-covering goes hand in hand with the possibility of a refusal to listen: Peter's confession also anticipates his denial, because, if the Transfiguration anticipates the Resurrection, it is only once the Passion is announced by Jesus, prepared by the "scribes and Pharisees" and rejected by the disciples.

Why then does Peter appear in the position of "first," as figurehead, first guarantor, first called, the prototype of the disciple?[34] Clearly because after negative or indecisive responses, he offers the first adequate (if not perfect) answer to an exemplary and already ancient question: "'Who is this,' they said, 'that even the winds and the sea obey him?'" (8:25) We must not forget here the rule according to which every call remains silent and unknown as long as the response does not make it explicit, at least in part: the call is understood only in the response that it evokes and to the extent that the response can receive it. Now, the confession of Peter according to Matthew is delivered in its longest formula, and the most profound as well: "You are the Christ, the son of the living God (σὺ εἶ ὁ χριστὸς ὁ υἱὸς τοῦ θεοῦ τοῦ ζῶντος)" (16:16). It is a New Testament *hapax*, since the other two Synoptics offer shorter and more summary formulas: "You are the Christ" (Mark 8:29), ". . . the Christ of God" (Luke 9:20). Matthew, on the other hand, calls Jesus not only by the titles of "Christ" and "Son of God" but specifies that he is the "Son of the living God" (16:16). In doing so, he takes up a first confession of Peter after Jesus walks on the water: "Truly, you are the Son of God" (14:33); but he anticipates also the solemn question of the high priest: "By the living God, I adjure you to tell us if you are the Son of God," to which Jesus only responds, "It is you [yourself] who say so" (26:63–64). Above all, he declares the almost involuntary recognition of the centurion and those who were "watching from a distance" the death of Christ: "Truly this man was the Son of God" (27:54–55). The identity that is here attributed to Jesus breaks with the significations of vetero- and inter-testamentary origins (recalled in 16:14) that had until then been in competition in order to pass over, in one stroke and for the first time, to a signification that directly refers in an already *Trinitarian* way to the Father (or see 28:19). What does Peter thus achieve, what does this linguistic performance accomplish? Nothing other than crossing the essential difference, opening an epistemological break: crossing the rift between points of view on the *mystērion*, passing from one interpretation (that of men of the world, who see in Jesus a carpenter, a prophet *redivivus*, an accomplice of Satan or a raging fool) to the one that Jesus hopes for and awaits, "The Christ, the Son of the living God." In short, Peter accomplishes the ultimate anamorphosis required by the *mystērion*, the saturated phenomenon *par excellence*.

We can understand Christ's great jubilation, for he truly "rejoices (ἠγαλλιάσατο)" (Luke 10:21),³⁵ with a "joy" already mentioned in another redactional passage, the parable of the discovery of treasure in a field: "in joy (ἀπὸ τῆς χαρᾶς)" (Matthew 13:44) the finder sells everything to buy the field. This joy burst out already in Matthew, in a pericope prior to the confession of Peter, but directly oriented around *apokalypsis*: "At that time, answering them, Jesus said: 'I thank you (ἐξομολογοῦμαί), Father, Lord of heaven and earth, because you have hidden (ἔκρυψας) these things from the wise and those who know, and you have un-covered (ἀπεκάλυψας) them to the little ones. Yes, Father, for thus it seemed good to you. All things have been handed over (παρεδόθη) to me by my Father, and no one knows the Son except the Father, and no one knows the Father except the Son and the one to whom the Son has decided to un-cover (ἀποκαλύψαι) him'" (11:25–27). Why this jubilation? Not only because Peter, by his confession, at last accomplishes the first anamorphosis awaited by Jesus since the beginning of the preaching of the Kingdom of God throughout Galilee and beyond, but because this anamorphosis does not depend only or originally on any man, who must nevertheless accomplish it, *nor even on Jesus*, who must nevertheless ask for it far and wide; it depends on the grace of the Father. This is confirmed by the mention here of "flesh and blood" (16:17). What comes "not from blood, nor the will of the flesh or that of man" comes "from God" (John 1:13); what is not "of flesh and blood," comes "from his grace, in order to uncover (ποκαλύψαι) his son in me" (Galatians 1:15–16). Peter becomes the prototype of the disciple not only because he succeeds in confessing "the Son of the living God," but because he does *not* succeed at it by himself: he succeeds because the grace and the will of the Father, thus the Holy Spirit, gives it to him. If Peter—alone among all the disciples in the New Testament—receives an individual and personal blessing from Christ (16:17), it is because this constitutes a grace of the Father *for Jesus himself*. In it, Jesus himself, the Christ, sees, and in a sense without having a hand in it, that certain men succeed in venturing the decision to accept the gift of the Father, as he himself does, always and perfectly. And this reception of the gift of the Father can only be produced starting from the Father himself, as Jesus knows by experience. Peter's recognition of Jesus as "The Christ, the Son of the living God" is, *for Jesus himself*, a gift of the Father, the Father's response to what

Jesus is waiting for, just like the "voice" at the baptism, the Transfiguration, and the Temple.

Confession as Blessing

Nevertheless, a question could arise here: What does Peter uncover in his confession, what does the Father give to him to un-cover? The adequate response to this question could only be Trinitarian and phenomenal, or rather phenomenally Trinitarian (see above, chapters 17–18), but we can now discern a shortcoming here.

First of all, because the un-covering of the sonship of Jesus, now recognized as "the Christ, the Son of the living God," implies that nothing separates the Father from the Son, since "All things have been handed over (παρεδόθη) to me by my Father" (Matthew 11:27).[36] Next and above all, because the disposition to receive is what characterizes the "little ones" and the "poor," as their privilege from God's point of view. In fact, they alone have a theological capacity proportional to their social incapacity: as they do not possess power, do not know what it allows, and therefore do not know persistence in and by themselves, they know, or at least they cannot ignore, what the *elsewhere* reveals: they know what this *elsewhere* means, for they depend on it every day. And so what is called Jesus's macarism towards Peter, "Blessed are you (εἶ) Simon, son of John" (Matthew 16:17), amounts to simply prolonging and exemplifying a genuine case of the first beatitude: "Happy the poor in spirit, because the Kingdom of God is (ἐστὶν) theirs" (5:3). The present tense of the verb (the only tense in all the beatitudes)[37] is confirmed in the present tense of the confession of Peter, who is one of these poor in spirit who are blessed. This un-covering, which must come from *elsewhere*, in this case from the Holy Spirit and thus from the Father, proves impossible for all who know and believe they know enough to (not) decide, who do not want to know except on the condition that they remain in their wisdom, who stay in the safety zone of their point of view; the un-covering becomes possible, on the other hand, for the "little ones (νηπίοι)" who know they have no wisdom of their own to oppose the *apokalypsis*.

This final moment becomes absolutely decisive: only a "little one," but he first, manages to accomplish the anamorphosis. This means: passing from significations *they* ("people," everybody) use to identify Jesus (John the

Baptist, Elijah, Jeremiah, or one of the prophets) to the question that will identify not only Jesus but also those who respond to it, the disciples ("And *you*, who do *you* say that I am?"); which means: one of the disciples eventually and finally passes to the point of view of the Father (of the "voice" coming from the heavens) on Jesus. It is nothing less than this that Peter accomplishes, or rather allows to be accomplished in him. He is the first of all men to respond in tune (as one might say it musically): "You are the Christ, the Son of the living God." He is the first to perceive the un-covering (*apokalpysis*) of the *mystērion*, because he allows himself to be placed in the very place of its phenomenalization, the Trinitarian site opened by the Spirit between the Father and the Son. In response, Jesus sanctions this Trinitarian accomplishment and names it as such: "this un-covering did not come to you (οὐκ ἀπεκάλυψέν) from flesh, nor from blood, but from my Father who is in heaven" (16:17). The primacy of Peter—even though he will tempt Jesus immediately after this moment (Matthew 16:23; Mark 4:13), will later betray him, and will understand the Resurrection less quickly than John (John 20:8)—is nevertheless definitively decided here; it is derived solely from the privilege of having been the first to confess the identity of Jesus as Son of the Father, of having been the first one to *know* and to *be able* to let himself be led into the site where the un-covering becomes visible and bearable by a human gaze. And it is why he receives, in return, his own true name, seen and given from the point of view of Christ—Peter.[38]

Yet one final question remains. If, in adequately confessing Jesus as the Christ, Peter accomplished the first un-covering by man, why then does Jesus ask the other disciples to be silent (Matthew 16:20; see also Mark 1:34 and 9:9; Luke 8:56 and 9:21)? Why maintain the "Messianic Secret" (all the more since it is very often broken)? If we do not wish to be bogged down in uncertain philological discussions, but try to follow the logic of un-covering, a response seems to impose itself: even and especially *after* the Transfiguration, where Peter "did not know what he was saying" (Mark 9:6), the disciples must not divulge what they themselves cannot yet accomplish, nor comprehend, nor thus make known to other people who are even less capable of it. A clear confirmation again comes from the reprimand of Christ to Peter: although he is the foundation stone of the community of all who will accomplish the un-covering in themselves and by the Spirit, Peter immediately becomes the stumbling block and "scandal" and is called "Satan," because he rejects the idea that the Son of man must endure his passion and die in Jerusalem (Matthew 16:32; see Mark 8:33). The proclamations of the passion to the disciples (the first here, Matthew 16:21ff) were badly received, even denied (the second at least, where "they were saddened") (17:23). The disciples, like Peter, find themselves in a strange and unstable situation: they have understood the right signification required to see Jesus as "the Christ," "Son of the living God"; but they do not yet understand the meaning (*signification*) of this signification: that he must suffer and die for sinners, in order to rise again, and that only in this way can the un-covering, the whole *apokalypsis* be accomplished. They have attained the right signification, but they have not yet rightly understood it. They lack what the event alone can make them conceive, and even then with great difficulty: the Trinitarian play of filiation implies that Jesus remain or become the Son "to the end (εἰς τέλος)" (John 13:1): he goes to death to receive his life as he gives it, from the Father alone (John 10:18). This un-covering is something that no one, except Christ himself, can accomplish.[39]

We can thus respond here to the second question, which asked *how* what gives itself un-covers itself: what shows itself gives itself in the mode of an anamorphosis, a displacement from the point of view of the witness on the *mystērion*, a crossing of the epistemological break—which makes Jesus seen as "the Christ, as the Son of the living God," which makes him show himself as he gives himself, as Son *from the point of view of the Father*. "All things have been given (παρεδόθη) to me by the Father, and no one knows the Son except the Father, and no one knows the Father except the Son, and the one to whom the Son has decided that he be un-covered (ἀποκαλύψαι)" (Matthew 11:27). Or: "All things have been given to me (παρεδόθη) by the Father, and no one knows who is the Son, except the Father, nor who is the Father, except the Son and the one to whom the Son has decided that he be un-covered (ἀποκαλύψαι)" (Luke 10:22). We are already facing the Johannine word: "No one has ever seen God. But a God, the only Son, turned toward the bosom of the Father, has in fact exegeted him [for us]" (John 1:18).

FOURTEEN

The "Mystery"—of Whom? (John)

Following the logic of un-covering, we can now approach the third question, which seeks not only *what* there is an un-covering of (chapter 12), or *how* it happens (chapter 13), but in the end *who* is uncovered there (chapter 14). For, to deem that the *mystērion* is truly revealed (un-covered) in giving itself, we will have to clarify the core of this question: it is about not only *what* uncovers itself, but ultimately *the one* who can perfectly give *himself*; it is thus a matter of determining *who* (τίς) is *the one* who asks: "*Who* do men say that I am (τίνα με)?" (Mark 8:27; see Matthew 16:13 and Luke 9:18). The Gospel of John, which offers no literal echo of this question, will nevertheless allow us to respond more directly than the Synoptics, because it penetrates the farthest into the identity of Jesus, to the point of manifesting his *Trinitarian* status as Son of the Father.

The Movement of Un-covering

There remains one initial difficulty on this path: John does not mention the principle of unveiling in the explicit terms of the Synoptics, most notably in Matthew: "Nothing, indeed, will be covered (κεκαλυμμένον) that will not be un-covered (ὃ οὐκ ἀποκαλυφθήσεται), nor hidden (κρυπτὸν) that will not become known (ὃ οὐ γνωσθήσεται)" (Matthew 10:26; see also Mark 4:22 and Luke 8:17, chapter 13 above). Where then could we find the equivalent of this *apokalypsis*? This difficulty is further confirmed if we note that the principle of un-covering in John is not accomplished in the confession of Peter, as it was in Matthew ("flesh and blood have not un-covered it to you, but my Father in heaven") (Matthew 16:17). Of course, this confession still takes place in John: "Simon Peter responded: 'Lord, to whom shall we go? You have the words of everlasting life. And we have believed, and come to know, that you are the Holy One of God.'" But Jesus does not celebrate it as a blessing or a jubilation, but instead foretells the betrayal of Judas, denouncing "a demon among you" (John 6:68–70). Thus the principle of un-covering and the confession that performs it seem in fact to be absent.

But this is only an appearance. First of all, because Peter's confession, at the end of the "scandal" (6:61) provoked by the "hard saying" (6:60) about the bread of life, serves as an explicit recognition of Jesus as the Christ—"We have believed, and have come to know, that you are the Holy One of God (ὁ ἅγιος τοῦ θεοῦ)" (6:69). Further, according to a strongly attested variant, "You are the Son of the living God (ὁ υἱὸς τοῦ θεοῦ τοῦ ζῶντος)" (ibid.), this phrase recalls the exact words of Peter according to Matthew ("You are Christ, the Son of the living God," Matthew 16:16), the same as will be used by the high priest (Matthew 26:63). Thus, in John, Peter confesses Christ by literally the same formula as Matthew, and just as clearly. Where then is the divergence from Matthew, and what is the source of John's reluctance to invoke the principle of un-covering?

The question is further complicated if we take note of evidence pointing in the opposite direction: unlike the Synoptics, John is unique in reporting many confessions about Jesus's identity well *before* that of Peter, such that the un-covering is ceaselessly being accomplished. Let us quote from the most striking cases. First of all, John the Baptist recognizes that "this is the Son of God" (John 1:34) and "the lamb of God" (1:36). Then Andrew acknowledges he has "found the Messiah (which is translated as Christ)" (1:41), as does Philip: "We have found the one written about in the Law of Moses and the prophets: it is Jesus, the son of Joseph of Nazareth!" (1:45); then Nathaniel: "Rabbi, you are the Son of God, you are the king of Israel" (1:49). Nicodemus does not hesitate either: "Rabbi, we know that you have come to teach from God" (3:2). But it is not only the disciples or quasi-disciples who "believed in him" from the first miracle of Cana (2:11), since, after the first ascent to Jerusalem, "many" others "believed in his name" (2:23). For example, the Samaritan woman (4:25–26) and the inhabitants of her village, who "told her,

'It is no longer because of what you said that we believe, for we have heard ourselves and we know that this truly is the savior of the world'" (4:42). And then the royal official "believed, he and all his household" (4:53). And *after* the confession of Peter, still more confessions follow: "many believed in him" (7:31; 10:42; 11:45) because of the signs; the man born blind, who "said, 'I believe'" provides the most detailed example of this (9:38). We must therefore conclude that the difficulty does not come from the confession itself, as in fact it happens frequently.

But then where does it come from? Namely, from this: that it is a matter of speaking the confession, but also of knowing what this confession really means, how it is valued in the depths of the hearts of those who utter it. For every time that some of those in the crowd believe and confess because of the "signs," others (the Pharisees, the "Jews") do not believe, at the same moment and before the same signs whose authenticity they do not call into question. The question is therefore not only or first of all about the difference between those who believe and confess and those who do not, but, more radically, about what is really believed by those who believe and what is really confessed by those who confess. It is undoubtedly in this way that we must understand the author's curious and, in a sense, surprising remark about Jesus's reserve toward those who believed "in his name at the sight of the signs that he accomplished" (2:23): "Jesus himself did not trust them (οὐκ ἐπίστευεν), because he knew them all; and because he did not need anyone to testify (μαρτυρήσῃ) to him about man; for he himself knew what was in man" (2:24–25). Man not only cannot confess, but, when he does confess, he may not know what he is confessing, nor what his own confession means. He cannot even know how far he believes what he confesses, nor even the meaning of what he says—this was the case for Peter at the Transfiguration, who "did not know what to say" (Mark 9:6). For man does not know what to say, since he does not even know who he is; and he knows it still less when he has to decide to say *who* is the one who is speaking to him, Jesus.[1]

To simplify, we can say that the Synoptics make the un-covering coincide with the confession (hence the primary function of the confession of Peter, paradigm of all the others), while John verifies and explains that no human confession of Jesus as Christ is enough, as such, to accomplish un-covering, because uttering the concepts of a confession does not yet in itself allow one to know what one is saying, to understand these significations and especially to see what one aims at in them. In this sense the accomplishment of a confession causes the real difficulty to arise, because it manifests what each hears and is able to understand of the significations it puts into action; it thus unveils more "what was in the man" who says them than what they aim at and what, most often, man does not yet see; in fact, he will not be able to catch a glimpse of the significations except from the Paschal event. The confession alone is not yet enough to manifest in truth what nevertheless is already un-covered. It is not enough to "truly (ἀληθῶς)"[2] confess Jesus as "Messiah," "Rabbi," "king of Israel," "Holy one of God," "Son of God," "Son of man," or "savior of the world" to understand and know what one is saying, still less to see it un-covered. To accomplish this, it will be necessary to understand all these titles as Jesus understands and fulfills them; that is, it will be necessary to understand them starting from the Father, and therefore to receive them as and by the will of the Father. This crucial difficulty will remain for the disciples until Pentecost: for Thomas, of course ("My Lord and my God," John 20:28), who must learn not only to see in order to believe, but to believe in order to see; for Peter as well, who still needs John to recognize the Risen One (21:7); and who must finally understand at the last moment what it means to love (ἀγαπεῖν/φιλεῖν, 21:15–17)—even if the Paschal "hour" (17:1) had allowed Jesus to say, by prolepsis, "Now and truly (νῦν), they [i.e., the disciples] have known that all the things that you have given me come from you" (17:7; see 17:25–26).

We understand, then, that the principle of un-covering (Matthew 10:26; also Mark 4:22 and Luke 8:17) can no longer be unconditionally imposed as the first principle. Indeed, since one can in fact see without believing ("But I said to you: you see me and do not believe," John 6:36), we must admit that seeing in full daylight does not yet determine an un-covering (above, chapter 10). It is not surprising, therefore, that the text of John that is the closest to the principle of un-covering from the Synoptics is paradoxically attributed to those who do not believe, and who, for that very reason, advise Jesus to go accomplish even more visible signs on the stage of Jerusalem to make himself more openly recognized there: "His brothers thus said to him: 'Pass from here into Judea, so that your disciples [from Judea and Jerusalem] may also see the works that you have done. No one acts in secret (ἐν κρυπτῷ) when he searches to be in presence and authority (ἐν παρρησίᾳ). If you do the same things, you will make yourself manifest in the world (φανέρωσον σεαυτὸν τῷ κόσμῳ).' For his own brothers did not believe in him" (John 7:3–5). The "brothers" are false brothers, who do not do the will of God (Mark 3:35), but believe they can achieve an un-covering by compensating for their lack of faith with a worldly visibility. In fact, they anticipate the onlookers who, before Jesus on the cross, railed at him out of defiance, but also out of worldly logic, "save yourself (σῶσον σεαυτὸν) and us!" (Luke 23:39) And so it is not surprising that Jesus, who will nevertheless later claim to have never "said anything in secret (ἐν κρυπτῷ)" and always to have "spoken openly (παρρησίᾳ)" (John 18:20), and of whom Paul will affirm that "it is not in a little corner (ἐν γωνίᾳ) that this was done" (Acts 26:26), here rejects this trivial staging, organized in the public square to promote him like an object: so "he went up [i.e., to Jerusalem] without being seen, but in secret (ἐν κρυπτῷ)" (John 7:10), not to make himself acclaimed and seen, but to see the Father in praying to him. And this refusal rests on a decisive criterion, namely, its temporality, its favorable time: "My moment (ὁ καιρὸς ὁ ἐμὸς) is not yet here (οὔπω πάρεστιν), where yours is always at hand (ἕτοιμος)" (7:6). Indeed, the moment of un-covering is not organized by human will, any more than one "organizes an event" (oxymoron!) in the world. It comes in its time (*kairos*), which does not depend on us, but which arises *from elsewhere*: from the will of the Father. The manifestation of the un-covering does not come any more from a decision of Jesus than from a worldly organization: it comes to Jesus from the Father, and as his Son. The un-covering of the Son, of Jesus as the Son of the Father, depends on the Father and on him alone. "About that day and that hour, no one knows anything, neither the angels of heaven, nor the Son, but the Father alone" (Matthew 24:36). The temporal criterion of visibility is deepened into a Trinitarian criterion of un-covering, which alone assumes the role of first principle (see chapters 15–18).

Because of this reversal, witnessed by the debates following Jesus's initial refusal to be made into a spectacle at the Temple (as "some of the people from Jerusalem," John 7:25, observed that in fact, despite his hidden arrival, Jesus "speaks openly" [παρρησίᾳ] there), they came to suspect that the "authorities" let him do so because they "knew (ἔγνωσαν) that he is the Christ" (7:25–26). However, a counterargument prevents them from recognizing Jesus as Christ: his supposed origin. "But we know *from where* he comes (οἴδαμεν πόθεν ἐστίν), whereas when the Christ comes, no one will know *from where* he comes (οὐδεὶς γινώσκει πόθεν ἐστίν)" (7:27–28).

This provokes a debate on the origins of Jesus. "In the crowd, many heard and said: 'It is really him, the prophet!' Others said, 'It is the Christ'! But others responded: 'Would the Christ come from Galilee then? Does not Scripture say that Christ must come from the offspring of David and from the town of Bethlehem?' (Micah 5:1). The crowd was divided because of him" (7:40–43). Yet this division (σχίσμα) still masks the heart of the matter; for if the inhabitants of Jerusalem did not know Jesus as Christ, it is not only nor primarily because they are not correctly informed of his birth "in Bethlehem of Judaea" and they imagine he was born in Nazareth, in Galilee; it is above all because they all assume they "know" that his origin is found on earth, and in this world, in short, that he comes, as all other men, from among men. Where do they draw this certitude from? In fact, the crowd and the Pharisees invoke Scripture (7:43), and therefore the Law (7:49) to form themselves into the position of subjects presumed as knowing. Here everyone knows, and knows that he knows (γιγνώσκειν, 7:26; εἰδέναι, 7:27, 29; διδάσκειν, 7:28); and Jesus denounces their illusion: "And [you say] you know me and know *from where* (πόθεν) I come. But I have not come from myself, but there is truly one who sent me, one that you do not know (ὃν ὑμεῖς οὐκ οἴδατε)" (7:28). Indeed, if one holds to the Scriptures, or rather their interpretation as certain knowledge at a human level, the question can be settled: "Search the Scriptures!" (7:52) Nicodemus is told. But there is something, or rather someone, whom everyone does not know; the origin (πόθεν ἐστίν) of Jesus *as* Christ is found neither in Bethlehem nor in Nazareth (nor even in Jerusalem!—4:21) but in the *elsewhere* of the Father. The concept is not summed up in such-and-such a title that could be recognized as belonging to Jesus, and that as such would suffice to confess him correctly; the adequacy of the confession does not in the final instance depend on such and such a concept, but on the *referral* of each concept, inadequate in itself, to the one who qualifies it and disqualifies it at the same time, to the *elsewhere* that opens onto the Father and comes from him. In other words, the concept must come from above, since its adequacy can only arrive *from elsewhere*. "He is true, the one who has sent me, and you do not know him (ὃν ὑμεῖς οὐκ οἴδατε)" (7:28). The secret origin of Jesus, which makes him a Son, is in the *mystērion*, the Name of the Father.

Un-covering "from Above": Nicodemus

The correct signification is thus not located in any of those that could have been literally known by adequation, but in its "true" location, its referral to the depth of the Father who gives it: I come *from elsewhere* than from myself. This is what Nicodemus tried, in vain, to make the Pharisees admit (John 7:50–52); and he only risked doing so before them because he had already heard it from Jesus (John 3:1–21). Now Nicodemus's dialogue with Jesus becomes retrospectively clear.[3] It consists in three questions by Nicodemus, which are met with three responses from Jesus; each is introduced by the double *amen, amen* (proper to Jesus in the Gospel of John; here 3:3, 3:5, and 3:11), which reverses the position of the master teacher from Nicodemus to Jesus (3:2 and 3:10) and three times lifts the prohibition of the impossible—"How can all these things happen?" (3:9, following 3:2; 3:4 and 5)

Consider the first moment. Nicodemus comes to visit Jesus; although a dissident (he has come in secret and at night), he stands as a de facto "authority (ἄρχων)" among the "Jews" (3:1). He does not belong (yet) to the number of the disciples,[4] but he concedes to Jesus the minimal dignity granted to him by the other Pharisees: he is a "master," as is confirmed by the signs he has accomplished (3:2). But this is precisely the reason for their quarrel with him, that his teaching authority (παρρησία) coincides with this power (ἐξουσία) that confirms it: "how in God's name is it possible" that God is with him, while he seems to flatly contradict the Law (3:3)? The debate finally rests on the point of knowing who, here, will teach the other: Will it be Jesus, whom Nicodemus greets *a minima* as a "teacher, a master, διδάσκαλος," or will it be Nicodemus, to whom Jesus ironically returns the compliment, "You are a master, διδάσκαλος, a teacher in Israel and you do not know these things?" (3:10) But the first response of Jesus radically modifies the question, which is transposed from the teaching to the origin of the one who gives it: "If someone is not born from above (ἄνωθεν), it is impossible for him to see (οὐ δύναται ἰδεῖν) the Kingdom of God" (3:3). Further, it is not only about teaching, but about seeing; better still, it is no longer about seeing, but the possibility of seeing: the possibility of seeing depends on the possibility (or not) of "being born from above, ἄνωθεν." In referring Nicodemus back to the vision of the "Kingdom of God" (the only use in John, here in agreement with the

Synoptics), Jesus refers him to the final break, to the frontier between the possible and the impossible: either one belongs to the world and comprehends all things from its point of view, or else one conceives all things "from above," in other words, *from elsewhere*. The question of hierarchy between the two "teachers" disappears; the question of the impossible and of the *elsewhere* arises.

In the second moment, Nicodemus tries to conceive this "above," but can only succeed in doing so (or rather does not succeed in doing so) by understanding it starting from the world: he understands *anōthen* temporally, as in being born "a second time (δεύτερον),"⁵ returning to his mother's womb to emerge from it by a kind of palingenesis. But being born of the spirit does not mean becoming someone "born again";⁶ the "possibility of entering (εἰσελθεῖν εἰς) the kingdom of God" (3:5) does not consist in being reborn (again, a second time), but in being born for the first time "from above (ἄνωθεν)"; in other words to be born at last and for the first time *from elsewhere*. This is not "amazing (θαυμάσῃς)" since we have "heard the sound of the breath" of the Spirit, even though we do not know "where it comes from (πόθεν ἔρχεται)" nor "where (ποῦ) it blows" (3:7–8). Our ignorance about the ends and results of the breath of the Spirit does not mean that the Spirit does not blow, but confirms and attests that it blows *from elsewhere*; if we knew from where or to where it was blowing, it would not be the spirit *from elsewhere*, but a worldly phenomenon, an object of a weather forecast. Like the people of Galilee and Jerusalem, our powerlessness to know "from where (πόθεν)" Jesus comes finds here its meaning and scope: it is a *felix ignorantia*, necessary to the experience of the *elsewhere*, which would not be un-covered as such if we knew its direction. We begin to recognize Jesus as such only when we receive what he says starting from his own place: "I know from where (πόθεν) I come and where (ποῦ) I am going; but you do not know from where (πόθεν) I come and where (ποῦ) I am going. You judge according to the flesh" (8:14). This positive ignorance, which alone opens the *elsewhere*, perhaps also allows us to conceive, in a certain way (probably not the only one), that it is by leaving that Christ comes to us: "You have heard that I said to you: 'I am going and I will come to you'" (14:28).⁷ The departure in fact opens the distance from which the *elsewhere* arises, and thus it un-covers the paternal origin of Jesus as Son.

In a third moment, the break with what the world can and cannot understand is marked by the exclamation of Nicodemus: "How can these things happen (πῶς δύναται ταῦτα γενέσθαι)?" (3:9), a bewilderment that anticipates that of many others, including that of Pilate, "What is the truth?" (18:38).[8] Nicodemus could not conceive that *anōthen* refers to the *elsewhere* of the Spirit, outside time and outside the world, outside of the time of the world (for there is no other); he understood only what the world meant by it, being born "a second time." And so he is exposed to the irony of Jesus, who is astonished that a teacher of the Law does not know what the Spirit is about (3:10), the same astonishment as that of the "Jews" who were "astonished (ἐθαύμαζον)" that Jesus "knew the Scriptures without having learned them (οἶδεν μὴ μεμαθηκώς)" (7:15); or as that of the man born blind toward the Pharisees: "What is astonishing (θαυμαστόν) is that you do not know *from where* (οὐκ οἴδατε πόθεν) he comes" (9:30). So it becomes clear that there is no access to the *elsewhere* by any other way than the *elsewhere* itself: one must enter it all at once, by anamorphosis, like one enters a hermeneutic circle.

From this follows another result as a corollary: we might find here the reason for the absence of every recourse to parable in John: "If you do not believe me when I tell you the things of earth (τὰ ἐπίγεια), how will you believe me when I tell you the things of heaven?" (3:12). Indeed, as we have seen in the Synoptics (above chapter 13), every parable supposes a continuity between the starting point of the story, which follows everyday life as closely as possible, and its end point in the *elsewhere*, which exposes the listener to his decision of interpretation. Yet here arises an impassable discontinuity between the "things of earth" and the "things of heaven"; this sharp and blunt break, which takes the name of a crisis ("the one who believes in him [i.e., the Son] is not judged, but the one who does not believe in him is already judged" 3:18), thus no longer allows progress along the way of parable; what is left is to proceed by way of paradox.[9] The first of these paradoxes is stated without ambiguity: no one can ascend to heaven except the one who descends from it (3:13). No one from the first Covenant (neither Abraham, nor Moses, nor Elijah, nor Enoch, nor "the prophet") could end up rising in a final ascent toward the *elsewhere*. Only the "Son of Man" (3:15) can open the heavens, because he comes from them; and he only comes from them, because he is from them; and he is from them as the "only Son" (3:16) of the only God. Humans therefore will only ascend to heaven by gazing at the one who comes from there, as the people gazed at the serpent erected in the desert by Moses (3:14–15).

And so, as a final culmination, the *elsewhere* constitutes the first gift of the Father—in the double sense of a gift made by the Father and a gift that consists in the very access to the Father. This gift comes "from above" as "every good givenness and every perfect gift" (James 1:17), but it comes first and preeminently. The Son comes *from elsewhere* like every gift of the Father, as the "wisdom from above" (John 3:15 and 17), as the one whom the Father gives ("God so loved the world, that he gave it his only Son," 3:16). And thus, because they "are one" (10:30, 17:11), the Son comes *from elsewhere* like "our Father in heaven" (Matthew 5:16) himself, as he gives. For *the Father, insofar as he gives, un-covers the Son, and the Son, insofar as he gives himself, un-covers the Father*. And thus to receive Jesus as such, that is, to receive him as Christ, means to receive him *from elsewhere*, as the very *elsewhere* of the Father. Unless this is the case—that the Son comes from the Father, only appears from him, and so makes the gift of the given, namely the Father—he does not un-cover himself.

Receiving the Bread Come from Elsewhere

The step that must be taken to reach the Son starting from the mere sight of Jesus can be identified on a number of occasions but probably nowhere more than in the "Bread of Life Discourse." It is thus unsurprising that it was received by the majority of its hearers as a "hard (σκληρός) discourse" (John 6:60). Its intellectual difficulty is not the problem: as always, everyone understands *on a certain level* what it is about; but it is precisely for that reason that the majority do not accept it. They understand it well enough to refuse it *knowingly*: "You have seen (with your eyes, ἑωράκατέ) but you have not believed" (6:36). What steps must be taken to be able to confess, like Simon Peter, that "we have believed and known that you are the Holy One of God" (6:69, the same formula as the demon in Mark 1:24)? Under the guise of a theoretical question (a request for information, the solution of an aporia, the reply to an argument), each step consists in a more or less voluntary decision to shift, or not, to the point of view of Jesus—which implies first of all conceiving this point of view, and thus attaining it.

The first moment (6:24ff) acknowledges their hunger; "the crowd" wants to know when Jesus arrived in Capernaum; and Jesus immediately corrects the terms of the question: the people were not seeking to understand the teaching that the "signs" (multiplication of bread) have just qualified, but only to once again eat their fill (6:26). He exhorts them to change foods, passing from perishable food to that which gives eternal life and which is given by the Son of Man. The second moment consists in changing hungers, thus identifying and confessing the true hunger. It ends in repeating, now with bread ("Lord, give us this bread always," 6:34), the discussion about living water with the Samaritan woman ("Lord, give me this water, that I will not thirst nor have to come here to draw water," 4:15).[10] Indeed, if Jesus desires to be recognized as bearing the "seal" of the Father (6:27), he must claim to show, by giving the multiplied bread, a sign at least equal to the manna that Moses had given to the people. Nevertheless, Jesus rejects this improper Mosaic paradigm, by reestablishing that the manna was a gift from the Father, and not from Moses. The bread of God thus comes down from God and God alone.

The third moment (6:35–40) consists in accepting Christ himself as this bread and this food: "I am the bread of life" (6:35 and 6:48). In what sense and by what right can Jesus claim this? In the sense that he himself is given to the world to save it, given from heaven like the manna that God gave to the people from heaven. But, once again, by what right can Jesus claim to give to the world nothing less than the bread of God, and thus to give himself as the gift of God? In this: that if on the one hand his will wants only the will of the Father ("I have not come down from heaven to do my will, but the will of him who sent me," 6:38); if, on the other hand, the will of the Father is sufficient to nourish him ("I have another food to eat that you do not know about.... My food is to do the will of him who sent me," he said to his disciples in Samaria, 4:32 and 34); then not only is Jesus nourished by the will of the Father, but, because he acts "in the same way" (5:19) as it, to the point that it becomes his "daily bread" (Matthew 6:11), he himself has also *become* this bread. He gives the bread that nourishes him, the only nourishing bread, and which he is assimilated to—the will of the Father, to do and to eat. The obstacle to receiving such a discourse can now be identified: if the majority "have seen, but have not believed" (6:36), it is not exactly because they did not see (they certainly saw the signs and heard the teachings), but because they did not *want to believe* (and therefore see) what they saw with their eyes—that Jesus was *not* the one "whose father and mother [they] know": that, although they did not understand "how (πῶς)" (6:42), he did not belong to the world as it is. To see him, one must believe he comes from *elsewhere:* "No one can come to me unless the Father who sent me draws him" (6:44, see above chapter 9). No one can see Jesus as such, and thus as the Son, if he does not believe that he comes from heaven, or in other words, that he lives only by the will of the Father.

The final moment (6:45–59) draws the final implication from the fact that Jesus gives (himself as) "the bread of life" (6:33): he can only truly do so (and only truly is) because he refers exclusively to the Father, such that he only gives life insofar as he accomplishes the will of the Father and comes from him. He only gives "the bread come down from heaven" (6:51) insofar as he comes down from heaven (continuously, one might venture to say), has seen the Father, and is one with him: "No one has seen the Father, except the one who is from the Father; he has seen the Father" (6:46). It is only on this condition that Jesus can in truth claim to appear as the Son and give himself as the bread of life. Here believing makes one see, because believing that Jesus gives the bread of life from the Father, that he comes down from the Father because he comes from him—this makes it possible to see him in his depth. The face of Jesus is no longer a screen at a visible depth, since we can, if we believe, see in it the work of his will doing that of the Father (and not his own), the work of another will that he makes all the more his own since he applies himself to conforming his will as closely as possible to the Father's. His face opens according to the filial depth onto the "mystery" of the will of the Father. In interpreting the face of Jesus as that of a perfect son, as that of *the* Son, we *see* in it the gaze of the Father on him and thus on us: "Whoever believes in me, it is not in me that he believes, but in the one who sent me" (12:44); such that in relating himself in this way in the will of Christ to that of the Father, the believer sees on the face of Christ the one face of the Father: "whoever sees me sees the Father (ὁ ἑωρακὼς ἐμὲ ἑώρακεν τὸν Πατέρα)" (14:9).

The debate over the bread that God gives as food to his people (manna) and to the whole world (the "bread of life") leads, through so many hermeneutic steps, first to the identification of the bread with Christ, then Christ with the will of the Father as his daily bread, and finally the depth of Christ's face [*visage*] with the very aim of the Father who is invisible, but targetable [*visable*] and seeing [*qui envisage*]. The final confession of Simon Peter, which recognizes Jesus as "the Holy One of God" (John 6:69), therefore takes on, more than in the Synoptics, the fullness of its already Trinitarian scope: Jesus appears as the Holy One of God because nothing in him differs, diverges, or deviates from the will of the Father. And we understand even better, in light of John, why Peter, after his confession in Matthew 16:17–20, is rebuffed and treated as "Satan" (Matthew 16:23). What fault did he commit? He refused Jesus's proclamation of his Passion. "May God forbid, Lord! It will never be so!"[11] His fault thus consists in not accepting to envisage the Passion (16:21) from the Father's point of view, but instead clinging to that of men: he understands it only as an excruciating and unjust death, without being able to conceive of it as the absolute and perfect accomplishment of the will to save humankind by doing the will of the Father. Peter rejects nothing less than the victorious act of Jesus, the glory of the Son, of having said, "Not as I will, but as you will" (Matthew 26:39–43), and of having done it. He thus clearly deserves to be treated by Jesus as an occasion of scandal (Matthew 16:23), even though he would nevertheless swear that if "everyone falls (σκανδαλισθήσονται), [he] will not" (Matthew 26:33). What is necessary to know how to see—that Jesus appears as the Son when his face opens up onto the depth of the Father—cannot be seen except by believing—precisely by entering into this depth.

Seeing the Son as He Is Seen and Sent by the Father

Now we see where the difficulty of the phenomenality of Jesus comes from: in order to see him as such, as the Christ, we must pass through a hermeneutic decision: when it is a question of recognizing Christ as "the bread of life" without stumbling over an obstacle ("does this scandalize you?"; John 6:61 and Matthew 16:23), we must cross the gap between the point of view of the flesh (σάρξ), which "is worthless," and that of the Spirit (πνεῦμά) (6:63).[12] This crossing implies a shift of the viewpoint of the gaze, in other words of the anamorphic point; and here in an anamorphosis so radical that no man can, of himself, accomplish it. So we must finally admit that only God can grant the accomplishment of anamorphosis that leads from the point of view of man to that of God. "No one can come to me, unless the Father who sent me draws him (ἑλκύσῃ αὐτόν, *traxerit*)" (John 6:44; see chapter 9 above); or again, "No one can come to me, unless it is given to him by the Father (δεδομένον αὐτῷ ἐκ τοῦ Πατρός)" (6:65). But if only the Father can make Jesus seen as the Son, what hope is there for the ordinary human being? Is it not a circle that presupposes itself: that only God grants the ability to take up God's point of view, which in turn would allow us to see God phenomenalize himself in Jesus? Clearly, we must see an aporia here, but at the same time the opening of a path. For one can reverse the objection and ask: If man cannot accomplish anamorphosis himself, what would be more logical than to infer that a path can only be opened up precisely if it comes to him *from elsewhere*, the *elsewhere* from which it comes, from that which (in this case, the one *whom*) the anamorphosis allows him to aim at? What is more: every anamorphosis *always* implies the traversing of a gap not only in view of an aim that remains inaccessible, at the beginning, according to the initial point of view; but it only crosses this gap in view of an unknown aim, which is defined little by little (or all at once) according to an elsewhere that, like a star, guides intentionality in this movement ("behold, the star went before them," Matthew 2:9). In fact, in *every* anamorphosis, even those of the world, the passage from one aim to another is *always* set in motion starting from the final aim: for it is the thing itself that makes *itself* seen as it gives *itself*; the one it calls to see can respond to it and follow it, but never constitute it or anticipate it. And the one who accomplishes anamorphosis (the lover, the genius, the *adonné*) does not succeed because he can or wants to, but because he has the strength to become *weak* enough, docile enough to let himself be drawn by a saturated phenomenon seizing him, guiding him across the desert on an anamorphic journey, leading him finally to the promised land—the heralded un-covering. And so, to break our powerlessness to see the phenomenon offered by Christ, we must no longer cling to our point of view in order to dodge a logical circle; we must rather strive to enter into the hermeneutic circle all at once (or little by little), but as resolutely as possible. To take the correct point of view on the phenomenon that God gives to be seen (in Jesus Christ) can indeed only come from God himself (the Father), who offers at the same time the phenomenon (that which shows itself) and the conditions of its visibility (what shows itself as it gives itself). And since this can only come from *elsewhere* (from the Father), it cannot be the object of our will, our decision, or any action that we could or should produce, but only of a will, a decision, and an action that remains for us to give, or in this case, to receive. *The one who shows himself, Christ, cannot be seen unless we place ourselves at the very point of view of the one who gives him, the Father.* Christ can thus only be seen if the Father gives access to this point of view. "For our God, Jesus Christ, appears better in being in the Father (ἐν πατρὶ ὢν μᾶλλον φαίνεται)" (Ignatius of Antioch).¹³ Hence this paradox, that the more Christ goes to the Father, the more he manifests himself *as such*: "That I am going away, this will be to your advantage" (John 16:7).

The question of the identity of Jesus ("Who do you say that I am?") thus finds its correct response in the point of view of the Father, who gives us to see the one that he gives, or more precisely, who gives us the self-showing of that which he gives. Recognizing Jesus as the Christ implies referring him to the Father, and in two ways. First because Jesus merits the title of Christ only as the Son of the Father, therefore by essential reference to the Father who *gives* him to himself; next because Jesus can only *show* himself, make himself seen and recognized to the one who sees him from the point of view of the Father. The Father establishes the condition of Christ, as he gives him and as the latter shows himself. The Father thus constitutes at the same time the depths of the unseen of the Son, the unseen manifested in the depth of the visibility of Christ, the face of Jesus, and the condition of un-covering of the Son as such, as his envoy. Hence the rule that governs the crossed phenomenality of the Father and of the Son: "No one knows the Son except the Father, no one knows the Father except the Son and the one to whom the Son has desired to un-cover him (καὶ ᾧ ἐὰν βούληται ὁ Υἱὸς ἀποκαλύψαι)" (Matthew 11:27; see Luke 10:22). Second, because, if it is not possible to see Jesus as the Son except by seeing him in his being sent by the Father, it becomes possible in return to see, in the sending of the Son, the Father as he sends him. In other words, following John, "'I am the Way, the Truth, and the Life. No one comes to the Father except through me. If you know me, you will know the Father. From now on you do know him and have seen him (ἀπ' ἄρτι γινώσκετε αὐτὸν καὶ ἑωράκατε).' Philip said to him: 'Lord, show us the Father and that is enough for us.' Jesus said to him: 'Have I been with you so long and you do not know me, Philip? Whoever has seen me has seen the Father (ὁ ἑωρακὼς ἐμὲ ἑώρακεν τὸν Πατέρα). How can you say, "Show us the Father?" Do you not believe that I am in the Father and the Father is in me?'" (14:6–10). Nothing is a better confirmation that the Father constitutes the depths of that which gives itself in the Son and the form that allows the Son to show himself, than a proof by contrast: without reference to the Father, the identity of Jesus—his status as Son—becomes immediately illegible: "you do not know me, nor the Father. If you knew me, you would know the Father also (εἰ ἐμὲ ᾔδειτε, καὶ τὸν Πατέρα μου ἂν ᾔδειτε)" (8:19).[14] This is how the Father and the Son "work" (5:17): the Father gives the one who shows himself (as the *ratio donandi* of the Son), and the Son shows the one who gives himself (as the *ratio manifestandi* of the Father). This is how to accomplish the anamorphosis which makes us pass from our point of view on Jesus to the Father's point of view on Jesus as his Son. This is how it becomes possible to cross the visibility of Christ and reach the invisibility that gives itself there, that of the Father.

The Obedience of the Son

This journey of anamorphosis therefore fixes, for the disciples, for us, for all who are called to see, the way of seeing Christ as such. But the one whom they can see in this way is himself defined also and first of all by the journey of anamorphosis: he lives and gives himself to be seen (to be recognized) to the extent that he is ceaselessly carrying out anamorphosis and accomplishes it to perfection. For all that, if the journey of anamorphosis makes it possible to shift the intentional aim's point of origin to the point where it can effectively aim at and see Jesus as Son, and, by the sending of the Son, refer him back to the Father, this approach clearly does not abolish the gap between the Son and the Father, because it plays out in it and attests it all the more. As a result, the Son, the role that Jesus assumes as Christ, is not only never confused with the Father, but he refers back to him all the more as he acknowledges that he depends on him, submits to him, and surrenders himself to him without measure. The Son makes the Father appear all the more because he acts as his true Son, that is, he identifies him as his other, as prior to him, as "greater" than him (John 14:18). This is established by a number of paradoxes.

The first paradox relates to the equality of Jesus with God. The condemnation of Jesus, at least the religious one, is based on a fact publicly witnessed by the Sanhedrin: in answer to the question "Are you the Son of God?" either he responds affirmatively, "I am" (Mark 14:62), or he allows his questioners to provide the obviously positive response themselves: "You have said so" (Matthew 26:64), "It is you who say that I am" (22:70). This convergence of narratives corresponds to what his listeners immediately understood: because Jesus purifies the Temple as the "house of [his] Father" (John 2:16), since he authorizes himself to "work" on the Sabbath like "[his] Father" (5:17), he claims a divine rank: "Not only did he unbind himself from the Sabbath, but he called God his own Father, making himself equal to God (ἴσον ἑαυτὸν ποιῶν τῷ Θεῷ)" (5:18). And Jesus confirms this when he affirms that "I and the Father are one" (10:39), when he claims that "All that is mine is yours, and what is yours is mine" (17:19; see also Luke 14:31).

Or rather he *almost* confirms it. For the debate on the potential blasphemy depends on the way this equality is conceived, which can vary tremendously. For Jesus's adversaries (as for us, in our natural presumptions today), the equality of Christ with God should be understood as at least the possibility of breaking free from the anteriority of God, exempting oneself from the primordial power of the Father, or in short, reclaiming possession of the self, in order to "be like God" (Genesis 3:5). For Jesus, on the other hand, becoming like God means to interpret God as a Father, thus becoming like the Father—as one who gives everything without holding anything back. Or better: this means to conform to God as Father, thus responding to his gift without reserve in recognizing that we have "nothing that we have not received" (1 Corinthians 4:7). Elevating oneself to the rank of God means, then, to *equal* the absolute gift given by the Father, by means of the Son's *equally* unreserved abandonment to this gift. For Jesus, equality of God only takes place in the play where God manifests himself as such, as the Father who gives everything. It is indeed a matter of equaling God, but equaling him according to his own logic, the logic of the gift. Equality means, for Jesus as for God, for the Christ as for his Father, only the equality in the process of the gift, received as it is given up, *to the full*. And Jesus receives the title of Son, the "name that is above every name," that of the "Lord Jesus Christ" (Philippians 2:9–11) for this reason alone—he equaled the gift given "without repentance" (Romans 11:29) by the Father in his surrender "to the end" (John 13:1; see 19:30). In other words, "While in the position of having a divine form (ἐν μορφῇ Θεοῦ ὑπάρχων), he did not consider [the fact of] being equal to God as something to cling to (οὐχ ἁρπαγμὸν ἡγήσατο τὸ εἶναι ἴσα Θεῷ)" (Philippians 2:6). For him (but not for his accusers, nor for us), equality allows the perfect path from the distance of the Father to the

Son and the Son to the Father; and thus it implies first of all recognizing the principal anteriority of the Father over the Son: "The Father is greater than I" (John 14:28); next it implies admitting that the Son must by definition receive everything from the Father: "I can do nothing on my own" (5:30). Moreover, not only does Jesus's equality with God not contradict the communion of the Son with the Father, but it reinforces it by the reciprocal distance of the gift, where the Father abandons everything to the Son in order to accomplish his fatherhood and thus allows him to accomplish his sonship; and where the Son accepts everything from the Father in order to thus recognize his fatherhood and to receive from him his own sonship: "All that is mine is yours, and what is yours is mine" (John 17:10).[15] The equality of divine conditions allows communion by gift, abandonment, and re-giving of the gift, without end. This, the world (and thus the adversaries of Jesus) cannot see: for them, equality with divine conditions, like the equality of conditions between men, can only lead to mimetic rivalry and the fight to the death. This is the paradox of equality as communion.

From this follows another paradox: Jesus, even when he asks to be recognized as the Christ, continually emphasizes that he does not say anything of himself: "The words I say to you, I do not say them of myself (ἀπ' ἐμαυτοῦ οὐ λαλῶ)" (John 14:10). Or again, "I have not come of myself (ἀπ' ἐμαυτοῦ), but it is he who sent me" (8:42). At first glance, Jesus compromises his request for recognition: because he does not speak "of himself," he does not say what he thinks and perhaps does not think what he says; how, in this ambiguity, could he inspire and receive the least acceptance? How could he even ask for a frank and good-faith engagement, if he himself is not speaking openly and in good faith? In this sense (ours, that of our time and our ideology), Christ lacks (good) self-awareness; he is not himself; he speaks and acts in perfect *inauthenticity*.

Unless here again everything must be reversed. For, from Christ's point of view, *our* way of speaking authentically amounts to speaking from oneself, saying *nothing except* what I think by myself and according to myself alone, thus not thinking what the Father thinks. Authenticity means that I think and speak directly from myself and from my own point of view; it excludes every anamorphosis; it precisely characterizes the one who *does not say* what the Father means, the one whose thinking screens and masks that of God; in a word, the one who covers up the word of God by his own. This is exactly the posture of Satan: "When he tells a lie, he speaks from his own [i.e., thoughts] (ἐκ τῶν ἰδίων λαλεῖ), because he is a liar and the father of lies" (8:44). To speak from oneself, from one's own resources, saying what one has on one's mind or heart, implies speaking from what one has *in* the heart; for "out of the heart come evil thoughts, murder, sexual immorality, fornication, theft, false witness, blasphemy" (Matthew 15:19). Speaking from oneself, with an open heart, *wholeheartedly*, amounts to lighting "the fire of the tongue, a world of wickedness," for the authenticity of Satan sets the forest on fire (James 3:5–6). It is "in the heart" that "the devil" comes to settle (John 13:2), "in the house of the strong man" who comes "to plunder" (Matthew 12:29) and "live there" (12:45). It is therefore necessary to leave one's own heart, one's own authenticity, to speak according to the word of another, the only true other, God as Father. Only the one who does not speak from himself *succeeds* at this, because he satisfies the most exacting condition: Jesus *speaks from elsewhere*, insofar as he "does not seek [his] own will, but that of the one who sent [him]" (John 5:30; see also 6:38); and people have trouble accepting him precisely because he does not speak of himself, as they do, because he does not have the same thought as them, because he does not want with the same evil will that they want: "I have come in my Father's name, and you have not received me; but if another came in his own name (ἐν τῷ ὀνόματι τῷ ἰδίῳ), you would receive him" (John 5:43). Framed in this way, inauthenticity defines the path across the gap between the human point of view and God's, a path that alone allows one to see Jesus as the Christ, thus as the Son of the Father. Understood in this eminent sense, inauthenticity (literally, disappropriation, impropriety) results in no longer belonging to oneself, but surrendering oneself to another than oneself, in being exiled *elsewhere*, in order to let this *elsewhere* grasp one's self. In a word, inauthenticity once again indicates anamorphosis and its achievement. And Jesus makes it known as such—as conformity of one's will to the will of the one who sent him—in making appear what decisively separates him from his adversaries: "Who among you will convict me of sin?" (8:46).[16] The gap between the two dispositions of authenticity and inauthenticity defines exactly the two possible poles of intentionality—the masterful point of view of the transcendental posture and the displaced point of view of anamorphosis: "The one who speaks from himself (ὁ ἀφ' ἑαυτοῦ λαλῶν) seeks his own glory; the one who seeks the glory of the one who sent him is truthful, and there is no injustice in him" (7:18). And in fact no one has accomplished anamorphosis as perfectly as Christ, insofar as he refers, as Son, absolutely and without ceasing to the Father's point of view. Human beings, starting with Peter, only follow in his footsteps, from a worldly place to a Trinitarian place and, by the same token, a phenomenally operative one. It was, then, a question of the paradox of inauthenticity as a feature of filiation.

These initial paradoxes perhaps allow us to touch on one more, if only indirectly: the old question of the awareness that Jesus had (or not) of his divinity. We note first of all that the seriousness of the Incarnation (or rather of the *Menschwerdung*, of the becoming man) of God in Jesus implies that, like every man, Jesus did not have the perfect awareness of what he was as a man from the outset, and in a sense never attained it; for this very fact is what defines man, to not know exactly who one really is for one's whole life.[17] However, to know oneself does not consist in capturing a clear, final, and reflexive consciousness of what one is, but rather in no longer being mistaken about what one cannot be, and, above all, what one can be as far as one ought. So it was for Jesus. Indeed, he learned who he was by discovering it as he did it; but he learned it from what he did *by obeying* his Father, in each of his varied encounters—with his family, his "brothers," the "teachers" at the Temple, John the Baptist, the tempter in the desert, the crowds, the disciples, the demons, the gentiles of Galilee and the scribes of Jerusalem, the trial and the cross; each time sensing more and more and achieving his destiny step by step. "Driven by the Holy Spirit" (Matthew 4:1; Mark 1:12; Luke 4:1), Jesus learned to act as the Christ and thus to become through our condition what he was from all eternity: he learned to perform in the flesh and among us his function as eternal Son. From baptism to agony, from death to Resurrection, he learned who he always was by accomplishing it in our terms, with our actions and our words. So there is not the slightest contradiction between this grasp of the temporal consciousness of Jesus and the perfect eternal consciousness of the Son. The perfect Trinitarian consciousness has accepted to lower itself to human consciousness of itself by taking the condition of man. For temporality belongs to the condition of the creature, and eternity to God. The Incarnation of Christ thus had to join together, without separation or confusion, the one and the other.

This learning process is not the result of an accidental pedagogical constraint on Jesus (the ancient and vulgar scholastic position), nor even a proleptic between the proclamation of the kingdom and its post-Paschal justification (the recent and superficial scholastic conception), but arises from what the Son had to un-cover to us by accomplishing it for and among us. Eternal sonship is played out, in a human way and in a situation of sin, under the form of obedience, obedience unto death, but the death of a Son un-covering the Father: "He, in the days of his flesh, offering prayers and supplications with a loud cry and tears, to the one who could save him, was heard for his piety (εἰσακουσθεὶς ἀπὸ τῆς εὐλαβείας, *pro sua reverentia*); and indeed being Son, he learned obedience (ὑπακοήν, *oboedientiam*) from what he suffered, and, thus fulfilled (τελειωθείς, *consummatus*), he became the cause of eternal salvation for all who obey him in return (ὑπακούουσιν, *obtemporentibus*)" (Hebrews 5:7–9). This text, as clear as it is precise, presents first of all the details of the Passion[18] as acts of piety toward God, who "can save" (see "Πατήρ, πάντα δυνατά σοι," Mark 14:36). However, "to save" does not necessarily mean saving *from* death (in this sense Jesus would not have been answered),[19] but can also indicate saving reverence toward God *even in* death (and in this sense Jesus was answered). From this, we see that the eternal Son accomplishes obedience to the Father even in the sinful condition of humanity; and, as he assumed it, he indeed "learned, ἔμαθεν, *didicit*" among us what he is eternally for the Father. The obedience fulfills (ὑπακοή and τελειωθείς), manifests, and confirms, this time in our finitude and in the situation of sin, eternal Trinitarian filiation. Evil and death are defeated "once and for all," because they have not been able to wipe out the eternal Trinitarian play. The humiliation of Christ on the cross repeats, through the distorting prism of evil, the Son's humility in the Trinitarian situation. In both cases, what clearly manifests the Son as Son of the Father consists in the fact that he never refers to himself, but always and first of all to the Father. Jesus manifests himself as the Son, in other words, the Christ appears as the Son, only by the perfection of his obedience (listening, ἀκοή), which causes the salvation of "those who obey him" (who listen, τοῖς ὑπακούουσιν) only because they imitate him precisely in this way. One could even conclude that the task of Jesus does not require that he succeed in making everyone believe in him or glorify him (in fact, that was not the case), but to make those who believe in him and those who do not believe in him always and in every situation (including death on the cross) refer to the Father, so that it thus becomes patently clear that he himself refers to the Father, and thereby manifests him. In this way, everything brought about by his words is referred to the one who sent him, to the Father: "Whoever believes in me does not believe in me, but in the one who sent me (Ὁ πιστεύων εἰς ἐμὲ οὐ πιστεύει εἰς ἐμὲ ἀλλὰ εἰς τὸν πέμψαντά με). And whoever sees me, sees the one who sent me (ὁ θεωρῶν ἐμὲ θεωρεῖ τὸν πέμψαντά με)" (John 12:44–45).[20] Jesus attests that he is the Christ to the extent that, by obeying until the end, he manifests another than himself, the Father—an other who then qualifies him as his Son. The glory of Jesus consists in being confounded with the glory of the Father that envelops him.

The Glory of His Father

The confession of Peter consists, then, in taking Jesus into view from the point of view from which the Father gives him and sees him—as the "Holy One of God," who comes down from heaven to do the will of another, the Father, and who thus shows himself by showing how to accomplish the one and only anamorphosis: for him, taking the Father's point of view (doing the will of the Father and not his own), for us, taking the point of the view of the Son doing the will of the Father (and thereby seeing the Son as coming from and going to the Father). When these two acts of anamorphosis coincide and the faith of the disciple finds its place within the movement of obedience of the Son to the Father, then the one who believes *in this way* obtains eternal life *as well*, because he sees the Son as Son of the Father, and thus enters into the vision of the Father. "This is the will of my Father, that everyone who sees the Son and believes in him should have eternal life (πᾶς ὁ θεωρῶν τὸν Υἱὸν καὶ πιστεύων εἰς αὐτὸν ἔχῃ ζωὴν αἰώνιον)" (John 6:40). It is enough to believe it in order to see it, for the anamorphosis of faith repeats the Trinitarian anamorphosis that makes Jesus appear as the Christ, Son to the Father. But "there are some among you who do not believe (οὐ πιστεύουσιν)" (6:64), or in other words, those who have not accomplished the anamorphosis by their own gaze, cannot see that which Christ accomplishes. Or we might say that they see without believing ("ἑωράκατέ με καὶ οὐ πιστεύετε," 6:36), but then they see in Jesus nothing more than the "son of Joseph" (6:42); that is, they do not see him at all as he shows himself, because they do not see him as the one whom the Father gives them.

Thus, we find ourselves provoked to see what shows itself by the excess of what gives itself. But, as what gives itself to us is given first between Father and Son, what shows itself to us *ad extra* rises from the *ad intra* phenomenality of the Trinity with itself. Or again: if what is manifested to us in Christ consists in nothing less than in the aim of the Son toward the Father and the Father's view on the Son, then we must admit that the Trinitarian play is opened even to our view, even in this world. Not because the Trinity would be worldly and thus go outside of itself (*alienated* from itself) but, just the opposite, because the world is open and raised up outside of itself, in a supreme play that it cannot see because it encompasses it, as Stephen attests: "I see the heavens open and the Son of man standing at the right hand of the Father" (Acts 7:56). Only from this opening can we hear and correctly understand the public *invocations* made to the Son from the voice of the Father, or those made by the Son to the Father, which punctuate the Gospel of John,[21] as just so many *provocations* coming from the Trinity toward men, so that they might believe in order to see, repetitions of the warning, "Look what you hear!" (Mark 4:24)

And so we have the thanks given publicly to the Father by Jesus, before the resurrection of Lazarus, in order to make manifest to "the crowd (τὸν ὄχλον)" what he himself knows "always (πάντοτε)" takes place: "I thank you Father that you have heard [answered] me (Πάτερ, εὐχαριστῶ σοι ὅτι ἤκουσάς μου)" (John 11:41–42).[22] Jesus's prayer goes directly to the Father, and in this sense, differs completely even from Martha's confession to him, "Yes, I have believed that you are the Christ, the Son of God, who is come into the world" (11:27); for she did not see him in the Father, nor consider his status as Son. It could not be more clearly suggested that, for John, a perfect confession involves not only the recognition of the concept of Jesus as Christ, but the un-covering of the Father who attests his sonship.

So too, during the final public arrival at the Temple for the last Passover, when "the hour had come where the Son of man must be glorified" (12:23), when it becomes clear that the grain must die in order to bear fruit (12:24) and that the one who does not lose his life "in the world" will not save it "for eternal life" (12:25), when the ultimate moment awaited since the beginning at last arrives ("now (νῦν) my soul is troubled," 12:27),[23] the moment of crisis (νῦν, 12:31), then Jesus publicly asks the Father to confirm him in his function as Son, who precisely "came for this hour" (12:27): "Jesus [says] 'Father, glorify your name.' Then a voice came from heaven, [saying] 'I have glorified it, and I will glorify it again (πάλιν)'" (John 12:28). This confirmation of the Trinitarian glory is accomplished in the world itself; it is why "the crowd" does not "see" what they have nevertheless "heard (ἀκούσας)" (12:29; see Mark 4:24), neither "from where" nor from what *elsewhere* it came to them: Is it a thunderclap or an angel (12:29)? And yet, in spite of or precisely because of this incomprehension, Jesus warns one last time: "It is not for me, but for you that this voice has come" (12:30). Here again, it is not only a matter of seeing Jesus as the Christ (or not), but of seeing the Trinitarian origin and the legitimacy of this title: "The one who believes in me, does not believe in me, but in the one who sent me, and [thus] the one who sees me sees the one who sent me" (12:44–45). Jesus only merits the title of Christ because he appears as the Son *of the Father*, which he carries out precisely by only doing the will of the Father, by making his own the Father's will, by manifesting the Father himself in the will that he unfolds as his Son.

And finally, the last prayer before the arrest. Christ asks in front of his disciples to receive, even and above all at this nadir, the glory of his eternal zenith: "Father, the hour has come. Glorify the Son [who is] yours, that the Son may glorify you (δόξασόν σου τὸν Υἱόν, ἵνα ὁ Υἱὸς δοξάσῃ σέ)" (John 17:1); and "Glorify me now with the glory (νῦν δόξασόν με σύ) which I had with you before the world was" (John 17:5). Clearly, it is nothing less than the intra-Trinitarian glory that must be manifested to men "in the world," that it may show itself everywhere where it is given, which is to say, precisely, everywhere and even where it is rejected: "I have manifested your name to the men whom you gave me (Ἐφανέρωσά σου τὸ ὄνομα τοῖς ἀνθρώποις οὓς ἔδωκάς μοι)" (John 17:6). Such a manifestation *ad extra* of the Trinity to men (even unbelievers) does not imply any diminishment of the *mystērion* into some sort of negativity of spirit or worldly profanation; on the contrary, it provokes the "crowd" and especially the disciples to believe that which shows itself as it gives itself, and therefore to *enter into* the Trinity, far from the Trinity being dissolved in exteriority. The Trinitarian uncovering opens itself "In order that you may know and learn that the Father is in me and I am in the Father" (John 10:38). This is what is accomplished in the one who keeps the commandments, and who therefore loves Christ and is loved by the Father as Christ is loved; thus Christ "shows himself to him (ἐμφανίσω αὐτῷ ἐμαυτόν)" (John 14:20-1); and thus, in the end, it is "the Father in person who loves (αὐτὸς γὰρ ὁ Πατὴρ φιλεῖ ὑμᾶς)" (John 16:27; see John 14:21) those who find themselves, in fact and even by right, included in the Trinity, "that they may be one, even as we are one (ἓν καθὼς ἡμεῖς)" (John 17:11), "that they may all be one; even as you, Father, are in me, and I in you, that they also may be [one] in us (ἵνα ὁ κόσμος πιστεύῃ ὅτι σύ με ἀπέστειλας)" (John 17:21); "that they be completed to their end in unity (τετελειωμένοι εἰς ἕν)" (John 17:23). As much as the stake of the un-covering, the Trinity becomes its very *place*: we can see that which shows itself only by receiving it as it gives itself, that is, only by receiving ourselves from the one who gives himself, and who gives everything—including our seeing of it.

The Icon of the Invisible

Knowing the one, the Father, thus means knowing the other, the Son, and vice versa, provided we preserve their divergence without separation, their union without mixture. For what joins them is precisely the referral of the one to the other—of the Father who *gives* the Son to himself, the Son who *shows* the Father in himself. Only with this precaution can we conceive of Christ being defined as the "icon of the invisible God" (Colossians 1:15).

This formula remains enigmatic. Or at least it should remain so, and not dissipate its difficulty and its power into the flattened yet almost universally received translation of an "image of the invisible God." First, to understand it in this way results in a patent aporia: How could an image, which is by definition visible, ever make an invisible come into view? How could the *in*-visible *resemble* the visible? It would certainly be a contradiction in terms to imagine a doubled visible that would claim to directly preserve the vestiges of the invisible by imitation or representation: from the visible to the invisible, there is no continuity, image or likeness. Further, other New Testament uses of *eikōn* imply neither similitude nor likeness, but exclude them. For example, when in the discussion about paying taxes to the Romans, Jesus shows a coin bearing the effigy of Caesar and asks: "This *eikōn*, whose is it?" (Matthew 22:20; Mark 12:16; Luke 20:24). This face does not show anything identifiable;[24] for neither Jesus nor any of his listeners (perhaps even none of the Romans) had ever seen the face of Caesar (Augustine, Claudius, or another). All who pay the tax or use this money must rely on an identification that is *invisible*, if recognizable by public convention. This is why Jesus also asks that the identity of the unknown face be confirmed by the "inscription" (ἐπιγραφή), which identifies by name what the visible face leaves anonymous and invisible. Even in this banal case (the coin), the *eikōn* is not captured by an image, because it does not presuppose any likeness of visible to visible, but a relation of a visible (the inscription, although it shows nothing, but semantically designates) to an invisible (the face, which shows, but designates nothing).[25] Let us conclude that here, even more than with the coin, we must understand the *eikōn tou theou tou aoratou* as the icon of the invisible God. And it is all the more necessary to hold to this paradox as it is found again in Paul in two other cases, "Christ, who is the icon of God (εἰκὼν τοῦ Θεοῦ)" (2 Corinthians 4:4) and "according to the icon of the one who created it (κατ' εἰκόνα τοῦ κτίσαντος)" (Colossians 3:10).

It is thus not a doubled invisible (of the visible), but an *inverted* visible, coming from the invisible *elsewhere*: Christ does not reproduce the prior visibility of the Father still sealed and forbidden—for "no one has ever seen God"; but he manifests in the first instance, for the first and only time, the Father, insofar as he lends him a visibility on his face as Son become man. Insofar as he is given by the Father (manifesting the gift of God in *incarnating* him) and gives himself as such (as sent by the Father into the visible), he consists only in this sending and, thus, by referring to the given, succeeds in manifesting the invisible giver in return. To see Christ amounts to seeing what, or rather *the one* whom the Father manifests by giving him, and who consists only in this gift seen (and to be seen) as given: "God so loved the world that he gave (ἔδωκεν) his only Son" (John 3:16). That Christ shows (himself as) the gift given by the invisible (the Father) in a visible icon, means, for the gaze of man, to see oneself seen by the Father, in the gaze of Christ seen visibly and invisibly *as* the Son. The iconification of Christ, which properly defines the work of the Spirit, is accomplished in this way.

What Colossians 1:15 allows us to conceive, another Pauline text sets out rigorously: "All of us, with faces un-covered (ἀνακεκαλυμμένῳ προσώπῳ), reflecting in a mirror (κατοπτριζόμενοι) the glory of the Lord, will be metamorphosed into his icon (τὴν αὐτὴν εἰκόνα μεταμορφούμεθα) from glory into glory, as following the Spirit of the Lord" (2 Corinthians 3:18). This can be read from the end of the verse to its beginning. If we accomplish the anamorphosis, by letting the Spirit loosen our point of view and leave the aim of our constituting ego, in order to let us take up the Father's point of view on Jesus, then our face, that is to say our intentional aim, will be uncovered, will be freed from the calculated targets of its shooting range, will set its sights on what is given and will finally *think in the open* [*à découvert*]. Exposing ourselves uncovered like an empty mirror, our face will become the place where the filial icon of the Father will be exposed, precisely because, by letting the anamorphosis be accomplished in us, we will accomplish the Trinitarian anamorphosis. At last we will see, because it will absorb us, will metamorphose us into it and, upon our un-covering, its visibility will shine forth.

V
The Icon of the Invisible

FIFTEEN

Monotheism and Trinity: An Ontic Model

The phenomenal approach to the "good news of Jesus Christ, Son of God" (Mark 1:1) has enabled us to unfold the moments of its un-covering. And it is indeed an un-covering that is at issue, which we have let unfold according to its own logic by distinguishing several of its stages. First, what initially and necessarily remains covered up, reserved, and inaccessible (the *mystērion* of the Father), that is, the hyperbole of charity surpassing all knowledge, can be understood as a *saturated phenomenon* par excellence (chapters 11–12). Second, this saturated phenomenon is implemented according to the principle that everything, however secret, must be un-covered in the evidence of Christ and in view of the recognition of Christ as Son of the Father; this discovery of the depth of Christ thus requires that the one who wishes to see it be transformed into a *witness*, judged by what he reports (chapter 13). Third, it is not only a question of seeing Jesus, but of looking upon his face as that of the Christ and crossing this surface according to the depths of the Son, that is to say, to know in it, by viewing it under a certain angle, the icon of the invisible Father, in a phenomenon that is both visible and invisible, a *paradox*. As a consequence, then, no witness can approach this phenomenalizing of the face of Christ if he did not traverse the depths—depths that allow him to aim at the invisible Father in his visible icon (chapter 14). It would be necessary, therefore, to acknowledge that what Christian theology calls the dogma of the Trinity belongs to the phenomenal field of the un-covering of

Christ as the paradox of the preeminent saturated phenomenon, Revelation. What is left for us now is to show it and conceive it (chapters 15–18).

A Multiplication of Trinitarian Models

To achieve this, we must yet again turn to the remark made by Barth: "*God* reveals Himself. He reveals Himself *through Himself*. He reveals *Himself*."[1] In other words, the triple dimension of the origin, mode, and result of the sole revelation of the one God attests that "in the That and the How of this revelation He also and specifically shows Himself to be this God. Indeed, *this God* will and can make Himself manifest in no other way than in the That and the How of *this revelation*."[2] The Trinitarian character of God does not result in the manifestation of the *mystērion*, as if it were one piece of information (among others); it defines the very mode of this manifestation, so that the form and depths exactly coincide, so that the Trinity is uncovered in a Trinitarian mode. "We are not saying, then, that revelation is the basis of the Trinity, as though God were the triune God only in His revelation and only for the sake of His revelation. What we are saying is that revelation is the basis of the doctrine of the Trinity; the *doctrine* of the Trinity has no other basis apart from this."[3] The audacity of Barth consists not only in considering that the three dimensions of revelation (the ternary of origin, mode, and result) already imply a triplicity of operations, but that for this triplicity of manifestations, the Trinity itself is revealed and thus phenomenalized. The triplicity of manifestation is indispensable because it unfolds the very triunity of God, the triunity of God is revealed by the triplicity of its manifestation. But in what sense? It is one thing to come to perceive (according to the Synoptics) that the Father constitutes the depths from which the face of Jesus can be recognized as the figure of Christ; it is another to conceive that the figure of Christ is uncovered as that of the Son, the only icon of the Father, because it opens the distance of sonship in God and thus, in turn, his eternal fatherhood (according to John); but it is again something entirely different to posit that these dimensions of the manifestation of the Son and of the Father *for us* are uncovered *in themselves* as Trinity, "God whom no one has ever seen." Shouldn't the unfolding of these moments of manifestations *for us* be enough to exhaust what a phenomenal approach to revelation can assure *us*? Can we really infer from this unfolding and this accomplishment an uncovering of God as God, *in himself,* a revelation of the Trinity as such? Yet it would be necessary to do so, since "The doctrine of the Trinity is what basically sets apart the Christian doctrine of God as Christian, and therefore what already sets apart the Christian concept of revelation as Christian, in contrast to all other possible doctrines of God or concepts of revelation."[4]

We have already amply witnessed the inability of any closed concept to even reach the logic of un-covering, even more so after having stigmatized the idolatrous illusions of such attempts (chapters 6–7); so we know too much to overlook the principle that, when it is a matter of God, claiming to understand him makes no sense. It is only a question of understanding as best as possible how we must enter and remain within a proper incomprehensibility— for if it became comprehensible, it would no longer be about God. The best that can be conceived is the best conception of the incomprehensible. By definition, no model of the Trinity is appropriate to the Trinity, still less to its revelation, assuming that we could approach it according to the uncovering of its own phenomenality, the phenomenality of charity (chapters 8 and 10). Thought about the Trinity that would be rational and sober, rather than raving or idolatrous, can at best only aim at conceiving how and why it remains accessible solely through an act of charity that aims at charity in action. Barth himself was not unaware of this reticence of principle, having corrected an initial formulation of the link between revelation and Trinity that he judged too cursory: "Logically they are quite simply questions about the subject, predicate and object of the short statement: 'God speaks,' '*Deus dixit.*'" He conceded that he obviously did not mean to deduce from the predicative form of judgment a model of intelligibility of the Trinity, nor to ground "a grammatical and rationalistic proof of the Trinity."[5] Yet he maintained, and rightly so, that this simple grammatical formula, once confronted with the Word of God, that is, provided it is related to Scripture, would make it possible to reconstitute a certain Trinitarian logic of its revelation as well. *As well,* because others, and perhaps a myriad of others, can be applied to it, precisely because none is adequately fit to the *mystērion.*

It seems legitimate therefore to introduce a new logic, the phenomenal model of the Trinity, which could, perhaps better than others, although by definition imperfectly, provide some access to the intrinsically Trinitarian manifestation of the uncovering of the *mystērion.* To develop it in a more compelling and precise way, we will sketch it by contrast with two other models, more developed in the tradition (chapter 17). One, the ontic model, was pursued by the first dogmatics of the ecumenical councils, even if theologians have pointed out its limits, and metaphysics (in the sense of modern *metaphysica*, the only kind that I mean by this term) tried to critique it (chapter 15). The other, the economic (or, if you will, the historical) model has often been privileged by contemporary theology, Catholic as well as Reformed, even if possible deviations could be very quickly identified (chapter 16). This itinerary, however rough its outline, will perhaps be able to open onto the final difficulty, which is inseparable from the final un-covering: the model of communion (chapter 18).

The Stake of Raising the Questions

The question of the Trinity is becoming urgent once again in the age of nihilism that we belong to; indeed, it is a symptom of it. For the question of God today no longer resides primarily in the question of his existence. And for good reason. Not only because *metaphysica* does not allow us to define an existence as anything other than a position, let alone prove or demonstrate it: even when it is a matter of a worldly being, we can only observe it, and by imprecise experience. But especially because we can no longer maintain without caution that being (in whatever sense we mean it) can relate to the holiness of God, or that it can unveil whatever that might *be*, short of a perfunctory, though metaphysical, idolatry. What is more: between the one who admits God and the one who rejects him, there is probably no difference in ontic knowledge and psychological experience: both *know* the same amount, and they only differ because of what they have decided and inferred. In short, the question of God shifts from the debate about his existence to the decision about his essence. Or rather about the fact that this essence, too, remains inaccessible, for if we knew it, once again it would not be God that we were speaking about. The real investigation is now focused around this point: Can we conceive of any thought that would deserve to be attributed to something like "God"; or rather, can we conceive of any thought that would not immediately disqualify itself if we related it to what we aim at, without understanding, under the name of "God"? The plight of our time is not felt primarily or only by the "death of God" but by the lack of words to speak about God and even to curse him: the failing of divine words.

Here, precisely, the authority and power of the Christian claim of God's Trinity are felt: that claim constitutes one of the rare attempts, if not the only serious one, to approach, aim at, and even state the incomprehensibility of God *as such*, and thus to free ourselves from idols, whether sensible or conceptual. This exception and this assertion also explain why the Trinitarian interpretation of God's manifestation is contested, and harshly, by two critiques opposed to each other, but allied against what has resisted them through the centuries, a stronghold that has been sometimes sidestepped, but never conquered. These two opposing sources of resistance nevertheless converge because they reject, in two different directions, what the Trinity gives us to think: that the unicity of God depends on the mode of his unity, communion.

In a preliminary sense, one can challenge what Athanasius defended under the title of the "holy preaching of the monarchy, ἅγιον κήρυγμα της μοναρχίας."[6] In its simplest form, this first of all has to do with a political objection raised by Erik Peterson: the monarchic interpretation of the Trinity, which begins from and grants preference to the Father, would have led in both "Greek Theology" and strict Arianism to confusion with the hierarchy of the power in the city of men; it would have endorsed or made possible absolutist and even totalitarian forms of political authority.[7] This political objection is itself added to a more ancient and more forceful challenge to the unicity of the Trinitarian God. By what right, in fact, could the God of the Hebrews claim the rank of the only God, when he himself was long in open competition with the gods of other nations, even and especially when the chosen people had taken possession of the land of Israel and had to fight against the deities of Canaan, that is, to confront them, often compromising with them and therefore recognizing them? By what right can we disqualify as null and void the religious experience of those who were then called pagans, when testimony abounds of their piety, their prayers and rites, even of their spirituality? The construction of the myth of the "virtuous atheist" by the "libertines," the comparative study of religions by the Enlightenment, and the reevaluation of mythology by the Romantics reinforced this challenge to the unicity of the divine. Nietzsche could evoke the amused smile of the gods of Olympus before the exclusive claim of Yahweh; Hölderlin could set Dionysius alongside the "One and Only" Christ as his brother in godhood; and finally Heidegger could submit every possible uncovering of a unique God to the uncovering of gods, the latter to the opening of the divinities, the former to the horizon of the hale, therefore of being.[8] In every case, the divine becomes too serious a matter—even and especially if we reject its *elsewhere*—to concede its exclusivity to Yahweh. Trinitarian revelation is thus itself called into question in the name of the plurality of the divine.

But conversely, it is also called into question because it would compromise the unicity of God. Judaism after the end of the Temple, then Islam, denounced (and have not ceased denouncing) the slow and difficult Christian development of the Trinitarian dogma as a return to idolatry and polytheism: if God begets a Son who is himself God, God would not be the Only God, and thus would no longer be God. In fact, in the debates between Christians, the denunciation of *polyarchy*, weakened by *bitheism* and even *tritheism* imposed by the two other persons,[9] underlies all the stages of the Arian controversy up to its final development, the question of two wills and the dispute over icons. This temptation has never ceased, lingering through the centuries, with the appeal of medieval thinkers to a *deitas* beyond the Trinity, with the various avatars of Socinianism (up through a number of liberal Protestants). The contemporary conflict with the Quran, ultimately too rudimentary to count as more than a symptom, is precisely the symptom of another difficulty, which is much more serious: if God remains God only insofar as he is the Only God (Christians grant this as much as others, even if they understand it *in another way*), the correct conception of the mode of this unicity remains to be conceived. Or rather, it remains to conceive whether and to what extent unicity will suffice to define the unity of God with himself.

Otherwise, we end up with a confused approximation that in fact covers up the simplistic character of its solution. A confused approximation leads us to use the disputable term *monotheism* to group Judaism, Islam, and Christianity as supposedly comparable, even compatible, under the title (which is false for Christianity) of the "religions of the Book," or under another title (itself disputable) of "Abrahamic Religions" (see John 8:39–40). In so doing, we forget or disguise the fact that the confession of Jesus as Christ necessarily implies his un-covering as the Son of the Father, who is simultaneously one with him and who remains, for that very reason, greater than him (chapter 14). In so doing, we do not reach any real conciliation with Judaism and Islam, because we eliminate the thesis that is properly Christian.[10] Implicitly but inevitably, we will end up with a simplistic solution: a generalized (and polymorphic) Arianism, which thinks it avoids polytheism and respects monotheism, but merely adopts an emanationist model of philosophy (in this case of Neo-Platonism, where a hierarchical ordering of hypostases follows from the One, here the Son and the Spirit), by adapting it to an intra-Trinitarian subordinationism ("there was a time where the Son was not") and a Christological adoptionism (the "man assumed" by the Word). The most pronounced refusals of Christianity share the same presupposition as humanist approvals of Jesus: there is no question that Christ would be the Son of the Father; anything can be admitted except that "he is the equal of God" (John 5:18). When Christ is rejected, it is always because of a refusal of his Trinitarian status, and when he is tolerated, it is on condition he be deprived of it.

In this refusal, as in the debates that led to it, a real question nevertheless plays out: under the supposedly divine title of the One lies the conflation of two different, if not diverging, notions: that of unicity and unity. Rejections of the Trinity, however opposed they seem, rest on the identification of divinity with unity, whether to deplore it or reinforce it. The very discussion of the theologians (whether the most traditional or the most critical) on the compatibility of unicity (of substance) with plurality (of persons) rests on this same identification. In every case, we admit, at least implicitly, that unicity *as such* defines something like the divine essence, exactly like being unbegotten (*agennēsia*) does for Arianism.[11] Christian "theology" (here understood in the terms of Trinitarian doctrine) draws both its originality and its difficulty from the fact that it breaks with this identification. For a negative reason, of course: it assumes that a divine essence knowable by a concept is pure and simple idolatry. For a positive reason too: divine unity, as it is uncovered by the Trinity, comes from and returns to union, thus implying the interplay of three poles of this union. After the manifestation of Christ as Son, as the one who only does the will of the Father and thus only consists in his accomplishment "unto the end" (John 13:1), the divine unicity enacts the communion of *agapē*. God's unicity is not closed in on itself, but exudes charity, which it diffuses and which it opens up even as the *elsewhere* from which all things arise. Unicity does not close God in an irremediable secret

(*Deus absconditus*),[12] it uncovers (itself) as a communion, which not only ensures its union, but unfolds it, gives it (*bonum diffusivum sui*). In a word, identity does not come from pure and simple unicity, nor can it be reduced to it; it comes from unity, and unity in turn comes from the exercise of love—by communion. This properly "theological" requirement has a consequence for the phenomenal understanding of the Trinity: the phenomenality of un-covering must not only contradict, but corroborate the unity of the communion of the only God. What this means here is that it must corroborate it by making it manifest in its *own way*—phenomenally, by making appear the unity of the communion of Trinitarian terms as a phenomenon.

Numerical Plurality, Unicity

We can now return to an initial, properly philosophical difficulty regarding the ontic model of the Trinity. In fact, the exclusive privilege granted to God in his unicity comes down to an ontic starting point: being means being *a* being, and, in turn, a man who is *one* is equivalent to a man *being*, because "being (*l'être/étant*; τὸ ὄν) is said in the same way as 'one.'"[13] Unicity thus applies to everything that falls within the horizon of being as a being. It brings into play what the system of metaphysics will establish as its first principle, the principle of identity; nothing can be non-identical to itself at the same moment and in the same respect. Therefore, since identity, which includes numerical identity, defines being, in order for God to be (in whatever manner he might be) he must remain identical to himself without differing from himself. His unity depends on his unicity: the Only God must above all remain one. We may then return to a first, properly philosophical objection (see chapters 5–6): if we approach God by his essence and his existence, the persons cannot be taken into account without compromising his unity, so in what way does this plurality of persons qualify the essence of God? The only correct answer to such a question is provided by Kant in his *Conflict of the Faculties*: seeing as how the Trinity does not allow any understanding of God as such, the question of *de Deo uno* must be examined before the tribunal of reason without reference to the *de Deo trino*, since the possible plurality of persons neither essentially nor substantially concerns the divinity of God. In other words, "The doctrine of the Trinity, taken literally, has *no practical relevance at all*, even if we think we understand it; and it is even more clearly irrelevant if we realize it transcends all our concepts.—Whether we are to worship three or ten persons in the Deity makes no difference: the pupil will implicitly accept one as readily as the other because he has no concept at all of a number of persons in one God (hypostases), and still more so because this distention can make no difference in his rules of conduct."[14] And further, if the plurality of persons is only an afterthought to the unity of essence, not only does it teach us nothing about the only God (the only one that metaphysics could consider, because it is bound to determinations of being alone, thus to substance or essence), but the number of this plurality remains itself undetermined, because it lacks any theoretical validity. As a result, there is nothing *to do* with the plurality of persons.

Clearly, this blasphemy (which it is in the literal sense, for Kant here *speaks evil* against the mystery of the Trinity) leads to a position that is at once obvious and deficient. Obvious, for all it does is draw the almost inevitable conclusion from a division, already admitted by the majority of modern theologians since at least Thomas Aquinas, between the treatises *de Deo uno* and *de Deo trino* (we will return to this). Deficient, too, because Kant does not for an instant suspect that the Trinity, precisely as a communion of persons, could, against his conclusion, un-cover God in the most radical way for practice itself ("*schlechterdings nichts für Praktische*"); but to conceive this, it would have been necessary to recognize that the plurality (in the number) of persons is not an optional and arbitrary appendix added on to the unicity of God, but the economy of an apocalypse of love, such that it constitutes the essence, the *practical* essence, of God. This is something that Kant, who eliminates love from theory and especially from practical reason, could not have even suspected. And so we must find another guide.[15]

Monotheism, Polytheism

The fact remains that Kant's position on the irrelevance of the plurality of persons marks a decisive moment in metaphysical theology, even more decisive than his assertion of the impossibility of proving the existence of the only God; for, as much as this latter thesis will still be contested after him, the indetermination of the Trinity itself will fix the horizon of the question of God, and still fixes it today. Hölderlin, Schelling, and even Hegel, each in his way, remained faithful to the essentially Kantian position that they outlined together in Tübingen in *The Oldest Systematic Program of German Idealism*: "*Monotheismus der Vernunft und des Herzens, Polytheismus der Einbildungskraft und der Kunst, dies ist's, was wir bedürfen*—Monotheism of reason and the heart, polytheism of imagination and art, this is what we need."[16] It could not have been better said: for philosophy (and for the natural religion which it eventually permits), in other words for the realm marked by Kant's first two *Critiques* (of pure reason and practical reason), we must stand by monotheism; by which we mean at the same time a single God and God as the One, according to what metaphysics is able to say about him when considering him in the horizon of being/beings and according to its logic. But this approach to God is not enough, when we try to approach the divine by imagination and art, in other words, by the domain barely opened by Kant's third *Critique* (the faculty of judgment): the realm of the beautiful, the sublime, and finality, that which is most often unfolded "without concept" and which comes close to saturated phenomena, exceeding the abstract and empty narrowness of monotheism. For Schelling and Hölderlin (after and before a number of others), it was necessary to return to, among other things, a renewed mythology of the Ancients, which takes up again the vast field of divinity and the sacred that had been rejected and abandoned by the system of metaphysics. We are still in this age today; its irrational and chancy nostalgias for other supposed wisdoms or undecided spiritualities attests to the radical inadequacy of the so-called "monotheist" approach of the one and only God, as the one who does not give himself and therefore does not manifest himself, who remains hidden from us.

Schelling will later formulate this question clearly. We must of course begin by monotheism, "The concept of *monotheism*, i.e., the highest concept of every true religion—but also precisely where one must begin if one wants to propose an objective explanation of false religion." But this monotheism can only be abstract, a simple numerical singularity of an essence perfectly identical to itself; we must therefore distinguish "the monotheism in concept from monotheism as dogma, or from actual monotheism. It is the latter where potencies mutually exclude each other, where an actual plurality is posited in God." Still to be conceived is what brings out the truth of this plurality in actual monotheism. In such an instance, to what authority do we entrust the idea "that God is not (as in mere theism) purely and simply singular, but the singular *as* God, or that the affirmation of the unicity of God is not simply a negative, and that it can only be positive, i.e., affirmative"?[17] In fact, it is a question of reintroducing *into* metaphysical monotheism a quasi-Trinitarian plurality. But Schelling, who does not think as a Christian theologian (despite certain appearances), only undertakes the thinking of this "affirmative" unicity starting from metaphysical resources (in this case dialectical and speculative), starting from the difference in "potencies (*Potenzen*)," and thus from being in its (positive or negative) moments, just as Hegel undertakes thinking based on the difference of logical figures (the concept, the negative), and therefore still on the basis of being. Nietzsche certainly remains within this horizon, when he attempts to raise up "new gods" starting from the will to power alone. Heidegger entrenches himself further in this track, when he awaits the *Ereignis*, the heart of being, the "last god," or the new one.

In reality, we should wonder, is it possible to surpass the limits of an ontic model of Trinitarian uncovering while remaining within the limits of being/beings (even by relying on the negative and on "potencies")? It remains to be asked how philosophy can, even and especially in its final attempts at speculation, overcome its metaphysical destiny. It certainly does not go without saying that philosophical reason can apprehend more in God than his essence (or his substance), in other words, more than his unicity according to the way being allows us to conceive of it; nor that it could conceive this unicity starting from a more radical unity—the unity of a truly "affirmative" communion.

The Distinction between the Treatises

But these questions become all the more daunting as they arise on the basis of another difficulty, a properly theological one, which as we have already seen appears with the epistemological interpretation of revelation (chapters 4–5): the distinction between, on the one hand, natural knowledge of God by the light of reason, and, on the other, supernatural knowledge by divine revelation, which is then quickly expanded into a distinction between the philosophical (i.e., metaphysical) knowledge of God's existence, and thus his unicity, on the one hand, and the revealed (supernatural, "theological") knowledge of his Trinity on the other. Thus, in orthodox Christian thought itself (including and in a sense especially after its Chalcedonian formulation), the lack of connection between the plurality of persons and the unicity of essence (or substance) would give rise to another distinction, itself apparently very clear, between two modes of knowledge, or two sciences (or quasi-sciences). These added differentiations resulted in the academic as well as the conceptual distribution of God's revelation into two separate treatises, *de Deo uno*, and then *de Deo trino*. Thomas Aquinas already admitted this ontic distinction (God as he is in his quasi-essence, and God as he is unfolded in his Trinity), which is immediately confirmed by an epistemological distinction (natural reason, supernatural science): "Now, the creative power of God is common to the whole Trinity; and hence it belongs to the unity of his essence, and not to the distinction of the persons. Therefore, by natural reason we can know regarding God what belongs to the unity of his essence, but not what belongs to the distinction of the persons."[18] The superimposition of these two distinctions could not avoid producing an effect as radical as those we have previously seen in the epistemological interpretation of revelation.

For Suárez, this effect comes down to nothing less than dividing the divine substance (precisely in the *Tractatus de divina substantia*) into two clearly distinct parts: "Therefore in this work we discuss God as one and as triune; and thus there will be two parts, the first of which, one might say, is on the Unity of God, the second on the Trinity."[19] The stakes of this division go even further: it is not only a matter of distinguishing two sciences, nor of marking the difference between unity and plurality; it is a matter of deciding what does *or does not* belong to the divine essence, that is, of considering the possibility that God could be and could be known as such without considering the Trinitarian communion. "I have always preferred the contrary thesis, according to which I affirm that the relations, whether the personalities or the persons, *do not fall under* the divine essence, nor under God as such."[20] In fact, the origin of this decision is outlined in Boethius: "So then, the divine substance contains the Unity, while the divine relation multiplies the Trinity."[21] In other words, as the Trinitarian persons do not define the essence of God, the divinity of God is therefore unfolded as such without the Trinitarian community in a unity that is summarized in (ontic) unicity and that does not uncover any hint of its union (of charity). These are the ontic terms of the model that must thus come under question, if not under suspicion.

Substance and Person: Ontic Aporias

How to evaluate this surprising (if hardly Christian) conclusion? In its most obvious sense, it is a kind of monotheism by subtraction, assigned to revealed knowledge, and which is exposed to two equally daunting objections. But at its basis it results from a single, early decision: to think the Trinitarian mystery starting from two concepts (or sets of concepts) with a decidedly ontic origin, *ousia/physis/substantia/essentia* on the one hand and *hypostasis/prosōpon/persona* on the other. The crucial and contentious point does not lie in the supposed "Hellenization" of the biblical heritage by the earliest Christian thinkers; for the translation of the books of the Bible and the Hebrew lexicon had become so inevitable that it began well before them in the ancient Judaism of the diaspora: Justin and Origen were already its heirs. The point in question is not so much a matter of a linguistic transfer (for everything can be translated, and well, even and above all the untranslatables),[22] but of the inevitably *ontic* horizon of the Greek lexicon. The question of being is spoken in Greek, and Greek spontaneously speaks the question of being. Jewish thought has felt the difficulty of saying in Greek what resists the thinking of being (Levinas), and Christian thought has not escaped it either. It could not, nor should it. Admitting this, we can clarify the terms of the question: To what extent could concepts designed for thinking or at least speaking being/beings (in Greek) speak or think the (Trinitarian) uncovering of the *mystērion* (of the Father)? What corrections and what precautions must we introduce, and when?

It should be noted that the ontic lexical terms were imposed on the Fathers of Nicaea and Chalcedon first of all by their Arian opponents, who themselves had no reservations about using philosophical vocabulary to expound the *mystērion*. Without hesitation they made use of *ousia*, the One, the procession of hypostases, their hierarchization, and their emanation, in order to draw out unscrupulous ontic consequences for "theology" that were all governed by subordination. The ontic choice of concepts thus inevitably, and for them obviously, resulted in supposedly Christian versions of Neoplatonism. Of course, from Athanasius to Maximus the Confessor, the Greek Fathers knew how to correct concepts of ontic origin in order to make them serve the orthodox requirements of "theology."[23] The question of the relation between Hellenism and Christianity remains open, but precisely because it is a question of measuring the Christianization of Hellenism, and not the Hellenization of Christianity: here Nietzsche and Heidegger were more perceptive than Bultmann. What remains to be determined, in each case, and especially when we arrive at the Trinity (and in fact we arrived at it from the beginning), is how far a concept with an ontic origin can go and from what moment it is no longer appropriate. It was perhaps the Latin Fathers, precisely because they remained more distant from the self-evidence of the Greek language, who clearly saw these limits, at least in two cases: *ousia/substantia/essentia* and *hypostasis/prosōpon/persona*.

Strangely, Boethius, although he had allowed the distinction between the unity of *substantia* and the plurality of *personae*, did not himself admit that the first of the categories of being, *substantia*, applied to God: "*Nam substantia in illo [sc. Deo] non est vere substantia sed ultra substantiam*—For substance in Him is not really substance, but is beyond substance."[24] In other words Boethius does nothing other than adopt the reticence of Saint Augustine: "*Unde manifestum est Deum abusive substantiam vocari, ut nomine usitatiore intelligatur essentia, quod vere ac proprie dicitur; ita ut fortasse solum Deum dici oporteat essentiam*—So it is clear that God is improperly called a substance, instead of understanding him by the more usual word essence, which is said truly and properly; such that perhaps only God ought to be called *essence*."[25] Indeed, *substantia* takes its primacy among the categories (*ousia*), and also its rank as one of the four senses of being, only because in the first case it allows us to predicate one of the other categories (quality, difference, quantity, etc.) of it, and in the second case to attribute accidents (*symbebēkota*) to it. Yet in God there are no predicates, nor attributes, according to the principle that in God everything is (of) God himself. In God, nothing is relative, because nothing is relatively God.[26] Thus, strictly speaking, God does not *lower* himself to the rank of a substance, even the first, but surpasses substantiality (*ultra substantiam*). Arianism and all its derivations assumed the opposite. But if *substance* is not appropriate for God, what does it mean to expound the divinity as a substance, and how can this substance without a trinity of persons expound the divinity of God? Or else, if the persons come to be added (by predication or by attribution, or by any other way we like) to the single divine substance, how could they amount to God himself?

The same non-adequation is repeated for the concept of *persona*. Augustine remarked that the Greeks say *hypostasis*, without being able to differentiate it from *ousia*, such that the formula, {to believe in} *mia ousian, treis hypostaseis* becomes rather confused in Latin: *unam essentiam, tres substantias*; so the preference is *unam essentiam vel substantiam, tres autem personas*. It remains to be determined what exactly this *persona* could mean. Certainly, we want to indicate that the Father is confused neither with the Son nor with the Spirit, that they remain distinct in one distance; but what qualifies this distinction itself? We think it and say it without being able to say it by a concept: "*Tamen, cum quæritur quid tres, magna prorsus inopia humanum laborat eloquium. Dictum est tamen: tres personæ, non ut illud diceretur, sed ne taceretur*—Yet when you ask, 'Three what?' human speech labors under a great dearth of words. So we say three persons, not in order to say that precisely, but in order not to be reduced to silence."[27] No "special or general name" allows us to "say something when asked what, or rather who, are these three that the faith declares to be three." By responding *tria personæ*, three persons, we do not have the least concept of *what* the three share in common (for they share their common divinity, and that is enough), nor *as what* they share it (for they share it as different, as Father, as Son, and as Spirit, and that is enough). We therefore think what we do not say, because we lack the concept. We think their triplicity without being able to say it by a concept. And this itself—the excess of what there is to be thought beyond our resources and concepts—is absolutely fitting for what it is we are thinking about.[28] If we examine it seriously, Boethius's definition of the person (now a proverb), "*naturae rationalis individua substantia*, an individual substance of a rational nature," brings into focus the difficulties.[29] First of all, an individual substance is only individual if it is an *ousia prōtē*, a first essence; but in this case, the principle of its individuation remains undetermined, and a *nature*, if it is indeed a second *ousia* (genus, species), is not immediately sufficient to individualize it. Next, even supposing we attain it in this world, can this individuation be transferred to God and multiplied in him? In order to keep *persona* as a concept, Thomas Aquinas will have to overdetermine it by the doctrines of relation and mission, and thus in a sense abandon it.[30] But such an abandonment is (fortunately!) a sign that he is taking a step back from the ontic model of the Trinity. The concepts intended to "search" being/beings can be and no doubt must be used, but we must also know how to use them only up to their breaking point, or rather their inaptitude. We can only affirm the observation of Louis Bouyer: "More than that . . ., once one begins from the vision of three equal, coeternal, inseparable persons, one can only, however much one may do, avoid falling into an inevitable tritheism by having at the back of one's mind a prior vision of a single essence in which the persons are *a priori*. Thus, even those who opt for the so-called 'Greek' Trinitarian scheme are bound sooner or later to fall back into the 'Latin' one, and so once again run up against its insurmountable aporias."[31]

Could modern theology, as the successor of *sacra doctrina*, undo, correct, and surpass what it had in the first place permitted—the distinction between unity (essence/substance) and plurality (persons) in God—and then provoked—namely, a God thinkable *without* Trinitarian communion, a unicity without unity or communion?[32] What we must understand, in turn, is this: Revelation is the basis of the Trinity, because the mode of un-covering (*apokalypsis*, *oikonomia*) of the *mystērion tou Theou* (of the "economic" Trinity) remains itself joined in a Trinitarian manner to the three of the Trinity as such ("immanent"); Revelation reveals the Trinity, and above all it reveals it *in a Trinitarian way*; the way the Trinity is un-covered remains so perfectly and integrally Trinitarian that the Trinity alone succeeds in revealing the Trinity, and wants only to reveal the Trinity itself. In a word, the Trinity offers not only the content of un-covering, but also its mode of manifestation. Or better: the mode of manifestation (the phenomenal *wie*) coincides exactly with what manifests itself (the *Sich-selbst-zeigende*). But this warning and repositioning is not enough to fix the place and the logic of a unity by communion that, in God, defines his unicity. It is not enough merely to recall a necessity to satisfy it, however unquestionable it may be (i.e., the un-covering of the Trinity happens in a Trinitarian way). In speaking of an economic revelation, we must still determine what kind of economy is in question.

SIXTEEN

Immanence and Economy: A Historical Model

The inadequacies of an ontic model of the Trinity must not surprise us. Why be astonished that the concepts designed to target the question of beings in their being (namely, *ousia*) are not suitable for accurately conceiving the *mystērion* of *agapē*? But at the same time, these inadequacies must not be underestimated: neither the unicity of the One nor the determination of beings through unity, nor the complications of monarchy by emanation, procession, or multiplication can in the final analysis help a *theo*logical approach to the Trinity. Consequently, we must put into question the decision that blocked the investigation, the distinction between the treatise *de Deo uno* (governed by the logic of beings in their being, and thus by the equivalence of *ousia* to unity) and the treatise *de Deo trino* (in quest of a union through communion, and thus of a plurality of the terms of this union).

Trinitarian Economy and Trinitarian Immanence

This is how we must take the thesis posed as a principle by Karl Rahner: "The Trinity of the economy of salvation *is* the immanent Trinity and vice versa."[1] In fact, this principle had already been outlined by Karl Barth, among others: "All our statements concerning what is called the immanent Trinity have been reached simply as confirmations or underlinings or, materially, as the indispensable premises of the economic Trinity."[2] The question would become that of thinking the forms and the moments of God's uncovering to humanity and within our history on the basis of the dimensions and figure of that which (or the one who) shows itself (or himself); in such a way that God uncovers himself exactly in the gestures of his uncovering; that the gestures of the uncovering happen not only as a means of communication of that which uncovers itself, but as their manifest placement into operation; and that the economy would directly bring to light and onto center stage the immanence of God himself. The style of the uncovering should coincide with the uncovering of the *mystērion*.

And yet it is enough to formulate this requirement to take note of its difficulty. Indeed, the style of the uncovering differs from the uncovering of the *mystērion* in at least two aspects. First, it differs in that the economy of the manifestation is uncovered according to the *gesta Dei*; God's deeds are inscribed in the moments of a history that, however holy it remains (and precisely in order for it to become so), is unfolded temporally; thus God's self-immanence must be transported and translated into our temporality, that is to say inseparably into our finitude, which it nevertheless exceeds. Of course, we do not know what the term *eternity* may signify conceptually, and, at best, we only conceive it as a contradiction (an instant that is indefinitely permanent). Nevertheless, even in understanding it as a pure and simple negation of temporality, even in confining ourselves to the paradox that "for God a thousand years are like a day," we must at least hold that the only time that we know, namely our own, as such does not concern God. The identity between the immanence of the Trinity and its economy would require, however, that God enter into this finite temporality, like he enters into our fleshly condition. And that is something we can conceive of only obscurely, or not at all.

But this first gap that separates the time of the economy and God's self-immanence causes another difficulty to arise: Between the one and the other, whence comes the *elsewhere* that we know characterizes every Revelation as such, and where is it situated (chapters 1–2)? Note that this *elsewhere* can be understood here in two opposed senses. First we could say that the "immanent" Trinity, which of itself remains in itself, is exteriorized in the economy and thus goes out of itself by entering into history. The historicity of the self-immanence of the Trinity would thus become the *elsewhere* in which its uncovering is unfolded. Temporality would open the *elsewhere* of the Trinity, as would the finitude that the Son assumes in and as Jesus.

In contrast to Trinitarian immanence, history appears as the *elsewhere* in which the deed of God is inscribed, a deed that would uncover itself by going out *elsewhere* than in itself, and would only be manifested by being exteriorized. Would this be *elsewhere* than in himself? Yet if God is God, his infinity leaves place for no other *elsewhere* outside of himself and every *elsewhere* still must dwell in him alone. Properly speaking, God as such admits no exteriority beyond his limits, since he admits no limits. *A fortiori* this unthinkable exteriority cannot be accomplished by the least alienation or alteration (*Entäußerung*), since if God is worthy of this title nothing is foreign to him, above all himself to himself. If then the immanent Trinity coincides with the economic Trinity, the economy must remain internal to the immanent Trinity; but then how can we still think seriously of the *elsewhere* of the Trinitarian uncovering?

Or instead it would be necessary to allow for the opposite: rather than the economic Trinity unfolding the immanent Trinity *elsewhere* than within itself, in the temporal *elsewhere* that our finitude would make room for outside of itself, it would be the economy that would open in our temporality and our finitude the stage upon which the immanent Trinity would uncover itself directly. Henceforth, the immanent Trinity—God himself— would appear as the *elsewhere* from which the economy would open the deeds of God among us. Which would amount to thinking the economic Trinity from *elsewhere*, and therefore *starting from* the immanent Trinity. In a word, it would be thinking the economy on the basis of the Trinity itself and not the reverse; on the basis of the immanence of God to himself, and not the reverse—beginning from *elsewhere* than our own point of view on the economy. To accomplish Revelation would mean to see the economy in which God is revealed not only from our point of view but, through a radically Trinitarian anamorphosis, as God sees it. To see Jesus as the Father sees him—as the Son. Coherent as it may be, this reversal seems definitively to exceed what a finite understanding can conceive and to postulate an anamorphosis that is even more extreme, even more *staggering* than the one that our examination of the biblical texts already postulated (chapters 11–14). And yet, would there *truly* be a Revelation if that which uncovered itself, or if the one who uncovered himself, did not come to us from *elsewhere*, if he came to us only by becoming other than himself, by being altered from himself? It is thus necessary to think from *elsewhere* that which comes to us only in order to make us see and live from *elsewhere* than our own point of view.

There should be no surprise, then, and precisely because it reaches the heart of the aporia, that Rahner's formula is not without ambiguity. To be sure, it seems unquestionable that "the economic Trinity *is* the immanent Trinity," that "no adequate distinction can be made between the doctrine of the Trinity and the doctrine of the economy of salvation," because our relation to the Trinity in itself is not reduced to "a copy or an analogy (*ein Abbild oder eine Analogie*)"; and that, on the contrary, "the Trinity is a mystery whose paradoxical character already resonates (*anklingt*) in man's *Dasein*." And yet, can we without any qualms complicate the rule that *"the 'economic' Trinity is the 'immanent' Trinity"* by adding *"and vice versa (umgekehrt)"*?³ Indeed, can one think this return without immediately reintroducing the auxiliary concepts that precisely must be surpassed in order to avoid maintaining the caesura that one claims to fill in—the "exteriorization (*Entäußerung*)" of the "intra-divine (*innergöttliche*)" in "the non-divine (*in das Nichtgöttliche*)"?⁴ Does the equivalence of the two versions of the Trinity, if we may so put it, also imply that the immanent must be temporalized without remainder in the economic, to the point of being dispersed there, thus risking that the accomplishment of the manifestation of God would both align him with the completion of universal history and place him on its margin? This is the first reservation, clearly expressed by Hans Urs von Balthasar⁵ and which corresponds to the first difficulty previously registered. The second question, which for us is more decisive, remains: Does adding "and vice versa" to the rule of the unquestionable identity between the two versions of the Trinity not mask or even completely annul the *elsewhere* that characterizes uncovering? And in so doing the anamorphosis as well, without which the *theo*logical uncovering founders in theo*logical* unconcealment, in reality metaphysical or philosophical?

Hegel and the Primacy of the Economic Trinity

This double difficulty would not surface in an author as well informed as Rahner if it did not come from afar and with significant weight. Its origin, like its final orientation, goes back to Hegel, who first thought through all the implications of Rahner's "and vice versa (*und umgekehrt*)." To better see this, we will follow the *Encyclopedia of the Philosophical Sciences* (1830), which crystallizes the economic declination of the Trinity more powerfully, in a sense, than do the *Lectures on the Philosophy of Religion* (1821 to 1831); and, to be more precise, we will focus on paragraphs 564–71, which gather the entire doctrine of Revelation into three syllogisms, and which all the interpreters hail as a summit.

The first moment (§564) relies on a foundation that we have already probed (chapters 5–6): the equivalence between the manifestation and the Revelation of God. In effect, "It lies essentially in the concept of religion,—the religion i.e. whose content is absolute mind—that it be *revealed (geoffenbart)*, and, what is more, revealed *by God*"[6]; but as this revelation of the divine "substance" is attributed to the mind (according to the principle posed ever since the *Phenomenology of Spirit*, that it is necessary to "grasp and express the True, not only as *Substance*, but just as much as *Subject*"[7]), and as the mind determines itself, this revelation "is an absolute manifesting *(schlechthin Manifestieren)*" that "manifests itself *(sich selbst manifestiert)*."[8] Without manifestation, and therefore without the concept through which the mind understands and understands itself, there is no Revelation.[9] Consequently, the knowledge of God demands going beyond "the homely pictures of faith" toward "thinking by concept *(begreifenden Denken)*" (§564), for the mind's self-resolution extends "not merely to the simplicity of faith and devotional feeling, but even to thought" (§571).[10] Otherwise, the "religion which is expressly called the revealed" would become a "religion in which nothing of God was revealed *(nichts offenbar)*, in which he had not revealed himself *(nicht geoffenbart hätte)*" (§564).[11] An unavoidable contrary consequence follows: every theology not aimed at the manifestation of God knowing himself and making himself known through concepts will result in men "'who know not God.'"[12] Three inseparable propositions must be set in sequence: "God is God *only so far (nur ... insofern)* as he knows himself; his self-knowledge is, *further (ferner)*, a self-consciousness in man; *and finally (und)* man's knowledge of God *proceeds to (fortgeht)* man's self-knowledge in God."[13] The transitivity of the three propositions rests on a single presupposition: whether it concerns the knowledge of God by himself, by himself in man, or by man, this knowledge always remains in the same sense a knowledge of self. The univocity of this knowledge of self rests in turn on the univocity of the mind's "thinking by concept": God and man know themselves in themselves and through one another according to the only possible logic, as "the system of pure reason, as the realm of pure thought," "the content" of which would be nothing other than *"the exposition of God as he is in his eternal essence before the creation of nature and of a finite spirit."*[14] The *science of logic* determines everything; it thus encompasses God and his Revelation, in the manifestation by concept.

This presupposition calls for two remarks. First, we must note that what are often referred to as the three "syllogisms" (§§567–69) clearly do not take the Aristotelian form (assumed to arise from the logic of the understanding); at issue, more precisely, are "three reasonings (*Schlüsse*)" (§571), which develop the "different moments of the concept" (§566),[15] and thus put into operation (like the *personae* and the *hypostaseis*) in three moments the henceforth conceptual essence of God. From this we must conclude that the whole of the Trinitarian question passes under the control of logic, and thus of philosophy, that is to say, of the completion, here, of metaphysics: "In this form of truth, truth is the object of *philosophy (der Gegenstand der Philosophie)*" (§571).[16] The eventual uncovering (*Offenbarung*) of the immanent Trinity henceforth plays out exclusively within the economic horizon of manifestation according to the logic of the concept.[17] Here is where the second critique comes in, put forward by Michel Henry: the transfer of Trinitarian authority to the concept and the mind presupposes that "negativity is the essence of manifestation"; but, as Henry demonstrates, negativity opens no region, no phenomenality, not even any mode of being, but remains a simple logical "category" that allows at best only a description of "the essence of manifestation starting with the fundamental process of objectification."[18] In fact, "*in Hegelianism, man does not have his own Being*," and "the Subject does not have its own Being; it is the *Being of substance*."[19] Hegel's ambition—to think the absolute not as substance but as subject—failed from the beginning, because, according to Henry, Hegel assumed, against all phenomenological evidence, that negativity and the negative were enough to define man by defining him as mind [*esprit*]. And, it is true, one could hold that the best of philosophy post-Hegel has endeavored to avoid thinking the ego from logical negativity (with the unhappy exception of Sartre). One can at least contest that the negativity of mind, already insufficient for characterizing the finite mind, could suit the infinite mind, the Trinitarian God, the uncovering of which it is the task to think.

Hegel: The Three Moments of the Economy According to the Concept

Having reached the point of its being taken up by the concept, the Trinitarian doctrine undergoes a double transformation. On the one hand, once man's knowledge of God is as one with God's knowledge of himself, the distinction between the immanence and the economy of the Trinity fades completely into the unique "object of philosophy." On the other hand, as the Trinity now follows the moments of the concept and the concept unfolds itself in dialectical discursivity, the lack of distinction between economy and immanence plays to the benefit of economy, henceforward reduced to the history of absolute consciousness. The treatise *de Deo uno* philosophically recapitulates everything that the treatise *de Deo trino* had safeguarded of the biblical Revelation.

The *mystērion* of the Father (§567) therefore no longer appears here except as the "moment of *Universality (Allgemeinheit)*," already mind, but still abstract, presupposed, and substantial, not yet subject. It is only a "*substantial power (substantielle Macht)*," that exerts its "causality" as "*creator (Schöpfer)* of heaven and earth." In this abstract differentiation, the Son "remains in original identity that from which he is distinguished." In Christian terms, one can say that the monarchy of the Father does not yet unfold a relation of paternity, that the Son does not yet receive the relation of filiation, and that his distance from the Father is still confused with the distance between the creation and the creator.

The Son will become Son, then, only in the "moment of the singularity of judgement" (§568), when "the production of the *appearance (Erschaffung der Erscheinung)*" will introduce a "fracture *(Zerfallen)* . . . of the only Son" into a double "opposition taking place in itself *(selbständigen Gegensatz)*." For the opposition that "inherent negativity" provokes does not assure the singularity of the Son by deepening it through his filial relation and his *missio*; on the contrary, by "autonomizing itself," negativity increases opposition to the universal, first as nature ("heavens and earth"); but also to "the extreme *(Extrem)*," to "wickedness *(zum Bösen)*." For only these two oppositions allow for radicalizing, at last, the filiation in an "external relation *(äußerliche Beziehung)*." Deepening the singularity, or rather suppressing it: the Trinity becomes actual only by opposing itself, by annulling unifying communion through alienating opposition.

280   *Chapter Sixteen*

The "moment of *individuality*" (§569) can at last enter in, but always "under the name (*nämlich*) of subjectivity and concept." The Son in effect "transposes (*versetzt*) the abstract substance of the *universal* into his *individual* self-consciousness"; he surpasses in himself the alienation of creation and the opposition of wickedness through an "*absolute return (absolute Rückkehr)* and a universal unity of the universal and individual essence" of his "universal subjectivity." In this way there appears the "witness of the [mind]" (§570), through a two-part supercession (§571) that "actualizes (*verwirklicht*)" (§569) the idea of the mind, this time "as eternal, but *alive* and present (*gegenwärtigen*) in the world" (§569). Nevertheless, this return takes place only on one condition: that the concept "transpose" the alienation "into the world of time (*in die Zeitlichkeit versetzt*)" (§569) through a very precisely identified mediation, the trial of "the pain of negativity (*Schmerz der Negativität*)" (§§ 569 and 570). This pain develops the labor of negativity; that is, it unfolds the depths of the mind: the authority of negation. From this we must conclude that all the repetition of the Trinity called immanent signifies not only its transposition into time and into the world (and in this sense also its absorption into the Trinity called economic), but above all that this displacement and replacement rest on the fact that the logical power of the concept and of the "pain of negativity" are substituted for Trinitarian communion.

In which case, another question arises: Is negativity according to the concept, even endured as a "pain" in implicit imitation of Christ entering "into an agony" (Luke 22:44) with "loud cries and tears" (Hebrews 5:7), sufficient? Does it allow for the "recapitulation" (Ephesians 1:10) from the depths of the economy of the communion of the Trinity in itself? Or must we await something "greater" (John 5:36)?

Hegel, Triteness, and Seriousness

The question becomes all the more insistent because, after the three "reasonings"—*after* the "result," *after* "the spirit *in itself* in which all mediation has superseded (*aufgehoben*) itself" (§571)—Hegel still admits that "the infinite subjectivity, the merely formal self-consciousness, knowing itself in itself as absolute" may arise again. In a strange anticipation of the objection that Kierkegaard will address to him, he calls it "*irony (Ironie)*," and defines it by "an arbitrary emptiness," but one that "can make every objective reality naught and *vain (zunichte, zu einem eiteln)*" (§571). Perhaps we could think that this irony would above all allow us to doubt, or indeed to challenge the claim that logical negativity is sufficient to accomplish the Trinity according to the concept alone; or that the concept and negativity, even in its "pain," is *sufficient* to put into operation (in the economy) the Trinity itself (in its immanence). Asked in another way: In order to move beyond the aporias of a propositional interpretation of Revelation, is it enough simply to rectify the proposition of understanding in a proposition that is henceforward "speculative"?

Here we must return to the presupposition that guides the "transposition" of the Trinity into the logic of the "speculative" proposition. Hegel articulates it in a famous passage in a celebrated preface whose ultimately scandalous character ought to have been more accurately measured by Christian thinkers. "The life of God and divine cognition might thus be expressed as a game love plays with itself (*als ein Spielen der Liebe mit sich selbst*). If this Idea lacks the seriousness, the suffering, the patience, and the labor of the negative (*der Ernst, der Schmerz, die Geduld und Arbeit des Negativen*), then it lowers itself into edification, even into triteness. *In itself*, that life is indeed an unalloyed sameness and unity with itself, since in such a life there is neither anything serious in this otherness and alienation (*Ernst mit dem Anderssein und der Entfremdung*), nor in overcoming (*Überwinden*) this alienation."[20] The contention proceeds in three moments. First, the life of God in itself (the immanent Trinity) can, if one insists, be conceived in terms of love (in an undetermined sense) as the union through communion of distinct terms; and yet this is only the representation of faith. Second: such a "life of God" remains abstract and indeterminate because the religious conception of the terms of the immanent Trinity (Father, Son, Holy Spirit) does not *in itself* reach an actual alterity, a difference that is radicalized to the point of opposition, rupture, indeed antagonism; this conception would require negativity, which implies that the divine would go *outside of itself* and that it would alienate itself, not only in an other self (the Son), but in an other *than* itself (the world, temporality, finitude), or even a non-self (evil, wickedness). The Trinity does not reveal itself and does not uncover itself henceforth as such except when it finds its true *elsewhere* outside of itself. The immanent Trinity only unfolds itself when it acquires its plural self through the only actuality that differentiates, namely, that of the negative, the final operator of the economy. The two worlds of the Trinity therefore coincide, but to the benefit of the economy, itself reduced to self-exteriority, like the alienation of a foreign *elsewhere*. We come to the third moment: this mutation of the Trinity assumes that it does not reach genuine communion in its immanence, since, in this "disporting of love with itself" it does not yet put into play an actual plurality; its plurality remains abstract, empty, leading to no reconciliation, because the very terms to reconcile are missing: love, in not separating, has nothing to put into communion. The primacy of the economic *elsewhere* and negativity implies the powerlessness of love to produce an *elsewhere* through love alone. God thus does not uncover himself in coming *from elsewhere* "to what is his own, εἰς τὰ ἴδια ἦλθεν" (John 1:11); he comes to seek in that which is not his own the *elsewhere* that he lacks in himself. The *elsewhere* is reversed and the anamorphosis becomes that of God taking upon himself the point of view and aim that is not his own.

Every Hegelian interpretation of the Trinity thus rests on this last moment: the *elsewhere* is located outside of God, because "the play of love" opens no *elsewhere*, not even for God. The heart of the argument doesn't even lie in the reversal of the *elsewhere*, but rather in that which makes it ineluctable for Hegel: the triteness and the edification of love, powerless to attain, accomplish, and endure "the seriousness, the suffering, the patience, and the labor of the negative (*der Ernst, der Schmerz, die Geduld und Arbeit des Negativen*)." God, while he remains *in himself* at home, dreams his Trinity in sentiment and sensation, without actualizing it: he bovarizes.[21] The concern is the misunderstanding of love that, deep down, comes from a blasphemy that even Nietzsche was careful to avoid: "I have never profaned the holy name of love (*Ich habe den heiligen Namen der Liebe nie entweiht*)."[22] For it may be that love, understood as *agapē*, in fact accomplishes precisely the four operations that Hegel thinks can only fall to the "negative." Indeed, according to Saint Paul, "Love... suffers all things (πάντα στέγει), believes all things (πάντα πιστεύει), hopes all things (πάντα ἐλπίζει), endures all things (πάντα ὑπομένει)" (1 Corinthians 13:7). We can take the risk of making the two lists correspond term by term: love suffers all "pain"; it believes all things with "seriousness"; it hopes through its "labor"; and it endures with its "patience." Far from lacking what negativity seemingly claims (in its way), love seems to accomplish it superabundantly. Superabundantly and not negatively, because love never denies anything, nor gives in to any negativity, and because nothing can oppose it, since it accepts no condition of possibility to succeed in loving. Without any condition of possibility, not even self-identity or sufficient reason, it becomes impossible that anything there may *be* could remain impossible for it. Earlier we asked if we should not await a "greater" (John 5:36) help than the negative. The answer comes here: "Now (νυνὶ) faith, hope, love remain, these three. But of the three love is the greatest (μείζων)" (1 Corinthians 13:13).

The aporias of the ontic interpretation of the immanent Trinity (chapter 15) are thus not dissipated with the logical interpretation of its economy according to negativity (Hegel). It fails to progress "higher," by thinking the Trinity on the basis of what it uncovers of itself: "No one has greater love (μείζονα ἀγάπην) than he who gives his soul for his friends" (John 15:13). And the Son did it in the economy for his adoptive brothers only because he does it eternally with the Father in the self-immanence of the Trinity. But that can be conceived only by overturning Hegel's entire enterprise.

Schelling, the A Priori, and the A Posteriori

One might venture that when Schelling gave his lectures on the *Philosophy of Revelation* during the winter of 1841–42, from the chair that Hegel had occupied in Berlin, it was precisely this overturning that he undertook. He undertook it in a solemn effort (in front of Kierkegaard, Engels, Burckhardt, Bakunin, and others) that doubtless constitutes the last *positive* advance of German idealism toward the completion of metaphysics.[23] It was destined to fail not only because it came too late after the Hegelian closure, but above all because in order to complete metaphysics *against itself*, it would have been necessary to redefine even more radically the question of being, or rather, to think *without being*. Nevertheless, although it is late and unfinished, this effort remains a decisive breakthrough in view of an approach to Revelation that is *theo*logically free. We already noted that Schelling had overturned the terms of the debate: no longer must we ask how to interpret Christian Revelation so that it may have meaning in metaphysics (chapter 6); on the contrary, we must ask what form of philosophy is required in order to recognize the meaning of Revelation.[24] This truly heroic decision, probably impossible to put into operation at *that* moment, nevertheless allowed Schelling to cross a frontier, to exit the closed sea of *metaphysica* and enter into the free waters of the ocean. Let us therefore briefly retrace the steps he took.

The first step passes from negative to positive philosophy. Negative philosophy must be understand as *metaphysica*, which "consists only in a deduction of the objects themselves,"[25] without referring to experience like Locke and Hume did, following, in their own way, Aristotle; for, since Kant (and in fact Descartes), these concepts were "reduced to mere subjective forms of the faculty of knowledge, which, to be sure, correspond to something in the objects, insofar as they are objects of our experience (*Objekten, sofern sie Gegenstände unserer Erfahrung sind*) but do not, however, correspond to the objects *in themselves*, independent of experience."[26] The being's being is reduced to the process that fixes and recognizes accomplishments of the *cogitabile*, and the truth is limited to the deduction through logical steps of one *cogitabile* from another, in a system. Referred to God, *metaphysica* can reach only an idea of him, certainly supreme, but as deprived of existence as every other *cogitabile*:

> reason . . . can *begin* nothing with this idea, and can never make this idea into the beginning of any knowing. Theoretically, with this negative result all real religion was basically negated since all real religion can only relate to a real God, and indeed to him only as the Lord of reality (*Herrn der Wirklichkeit*) and because a being (*Wesen*) that is not this can never become the object of a religion, much less the object of a superstition. . . . Revealed religion presupposes a God who reveals himself, thus an active and real God (*wirkend und wirklich*). . . . Of the God who is just the highest idea of reason, it could only be said that he reveals himself to consciousness in a very improper sense, completely different from that in which those who believe in revelation speak of revelation.[27]

Negative philosophy is characterized by what it lacks or seeks not to know—by the incapacity of the concept to ever reach real existence—because it is limited to the essences and representations of objects. Under the title of existence it does not conceive real being, which precisely does not show itself through a concept, but maintains "none other than a *negative* concept of that which being itself is (*von dem, was das Seyende selbst ist*),"[28] that of logical possibility, of non-contradiction, of the property of not being a non-entity.

Because existence is demonstrated to the extent that it is represented, and one therefore cannot meet up with it *in the end*, it is necessary either to renounce attaining it (as negative philosophy did), or *to begin* with existence. And only positive philosophy has the means to a real beginning. However, beginning with existence does not consist in supposing we could find it already there and available in experience, as classical empiricism would have it. For in this case the *quod* of existence (*daß*) would once again be confused with the *quid* (quiddity, such and such essence, *Wesen, ousia,* entity). If there is being here, it must be understood verbally and not attributively: "Existence, which appears as accident in everything else, is here the essence (*Wesen*). The *quod* is here in the position of the *quid*." In this "inverted idea (*Umgekehrte Idee*)," it must be admitted that "reason is set *outside* itself (*außer sich*)."[29] Thought does not find real experience by itself, for in this case, it would once again accomplish the beginning. "If positive philosophy does not *start out* (*ausgeht*) from experience, then nothing prevents it from going toward (*zugehe*) experience, and thereby proving a posteriori what it has to prove, that its *prius* is God." Why maintain in this way the paradox that "it does not start out from experience but goes *toward* experience (*nicht von der Erfahrung aus, aber der Erfahrung* zugeht)"?[30]

Without the Concept, the Unprethinkable

For a clear motive worth reflecting upon. To begin at the beginning assumes beginning from that which is deduced from nothing else; it assumes beginning from a fact, and an absolute fact, and thus not an *a priori* where reason would be found already itself in the first position, because it would conceive the *a priori* by a concept: "what it begins with is a priori—but a priori it is not God, only a posteriori is it God. That it is God is not a *res naturae*, something that is self-evident, but is a *res facti*, and can therefore only be proved factually. It is God/God is (*es ist Gott*). This proposition does not mean the concept of this *prius* is equal to the concept of God. It means that this *prius is* God, not according to its concept, but according to its reality."[31] It is an event, it *happens*, God happens, or better: it *happens* God (*ein Geschehen*).[32] Positive philosophy

can only start out from that which is before and external to all thought (*ausgehen von dem, was vor und außer allem Denken ist*), consequently from being, but not from an empirical being. . . . If positive philosophy starts out from that which is external to all thought, it cannot begin with a being that is external to thought in a merely relative sense, but only with a being that is *absolutely* external to thought. The being that is external to all thought, however, is just as much beyond all experience as it is before all thought: positive philosophy begins with the *completely transcendent being* (*schlechterdings transcendente Seyn*).³³

The beginning must be absolute and happen absolutely; thus it can only be manifested absolutely *a posteriori*. As for other *a posteriori* situations in the everyday experience of the world, they do not bring about the truly *a posteriori*, because for them reason remains in principle *a priori*, through the authority of the concept and the representation that it puts into operation, so that reason knows *a priori* that everything that will happen to it will become for it an object through concepts. But here, where the absolute *prius* is at issue, we are dealing with an *a posteriori* that is also absolute—"*das absolute Prius . . . nur a posteriori Erkennbares.*"³⁴ Because it poses itself as first in itself, it can be known only *a posteriori*. "To be known a priori means just this: to be known from and out of the *prius*; what is known a priori is, thus, that which a *prius* possesses and from which it is known. The absolute *prius*, however, is what has no *prius* from which it can be known. To be the absolute *prius* means, therefore, not to be known a priori."³⁵ From this point on, the *prius* to know no longer coincides with the *a priori* of knowledge, it precedes it and thus inverts it in an irreducible *a posteriori*.

When Schelling states that "the entire history of philosophy . . . presents a struggle between the negative and positive philosophies,"³⁶ he thus formulates exactly what we have aimed at in our persistent polemic against the *a priori* (chapters 6, 8–10). In fact, he even radicalizes it. For if on the one hand God imposes himself as an absolute *prius* who becomes conceivable to us only absolutely *a priori*, and if, on the other hand, the metaphysical authority of the concept holds to its claim to fix the *a priori* starting from our transcendental point of view, then the event and the fact of God revealing himself disqualify every concept, because he precedes them all. If he can and must be known, he will be known as he is: "*if* he exists, he can only be *in* and, as it were, *before* himself, that is, *he can only* be that which is *before* his divinity; but if before he is divine he is that which is, then for this very reason he is that which precedes his concept, and, thus, all concepts (*das seinem Begriff, also allem Begriffe voraus Seyende*)."³⁷

Thinking without beginning with the concept: it is on this condition alone that God can be thought, God as such, that is to say unconcealing himself from himself alone. God begins before the concept conceives him. Thinking the manifestation of God requires thinking clearly this originary delay; for this delay is precisely what defines the origin. The beginning only inaugurates if it precedes everything, including every concept that would seek to think it; the "concept" of the beginning consists in the delay that it imposes on every concept in relation to its beginning. The concept differs from the beginning because this delay defers the concept. Schelling formulates thought's essential delay from the beginning, and thus of the created from God, with a perfect neologism: God makes himself known as un-pre-thinkable (*unvordenklich*), as that which the concept cannot think in advance, nor foresee, nor pre-think.[38] One could also name it the new, the unexpected, "*Neues, Unerwartetes.*"[39] At issue here is what we have designated since the beginning (chapters 1–2) as the *elsewhere*, that which arises from *elsewhere* and allows (or requires) an anamorphosis. Here it is the anamorphosis of a *prius*, the fact of which shifts all knowledge of the *a priori* to the *a posteriori*, turns the negative philosophy into the positive, and in this way opens the possible of a Revelation. And indeed Schelling ends up at the heart of the biblical Revelation when he concludes, "For, of itself, the One is unknown, it has no concept through which it could be designated, but rather only a *name (keinen Begriff, durch den es zu bezeichnen wäre, sondern nur einen Namen)*—therefore, the importance placed on the name—in name *He* is *himself*, the Singular, he who has no equal."[40] God, he whom we all know at least by name, but singularly by Name.

Schelling: Being on the Other Side of Being?

One cannot underestimate what the *Philosophy of Revelation* accomplished by overturning the *a priori* of the concept and by liberating the possibility of an *elsewhere* for thought, and thus by opening the site for a Revelation as such. But this result, while it bears the title of positive philosophy, remains, in another sense, merely negative: the recognition of the unprethinkable concerns solely the question *de Deo uno*, without yet saying anything *de Deo trino*. It remains for us to see what the recognition of God as "Lord of being" allows us to conceive of the *mystērion* of charity in him.

In order to sketch an answer to this question, it is first fitting to clarify how and at what point being is surpassed, and by what "lordship." The breakthrough from the negative to the positive in philosophy is remarkably explained in a passage from Lecture V:

At some point and time in its development the human spirit will feel the need, to express myself in such a manner, to get to the bottom of being (*hinter das Seyn zu kommen*) . . . , one would very much like, as one says, to get to the bottom of an issue. But what is here, at "the bottom of the issue"? Not being, for this, on the contrary, is what lies on the surface of the issue (*das Vordere der Sache*), that which immediately comes to mind, and, thus, what is already presupposed in all this: if I want to get to the bottom of an issue, for example, an event (*Ereignis*), then the issue—in this instance, the event (*Ereignis*)—must already be given (*schon gegeben sein*). At the bottom of this issue is, therefore, not being, but the essence (*Wesen*), the potency, the cause (*Ursache*) (properly speaking these are all just synonymous concepts). Thus, at the highest point of its development, the propensity to understand that is so deeply embedded and insurmountable in humanity will also demand to get to the bottom of not merely this or that issue but to the bottom of being in general (*hinter das Seyn überhaupt zu kommen*). Not to see what is above being, for this is an entirely different concept, but to see what lies *on the other side* of being.

What do we encounter beyond this frontier? What do we find "given" there, what does the "event" bring that is new? Here, we find an indication: "to flee into a complete wasteland devoid of all being (*in eine völlig Wüste alles Seyn*)"; and then another positive one: "that *inner organism* of successive potencies through which it [i.e. reason?] possesses the key to all being, and which is the inner organism of reason itself."[41] But, the potency or potencies join together "being (*das Seyende*)," which "itself exists," even if it is "above (*über*) that being."[42] The ambiguous yet constant usage of the same terms (*Seyn* and *Seyende*), sometimes negative according to the concept of beings, sometimes positive according to the actuality of the fact happening, separated only by often imprecise polemical explanations, betrays the indetermination of the surpassing "beneath" and "on the other side of" being that the "potencies" are claimed to accomplish. In other words, can the one who has lordship over being simply be defined in relation to this being, as "no longer just the being (*bloß das Seyende*), . . . but rather the Over-being (*das Überseyende*)"?[43] The being beyond being remains, like the God without being, understood, and only *negatively* so, on the basis of what it would like to surpass and believes it surpasses. In order to go beyond, it is necessary to forget and leave behind ourselves what we transgress. Such is not the case here.

Schelling: Impotency of the Potencies

The goal then is to measure whether "the doctrine of potencies," after having "been enough to explain mythology," also allows one to "lay the ground (*den Grund . . . legen*) for the future philosophy of Revelation" by explaining "the idea of the unitrinity in God."[44]

In an initial moment, the potencies play out in an opposition between being in itself and being for itself, and determine, in a quasi-Hegelian sense, "the absolute" or "perfect spirit."[45] To begin with, take "the spirit being *in itself*," never an object even for itself, "the absolutely non-objective": in itself, that is, not "going beyond itself," a "pure self, in the complete destitution of self, in the absolute unknowing of oneself." We note that the primacy of this first potency (in fact, the Father) is defined first of all in terms of knowledge (of self), of thought (of self), certainly by contrast, but referring itself in this way all the more to the logic of negative philosophy. Whence it follows that the "purest aseity" is once more defined as "that from which the understanding can appropriate nothing"; whence comes also the "deepest, most intimate and equally the most withdrawn" "silence" and "rest" of the divinity, "hidden" and "invisible." We cannot avoid concluding that this determination of being-in-itself as in-itself does not manifest, indicate, or tell anything about the paternity of God.

Next, take "the spirit being *for itself*." Being for itself it is not in-itself, and therefore, obviously, it is "far from itself, *von sich weg*." And, like Hegel before him, Schelling must assume that it can find a space (but which, and where?) that allows the spirit to take place as "the exterior, *das Äußere*." The *for-itself* would so to speak bring about this exteriority from itself, because it is not more necessarily "with itself, *bei sich*" than it is "apart, *weg*" from itself; it is freely both the one and the other through its property (opposed to that of the *in-itself*) of "going far away from itself, *von sich weggehen*." Thus we could conclude that such an indetermination of being for-itself manifests, indicates, and says nothing of the filiation that is in God, but we note that sometimes here another vocabulary operates; for example when Schelling remarks:

> The nature of the spirit *for*-itself is precisely to be solely for *itself*, that is, it consists in being for the spirit existing in-itself, in *giving itself* (*sich geben*) totally to it. And at the same time, from the other side, we can say that the nature of the spirit existing *in-itself* consists solely in being the one for which the other is there. In a sense, the one is forgotten in the other; neither of the two, we can say, is in view of itself: the entity *in-itself* is only in order to be possessed as spirit existing for-itself, and the spirit existing for-itself (and thus not in-itself) only is in order to give itself (*geben*) to that one (the spirit existing *in-itself*).

How do we understand that the doctrine of potencies and the antinomy of the entity *in-itself* with the *for-itself* operate unexpectedly with the help of the logic of the gift? Obviously, in belonging to totally different registers they cannot merge. Can they be organized hierarchically? Or rather should they be opposed and exclude one another?

Finally, there comes "the spirit *close to* itself (*bei sich*)." It is defined as "that which can be apart (*weg*) from itself, go far away from itself (*von sich weggehen*), exteriorizing itself (*sich äußern*, estranging itself), without however being less in itself, and inversely being in itself without however being any less able to go far away from itself (*von sich weggehen*)." How the spirit arrives at the status of "perfect spirit" would remain to be shown. But the foundation of this unity "in the concept, *im Begriff*" seems at best vague and weak, at worst a regression into the negative philosophy. Resorting to "the spirit free even from itself," to the "freedom that is what is the highest for us in our divinity" only postpones the difficulty: How and from where is this freedom exercised, even toward oneself? Here we cannot avoid asking what is lacking in the reconstitution of the Trinitarian life starting from the doctrine of the potencies.

Schelling: Love Missed, and the Indecision of the Gift

To respond to this question it would be necessary to examine Schelling's entire Christology, a work that goes beyond my aims here, and which has been accomplished quite well by others.[46] I will content myself with insisting on one point, which in fact is decisive for every interpretation of the

Trinity. Indeed, Schelling gave a commentary on the hymn quoted in the Letter to the Philippians (2:6–8): "Jesus Christ, who subsisted (ὑπάρχων) in the form of God (ἐν μορφῇ θεοῦ), in no way regarded being equal to God (τὸ εἶναι ἴσα θεῷ) as a good to be possessed (οὐχ ἁρπαγμὸν ἡγήσατο), but he emptied himself (ἐκένωσεν) [of] himself, taking the form of a slave (μορφὴν δούλου λαβών) by becoming alike to man; and found like a man, he humbled himself by becoming obedient to death, even death on a cross." In order to understand it, Schelling seeks to measure the economic gap between Jesus and the Father and assumes that he fixes *at the same time* the norm of the relation of the Son to the Father in the immanent Trinity. This interpretation, which proceeds by several fairly questionable arguments, reaches a rather detrimental conclusion.[47] For Paul, clearly the point is to emphasize the parallel between the immanent Trinitarian relation of the eternal Son to the Father (in the Spirit) and the economic repetition by Christ of this same relation in finitude (becoming man), In obedience, and finally in death; it is only by presupposing this likeness between the Trinitarian situation of the Son and the economic situation of Christ that one understands why the apostle would recommend to the community of believers to have "in yourselves the very same thought (τοῦτο φρονεῖτε ἐν ὑμῖν) that is found in Christ Jesus" (Philippians 2:5). Schelling, however, holds on the contrary that the μορφῇ θεοῦ here defines "a third state, in which he [Jesus Christ] is posed as an extra-divine personality, without however already being a man."[48] In this way, the Son would be, *before* the Incarnation and *a fortiori* his death on the cross, essentially different from the "essential" divinity, according to a "*rupture (Abgeschnittenheit)* of the Son from the Father, . . . in a total *freedom* and independence with regard to the Father."[49] Thus even in the immanent Trinity, freedom with regard to being would render the Son free with regard to his own divinity, and thus autonomous with regard to the Father. The Son would be divine, but without, or indeed "against, *gegenüber*" the Father, "not inwardly, but externally, *äußerlich.*"[50]

From this follows an inevitable question: Why must the immanent Trinity be understood as a rupture placing the Son outside of the Father? Answer: Because, without this rupture, the distinction of the Trinitarian persons could not truly be accomplished. Why is that? Because no other differentiation between the Father and the Son is considered; because *agapē* is never seen as a logic allowing for distance, as a distinction through and in view of communion. The logical distinction forces Schelling, as it already did Hegel, to introduce into the immanent Trinity the only principle that they can envisage to accomplish it: the rupture. Little does it matter that this rupture comes from the negative in the speculative proposition (Hegel), and from the freedom of the spirit or the play of the in-itself/for-itself (Schelling), provided that it remains the work of the sole concept. And never that of *agapē*. This mistake of grammar—to want to think the Trinity according to the logic of the concept and never according to the logic of *agapē*—is detected in Schelling, as it was previously in Hegel, through the unintelligence of what nevertheless is sometimes hailed as the "wonder of love, *Wunder der Liebe*."[51] More precisely, through the unintelligence of the *gift* in its Trinitarian function.

At least one text indicates this clearly.

> Then comes the moment when it [a potency that makes creation possible] is again raised, in human consciousness [that of Christ], to the status of the Lord of this being, when it again has a sovereignty and is therefore also *in this way* again (externally) a divine personality. But it is a divine personality as Lord over the being that the Father *did not* give it (*das* nicht *der Vater ihr gegeben hat*)—the being that it possesses independently of the Father. As a result, it is *independent* of the Father and therefore must, at this moment, be determined according to its being as a personality at once extra-divine and divine (*außergöttlich-göttliche*): divine because it is the Lord of being, extra-divine because it possesses this being as a being *not* given by God (*von Gott* nicht *gegeben*), and thus independent of the Father. Its freedom consists *in this*. One must know this in order to understand this *obedience* of Christ, of which so much is said (Philippians 2:8; Hebrews 2:9 and 5:8, etc.) and on which at the same time so much depends. The Son *could* exist independently of the Father in his *own* (*eigner*) sovereignty; he certainly could not be the *true* (*wahre*) God apart from the Father, but he could nevertheless, apart from the Father and without him, be *God*, namely the Lord of being; he of course could not be God in *essence* (*Wesen*), but he could be God in *actu*. But *this* sovereignty, which he could have independently of the Father, the Son despised, and *in this* he is Christ. That is the fundamental idea of Christianity.[52]

It is clear: the Father *gives* divinity to the Son (and Christ understands it this way) as a mere divinity *in actu*, but not as essential; this divinity, because given, remains independent of the Father and is therefore limited: the Son "cannot possess true divinity (*wahre Gottheit*)," but only an "accidental being (*zufällig*), an "*inessential, unwesentliche*" divinity, or even a "*false* (*falschen*) divinity."³³ Shouldn't we therefore say instead that the Father *does not give* divinity to the Son, at least, not his own? And therefore neither does he give the Son independence, for whom "all that is mine is yours and all that is yours is mine" (John 17:10 and Luke 15:31)? Does the Father's gift give or *reserve* the being, sovereignty, and independence that he purportedly gives without *truly* giving them? Schelling seems, two pages later, to hesitate or sense the difficulty when he writes, after having mentioned "the being that the Father has *not* given" to the Son, that the Son "possesses being . . . not originally like the Father, but insofar as it was given to him (*als ein ihm gegebenes*), as Son."³⁴ The question becomes clear: Does the Father give all things to his Son, as one gives paternally—totally and without return—or does he give without giving all (all divinity, all independence, all freedom), or in other words, without giving at all? Does he give with the reserve of the concept, according to which what *is* apart from the Father is apart from God, and what *is* different from God the Father is alienated from him, or in short, where difference is conceived only as rupture? Or does he give in the communion of *agapē*, where the distinction between the poles of love makes the union *grow*, where the Son abandons himself all the *more* to the Father as the Father abandons everything to him, the one and the other giving without reserve, such that this non-reserve itself appears as their Spirit?

Schelling was not unaware of this other hypothesis, and sometimes did more than touch upon it. A magnificent interpolation, for instance, considers that "if by being one understands merely that which gives itself (*wenn man unter dem Seyn bloß das sich gebende*), the revealed, that which is outside itself and moves away from itself (*das offenbare, das außer sich, von sich weggehende*), then the spirit *for*-itself is the pure entity."³⁵ Could being be conceived, or could it have been conceived, on the basis of the gift that delivers it from itself and hands it over as itself, as *being given*? Schelling came awfully close to doing so, even if he finally fell short, perhaps perceiving that crossing this limit would have led in principle to the site where a *theo*logical thinking of the Trinity would become, or at least could have become, possible. Another text suggests this as well, seeming to *renounce* the strict doctrine of the potencies:

With the persons, our reflection rises to a higher level, we can even say to another *world*. In the potencies, for as long as they are in tension, we see only the natural side of the process (we see it only as the process of the birth of the concrete). With the persons there opens another world, the divine world as such; and it is precisely in this way that for the first time there appears the superior meaning, namely the divine meaning of the process. Indeed, with regard to divinity it has *this* sense, that being, which originally is only with the Father, who possesses it as mere possibility, is *given* (*gegeben*) to the Son, and even communicated to the Spirit, for to the Son being is *given* (*gegeben*) by the Father, but to the Spirit it is given (*gegeben*) by the Father and the Son.[56]

Schelling deserves credit, then, for his indecisions.

Schelling, the Higher History

The one and only rupture in conformity with the concept thus governs both the immanent Trinity and the economic Trinity. Hegel and Schelling end up with the same result and the same aporia left exposed by Rahner's judgment. As a result, the economy includes history, even if it is not reduced to the common (metaphysical) concept of history, since it has to do not with a succession or an ensemble of objects, but with a discontinuous diachrony of events. But invoking a "higher history"[57] here does not dispel the aporia; for in order to conceive (or rather, receive) events correctly, it is not enough to substitute for the *logia* of a propositional interpretation of Revelation (chapters 4 and 15) the *gesta Dei* of an imprecise (linear, chronological) historical interpretation of Revelation (chapter 16). Moreover, strictly speaking, Revelation does not belong to history (neither in the sense of the *Historie* of the historians nor that of the philosophical *Geschichte*), but is inscribed in or rather *through* events, that is to say saturated phenomena, unobjectifiable by concepts, the occurrence (unexpected arrival) of which therefore imposes on their witnesses an unlimited hermeneutic. Without this phenomenological specificity, the historical interpretation of Revelation fails to get beyond the aporias of its propositional interpretation, but repeats its idolatry—no longer that of the concepts, but that of the "facts" or, worse, of the "meaning of history." There is nothing modern or postmodern about this temptation.

When Schelling was concluding the *Philosophy of Revelation* by assigning the three successive Churches to the three persons of the Trinity ("Peter ... is the apostle of the Father; Paul, of the Son; John, of the Spirit"[58]), not only did he give in to a *weak* (because merely chronological) historical interpretation of the revelatory function of the Trinity; not only did he completely miss the identity here between the revealed and the mode of Revelation (between the phenomenon and the "how, *wie*" of its phenomenalization); but above all, echoing Joachim de Fiore, he came back to a famous but already insufficient interpretation made by Gregory of Nazianzus: "[T]he old covenant made clear proclamation of the Father, a less definite one of the Son. The new covenant made the Son manifest and gave us a glimpse of the Spirit's Godhead. At the present time (*nyn*), the Spirit resides amongst us, giving us a clearer manifestation of himself than before."[39] Taken literally, the narrowly historical temporalization of the Trinity flattens the economy into chronology rather than consecrating history as revelatory in a Trinitarian manner. No objectivity can define what is put into operation in the economy, even less so if this economy must be able to unfold itself in a Trinitarian manner, in its phenomenal given as well as, and perhaps first of all, in its mode of phenomenalization.

SEVENTEEN

The Trinity as Icon: A Phenomenal Model

Two Shortcomings

Thus, the two primary models of interpretation of the Trinity display their shortcomings. It is not a question of their powerlessness "to speak the wisdom of God in his mystery" (2 Corinthians 2:7), the inevitable and indispensable powerlessness that authenticates every correct conception of what can only be understood by not understanding it (according to a theological rule that has no exception). Rather, it is a question of their twofold claim to understand more than is possible of the Trinitarian mystery, and thus to lack decisive determinations of it—decisive because they indicate the ways of access to what cannot and must not be conceived by concept.

The first model attempts to lower the three *nescio quid* of the Trinity to the horizon of being and beings (*être/étant*) by imposing on them the lexicon of being, above all the principle of its identity. In this way it dislocates the unity by communion in a triplicity and a wrongly juxtaposed and thus wrongly reconciled unicity, because it wants to think them according to *ousia* (whether primary or secondary). The error comes from approaching the Trinity starting from a point of view other than its own, deporting it from its center to displace it somewhere else. Or more exactly, it is banished to a place of interpretation that is suited to *our* metaphysics (whether spontaneous or sophisticated), but which remains foreign to it. Considered outside itself, it aligns with our perspective, which thus banishes it elsewhere, but an elsewhere which exactly inverts what defines every revelation—that it come from *elsewhere* to the one who receives it. The first model of the Trinity ontically cancels out the *elsewhere* of its uncovering.

The second model attempts to unfold the Trinity's unity by communion within the logical horizon of the sequence of the concept, whether according to the speculative proposition, following the link between subject and predicate, and thus by the operation of the negative (Hegel); or by the articulation of the spirit between its in-itself and its for-itself, therefore by the power of its freedom towards its own being (Schelling). In both cases, the unity no longer rests on the communion of the *nescio quid* in the single act of charity, but results from a discursive unfolding, which ultimately comes under the heading of history more than the Trinitarian "economy." The realization of communion even remains inchoate, since it is attested only in its unfolding, if not its historical disarticulation in the progression of the world. The error once again comes from the fact that the Trinity is approached here from another point of view than its own and removed from its center, by inverting the elsewhere. Considered from the logic of the spirit or (what comes down to the same thing) from the speculative proposition according to its metaphysical understanding, the Trinitarian communion is torn apart from the mystery of charity and, stateless from itself, displaced into a desert devoid of love, recorded under other names and other skies, elsewhere, in the immanence of our worldly logic. This other place, ours, constrains it to live in an elsewhere that is not its own, but which alienates it: it is no coincidence that alienation (*Entäußerung*) becomes the primary operator of these reappropriations and misappropriations of the Trinity. For it is a matter of nullifying its true *elsewhere*—the place from which it must come to arrive in its uncovering—so that it no longer uncovers itself, but recovers itself *among us*: "and his own did not receive him" (John 1:11).

The common flaw of these two models now becomes obvious: they neutralize the *elsewhere* from which the Trinity reveals itself, by deporting it from charity, into our temporality and our world—thereby claiming to save it, but saving it under our conditions. Neutralizing the *elsewhere*, refusing anamorphosis—here we are.

How can we break free from this captivity? Two negative conditions immediately stand out. Against the first model, one must admit that being/beings [*l'être/étant*], even if it *can* also denote God, can only do so by renouncing its fundamental intention: to adequately know by concept. In other words, one must scrupulously heed the warning of Thomas Aquinas: "just as the substance of God is unknown, so it is for his being (*sicut Dei substantia ignota, ita et esse*)."[1] It is also necessary, against the second model, to draw out the consequences of the warning given by Basil of Caesarea: "Each of the hypostases we proclaim as unique (μονοχῶς); and if it is ever necessary to count them one after another, we do not let ourselves be carried away by ignorant enumeration (ἀπαιδεύτῳ ἀριθμήσει) towards a polytheistic conception."[2]

But to these two negative injunctions, one must further add two positive ones. First, the one already formulated by Barth (chapters 7 and 15): the dimensions of the Trinity must govern the acts [*gestes*] of its revelation and the acts of revelation must correspond to the dimensions of the Trinity. In other words, it is fitting that the three terms of (immanent) communion are also found at play in the moments of its (economic) manifestation, in other words, the communion and manifestation put into play exactly the same logic of charity. The immanent unity of communion should not, therefore, be manifested economically by unfolding itself, by disconnecting itself into moments that are different than it, or even contradictory to it. The Trinity must unfold itself in moments that always belong to a union of communion and that ensure, in this very communion, the conditions and dimensions of its manifestation. It is necessary that the three *nescio quid* are required as intimately in the exercise of manifestation as they are united in their immanent communion: in this way alone will the "and vice versa" (*und umgekehrt*) be accomplished correctly, by a manifestation that is not triple (where economy would contradict immanence) but triune (where the manifestation follows the exact rhythm of the communion). The immanent Trinity and the economic Trinity remain isomorphic, because charity gives itself as it is accomplished, precisely because it is accomplished in itself as gift—*dando revelat, revelando dat*. There remains finally a last injunction, which we have just formulated *a contrario*: since the previous models fail because they cancel out the *elsewhere* of the Trinity by imposing their own elsewhere on it (the ego's point of view and its master concept), and since they reject the very possibility of an anamorphosis, and therefore of a revelation, a third model would have to reestablish the pivot and turning point of the *elsewhere*. And this *elsewhere* must be established in its clearest radicality, as that which does not come from us, does not speak the words of our tribe, remains impracticable to us *as such*, as the condition always *a posteriori* for us of the *a priori* manifestation of the other.

The Spirit and the Elsewhere

How to arrive at such a Trinitarian model? Perhaps by revealing a trait common to the two other models: their shared *retreat* before the Spirit. They were, in effect, first built to conceive the relation of Jesus to God, and thus of the Father to the Son; and, in practice, we have scarcely invoked the Trinity until now except by naming the Father and the Son. In this way, in the three persons of the Trinity, it would seem that the Spirit only arrives late, as a complement and a repetition of what is played out prior to him between the first two; this has often been deplored, sometimes to the point of polemic; but there is some naïveté in being astonished by it. Not only does the history of dogma show that the Trinitarian debate was provoked by the question of the Son's equality (or not) with the Father, but it was only after a century of latency that Arianism (especially the followers of Macedonius) brought the Spirit to the debate, questioning his Divinity. This reluctance or this delay before the third term is explained all the more by the fact that the Spirit does not appear in biblical testimonies except in an auxiliary way, as the Spirit *of God* (Matthew 3:16; Romans 8:14; 2 Colossians 3:3; Ephesians 4:30), the Spirit *of the Father* (Matthew 10:20), the Spirit *of the Son* (Galatians 4:6), or the Spirit *of Jesus Christ* (Philippians 1:19); not to mention in a veiled way, because his divinity is not explicitly attested; for if "God is spirit" (John 4:24), nowhere do we read the reverse. Where then to situate the Spirit in God: in the Trinity, or in some margin, and which one?

However, the conclusion that would almost go without saying—that the Spirit is not revealed as God—would here be a complete misinterpretation. The Spirit is situated in the immanent Trinity, because he situates it in its economy. The Spirit belongs to what is revealed in a Trinitarian way, because he operates by *revealing in a Trinitarian way* what is revealed. It is even this that distinguishes his divine function from that of the Father and the Son.

"Beloved, do not have faith in any spirit, but test the spirits, [to know] if they are of God.... The spirit of God is recognized by this: every spirit which confesses that Jesus Christ has come into the flesh is of God; and every spirit that does not confess Jesus is not of God" (1 John 4:1–3). His Trinitarian function does not consist in revealing *himself* directly, but in revealing the Father in Jesus Christ manifested as the Son. The Spirit participates intrinsically in the revelation of the Trinity as its revealer [*révélateur*] (in the sense that without a chemical developing agent [*révélateur*], an image impressed on the film negative could not be developed, and thus would not appear). "Therefore I make it known to you: no one has said in the Spirit of God, 'Anathema to Jesus,' and no one can say 'Lord Jesus,' except in the Holy Spirit" (1 Corinthians 12:3). The Spirit causes the confession of Christ as Son of the Father; this confession is only performed in and by him, even and especially if it is up to man to perform it; for a human being, by confessing Christ as Son of the Father, recognizes at the same time (as tremendous as this leap appears to us) this Father, of this Son, as his own: "You did not receive a spirit of slavery, to fall back into fear, but you have received the Spirit of sonship, in which we cry 'Abba, Father!' The Spirit himself joins his testimony to our own (αὐτὸ τὸ Πνεῦμα συνμαρτυρεῖ τῷ πνεύματι) to testify that we are sons of God" (Romans 8:15–16). The Spirit reveals the Father in the Son by making us, too, Sons of the Father—the economic Trinity coincides with the immanent Trinity, because it is accomplished in itself and according to its one Spirit. "Because you are sons, God sent (ἐξαπέστειλεν) the Spirit of his Son into your hearts to cry, 'Abba, Father!' So you are no longer a slave, but a son. And if you are a son, you inherit through God (διὰ θεοῦ)" (Galatians 4:6–7). The Spirit makes us sons, not only because he makes us dare to confess God as Father and makes us achieve this, but also because he introduces us into the position and filial condition of Christ; indeed, what he confers on us, he borrows directly from the Son: "When he comes, the Spirit of Truth, he will open the way (ὁδηγήσει) toward the whole truth.... He will glorify me, for he will take from what is mine (ἐκ τοῦ ἐμοῦ) and will proclaim it to you" (John 16:13–14). Thus, the Spirit manifests the fatherhood of God by making Jesus recognized as the Son, but by one and the same gesture that, at the same time, glorifies the (immanent) Trinity as such, uncovers it to us economically, and finally enables us, too, still caught in an economy oozing sin, to perform sonship in the name of Christ. For this is the case according to another paradox, stated by Christ himself: "Whoever believes in me will also do the works that I do, and he will do greater ones, because I am going to the Father" (John 14:12). He will do greater works, because Christ, having returned to the Father, restoring everything and definitively accomplishing the (immanent) Trinity, definitively absorbs the (economic) play of the adoptive sons within it.

The Possibility of an Anamorphosis

The idea that the Holy Spirit comes to say "Abba, Father!" in us and manifests the (immanent) Trinity by making us a part of its economy can and should surprise us, as a paradox. Yet this paradox must be received correctly, for it is not a matter of hyperbolical exaltation due to *Schwärmerei* or supposed "mysticism." It is a question of an operation that we have already described at least as a sketch under the term *anamorphosis*, but this time in soberly biblical terms. Anamorphosis designates the transfer of the anchor point of the intentional aim from one place (the zero point, *Nullpunkt*) to another that is distant and different, the displacement of the intentional ego from one point of view to another, according to mostly silent but all the more binding requirements of the phenomenon that gives itself to be seen; for some give themselves in such a way that they show themselves only if the one who claims to see them accepts to place himself at (thus to move toward) the site where the diverse character of intuitions, up until then scattered, chaotic, and confused, is organized from itself (and no longer from our *a priori* concepts) under a coherent, organic figure, which is in *a* sense (its own, not mine) born from itself. Here, the phenomenality of Christ is given, but not in a way that our gazes, restricted by their history, their destiny, and their shame, could immediately receive him, or foresee him, or see him as the Son of the Father; they will only be able to see what gives itself by relinquishing their foresight, thus by shifting from one point of view (religious, cultural, political, etc.) to another, to *this* other that will open up to them all at once the confession of Jesus as Christ, and thus as Son of the Father (chapters 13–14). This is indeed an anamorphosis. But *here* we understand that the place required by anamorphosis is exclusively defined by the Spirit, who "makes and clears the way (ὁδηγήσει)" (John 16:13).

Clearing the way consists in guiding the steps of the one who does not know in advance where to go and relies on the guide (*hodēgos*) who alone knows where to go. Such guidance (*hodēgia*) blazes a trail that does lead somewhere, but without the one who takes it knowing where it leads, or if it leads anywhere to begin with. The guide who opens the way thus proceeds (moves ahead and ventures forward) by the exact inverse of method (*methodos*) that knows in advance where it is going (and moves ahead without ever venturing anywhere, without risking anything). Blazing a climbing route or a ski trail does not consist in building a marked path, which transforms the mountain face or the slope into a *via ferrata* or an express lane that one can then travel at will. It consists in *working* to see the mountain or the trail as a possible path *at that moment*; thus to go see for oneself how to place oneself at the point of view where the landscape shows the road that it was already giving, but that is hidden for anyone who is not sighting it from the right place. As soon as this point is reached, then, the path and the trail are clearly opened to the gaze. The phenomenon of the trail made its path, that which was giving itself ends by showing itself, because I came to its point of view, because I *surrendered* myself to it. Surrendering to what is given, allowing it to show itself: this is what anamorphosis demands and method refuses. The methodical ego strives to keep the same point of view on its journey; it advances from a known place toward another place, foreseen from the outset so that it can be known (or re-cognized) by the same gaze that kept the prior place under its guard: the ego has mapped its journey, progresses from the known to the knowable, and thus to the known by anticipation. It knows where it is going, as much as it only goes where it knows and where it will be able to know; it safeguards its gaze and explores so as to not expose itself. In contrast, a serious anamorphosis involves walking toward discovery, walking without a map, "by the stars" (Matthew 2:2), on the lookout with each step to see if it might not be here, or rather *there*, or in any case *elsewhere*, that, "suddenly (ἐξαίφνης)," the given phenomenon will show itself, spring forth like a "multitude of the heavenly host that praised God" (Luke 2:13), like a master returning without notice (Mark 13:36), like a blinding light on the road to Damascus (Acts 9:3 and 22:6).

The Spirit, guide of anamorphosis, thus leads the ego out of its site, out of its zone of security (as one says), or better, out of its methodical certainty along an *elsewhere* that, at first, seems to him an exile, a *terra incognita*, merely promised. This exit from self is marked by the loss of speech. Like Peter, who "did not know what to say" (Luke 9:33), we no longer know how to speak; and so the Spirit speaks in our place. Not that he takes the words out of our mouths and we cease to define ourselves, as humans, as "having *logos*," but that we receive another *logos*, when his *logos* replaces ours. He speaks for us like an advocate called to the rescue (*paraklētos*) to lend us a voice that says what we do not know how to say: "Do not worry yourselves in advance (μὴ προμεριμνᾶτε) what to say, but whatever is given to you in that hour (ὃ ἐὰν δοθῇ), say it; for it is not you who speak, but the Spirit, the Holy One (τὸ Πνεῦμα τὸ Ἅγιον)" (Mark 13:11), "... but it is the Spirit of your Father who will speak" (Matthew 10:20). And this *logos*, which does not come from us, nevertheless makes us understand those who do not speak our native language: "They began to speak in other tongues, as the Spirit had given (ἐδίδου) them to speak out . . . and each of them heard them speaking in his own dialect" (Acts 2:4 and 6). It could not be more clearly shown that, when it is a question of the uncovering where God reveals himself, anamorphosis goes so far as to transfer the ego to a site given by God himself, making it speak and see from the Spirit's point of view. Still, for our ego to be situated in the Spirit, it is necessary that "the love of God has been poured into our hearts through the Holy Spirit who has been given to us (τοῦ δοθέντος ἡμῖν)" (Romans 5:5). The outpouring of the Holy Spirit thus has a properly phenomenal function here: it allows an anamorphosis commensurate to the economic phenomenalization of the Trinity. But, one might ask, can such an anamorphosis really be accomplished? Doesn't it remain, at best, an extreme hypothesis, possible for a few, at most, and in exceptional occasions, but so marginal that it does not enter into the field of common phenomenality? We do not have to take the step that leads from possibility to actuality here, but at least to corroborate this possibility itself, and to corroborate it as it gives itself, theologically, therefore by arguments that are themselves theological, or in a word, biblical.

Let us begin from the position that has thus far been determined: anamorphosis comes from the Holy Spirit who pours out in us "the love of God" (Romans 5:5) and the "greatest" *elsewhere* can only be attained at this price, nothing less than love or charity: "Now (νυνὶ) three things remain, love, faith, and hope. But among them, the greatest is love" (1 Corinthians 13:13). Must faith and hope be thus subordinated to love to disappear in the end? "Now," in the economy, they still remain; but they remain already in their relation to charity, whose operations they deploy. Of course, "now" no ego can succeed in accomplishing anamorphosis "up to the end (εἰς τέλος)" (John 13:1), except Christ—and that is enough.

For us, in the approach that must be ceaselessly taken up and continued, charity remains imperfect, and our tongue parrots the words when we lend it to the voice of the Spirit; our anamorphosis stops short and must thus resort to faith. However faith is not defined simply as an arbitrary and insecure belief (a non-knowledge, says metaphysics), but as "the substrate of things that one hopes for (ὑπόστασις τῶν ἐλπιζομένων), the argument for things we do not see (πραγμάτων ἔλεγχος οὐ βλεπομένων)" (Hebrews 11:1). Love *for us* must certainly believe what it does not yet love enough to have seen it, but it believes what it does not know yet, because it knows what it has already experienced and accomplished through love; it has already experienced enough and seen enough accomplished in it, since "God has placed into our hearts the deposit of the Spirit" (2 Corinthians 1:22); we have already secured and received enough advances on the inheritance to know that the rest will surely follow.[3] Faith therefore has hopes. Faith hopes, and love in us believes, but because it is no longer ignorant and already *sees*. The anamorphosis of charity is still ongoing, but it proceeds and progresses; what it does not yet see and what is not yet shown to it, charity already knows that it has been given to it: "We are sanctified . . . once for all" (Hebrews 10:10). Of course we still only see "in a mirror and in enigma" and not yet "face to face," but in fact "we do see (βλέπομεν)" (1 Corinthians 13:12). The noema does not reach its perfect fulfillment, but the noematic core has emerged, has taken shape; the noesis does not yet reach adequation, the thing itself does not yet appear as such, but noesis is continually constituted. "That which is to be seen is born from things that have not yet appeared (τὸ μὴ ἐκ φαινομένων τὸ βλεπόμενον γεγονέναι)" (Hebrews 11:3).

We can thus admit the possibility of a *phenomenal* model of the Trinity, constituted starting from the Spirit, and which satisfies better than the two prior models the negative and positive conditions of formal identity in the Trinity, between its economy and immanence.[4]

Basil of Caesarea and the Phenomenal Model

At the margins of the most well-known models (ontic, historical, etc.), it thus seems possible to discuss another, which has remained more marginal, but is now more pertinent. The clearest effort to develop this model probably comes from Basil's treatise *On the Holy Spirit*. Of course, it can be read as a defense of the ontic model (in the flawless style of the *Theological Orations* of Gregory of Nazianzus and *Quod non sint tres dii* by Gregory of Nyssa), which expands into an illustration of the divinity of the Holy Spirit. It must also be understood as an essay on thinking the immanent Trinity on the basis of its economy as coming from *elsewhere*, in order to break as radically as possible with the logicism and emanantism of the Arians, or in short, with their *a priori* delusions. But to accomplish this, Basil tries to conceive this economy as setting up the process of the *phenomenal* uncovering of the Trinity. This phenomenal turn of the Trinity attempts to model the process of economic manifestation on the dimensions and conditions of immanent communion. Such a coincidence is itself made possible by the intervention of a concept as crucial for the economy as for immanence, that of the icon: the immanent Trinity is accomplished iconically, as exactly as the economic Trinity is manifested iconically. And, if he must intervene, the Holy Spirit will then intervene as the phenomenal operator of this single icon.

One text in particular anchors this idea:

> We do not count by addition, going from one to many by accumulation, saying "one, two, three," or "first, second, third." For, "I, God, am the first and I am the last" (Revelation 1:8). And even to this day, we have not yet heard of a second God. By worshiping God from God (θεὸν ἐκ θεοῦ), we confess what is proper (τὸ ἰδιάζον) to each of the hypostases and we remain within the monarchy, without scattering theology (i.e., the Trinity) into a plural accumulation, because of (διά) this: contemplating, so to speak, one and the same form (μίαν ... τὴν οἱονεὶ μορφὴν θεορεῖσθαι) in God the Father and God the Only Begotten, [a form] iconified (ἐνεικονιζομένην, *mise en icône*) by the unchanged [mirror] of divinity. The Son is indeed in the Father, and the Father in the Son, since such as [is] the latter, such [is] the former, and in this [they are] one.[5]

This sequence calls for a remark. Indeed, if we want to be freed from an arithmetical model of the Trinity (presupposed by those who, in the name of their conception of "monotheism" do not want to, or rather *are not able to* see in it anything but a hierarchy, an emanation, and thus a polytheism), it is necessary to pass to a model where it is a question of an icon, or more exactly, of "one and the same icon, so to speak." What icon is this? All the difficulty lies in this implicit reservation: How could one and the same form (*morphē*) be valid for the Father and the Son—and what then of the Spirit?

Right away we find several confirmations that it is essentially a question of the icon here, and thus of phenomenality. First in the discussion that immediately follows, to know if the Father and the Son are one or two; they are *both* one, *and* two according to whether we consider the person (*prosōpon*) or nature (*physis*), or also whether we consider "the icon (εἰκών)" of a king, for example his image on a coin or a statue; and indeed, in the icon of the king, we do not see a second king, but "one single authority (ἡ ἐξουσία μία)." This classical argument no doubt alludes to the "icon" of Caesar that Christ commands to be given to Caesar (Matthew 22:15–22). Thus the icon designates the phenomenal visibility of a hypostasis. From this follows a second confirmation of this concept; for Basil concludes his argument by introducing a formula that will become decisive several centuries later, when the Council of Nicaea II will take it up in order to settle the iconoclast quarrel: "The honor paid to the icon is transferred to the prototype (ἡ τῆς εἰκόνος τιμὴ ἐπὶ τὸ πρωτότυπον διαβαίνει)."[6] If the formula of Basil does not relate to the precise concept of the icon, it would be difficult to understand why the Fathers of such a precise and learned council invoked its authority; thus we cannot seriously doubt that it does relate to such a concept.

But, we might ask, how and why does the honor pass from the icon to its original? Because, from a phenomenal point of view, the visibility of the icon is distinguished by a remarkable property: it concerns not only itself, but also, or even *first of all*, bears on another. As a kind of double visible, or visible with a double effect, the icon has the property of not appropriating its own proper visibility alone, of not showing only itself in it, of not making seen what every other visible is limited to showing—that is, a visible that shows only itself, as one numbered among all the others. By contrast, the visibility retained by the icon refers it back to another term, puts it at the beck and call of that which, without it, would remain invisible, and which does not allow itself to be seen or aimed at except through it, the icon. This other term certainly appears *like* itself, yet without showing itself directly *through* itself, since it borrows its visibility from the icon, with which it is nevertheless not identified. This phenomenal arrangement (the iconic model) can enter in here, in "theology," because it corresponds formally to the Trinitarian model of the manifestation of the Father in the Son, himself understood *as* the Christ: "He who is the icon of the invisible God (εἰκὼν τοῦ Θεοῦ τοῦ ἀοράτου)" (Colossians 1:15; see Romans 8:29). Christ appears as the visible icon of the Father, who remains invisible, because by looking at his face *as he should*, the believer not only sees Jesus, the son of the carpenter of Nazareth, *as* the Christ, but also Christ *as* the Son, and thus, finally, the Son *as* the Father. Because the Father and the Son share the same face, or precisely, the same icon with double visibility, they not only manifest themselves "in one and the same form, so to speak," but their Trinitarian identity is uncovered in the process of their common manifestation, or rather, their communion in the manifestation. In this way we find accomplished, iconically and in a Trinitarian way, what is to be conceived in the foundational paradox of Revelation understood as an un-covering: "Whoever sees me, sees the Father (ὁ ἑωρακὼς ἐμὲ ἑώρακεν τὸν Πατέρα)" (John 14:9). Seeing the Father consists in seeing him in the Son, seeing sonship in the Son (toward the Father), and thus inseparably the paternity that sees me (starting from the Father).

Iconification

There remains a third confirmation of this function here, from the concept of the icon. That is, this "one and the same form, so to speak," for contemplating the Son and the Father is described as an "iconification (ἐνεικονιζομένη) by the invariable mirror of the divinity."[7] This term *eneikonizomenē*, whose participle I am rendering literally here by the term "*iconification* [*mise en icône*]"[8] has few uses,[9] so that this translation cannot be corroborated by other occurrences, and therefore is not self-evident. The difficulties nevertheless come down to deciding if the verbal form *eneikonizomenē* should be understood from the strict concept of *eikōn*. One could judge that it should not, and speak instead of a "form reflecting itself as in a mirror" or a "reflexive condition."[10]

But then we are exposed to patent objections: on the one hand, §45 never mentions a "mirror (κάτοπτρον)"; on the other hand, the icon does not proceed by reflection, and even less by reciprocal reflection between the hypostases, because the icon unilaterally "refers to (διαβαίνει)" its archetype without the latter relating to it, so there is no reflection as understood in its subjective and modern sense. Basil suggests instead that the "form" of Son and Father remains "one and only one (μία)," because it functions as an icon, and because it is put *into* an iconic situation [*se met dans une situation iconique*], *en-eikonozomenē*. The Father and the Son offer one single form as long as this form assumes the status of an icon, and the Father projects himself into the figure (*Gestalt*) of the Son, precisely because Christ acts perfectly according to sonship, and, by consequence, makes fatherhood, and thus the Father, manifest. Basil also evokes "a timeless (ἀχρόνως) givenness of will (θελήματος διάδοσιν) from the Father toward the Son, like some form appearing in a mirror (τίνος μορφῆς ἐμφάσιν ἐν κατόπτρῳ)."[11] This "iconification" does not make two visible things interact, nor reflect one another, but the two enter into one visibility there, that of the depth of reference of the icon. In other words, "the image is not a copy, but the incorporation of a form, the shaping or structuration of what does not have form."[12] To see the face of the Son *as* the face of the invisible Father, it is necessary to cease looking at the face of Jesus simply as such, and to see it *in a certain way*, according to a double visibility, *as* putting into view the in-visible of the Father. The iconification of the image, as Basil describes it, thus consists not only in qualifying the face of the Son as an icon, but inscribing in turn the invisibility of the Father in the very same icon.

It is in this way that John of Damascus explicitly understands it when he comments on the formula borrowed by the Second Council of Nicaea from this text of Basil: "the prototype is that which is iconified (τὸ εἰκονιζόμενον), [the prototype] from which comes the one who directs (τὸ παράγωγον)."[13] We can therefore say that the Father and the Son are both iconified, precisely because only one of them is necessary for both, one and the same form for two, a visibility with double entry. Basil thus includes himself in the consistent interpretation that "No one knows the Son except the Father, no one knows the Father except the Son and those to whom the Son wanted to uncover him (ἀποκαλύψαι)" (Matthew 11:27). Irenaeus, too, had perfectly formulated this Trinitarian function of the icon: "*Invisibile etenim Filii Pater, visibile autem Patris Filius*—for the Father is the invisible of the Son, but the Son the visible of the Father." Indeed, he continues: "and the Father, of course invisible and without any possible determination for us (*indeterminabilem quantum ad nos*), is known by his own Word, and as he [the Father] cannot be said (*innarrabilis*), it is he [the Son] who tells it to us; but in return only the Father knows his Word: the Lord has indeed manifested that these two things were so (*utraque autem hæc sic se habere*). For the recognition of the Father is the manifestation of the Son (*Agnito enim Patris est Filii manifestatio*): for all things are manifested by the Son."[14] As did Saint Augustine: "The invisible Trinity produced what is the visible person of the Son alone (*Visibilem namque Filii solius personam invisibilis Trinitas operatis est*)."¹⁵ But does the Holy Spirit participate in this iconification of the Father in the Son?

The Functions of the Spirit

This remains a question, however, or even an overwhelming objection: unlike Saint Augustine, who adds that "This action, visibly expressed and presented to mortal eyes, is called the sending of the Holy Spirit,"¹⁶ and also unlike Origen, who clearly stated that "every knowledge of the Father is acquired through the revelation of the Son (*revelante Filio*) in the Spirit,"¹⁷ neither the text cited by Basil nor the argument that we have drawn from it mentions the Holy Spirit. Of course, the Trinitarian communion of the Son and the Father is un-covered here in the visibility of the unique "form," but where is the Holy Spirit in the phenomenal model of the icon? Can we assign to this model an authentically *Trinitarian* function if it only puts into operation a *double* visibility (of the Son *as* the Father), while the Spirit remains by contrast the *non-visible* (neither directly visible like the Son, nor indirectly visible like the Father)?

We have seen that the biblical texts suggest another conclusion (chapters 13–14). Summoned by Jesus to respond to the question, "And you, what do you say about me?" Peter confesses, "You are the Christ, the Son of the Living God." In other words, he is the first of all the disciples to succeed in performing the iconic double visibility of Jesus, verifying the rule that "Whoever has seen me has seen the Father" (John 14:7). And Jesus recognizes this very confession as a grace, for "neither flesh nor blood have revealed (un-covered, ἀπεκάλυψέν)" his Trinitarian identity, "but my Father who is in heaven" (Matthew 16:15–17). Which indicates that, in order to accomplish the phenomenal function of the icon, beyond the double visibility, we need grace, which is to say, we need at the same time the gift, the art, and the knack of taking it into view: it is necessary to know how to see the icon *as* such. And it is this grace, this gift, and this art that Christ himself receives and experiences through the action of the Holy Spirit: "In that same hour, the joy of the Holy Spirit filled him and he said, 'I thank you, Father, Lord of heaven and earth, because you have *covered over* (ἀπέκρυψας) these things for the wise and learned, and *un-covered* them for the simple'" (Luke 10:21). The icon shows the Son *as* the Father only if God gives the grace, the art, and the manner of seeing it *as it should be* seen; and God gives it *as* the Holy Spirit, as *the one who remains invisible in the icon because he shows it*: "When the Paraclete comes, whom I shall send to you from the Father, the Spirit and truth, who proceeds (ἐκπορεύεται) from the Father, he will bear witness to me" (John 15:26).

Yet, against what we had been led to believe by the first text we have just studied, the powerful originality of Basil of Caesarea in his treatise *On the Holy Spirit* consists in showing the indispensable function of the Holy Spirit *as itself invisible* in the phenomenal model of the Trinity. Faced with the reticence of some to recognize the divinity of the Spirit (for, in fact, the Scriptures never literally attribute to him the title of "God"), Basil undertakes to resolve this difficulty surrounding the Spirit's status in the immanent Trinity (the Spirit's ontic status, if we dare to put it that way) by demonstrating the Spirit's role in the divinization of man through the Incarnation of the Son (according to the "economy"); and, in particular, by establishing the Spirit's phenomenal function—his function of bringing to light Jesus *as* the Christ and *as* the Son, and thus Jesus's iconification *as* the revelatory instance of the Father. The divinity of the Spirit absolutely must be admitted first, because the Spirit divinizes particularly in baptism, but also because he divinizes by showing the Father in the Son—putting on stage the icon of the Father, the Son as the Christ, on the face of Jesus. The Spirit is "fount and cause (αἰτία, *réquisit*) of the good,"[18] precisely as the "necessary condition for the fulfillment (αἰτία τελειωτική, *réquisit pour l'accomplissement*)"[19] of this divinization through iconification of Christ's face *as* the gazing face of the Father. The Spirit establishes himself as the phenomenal way of access to the iconic vision of the Father in the Son, functioning as the stage director of the Trinitarian un-covering of God, the only economy of theology.

This function is described and explained in several moments. First, it must be recognized that without the Spirit no vision or revelation could take place: "As for the one appointed to announce the mysteries of the vision (ὀπτασία) to 'the man of desires' (Daniel 10:11), where did he derive the wisdom to teach hidden things, if not from the Holy Spirit? The uncovering of mysteries is particularly suited to the Spirit (τῆς ἀποκαλύψεως τῶν μυστήριον ἰδίως τῷ Πνεύματι προσηκούσης). . . . It is not possible to see it without the Spirit (τὸ δὲ βλέπειν, οὐκ ἄνευ τοῦ Πνεύματος)."[20] Second, the Spirit allows the showing (the un-covering, the revealing) *in himself* of

The Trinity as Icon: A Phenomenal Model 311

Christ *as* the power and wisdom of God. The Spirit shows Christ *as* God because he acts as a developing agent [*révélateur*] (again in the photographic sense of the term)—with him, *in him*, the face of Christ suddenly appears as the imprint of the Father, whose character it then bears visibly: "Hence he [i.e., the Holy Spirit] alone worthily glorifies the Lord. For, [Christ] says, 'he will glorify me' (John 16:14), not as creation, but as the Spirit of truth, he who makes the truth clearly shine forth in himself (τρανῶς ἐκφαῖνον ἐν ἑαυτῷ); and also as a Spirit of Wisdom who uncovers in his own greatness (ἐν τῷ ἑαυτῷ μεγέθει ἀποκάλυπτον) Christ [as] the Power of God and [as] the Wisdom of God. And, as Paraclete, he bears in himself the stamp (ἐν ἑαυτῷ χαρακτηρίζει) of the goodness of the Paraclete who sent him, and in his own dignity he manifests the greatness of him from whom he came forth."[21] The Spirit ensures this is taken as a "single form" and thus the entry of the Father into the *figure* (*Gestalt*, in Hans Urs von Balthasar's sense, as in chapter 7) of Christ.

Third, and above all, we can describe the way that the icon of Christ is brought to light and taken into view *as* the gaze of the Father in a mode that is, so to speak, optic, or even phenomenological.

When, through an illuminating power (δύναμις φωτιστική), we fix our gaze on the beauty of "the icon of the invisible God" (Colossians 1:15), and impelled by it we are led up to the more-than-beautiful vision (ὑπέρκαλον . . . θέαμα) of the archetype, the Spirit of knowledge is inseparably present there (πάρεστιν ἀχωρίστως), in himself bestowing on those who love to see the truth the icon's power to make seen (τὴν ἐποπτικὴν τῆς εἰκόνος δύναμιν); not by making the [de-]monstration from without (οὐκ ἔξωθεν τὴν δεῖξιν ποιούμενον), but leading to recognition in himself (ἐν ἑαυτῷ). . . . and so, it is in himself (ἐν ἑαυτῷ) that he shows the glory of the Only Begotten and furnishes the knowledge of God [i.e., the Father] to true worshippers.[22]

This can be understood in the following way: the visible manifests to the human gaze the face of Jesus in the world; but the un-covering (the revelation) consists in apprehending this visible face *as* that of the Christ, *as* that of the Son; and in turn, this apprehension of the visible face of the Son must allow for targeting there [*d'y viser*], as an "icon," the invisible gaze of the Father. In short, it is a question of aiming at, in the visible face of Jesus, the iconic invisibility of the Father. This hermeneutics (see Luke 24:27), or rather, this exegesis (John 1:18), cannot be carried out by any human, for "God, no one has ever seen" (John 1:18). And yet, the rule remains: "Whoever has seen me has seen the Father" (John 14:9), and no one sees the Father except through the Son. How then can this be possible? Because nothing is impossible for God (Luke 1:37)—here, for the Spirit—who "makes the way" (John 16:13), in other words, gives the Trinitarian *method* of "iconification." It is what Basil sums up in a formula: "For our mind being illuminated by the Holy Spirit fixes its gaze on the Son (πρὸς Υἱὸν ἀναβλέπει), and in Him as in an icon (ὡς ἐν εἰκόνι θεωρεῖ) he contemplates the Father."[23]

The One and Only Trinitarian Form

Indeed, the Spirit positions the human gaze at the exact point of view and in the exact alignment where the visible face of Christ (Jesus *as* Son) can, at once and with perfect precision (a *definition*), be uncovered as the very axis of passage of the Son's gaze on the Father *as well as* the Father's on the Son; yet this place of aim and this point of view remain inaccessible to man, who is always the prisoner of his organization of the visible, which is not only finite, but above all *closed*; the hold of his perspective on the opening of the visible condemns him to remain at the center of a spectacle that consequently brings to him only objects, common law phenomena, invisible mirrors of his own solitary gaze. To reach another point of view and an axis for the gaze other than this necessarily idolatrous perspective implies an overturning of the entire phenomenal arrangement: crossing to a complete anamorphosis. Anamorphosis, or the arrangement wherein the human gaze would be placed at the exact site that the icon itself requires in order to be recognized in full manifestation. It would be necessary to be placed at the axis of the iconic gaze, which, suddenly and all at once, comes forth from the face of Christ at last apprehended *as* Son, and thus *as* the manifestation of the Father. To place the gaze of a human at this point of anamorphosis is a work that only the Spirit can do: he "guides" and orients, "leads" the human gaze and places it at the precise point where (like a two-dimensional image that, under a precise angle of view with the light reflected just so, suddenly appears in three dimensions), his "optic" or "illuminating power" once and for all "iconizes" the visible face and makes "the more-than-beautiful vision of the Archetype" burst forth *in depth*. The Holy Spirit puts on stage, or in view; in a word, he uncovers and brings forth the filial glory of the Father in the paternal glory of the Son.

Those who opposed the divinity of the Holy Spirit did not understand that the Spirit does not appear as a third spectacle in the iconic arrangement of the Trinity, because he *must* not, precisely due to the essential phenomenological function that he assumes within it. And this is so for at least two reasons.

First, because already there are not *two* spectacles; the Son and the Father are "iconified in *one* and the same form," constituting only one single visible *in depth*—that of the Father *through* or rather *as* the Son, Son and Christ, the unique, unsurpassable and completed "radiance of the glory and the exact stamp of the person (ἀπαύγασμα τῆς δόξης καὶ χαρακτὴρ τῆς ὑποστάσεως)" (Hebrews 1:3) of the Father.

Next, the Spirit does not appear because, "as Paraclete, he bears in himself the imprint (ἐν ἑαυτῷ χαρακτηρίζει)"[24]: not as a second imprint, but the only imprint, that of the Father in the Son, whose seal only he can allow to be received, and with which he seals man in baptism. "For, indeed, it is impossible (ἀδύνατον) to see the 'icon of the invisible God' (Colossians 1:15) except in the illumination (ἐν τῷ φωτισμῷ) of the Spirit, and there is no way (ἀμήχανον) for him who fixes his eyes on the icon to separate the icon from the light. The condition of seeing (τοῦ ὁρᾶν αἴτιον) must be seen together with the thing seen (τοῦ ὁρᾶν αἴτιον ἐξ ἀνάγκης συγκαθορᾶται). And so, in all suitability and consistency, we see the radiance of the glory of God through (διὰ) the illumination of the Spirit."[25] *The Spirit, then, is not seen precisely because he makes us see*, as he alone can do. But already the Father was not seen otherwise than in the unique icon, the one offered in the face of Jesus, seen *as* the Christ and thus *as* the Son. There is *only one visibility* in the manifestation of the Trinity, which is shown as one insofar as it shows by the triple work of its *nescio quid*. And the work of the Spirit, this staging by the Spirit, while himself invisible, is called sanctification, operated by the phenomenal operator of holiness himself: "not made holy, but making holy (οὐχὶ ἁγιαζόμενόν ἐστιν, ἀλλ' ἁγιάζον)."[26] Just as he is not seen, but makes us see, he is not sanctified, but sanctifies, which is confirmed by the parallel formula of Gregory of Nazianzus: "The Spirit is truly holy, the Holy One (τὸ ἅγιον) . . . holiness in person (αὐτοαγιότης)."[27] And so, precisely because his concern for the unity of the Church, for good or for ill, had held Basil back from innovating against the Pneumatomachs, and because he had avoided a repetition of the *homo[i]ousios* quarrel concerning the divinity of the Holy

Spirit, he successfully formulated his *equality of honor (isotimia, homotimia)*. The Spirit receives the same honor and the same glory as the Father and the Son, because he alone gives us to see the one in the icon of the other. By this formula, which will be taken up literally at the First Council of Constantinople, he enters the tradition (recalled in fact throughout *On the Holy Spirit* XIX), which begins, at least, with Irenaeus: "Without the Spirit there is no seeing the Word of God, and without the Son there is no approaching the Father; for the Son is knowledge of the Father (*cognitio enim Patris Filius*), but the Son's knowledge of God is only through the Holy Spirit (*cognitio autem Filii Dei per Spiritum sanctum*). As for the Spirit, it is according to the Father's good pleasure, that the Son, as his minister, dispenses to those whom he [the Father] wills and as he wills."[28] And this extends at least up to John Chrysostom: "For it is not possible that where the Spirit is present Christ would not be (Οὐ γὰρ ἐστι Πνεύματος παρόντος, μὴ καὶ Χριστὸν παρ εἶναι)."[29]

The Phenomenal Model as Confession

The breakthrough accomplished by the phenomenal model now appears clearly: the Trinity is only uncovered as it gives itself, that is, its holiness is only revealed to holiness, the holiness that receives it, and therefore the holiness that the Spirit "pours out in our hearts." This advance dispels the debate from the presuppositions of the two prior models. First, from the ontic model. We have observed that Basil, no doubt because he did not want to revive the *homo[i]ousios* disputes, shows "a certain reluctance to use the term *ousia*," and even practices an "avoidance of the vocabulary of *ousia*"; in any case, he prefers relation, and "makes use of . . . relation to de-substantiate, as it were, the status of the hypostases in their relation to the divine essence."[30] The same is true of the historical model: the Holy Spirit remains in God and thus, as God, does not remain in any place of the world; himself a non-place (*achōrētos*) that contains nothing, he is established as "the place (*chōra*) of the sanctified . . . the proper place for true worship."[31] From this it follows that those who receive him receive themselves thereby, and what is uncovered to them—the Trinity—is not uncovered in the world, since they themselves are found in the Spirit. The immanence of the Trinity submerges its economy in the Spirit and relocates itself in it, since everything happens from now on in the one and only Spirit. The two first models lose their principles, or rather, must submit them to the Spirit, who breathes where he will, outside of *ousia* as outside of worldly history. These two principles remain, but taken up in "a certain [glory] come from *elsewhere* (ἔξοθεν),"[32] put out of play by this beyond-place. This conclusion may be surprising, since, in Basil's strategy, the entire demonstration of the divinity of the Holy Spirit passes by substitution of the particle *in* for the particle *with* (*syn*) in order to inscribe the Spirit in the Trinity: "Glory to the Father, *through* the Son, *with* the Holy Spirit." Doesn't he accomplish *that in which* the Trinity uncovers itself, the *chōra* of sanctification? Why then does he appear as *that with which* it is uncovered?

In order to conceive of this, in the case of the divinity of the Spirit, we must return to the substitution of the equality of honor for the identity of *ousia*. How and *when* do we give the same honor to the Spirit as to the Father and the Son? When and by passing from the (supposedly) theoretical knowledge of the Trinity to its practical implementation, that is, in the act of baptism, an act that is performed by pronouncing on the catechumen, with his complete approval, the originally Trinitarian baptismal formula: "teach all the nations, baptizing them in the Name of the Father, the Son and the Holy Spirit" (Matthew 28:19). To praise and honor God as God means to confess his name, his Trinitarian name. To uncover the Trinity means performing it by confessing it as a whole—to see the Son as the icon of the Father thanks to and with the Spirit who gives us to see according to the correct anamorphosis of charity. And so "faith and baptism, two ways of salvation, are united with each other, and indissolubly. While faith is fulfilled by baptism, baptism is fulfilled by faith; each attains its fulfillment by the same names. For we believe in (εἰς) the Father, in the Son and in the Holy Spirit, so also are we baptized in (εἰς) the Name of the Father, and the Son, and the Holy Spirit."[33] The Trinity uncovers itself when it is performed in our baptism and the economy gives its immanence, because it gives *itself* to see in giving *itself* in itself. "We have made the confession of faith (ὁμολογίαν τῆς πίστεως) a kind of principle and the mother of praise (οἷον ἀρχήν τινα καὶ μητέρα τῆς δοξολογίας ἐποιησάλεθα)."[34]

The Trinity, the *mystērion theou*, is not only uncovered by the anamorphosis of the Spirit in us, but *with* the act of this anamorphosis.

EIGHTEEN

The Trinity as the Phenomenality of the Gift

Saint Augustine's Reworking of the Phenomenal Model

At the point where our research has arrived—the uncovering of the Trinity is brought about by the Holy Spirit that pours out *agapē* in our hearts, so that we may aim at the Father in his one and only icon, the Son—two difficulties immediately arise. First, one may ask how the Spirit succeeds at accomplishing in us (or better, at making us accomplish in him) the act of anamorphosis (one could also say confession, baptism). And this is a question about the possibility *for us* of an anamorphosis that nevertheless can be performed only from *elsewhere*. Next, one may ask how the Holy Spirit can allow this anamorphosis in such a way that one and the same *economic* performance (for us) coincides exactly with the *immanent* deployment (in itself) of the Trinity. And so the question is about the univocity of *agapē*, which is at once both what is at stake in the Trinity and the operator of its uncovering; for the patristic principle according to which "the unassumed is the unhealed, but what is united with God is also being saved" implies its inverse: that that which assumes remains univocally that which saves.[1] These two questions probably combine into one: How does the possibility of *our* iconification by the Holy Spirit result from the Trinity's accomplishment *in itself* in the *same* Holy Spirit? As summed up by Ambrose, in speaking of baptism, "Things impossible

The Trinity as the Phenomenality of the Gift 317

with men (*impossibilia . . . apud homines*) are possible with God (*possibilia sunt apud Deum*); God has the power, when he wishes, to forgive us [*quitus*] (*donare*) of sins, even of those which we think cannot be granted (*concedi*). And so it is possible for God to give us (*Deo donare possibile est*) that which it seems to us impossible to obtain."[2] The act of anamorphosis allows for our aim at the unique icon only because the Holy Spirit *gives* it. For the gift given (economy) remains exactly the giving gift (immanence), precisely when it gives *itself* to an other than itself. Basil had already done more than simply outline the possibility of anamorphosis in its connection to the necessity of the gift: "there is absolutely no gift (Οὐδὲ . . . ὅλως δωρεά τις) without the Holy Spirit."[3] But, provided that we avoid adhering to the commonly accepted account of a dissension between the Latin and Greek "theologies," we can recognize Saint Augustine as having found this phenomenal model, even to the point of conceiving the Father's taking figure in the Son (icon) as the very gift that unites them. For Augustine, who knew Basil's work, follows him closely, and extends his reach.[4]

And he does so in several ways. To begin, Augustine takes up from Basil the phenomenal model of the Trinity. Indeed, echoing the "iconification" of the Father in the Son in "one and the same form, so to speak," Saint Augustine underscores that the visibility of the Son is one with that of the Father, who validates it in return: "*Cum Pater* ostenditur, *et Filius* ostenditur *qui in illo est*; *et cum Filius* ostenditur, etiam Pater ostenditur *qui in illo est*—when the Father *is shown*, the Son who is in him *is shown also*, and when the Son *is shown*, the Father who is in him *is shown too*."[5] There is and there need be only one visibility, and thus only one phenomenon in and for the entire Trinity: the *persona* of Christ: "*Visibilem namque Filii solius personam, invisibilis Trinitas operata est*—For the invisible Trinity produced what is the visible person of the Son alone."[6] Indeed, only the Son can show himself to us, because he alone took on a visible body for us: "*solus in Trinitate corpus accepit.*"[7] Pushing precision even further, he adds that it is even necessary to distinguish and conjoin in the iconic model of the Trinity not only the Son and the Father (each equally invisible in the immanent Trinity), but, on the one hand, the Son, just as invisible as the Father, and, on the other, the Son made visible: "So it is that the *invisible* Father, together with the jointly *invisible* Son, is said to have sent *this same Son made visible*. . . . As it is, the 'form of a servant' was so taken on that the 'form of God' remained immutable (Philippians 2:7, 6), and thus it is plain that what was *seen* in the Son was the work of Father and

Son *who remain unseen*, that is, that *the Son was sent to be visible by the invisible Father together with the invisible Son*."[8] The invisible (immanent) communion of Father and Son is thus extended in an economic communion between the invisible (where of course the Son dwells with the Father) and the visible (where the Son appears in flesh and blood, in this very way uncovering the Father): the visible becomes, in the body of Christ made visible, the only place of manifestation for the entire Trinity, without the passage from the invisible to the visible inflicting upon him the least bit of extraterritoriality, exteriority, or alienation. Christ, the visible Son, makes the invisibility of the Father (and of the eternal Son) seen, because he himself sees it: "the work of Father and Son is indivisible, and yet the Son's working is from the Father just as he himself is from the Father; and the way in which the Son *sees* the Father is simply by being the Son. For him, being from the Father, that is being born of the Father, is not something different from *seeing* the Father; nor is *seeing* him working something different from his working equally."[9] The power of making the Father seen is based exclusively, for the Son, in filiation, which itself consists in seeing him; whence it follows that the (economic) Trinity makes itself seen only in exact consequence of the fact that it consists in seeing the Father in filial immanence. The divide, or rather, the span of all phenomenality, namely the transition from the visible to the invisible, is thus taken up and comprised precisely *inside* the Trinity, and in no way forced to exteriorize itself (after all, to what place other than himself could God ever go?) in order to be phenomenalized. In recapitulating in itself the space and the opening of the visibility of the invisible, it thus refutes the historical model, ahead of its time yet definitively. Augustine, just as much or even more clearly than Basil, established in this way the possibility or even the necessity of a phenomenal approach to the Trinity, according to the unique visibility of the Father in the Son (and vice versa) in the mode of their one and only icon.

The Completed Model of Trinitarian Phenomenality

Consequently, Augustine confirms and elaborates, perhaps better than Basil, why it is fitting that the Spirit remain necessarily invisible within this iconic model of phenomenality. For, when examining the mission of the Spirit and its always indirect manifestation (intervening *as* a dove, or *as* a clap of thunder), Augustine emphasizes his essential non-appearance: "This action, *visibly* expressed and presented to mortal eyes, is called the sending of the Holy Spirit. Its object was *not that his very substance might be seen* (*ut appareret*), since he himself remains *invisible* and unchanging like the Father and the Son; but that the hearts of men, stirred by outward sights (*exterioribus visis*), might in this way be converted *starting from the public manifestations of his coming in time* (*a temporali manifestatione*) to the hidden eternity of he who is ever present."[10] The phenomenal model of the Trinity is completed and radicalized here, because it encompasses explicitly the three moments of the un-covering (of the *apokalypsis*). First, the Father, ever invisible, takes figure (again always invisible) in the eternal (invisible) Son, who derives all his sonship from the fact that he sees the invisible Father (being *toward* him). Then, this "icon of the invisible God," in which the Son makes himself targetable [*visable*] and visible in Jesus Christ. And, finally, the Spirit, who remains invisible, because his operation consists entirely in making us aim [*viser*] (according to the right anamorphosis, the exact orientation of intentionality) at the "icon of the invisible God," so as to see, in it, in the human figure of the Son, the invisible Father. In other words, the model of the Trinity lays out within strict phenomenality, according to the interplay of the visible and the invisible, in a single arrangement and therefore all at once, the ever invisible Father, but *aimed at* through the Son; the Son, invisible yet visible as the "icon of the invisible God," as Jesus Christ inasmuch as he will be seen as the Son aiming at the Father and seen by the Father, and thus as *transparent* (making the Father show through in him, letting him be seen clearly); and the Holy Spirit, ever invisible, because he allows the gazes that accomplish the anamorphosis to aim at the invisible Father in the visible icon offered by the Son, to the extent that he adjusts the aim. In sum, the Trinity uncovers itself according to the three dimensions of a single phenomenality: as the *invisible aim*, as the *visible transparent to the invisible* and aimed at as icon of the invisible, and as the *invisible who targets* [*l'invisible visant*]. In this way the Trinity's phenomenal model is accomplished in a more complete, if not completely adequate, formula.

The Spirit as Gift

Of course, the Spirit, whose function is to make us aim at the Father through the icon of the invisible God, the Son, *can* very well not appear himself. Indeed, the director can decline to mount the stage, show himself, and play a role; similarly, the shooting instructor can remain behind the shooter, to adjust the aim; but they can also come forth to take a bow at the end of the performance, or gather the targets and the scores after each discharge. Things are different for the Spirit, and one may rightly ask why he himself *must not* appear precisely when he makes seen what can appear. What is the motive for the non-appearance, reflected even in the name Holy Spirit, of his relation to the Father and the Son (this relation that, according to Augustine, alone identifies him), while the relations of fatherhood and sonship appear manifestly in the names of the Father and of the Son ("*ipsa relatio* non apparet *in hoc nomine*")? The same sentence immediately delivers the motive for this particularity: "it is apparent when he is called the gift of God (*apparet autem cum dicitur donum Dei*, δωρεὰν τοῦ θεοῦ)" (Acts 8:20).[11] This is a strange response: the relation, which does not appear, appears nevertheless under the title of "gift"; if this is not a contradiction, should we not suppose that the "gift" appears here as the motive of the non-appearing of the Holy Spirit? At base, what is the meaning of the displacement that makes us pass from the name "Spirit" to *donum Dei*?

A preliminary remark is necessary: the text of Acts 8:20 invoked here concerns the economy, since it has to do with the reprimand Peter makes to Simon Magus, who believed he could "obtain God's gift with money"; it has to do with the Spirit's giving to men and women the means to gain access to God, and witnessing to this possibility by conferring on them the power to accomplish signs (miracles). Augustine understands the term *donum Dei* as the immanence of the Father to the Son, referring it to John 15:26, "He is the gift of the Father and of the Son, because 'he proceeds from the Father' (παρὰ τοῦ πατρὸς ἐκπορεύεται)." Must we see a forced reading here? Probably, but at this level, a forced reading indicates a decisive breakthrough—the perfect identification of the immanent Trinity and the economic Trinity, which, thanks to the Spirit as gift, gives to men and women the very gift in which God consists and, by giving him, reveals him. "*At vero dando Spiritum per quem revelat, etiam ipsum revelat: dando revelat et revelando dat*—It is by giving the Spirit, through whom he [Christ] reveals, that he shows us himself; in giving he reveals, and in revealing he gives."[12] If then we can ever conceive the economic invisibility of the Spirit (invisible, because he allows for the aim that lets one see what shows itself), it will be by thinking it on the basis of the immanent Trinity, in which this Spirit assures, as gift and in the form of a gift, "a kind of inexpressible communion or fellowship of Father and Son—*ineffabilis quædam Patris Filiique communio.*"[13] Would the logic of the gift shed light then on the relation of visibility to invisibility in the Trinity? Unless the reverse were true: that the terribly complex plot of visibility and invisibility in even the most common gift might be conceived in its depth only by starting from the Trinitarian communion. Indeed, this will be our hypothesis.

Here again, Augustine continues along the path of Basil.[14] Basil had already tied the question of the visibility (or the invisibilities) of the Holy Spirit to the terms of the gift: "When we receive gifts (τὰ δῶρα), we first encounter the one who distributes them, then we consider the one who sent them, and then we lift our thoughts to the fount and cause of the goods (ἀγαθῶν) [given]."[15] We find in Augustine a similar distinction between the gift's modes of visibility: "a fiancé gives a ring to his betrothed; but she loves (*diligeret*) the ring thus received more than the fiancé who gave it to her. Wouldn't we consider her adulterous in the very gift (*in ipso dono*) made to her by her fiancé, even while she loves what her fiancé has given her (*amaret quod dedit*)? . . . You love gold instead of the man, you love the ring instead of your fiancé."[16] Let us try then starting from the gift of the invisibility (or the indirect and *a contrario* visibility) of the Spirit. Augustine's innovation regarding the Holy Spirit as a gift is clearly formulated: "For whether he is the unity of both the others (*unitas amborum*) or their holiness or their charity, whether he is their unity because their charity, and their charity because their holiness, it is clear that [the Holy Spirit] is not one of the two (*non aliquis duorum*), since he is that by which the two are joined each to the other. . . . So the Holy Spirit is something common to Father and Son, whatever it is (*commune aliquid est Patris et Filii, quidquid illud est*)."[17] If the Father gives everything to the Son and if the Son, who receives himself completely from the Father, gives (himself) in return ceaselessly to the Father, their communion is accomplished through the gift and in a union *through communion*. "So the Holy Spirit is a kind of inexpressible communion or fellowship of Father and Son (*ineffabilis quædam Patris Filiique communio*)," or, "their very commonness or communion, consubstantial and coeternal (*ipsa communio, consubstantialis et coæterna*). Call this friendship, if it helps, but a better word for it is charity (*sed aptius charitas*)."[18] As communion of charity through the gift, the Trinitarian God is accomplished in the reciprocal gift, a "Gift which is not said except of the Holy Spirit (*Donum quod non dicitur nisi Spiritus sanctus*)."[19] Indeed the accomplishment of the gift comes down to the Holy Spirit because *he alone* gives its result (a gift, in this case charity) as well as the complete process of the gift. The Spirit "is called the gift of both (*vocatur donum amborum*)" because he conjoins the two dimensions of the gift in them, "the gift of the giver [the Son] and the giver of the gift [the Father] (*donum ergo donatoris, et donator doni*)."[20] The Holy Spirit gives eminently because he gives not only what he gives (just as a deliveryman— the simple intermediary between the given and the addressee—frees himself from what he delivers, delivers himself from what he delivers), but gives in giving *himself*; and thus gives knowing how to give, the practicing of the gift according to the logic of giving.

This unique privilege is explicitly marked by another specification introduced by Augustine: the *givability* of the gift.[21] For one might object that the Holy Spirit *is not* a gift in the final instance, since he first takes after the Father (and the Son) in being, and thus in being *before* being given; the giving function would come to him immediately after, in an adventitious and accidental fashion, once and for all only after he would actually be given. The Spirit would become the gift only after a time, while the Son is Son by the very fact that he is born (thus, *is*) of the Father, as the Father is eternally such. This would be the Spirit about which one could *almost* correctly say that there was a time when he was not—not given. A response, though presented as conjectural, nevertheless lifts the ambiguity: the Spirit proceeds eternally as gift, because he is constituted from all eternity as *givable*, and because he occupies himself essentially and exclusively with *giving (himself)*, even before finding himself giving (himself) as a given gift: "Or is the answer that the Holy Spirit always proceeds and proceeds from eternity, not from a point of time; but because he so proceeds as to be *givable (donabilis)*, he was already gift *even before there was anyone to give him to (antequam esset cui daretur)*? We must conceive the gift (*donum*) differently from the given (*donatum*); it can be a gift (*donum*) even before it is given (*et antequam detur*), but it cannot be called in any way a given (*donatum*) unless it has been given (*nisi datum*)."[22] In other words, the difference between time and eternity implies radical modification of the understanding of the gift. Other gifts, temporal ones, are accomplished only in the contingent act of their giver, so that the given is not identified essentially with the givable itself, and does not deliver up all of the givable, but instead a part of the gift remains in itself resistant to the act of giving. In contrast, the Holy Spirit attests (himself) eternally (as) a perfect gift by ordering himself without reserve to giving, and because the given gives the givable completely without anything remaining to be given: essentially *givable*, he leaves nothing behind him to subsist, neither being nor substance, that cannot pass into a gift. In him, what he gives (*donum* as *datum*) coincides exactly with the very process of the gift (*donum donabile*): not only does he accomplish the gift but manifests the principle of giving. And this identity in him of the gift given along with giving itself therefore sanctions in a single "communion" the two other dimensions of the immanent Trinity: the Father, "giver of the gift," and the Son, "gift of the giver." The Holy Spirit gives *himself* and consists only in so doing: *giving himself*: "So he is the gift of God insofar as he is given to those he is given to (*in quantum datur eis quibus datur*). But in himself he is God even if he is not given to anyone (*etsi nemini detur*), because he was God, co-eternal with the Father and the Son, even before he was given to anyone (*antequam cuiquam daretur*). Nor is he less than they because they give and he is given. He is given as God's gift in such a way that as God he also gives himself (*datur sicut Donum Dei, ut etiam se ipsum det sicut Deus*)." For there (*illic*), in the Trinity, the Holy Spirit is not found "in the subject condition of the one given and under the domination of the givers (*conditio dati et dominatio dantium*), but as the concord of the one given and the givers (*concordia dati et dantium*)."²³ If then the Holy Spirit not only unfolds a gift but the principle of giving in the immanent Trinity (the communion of the two, the concord among givers), then, when he comes to give (himself) in the very economy of our temporality, he *thus* gives not only a gift but the principle of giving, because he cannot give the one without manifesting the other.

The Gift in Its Invisibility

A final difficulty remains, or rather another paradox. We must ask: Why does the fact (no longer to be contested here) that the Holy Spirit perfectly accomplishes himself—giving at once not only the given gift but the principle of giving, not only the *donum datum* but the process, the art, and the way of giving—at the same time forbid him from appearing himself in the "one and the same [iconic] form" of the Trinity? If he thus *gives himself* absolutely, why can he not also *show himself*? The most obvious responses (the inevitable failure to accomplish the anamorphosis, the saturation of the phenomenon, and the irreducible gap between what shows itself and what gives itself) are not sufficient, first because they all presuppose a taking aim at the invisible, guided or oriented by the Spirit. And further, because the invisibility of the Spirit constitutes neither an obstacle nor a limitation to taking aim at the "sole form" of the icon, but rather the ultimate condition of this taking aim. In order to conceive this impossibility, we must push on further, as far as the very phenomenality of the gift, and then as far as the phenomenality of the Trinitarian gift.

I have already laid out in detail on other occasions[24] what is proper to the gift reduced to givenness: the more it is perfectly accomplished, the more it delivers what it gives without return and in perfect abandonment, so that the gift *datum* is found to be irreversibly put at the disposition of the receiver, the more the giver and with her the whole process of giving must withdraw from presence. Two reasons explain this paradox. The first, which is obvious and part of daily experience, lies in the fact that a gift that retains in its depths the still visible face of the giver, like a jewel in a case or setting, is not absolutely given or abandoned to the recipient. In effect, the face of the giver, even dimmed or blurred, remains watching over the given gift, demanding (even in silence, perhaps all the more so) a counter-gift, if only in the form of a recognition of debt, or a simple sign of gratitude, or indeed a (probably guilty) awareness of dependence. The visibility of the giver lying behind the gift makes it a conditional gift, granted by favor; in short, it prevents its appropriation by the receiver. The gift thus becomes its opposite, a counter-gift, an exchange—and this is exactly what the common mentality understands by the word *gift*. The gift that remains under the visible shadow of the giver, the gift often deemed gracious, precisely *lacks the grace of an abandonment*. A truly accomplished gift can only come from *elsewhere* and, therefore, like a miracle, it must come about without a cause, without a known origin, without a visible giver. The giver only makes her gift visible if she herself becomes invisible; she only gives the gift if she gives over all its use (and thus also its abuse) to the recipient.

The second reason explaining this paradox derives from a more conceptual approach. The gift leans on and finds support in a being, a thing or an object that *is*, and even *is* at the same time available and usable. As it appears, I always give *something*; and the one who receives my gift accepts it in most cases quite willingly, precisely because he recognizes in it the availability and the utility of this entity. The gift being first of all and most often a *given being*, it appears receivable and is received above all for as long as it presents itself as a present entity. This entity is better than *nothing* (availability), for even a *little nothing* can serve as something (utility, useful things, equipmentality). The visibility of the gift is inevitably concentrated in its *ontic* evidence. Not only does the evidence of the gift conceal it as gift, since it offers it to a taking possession wherein the disappearance of the former possessor (the giver) in turn frees up the right of the new one (the recipient) to see and receive in it only an entity to possess; but above all this entity given to be possessed now occupies the entire stage of the visible and appropriates to itself all visibility: it captures everyone's gaze, attracts all the light. In return, what does the evidence of the entity thus given to be possessed conceal and push off stage? It obscures this entity *as given*, as ontic support of the gift and as that which the gift has raised to the possible by making it givable. And the evidence of the thing given obscures even more: it makes invisible the giving itself, the process of putting the gift on stage, the logic that overdetermines the being in a given entity and transmutes it into a gift abandoned by the giver to the recipient; in such a way that the dispossession becomes the (in-)sufficient reason of the transfer of possession, and there opens the possibility that the gift no longer gives rise to a counter-gift (which would degrade it into an exchange), but, in return, an abandonment, a communion. As such, the evident visibility of the gift thus renders invisible the process of giving.

For these two reasons, the phenomenality of the gift can provoke at least the possible invisibility of its terms (or even the invisibility of all of them), and furthermore implicate the invisibility of the logic of giving. To what extent can that which holds in general for the phenomenality of the gift and the logic of giving extend to the phenomenality of the Trinitarian gift? Or, on the contrary, might it be that, in the single case of the Trinitarian *mystērion*, *agapē* allows for the situating, correction, and accomplishment of the invisibility of the gift?

The Invisible Place of the Holy Spirit

We come, then, to the conclusion of the argument: the Holy Spirit is not seen, because he makes it possible to see; through anamorphosis he allows one to aim at "the icon of the invisible God." Thus he himself does not allow himself to be targeted; by taking aim, he remains untargeted and thus invisible. In the phenomenal model of the Trinity, the Spirit puts into operation the system of vision by putting—that is, *displacing*—she who must see into the exact place (through anamorphosis) where the face of Christ will be seen as the face of the Son, and thus as the icon of the Father. The goal is not for the Spirit, any more than it is for the Son, to make himself seen, since each of them is ordered to the unique manifestation of the Father, the one as his *transparent* face, the other, *taking aim*, as the *invisible* point of aim. The invisibility of the Spirit flows inexorably from his function as promoter, producer, and protector. He who puts others on the stage does not himself mount it, the light does not shine on him who directs the lighting, he who puts words in the mouths of the actor does not speak them himself. In the economy, the Holy Spirit *places* us exactly in the right place to confess and to see; and he places us there by *displacing* us: "My friend, move up higher!" (Luke 14:10) Thus displaced, replaced, and placed perfectly, we see and confess there and from where the Spirit wishes, he who goes where we do not know (John 3:8), but who shows us the place by making us go there ourselves. We see what he wants to show us; we operate like him, in place of him, or rather *in* his very place. The Holy Spirit carries out his task when he succeeds in having us replace him, directly, in his place, or rather *in* his place. We carry out our task when we speak and it is his words that our mouths say, when our eyes see what he aims at and makes us target: "You have received a Spirit of sonship, in which we cry, 'Abba, Father!'" (Romans 8:15); or further: "God has sent the Spirit of his Son into our hearts, crying, 'Abba! Father!'" (Galatians 4:6) If the Holy Spirit "is the gift of God, in that he is given to those who love God *through him* (*in quantum datur eis qui per eum diligunt Deum*),"[25] then we succeed in loving God only insofar as he gives himself absolutely to us, transferring to us his privilege (the grace of the anamorphosis that displaces us) to the point where he *replaces* us enough so that in return (*umgekerht*) we *replace* him: he inspires our words to such an extent that we speak like him, in his places, and in his place.

Consequently, his invisibility bursts forth and becomes paradoxically manifest; the Spirit makes himself invisible, because he has put us forward, out in front of him, so to speak; he pushed us to the front, to the better place for aiming at and then seeing "the icon of the invisible God" and, at last, glorifying the Father through the transparency of the Son. Of course, we do not see the Spirit, but he becomes *positively* invisible to us, since his invisibility signifies that *we* are, in short, placed in a place that we no longer regard and that we forget, for it is *from* this place that we aim at the Son and see the Father. Consequently, we live as we aim and see, no longer in ourselves, but in the icon itself: "I no longer live myself (οὐκέτι ἐγώ), but [there] lives in me—Christ" (Galatians 2:20). Or, "If we live, we live through Christ" (Romans 14:8). This displacement of the ego, in the end truly other in Christ, its true place, puts us in the situation of taking the role of Christ *in* the Spirit: "But you, not being in the flesh but in the Spirit, thus the Spirit of God dwells in you" (Romans 8:9). The invisibility of the Spirit introduces us into the visibility of the icon and thus also into its eschatological tension: "Our life is hidden in God with Christ. When Christ who is our life will be manifested, then you also will be manifested with him in glory" (Colossians 3:3–4). And we are not only introduced through the Spirit into Christ (the Word made man), as if the economy closed on its sole incorporation; we are introduced *into the very place* of the Spirit, into *the place*, into the immanent Trinity, because by living the life of Christ we commune in the eternal communion of the Son with the Father, there too and first of all, *in* the place of their common gift: "And I have given them the glory you gave me, so that they may be one, as we are one, I in them and you in me, that they may be completed in one (τετελειωμένοι εἰς ἕν), that the world may know that you sent me, and that you loved them even as you loved me" (John 17:22–23). The immanent Trinity comes to the economy so that the economy returns to the immanent Trinity. Such is the work of the invisible Spirit.

Consequently, we understand that charity must similarly remain invisible in us in its own manner. It gives without rendering itself visible; therefore it can alert a man that his left hand does not know what his right hand is doing, "so that your alms may be done in secret" (Matthew 6:4); the prayer remains preeminently "in secret," invisible to humans, so that "your Father who sees in secret" will reward it (Matthew 6:6). And in a sense, one neither knows nor sees how one receives what is given. The Spirit operates through charity and thus remains invisible. Which indicates that, in a sense at least, charity also remains invisible. Here we must consider literally a decisive remark made by Hilary: "Concerning the Holy Spirit, we should neither be silent nor should we speak. Of course, we cannot remain silent because of those who do not know Him. But there is no need to speak of the one whom we are bound to confess, because the Father and the Son qualify him (*Patre et Filo auctoribus*). For my own part, I think it wrong to discuss the question of whether He is (*an sit*). He does exist, for He is given, accepted, obtained (*donatur, accipitur, obtinetur*). He who is joined (*connexus*) with the confession of the Father and the Son cannot be excluded from the confession of the Father and the Son."[26] The Spirit appears in his very invisibility, for, in this unique case, his office consists in doing and making done; he appears by making one take aim at and see the invisible Father in the transparency of the Son. Not only does he not make himself seen, and disappear into what he makes seen; but he makes seen the logic of giving manifesting itself in the gift, given, received, and returned. There is nothing to say about the Holy Spirit; he only has to be allowed to work: "I will say nothing else about the Holy Spirit except that he is your Spirit."[27] We must let him work, allowing him as it happens to guide our aim and make us *speak* (and thus do by speaking) what we could not say by ourselves. Whence this magnificent yet almost untranslatable formula from Hilary: "Your Holy Spirit, as the Apostle says, searches your depths (1 Corinthians 2:10–11) and knows them, and as your advocate speaking for me [by interrupting what I say] (*interpellator pro me tuus*), [he makes it so that] to you are spoken by me things I could not utter (*inenarrabilia a me tibi loquuntur*)."[28]

Re-giving the Gift

It is notable that Thomas Aquinas, in a quite different register, approaches this same conclusion. After having tortuously validated some concepts (subsistent relation, *persona*, mode of the will, etc.) that are probably ill-fitted for conceiving the "specific name" that the Holy Spirit lacks, he concludes, in a final effort, by designating him as gift. What sort of gift? A gift taken "personally (*personaliter*)," in a sense found only among "divine things," and that ends up in love: "a gift is properly an unreturnable giving (*datio irreddibilis*), . . . a thing which is not given with the intention of a return; and it thus contains the idea of a gratuitous giving (*gratuitam donationem*). Now, the reason for gratuitous giving is love (*ratio autem gratuitæ donationis est amor*), since therefore do we give something to anyone gratuitously inasmuch as we wish him well (*volumus ei bonum*). So what we first give him is the love whereby we wish him well. Hence it is manifest that love has the nature of a first gift, through which all free gifts are given. So, since the Holy Spirit proceeds as love, ... He proceeds as the first gift."²⁹ While love characterizes the entire Trinity, it nevertheless properly denominates the Holy Spirit because by giving through love he allows for every gift. That is to say, he allows for every gift in the immanent Trinity *and* the economic Trinity, every gift made to men, and thus *also* made by them. He gives the gift of giving. He loves in such a way that he *makes* loving. In other words, he appears not only as a gift, nor as the one who gives the gifts (the "seven gifts" of the Spirit), but above all as the one who inaugurates giving. He gives gifts because his giving gives the first gift, gives first of all and above all. He gives by delivering and opening the "reason of free giving (*ratio autem gratuitæ donationis*)." He makes giving itself appear in each gift, while in the experience of human things, as we have seen, the manifestation of the given gift on the contrary makes the manifestation of giving disappear. The Spirit is named *gift* because he alone makes the logic of the gift appear.

Thus the revelatory work of the one Trinity, immanent *as well as* economic, operating among men is defined as no longer masking the process of giving through the evidence of the given, as in the experience of the world (unconcealment, *alētheia*), but instead reestablishing each and every time the manifestation of the process of giving in the evidence of the gift (uncovering, *apokalypsis*). The phenomenal model of the Trinity thus accomplishes all the un-covering that we were seeking. This phenomenal reversal can be thematized as the re-giving of the gift,³⁰ or, to put it *almost* as Richard of Saint-Victor does, "in the Father is found the fullness of gratuitous love, in the Holy Spirit the fullness of love owed, and in the Son the fullness of love that is both owed and gratuitous."³¹ *Almost* and not exactly, for, as we shall see, the "fullness of the gift that is both owed and gratuitous" in the end characterizes the Holy Spirit. Let us take up once more the three moments, which are in fact simultaneous, in every accomplished act of giving.

There is the un-covering of the *ratio donationis* starting from the Father. In the gift according to the world, this gift appears, as we have seen, only if it occupies the entire stage of visibility and unfolds itself there as such, autonomous, without condition or restriction; that is, only if it obscures by its evidence the figure of the giver. In contrast, in "divine things" (and thus *also* in the economy taken up by the Trinity), the giver puts the first gift into parentheses, because it could interfere with the process of giving and its un-covering; but this putting into parentheses does not suppress the gift, or take it back or annul it; rather it re-gives it. This is called forgiveness. Forgiveness re-gives, and in this re-giving the gift given a second time appears for the first time as all the more perfectly gratuitous (*plenitudo amoris gratuiti*), since the giver does not control it or manage it underhandedly; he does not give it under the appearance of a dispossession that is still contained within the ambit of possession. He truly re-gives it *for nothing*, not in order to manifest the dispossession of the gift or only himself as giver, but in order to un-cover the *ratio donationis* itself. The re-giving of forgiveness gives solely for the love of giving.

Next there is the un-covering of the *ratio donationis* starting from the Son. In the gift according to the world, as we know, this gift appears to the recipient only if it occupies the entire stage of visibility and unfolds itself there without condition or restriction, like an entity to be possessed; that is, only if it obscures by its evidence the very fact that it was given and erases its givenness. In contrast, in "divine things" (and thus *also* in the economy of the Trinity), the recipient puts or can put into parentheses the first gift, the entity in itself that could annul the un-covering of the process of giving; but this putting into parentheses does not consist in challenging or distancing the gift, but rather in recognizing it *as given*. Which is called sacrifice. Sacrifice recognizes in the apparently available entity, free of seizure and open to any act of possession—that is, in the thing lacking origin or giver, in this *nullius*—a gift that was given and which *remains* so. The sacrificed gift reappears. Or rather, it appears for the first time as such, a gift seen henceforth according to the logic of giving, all the more received as gift as the recipient receives it as he ought, like a gift owed (*plenitudo amoris debiti*). The sacrifice does not do away with anything, does not destroy anything; it doesn't even render anything or reestablish any exchange. Rather, it does more, and better: it re-gives a gift that was not received as such, so as to recognize it and thus manifest it as given. The sacrifice accomplishes this re-giving of the gift *for nothing*, not even to express a belated gratitude to the giver, but instead to un-cover the *ratio donationis* itself. The re-giving of sacrifice gives solely for the love of giving.

Finally, there remains the un-covering of the *ratio donationis*, starting from the Holy Spirit. I propose to conceive of it using what Richard of Saint-Victor nevertheless attributed to the Son: "the fullness of love that is both owed and gratuitous (*plenitudo amoris debiti simul et gratuiti*)." Perhaps I will be humored for this audacity, for two reasons. First, because as a general rule it is necessary to hold a certain apophatic reserve with regard to Trinitarian appropriations. Thus the love "that is both owed and gratuitous" can in principle qualify the three members of the Trinity for the excellent reason that the *ratio donationis* always mobilizes these two qualifiers: from whatever point of view one looks upon it (gift given, giver, or receiver), the giving implies gratuity and gratitude; these notes can therefore apply to the Holy Spirit. Second, and above all, they perhaps would also allow for the resolution of a difficulty concerning at once both the gift given and the Holy Spirit.

In the gift given according to the world, it is clear that it seizes the entire stage of the visible without sharing and without any reserve, like a being in itself, offered for possession, for *usus* and *abusus*; otherwise it would quite simply not be given at all. Consequently, by the very fact that it was given, it erases in itself the least trace of givenness. Can one avoid this consequence? I once proposed a response in phenomenological terms, which remains valid.[32] It resorts once again to a bracketing: the gift given is an entity, thing, or object only in appearance, and provisionally. Indeed, contrary to the commercial exchange, the gift is not summed up in the entity that changes possessors by changing hands; of course, most of the time it happens that the process of donation mobilizes something that subsists in itself and that remains available (for consumption, for usage, as patrimony, etc.) to its beneficiary. But in this case, either it has to do purely with an economic transaction (a notarized act, accountable, monetized), which does not have to do with the gift or giving; or if it has to do at least in part with a true gift and giving, the entity put into play fulfills only a subsidiary and pretextual role. In fact, it furnishes the occasion for a much larger process, that of an immaterial sign or symbol of the gift that is truly being given. And the greater the gift's importance the less the entity that it puts into operation matters in itself; a marriage engagement does not consist in exchanged rings, nor in a contract signed before a notary; investiture with power is not summed up by what signals it (the collar of the *Légion d'honneur*, the nuclear codes, the oath on the Bible, etc.); taking possession of a piece of real estate or a business is not identical to signing an agreement, or "having" the signature for an account. In what, then, does the gift actually consist, if it is equivalent to nothing real, to no thing, no object? It consists in the modification of the phenomenality of that which becomes a gift: it happens, suddenly or after calculations, that an object or a thing appears no longer as static and subsistent in itself, but veers about under the aspect of that which proposes *to give* or *to receive*; it shows itself under the allure of givability or acceptability. In the two cases, it proposes itself to the potential giver and receiver as soliciting to enter into the phenomenality of givenness [*donation*], to become a gift. The object or thing asks of the other terms of the gift to appear as a gift given. The rendering unreal of the entity given becomes the very trait of its entrance into giving [*donation*].

This paradox is of great consequence, for it allows us to understand why the gift, even if returned just as it was given, even if redoubled in re-giving, never restores an exchange. When the three terms of the gift are reduced to givenness through their triple bracketing, no exchange whatsoever results because, literally, *nothing*, no thing or object, passes, like a weaver's shuttle, from one hand to the other and back again. The *ratio donationis gratuitæ* does not put into place something intermediary, but gives rise to two intentions to give and to receive, which run across each other but do not compensate for or cancel one another out. And furthermore, when the gift turns toward abandonment, one of the two intentions can be perfectly accomplished without the other, and yet the gift remains valid—an unreceived or rejected gift remains a gift truly given, just as a vain attempt remains within the logic of the gift. The given gift appears fully, no longer as the content or stake in an eventually reciprocal process but as the very movement that manifests givenness and phenomenalizes it. The redounding of the gift, precisely because it renders each of the terms unreal, makes manifest the logic of giving.

What becomes of this result if we pass to "divine things," to the immanent Trinity and therefore *likewise* to its economy? Right away we see how the Holy Spirit responds to its name as *plenitudo amoris debiti simul et gratuiti*. Let us understand owed and gratuitous love here as the redounding of the gift, wherein the three terms have been placed in parentheses so that they could appear as such: pure phenomena of themselves, without objectification. The Spirit accomplishes the gift of the giver (the Father) through the redounding of forgiveness (gratuitous gift); he accomplishes the gift of the receiver (the Son) through the redounding of sacrifice (owed gift); and he himself accomplishes the union of the two not by imposing himself as their summation, their center or their ground, but instead, put in parentheses himself, he finds his name seemingly missing: communion. Even the traditional question of knowing whether the gift qualifies the union of the Father and the Son, or the whole Trinity, or particularly the Holy Spirit, finds its response here: it is only because the Holy Spirit has as his proper task to accomplish the gift of the Son and of the Father in its fullness that, by performing this "first gift," he manifests not such or such particular gift but giving itself. Once again, "there is absolutely no gift (Οὐδὲ ... ὅλως δωρεά τις) without the Holy Spirit."[33] Put another way, there is absolutely no gift manifesting the logic of giving.

The uni(ci)ty of the Trinity only makes itself seen in three points, three operators of its manifestation, three works of its revelation: the invisible Father, to be un-covered in the transparency of the Son, visible as "icon of the invisible," according to a point of view defined by anamorphosis (the displacement of the point of intentionality), where only the invisible Spirit's targeting can lead. It is not *in spite* of there being three that the Trinity manifests itself as communion, but precisely *because* it unfolds in these three operators of the *ratio donationis*. The path of the knowledge of God opens "*from* (ἀπό) the one Spirit *through* (διά) the one Son *to* (ἐπί) the one Father ... and the pious dogma of the monarchy does not fall away."[34] These three prepositions here do not approach the Trinity from the Father, through the Son, and in the Spirit (according to a more habitual ontic formula), but, according to the phenomenal order of the operations, from the aiming point of man in contemplation, from the point of view, dare we say, of his view; or, even more precisely, of his coming into vision according to the economy of un-covering. "To give glory from ourselves in the Spirit does not confess the dignity of the Spirit, but rather confesses our own weakness, indicating that we are not sufficient to glorify Him of ourselves; rather, our sufficiency (ἱκανότης, 2 Corinthians 3:5?) is in the Holy Spirit."[35]

VI
The Opening

NINETEEN

Being, Uncovered from Elsewhere

The elaboration of a phenomenological model of the Trinity (at least in outline) allows us to put into operation a properly *theo*-logical concept of Revelation: the invisible (the Father) targetable [*visable*] in the transparency of the visible (the icon, the Son) is un-covered through the invisible aiming [*visée*] that the Holy Spirit grants to the one who accomplishes the anamorphosis. The entire un-covering plays out in the end with the anamorphosis, the displacement from the point of intentionality. But no human being could perform such a displacement if it were not permitted, taught, and repeated to him by the Holy Spirit, who guides the ego away from itself, into exile from itself, toward the hermitage of the *elsewhere* required for the new aiming point. In other words, and as we have already seen, the un-covering *for us* according to the economic Trinity could not occur if our *elsewhere* did not coincide with the *elsewhere* that the Holy Spirit ceaselessly maintains in the immanent Trinity: we aim correctly at the invisibility of the Father because the Holy Spirit introduces us into the exact place of the Son, who himself is eternally situated in the *elsewhere*, and who goes to the Father because he comes from him. We can henceforth rightly say that the economic Trinity amounts to the immanent Trinity and assume the adverbial expression "*and vice versa*" since we have observed that these two specifications share the sole same *elsewhere*: the logic of the un-covering *for us* of the Trinity in its phenomenal model stems from the communion of the Trinity in itself. This is not the immanent Trinity that comes to transcribe itself into our presumed logic, but rather the economy of its dispensation that comes to unfold among us the unique *elsewhere* of its communion. We enter into the place, the Trinitarian place, the place of the Son *from which* the Holy Spirit makes us aim at the invisibility of the Father—and we enter there by repeating the same path from *elsewhere*, the path of the same *elsewhere* that Jesus traveled among us when he showed us how and why he was the Son of the Father in the Spirit.

The Advent from Elsewhere

We still need to make an inventory of the requirements concerning our fundamental concepts of the anamorphosis that the Holy Spirit demands, and of the journey toward the *elsewhere* that he allows. By these fundamental concepts we understand those precisely that, when we admit them without precaution or critique as *a priori*, *forbid* us to conceive even the possibility of Revelation (see chapters 3–6). Indeed, these *a priori* concepts (or forms) must be decentered by virtue of the phenomenological rule that the given imposes itself *a posteriori*,[1] but above all in consequence of the contrast between un-concealment (*alētheia*) and un-covering (chapter 10). Or again, we could say that the attempt to think starting from *elsewhere* implies rethinking all phenomenality, possible *as well as* impossible, including that of God, according to an absolutely radical *a posteriori*. If everything comes from *elsewhere*, then God as possible necessarily follows. Therefore, in order to receive or perceive him, it is only necessary to take that point of view, to be exiled from ours and travel the distance of the *elsewhere*. And therefore, in order to receive or perceive him, it is necessary to attempt to rethink being and time *a posteriori* on the basis of the *elsewhere*, the only original *a priori*. Here, as a conclusion (chapters 19–20), we will venture to undertake this almost inconceivable task.

First, being. In following Heidegger (chapters 10 and 17), we have seen the aporia that puts a strain on the phenomenality of being, even when one has ceased to conceive it following its persistent subsistence (as *ousia* and *parousia*) and begun to conceive its advent according to the unfolding of the "it gives, *es gibt*." Indeed, even *and above all* in this case, the phenomenality of that which gives itself—in this case the being that springs forth onto the stage of the visible and completely occupies it—must close up in the invisible not merely what or who (sometimes but not always) gives it (the giver), but also the very process that allowed for its appearing. For that which comes, the arrival, that which "has arrived" (*Ankunft*), the entity given like the gift of the phenomenon can manifest itself without reserve or restraint only by rejecting and obscuring the arriving (*Überkommnis*) across which its arrival advanced. The phenomenality of being implies that the being that is given through its visibility alone erases, outside of presence, the process of being that gave it the power to come forth: the more the manifestation of the given entity, the less the manifestation of giving being [*de l'être donnant*]. This aporia led Heidegger himself to give up on thinking phenomenality starting from "being," this provisional and deceptive term that closes access to that which it nevertheless points out. Beyond or next to "being" then looms the *Ereignis*, more as a dark point than as a clearing; at least it would indicate an arrival (*Ankunft*) that holds in its visibility the process of its arriving (*Überkommnis*), a phenomenon that unfolds the depths of its welling up instead of ridding itself of them—that attests both its own event (*Ereignis* in the current sense of that which happens, comes about) and which lets itself be appropriated by what it is coming to be (*Ereignis* as appropriation or reappropriation of the advent).² Heidegger saw this aporia better than anyone, and it is in order to arrive there that he had to undertake nothing less than the "destruction of ontology," to the point of suggesting we pass beyond the "question of being" itself; for to be sure the *Seinsfrage* unmasks the ontology of metaphysics, but it further masks that it only presents the symptom of something it has no access to—the *Ereignis*. Barely, and with difficulty, being poses a question it cannot answer. For in order to answer it, being would actually have to know how to hear a call or appeal. Not an appeal to the self from the self (like that which comes to *Dasein* only from itself), but a call coming from *elsewhere*. No call is heard except from *elsewhere*: there is no tautology or banality here, for the transcendental autism of the ego grants it at first only the hearing of itself in echoes, then, most of the time, forbids it the ordeal from *elsewhere*, and finally closes it to every appeal.

To hear a call from *elsewhere*: now another way opens, because another voice is heard—the voice of the exemplary other. It is fitting here to turn to theology, and more precisely to Trinitarian theology (a pleonasm for the Greek Fathers), because nothing speaks to us of the other more strangely than the Trinity. Indeed, we have reached the result that the immanence of the Trinity itself implies that its *elsewhere* also becomes, in its economy, our own. And further, this *elsewhere* is at play in the gift, the name of the communion between Father and Son, with which the Holy Spirit associates us. And yet, precisely what gift is at issue *here*? In a sense, it is the gift of the ethnologists and sociologists (Marcel Mauss and MAUSS), as well as the gift according to the phenomenological "*es gibt*" (Heidegger); but above all it is the gift according to the Trinity (immanent and economic), which reinterprets and accomplishes from *elsewhere* what we understand by "gift." For, as we have seen (in chapter 18), the logic of the Trinity does not consider only the terms of the gift for us (the giver and his giving, the receiver and his reception, the gift in its presence) and, consequently, it does not subject itself to the aporias that these terms cannot fail to provoke (the symbolic retaking possession of the gift by the giver, the denial of giving by the absent or ungrateful recipient, and the clouding over of the process of giving by the presence of the given gift). Here, in the gift taken up from the Trinitarian *elsewhere*, at least three new terms enter in, or more precisely, three new actions, which at once completely accomplish the gift and perform phenomenality in general as such.

The first of these actions is called *sacrifice*: the Son receives the gift in such a way that he recognizes it always and absolutely as coming to him as given, without ever claiming it or venturing to appropriate it to himself. This implies that the given gift is bracketed, so that it no longer functions as a screen for the manifestation of the giver. Thus Abraham renders Isaac to God not by killing him but by *binding him*, in that way forbidding himself possession of his son, which is to say, admitting the strict truth: Isaac is not his natural son, is not his, but comes from a pure gift (a miracle) of God; concerning Isaac, God provides, not only in the moment by making a ritual sacrifice (substituting the ram for him), but already in the fact of the (fulfilled) promise of his birth to a sterile woman. Similarly, Jesus constantly confesses that all he has comes from his Father, that this Father is greater than he (chapter 13), and that he is nourished only by his Father's will (chapter 14). Here the giver appears as such because the recipient suspends the given gift. This bracketing thus manifests, as much as the gift, the giver in the gift and therefore the advent of giving in him. The recipient no longer receives the gift given by crossing out the giver and the process of giving, but by underlining them in crossing out the gift, which has been sacrificed.

The second action is called *forgiveness*: the Father gives the gift absolutely and without return, in such a way that he never allows himself to appear in it, nor to remain at base its owner (through recognition of debt or, symbolically, by demanding gratitude, etc.); he succeeds in this by bracketing the first visible gift and every demand for recognition. And, by giving anew the gift to the one who did not want to recognize it (the prodigal son), will never do so (the enemy), or could never do so (the unknown), the giver appears in full light, because he exempts himself from any return on the gift. He makes even the giving seen by dispossessing himself of the gift a second time, and for good, and by thus abandoning his primacy. He proves that he has given for nothing by re-giving for nothing, by forgiving.

The third action names the gift as nothing if not a pure and simple *communion*. We have already seen that, from worldly experience, the gift is summed up only apparently in a thing or an object: the more the gift gives, the less it amounts to the transfer of possession of some *thing* or whatever may *be*, and the more it becomes symbolic of another reality, neither objectifiable nor even, sometimes, existing. What more can one give than one's time, one's life, or one's faith and one's love? Properly speaking they are nothing, nothing that *is* nor can serve as an *object*. On the contrary, they give only by giving *themselves*, like so many promises to come; in fact, they give only the assurance, still to be confirmed, that they will give themselves to the end. They give the fact and the promise that they will give themselves, and that between the giver and the recipient there will remain a communion. They give the fact that the two actors will remain in communion. And these two actors receive this communion only on the condition of never confusing it with what could symbolize it, whether object or entity: the bracketing of the gift becomes the condition of the communion's apparition.

Taken into view from *elsewhere* in this way, the gift is accomplished in its *redounding*. Unlike the gift as practiced by the world, the gift according to the Trinity escapes from the aporia of a dissimulation of the process of the advent (*Überkommnis*) through the evidence of the gift (*Ankunft*). The arriving of the giving shows itself all the more as the redounding of the gift brackets its suffocating presence. But if, *here* and here only, the process of appearing itself appears in the appearing of the phenomenon, would it be necessary to conclude that the Trinitarian *elsewhere* leads to something like the *Ereignis*? We cannot respond to this question without at least going back to the one it is symptomatic of, namely the "question of being." Can we consider the symptom ("being") and that to which it points (*Ereignis*) on the basis of the redounding of the gift? Can we read or guess at an anti- or counter-ontology, or in short an approach to the question of being beginning from the *elsewhere*? As surprising as this hypothesis may seem, perhaps we could pursue it.

The Redounding of Being

And more surprising still, we could pursue it by reading one of the texts that illustrates in an exemplary way what we have called the redounding of the gift, where its full phenomenality is accomplished beginning from *elsewhere*, under the title of *kenosis*, as cited in Philippians 2:6–11. The redounding or re-giving of the gift is indeed the concern, since Paul proposes Christ to the Philippians as an example for having bracketed the gift that he holds from the Father, having therefore sacrificed it, and in this way having received it through the re-giving of the gift of the Father, manifesting between them the perfect communion of the Spirit. But—and this point is very important for our hypothesis—the first two verses (2: 6–7) mobilize several terms from the philosophical lexicon broadly understood:

> he, though he was in the form of God (ἐν μορφῇ θεοῦ ὑπάρχων),
> did not regard as a possession to snatch and defend (ἁρπαγμὸν)
> to be equal with God (τὸ εἶναι ἴσα θεῷ),
> but he emptied himself (ἑαυτὸν ἐκένωσεν),
> taking the form of a slave (μορφὴν δούλου),
> becoming in likeness to men (ἐν ὁμοιώματι ἀνθρώπων γενόμενος) and,
> found as a man by his figure (σχήματι εὑρεθεὶς ὡς ἄνθρωπος)....

The often lively and probably interminable discussions about the correct translation of these terms (*form* or *condition*, *exist* or *subsist*, *to be equal* or *equality*, *likeness*, *aspect*, *figure*, etc.) of course have their importance; but their interest remains limited, because the potential differences have meaning only by presupposing the legitimacy of subsequent and metaphysical distinctions, which are anachronistic and therefore unsuited, and above all are distinctions that must be redefined from *elsewhere*. What is more, however one decides to translate the two occurrences of *morphē*, the essential does not change: the *morphē tou theou* is always bracketed by the kenosis; and whether this kenosis concerns the Incarnation alone or also the death on the cross, it results from "obedience" (2:8), and thus once again comes under the redounding of the gift through the bracketing of the gift given (here, the sacrifice). To the re-giving through the recipient (the Son and the sacrifice) there responds the re-giving by the giver (the Father and forgiveness), wherein

> God highly exalted him (ὑπερύψωσεν)
> and gave to him the gracious gift (ἐχαρίσατο) of the name
> that is above every name,
> so that at this name, *Jesus*,
> every knee should bend,
> in heaven, on earth, and in Hell
> and every tongue confess (ἐξομολογήσηται)
> "Jesus Christ—Lord"
> to the glory of the Father. (2:9–11)

To the kenosis (v. 7) that sacrifices the gift of equality with God there responds the "grace" that re-gives (forgiveness) the name of Lord (Κύριος), that is to say, the very name of the Father, and both moments (sacrifice and forgiveness) occur under the same sole "obedience." The "glory" of God stems from the fact that the double redounding or re-giving of the gift happens within the single "obedience," or put another way, in the single communion.

The redounding of the gift therefore structures the entire hymn in Philippians 2:6–11, but more particularly two of its terms: kenosis and obedience consist first of all in not holding a gift as a good to possess and defend (ἁρπαγμὸν), but instead in bracketing it so that the grace that (re)-gives it may appear; and then in that this good (given, sacrificed, and re-given) may consist in *being*, or more precisely, in "being-equal-to-God." We must examine these two points.

Equal to God

What does εἶναι ἴσα θεῷ mean? First let's consider *einai*: the usage of the infinitive is extremely rare in the New Testament.[3] Most of the time, it still has the function of a copula: "the fact of being without excuse, τὸ εἶναι αὐτοὺς ἀναπολογήτους" (Romans 1:20), or "being righteous, εἶναι δίκαιον" (3:26).[4] And, when position is at issue, the verb is conjugated: "for in him we live, we move, and we are (ἐσμέν)" (Acts 17:28).[5] Sometimes we find the position in the infinitive: "before the world was, πρὸ τοῦ τὸν κόσμον εἶναι" (John 17:5); "λέγων ἐν φωτὶ εἶναι" (1 John 2:9), but also with a copula value: "It is good for us to be here, καλόν ἐστιν ἡμᾶς ὧδε εἶναι" (Matthew 17:4 = Mark 9:5); or "What do men say [about what] the Son of man is? Τίνα ... εἶναι" (Matthew 16:13, 15). The occurrence in Philippians 2:6 remains all the more remarkable because it, probably alone, reinforces the absolute position of the infinitive first through the article *to einai*, and then through the adverbial locution *isa theō*—the fact of being equal to God. It is the fact of being in the absolute sense (whence the two occurrences of ὑπάρχειν), but also in a *mode* of being that is very particular, consisting of claiming to-be-equal-to-God. This mode of being is found only in a few rare other texts; for instance, Heracles finds himself honored with the title of "equal to the gods, ἰσοθέων," but Philo judges that this pretention is the mark of a man who "loves himself [too much] and is atheistic."[6] But hasn't Jesus precisely and constantly claimed this equality to God? "I and the Father are one" (John 10:30). Appropriating the rank of God: Is this not exactly what Christ was accused of doing? If they sought to kill him, it was "for blasphemy, because you, being a man, make yourself God, σὺ ἄνθρωπος ὢν ποιεῖς σεαυτὸν θεόν" (John 10:33), for a crime formulated nearly in the same (and rare) terms used in Philippians 2:7: "This was why the Jews sought all the more to kill him, because he not only broke the sabbath but called God his own Father, making himself equal with God, ἴσον ἑαυτὸν ποιῶν τῷ θεῷ" (John 5:18). It is astonishing that exegetical science has not underlined this patently evident connection: it is as if, despite the supposed incompatibilities of the dates, the hymn from the Letter to the Philippians answered, literally, to the accusation made against Jesus, refuting it. For there can be no argument about Christ having proclaimed himself to be on equal terms with the Father, to be God: "We have a law, and by that law he ought to die, because he has made himself the son of God, ὅτι υἱὸν θεοῦ ἑαυτὸν ἐποίησεν" (John 19:7). Always and everywhere, the issue is only this claim: "All things have been delivered to me by my Father" (Matthew 11:27 = Luke 10:22). And: "For he said, 'I am the Son of God'" (Matthew 27:43). Or: "Jesus said to her, 'I who speak to you am he'" (John 4:26, and see v. 42). And further: "I am in the Father and the Father in me" (John 14:10, confirming 10:30). The accusation is indeed valid, the crime founded. And yet the condemnation reveals itself to be unjust.

For the question does not consist in knowing if Christ is the Son of God and "one" with the Father, but instead in knowing how he is on an equal footing with God: everything depends on the manner in which this is so. The accusers from the Temple, the scribes and the Pharisees, understand this *manner* only according to their way of understanding the being that one is—as a *taking* possession, a possession to hold and above all to keep, an appropriation that is likely violent, or in any case demanding; in short, as an appropriation in the mode of jealousy (toward God), which assumes in turn a God who himself is jealous, in the mode of demonic temptation: "God knows that the day when you eat of it [the fruit of the tree], your eyes will be opened, and you will be like gods, knowing good and evil" (Genesis 3:5). What is more, when those who oppose him loudly and forcefully claim their "descendance from Abraham," Christ reproaches them not only for conceiving of that descendance as a "seeking for glory," but above all he makes of their claim a possession of demonic origin: "You are of your father the devil, and your will is to carry out your father's greediness (ἐπιθυμίας)" (John 8:33, 50, 44). His adversaries thus naturally interpret Christ's claim to divine sonship as they understand their own descendance from Abraham: as a taking possession. Never as a gift, which would appear *all the more* so as one allows oneself to be dispossessed of it.[7]

Being through Possession, Being through Dispossession

And so the question is transformed: in order to understand the unique occurrence of *to einai isa theō*, it is necessary to comprehend it through the opposite of what, according to Christ's adversaries, it signifies, namely a possession characterized by jealous appropriation. The hymn from Philippians very precisely identifies what equality with God *does not mean* in the case of Christ and his manner of being, his *to einai*. In order to say it, the hymn uses a significant, yet enigmatic, term that only appears here in the Scriptures, and remains quite rare in Greek texts: ἁρπαγμὸν, *harpagmon*. By drawing on two other substantives found in the New Testament, *harpax* (the ravisher) and *harpagē* (the prey, the plunder), and on the verb *harpazein* (to snatch away, to take by force), we can approach a plausible translation. Positively, it can refer to snatching someone from the fire (Jude 23), or a rapture that catches one up to heaven, such as Paul (2 Corinthians 12:2), or the faithful (1 Thessalonians 4:17), or the child threatened by the dragon at his birth (Revelation 12:5), or Philip from the sight of the eunuch (Acts 8:39). Negatively, it can also have to do with taking Jesus by force to make him king (John 6:15), or Paul in order to put him in the fortress (Acts 23:10). But in the majority of occurrences it is a matter of plundering (Hebrews 10:34), ravenous wolves (Matthew 7:15, and see John 10:12), the cupidity of the wicked (1 Corinthians 5:10; 6:10; Luke 18:11), the robber (Matthew 12:29), or the Pharisees' "rapaciousness beyond self-control, ἁρπαγῆς καὶ ἀκρασίας" (Matthew 23:25) or their "obscene rapacity, ἁρπαγῆς καὶ πονηρίας" (Luke 11:39). Whatever may be the ultimate aim of the formula "the kingdom of heaven has suffered violence," it is clear that in any case "the violent take it by force (ἁρπάζουσιν)" (Matthew 11:12). The term *harpagmon* thus designates that which one snatches up violently in order to possess it and persevere in that possession for as long as one has the strength to do so. It is not simply a "usurpation" that can only be made by force; nor is it "pursuing," because the possession is already an established fact; nor is it "restraining with jealously," which omits the gesture of violent appropriation.[8]

We find the point of disagreement here. For Jesus's adversaries, the aim is to possess one's rank, which for them means their descendance from Abraham and its privileges. For the disciples, the aim is to possess the positions of power in the Kingdom to come, with the accruing privileges. Neither the adversaries nor the disciples believe it should be any different for Christ, whom they imagine *possessing* the sonship that makes him equal to the Father, with the corresponding privileges. He would consider this sonship as a possession, if not to be taken by force, at least to be conserved and defended—doubtless as they themselves would do if they could. In order to settle this conflict of interpretations, at precisely its acme during the discussion with the disciples about their rank in the kingdom of heaven, Christ poses the contrary principle: "Whoever humbles himself like this child, he is the greatest in the kingdom of heaven" (Matthew 18:4), using moreover on this occasion the very precise verb "to humble oneself (ταπεινώσει ἑαυτὸν)" that is applied to him in the hymn ("he humbled himself, ἐταπείνωσεν ἑαυτὸν") (Philippians 2:8). Not only "if anyone would be first, he must be last of all" (Mark 9:35), but this inversion of values demands a radical humbling that will begin to be fulfilled in, among other acts, the washing of feet: "'Do you realize what I have done for you? You call me Teacher and Lord, and you are right, for that is what I am. So if I, your Lord and Teacher, have washed your feet, you also ought to wash one another's feet'" (John 13:12–14). In this way primacy in the Kingdom of God lies not in possession but in dispossession, not in conservation but in abandonment (the re-giving of the gift through sacrifice).

This goes to the point that here we see opposed to the principle of (metaphysical) conservation of one's being by each entity (*conatus in suo esse perseverandi*), as it puts into operation the principle of non-contradiction (no thing can differ from itself), what we might call the principle of self-contradiction: "If anyone wants to become my follower, let him deny himself (ἀπαρνησάσθω ἑαυτὸν) and take up his cross and follow me. For he who wants to save (σῶσαι) his life will lose it (ἀπολέσει), and he who loses his life for my sake will find it."⁹ In order to save and thus find oneself perhaps saved, one should in fact *not* try to save *oneself* at any price, contrary to the spontaneous opinion of those who challenge Christ on the cross to come down: "Save yourself (σῶσον σεαυτόν)!" (Matthew 27:40 and Mark 15:31). To save oneself: this is what Christ on the cross above all had *not* to attempt, since he had to manifest that all resurrection comes from the Father alone, who created *de nihilo*. The savior is not the one who saves *himself*, but rather the one through whom others are saved, and even the one who finds himself saved by another: here, the Father. And Jesus, the one who saves, only saved others because, in saving them, he *did not* do his own will but that of the Father to whom he handed over his will. In other words, in saving others he did not save himself first of all or in addition, but gave witness to the Kingdom to come and the signs that accompany it. The one who was saved and allows others to be saved appears as the one who precisely did not want to save himself by keeping possession of his being, but who "offered up prayers and supplications, with loud cries and tears, to the One who was able to save him (τὸν δυνάμενον σῴζειν αὐτὸν) from death, and he was heard (εἰσακουσθεὶς) because of his reverent submission. Although he was a Son, he learned, through what he suffered (ἔμαθεν ἀφ' ὧν ἔπαθεν), obedience (ὑπακοήν); and having been made perfect, he became the source of eternal salvation for all who obey him (τοῖς ὑπακούουσιν)" (Hebrews 5:7–9). What does "obedience" mean here? In Greek, it is equivalent to listening, to listening to a call, and thus to the reception of a gift. Salvation comes like a gift, received as such (through the re-giving of the gift, sacrifice), not possessed through the violence of appropriation.[10] Thus one can go so far as to "hate one's own soul" (Luke 14:26: μισεῖ ... τὴν ψυχὴν ἑαυτοῦ, and Luke 17:33; or John 12:25: ὁ μισῶν τὴν ψυχὴν αὐτοῦ ἐν τῷ κόσμῳ τούτῳ εἰς ζωὴν αἰώνιον φυλάξει αὐτήν). On the condition of not confusing the "hateful self"[11] with the resentment of a self-hatred, conceiving it as the opposite of the love of self—to the point of scorn for God. To love God to the point of scorn for oneself—to the point of leaving up to God one's care for oneself. Before God I am more responsible for my brother than for myself. Indeed, I can do much to save my brother, but nothing to save myself—nothing if not await salvation from God and not from myself. To be in transit toward the anamorphosis, not toward the *elsewhere*, but *on its basis*. In this way we understand "how the lofty came to be in humiliation, and is seen in humiliation, without falling from his elevation."[12]

Giving up on saving *oneself* becomes the very condition for receiving salvation. Self-conquest of one's own salvation, like every taking possession through appropriation, masks—and this is its original defect and failure—that the essence of salvation consists in the gift, in the fact *that* it happens *if* at least it happens *to me* from elsewhere than myself. And this gift can only happen if it can let itself be received by its addressee, thus solely if the possible addressee has given up on the mortal illusion of making it happen him or herself. Salvation can come only from elsewhere, coming to me like a gift; it therefore presupposes that I have abandoned to it the possibility of its happening *to me*, and the care to that end. I can receive only what I do not possess, what I do not produce, or conserve. I can receive only to the extent that I abandon the mastery of what I receive, and return the measure of salvation to the gift itself. Consequently the gift can be received only to the extent of the abandon that she who receives it concedes to it—who receives it precisely as what she does not possess, but what comes *to her* from elsewhere. No gift arrives without happening in possibility; possibility opens expectation, allows reception, and thus also disappointment; it assumes that I expose myself to possibility and do not close it through my taking possession or through my claim to possession (*harpagmon*). The gift gives and asks for nothing—other than that I abandon myself to it. Abandonment to the possibility of the gift fixes the only measure of the reception of the gift. With the measure by which Christ "emptied himself" and "lowered himself"—that is to say, abandoned himself to possibility to the point of exposing himself three times, first to humanity ("taking the form of a slave, passing into the figure of a man"), then to obedience ("he became obedient to the point of death"), and finally to the cross ("even death on a cross")—his immense abandonment opened the space of an immense gift: "God highly exalted him and granted him the grace (ἐχαρίσατο) of the name that is above every name" (Philippians 2:9). What is possessed is lost, along with the one who seized hold of it. For that which does not end up as something given, and something given that is received, is lost with its possessor. Only that which finds itself given ends up saved. Saved by the one who gives it to the one who receives it, to the extent that she abandons herself to it. Through the death of Christ there is revealed, even in the abyss that the fossilized thickness of sin gouges into the depths of the world, the principle that everything is lost, except that which finds itself given, that nothing survives if it does not pass into a gift, and that only the gift saves from abandonment, because only the gift makes of abandonment the paradoxical condition of the gift. Christ on the cross proves, for evermore, that only she who holds on to her soul loses it, and that she who abandons it saves it.

Being in Terms of the Elsewhere

Can this overturning of the mode of being, or more exactly this overturning of the manner in which *being* (here, τὸ εἶναι) happens in the case of the kenosis of Christ, be understood seriously as a position taken on the "question of being"? Can the dispossession regarding *to einai* as Christ accomplishes it seriously concern what metaphysics conceives as the being of beings, or even what the *Ereignis* awaits beyond being?

Instead of answering this line of questioning directly, we find ourselves at least in a position to understand it from *elsewhere*, and thus to argue that the question of the ontological difference does not stem from being, but from the gift: for, just as the arriving (*Überkommnis*) of being obscured by the arrival (*Ankunft*) of beings is conceived through the logic of the gift (*es gibt*), so too the full liberation of the logic of giving comes about only through the redounding of the gift.[13] Taken up economically in the phenomenal model of the Trinity, the gift bestows being because it precedes it and thus is exempt from it. The (supposed) ontological difference between beings and being in fact cannot be thought or even dispensed with or cleared up on the basis of itself. Indeed, through a required follow-up to the definition of the entity *in its being* (its beingness) as a persistent presence (Kant called it *Beharrlichkeit*), this entity masks and obscures being; so being disappears from the stage of the visible, as the destiny of metaphysics has proven. At the level of the being of entities, such as it is measured by the "level of reason," the entity rules out being, because, more originally, the gift censures giving. Responding to the "question of being" therefore no longer comes under being, or even the given entity *as such*, but henceforth asks that the entity dispossess itself of the visibility it preys upon, and thus that to begin with the gift abandon its evidence and render it to the process of giving. Schelling in his own way caught a significant glimpse of this. If God, as Son, reveals himself as the "Lord of being," he can do so not because he seizes hold of it (as every entity would ordinarily like to do), but because he rids himself of it.[14] He rids himself of it so that *such a being* appears at last as what it *is*, in "the total creaturization of this being as extra-divine."[15] Nothing less than "to unlord (*entherrlichen*) his being, to lower it" is necessary; and, thinks Schelling, not "in relation to a still higher being,"[16] but because above being there is no other being, no other way of being, if not the Trinitarian redounding of the gift without being. It is necessary to "unlord being" because it is proper to denounce its irreducible finitude. The finitude of being destines it for the finitude of man, and thus erases it before the holy infinity of God. The Son empties himself of his being, of being (τὸ εἶναι), so that "being strips off its divinity"[17] and the holiness of God frees itself from being.

The goal and the meaning of kenosis, otherwise called the bracketing of "being equal to God, τὸ εἶναι ἴσα θεῷ," is not to manifest that the Son can freely renounce his divinity (and perhaps keep possession of his being as being), but to reveal that he owes his divine filiation not to *his* being, nor to being (*to einai*), nor to the least possession (*harpagmon*), nor to the least persistence attached to his substance (*ousia*), but to the Trinitarian redounding of the paternal gift. To testify that the Father gives him everything, the Son makes no recourse to being—being is powerless here, it literally can do *nothing*—but instead to "the hyperbole of the gracious gift (τὴν ὑπερβάλλουσαν χάριν) of God" (2 Corinthians 9:14). Kenosis empties the Son of his being, and extends the brackets even as far as Being, so as to manifest that grace alone gives, redoundingly so, the rank that makes him equal to God. The Son un-covers that his being equal to God comes to him from *elsewhere*. To him as the first born of all filiation, and then to all, but always from *elsewhere*.

The Reversal of Beings

There follows a reversed determination of the entity: it finds its site not in its being or in being, but henceforth located in the gaze of God. The entity comes to be understood as ever qualified and overdetermined theologically. For each entity the final (or first) question asks not whether it is or is not, but how and in what way what it is (or is not) un-covers itself in the light of God. Numerous occurrences of "being, ὄν," mark this new turn, where the theological qualifier that is joined to the present participle and quasi-substantive *being* becomes in fact the substantive. For example, "πονηροὶ ὄντες, being evil" indicates evil ones, who are (Matthew 7:11); "ἁμαρτωλῶν ὄντων, being sinners" designates a sinner, and who is (Romans 5:8); "being enemies, ἐχθροὶ ὄντες" identifies enemies, who are found to be (Romans 5:10); those whom one designates "κατὰ σάρκα / ἐν σαρκὶ ὄντες, being according to/in the flesh" draw attention to themselves as acting according to the logic of the world and who also are in the world (Romans 8:5, 8:8). Inversely, if "the one not being with me against me is, ὁ μὴ ὢν μετ' ἐμοῦ κατ' ἐμοῦ ἐστιν" (Matthew 12:30 = Luke 11:23), what defines him is not his beingness, but first of all his decision concerning Jesus. Beingness becomes indifferent when the concern is to un-cover "ὁ ὢν ἐκ τοῦ θεοῦ, the one being *of* God" (John 18:37), or "ὁ ὢν ἐκ τῆς ἀληθείας, the one being *of* the truth" (John 18:37). The adjective qualifies more than the substantivized participle of being; "being" becomes the adjective, the adjunct, the attaché of the qualification, originally theological.

The neutralization of being and of the entity (*to einai, to on*) is confirmed by the uses of *ousia* and its derivations or compounds. We shall not return to the unique usage of *ousia* in the New Testament (Luke 15:12, 13), which I have analyzed elsewhere,[18] except to underline that it has to do with real estate, landed property to be possessed, a meaning that subsists in Aristotle's *substance* (*ousia prōtē*) as the first determination of entities. When the younger son claims it as his part of the inheritance and the father gives it to him by "realizing" it in good round coin, the son spends it right away and loses it. The loss here comes not so much from the dissipated life of the son as it does from his taking possession: substance (*ousia*), contrary to expectation and appearances, does not hold up over time, allowing neither for persisting in presence nor even remaining alive. Pure and simple loss, its detriment and its cancellation, results from the illusion that being a being to be possessed can save. And what is important in the end, what gives life back to the lost son, will come not from another possession, nor from another *ousia*, but from forgiveness, which is to say from the re-giving of the gift, where the father gives him the rank of a son rather than this *ousia*. The son could never count on the *ousia* because it quite simply doesn't count, it is illusory because indifferent. By contrast we note the strangeness, more discrete but no less significant, of *parousia*. Paul sometimes uses the word in its current sense of the physical presence of someone (that of Stephanas, 1 Corinthians 16:17; that of Titus, 2 Corinthians 7:6; his own, 2 Corinthians 10:10–11), but at least one time he uses it more specifically: "Therefore, my beloved, just as you have always obeyed me, not only in my presence, but much more now in my absence (μὴ ὡς ἐν τῇ παρουσίᾳ μου μόνον, ἀλλὰ νῦν . . . ἐν τῇ ἀπουσίᾳ μου)" (Philippians 2:12). We see clearly here that absence (*apousia*) brings about or can bring about more obedience than presence (*parousia*); and, consequently, that the immediate insistence on the fact of *ousia* (for this is indeed at stake in *parousia*) not only sometimes fails to make an impact (and Paul's encounters with the Corinthians were the tangible proof), but it can have less impact than absence. This is not a negligeable anecdote, but rather the definition of authority and a useful discovery for any apostle. As for the uses of *parousia* to evoke the eschatological presence of the risen Lord returning in glory, they always and by definition occur in the mode of absence *right now*, as what "hope" is awaiting (1 Thessalonians 2:19), and what demands that we become "blameless" (5:23). In fact, *parousia* depends on God alone: "the manifestation of his *parousia*" (2 Thessalonians 2:8) will put an end to the reign of the "lawless one, ὁ ἄνομος." Thus, God's *parousia* even and above all evades any subsistent and persistent presence of beings in their being, and bursts forth (or will burst forth) like "lightning, ἀστραπή" that flashes from the East to the West (Matthew 24:27), neither present nor absent, but happening.[19] Here, for the persistent presence of beings there is substituted the flash of lightning (an image that Nietzsche privileged),[20] which is to say, an event without *ousia*.

To be or not to be, such is therefore not the question, because the difference between the two states of being is canceled in front of another difference, the recognition, or not, of the giving of the gift and its redounding. It is not a question of summarily privileging being over having (or the inverse), or of playing non-being against being in a game of "loser wins all"; rather, the point is to measure the vanity of the criteria of being (or not) in front of the un-covering of the hyperbole of charity. Whether rich or wretched it matters not: everything lacking "God's mystery, that is, Christ himself, in whom are hidden all the treasures of wisdom and knowledge" (Colossians 2:3), appears as deficient, and thus a useless possession. Ordering one's life according to being, the persistent possession of a present entity or the obsessive pursuit of an absent entity, amounts to selling life short: "What profit is there for a man to possess like loot the world in its entirety (κερδήσας τὸν κόσμον ὅλον), yet lose or forfeit himself (ζημιωθείς)?" (Luke 9:25 = Matthew 16:26). In an argument that closely follows the hymn from the Epistle to the Philippians, Paul applies to himself the logic that kenosis manifests in identifying very explicitly that which it sheds precisely as loss; for kenosis consists in a loss of loss, a liberation from that which causes the loss of the un-covering of the "mystery of charity," namely that which is in its being: "Whatever was loot for me (ἦν μοι κέρδη) I have come to consider a loss (ζημίαν) with regard to Christ (διὰ τὸν χριστὸν). More than that, I considered all things that are *to be* a loss (πάντα ζημίαν εἶναι) with regard to the excess (ὑπερέχον) of knowledge [of and through] Christ Jesus, my Lord, with regard to whom I have taken everything as a loss (ἐζημιώθην) and considered them so much rubbish (σκύβαλα), that I may possess Christ and find myself in him" (Philippians 3:7–9). Being (*metaphysica generalis?*), even with all beings, with beings in totality (*metaphysica specialis?*), becomes rubbish, a loss compared with finding oneself in the gift, or rather in the excess (ὑπερέχον) of the redounding of the gift.

Elsewhere than Being

Being as rubbish? Paul does not exaggerate, nor is he mistaken; and he anticipates Nietzsche. Taking note that a being (*ens*) was defined by the concept and exclusively as what the concept conceives without contradiction, to the finite extent of its definition, Nietzsche observes that a being in *this* state of being is reduced to what is purely and simply thinkable (*cogitabile*).[21] Concerning beings and following *this* being [*être*] (the only one known), Nietzsche (after a few others, including Hegel) recognizes "the deception of beings (*Täuschung des Seienden*)."[22] These beings, thus thought as pure thinkables, no longer think anything of being, which itself stoops to the rank of an "idol," to its own waste product. Thus "the 'highest concepts,' i.e., the most general, emptiest concepts, the last wisp of evaporating reality (*letzten Rauch der verdunstenden Realität*)."[23] This last breath, in which metaphysics breathes out all that remains of its being and of being—as its current state confirms with a funereal glimmer—exhausts itself from having wanted to make off with being by apprehending it as loot to possess, conserve, and reproduce. Metaphysics lost and undid being, the persistent substance in presence. Nietzsche sees it perfectly well: "It is *change* that is inherent in representing, not *movement*: passing away and springing up, and in representation all that remains-in-persisting (*alles Beharrende*) is lacking; on the contrary, it [representation] introduces two persistences (*zwei Beharrende*), it *believes* in the persistence (*Beharren*) of 1) an *I*, 2) a content."[24] In other words, the illusion of being as that which remains-in-persisting depends on the illusion that *I* can persist and that the thing known can as well.

Paul denounces these two illusions, with brevity and clarity. Representation, that is, what man believes he possesses by thinking it, lacks the persistence of the *I*. "If it seems to someone that he is something (δοκεῖ εἶναί τι), being nothing (μηδὲν ὤν), he deceives himself" (Galatians 6:3). My thought is not enough to think on its own basis, but it thinks what it receives to think; it thinks from *elsewhere*: "Not that of ourselves we are capable of reckoning something (ἱκανοί ἐσμεν λογίσασθαί τι) as coming from us; rather, our capacity comes to us from God (ἡ ἱκανότης ἡμῶν ἐκ τοῦ θεοῦ)" (2 Corinthians 3:5).[25] Furthermore, since thought does not think on its own basis, the thought of the *I* cannot be thought of itself. No one attains a self-consciousness nor the existence of self through the mere thought of oneself: "But by the grace of God I am what I am, χάριτι θεοῦ εἰμι ὅ εἰμι" (1 Corinthians 15:10). The anamorphosis shifts the *I* away from the approach of the self. It cannot reach itself like a presence that is self-identical, in which it would persevere in itself. It comes only from *elsewhere*. Put another way, "My grace is sufficient for you" (2 Corinthians 12:9). As to content, he who does not squander himself like the *ousia* of the lost and losing son cannot stand up and give anything at all unless he too finds himself given from *elsewhere*. This is not only because what is not given is lost, but because nothing can appear unless it is received: "What have you that you did not receive? τί ἔχεις ὃ οὐκ ἔλαβες;" (1 Corinthians 4:7). "Man can take nothing (λαμβάνειν) that was not given him (δεδομένον) from heaven" (John 3:27).

These paradoxes can be admitted only if they are indeed received. But it only becomes reasonable to receive them if one conceives them starting from *elsewhere* rather than from being, such as it consists in not receiving, but in maintaining itself in persistent presence. This *elsewhere* must then come from outside of being, from the site where the difference between that which is and that which is not is no longer decisive or evident. This site has only one name, which we have always known by name but which we challenge in the depths of our hearts: "God who gives life to the dead and calls the non-beings as well as the beings, θεοῦ τοῦ ζωοποιοῦντος τοὺς νεκροὺς καὶ καλοῦντος τὰ μὴ ὄντα ὡς ὄντα" (Romans 4:17).[26] In the end perhaps we all think like Parmenides: "It is necessary to say and to think the being being; for it is indeed being, and nothing is not, Χρὴ τὸ λέγειν τε νοεῖν τ' ἐὸν ἔμμεναι; ἔστι γὰρ εἶναι, μηδὲν δ' οὐκ ἔστιν" (*Poem*, fragment VI).[27] And yet, it could be, indeed it is certain, that "[God chose] the non-beings to annul the beings, τὰ μὴ ὄντα ἵνα τὰ ὄντα καταργήσῃ" (1 Corinthians 1:28). And that we must think beings from *elsewhere* than being.

TWENTY

Time, Uncovered from Elsewhere

This investigation had begun by seeking, through the incessant flow of what comes forward, carries me away, and surpasses me, what I could retain of it—what I could keep as a solid and steady point in space, and so, too, as an unforgettable point in the flow of consciousness. From the outset, the unforgettable established itself as the figure of what reveals itself, at least in a sketch: and thus revelation was uncovered temporally (chapter 1). What remains for us to determine here is according to which present, and thus which temporality.

Next, as soon as we tried to clarify the theological use of Revelation, its fundamental traits (witness, resistance, paradox) identified the phenomenal gap between that which *gives itself* and that which *shows itself*: for, if everything that shows itself gives itself, not everything that gives itself shows itself, since nothing shows itself except to the extent that it has been received. This gap is a matter of a certain temporality, since what gives itself is *already* given, while what shows itself is *not yet* received (chapter 2). What remains for us to determine here is according to what past and what future, and thus according to what temporality.

And so the same question arises for time as it did for being: From what *elsewhere* must they be understood? And, since being and time go hand in hand (not only with the conjunction "and," but especially in the one "it gives, *es gibt*" that bestows them), the *elsewhere* that being is detached from should be found within an *elsewhere* from time. However, it is not so self-evident that time could allow an *elsewhere*, for a number of reasons.

The Death of the Present

The common (that is, metaphysical) analysis of temporality is characterized first by its obstinate effort to remove from it every possible *elsewhere*. Indeed, the concern to separate what happens (accident, attribute, predicate) from what remains (substance or even essence) in the being of beings leads to thinking *ousia* along the lines of *parousia*, or more precisely, thinking *ousia* along the lines of presence reduced to the present. But what does the present, understood in this way, give without *elsewhere*? Time by definition passes in an extended flow: it does not cease to rise up from an original impression and surpass it, or more exactly, has itself covered over by another impression that is more originary and just as passing; in the bandwidth of presence, each of the presents only presents itself *by not lasting*—the present time will last neither a day, nor an hour, nor a minute, nor a second, nor a fraction of a second; strictly speaking, physically speaking, it *is* only insofar as it ceaselessly disappears. Metaphysics registers this present, at best, as an instant; the instant, an atom of presence concentrated in its nucleus, a nucleus that is obviously indefinitely separable. As a result, the present reduced to the instant can only establish itself as a possession to be kept (*harpagmon*) by colonizing and eating away at the two other exstases of time, because, in view of the present, they are not—the future is not yet, and the past is no longer—such that not only is the present atomized in the instant, but it also cancels out its other dimensions. The whole of time disappears, not only because it passes in a flow, but because it escapes every definition by being swallowed up in what should have assured it as a possession. Reduced to the atomic present, *chronos* devours not only its child (the future) but its ancestor (the past). Hence this strange situation, in which time has no duration whatsoever (*nulla mora*), not even the tiniest duration—*nulla morula*, as Saint Augustine writes.[1] This time, reduced to the "contained presence" (Mallarmé)[2] of common temporality (in fact its metaphysical comprehension, from Aristotle to Hegel and Bergson), is closed up in its nothingness and shuts out anything that would come to it from *elsewhere*. Incapable of the unforgettable, it can reveal nothing.

Yet, what remains is what will arrive, whether I will it or not, and for that very reason from *elsewhere*: my death. Not death in general, such as I observe it, when other human beings around me fade away, a sight both inexplicable (where are they going?) and familiar (we must all pass through it, because *"c'est la vie,"* as those say who are not yet dead). Not that, but death as my death, mine, the one which no one will experience in my place. This death constitutes my ultimate possibility, at the same time absolutely inevitable and undefined in its date and its modalities. Here is my ultimate possibility, but also in a paradoxical sense my only possession of a present time; for, *in articulo mortis*, in this lapse of duration, which I do not even know to last (and which, since in the end I know nothing about it, could perhaps open an eternity), I will be finally what I am, for the first time, since there will be no time after it. Then I will be what I am, except in one sense I already am, since from now on the possibility of dying retrospectively governs my partial actuality and attracts me toward it. I can thus consider that this death, this possible and certain death that I am already, constitutes the approach that is the least distant from the presence of time. My death offers at least the privileged moment of time: no other will come to substitute for it, nor abolish it, nor complete it; we could even suppose that it summarizes all the other moments by ending their flow, which was up until then elusive; at least it certainly seems the only one *without equal*. Must we then conclude that the unforgettable, the moment of revelation, would be in my death?

The Present of My Death

However, the death (according to the metaphysics of the concept) of the present does not even allow me to access the present of my death, for a reason too obvious to explain at length: my death, which I still know nothing about, could come without me experiencing or learning anything about it. At least if we suppose that death destroys the living, body and spirit, then when it intervenes, it will prevent my every experience of this death. Of course, such a definition of death remains by law a simple supposition, strictly speaking a prejudice, a judgment before an experience that no one has ever been able to return from to give us a report. This prejudice still keeps enough plausibility to forbid feigning any hypothesis about what death would teach me about my time, about what it was, about what it is at the end. Many will be witnesses or spectators of my death, but it could be that I am the only one to see nothing of it, to know nothing, to experience nothing; exactly like for my birth, an event about which I alone know nothing. Hence the conclusion of popular philosophy: there is nothing to fear in death because I will never experience it, for as long as I can experience anything, it is not there, and, when it will be there, I will no longer be there to experience it. Yet this is a weak and specious argument. Specious, first of all, because once again, nothing assures us that death, my death, eliminates mind as well as body (nor even its materiality, which, who knows, could change "in the twinkling of an eye" 1 Corinthians 15:52). Weak, especially because it does not describe death *for me*, but holds to death in general, that of everyone and thus of no one. I have indeed no need to experience death as *actual* (supposing, once again, that it involves an actuality that I have absolutely no knowledge of); it is enough to feel the *possibility* of it.[3] Long before I disappear from the radar of this world, *my* death determines me as possibility, and it determines me at each moment; and this is also the reason why these instants disappear as soon as they rise up. Having to die shapes and destines all my time, from the beginning. For, if the nature of my death remains undetermined, the certitude of dying is not in doubt, although paradoxically nothing demonstrates it to me in fact, at least *thus far*. I will not die because one day I will die, I will not die on the day of my death, but I will die because from the start my life itself was mortal, because I am insofar as destined to die (*moriturus*). Life must be understood as the undetermined but certain possibility of dying; or, in a more vulgar way, like a genetic disease, incurable and sexually transmissible. Thus, there is no other definition of life, or even access to it, than survival.[4] The finitude of my being (especially the finitude of being itself) is marked because death governs my life as its original and final possibility, lived in each instant, caught in a flow whose stubborn, ceaseless, and absurd passage bears its seal. It is thus necessary to conclude from this that even my death offers no access to the present, nothing unforgettable, but closes a senseless tale without even an idiot to tell it. Time does not give access to any *elsewhere*.

To this conclusion, one might object: my death, if considered as a possibility, would remain neither closed nor muted for me. The possibility would remain for me to assume this possibility myself, by anticipating it. I would no longer let death come to me, without being able to see it coming or come to see it. I would anticipate this unbridled possibility in order to make it mine. This anticipation of certain and indeterminate death, now admitted as the opening of a pure possibility (without object, without obtainable objective, free from the supposed actuality of the present), would confer its freedom on the *Dasein* that I would then finally become in truth: to decide oneself, to decide on this possibility as what must happen to oneself, to temporize oneself no longer by the present (according to the metaphysical aporia), but by the future (following a phenomenologically corrected temporality). We will not discuss here either the strength or the difficulties of Heidegger's obviously decisive step forward.[5] For what concerns us—access to an *elsewhere* in time—it is enough to concentrate on a single difficulty. Whatever the future that this anticipation launches toward (and we are right to doubt that Heidegger had ever defined it, or even pinned it down), this anticipation requires a *decision*, which will belong to *Dasein* as well as to the ego (whatever its variations, following Descartes, Kant, or Nietzsche). Anticipation reappropriates the possibility of death to this ego and transmutes it into its free possibility precisely because it is the ego's *own* decision. This anticipatory decision thus opens up two objections. First, when and how can I ever make this decision? What content and what other goal can I assign to it, if not precisely my freedom itself, thus the spontaneity of its anticipation? In other words, if my decision allows my freedom, will my freedom be enough to trigger my decision? Above all, how long will I be able to hold this anticipation? In a word, since in fact the anticipatory decision anticipates *nothing*, precisely because the nothing of every being introduces it into being, as is the case for *Dasein*, then we must conclude that *Dasein* anticipates only itself, and only by itself. From this result, which is positive for the existential analytic, there follows for us a second objection: *above all*, if *I* ever succeed in anticipating my death as the possibility of my being, this ecstatic temporality, as oriented as one would like toward the future, does not yet open any *elsewhere*. For it comes from me, it comes back to me and makes me come back to myself without ceasing, in the authenticity that appropriates me to myself (following the double meaning of *Eigentlichkeit*). Of course, this temporarily defines the present and the past from the future, but this future remains closed, because *I* still anticipate it as based on myself, in the (necessarily present) instant of my decision.[6] If I anticipate, then I even command the future. I close the possibility of a future that arrives to me from *elsewhere*. Because, for us, it is not a matter of anticipating the future in order to redefine presence, but to let the future drain the present and in this way imbue it with presence.

It would thus take a manna come from *elsewhere* than *parousia*, like the *epiousios* bread.[7] We know that the different interpretations of this rare term do not contradict each other, but decline each other. Of course this daily bread comes to provide for my present being (the bread necessary to *ousia*), which cannot pass it up without passing away: but it comes for the day which is today, for this day (ἐπὶ τῆν οὖσαν ἡμέραν), as the bread of the day (καθημέραν ἄρτος); finally, this bread surpasses my *ousia* because it arrives to me, day by day, once per day, and for the day that comes. What is essential, or rather superessential, about this bread comes from its arrival, the bread happens [*m'advient*] to me, it *events to me* [*m'évient*], as Péguy would say. In this sense, it opens for me an *elsewhere*. We should receive its unforgettable moment, its death, like we eat our daily bread.

Death on Hold from Elsewhere

In order for another death to come for me from *elsewhere*, it would be necessary not to anticipate its possibility by my resolution, but for it to come to me in fact from itself. It would thus be necessary to avoid compromise over the confrontation with death as the possibility of impossibility and really receive it as the "great Perhaps."[8] Where to find such a death, which reveals the *elsewhere*?

The death of Christ and its temporality can offer here a new paradigm, because Christ operates in the world as the Son who receives everything from the Father, and thus as the one to whom everything happens from what precedes him, from the *elsewhere* of the Father. As a consequence, the obedience of the Son rejects on principle every anticipatory resoluteness of an ego or *Dasein*. The very thing that the Arians stigmatized as Christ's ignorance itself indicates and confirms the Son's sonship: "Concerning that Day and that Hour, no one knows them, neither the angels in heaven, nor the Son; but the Father only" (Matthew 24:36). Here, it is not a question of Christ first renouncing knowledge of the future (his own and that of the world), nor even of recognizing the Father's mastery of time, but of manifesting that this time, given by the Father, must be received as he gives it, from *elsewhere*. *Time is not anticipated, it is received.* And Christ demonstrates this by renouncing every decision or anticipation" of death, all the more divinely as he renounces it *in a filial way*, as only the Son can do. And so, even when he gives his life freely while keeping the power of taking it up, he does not give it of his own initiative and does not take it back by his own decision; rather, in both cases, he acts in obedience to the Father: "For this reason the Father loves me: because I hand over my life (my soul, ψυχή) in order to take it up again. No one takes it from me, but I hand it over of myself. I have the power to hand it over and the power to take it up again: this is the command of my Father" (John 10:17–18). Two points must be stressed. First, Christ remains free to give his life, precisely because he receives it from the Father. "As the Father has life in himself, so he has given the Son to have life in himself" (John 5:26); Christ gives what he has, but he gives it insofar as he has received it. Next, this reception of life up to death constitutes a listening to the Father's command, exactly like the power of resurrecting ("For, as the Father raises the dead and makes them live, so the Son makes alive whom he wills," 5:21); the Son does not anticipate anything, but behaves as Son, that is, obeys. Christ therefore differs radically from Socrates, because he gives his life, rather than giving himself death or abandoning himself to it. Nor is the cross anything like a suicide, where decision anticipates death in order to appropriate it in reverse, and take possession of its future by suppressing its possibility.

In his death, Christ does not want death, but the will of the Father within it: he anticipates nothing of the Father's will and makes no guesses about it, but receives it as "food" (John 4:34) in the possibility that the Father opens to him. He receives this death exactly as he receives life from the Father, not because he wills it, but because he admits it as the will from *elsewhere*. He maintains, *up to death*, the possibility of the *elsewhere*, of the Trinitarian exchange outside of the world and outside history (chapter 16), the absolute *elsewhere*, that of the Father: "Kneeling, he prayed, saying: 'Father, if you will it (εἰ βούλει), take away this cup from me. But, let not my will, but yours be done.' And there appeared to him an angel coming from heaven, who strengthened him" (Luke 22:42–43).[9] What "comes from heaven" is "what eye has not seen and what ear has not heard" (1 Corinthians 2:9, following Isaiah 64:3). In the play of this drama, it is a question of manifesting on earth and in time what is accomplished outside time in heaven, by a grace of Revelation that surpasses everything that humanity could have hoped, everything it will ever be able to, because "behold the heavens were opened" (Matthew 3:16); and they have been open ever since, even for men like Stephen (Acts 7:55–56). What bursts forth here into the visibility of the world, by pure grace offered to the disciples, no longer belongs to the world, in this moment where we hear it, but to the unthinkable and unimaginable Trinitarian communion: "Father, the hour has come! Glorify your Son, so that the Son glorify you.... And now, you, Father, glorify me in your presence, with the glory that I had with you before the world was.... And I am no longer in the world ... but now I am coming toward you.... Like you, Father, are in me and I am in you, may they all be one in us, in order that the world may believe that it is you who sent me" (John 17:1, 5, 11, 13, 21). The hour comes to Christ from the Father and he receives it as such: "The hour is coming (ἔρχεται) and is now (νῦν) here" (4:23; see 5:25 and 16:32). The world receives the performance of divine glory, or perhaps to the contrary, the divine glory pervades and visibly saturates at last the scene of the world; the possibility arises from *elsewhere*. Instead of presentifying the future by an anticipation coming from the present, what is to come *futurizes* the present moment, and restores to it a presence that is received.

The will of the Father thus accomplished in the will of Christ therefore fixes, in the dispersion of our history, the only temporal moment that holds, the only *nunc stans* ever established in the inconsistent time of finitude and also death. In other words, we can observe, in time, the weight and the power of a moment (νῦν, *nyn*) that excepts itself from common time, woven of instable nothings and anticipations to be repeated. And so the *nyn*, where Christ performs his act of will in the name of the Father, makes the Trinity resound on earth, so to speak, and regains the *ephapax* in lost time. This is powerfully attested in the episode of Trinitarian dialogue made *public* in Jerusalem, before the Passion: "'Now (νῦν) my soul is troubled. And what to say? Father, save me from this hour? But for this I have come—for this very hour. Father, glorify your name.' And a voice came from heaven: 'I have glorified it and I will glorify it again.' ... Jesus responded [to the opinion of the crowd on the origin of such a voice]: 'it is not for me that this voice came, but for you. For now (νῦν) is the crisis [κρίσις, *krisis*, the calling to judgment of this world]. Now the ruler of this world will be cast out. And I, when I am lifted up from the earth, I will draw all men towards myself'" (John 12:27–33). It seems obvious here that the same moment (*nyn*) refers, as if by a double face, to two domains. One is strictly Trinitarian, where the Son and the Father are united in the *admirabile commercium* of communion of wills (the Spirit), a union that transcends our history and the dispersion of its senseless time. Here *nyn* designates the decision ("for good"). The other refers this time to our history, where the decision (the crisis) always is lacking, while nevertheless a decision is accomplished "once for all," which settles on and within history, to the point that it settles it more than it takes place in it—it is indeed now that the "ruler of this world" is driven out. The lost time of history and the moment of Trinitarian decision cross indissolubly and the same *nyn* determines them.

Two Judgments in One

But, one might ask, what is common between him and me, between the absolute moment of the Son, the hour received from the Father, and my death, which remains first of all closed in on itself, and which most often does not open up to any decision from *elsewhere*? Precisely because the death and the temporality of Christ proceed from *elsewhere* (from the Father, by sonship and obedience), they are opposed to my project of anticipatory resolution—and they oppose it not with a decision starting from myself and my own intentionality (centrifugal), but a decision (centripetal) in response to a "commandment" from *elsewhere*. This opposition is enough to provoke a crisis: "Now is the crisis of the world, it is now that the ruler of this world will be cast out" (John 12:31). This crisis calls my incoherent temporality, which seeks to attain presence by appropriating the present in vain, into judgment by the temporality abandoned to the "hour" that the Father gives from *elsewhere*. It is a crisis of my temporality before the first real *nyn*, the first *now* that has happened in it. The crisis arrives now, but because now the first *nyn* arrives, the first "now" that stands, that does not pass, that no one will forget, because it happens from elsewhere. This judgment bears on the world "for good" (since that is the other sense of *nyn*) at the heart of its apostasy, only because it bears on it "once for all" (*ephapax*), from the depth of the now (*nyn*) of the definitive and original glorification: "Now (*nyn*) the Son of Man has been glorified, and God has been glorified in him" (John 13:31; see 4:23). Before this glory, we must decide for ourselves, for it is already, forever and ever, from the moment when "every tongue will confess Jesus

Christ [as] Lord in the glory of God the Father" (Philippians 2:11), that is, from the moment (nonchronological) outside time, where the Son can and must say of himself, in the name of the Father, "I am (νῦν ἐγώ εἰμι)" (Luke 22:69–70; see Matthew 22:44). The same name, the Name of the Father, forever manifests for us the Son. If Christ indeed proclaims, "I am the life and the resurrection" (John 11:25), he can do so because he always receives it from the Father: "When you have lifted up the Son of man, then you will know that I am (ἐγώ εἰμι) and that I do nothing on my own" (John 8:28): he merits the very name of the Father precisely because he does the will of the Father, and never his own.[10] He never proclaims this *egō eimi* more freely than at the moment of his arrest (John 17:5–6). Death and resurrection therefore constitute the unconditional and intemporal *nyn* (eternal, to say it abstractly), but anchored in time, the absolute *ephapax* of the opening and of the manifestation of the "mystery hidden for ages in God" (Ephesians 3:9), "mystery held under silence for endless ages, now manifested (φανερωθέντος δὲ νῦν)" (Romans 16:25–26).[11]

In this crisis where I must make a decision in front of the *now*, which has come from *elsewhere* and is accomplished once for all, we can speak of something like an individual judgment manifested in this individual end: I will know what I am, when I decide for myself in front of the death of Christ. But what characterizes the properly Christian vision of the end comes from the anticipation of the moment where "the Son of man 'comes' in his glory and 'all the angels with him' (Zachariah 14:5), and then he will sit on his throne of glory. All the nations will be gathered before him, and he will separate them one from another" (Matthew 25:31). It is a question of one end *for everyone*, of a judgment that "recapitulates all things in Christ, in heaven and on earth" (Ephesians 1:10). We will know what the world is, what it merits and what will be saved in this global recapitulation, which we can conceive as a universalization of what my death means for me, and call a universal and final judgment.

The answers that remain here are twofold: in front of the death of Christ, each person is in crisis, depending on whether or not he sees in it the life received from *elsewhere*; but the final presence of the resurrected Christ exercises a global judgment on all mankind and on the entire world. This is enough to reveal an indecision: it is not self-evident that we could make *both* judgments coincide, nor even that they must be harmonized (the debate still divides the best theologians today).[12] Above all, the presupposition of this possible duality could lead to a questionable, or even dangerous, conception of the economy of salvation. We can agree that God, from the Creation up to the Incarnation, enters into history—this is not contested. Often it is concluded from this that he himself becomes historical, and this, on the other hand, must be debated. For if, in order to assume humanity in its totality and its seriousness, and bearing its "likeness in all things but sin" (Hebrews 4:15), God in Jesus Christ does indeed assume a history (which he himself brings about in choosing his people) and finally history as a whole (that of the universe as created), if therefore in making himself historial, he confers on this history its meaning, this would in no way imply that the meaning thus conferred on history remains itself historial. To the contrary, God only enters history to give it another meaning than the one that it is believed to have, or, more simply, to give it the meaning that it does not have by itself.[13] For *our* history remains determined by common time and its inevitable aporias, without being able to envisage any longer an end that can know its beginning. As such, it remains only historical in its *meaning* or *direction* [*sens*], closed in on itself, condemned to an indefinite flow of incoherent instants, or even (in the best or worst hypothesis) a repetition of the same, neither of which could claim any *meaning* whatsoever. Or, what comes down to the same thing, either it believes it is delivered from *meaning* of any kind (Eternal Return), or it claims to define meaning by continually putting off the final goal (ideology of progress, economic growth, etc.). The two last centuries have excessively boasted about their acting in accord with the meaning of history, but nihilism will have at least convinced us that, supposing we could invoke a global meaning for the human condition, history would certainly not be the place for it. Meaning has no place in history, for history has no meaning, any more than time does. And thus, if God comes into our history, he does not come to find the meaning of history there, or still less to find his own divine meaning, thanks to the (supposed) meaning of history; rather, he comes to give to history the meaning that it cannot itself give, nor give itself. By Creation and the Incarnation, God comes to give a meaning to *meaningless* human history—his own meaning, a divine and not a historical one, that we can only name the "meaning of history" by understanding it as the ahistorical or transhistorical meaning of God himself. The Trinity (the *theologia* of the Greek Fathers, the logic of divine *agapē*), constitutes the only meaning (in other words the only *logos*) of Redemption (the *oikonomia* of the

Greek Fathers), and thus of *our* history. The entire modern debate between a so-called "consequential" eschatology, where the immediate expectation of the end is delayed so long that it ends up disappearing, and a "realized" eschatology, where the irruption of the fact of Christ accomplishes in itself the Kingdom of God, supposes to the contrary that history, in the sense of *our* linear conception of history, remains the place of meaning and actuality for Christ. Consequently, this debate cannot guide us any longer.

With this in mind, we could simplify the responses to the question that is so common, and at the same time so imprecise, regarding the relation between the individual judgment (upon my biological death) and the collective judgment (at the end of history). The fact is that, "according to the Bible, there are not two judgments or judgment days, but only one, and, therefore, we must see the particular judgment after death in some kind of dynamic connection with the last judgment."[14] How should this be understood? We can certainly claim that the first judgment still only concerns the soul, while only the final judgment will include the body of flesh; or that the first, precisely because it is individual, can only truly be carried out by including the community that lived with the individual, which entails the Final Judgment; or that the whole of creation must pass through a global decision. But, whatever the arguments in favor of reconciling the two judgments, they all rest on the presupposition that the time of global history continues after individual death. This presupposition does not withstand an obvious and more radical consideration: once my death arrives, I will immediately leave the time of *our* history. Therefore the gap between the individual judgment and the Last Judgment, *if there is one*, cannot in any way be explained in terms of the temporality of the world, according to a chronological difference.[15] There is no more sense in asking what happens between the end of my time and the end of time (precisely when no more time takes place) than in asking what God was doing before creating the world (because time was also created only with and for the world). The gap "between" the two judgments, *if there is one*, does not in any case belong to our time. And if they coincided, it would neither be a temporal coincidence (which is only valid for the creature), nor even an eternal one (an eternity too abstract to say anything about it). To investigate this gap results in absolutizing *our* history, to the point of imposing the chronological aporia on the wisdom of God. In fact, the appearance of a gap between the two judgments indicates that we are in suspension [*en souffrance*] (as in Romans 8:22) from the crisis: we suffer the suspense of having to wait for the decision to fully come about (in suspension, like a letter already sent out and not yet received, like a decree already made and not yet published, like a law already voted but without ordinances implementing it). This *suspension* [*souffrance*] reflects, in our finitude and our unstable temporality, the two dimensions of what, from the point of view of God, remains one and the same crisis—the decision of each creature and of all creation for or against its recapitulation in Jesus Christ. And from this point of view, now (*nyn*), the ruler of this world is cast out and Christ judges all creatures once for all (*ephapax*). In other words, "Christ, who is judge, according to one and the same most simple and undivided judgment, at one moment and for all (*secundum unicum simplicissimum atque indiversum judicium in uno momento omnibus*)."[16]

History as Idol

But, we might perhaps object, why then can't *our* history produce meaning by itself, or discover it in itself? Yet, between teleology and eschatology, we must choose (Teilhard de Chardin demonstrated this by contrast and in spite of himself). For if we wanted to demote eschatology to teleology, as the dogmatic theology of the past century was unreasonably inclined to do, we would end up understanding the universal and final judgment in a way that is undeniably absurd as well as idolatrous. Absurd, because it would be necessary for a temporal interruption to arise within chronological history, completely unconceivable following its own (common) concept of temporality, which would only open on to an eternity that is itself totally undetermined, an empty suspension of a time which is not. History would be interrupted in an abstract permanence, itself just as contradictory as the present in the instant, which it would claim to sublate.[17] Idolatrous above all, because the Last Judgment would itself take place in history (and temporality), whose supposed meaning it would borrow and therefore validate. By crowning the "meaning of history" (a crowning whose divine character would itself remain completely indeterminate), Christ would inscribe his ambiguous triumph (and God knows how far millenarianism pushed this ambiguity!) in a now worldly glory in common temporality, as, at best, the final triumph of the final *imperator*, realizing the dream of all the Great Inquisitors. Without going as far as evoking the Antichrist, we can recognize here a much more pressing risk, which threatens all believers and especially the most faithful: if the final victory of Christ the King must truly enter into the "meaning" of *our* history, then it has not yet happened; so the second *parousia* remains to come, and without it the first remains fragile, provisional, in short, awaiting its definitive confirmation.

If we thus admit two judgments, it will also be necessary to admit that my own, linked to my individual death, does not decide the whole of history any more than the individual death of Christ (even his singular Resurrection in *our* history) recapitulates its totality; by consequence, we would still have to await another judgment, collective and recapitulative, that would intervene at the end of history, after me. In fact, only the latter would accomplish all things and decide the end—the victory of Christ over evil. The second *parousia* would be the only true one, and the end of the world would conclude the economy of salvation, which, as long as *our* history lasts, remains undecided. During "this remarkable postponement of 'Victory Day,'"[18] it would still be necessary to fight and struggle, so that Christ the King finally might accomplish his reign and establish his kingdom for good.

We find again, inevitably, the obsessive and anxious questions that the disciples (on behalf of all of us) addressed to the Risen One: "Lord, is it at this time (ἐν τῷ χρόνῳ τούτῳ) that you will restore the kingship to Israel?" (Acts 1:6) This question calls for two remarks. First, since "at this time" can mean not only the present moment, but also time according to the common temporality, the question in fact asks: Is it in chronological temporality, in the present non-being of the instant, in the meaninglessness of *our* history, that the reign of God can and must be restored? Next, as this question does not come from Zealots or Pharisees, nor suspicious adversaries, but from the apostles (the best of the believers, the pillars of the Church, here standing before the Risen One, whom they recognize as such), must we conclude that, for them and in this moment (before the outpouring of the Spirit), the reign of God is not yet established, that its fulfillment remains still to come, that the Resurrection is not enough?

Everything Is Accomplished in Heaven and on Earth

But then, how can we conceive the fact (if it is one) that, since the Passion, "everything has been accomplished to its end, τετέλεσται" (John 19:28–30)? If the last "great cry" of Christ (Matthew 27:50 and Mark 15:36) does not proclaim that *already* "it is done (γέγοναν)!" (Revelation 16:17 and 21:6), that he has *already* "accomplished the work that [the Father] gave him to do" (John 17:4), then his "death on the cross" was not yet enough for "God [to] exalt him and favor him with the Name above every name" (Philippians 2:9), nor for him to proclaim, after this cross, "I am the alpha and omega, the principle and the end (τέλος)" (Revelation 21:6 and 22:13).[19] Of course, if Christ has not risen, "our proclamation is empty" (1 Corinthians 15:14); but if his Resurrection does not accomplish all things, if there must be a second coming to ratify, confirm, and validate it, "our faith, too, is empty" (ibid.). Paul's response to this difficulty appears as explicit as it is surprising: if Christ's Resurrection occurred without the final resurrection of the dead, then it would not be real and effective (1 Corinthians 15:12–13 and 16). In good theology, we cannot but admit therefore that the Resurrection of Christ, which is the only thing that has already been accomplished in our time, implies, encompasses, and *already* includes the resurrection of the dead, which in our time, remains to come—"But Christ is in fact (νυνὶ) risen (has been raised, ἐγήγερται) from the dead, first fruit of those who have fallen asleep" (15:20). The double meaning of the adverb must be understood: it is both (as of) now and in fact (*nyni*) that the risen Christ initiates and begins (*ap-archē*) the awakening and raising of those who have fallen asleep in death. One and the same moment (*nyn*) includes more than the present (thus absent) instant of the time as chronology; it governs and commands (*archein*), so to say, in advance (*apo*), the new life outside of chronological time. What for us (in the chronological time of *our* senseless history) remains still to come (resurrection of the dead) is from now on (still in the chronological time of *our* meaningless history) included in what Paul calls a recapitulation.

This *anakephalaiōsis* (Ephesians 1:10) should perhaps be understood literally: bringing under one head, certainly, in the sense of turning over (*ana-*) the hierarchy by putting the head at the top:[20] or rather by putting the head at the head of the body, ordering the whole under one single *archē*, such that what is true for the head (the Resurrection of Christ) is true also, by the same stroke, for everything that follows from it (the resurrection of the dead). This "single-mindedness" [*entêtement*] grafts the meaningless history of the living and dead under the moment (*nyn*) accomplished by Christ, saving it from chronological dispersion. To respond to our initial question—how to understand the fact that, *since the Passion*, "everything has been accomplished to its end, τετέλεσται" (John 19:28–30)—it would thus be necessary to conceive of this moment (*nyn*) where Christ recapitulates once for all (*ephapax*) what he accomplishes in *our* scattered history, from one end to the other.

But we can conceive it only faintly and in a confused way. First of all because we always lack faith and its understanding, even supposing we are willing to risk it: "Oh unintelligent hearts and slow to believe!" (Luke 24:25) But also because the common understanding of time, as has been said, holds us back with a metaphysical constraint: that is, if *our* time offers the only theater of the economy of salvation, a once-for-all (*ephapax*) recapitulation remains impossible, for no decision (no crisis) can occur in temporality that is at once without permanence (the instant, a *nunc* never *stans*, provides no duration) and without consequence (nothing holds *for ever*, because nothing unforgettable *ever* happens).[21] Time, according to its common conception, cannot offer the least place for the economy of salvation. It is necessary to first save time from its literally senseless dispersion, so that it welcomes the possibility of a decision. If nothing is decided in time, nothing is saved in time. Time must therefore be saved from its indecision. To do this, we must start with a death, where a genuinely present moment would accomplish a definitive decision, where therefore a moment (*nyn*) would deliver an event (*ephapax*).[22] It is thus the death and the Resurrection of Christ that we must investigate.

Once for All

From now on, the chasm no longer lies between time and eternity, nor between particular and universal judgment, but between the time that passes and passes of itself without ever being decided, and the time, or rather the moment, or more exactly "the hour," that allows the decision, because it opens up a possibility. In other words, between the time of repetition and the moment of decision, between worldly hope (which awaits what could arrive) and theological hope (which waits *for* something to happen and *because* it has already happened), between what is passing and the unforgettable.

The Scriptures use the adverb *ephapax/hapax* almost exclusively to characterize Christ, whose acts occur "once for all" and indissolubly "for good," definitively. Thus he appears "to more than five hundred only one time" (1 Corinthians 15:6); he has "died to sin once for all" (Romans 6:10), "died for sins once for all" (1 Peter 3:18). This term plays such an important role that the writer of the Letter to the Hebrews feels the need to comment on it as such: "The word *'ephapax'* indicates the transposition (μετάθεσιν) of mutable things, which can be shaken (σαλευομένων) as created things (ὡς πεποιημένων), so that the immutable things, which are not shaken (τὰ μὴ σαλευόμενα), remain" (Hebrews 12:26–27).[23] It is no longer a question of an instant, but of a moment that, instead of fading away as soon as it appears while vainly pretending to last, manages to decide for good: this "hour" makes the decision (as if by a theological reduction), in order to dissipate what changes and is shaken, in order to leave in play that which, unlike "a reed swayed (σαλευόμενον) by the wind" (Matthew 11:7), does not falter; that which is not shaken, that which does not stumble. It is by virtue of this reduction that Christ, in contrast to the repetitive great priest, can accomplish a singular sacrifice, valid once and for all. And he succeeds in this singularity because he pays for it with his own person, by offering himself without reserve, wholly, "for good": "This he did once for all, by offering himself once for all" (Hebrews 7:27).[24] Christ leaves *our* history (and takes us out of it), precisely to save us there.

But how can the will of man will in a decisive, irreversible, and whole manner, "once for all"? Does it not remain irremediably submitted to the chronological dispersion of *our* history, where every instant must be repeated because it never accomplishes anything? Can the will hope for more than the repetition of the similar? The will of Christ can nevertheless succeed in doing so, because it does not will what, in the repetitive and vain time of *our* history, one cannot help but will: to affirm one's own will by repeating it as much as possible, by striving to be the same in an attempt to persist in the flow of the present nothingness; in short, by willing its own will. On the contrary, Christ succeeds in willing *ephapax*, because he does not will his own human will, but wills the will of the Father, which comes from *elsewhere* than *our* scattered time, an *elsewhere* that alone is now and always. He decides not to will with an unstable, inconsistent, and therefore frenetically repetitive *will*, but that which comes from *elsewhere*, before all time, before Abraham was, the will of the Father "before endless ages" and "who does not lie" (Titus 1:2). Because this decision to pass from a vain will to another will comes from another, from the other *par excellence*, the Father, it alone gives the depth of field and the irrevocable seriousness that the bandwidth of the instant, nothingness in itself, lacks. The will that Christ wills and with which he wills sinks so deeply into our time (to the point of cutting it in two, Matthew 27:51) only because it falls from on high, from the height of the Father in the heavens, definitively "effective and sharper than any two-edged sword" (Hebrews 4:12; see Isaiah 55:11). Since God does not want material sacrifices (things or animals, etc.), sacrifices in appearance, made through an intermediary and unable to personally commit the one who offers them, it is appropriate that someone come in person to make a sacrifice, that is, that he give himself in person, body and soul. The only one capable of this can do it in only one way: to give oneself in person amounts to doing another's will rather than one's own, the will of the one to whom he wills to give himself: "And so I said, 'Behold, I have come—in the scroll of the Book it is written of me—to do your will, O God'" (Psalms 40:7–8, LXX).

The Kingdom of God comes among us strictly to the extent that the will of the Father is done on earth (amidst *our* vain dispersion) as it is in ageless heaven; but only Christ accomplishes what we ask in his name in the prayer that he has taught us. And, as he alone has succeeded in willing once for all and "for good" (*ephapax*) the other will of the Father, it is also "in this 'will' that we are 'sanctified' by the 'offering' of the body of Christ once for all (*ephapax*)" (Hebrews 10:10). Under our eyes, in the depths of *our* history chronologically destitute of every decision, even as far as the pit of our filth, a perfect will was accomplished, "what is good, pleasing, and perfect" (Romans 12:2). And so, it is "in the knowledge of God's will" that we find "every spiritual wisdom and understanding" (Colossians 1:9). Finally, for the first time and in fact, one of ours (but who was God) has really willed once for all. And therefore, we along with him: "Christ suffered once (ἅπαξ) for sins, the just for the unjust, in order to bring us to God, was put to death in the flesh, brought back to life by the Spirit" (1 Peter 3:18). And therefore, as a result of this, we live by willing: "Christ, once raised from the dead, will never die again (οὐκέτι), death no longer (οὐκέτι) has power over him. For in dying, he died to sin once for all (ἐφάπαξ); but in living, he lives for the Lord" (Romans 6:10).

Making My Time

If therefore I, too, can will effectively enough that my will decides anything "once for all," I will have to will in the only moment (*nyn*) where, to my knowledge, such a decision has ever been made—in the moment of Christ: "Truly, now (νυνὶ) Christ is raised from the dead, principle (ἀπαρχὴ) of all who sleep" (1 Corinthians 15:20). Every decisive moment is inscribed there as in its principle. Christ thus offers the sole place and the single moment wherein we must be if we want to make a decision for good. "It is no longer I who live, but Christ who lives in me. The life that I actually live now (*nyn*) in the flesh, I live in faith in the Son of God, who loved me and gave himself up for me" (Galatians 2:19–20). As long as we are able to situate ourselves in this moment, we glimpse the possibility of accessing the precise point where *our* history is drawn up into the alpha and the omega, into the Trinitarian communion such as the Son ceaselessly accomplishes it. Here is the crisis, to put an end to *our* history, on the condition that we receive it as such: "my crisis is the real one" (John 8:16), that is to say, received as the will of the Father, who frees us from the space of a decision "once for all" by allowing us to not will our own will: "My crisis is just, because I do not seek my own will, but the will of the One who sent me" (John 5:30). And so this crisis becomes ours, potentially, because Christ himself "does not judge the world" (John 3:17), just as "the Father judges no one" (John 5:22); and especially because it is "the word (*logos*) that I said which will judge on the last day" (John 12:48). In fact, I will judge myself according to what I will have decided before the crisis which the word of the *logos* provokes in me. The crisis, because it is true and just, comes down to me alone: I *decide for myself*, in full awareness, once for all and the first time for good. This is how we must understand the warning: "Judge not that you be not judged. For it is with the judgment (*krisis*) that you judge that you will be judged (ἐν ᾧ γὰρ κρίματι κρίνετε κριθήσεσθε) and it is with the measure with which you measure that you will be measured" (Matthew 7:1–2). It would be a misinterpretation to imagine I could decide anything whatsoever by myself, as if my will could ever decide anything by itself, without a crisis allowing it to do so from *elsewhere*. The right understanding consists in receiving the crisis from *elsewhere*, from the will of the Father, given in the word of the Son and seen in the obedience of Christ, to decide for *oneself* finally and in truth.

Then alone does the decisive moment open, the one allowed by the depth of field that the Trinity bestows, the heavens entirely opened onto *our* history and in our vain time. The irremediable moment, which can change sinners into fishers of men: "Now (νῦν), it is men that you will catch" (Luke 5:10); or make Simeon see salvation, ("Now [νῦν], O Master, you can let your servant go in peace, for my eyes have seen your salvation," Luke 2:29–30), which can make blessed from now on those who weep (νῦν, in Luke 6:2, 21, 25), and in a single present (Matthew 5:3: "Happy the poor in spirit, the kingdom of heaven *is* in them"). But also the irremediable *nyn* of the crisis extending to divided families (ἀπὸ τοῦ νῦν, Lk 12:52 and Matthew 10:30) or the gulf between the poor Lazarus and the rich man (νῦν δὲ, Luke 16:25). This moment, which offers the gift of the crisis, this *nyn* that *our* history proves itself incapable of, provides us with the singular opportunity to accomplish a decision "once for all (*ephapax*)" (Hebrews 12:26, sq).

The *nyn*, once restored by Christic temporality, can bear the *ephapax* of the eschatological crisis—of the decision that makes appear what remained hidden. Not the atemporal eternity, but the *ephapax* of the question always undecided in our time, the *nyn*, the moment that allows the decision for (or against) the discovery of this "mystery." It is thus a matter of the drive toward the end, the final separation, where, "no longer seeing (ἐπιλανθανόμενος) what is behind me, stretched out ahead (ἔμπροσθεν ἐπεκτεινόμενος), I run straight toward the goal" (Philippians 3:13–14). And what is true for each person is true for all of creation: "the waiting (ἀποκαραδοκία) of creation awaits (ἀπεκδέχεται) the uncovering (ἀποκάλυψιν) of the sons of God" (Romans 8:19).[25] From now on everything is played out here and now; and "in this moment (νῦν) the kingdom that is mine is not from there (ἐντεῦθεν)," with Pilate or the Sanhedrin, or in short, from this world (John 18:36), but indeed "in the midst of you" (Luke 17:21). As a result, this moment becomes a "here and now" that settles us and maintains us in the crisis, in front of the decision to decide for ourselves. *To decide to decide*, here is the crisis, the possibility of the *ephapax*. It is here and now that we must say yes or no, so that the crisis does not make us fail, so that we do not fail for lack of the crisis: "Let your *yes* be *yes*, your *no*, *no*, in order to not fall under the crisis" (James 5:12). And so in this way we only conform to the paradigm of Christ, "in whom came the *yes*. For all the promises of God [find their] *yes* in him; it is therefore also by him that our *amen* [is made] to God for his glory" (2 Corinthians 1:19–20). The

Resurrection begins for us in this awakening. "For you know the moment where we are (τοῦτο ... τὸν καιρόν), it is already the hour for us to arise from sleep. For in this moment (νῦν), salvation is nearer than when we [first] believed. The night is advanced, the day is approaching" (Romans 13:11–12). And what follows will only be the unfolding of what from now on is already accomplished: "We are now/actually (νῦν) the sons of God, but what we will be has not yet (οὔπω) been manifest" (1 John 3:2). The result of *our* horizontal history and the vertical crisis (*ephapax*) traces the diagonal of the *nyn*.[26]

Let us conclude: my personal judgment is one with the universal judgment, because my personal *nyn* is decided for, in front of and in the *ephapax* of God, contemporaneous to each of our moments. All of them constitute so many *occasions* of a decision of the will from *elsewhere*. Eschatology transpierces our time, but does not allow itself to be swallowed up by it any more than it vanishes into abstract eternity. According to the diagonal of the *nyn*, each instant *can* (and should) be lived as the last—as the occasion of the decision for or against Christ, as the opportunity to end the time of indecision. The Last Judgment can take place at any moment where this decision can be made, at any instant whatsoever of our senseless time. "Behold, now (νῦν) is 'the favorable time,' behold, now is 'the day of salvation' (Isaiah 49:8)" (2 Corinthians 6:2). Upon my death, suddenly, I am introduced into the absolute, where everything has *already* played out.

Bringing Up to Date, Bringing to Light

Between teleology and eschatology, one must choose. Either to include the absolute in history, or to include history itself in the absolute, the only one: the Trinity. For "during the earthly life of Jesus, in his divine person incarnate in our common humanity, the age to come was found to coexist with the present age. In the Church, however, which is his body and to which he has sent his own Spirit, the age to come is already really present under the appearances of the present age which carries on, not unlike it did before his Passion itself" (Louis Bouyer).[27] One must not, if we might dare such neologisms, presentify (make eternally present) the future, but futurize (orient toward the future, the yet-to-come) the present, or eventialize it less poorly toward the future.[28] For eternity will be made, for each of us, by what awaits us. But what awaits me is nothing other than what I am awaiting—deep down. Not another history, but an exit from history. In such a way, however, that only what enters into history and passes through, coming from *elsewhere*, can take its leave from it. "No one has gone up to heaven, but the one who has come down" (John 3:13). No one comes out of *our* history, brings us out of this history, but the one who does not come from it, but arrives in it as the absolute *ephapax*. By bringing all that is in me and everything in the world up to date, uncovering brings all things to light.

Notes

Foreword

1. Jean-Luc Marion, *God Without Being: Hors-Texte*, trans. Thomas A. Carlson (Chicago: University of Chicago Press, 1991), 1.

2. Karl Barth: "Nur Vorarbeit ist alles menschliche Werk, und ein theologisches Buch mehr als jedes andre Werk!" *Der Römerbrief* (Munich: Chr. Kaiser, 1922), vi. English translation: *The Epistle to the Romans*, translated from the sixth edition by Edwyn C. Hoskyns (Oxford: Oxford University Press, 1933), 2–3, modified.

3. Jean-Luc Marion, *Givenness and Revelation*, trans. Stephen E. Lewis (Oxford: Oxford University Press, 2016).

4. Jean-Luc Marion, *Das Erscheinen des Unsichtbaren. Fragen zur Phänomenalität der Offenbarung*, trans. Alwin Letzkus (Freiburg im Brigau: Herder, 2018).

5. But it is important to guard against "going through the window": that is, to stop on the steepest slope, to get off the bike and claim to have reached the summit; such simplification of the question to fit the partiality of the answer leads to crossing out the question, to scaling it back to fit the chosen answer, in short to rationalizing defeat in order to justify it. This serves fairly well to define heresy, a facile excuse for the failure to reach the goal that seeks to deceive others into believing that the summit was not higher than the point where you threw in the towel.

6. Nicholas of Cusa, *De visione Dei* XVII.79, in *Opera omnia*, vol. 6, ed. Adelaida Dorothea Riemann (Hamburg: Felix Meiner, 2000), 63; English translation: *Selected Spiritual Writings*, trans. H. Lawrence Bond (New York: Paulist Press, 1997), 270.

Chapter One

1. Charles Baudelaire, "Correspondances," *Les Fleurs du mal*, in *Œuvres complètes*, ed. Yves-Gérard Le Dantec and Claude Pichois (Paris: Gallimard, Pléiade, 1966), 11.

2. "Tout s'enfle contre moi, tout m'assaut, tout me tente": Jean de Sponde, "Sonnet," in *Poètes du XVIe siècle*, ed. Albert-Marie Schmidt (Paris: Gallimard, Pléiade, 1953), 898; English translation: *Sonnets on Love and Death*, trans. Robert Nugent (Westport, CT: Greenwood Press, 1979), 77.

3. "Dans la nuit éternelle emportés sans retour, / Ne pourrons-nous jamais sur l'océan des âges / Jeter l'ancre un seul jour?": Alphonse de Lamartine, "Le lac," *Premières méditations poétiques*, in *Anthologie de la poésie française*, ed. André Gide (Paris: Gallimard, Pléiade, 1953), 412; English translation: E. H. and A. M. Blackmore, eds., *Six French Poets of the Nineteenth Century: Lamartine, Hugo, Baudelaire, Verlaine, Rimbaud, Mallarmé* (Oxford: Oxford University Press, 2000), 11.

4. Arthur Rimbaud, "Chanson de la plus haute tour," *Une saison en enfer*: "Qu'il vienne, qu'il vienne, / Le temps dont on s'éprenne," in Rimbaud, *Œuvres complètes*, ed. Antoine Adam (Paris: Gallimard, Pléiade, 1972), 108; English translation: *Rimbaud: Complete Works, Selected Letters*, trans. Wallace Fowlie (Chicago: University of Chicago Press, 1966), 195, modified.

5. Among many testimonies, there is that of Christophe Lemaitre, a timid child often bullied at school, who in 2010 became a triple European champion (100, 200, and 4x100 meters relay), and a bronze medalist in the 200 meters at the World Championships of 2011 and the 2016 Olympic Games: "Track and field didn't only bring me performances and medals. It also allowed me to reveal me to myself." *L'Équipe Magazine*, no. 1894, supplement to November 3, 2018. With one correction: he did not reveal himself to himself, but was revealed by the event and the athletic movement.

6. "ce rêve étrange et pénétrant / D'une femme inconnue, et que j'aime et qui m'aime": Paul Verlaine, "Mon rêve familier," *Poèmes saturniens*, in *Œuvres complètes*, ed. Yves-Gérard Le Dantec (Paris: Gallimard, Pléiade, 1962), 63.

7. See a more explicit development in Jean-Luc Marion, *The Erotic Phenomenon*, trans. Stephen E. Lewis (Chicago: University of Chicago Press, 2007), §§23–25, 112–35.

8. See *The Erotic Phenomenon*, §§3–7, 19–40. Levinas saw this more than others, explaining that I come from "a word coming from *elsewhere*, from outside and simultaneously dwelling in the one who welcomes it." "Revelation in the Jewish Tradition," in *Beyond the Verse: Talmudic Readings and Lectures*, trans. Gary D. Mole (Bloomington and Indianapolis: Indiana University Press, 1994, 1982), 133, modified. See the analysis by Raphael Zagury-Orly, which locates here an "intrusion," "that can be referred neither to a subjective stance or regulatory idea of reason, nor to an objective or spatial exteriority," for it concerns "that which is given to the subject but cannot be lodged in him." "Approche de la révélation. Kant et Lévinas,"

Questionner encore (Paris: Galilée, 2011), 84 and 88. In fact, "The idea of Infinity *is revealed*, in the strongest sense of the term." Emmanuel Levinas, *Totality and Infinity: An Essay on Exteriority*, trans. Alphonso Lingis (Pittsburgh: Duquesne University Press, 1969), 62, Levinas's emphasis.

9. Charles Péguy, *Note conjointe sur M. Descartes et la philosophie cartésienne*, in *Œuvres en prose complètes*, ed. Robert Burac, vol. 3 (Paris: Gallimard, Pléiade, 1992), 1408; English translation: *Notes on Bergson and Descartes: Philosophy, Christianity, and Modernity in Contestation*, trans. Bruce K. Ward (Eugene, OR: Cascade Books, 2019), 173, modified.

10. "In this singular workshop that the world becomes when considered in this way, the work is piecework, but (becomes, *events*, goes by) happens on time. The work is done piece by piece, with everything that piecework implies and requires that is fragmentary, discontinuous, precarious, exposed, proud, risky, accidental, free, chancy, competitive, human, secular, adventurous, *audax*, ingenious, ambitious, profitable, Hellenic, fortuitous, fatal too, altogether industrious, Odyssean and Promethean.... The event is done on time, imperturbably, irrevocably on time." Charles Péguy, *Texte posthume* (1907), in *Œuvres en prose complètes*, ed. Robert Burac, vol. 2 (Paris: Gallimard, Pléiade, 1988), 1493, a text brought to light by the scholarly meticulousness of François Fédier, *Regarder voir* (Paris: Les Belles Lettres, 1995), 115.

11. "Elle est retrouvée! / Quoi?—L'Éternité. / C'est la mer allée / Avec le soleil." Arthur Rimbaud, "L'Éternité," in *Œuvres complètes*, 79; English translation: *Rimbaud: Complete Works*, 141.

12. *Gestalt* comes from *stellen*, to place, like *Gestell*, scaffolding.

13. Friedrich Hölderlin, "In lieblicher Bläue," *Sämtliche Werke*, ed. F. Beißner, Bd. II/1 (Stuttgart: Kohlhammer, 1951), 372; English translation: *Poems and Fragments*, trans. Michael Hamburger (Ann Arbor: University of Michigan Press, 1966), 600, 601, modified. For another, more complete commentary, see Jean-Luc Marion, *The Idol and Distance: Five Studies*, trans. Thomas A. Carlson (New York: Fordham University Press, 2001), §8, 81–91.

14. Edmund Husserl, *Ideen zu einer reinen Phänomenologie und phänomenologischen Philosophie, I: Allgemeine Einführung in die reine Phänomenologie*, Hua III/1 (The Hague: Martinus Nijhoff, 1950), §24, 52; English translation: *Ideas for a Pure Phenomenology and to a Phenomenological Philosophy, First Book*, trans. Daniel O. Dahlstrom (Indianapolis: Hackett, 2014), 43, modified.

15. Martin Heidegger, *Being and Time*, trans. Joan Stambaugh, rev. Dennis Schmidt (Albany: SUNY Press, 2010), §7, 32. For a detailed exposition of this first principle, see Jean-Luc Marion, *Being Given: Toward a Phenomenology of Givenness*, trans. Jeffrey L. Kosky (Stanford, CA: Stanford University Press, 2002), 7–70; and Jean-Luc Marion, *Reprise du donné* (Paris: PUF, 2016), chapter 1, 19–58.

16. Immanuel Kant, *Critique of Pure Reason*, trans. Paul Guyer and Allen W. Wood (Cambridge: Cambridge University Press, 1998), A111, 234. Or in other

words, "*Revelation* constitutes a veritable inversion of *objectifying cognition*." Levinas, *Totality and Infinity*, 67, modified, Levinas's emphasis.

17. See Jean-Luc Marion, *Negative Certainties*, trans. Stephen E. Lewis (Chicago: University of Chicago Press, 2015), 173–81; and Marion, *Reprise du donné*, 147–89.

18. On these distinctions, see Marion, *Being Given*, §§21–24, 199–247; *In Excess: Studies of Saturated Phenomena*, trans. Robyn Horner and Vincent Berraud (New York: Fordham University Press, 2002), 1–29; and *The Visible and the Revealed*, trans. Christina M. Gschwandtner (New York: Fordham University Press, 2008), 119–44.

Chapter Two

1. So it is that the investigator, when he interrogates the witness, can understand more than what the witness says, because he knows the whole of the affair, tallies information, compares reports. See Marion, *Being Given*, 212–21.

2. See the formally perfect response of his parents, most likely frightened by this inquisition: "We know (οἴδαμεν) that this is our son and that he was born blind. But how he sees now we do not know (οὐκ οἴδαμεν), nor do we know who opened his eyes (οὐκ οἴδαμεν)" (John 9:20–21). Similarly, the paralytic from the pool of Bethesda, "the pool with five porticoes": "They asked him: 'Who is the man who told you, "Take up your mat and walk?"' But the man who was healed did not know (οὐκ ᾔδει) who it was" (John 5:12–13).

3. On the logic of this story see Paul D. Duke, who organizes it perfectly into seven moments that reply to one another in a chiasmic pattern: (1) 9:1–7, Jesus and the blind man: natural blindness = (7) 9:39–41, Jesus and the Pharisees: spiritual blindness; (2) 9:8–12, the blind man healed and those around him: the identity of Jesus = (6) 9:35–38, Jesus and the healed blind man: Jesus son of man; (3) 9:13–17, the healed blind man and the pharisees: Is Jesus from God? = (5) 9:24–34, Jesus is from God. These three couples are reversed in (4) 9:18–22, at the confrontation between the parents of the healed blind man and the Pharisees, over the indisputable miracle. In *Irony in the Fourth Gospel* (Atlanta: John Knox, 1985), especially 126 and following. On the witness, also see below, chapter 14.

4. On this concept, see Marion, *In Excess*, 49–53.

5. Hans Urs von Balthasar: "by exercising himself in extroversion to God's historical form, [the believer] must allow himself to be initiated to the fundamental extroversion of faith's attitude toward God." *The Glory of the Lord: A Theological Aesthetics*, vol. 1, *Seeing the Form*, trans. Erasmo Leiva-Merikakis (San Francisco: Ignatius Press, 1982), 181.

6. In this way, because "I am not alone, but it is I and the Father who sent me" (John 8:16), the principle is confirmed that "in your law it is written that the testimony of two men is true" (8:17). The gap between the witness and what he aims at still remains in our world, but in light of the Trinity it is overcome through the communion of Christ as Son with the Father.

7. Blaise Pascal, *Pensées*, L 318, trans. A. J. Krailsheimer (Harmondsworth: Penguin Books, 1995), 99.

8. Dionysius the Areopagite, *Letter III*, PG 3, 1069b; English translation: *Pseudo-Dionysius: The Complete Works*, trans. Colm Luibheid (New York: Paulist Press, 1987), 264, modified.

9. John Locke's attempt, in *The Reasonableness of Christianity* (London, 1695, 1696), seems exemplary of this effort, as confirmed by his *A Vindication of the Reasonableness of Christianity* (London, 1696) and *A Second Vindication of the Reasonableness of Christianity* (London, 1697). See John Locke, *Vindications of the Reasonableness of Christianity*, ed. Victor Nuovo (Oxford: Clarendon Press, 2012).

10. F. W. J. Schelling, *Philosophie der Offenbarung*, in *Schellings Werke*, ed. Manfred Schröter, Ergänzungsband VI (Munich: Beck, 1983), 142, 143; English translation: *The Grounding of Positive Philosophy*, ed. and trans. Bruce Matthews (Albany: SUNY Press, 2007), 189.

11. Stéphane Mallarmé, "Quant au livre," *Divagations sur un sujet*, in *Œuvres complètes*, ed. Bertrand Marchal, vol. 2 (Paris: Gallimard, Pléiade, 2003), 223; English translation: *Divagations*, trans. Barbara Johnson (Cambridge, MA: Belknap Press of Harvard University Press, 2007), 225.

12. Balthasar, *Herrlichkeit*, I, *Schau der Gestalt* (Einsiedeln: Johannes Verlag, 1961), 439; *The Glory of the Lord*, 1, 457.

13. Josef Simon, "Das philosophische Paradox," in *Das Paradox. Eine Herausforderung des abendländischen Denkens*, ed. Paul Geyer and Roland Hagenbüchle (Tübingen: Stauffenburg Verlag, 1992), 46. Simon draws out the two criteria of self-reference and undecidability and concludes, "For this reason, what are called 'logical paradoxes' are not authentic paradoxes, to the extent that it is on principle that they cannot be resolved, and not by virtue of a power of enlightenment that is subjective and limited. In practice, they irritate no one" (47); and in fact, the paradox, far from remaining unintelligible, is intelligible to such a degree that it irritates; those who listened to Socrates and above all to Jesus prove this well. See also Henning Schröer, "Das Paradox als Kategorie systematischer Theologie" (ibid., 61–70). We will come back to the question of the paradox in the situation of Revelation later, in chapter 10.

14. Tertullian, *De Carne Christi* V.4, ed. and trans. Jean-Pierre Mahé, SC 218 (Paris: Cerf, 1975), 228. It is deplorable that even an expert translator continues the absurdity of translating *ineptum* by *absurd*. The immense majority of readers (and especially of nonreaders) of Tertullian refer to a supposed *credo quia absurdum*: Karl Jaspers, who rejects it (*Der philosophische Glaube* [Munich: Piper, 1948], 113), and even Karl Barth, who approves of it: "the Word of God, if it be rightly proclaimed, must always out-distance other words, and, since the mission of the Son of God is the divine reaction against sin, it can be described only in weighty negations, preached only in paradoxes, understood only as that *absurdum* which

is, as such, *credibile*—nur als das *Absurdum*, das als solches das *credibile* ist)." *Der Römerbrief*, 261; English translation: *The Epistle to the Romans*, 278. In fact, *absurdum* is not the word here but *ineptum*, which has never meant anything else in Latin than "that which is inappropriate, uncalled-for, inopportune, maladroit, awkward, impertinent." Félix Gaffiot, *Dictionnaire latin-français* (Paris: Hachette, 1985). The absurd persistence of this *absurdum* across the centuries and the libraries, under the pen of supposed authorities, is terrifying. The misinterpretation of the alleged *credo quia absurdum*, so widely spread, nevertheless has found a definitive refutation thanks to Bernard Williams, "Tertullian's Paradox," in *New Essays in Philosophical Theology*, ed. Antony Flew and Alasdair McIntyre (Oxford: SCM Press, 1955), which concludes that "people who express themselves in paradoxes are in a strong position" (190).

15. Luke 1:37 (quoting Genesis 18:14) and Matthew 19:26. On this point, see Marion, *Negative Certainties*, 71–82.

16. Gilbert of Poitiers: "Haec igitur sunt sapientiae in qualibet facultate, sed maxime in theologica, paucis nota secreta. Quorum, quia gloria dignitatis summorum etiam philosophorum trahit admirationem, ab ipsis 'paradoxa' vocantur." *Expositio in Boethii librum 'De Bonorum Hebdomade', Prol.*, §9, in PL 64, 1315a. See some indications in Marion, *Being Given*, 225–28.

17. William of Saint-Thierry: "Idcirco cum de Deo verbis agitur, rationes verborum rebus coaptande sunt; non ille illis." *Ænigma Fidei*, §64, in *Deux traités sur la foi*, ed. and trans. Marie-Madeleine Davy (Paris: Vrin, 1959), 146; English translation: *The Works of William of St. Thierry*, vol. 3, *The Enigma of Faith*, trans. John D. Anderson (Washington, DC: Consortium Press, 1974), 87, modified.

18. Let us note that ἔκστασις is also used for the awakening of Jairus's daughter (Mark 5:35–43), for the Resurrection of Christ (Mark 16:8, with the same fear, ἐφοβοῦντο), and for the healings carried out by Peter (Acts 3:10).

19. Ludwig Wittgenstein, *Tractatus Logico-Philosophicus*, 6.432, in *Schriften I* (Frankfurt: Suhrkamp, 1980), 81; English translation: *Tractatus Logico-Philosophicus*, trans. David Pears and Brian McGuinness (London: Routledge, 2014), 89, modified.

20. "Certains jours il ne faut pas craindre de nommer les choses impossibles à décrire": René Char, *Recherche de la base et du sommet*, in *Œuvres complètes*, ed. Jean Roudaut (Paris: Gallimard, Pléiade, 1983), 631.

21. The strangeness is apt here in two senses, for a theologian (who is surprised that the Word of God can also *appear*) as well as for a strict philosopher (surprised that one seeks to *see* anything having to do with faith). Whence the importance of a remark made by one of the first phenomenologists to apply himself to theology: "If one makes the objection to the phenomenologist that certain givens are not objects of Experience, but of Revelation, he will reply that the intrinsic meaning of

a 'Revelation' implies the unveiling of a given before or for Consciousness; consequently, the given and the manner of its apparition will be susceptible to description, as well as the particular genus of certitude that accompanies it." Jean Hering, "La phénoménologie de Husserl il y a trente ans. Souvenirs et réflexions d'un étudiant de 1909," *Revue internationale de philosophie* (1939): 366–73, 372n1, quoted in Dominique Pradelle and Claudia Serban, eds., "De l'éidétique à la phénoménologie de la religion. Présentation du dossier," *Revue de théologie et de philosophie*, no. 148 (2016): 400–407, 405. And this faithfully echoes a remark made by Husserl himself: "Here, as everywhere in phenomenology, one must simply have the courage (*der Mut*) to accept what is actually to be seen in the phenomenon precisely as it gives itself (*wie es sich gibt*) rather than interpreting it away (*umdeuten*), and to describe it *honestly* (*ehrlich*)." Edmund Husserl, *Ideen I*, §108, Hua III/1, 221; *Ideas I*, trans. Dahlstrom, 212–13, modified. According to Hering, there indeed is an eidetic of Revelation, for the thesis that the religious given "is not given, or that it is 'in reality' (*eigentlich*) something immanent, cannot be affirmed without falsifying radically every religious philosophy. . . . Analysis can furnish a theory of religious experience, not only of subjective states or acts alone, but of the intentional object as well, which must be described by its research." *Phénoménologie et philosophie religieuse* (Paris: Alcan, 1926), 129 and 130; see Sylvain Camilleri, "La théologie et l'exégèse biblique de Jean Hering sont-elles phénoménologiques?" *Revue de théologie et de philosophie*, no. 148 (2016): 449–65. This is the best refutation of the "pragmatic rule" of William James: "As far as this goes I probably have you with me, for I only translate into schematic language what I may call the instinctive belief of mankind: God is real since he produces real effects." *The Varieties of Religious Experience*, "Conclusions," in *Writings 1902–1910*, ed. Bruce Kuklick (New York: Library of America, 1987), 1–478, 461; see below, chapter 9. God certainly brings about real effects, because the "beliefs" that he arouses concern the consciousness of the believers who experience them; but above all, these believers believe first of all that, through these "beliefs," they experience God himself. Otherwise, they would quite simply not believe that they have to do with God, and God would quite simply not produce any "real effects" through them.

22. See my commentary, "'They Recognized Him, and He Became Invisible to Them,'" in Jean-Luc Marion, *Believing in Order to See: On the Rationality of Revelation and the Irrationality of Some Believers*, trans. Christina M. Gschwandtner (New York: Fordham University Press, 2017), 136–43.

23. See "The other disciples told him, 'We have seen (ἑωράκαμεν) the Lord'" (John 20:25); "for we cannot but speak of what we have seen (εἴδαμεν) and heard" (Acts 4:20); "I, John, am he who heard and saw (βλέπων) these things. And when I heard and saw (ἔβλεψα) them, I fell down to worship at the feet of the angel who showed them to me (δεικνύοντός)" (Revelation 22:8).

24. See my outline, Jean-Luc Marion, "Qu'attend la théologie de la phénoménologie?" in Nicolas Bauquet, Xavier d'Arodes de Peyriargue, and Paul Gilbert, eds., *"Nous avons vu sa gloire": Pour une phénoménologie du Credo* (Brussels: Lessius, 2012), 13–31.

25. Friedrich Hölderlin, "Friedensfeier / Celebration of Peace," trans. Michael Hamburger, in *Hyperion and Selected Poems*, ed. Eric L. Santner (New York: Continuum, 1990), 231.

26. Bernard of Clairvaux, *Sermons sur le Cantique des Cantiques* VIII.5, ed. Jean Leclercq et al., SC 414 (Paris: Cerf, 1996), 180; English translation: *The Works of Bernard of Clairvaux*, vol. 2, *Song of Songs I*, trans. Kilian Walsh OCSO (Kalamazoo, MI: Cistercian, 1981), 48, modified.

Chapter Three

1. Nicolas Malebranche, *Dialogues on Metaphysics and on Religion*, VI, §3, trans. Nicholas Jolley and David Scott (Cambridge: Cambridge University Press, 1997), 94.

2. Michel de Montaigne, *Essais*, II.32, ed. Pierre Villey (Paris: PUF, 1988), 724; English translation: *The Complete Essays of Montaigne*, trans. Donald M. Frame (Stanford, CA: Stanford University Press, 1965), 547.

3. Malebranche, *Dialogues on Metaphysics and on Religion*, VI, §8, 100.

4. Charles-Louis de Secondat, baron de Montesquieu, *Discourses, Dissertations, and Dialogues on Politics, Science, and Religion*, edited and translated by David W. Carrithers and Philip Stewart (Cambridge: Cambridge University Press, 2020), 237.

5. Nicolas-Sylvestre Bergier, *Dictionnaire de théologie* (1788; Paris: Migne, 1851), vol. 4, 175 (emphasis added). Through this lens, "natural" revelation is confused with the biblical Revelation, because the natural contains the biblical: "The comparison is therefore not difficult to make between the true revelation and those that are false. Properly speaking, there is only one; it began with the world, and it remains until the end, because man has an essential need of it" (187). As for the biblical Revelation in the strict sense, it has only a supplementary and confirming role: "The revelation of the mysteries serves to exercise the docility and the submission that we owe to God, to *confirm* the demonstrable truths, to quell the temerity of the philosophers, to ground the holiest and most sublime morality" (188, emphasis added).

6. Respectively: Heinrich Fries, "Offenbarung, III. Systematisch," in *Lexicon fur Theologie und Kirche*, 2nd ed., ed. Josef Höfer and Karl Rahner, vol. 7, col. 1110 (Freiburg im Breisgau: Herder, 1962): "zwar in grundsätzlicher Sicht zu relativ später Zeit"; Avery Dulles, *Revelation Theology: A History* (New York: Herder, 1969), 31, with similar judgments by Dulles in *New Catholic Encyclopedia*, vol. 12 (New York: McGraw-Hill, 1967), 441, and *Models of Revelation* (New York: Orbis Books, 1983),

19; Bernard Sesboüé, in Bernard Sesboüé and Christoph Theobald, *Histoire des Dogmes*, vol. 6, *La Parole du Salut* (Paris: Desclée de Brouwer, 1996), 109.

7. The discovery of this delay would surprise us less if we recognized that the term *theology* itself was gloriously unknown (when it was not explicitly rejected) to the first twelve centuries of Christian thought, which we nevertheless view, and rightly so, as the centuries of the greatest *theology*. See the still relevant clarification by Jean Rivière, "Theologia," *Revue des sciences religieuses*, 16/1 (1936): 47–57. Saint Augustine impugns the term as proper to the pagans and prefers *philosophia* (*De civitate Dei* VI.5–8, VIII.8). Saint Bernard savagely denounces it in Abelard: "in the first chapter of his theology, or rather his stupidology (*Theologiæ, vel potius Stultilogiæ suæ*), he defines faith as an estimation (*æstimatione*). As if just anyone could think and say whatever he pleases." *Contra Quaedam Capitula Errorum Abaelardi* IV.9, PL 182, 1061b.

8. Jean-Yves Lacoste, "Révélation," in Lacoste, ed., *Dictionnaire critique de théologie* (Paris: PUF, 1988), 999. He puts it differently in the latest edition: "The *lexicon* of revelation (Greek *apokalypsis, epiphaneia, delōsis*, Latin *revelatio, manifestatio*) figures in Christian literature since its origin, but Christianity waited a long time to furnish a structured *concept* of revelation." *Dictionnaire critique de théologie* (Paris: PUF, Quadrige, 2007), 1215.

9. Augustin Léonard, "Vers une théologie de la parole de Dieu," in *La Parole de Dieu en Jésus-Christ* (*Cahiers de l'actualité religieuse*, 16) (Tournai: Casterman, 1961), 12 (emphasis added), quoted by René Latourelle, *Théologie de la Révélation* (Bruges: Desclée de Brouwer, 1963), 10, who himself formulates the difficulty: "It is the first time that a council [Vatican II] studies, in so conscious and methodical a manner, the *fundamental and first categories* of Christianity: namely, those of Revelation, Tradition, and Inspiration. These notions, omnipresent in Christianity and implied in every theological approach, are also the most difficult to define, precisely because they are *primary* notions. . . . [W]e live by these realities, but they are the last to become the object of a critical reflection" (369). Has this reflection truly been undertaken? And have we truly acquired the means to do it? Is a "critical reflection," in the modern sense of "critical," enough, in any case? For who must *critique* what?

10. Thomas Aquinas, *Summa Theologiae* Ia, q.1, a.1, *resp.*; English translation: Anton Pegis, ed., *Basic Writings of Saint Thomas Aquinas*, vol. 1 (Indianapolis, IN: Hackett, 1997), 6.

11. Thomas Aquinas, *Summa Theologiae* Ia, q.1, a.1, *ad 2m*; Pegis, *Basic Writings 1*, 6.

12. Thomas Aquinas, *Expositio super librum Boethii De Trinitate*, q.5, a.4, *resp.*, ed. Bruno Decker (Leiden: E. J. Brill, 1965), 195; English translation: *The Trinity and the Unicity of the Intellect*, trans. Sr. Rose Emmanuella Brennan, SHN (St. Louis and London: B. Herder, 1946), 164.

13. Ibid., 194, 195; English translation, 164, 165.

14. Ibid., 195; English translation, 164.

15. Ibid., 195; English translation, 164: "that theology which the philosophers sought to master, which, according to another name, is called metaphysics."

16. Ibid., 194; English translation, 164: "as they are made manifest through their effects."

17. Ibid., 194; English translation, 163–64.

18. Ibid., 194, 195; English translation, 163, 164, modified.

19. See: "Sed divinorum notitia *dupliciter* potest aestimari. Uno modo ex parte nostra, et sic nobis cognosciblia non sunt nisi per res creatas, quarum cognitionem a sensu accipimus. Alio modo ex natura ipsorum, et sic ipsa sunt ex se ipsis maxime cognoscibilia, et quamvis secundum modum suum non cognoscantur a nobis, tamen a Deo cognoscuntur et a beatis secundum modum suum—But knowledge of divine truths can be thought of in *two* ways. In one way, as on our part, such truths are not knowable except from created things, of which we have a knowledge derived from sense experience. In another way, on the part of the nature of these things themselves, they are, in themselves, most knowable; and although they are not known by us according to their essences, they are known by God and by the blessed according to their proper mode." Thomas Aquinas, *Expositio super librum Boethii De Trinitate*, q.2, a.2, *resp.*, 86–87, emphasis added; *The Trinity and the Unicity of the Intellect*, 52. Other confirmations: "hoc modo [*sc.*, procedere ex principiis notis lumine superioris scientiae] sacra doctrina est scientia: quia procedit ex principiis notis lumine superioris scientiae, quae scilicet est scientia Dei et beatorum—So it is that sacred doctrine is a science because it proceeds from principles made known by the light of a higher science, namely, the science of God and the blessed" (*Summa Theologiae* Ia, q.1, a.2, *resp.*; Pegis, *Basic Writings 1*, 7); and "Est etiam in his, quae de Deo confitemur, duplex veritatis modus. Quaedam namque vera sunt de Deo quae omnem facultatem humanae rationis excedunt, ut Deum esse trinum et unum. Quaedam vero sunt, ad quae etiam ratio naturalis pertingere potest, sicut Deum esse, Deum esse unum, et alia hujusmodi; quae etiam philosophi demonstrative de Deo probaverunt, ducti naturalis lumine rationis—There is a twofold mode of truth in what we profess about God. Some truths about God exceed all the ability of the human reason. Such is the truth that God is triune. But there are some truths which the natural reason also is able to reach. Such are that God exists, that He is one, and the like. In fact, such truths about God have been proved demonstratively by the philosophers, guided by the light of natural reason." Thomas Aquinas, *Summa Contra Gentiles* I.3, and see I.9; English translation: *On the Truth of the Catholic Faith, Bk. 1*, trans. Anton C. Pegis (Garden City, NY: Image Books, 1955), 63. On this double status of theology, see the excellent account by Michel Corbin, *Le Chemin de la théologie chez Thomas d'Aquin* (Paris: Beauchesne, 1974), chapter 2, especially section 2, 359–72.

20. This principle, presented by Saint Thomas Aquinas under the form "Nullus posset amare aliquid incognitum—none can love what he does not know" (*Summa Theologiae* IaIIae, q.27, a.2, *sed contra*; trans. Fathers of the English Dominican Province, vol. 1 [New York: Benziger Brothers, 1947], 707), comes from Saint Augustine: "Certe enim amari aliquid nisi notum non potest—It is quite certain that nothing can be loved unless it is known." *De Trinitate* X.1.2, ed. Paul Agaësse, BA 16, 118; English translation: *The Trinity*, trans. Edmund Hill, OP (Brooklyn, NY: New City Press, 1991), 287. But, while Thomas Aquinas here determines a principle, Saint Augustine has instead stated a problem; for, in the case of the love of God, the *appetitus* already constitutes a manner of knowing: the love of what one does not know becomes possible as soon as one understands that in fact it has to do with loving a thing on account of which one wants to know what one does not yet know: "omnis amor studentis animi, hoc est volentis scire quod nescit, non est amor ejus rei quam nescit, sed ejus quam scit, propter quam vult scire quod nescit—all the love of a studious spirit, that is of one who wishes to know what he does not know, is not love for the thing he does not know but for something he knows, on account of which he wants to know what he does not know." *De Trinitate* X.1.3, BA 16, 122; *The Trinity*, 288–89; see *Confessions* X.20.29, ed. M. Skutella, BA 14, 192–96, and the commentary in my *In the Self's Place: The Approach of Saint Augustine* (Stanford, CA: Stanford University Press, 2012), 101–7. For Saint Augustine, the science of God does not condition the love of God, but rather results from it, in contrast to Saint Thomas, who must assume a science of God *prior* to the love of God. This discrepancy will have decisive consequences (see below, Part III, chapters 8–10).

21. Thomas Aquinas, *Summa Contra Gentiles* I.4; *On the Truth of the Catholic Faith, Bk. 1*, 67.

22. Thomas Aquinas, *Quaestiones disputatae de malo*, q.5, a.1, *resp.*, in *The De Malo of Thomas Aquinas*, with facing-page translation by Richard Regan; ed. Brian Davies (Oxford: Oxford University Press, 2001), 408–9 (modified). See: "Et ideo creatura rationalis, quae potest consequi perfectum beatitudinis bonum, indigens ad hoc divino auxilio, est perfectior quam creatura irrationalis, quae huiusmodi boni non est capax, sed quoddam imperfectum bonum consequitur virtute suae naturae— And therefore the rational creature, which can attain the perfect good of happiness, but needs the Divine assistance for the purpose, is more perfect than the irrational creature, which is not capable of attaining this good, but attains some imperfect good by its natural powers." *Summa Theologiae* Ia IIae, q.5, a.5, *ad* 2; trans. English Dominican Province, vol. 1, 613. Here I am following Henri de Lubac, *Surnaturel. Études historiques* (Paris: Aubier-Montaigne, 1946) and *Le Mystère du Surnaturel* (Paris: Aubier, 1965) (with *Augustinisme et théologie moderne* [Paris: Aubier, 1965]).

23. *Summa Theologiae* Ia, q. 1, a.1, *resp.*; Pegis, *Basic Writings 1*, 6. See also *Summa contra Gentiles* I.4, and *Summa Theologiae* IIa IIae, q.11, a.4. Paul Synave provides a good analysis in "La révélation des vérités divines naturelles d'après saint Thomas

d'Aquin," in André Wilmart, ed., *Mélanges Mandonnet. Études d'histoire littéraire et doctrinale du Moyen Age*, vol. 1 (Paris: Vrin, 1930), 327–70. Maimonides already was on this track: "Accordingly, if we never in any way acquired an opinion through following traditional authority . . . , but were obliged to achieve a perfect representation by means of essential definitions and by pronouncing true only that which is meant to be pronounced true in virtue of a demonstration—which would be impossible except after the above-mentioned lengthy preliminary studies—this state of affairs would lead to all people dying without having known whether there is a deity for the world, or whether there is not, much less whether a proposition should be affirmed with regard to Him or a defect denied. Nobody would ever be saved from this perdition except 'one of a city or two of a family' (Jeremiah 3:14)." Maimonides, *A Guide of the Perplexed*, I, §34, trans. Shlomo Pines, in Isadore Twersky, ed., *A Maimonides Reader* (Springfield, NJ: Behrman House, 1972), 261–62, in a long warning about the inherent difficulties in the study of God through philosophy (§§31–36). In addition to arguments that go back to the apologetic Fathers, we can recognize here the description of the knowledge of the principles which the probable syllogisms are based (ἔνδοξα) on, according to Aristotle (*Topics* I.1, 100b20).

24. *Summa Theologiae* Ia, q.1, a.1, *ad 1m*.

25. *Summa Theologiae* Ia, q.1, a.1, *ad 2m*; Pegis, *Basic Writings 1*, 6.

26. Thomas Aquinas, respectively *Scriptum super libros Sententiarum* I, q.1, a.3, Latin original with English translation by Hugh McDonald in *On the First Book of the Sentences*, prologue and question 1, articles 1–5, emphasis added; and *Expositio super librum Boethii De Trinitate* q.2, a.2, *resp.*, 87, emphasis added; translation in *The Trinity and the Unicity of the Intellect*, 53 (modified). See the full passage: "ut sic ipsa, quae fides tenemus, sint nobis *quasi* principia in hac scientia et alia sint *quasi* conclusiones" (ibid., emphasis added). Marie-Dominique Chenu, while insisting on the importance of this *quasi*, interprets it as a confirmation (*La Théologie comme science au XIIIe siècle* [Paris: Vrin, 1927, 1969], 13) and, perhaps, gets carried away about it, as if it went without saying that revealed theology has much to gain from claiming to be a rigorous science. Étienne Gilson remains more moderate. *Le Thomisme. Introduction à la philosophie de saint Thomas d'Aquin* (Paris: Vrin, 1945], 27 and following. Likewise for Jean-Pierre Torrell: "One cannot emphasize too much this *quasi*, which signifies that Saint Thomas was conscious of the limits of his transposition. The scholar who practices a subaltern science must be able, at least theoretically, to raise himself to the level of the superior science and acquire in turn, if he so desires, the evidence of the principles that he made use of to that point in a pragmatic fashion. This, however, is impossible for the theologian." *Recherches thomasiennes* (Paris: Vrin, 2000), 150.

27. Olivier Boulnois concludes, "Theology is thus a science 'as subalternated' (*quasi subalternata*) to divine science, with all the ambiguity of the *quasi* . . . , which leaves it understood that the model is not perfectly adequate." Philippe

Capelle-Dumont, ed., *Philosophie et théologie*, vol. 2, *Philosophie et théologie au Moyen Âge*, under the direction of Olivier Boulnois (Paris: Cerf, 2009), 219, which on 317–20 cites the two authors from our previous endnote. And the objections to this doctrine have not been lacking; Henry of Ghent contested that the *scientia beatorum* might furnish a veritable knowledge of the cause (of the *propter quid*) of *sacra doctrina*, as the Aristotelian model had required (*Summa quaestionum ordinarium*, a.7, q.4–5); and Godfrey of Fontaines refused that the certainty of evidence of the *beati* could help believers who had available only a certainty of adhesion (*Quodlibetum IV*, q.10). See the French translations and the commentary by Stephen F. Brown, "La subalternation et ses critiques d'après saint Thomas. Henri de Gand, Godefroid de Fontaines, Jean de Paris, Pierre d'Auriole," in Olivier Boulnois, ed., *Philosophie et théologie au Moyen Âge*, 311–26, 317–20.

28. According to the *Index Thomisticus* (ed. Roberto Busa, SJ, et al., web-based version https://www.corpusthomisticum.org/it/index.age, accessed July 18, 2023), the entry "*revelabilia*" in fact points to two occurrences, drawn from the same text, *Summa Theologiae* Ia, q.1, a.3, *resp.* and *ad 2m*.

29. Thomas Aquinas: "omnia quaecumque sunt divinitus revelabilia communicant in una ratione formali obiecti huius scientiae." *Summa Theologiae* Ia, q.1, a.3, *resp.*; Pegis, ed., *Basic Writings 1*, 8 (modified). See Étienne Gilson, "Note sur le *revelabile* selon Cajetan," *Medieval Studies*, no. 15 (1953): 199–206, collected in *Humanisme et Renaissance*, ed. Jean-François Courtine (Paris: Vrin, 1983), 37–44. Gilson shows clearly that Cajetan established, in patent opposition to the intention of Thomas Aquinas, a formal distinction between the *demonstrabilia* and the *revelabilia*, so as to ground a distinction between man's (natural, philosophical) end according to simple *esse* and his supernatural (revealed, "theological" in the modern sense) end according to *esse bonum*. But Gilson neither explains nor justifies the point that to my mind is crucial: the integration in Thomas's work of the *demonstrabilia* into the *revelabilia*, such as it is solely made possible by the epistemological interpretation of Revelation itself.

30. Étienne Gilson, *Thomism: The Philosophy of Thomas Aquinas*, trans. Laurence K. Shook and Armand Maurer (Toronto: Pontifical Institute of Mediaeval Studies, 2002), 9. He specifies further: "The 'revealable' in itself is philosophical but it is drawn, so to speak, into the orbit of theology because knowledge of it, like knowledge of the revealed, is necessary for salvation. Unlike the 'revealed,' the 'revealable' does not belong to revelation rightfully and in virtue of its own essence. However, it is included in theology, which assumes it in view of its own end," following a "permanent availability of all knowledge for the work of the theologian" (13, 15).

31. Balthasar, *The Glory of the Lord*, vol. 1, 168.

32. Thomas Aquinas, *Summa contra Gentiles* IV.1, respectively 416, 416, 415, 416, 415; *On the Truth of the Catholic Faith*, Bk. 4, trans. Charles J. O'Neil (Garden City, NY: Image Books, 1957), 39, 39, 37, 39, 38.

33. Here I follow the *Summa Theologiae* Ia, q.1, a.2, successively *obj.* 1; *conclusio*; and *resp.*

34. Thomas Aquinas had already recognized this: "in scientiis subalternatis supponuntur et creduntur aliqua a scientiis superioribus subalternantibus, et huiusmodi non sunt per se nota nisi superioribus scientiis. Et hoc modo se habent articuli fidei, qui sunt principia huius scientiae, ad cognitionem divinam, quia ea quae sunt per se nota de scientia, quam Deus habet de se ipso, supponuntur in scientia nostra et creditur ei nobis haec indicanti per suos nuntios, sicut medicus credit physico quatuor esse elementa—In subordinate sciences certain things taken from superior sciences are assumed and believed to be true; and truths of this kind are not *per se nota* except in the higher sciences. This is the case with the articles of faith; for they are principles of that science leading to knowledge of divine things, since those truths which are *per se nota* in the knowledge which God has of Himself, are presupposed in our science; and He is believed as the one manifesting these truths to us through His messengers, even as the doctor believes from the word of the physicist that there are four elements." *In Boethium De Trinitate* q.2, a.2, *ad* 5*m*; *The Trinity and the Unicity of the Intellect*, 54–55. Thus, on the one hand, our (or our two) way(s) of knowing God find themselves subordinated to the science that God has of himself, which we naturally *do not have*. How then does he conclude that this subalternation reproduces that of the doctor to the physicist? The strictest Thomists often agree: "When the theologian is no longer *viator*, when he will have received the beatific vision, he will immediately see *in Verbo* the inner life of God, the Deity or divine essence; he will attain in full light the truths that he first knew by faith, and he will be able to see *extra Verbum* [where?] the conclusions that can be deduced from them. In heaven theology will exist in the perfect state, with the evidence of the principles, while *in via* it exists in the imperfect state, it has not yet reached adulthood, so to speak." Réginald Garrigou-Lagrange, "Thomisme," in Alfred Vacant and Eugène Mangenot, eds., *Dictionnaire de théologie catholique* (Paris: Letouzey et Ané, 1946), vol. 15, cols. 823–1023: col. 848. More soberly, Jean-Pierre Torrell writes, "Thomas distinguishes carefully between the wisdom of the saints and that of the theologians." *Recherches thomasiennes*, 136.

Chapter Four

1. Yves M. J. Congar, OP, *Tradition and Traditions: An Historical and a Theological Essay* (New York: Macmillan, 1967), 93. One could even correct this excess of optimism since, even "in modern times" and even "in his school," the neo-Thomists of the nineteenth and twentieth centuries hardly "followed" him on essential points of doctrine.

2. Yves Congar, "Théologie," in Alfred Vacant and Eugene Mangenot, eds., *Dictionnaire de théologie catholique*, vol. 15/1, cols. 342–502: col. 409.

3. Hermann Dieckmann: "*Objectum* [revelationis] sunt veritates, i.e. spectat ad ordinem *cognitionis intellectualis; finis* est religiosus." And: "Revelatio igitur est veritatum; hinc pertinet ad ordinem *cognitionis intellectualis.*" *De Revelatione Christiana. Tractatus Philosophico-Historici*, §196 (Freiburg im Breisgau: Herder, 1930), 136.

4. Dieckmann: "Haec manifestatio mentis divinæ sua natura est *intellectualis* et conceptualis, quae pro objecto habet veritates et ab homine percipi nequit nisi intellectu." Ibid., §199, 138. And see, "Locutio natura sua tendit in communicandam propriam cognitionem alteri, i.e. ad *docendum* alterum" (§202, 140). Or, "Et haec quidem auctoritas recte vocari potest *theoretica* vel, si ut talis constat, scientifica" (§203, 141).

5. Dieckmann, ibid., §196, 136.

6. Francisco Suárez: "Sed quaeret aliquis primo, quid nomine revelationis intelligamus. Respondeo breviter intelligi omnem *sufficientem fidei propositionem*, sive interius tantum fiat, sive per exteriorem praedicationem. Ut hoc autem magis intelligatur, adverto ad cognitionem fidei duo esse necessaria: unum est apprehensio rerum credendarum, quatenus homini proponuntur ut dicta a Deo, et consequenter ut credibilia ex testimonio divino; aliud est assentio ad res propositas, in quo proprie fides ipsa consistit." *De Necessitate gratiae* II.1.8, in *Opera omnia*, ed. C. Berton, vol. 7 (Paris: Vivès, 1857), 588, emphasis added.

7. Suárez: "qui cum hac revelatione stat, hominem non assentire veritati revelatae, et tunc dici non potest cognoscere illam, sicut qui audit, astra esse paria et non assentit, nec judicat esse paria, non cognoscit esse paria, sed tantum apprehendit et audit, id affirmari." *De Trinitate* I.12.4, in *Opera omnia*, vol. 1, ed. M. André (Paris: Vivès, 1857), 571.

8. Suárez: "posset enim primus fidei praedicator doceri a Deo per scientiam infusam vel beatam, et tunc non esset necessarium proprium objectum fidei, quatenus tale est, alicui proponi a Deo immediate, sed solum ut *objectum scientiae vel visionis.*" *De Fide* IV.1.5, *Opera omnia*, vol. 12, 113, emphasis added.

9. Suárez: "solam objecti revelati *sufficientem propositionem*, sive credatur ab eo cui fit talis revelatio, *sive non*, et sive revelatio fiat mere interius an ipso Deo per se ipsum, vel per angelos, sive fiat exterius per hominum praedicationem." *De Trinitate*, I.12.4, 571, emphasis added. Or: "Sic enim contingit multis revelari fidem qui *non* credunt, quamvis sine praevia revelatione nemo credat—Thus, in fact, it happens that faith is revealed to many who do *not* believe, although no one believes without revelation leading the way." *De Necessitate gratiae*, L. II.1.8, 588, emphasis added.

10. Suárez: "hunc modum propositionis fidei posse esse sufficientem—it is possible for this mode of proposing the faith to be sufficient." *De Fide*, d. IV.1.4, 113.

11. Suárez, *De Fide*, d. III.11.5, 96.

12. Suárez: "assero omnem assensum theologiae, per se fundatum in discursu tanquam in propria ratione assentiendi, esse actum non solum a fide distinctum, sed etiam in substantia sua naturalem, et consequenter certitudinem illius non excedere certitudinem naturalem illius principii, a quo pendet." *De Fide*, d. VI.4.10, 178.

13. Suárez: "Revelatio tantum virtualis seu mediata non sufficit ad objectum formale fidei, et consequenter assensus in illa fundatus cum juvamine alicujus principii naturaliter evidentis non sufficit ad proprium assensum fidei, sed tantum ad theologicum." *De Fide*, d. III.11.7, 97.

14. Suárez: "recte loquuntur Theologi, qui dicunt Theologiam esse scientiam in Catholico, non in haeretico—the Theologians speak rightly who say that Theology is a science for the Catholic, not for the heretic." *De Fide*, d. III.11.9, 98. Which means that, since theology is a science, the statement can change status according to whether one believes or not, but it remains, in its "scientific" sense, unchanged.

15. Suárez respectively: "Ergo hac ratione propositio illius objecti antecedere debet, saltem est conditio necessaria ad credendum"; and "objectum fidei in se non videntur, neque etiam revelatio ipsa evidenter cognoscitur et emanans a Deo." *De Fide*, d. IV, *prooemium*, 111.

16. Suárez: "alio modo, solum actualiter, quantum ad certitudinem illius doctrinae quam sufficienter proponit, ut a Deo traditam. . . . Ratio autem propria est, quia res fidei proposita ab aliquo praedicante non habet auctoritatem ab ipso secundum se spectato—in another, solely actual, way, as to the certainty of that doctrine which he sufficiently proposes, as handed down from God. . . . But the reason is proper, because the matter of faith proposed by any preacher has no authority from him when viewed in its own right." *De Fide,* d. V.1.3, 139. The proposition of faith that is taught does not draw its authority from the one who proposes it.

17. Suárez: "Unde dico evidentiam credibilitatis non fieri a lumine fidei, tanquam ab habitu eliciente judicum evidens. . . . [H]aec autem credibilitas non revelatur a Deo, sed ex signis per experientiam cognitis sumitur ; nec etiam obscura, sed clara est ; ergo non est ex objecto formali fidei." *De Fide*, d. IV.6.2, 136.

18. Suárez: "Responsio ergo generalis est, sufficere evidentiam credibilitatis, quae tam in propositione externa quam in mere interna inveniri potest." *De Fide*, d. IV.1.8, 115.

19. Suárez, *De Fide*, d. IV.2.1, 115.

20. Suárez, *De Fide*, d. III.2.6, 44. To be sure, *informatio* here *also* has the Aristotelian meaning of "giving a form"; but, as the form in question consists in nothing more than the *propositio sufficiens* without *assentio*, the *informatio* is well and truly limited to transmitting what we today call information, which one may *or may not* accept.

21. William of Ockham: "Puerile est dicere, quod ego scio conclusiones theologiae, qui Deus scit principia quibus ego credo, quia ipse revelat ea." *Ordinatio*

sive Scriptum in librum primum Sententiarum, prol. Q.7, ed. G. Gal, S. Brown, G. I. Etzkorn, and F. E. Kelley (New York: Saint Bonaventure Institute, 1967), vol. 1, 199.

22. Ockham, "Praeter autem istum habitum et de facto in majori parte studens in theologia, sive sit fidelis, sive haereticus, sive infidelis, adquirit multos habitus scientiales, qui in aliis scientiis possunt adquiri.... Respectu autem omnium... quilibet studens in theologia potest adquirere habitum apprehensivum." Ibid., 197. Here we find the origin of Dieckmann's declaration, which is rather stupefying but was nevertheless relatively current not so long ago: "Therefore, in the order of fact in effect (supernatural), someone who is unbelieving and deprived of grace can understand what the Catholic Church teaches in the treatise *On the Holy Trinity* about this mystery, even while he does not accept its truth or recognize it—Ita in ordine de facto vigente (supernaturali) possit qui, alioquin incredulus gratiæque expers, intelligere quidnam in tractatu *De SS. Trinitate* de mysterio isto ab Ecclesia catholica doceatur, licet ejus veritatem non admittat vel agnoscat." Dieckmann, *De Revelatione Christiana*, §208, 145. Also see Juan Muncunill: "Infideles et hæreticos, licet supernaturali lumine destitutos, omnia in Sacris litteris contenta cognoscere posse et nonnuli eorum revera cognoscere—Infidels and heretics, though destitute of supernatural light, are able to know all that is contained in the Holy Scriptures, and some of them indeed really do know it." Muncunill, *Tractatus de vera religione* (Barcelona: Gustavo Gili, 1909), 13, quoted by Dieckmann, §13, 8. But what does "to know" mean here?

23. Ockham, "habitus qui facit aliquid imaginari melius per intellectum absque omni adhaesione." *Ordinatio sive Scriptum in librum primum Sententiarum, prol.* Q.7, vol. 1, 195. Is this the *habitus* that Réginald Garrigou-Lagrange meant when he evoked the "habitus *naturalis* theologiae"? R. Garrigou-Lagrange, *De Revelatione per Ecclesiam catholicam propositia* (Paris and Rome: Desclée/Libreria Ferrari, 1924), 15.

24. Ockham, "omnem habitum naturaliter adquisitum quem potest habere fidelis, potest habere infidelis." *Ordinatio sive Scriptum in librum primum Sententiarum, prol.* Q.7, vol. 1, 191; and see 193.

25. Ockham, ibid., 187 and 194.

26. William of Saint-Thierry: "Multi enim hujusmodi multa sciunt de Deo, vel scire student; seu ut tantum sciant, curiose agentes seu ut scire vel videantur vel sciantur, gloriam suam querentes, et non Dei." *Ænigma fide*, §42, in *Deux traités sur la foi*, trans. Davy, 128; English translation: *Works*, vol. 3, *The Enigma of Faith*, trans. John D. Anderson, 69–70, modified. Or see Hugh of Saint-Victor, who distinguishes three "dwelling places": knowledge that, even if exact, serves for nothing (*recta ... et inutilis*), the imitation of what one knows, and finally its putting into practice: "In prima ergo mansione est cognitio, in secunda opus, in tertia virtus, in suprema praemium virtutis: Dominus Jesus Christus." *De Archa Noe* II.7, ed.

P. Sicard, in *Corpus Christianorum, Continuatio medievalis*, vol. 176 (Turnhout: Brepols, 2001), 41. Sometimes, one almost agrees with Heidegger: "Only the theologians, that is to say the true unbelievers (*Ungläuber*), concoct idle talk (*Gerede*) on faith and knowledge." Martin Heidegger, *Anmerkungen I-V* (*Schwarze Hefte 1942–1948*], GA 97 (Frankfurt: V. Klostermann, 2015), 204.

27. Suárez, *De Necessitate gratiae*, II.1.7, 588.

28. John Locke, *An Essay Concerning Human Understanding* IV.18, §4, ed. Peter H. Nidditch (Oxford: Clarendon Press, 1975), 690–91.

29. Must we recall that Thomas Aquinas's admittedly numerous uses of the word *metaphysica* do not refer to philosophy as *metaphysica*, but, in the great majority of cases, to the books of Aristotle grouped together by the editorial tradition under the title *Metaphysica*, or rather *Libri Metaphysicorum*?

30. Suárez, *Disputationes Metaphysicae, Proemium*: "Divina et supernaturalis theologia, quanquam divino lumine principiisque a Deo revelatis nitatur, quia vero humano discursu et ratiocinatione perficitur, veritatibus etiam naturae lumine notis juvatur, eisque ad suos discursus perficiendos, et divinas veritates illustrandas, tanquam ministris et quasi instrumentis utitur. . . . Cum enim inter disputandum de divinis mysteriis *haec metaphysica dogmata* occurrerent, sine quorum cognitione et intelligentia *vix, aut ne vix quidem*, possunt altiora illa mysteria pro dignitate tractari, cogebar saepe . . . divinis et supernaturalibus rebus inferiores quaestiones *admiscere*. . . . Ita enim haec principia et *veritates metaphysicae cum theologicis conclusionibus ac discursibus cohaerent*, ut si illorum *scientia ac perfecta cognitio* auferatur, horum etiam scientiam nimium labefactari necesse sit." *Opera omnia*, vol. 25, 1, emphases added; for an English translation with facing page Latin text, see Francisco Suárez, *Metaphysical Disputation I: On the Nature of First Philosophy of Metaphysics*, trans. Shane Duarte (Washington, DC: Catholic University of America Press, 2021), 10–13. We find this same position, taken to its fulfillment, in Malebranche, who nevertheless called himself a resolute adversary of medieval thought: "I do not plan to abandon metaphysics. . . . This general science rules over all the others. . . . For by metaphysics I do not mean those abstract considerations of certain imaginary properties, the principal use of which is to furnish the wherewithal for endless dispute to those who want to dispute. By this science I mean the general truths which can serve as principles for the particular sciences. I am persuaded, Aristes, that it is necessary to be a good philosopher to gain understanding of the truths of faith; and that the stronger we are in the true principles of metaphysics, the stronger we are in the truths of religion." *Dialogues on Metaphysics and on Religion*, VI, §2, trans. Nicholas Jolley and David Scott, 92. See Jean-Christophe Bardout, *Malebranche et la métaphysique* (Paris: PUF, 1999), especially 56 and following.

31. "Nota est omnibus essentiae ab existentia distinctio." René Descartes, AT VII, 194. See Vincent Carraud, "L'invention de l'existence," and Jean-Christophe

Bardout, "Causalité ou subjectivité: le développement du sentiment d'existence, de Descartes à l'"Encyclopédie,'" in Costantino Esposito and Vincent Carraud, eds., *Quæstio*, 3 (Turnhout/Bari: Brepols/Pagina, 2003), 3–25 and 163–205, respectively; as well as Jean-Christophe Bardout, *Penser l'existence. I. L'existence exposée. Époque médiévale* (Paris: Vrin, 2013).

32. Thomas Aquinas, *Summa contra Gentiles* III.49; Pegis, *Basic Writings 2*, 89. See "Sed quia hoc ipsum quod Deus est mente concipere non possumus, remanet ignotum quoad nos—Yet, because we are not able to conceive in our minds that which God is, that God exists remains unknown in relation to us." Ibid., I.11, 9; *On the Truth of the Catholic Faith, Bk. 1*, 81. Or, "in hac vita non cognoscamus de Deo *quid est*, et sic ei quasi ignoto coniungamur—in this life we do not know of God *what He is*, and thus are united to Him as to one unknown." *Summa Theologiae*, Ia, q.12, a.13, *a 1m*; Pegis, *Basic Writings 1*, 111. On these points, see Marion, *God Without Being*, 225–32.

33. Hermann Dieckmann's magnificently symptomatic formula, "the metaphysical account of Revelation" (*De Revelatione Christiana*, §197, 137), was spotted by Henri de Lubac (*La Révélation divine*, in *Œuvres complètes* [Paris: Cerf, 2006], vol. 4, 188), but without commentary. The issue here is exactly that of *metaphysica* in the modern sense (the only sense there is, as we know), since one undertakes to ground Revelation not on itself but on possibility: "possibilitas . . . interna sive metaphysica—internal or metaphysical . . . possibility" (§222, 156).

34. As Augustine recalls: "De Deo loquimur, quid mirum si non comprehendis? Si enim comprehendis, non est Deus—We are talking about God; so why be surprised if you cannot grasp it? I mean, if you can grasp it, it isn't God." *Sermon* 117.3, PL 38, 663; English translation: *Sermons 94A-147A on the New Testament*, trans. Edmund Hill, OP (Brooklyn, NY: New City Press, 1992), 211.

35. See René Descartes, *Meditationes de prima philosophia*, AT VII, 3, line 5; CSM 2, 4.

36. See Jean-Luc Marion, *On Descartes' Metaphysical Prism: The Constitution and the Limits of Onto-Theo-Logy in Cartesian Thought*, trans. Jeffrey L. Kosky (Chicago: University of Chicago Press, 1999), 244–76.

37. The respectable attempt by Richard Swinburne to defend the propositional interpretation of Revelation rests upon a remark that is quite right: "It is in any case very hard to see how God could reveal himself in history . . . without at the same time revealing some propositional truth about himself. . . . If God did really reveal himself to us in Christ, then he must have revealed some propositional truth, minimally the truth that Christ's acts were his acts." *Revelation: From Metaphor to Analogy* (Oxford: Clarendon Press, 1992), 4, and see 2, 3, 73, 83, 101. But the question immediately becomes: In what sense can the acts of Christ and even their significations be transcribed into propositions, conforming to the logic of those

that we construct on the basis of the experience of things of the world and our finite (if not created) rationality? Can and must the *logos* of Christ coincide with the *logos* of the world? See the remarks, Thomist in origin, of Thomas J. White, OP, "Monotheistic Rationality and Divine Names: Why Aquinas' Analogy Theory Transcends Both Theoretical Agnosticism and Conceptual Anthropomorphism," in Anselm Ramelow, ed., *God: Reason and Reality* (Munich: Philosophia Verlag, 2014), 37–80. One can make almost the same objections to the polemical project of Roger Pouivet, *Épistémologie des croyances religieuses* (Paris: Cerf, 2013); Camille Riquier reminds us that faith is not a (weak) knowledge, but a trust in the given word, an engagement; and above all, that if one wants "the object of belief to be made accessible and subject to debate independently of the fact of believing or not," then the believer will make for himself a religion of onto-theo-logy. Camille Riquier, "L'incroyable Dieu. Note conjointe sur Bergson et la philosophie réaliste," in Emmanuel Alloa and Élie During, eds., *Choses en soi. Métaphysique du réalisme* (Paris: PUF, 2018), 549–62.

38. See Yves Congar, "Tradition et 'Sacra Doctrina' chez saint Thomas d'Aquin," in J. Betz et H. Fries, eds., *Église et Tradition* (Lyon/Le Puy: X. Mappus, 1963), 157–94, reprinted in Yves Congar, *Thomas d'Aquin: sa vision de la théologie et de l'Église* (London: Variorum Reprint, 1984), 157–94.

39. See "die materiale Suffizienz der Schrift" studied by Josef Rupert Geiselmann (*Die heilige Schrift und die Tradition* [Freiburg: Herder, 1962], 72), and in "Das Konzil v. Trient über das Verhältnis der heiligen Schrift und der nicht geschriebenen Traditionen," in Michael Schmaus, ed., *Die mündliche Überlieferung* (Munich: Herder, 1957), 123–206, and then discussed by Yves Congar in "The Sufficiency of Scripture According to the Fathers and Medieval Theologians," *Tradition and Traditions: An Historical and a Theological Essay*, trans. Michael Naseby and Thomas Rainborough, 107–18, and by Joseph Ratzinger in "Revelation and Tradition," in *Revelation and Tradition*, Karl Rahner and Joseph Ratzinger, eds., trans. W. J. O'Hara (New York: Herder & Herder, 1966), 26–49.

Chapter Five

1. Heinrich Denzinger, *Enchiridion symbolorum definitionum et declarationum de rebus fidei et morum / Compendium of Creeds, Definitions, and Declarations on Matters of Faith and Morals*, ed. Peter Hünermann, 43rd ed. (San Francisco: Ignatius Press, 2012), *Decretum de libris sacris et de traditionibus recipendis*, no. 1501, 370. René Latourelle insists on this point: "We note first that the word *revelation* does not appear in this entire paragraph" (*Théologie de la Révélation*, 276), and "without making an appeal to the term revelation" (274).

2. On these points, see Bernard Sesboüé ("For the first time, this word will enter into the magisterial vocabulary," in B. Sesboüé, C. Theobald, eds., *Histoire*

des dogmes, vol. 4, 207) and René Latourelle ("But, through a new precision that did not appear in the Council of Trent, the Vatican Council expressly employs the term revelation to designate the content of the word of God: *haec porro supernaturalis porro supernaturalis revelatio*," *Théologie de la Révélation*, 286). Henri Bouillard registers (a) that Vatican I is the first council to explicitly address Revelation, and (b) that it could only get support from the two sole magisterial texts (Gregory XVI, *Dum Acerbissimas*, 1835, and Pius IX, *Qui Pluribus*, 1846) that designated the object of faith by this name. Henri Bouillard, "Le concept de révélation de Vatican I à Vatican II," in Jacques Audinet et al., *Révélation de Dieu et langage des hommes* (Paris: Cerf, 1972), 35–49.

3. *Dei Filius*, in Denzinger, *Enchiridion*, no. 3004, 601–2. Christoph Theobald comments, "But 'The gospel as source of all truth and all morals' is replaced here by the concept of 'supernatural revelation.'" "Dogmatisation progressive des fondements de la foi," in Sesboüé and Theobald, *Histoire des Dogmes*, vol. 6, *La Parole du Salut*, 274. And "Vatican I will replace in its own quotation of Trent the term *Gospel* with that of *revelation*" (207). See Latourelle, *Théologie de la Révélation*, 274.

4. *Dei Filius*, in Denzinger, *Enchiridion*, no. 3005, 602. The thesis is maintained in *Humani Generis*: "divina 'revelatio' moraliter necessaria dicenda est—divine 'revelation' must be considered morally necessary" (1950, see ibid., no. 3876, 800), and in *Dei Verbum*: "Divina revelatione Deus seipsum manifestare ac communicare voluit—Through divine revelation God chose to show forth and communicate Himself" (ibid., no. 4206, 920).

5. *Dei Filius*, ibid., no. 3006, 602. See also chapter 3 (*De fide*), ibid., nos. 3009–11, 603–4.

6. *Dei Filius*, chapter 3 (*De fide*), ibid., no. 3008, 603, translation modified.

7. Avery Dulles qualifies *Dei Verbum* as "the most important official statement ever issued by the Catholic Church on the subject of Revelation." Dulles, *Revelation Theology: A History*, 156. Henri de Lubac insists on this: "This was the first time that a Council studied" Revelation head-on "and was doing it by climbing back up the slope on which almost the whole of our classic theology had taken a stand." De Lubac, *La Révélation divine*, 192. The same for René Latourelle: "This is the first time that a council studies, in so conscious and methodical a manner, the fundamental and first categories of Christianity: namely, those of Revelation, Tradition, and Inspiration." Latourelle, *Théologie de la Révélation*, 369; see above, chapter 3, n9, page 387. On the history of this text, also see Bernard-Dominique Dupuy, ed., *La Révélation divine. Constitution dogmatique* Dei Verbum. *Texte latin et traduction française, commentaire par de nombreux collaborateurs*, 2 vols. (Paris: Cerf, 1968); Christoph Theobald, *"Dans les traces . . ." de la Constitution "Dei Verbum" du concile Vatican II. Bible, théologie et pratique de lecture* (Paris: Cerf, 2009) (here 37);

and Matthew Levering, *Engaging the Doctrine of Revelation: The Mediation of the Gospel Through Church and Scripture* (Grand Rapids, MI: Baker Academic, 2014), 5–33.

8. Henri de Lubac, who was not unaware of Barth (*La Révélation divine*, 74), mentions instead the precedent of Guitmond d'Aversa: "Christus seipsum significat." *De corpore et sanguine Domini*, 2, PL 149, 1461, cited by de Lubac, ibid., 126. See the study by Hans Urs von Balthasar, *Karl Barth. Darstellung und Deutung seiner Theologie*, first published in Cologne in 1951 (republished in 1976); English translation: *The Theology of Karl Barth: Exposition and Interpretation*, trans. Edward T. Oakes, SJ (San Francisco: Ignatius Press, 1992); on this topic, see Manfred Lochbrunner, "L'incroyable histoire de la genèse du livre de Hans Urs von Balthasar sur Karl Barth," as well as the dossier "Barth-Balthasar. De l'analogie à l'oecuménisme," *Revue catholique internationale Communio*, 36/3, no. 215 (2011): 23–36.

9. *Dei Verbum*, chapter 1, in Denzinger, *Enchiridion*, no. 4202 and no. 4203, respectively, 918, 919, and 918. See "Divina revelatione Deus Seipsum atque aeterna voluntatis suae decreta circa hominum salutem manifestare ac communicare voluit—Through divine revelation, God chose to show forth and communicate himself and the eternal decisions of his will regarding the salvation of men." Ibid., no. 4206, 920.

10. *Dei Verbum*, chapter 3, ibid., no. 4217, 923 (translation modified). Let us note, however, that there is already a formula that is almost the same in *Dei Filius* in 1870: "placuisse ejus sapientiae et bonitati, alia eaque supernaturali via se ipsum ac aeterna voluntatis suae decreta humano generi revelare—it has pleased His wisdom and goodness to reveal Himself and the eternal decrees of His will to the human race in another and supernatural way." *Dei Filius*, ibid., no. 3004, 602. But from this formula, Vatican I focuses more on developing the "eternal decrees of His will" than the "Himself" that is revealed.

11. Paul VI, *Ecclesiam suam* (August 6, 1964), *Acta Apostolicae Sedis* 56 (1964), 632. The connection (*Dei Verbum*, chapter 1, ibid, no. 4204, 918, also quoting Baruch 3:38) is underscored by René Latourelle, who points out here the "dialogic character of Revelation" (*La Révélation*, 332).

12. *Dei Filius*, chapter 3, Denzinger, *Enchiridion*, no. 3009, 605.

13. Cited in *Dei Verbum*, chapter 1, ibid., no. 4203, 919.

14. *Dei Verbum*, chapter 1, ibid., no. 4202, 918. On this reversal of the two authorities, see below chapter 12.

15. Among the authors who understood Romans 1:18–20 in this way, let us note (a) John Scotus Eriugena: "Proinde non duo a seipsis distantia debeamus intelligere Deum et creaturam, sed unum et id ipsum. Nam et creatura in Deo est subsistens, *Deus in creaturis, mirabili et ineffabili modo creatur, seipsum manifestans*, invisibilis visibilem se faciens et incomprehensibilis comprehensibilem et occultum apertum . . . et infinitus finitum—It follows that we ought not to understand God

and the creature as two things distinct from one another, but as one and the same. For both the creature, by subsisting, is in God; and *God, by manifesting Himself, in a marvellous and ineffable manner creates Himself in the creature*, the invisible making Himself visible and the incomprehensible comprehensible and the hidden revealed . . . and the infinite finite." *De Divisione Naturae* III.17, PL 122, 678, emphasis added; English translation: *Periphyseon (The Division of Nature)*, trans. I. P. Sheldon-Williams, rev. John J. O'Meara (Montreal: Éditions Bellarmin/Washington, DC: Dumbarton Oaks, 1987), 305, emphasis added. See my article, "*Veluti ex nihilo in aliquid*. De l'*apophasis* à la *divina philosophia* chez Jean Scot Erigène," in P. Büttgen and J.-B. Rauzy, eds., *La Longue Durée: Pour Jean-François Courtine* (Paris: Vrin, 2016), 77–92. (b) William of Saint-Thierry: "Deus illis *revelavit*; qui sic eos creavit, ut in seipsis habeant, unde *naturaliter* Deum cognoscant." *De Natura et Dignitate amoris*, §41, in *Deux traités de l'amour de Dieu*, ed. Marie-Madeleine Davy (Paris: Vrin, 1953], 128, emphasis added; English translation: "For God, who so created them that they might have within themselves the means of recognizing God naturally, has revealed Himself to them," in *The Nature and Dignity of Love*, trans. Thomas X. Davis (Kalamazoo, MI: Cistercian, 1982), 103. (c) Nicholas of Cusa: "Quid igitur est ergo *mundus*, nisi invisibilis *Dei apparitio*?—What, then, is the *world* except the *manifestation* of the invisible God?" *De possest*, §72, in *Philosophisch-theologische Schriften*, ed. Leo Gabriel, vol. 2 (Vienna: Herder, 1966), 354, emphasis added; English translation in Jasper Hopkins, *A Concise Introduction to the Philosophy of Nicholas of Cusa*, 3rd ed. (Minneapolis: Arthur J. Banning Press, 1986), 952. On this argument, see André Feuillet, who does not situate the knowledge of God through nature within the horizon of philosophical theology but relates it to the "ἐκ γὰρ μεγέθους καὶ καλλονῆς κτισμάτων ἀναλόγως [. . .] θεωρεῖται—For from the greatness and beauty of created things comes a corresponding perception of their Creator" of Wisdom 13:5; thus he points out "the fall of humanity into paganism . . . the cause of this fall, was the pride that darkened the intelligence." "La connaissance naturelle de Dieu par les hommes d'après *Romains* 1,18–29," *Lumière et vie* 14, (1954): 207–24, 219.

16. See, among other texts, Étienne Gilson, *The Spirit of Medieval Philosophy*, trans. A. H. C. Downes (Notre Dame, IN: University of Notre Dame Press, 1991), chapters 3 and 4, here 71. See the discussion by Paul Clavier, *Ex nihilo*, vol. 1, *L'Introduction en philosophie du concept de création*, vol. 2, *Scénarios de "sortie de la création"* (Paris: Hermann, 2011), and his thesis presentation, "La création est-elle soluble dans la philosophie ?" *Revue philosophique de la France et de l'étranger*, no. 137 (2012): 307–24.

17. Thomas Aquinas, *Summa Theologiae* Ia, q. 46, a.2, *conclusio*.

18. Surprising though it may be, let me suggest that here Jan Patočka could be a great help, by thinking of the world as an advent and starting from the possibility of a given that is never exhausted in an adequate knowledge. See Émilie Tardivel,

La liberté au principe. Essai sur la philosophie de Patočka (Paris: Vrin, 2011), and my analysis in *Reprise du donné*, chapter 3, §§22–25, 126–46.

19. Franz Rosenzweig, *The Star of Redemption*, trans. William W. Hallo (Notre Dame, IN: University of Notre Dame Press, 1985), 159, 161, with emphasis added, 135. Emmanuel Levinas took up and deepened this critique: "Theology imprudently treats the idea of the relation between God and the creature in terms of ontology. It presupposes the logical privilege of totality, as a concept adequate to being. Thus it runs up against the difficulty of understanding that an infinite being would border on or tolerate something outside of itself, or that a free being would send its roots into the infinity of a God. But transcendence precisely refuses totality, does not lend itself to a view that would encompass it from the outside. . . . What embarrasses the traditional theology, which treats of creation in terms of ontology—God leaving his eternity, in order to create—is incumbent as a first truth in a philosophy that begins with transcendence." Levinas, *Totality and Infinity*, 293.

20. Exodus 20:18, according to the literal translation of the Hebrew and of the Septuagint (see below chapter 11).

Chapter Six

1. Descartes, *À Mersenne,* April 15, 1630, AT I, 144; CSMK 3, 22, modified. A use confirmed by Spinoza: "Atque hic per Theologiam praecise intelligo revelationem— By theology here I mean precisely revelation)." Baruch Spinoza, *Tractatus theologico-politicus* XV. 6, in *Opera*, ed. Carl Gebhardt (Heidelberg: Carl Winter, 1925, 1972), vol. 3, 184; English translation by Michael Silverthorne and Jonathan Israel, in *Theological-Political Treatise,* ed. Jonathan Israel (Cambridge: Cambridge University Press, 2007), 190. And by Locke: "Faith, on the other hand, is the assent to any proposition, not thus made out by deduction of reasons; but upon the credit of the proposer, as coming from God, in some extraordinary way of communication. This way of discovering truths to man, we call Revelation." *An Essay concerning Human Understanding* IV. 18, §2 (1689), 689.

2. Descartes, *Discours de la Méthode,* AT VI, 8; CSM 1, 114. This formula comes, almost word for word, from Montaigne: "It is very necessary that he [God] still lend us his help, by extraordinary and privileged favor." *Essais,* II. 12, "Apologie de Raymond Sebond," ed. P. Villey, 441; English translation: *Complete Works*, trans. Frame, 321.

3. G. W. Leibniz, *Nouveaux Essais sur l'entendement humain* IV.7, §11, in *Philosophischen Schriften,* vol. 5, ed. C. J. Gerhardt (Hildesheim: Olms, 1965), 396; trans. Peter Remnand and Jonathan Bennet as *New Essays on Human Understanding* (Cambridge: Cambridge University Press, 1981), 416.

4. Edward Herbert of Cherbury: "Quando igitur, quod datur, humanum superat captum, et *conditiones* supra enumeratae adsunt, et in opere perficiendo

denique divinum persentis auxilium, propitium numen venerare!" *De Veritate prout distinguitur a revelatione, a verisimili, a possibili et a falso* (London, 1624), ed. H. Scholz, *De Religionsphilosophie des Herbert von Cherbury. Auszüge aus "De Veritate"* (Gießen, 1914), 56; "When therefore, what comes to us surpasses human understanding and all the preceding conditions are present, and we feel the Divine guidance in our activities, we must recognize with reverence the good will of God!" Trans. Meyrick H. Carré, in Edward Herbert of Cherbury, *De Veritate* (London: Routledge/Thoemmes Press, 1992), 308.

5. Descartes already observed that Cherbury was better in metaphysics than in theology: "He was clearly above average in his knowledge of metaphysics, a science that hardly anyone understands. But I thought that later on he mingled religion with philosophy, something that goes quite against the grain with me; so I did not read it to the end." *À Mersenne,* August 27, 1639, AT II, 570; CSMK 3, 137.

6. Thomas Hobbes, *De Cive* XV.3, *The English Works of Thomas Hobbes,* vol. 1, ed. Howard Warrender (Oxford: Oxford University Press, 1983), 185. [Translators' note: Marion here cites the Latin, in *Malmesburiensis Opera Philosophica quae Latine Scripsit Omnia,* ed. Sir William Molesworth (London: John Bohn, 1839), vol. 2, 333: "*Verbum* Dei *sensibile* ad paucos factum est, neque Deus per revelationem hominibus loquutus est, nisi viritim et diversis diversa; neque ullæ leges regni hoc modo populo ulli promulgatæ fuerunt."]

7. Thomas Hobbes, *Leviathan* I.7, ed. Edwin Curley (Indianapolis: Hackett, 1994), 37. Scripture alone, without private *revelatio,* thus becomes timeless, resulting in its complete reduction to propositions. See Dominique Weber, *Hobbes et l'histoire du salut. Ce que le Christ fait à Léviathan* (Paris: Presses de la Sorbonne, 2008), 270ff.

8. Thomas Hobbes: "Triplex ergo quodammodo dici potest esse verbum Dei, nimirum *rationale, sensibile* et *prop heticum*; cui respondet triplex genus autem audiendi Deum, nempe *recta ratio, sensus supernaturalis* et *fides.* Sensus autem *supernaturalis,* cum sit nihil aliud quam *revelatio* homini singulari facta, illum solum obligat cui facta est. A differentia inter reliqua duo verbi divini genera, *rationale* et *propheticum,* attribui Deo potest regnum duplex, *naturale* et *propheticum. Naturale,* quatenus illos regit, qui providentiam ejus agnoscunt, per dictamen rectæ rationis: *propheticum,* quatenus populum suum electum . . . regit." *Leviathan* XXXI, in *Malmesburiensis Opera,* vol. 3, 255–56; Hobbes's English version: "From hence there ariseth a triple word of God, *rational, sensible,* and *prophetic,* to which correspondeth a triple hearing, *right reason, sense supernatural,* and *faith.* As for sense supernatural, which consisteth in revelation, or inspiration, there have not been any universal laws so given, because God speaketh not in that manner but to particular persons, and to divers men divers things." *Leviathan,* ed. Curley, 235. It has been suggested (Levering, *Engaging the Doctrine of Revelation,* 95) that Hobbes is depending here on Bacon, who deplored what Saint Augustine praised—the fact that

Christianity has established another liturgy than that of the civic cult, and other doctors than the poets. Francis Bacon, "Of Unity in Religion," 1597, published in 1625, in *The Essays*, ed. J. Pitcher (New York: Penguin, 1985), 67.

9. John Locke, *An Essay concerning Human Understanding* IV.18, §8, p. 694. See *The Reasonableness of Christianity* (1695), ed. I. T. Ramsay (Stanford, CA: Stanford University Press, 1958), not to mention John Toland, *Christianity not Mysterious* (1696), and Matthew Tindal, *Christianity as Old as the Creation: Or, The Gospel, A Republication of the Religion of Nature* (1730).

10. John Locke, *An Essay concerning Human Understanding* IV.18, §10, 695. See also: "*Reason* must be our last judge and guide in everything. I do not mean, that we must consult Reason and examine whether a proposition revealed from God can be made out by natural principles, and if it cannot, that then we may reject it. But consult it we must, and by it examine, whether it be a *Revelation* from God or no. And if *Reason* finds it to be revealed from God, Reason then declares for it, as much as for any other truth, and makes it one of her dictates." Ibid. IV.19, §14, p. 704.

11. Or, more explicitly: "a miracle may be accurately defined, *a transgression of a law of nature by a particular volition of the Deity, or by the interposition of some invisible agent*." David Hume, *An Enquiry concerning Human Understanding* X.1, in *Enquiries concerning Human Understanding and concerning the Principles of Morals*, ed. L. A. Shelby-Bigge, 3rd ed. revised by P. H. Nidditch (Oxford: Clarendon Press, 1975), respectively 114 and 115nK.

12. Ibid. X.2, 127.

13. Ibid., 131.

14. David Hume thus confirms, by the reverse, what I have recognized as the first formal characteristic of every revelation (and therefore also of Revelation), namely its coming from *elsewhere*: "Nothing is esteemed a miracle, if it ever happen in the common course of nature." *Enquiry* X.1, 115.

15. Hume puts it in his own way: "The maxim, by which we commonly conduct ourselves in our reasonings, is, that the objects, of which we have no experience, resemble those, of which we have; that what we have found to be most usual is always most probable." Hume, *Enquiry* X.2, 117.

16. On this status of the impossible *for us,* yet possible *for the gods and God,* see my analysis in Marion, *Negative Certainties*, chapter 2.

17. See Johann Clauberg: "Ens est quicquid quovis modo est, cogitari ac dici potest," and "Nam eo ipso quo quid apprehendimus, jam est intelligibile et per consequens Ens in prima significatione." *Metaphysica de Ente, quæ rectius Ontosophia ...*, §6 and §10, respectively; in *Opera omnia philosophica* (1691; repr. Hildesheim: Olms Verlag, 1968), vol. I, 283.

18. Friedrich D. E. Schleiermacher, *Über die Religion. Reden an die Gebildeten unter ihren Verächtern,* ed. Hans-Joachim Rothert (Hamburg: Felix Meiner, 1958), 10; English translation: *On Religion: Speeches to Its Cultured Despisers,* trans. Richard Crouter (Cambridge: Cambridge University Press, 1988), 86, modified.

19. Schleiermacher, *Über die Religion*, 37; *On Religion*, 109

20. Schleiermacher, *Über die Religion*, 29; *On Religion*, 102: "It [i.e. religion] does not wish to determine and explain the universe according to its nature as does metaphysics; it does not desire to continue the universe's development and perfect it by the power of freedom and the divine free choice of a human being as does morals. Religion's essence is neither thinking nor acting, but intuition (*Anschauung*) and feeling. It wishes to intuit (*anschauen*) the universe." *Über die Religion*, 29; *On Religion*, 101–2.

21. Schleiermacher, *Über die Religion*, 31; *On Religion*, 104. "I entreat you to become familiar with this concept: intuition of the universe (*Anschauen des Universums*). It is the hinge of my whole speech; it is the highest and most universal formula of religion." *Über die Religion*, 31; *On Religion*, 104 modified.

22. Schleiermacher, *Über die Religion*, 41; *On Religion*, 102, an obvious echo of Kant's formula: "Thoughts without content are empty, intuitions without concepts are blind." *Critique of Pure Reason*, A 51/B 75, 193–94.

23. Schleiermacher, *Über die Religion*, 66; *On Religion*, 113. Or: "Look upon the *Dasein* of each as a revelation (*Offenbarung*) which is given to you of this humanity." *Über die Religion*, 51; *On Religion*, 120, modified.

24. Schleiermacher, *Über die Religion*, 68; *On Religion*, 136, modified. See Ludwig Feuerbach: "Man is the original (*Urbild*) of his idol," *Das Wesen des Christentums*, in *Gesammelte Werke*, ed. Werner Schuffenhauer (Berlin: Akademie Verlag, 1973), vol. 5, 11.

25. Schleiermacher, *Über die Religion*, 70; *On Religion*, 136.

26. Schleiermacher, *Über die Religion*, 74 and 70, respectively; *On Religion*, 140 and 137, respectively. See also, "In religion, therefore, the idea of God does not rank as high as you think" (72 =138). Whence his complete lack of interest in the Trinity, a simple question of "number": "that [God] be one or whether he be many, I despise nothing in religion as much as numbers" (70 =136, modified), in this way prolonging Kant's remarks in *Streit der Fakultäten*, I, 1, Appendix II, Ak. A. VII, 38ff; translated by Mary J. Gregor and Robert Anchor as "The Conflict of the Faculties," in *Religion and Rational Theology*, ed. Allen W. Wood and George Di Giovanni (Cambridge: Cambridge University Press, 1996), 233–393, at 264ff. See also chapter 15, below.

27. "Religion is the sensibility and taste for the infinite." *Über die Religion*, 30; *On Religion*, 103. Thus the impeccable diagnosis of Schelling reproaching Schleiermacher for having "wanted all the more to ground the greater claims of all higher convictions entirely in a blind feeling, in faith, or even in revelation"—except that it precisely no longer has anything at all to do with a Revelation. Schelling, *Philosophie der Offenbarung*, Lecture V, *Werke*, vol. 6, 85; English translation: *The Grounding of Positive Philosophy*, 148. In this way, I echo the conclusion of Avery Dulles on Schleiermacher, denouncing "a narrow concept of experience . . . , immediate, individual, instantaneous and self-evidencing" (Dulles, *Models of Revelation*, 81);

of Emilio Brito ("Le sentiment religieux selon Schleiermacher," *Nouvelle Revue de théologie*, no. 114 [1992]: 186–211); as well as that of Tilliette ("Raison et révélation chez Lessing et dans l'idéalisme allemand," in M. M. Olivetti, ed., *Filosofia della Rivelazione, Archivio di Filosofia* [Padua/Rome, 1994], 259–71).

28. Spinoza, *Tractatus theologico-politicus* I.1, 15; *Theological-Political Treatise*, 13.

29. Spinoza, *Tractatus theologico-politicus* I.28, 110 (and I.2, 80); *Theological-Political Treatise*, 26 (and 13–14), on the one hand; on the other, *Tractatus theologico-politicus* I.5, 82; *Theological-Political Treatise*, 14.

30. Spinoza, *Tractatus theologico-politicus* I.27, 108; *Theological-Political Treatise*, 24, modified. See *Tractatus theologico-politicus* II.1, 112; II.6, 118; and XIII.1, 448 (*Theological-Political Treatise*, 28, 30, and 172, respectively).

31. Spinoza, *Tractatus theologico-politicus*, II.1, 29; II.3, 30; II.6, 32; *Theological-Political Treatise*, 13, 14, 15. Spinoza overturns a distinction introduced by Descartes, who, like Kant, holds that, unlike metaphysics, which proceeds by the understanding alone, mathematics necessarily uses the imagination, and so it only attains certitude conditionally (by the metaphysical demonstration of the existence and goodness of God). Spinoza of course maintains the distinction between imagination and understanding, but he inadvertently attributes pure understanding to mathematics, downgrading imagination to the rank of a knowledge that is not only inadequate, but pre-theoretical.

32. Spinoza, *Tractatus theologico-politicus* XV.7, 186: "*nihil morale . . . quod cum ratione planissime non conveniat*—they offered no moral teaching which is not in accord with reason." *Theological-Political Treatise*, 192.

33. Spinoza, *Tractatus theologico-politicus* I.6, 83; *Theological-Political Treatise*, 15.

34. Spinoza, *Tractatus theologico-politicus* XV.6, 184: "*nec theologia rationi, nec ratio theologiae ancillari teneatur*—theology should not be subordinate to reason, nor reason to theology" (*Theological-Political Treatise*, 190), and "*nec Scriptura rationi, nec ratio Scripturae accommodanda*—Scripture is not to be accommodated to reason nor reason to Scripture," 185 (=191). This is opposed to the efforts of conciliation attempted by Maimonides, ibid. XIII.6, 170; *Theological-Political Treatise*, 175.

35. Spinoza, *Tractatus theologico-politicus* I.31, 29; *Theological-Political Treatise*, 26.

36. Spinoza, *Ethica*, II, §17, Scolium, in *The Collected Works of Spinoza*, vol. 1 (Princeton, NJ: Princeton University Press, 1985), 464–65. See also II, §28, Proof, ibid., 470, and already *De Intellectus Emendatione*, §82 and §92 (*Opera*, II: 31 and 34); trans. Edwin Curley as "Treatise on the Emendation of the Intellect," in *Collected Works 1*, 36 and 38. Spinoza clearly depends here on Aristotle (*De Anima* III.2, 425b25 and III.3, 428a8) and Thomas Aquinas (*Summa Theologiae* Ia, q.50, a.1, *c.*, q.78, a.4, *c.* and q.85, a.2, *ad* 3) as well as Descartes, *Meditatio* V (AT VII, 62; CSM 2, 44).

37. Spinoza, *Ethica* II, §28, Proof, 470; *Opera*, II:113. See also II, §35, Scolium: "men are deceived in that they think themselves free, an opinion which consists only

in this, that they are conscious of their actions and ignorant of the causes by which they are determined—Nempe falluntur homines, quod se liberos esse putant, quae opinio in hoc solo consistit, quod suarum actionum sint conscii, et ignari causarum, a quibus determinantur." Ibid., 473; *Opera* II:117.

38. Spinoza, *Ethica* II, §47: "The human mind has an adequate knowledge of God's eternal and infinite essence (Mens humana adæquatam habet cognitionem æternæ et infinitæ Dei essentiæ)." *Collected Works 1*, 482; *Opera,* II:128. That the human mind ever attains an *adequate* knowledge of the eternal and infinite essence of God, especially *in via*, but even in the beatific vision (*scientia beatorum*), seems refuted by the facts, just like the claim to "feel and know by experience that we are eternal (*sentimus experimurque, nos æternos esse*)." *Ethica* V, §23, Scolium, *Collected Works 1*, 607–8; *Opera*, II:296. Here the practice takes its revenge on the theory, for who, as pure philosopher, can claim these two accomplishments? See Ferdinand Alquié, *Le rationalisme de Spinoza* (Paris: PUF, 1981), 321ff.

39. Immanuel Kant, *Religion innerhalb der Grenzen der bloßen Vernunft*, Ak.A. VI, 144; translated by George di Giovanni as "Religion within the Boundaries of Mere Reason," in *Religion and Rational Theology*, 55–215, at 169, modified.

40. Kant, *Religion innerhalb der Grenzen*, 111; "Religion within the boundaries," 143, modified.

41. Kant, *Religion innerhalb der Grenzen*, 112; "Religion within the boundaries," 144, modified.

42. Kant's argument is so astonishing that the original deserves to be cited: "Denn das Theoretische des Kirchenglaubens kann uns moralisch nicht interessieren, wenn es nicht zur Erfüllung aller Menschenpflichten als göttlicher Gebote (was das Wesentliche aller Religion ausmacht) hinwirkt. Diese Auslegung mag uns selbst in Ansehung des Textes (der Offenbarung) oft gezwungen scheinen, oft es auch wirklich sein, und doch muß sie, wenn es nur möglich ist, daß dieser sie annimmt, einer solchen buchstäblichen [*sc.* Auslegung] vorgezogen werden, die entweder schlechterdings nichts für die Moralität enthält, oder dieser ihren Triebfedern wohl gar entgegen wirkt," *Religion innerhalb der Grenzen,* 110; "Religion within the boundaries," 142. Kant provides an example of such a correction by interpreting Psalm 59 (which calls on divine vengeance against evildoers) according to an exclusively moral sense (the enemies to be destroyed would be our evil inclinations, etc.), that is, following the traditional spiritual sense (in this case anagogical) of the Scriptures. See Kant, *Religion innerhalb der Grenzen*, 112, "Religion within the boundaries," 143–44. Yet let us observe (with Matthew Levering, *Engaging the Doctrine of Revelation*, 222ff) that Kant is still, in a certain way, included within the exegetical tradition that favors the spiritual sense in every case. For instance, this is how Origen corrects Joshua 8:24–26: "he who is 'outwardly a Jew' (*in manifesto Judeus*) (Romans 2:28) . . . thinks it is nothing else but wars being described, the destruction of enemies, and Israelites conquering

and seizing the kingdoms of nations. . . . But the one who is 'a Jew secretly' (*in occulto Judeus*) (2:29), that is, a Christian, . . . understands that all these things are mysteries of the kingdom of heaven and that even now my Lord Jesus Christ wars against opposing powers and casts out of their cities, that is, out of our souls." Homily XIII.1 in *Homilies on Joshua*, trans. Barbara J. Bruce, ed. Cynthia White (Washington, DC: Catholic University of America Press, 2002), 125. The Protestant rejection of the four senses of Scripture ("Littera gesta docet, quid credas allegoria / Moralis quid agas, quo tendas anagogia," Nicolas de Lyre) here shows its consequences. See Henri de Lubac, *Medieval Exegesis: The Four Senses of Scripture*, vol. 1, trans. Mark Sebanc (Grand Rapids, MI: Eerdmans, 1998), especially chapter 3, §§4–5, 142–59.

43. Kant, *Der Streit der Fakultäten*, I, 1, Ak. A. VII, 48; "The Conflict of the Faculties," in *Religion and Rational Theology*, 271, modified. The biblical text becomes *at best* a pretext reinforcing the text of the moral law, which is the only truly practical text; that is, it is fitting to "treat the text *only* (or at least *primarily*) as a contribution (*Veranlassung*) to any improvement of morals" (ibid., section I, Appendix, Ak. A. VII, 69; "The Conflict of the Faculties," 288, modified). See too, "[I] ask whether morality must be interpreted in accordance with the Bible, or the Bible, on the contrary, in accordance with morality." *Religion innerhalb der Grenzen*, 111, note; "Religion within the boundaries," 142.

44. Kant, *Der Streit der Fakultäten*, I, 1, Ak. A., t. VII, p. 45; "The Conflict of the Faculties," 270.

45. Kant, *Der Streit der Fakultäten*, 48; "The Conflict of the Faculties," 271–72, emphasis added.

46. J. G. Fichte, *Versuch einer Kritik aller Offenbarung*, §4, *Werke*, ed. F. Medicus after J.-H. Fichte, *Sämtliche Werke* (Berlin, 1845), *Fichtes Werke. Auswahl in sechs Bänden* (Leipzig: Meiner, 1922), vol. 1, 33; English translation, *Attempt at a Critique of all Revelation*, ed. Allen Wood, trans. Garrett Green (Cambridge: Cambridge University Press, 2010), §6, 144. See the patent "contradiction" of "want[ing] to employ *sensuous* stimuli as determining grounds for *pure morality*," *Versuch einer Kritik*, §5, 40; *Attempt at a Critique*, §7, 64.

47. Fichte, *Versuch einer Kritik*, §2, 22; *Attempt at a Critique*, §3, 40.

48. Fichte, *Versuch einer Kritik*, §8, 74; *Attempt at a Critique*, §10, 94. See also: "The concept of God (*der Begriff von Gott*) is already given to us by our reason alone, and is realized by it alone, insofar as it commands a priori; and there is simply no other conceivable way in which we could arrive at this concept (*Begriff*)." *Versuch einer Kritik*, §2, 21; *Attempt at a Critique*, §3, 52.

49. Fichte, *Versuch einer Kritik*, §2, 24; *Attempt at a Critique*, §3, 41, modified.
50. Fichte, *Versuch einer Kritik*, §10, 92; *Attempt at a Critique*, §12, 110, modified.
51. Fichte, *Versuch einer Kritik*, §10, 93; *Attempt at a Critique*, §12, 111.

52. Fichte, *Appellation an das Publikum* (1799), in *Fichtes Werke*, vol. 5 (Berlin: De Gruyter, 1971), 219, 220; English translation in *J. G. Fichte and the Atheism Dispute (1798–1800)*, ed. Yolanda Estes, trans. Curtis Bowman (Farnham: Ashgate, 2010), 111 and 112, modified, emphasis added. See also, "This is the true faith. This moral order is what we are assuming to be *divine* (*das Göttliche, das wir annehmen*). . . . The living and active moral order is itself God; we require no other God and can grasp no other." Fichte, *Über den Grund unseres Glaubens an eine göttliche Weltregierung* (1798), *Werke*, vol. 5, 185 and 186; *J. G. Fichte and the Atheism Dispute (1798–1800)*, 25 and 26.

53. Nietzsche, *Nachgelassene Fragmente*, 1886–87, 5 [71], §7, *Nietzsche Werke*, ed. Colli-Montinari, vol. 8/1 (Berlin: De Gruyter, 1974), 17; English translation: *Will to Power*, trans. Walter Kaufman and R. J. Hollingdale (New York: Vintage Books, 1968), 36. See my commentary in Marion, *The Idol and Distance*, §4, 27–36.

54. "The statements of Kant and of the young Fichte concerning the concept of Revelation still take place entirely within the opposition between reason and Revelation, as construed by Enlightenment philosophy. Reason is the ground on which and from which the possible content and validity of Revelation are determined." Karlfried Gründer, in Joachim Ritter, Karlfried Gründer, and Gottfried Gabriel, eds., *Historisches Wörterbuch der Philosophie* (Basel: Schwabe Verlag, 1984), vol. 6, 1121.

55. G. W. F. Hegel, *Vorlesungen über die Philosophie der Religion*, vol. 3, *Die vollendete Religion*, ed. W. Jaeschke (Hamburg: Meiner, 1984), 3; English translation: *Lectures on the Philosophy of Religion*, vol. 3, *The Consummate Religion*, trans. R. F. Brown, Peter C. Hodgson, and J. M. Stewart with H. S. Harris (Oxford: Clarendon Press, 2007), 63, modified to follow the very precise translation of Pierre Garniron (with Gilles Marmasse), *Leçons sur la philosophie de la religion*, part 3, *La religion accomplie* (Paris: PUF, 2004), 5.

56. Hegel, *Vorlesungen über die Philosophie der Religion*, 106; *Lectures on the Philosophy of Religion*, 3: 170, modified. I follow here Garniron's French translation, which marks very clearly the ambiguity between *Offenbaren* and *Manifestieren*, but also between *offenbar* and *sich offenbaren* (*Leçons sur la philosophie de la religion*, 103). See again: "This absolute religion is the *revelatory* (*offenbar*) religion, the religion that has itself as its content and fulfillment. But it is also the religion which is called revealed (*die die geoffenbarte gennant wird*)—which means, on the one hand, that it is revealed by God (*von Gott geoffenbart*), that God has given himself for human beings (*Gott sich selbst dem Menschen gegeben hat*) to know what he is; and on the other hand, as being revealed (*geoffenbart*), it is a *positive* religion in the sense that it has come to humanity from outside (*von außen gekommen*), that it has been given to it (*gegeben worden*)." *Vorlesungen über die Philosophie der Religion*, 179; *Lectures on the Philosophy of Religion*, 3: 252, modified. The irreducibility between

Offenbaren/offenbar and *geoffenbart* shines out all the more when it ends up in opposing (as in Kant and Fichte?) the (conceptual) knowledge of God by and as spirit and the gift by God himself in a positive religion.

57. "In dieser Religion ist deswegen das göttliche Wesen *geoffenbart*. Sein Offenbarsein besteht offenbar darin, daß gewußt wird, was es ist. Es wird aber gewußt, eben indem es als Geist gewußt wird, als Wesen, das wesentlich *Selbstbewußtsein* ist. . . . Dies—seinem *Begriffe* nach das Offenbare zu sein—ist also die wahre Gestalt des Geistes." *Phänomenologie des Geistes,* ed. Wolfgang Bonsiepen and Reinhard Heede, *Gesammelte Werke,* vol. 9 (Hamburg: Meiner), 405; English translation: *The Phenomenology of Spirit,* trans. Terry Pinkard (Cambridge: Cambridge University Press, 2018), 435, modified. This equivalence, never explained, punctuates Hegel's analyses.

58. Fichte, private letter, *Werke,* vol. 5, 387; *J. G. Fichte and the Atheism Dispute (1798–1800),* 258. A more general view of Fichte's theology and its evolution can be found in Björn Pecina, *Fichtes Gott. Vom Sinn der Freiheit zur Liebe des Seins* (Tübingen: J. B. C. Mohr Siebeck, 2007).

Chapter Seven

1. Paul Tillich, "Offenbarung als Idee ist so alt wie die Religion. . . . Offenbarung als Begriff ist sehr viel jünger." "Die Idee der Offenbarung," *Zeitschrift für Theologie und Kirche,* 8/6 (1927): 403–12, here 403. This is Tillich's inaugural lecture at the University of Leipzig.

2. See Yves Congar: "These words [*revelare, revelatio*] are sometimes used a propos of the *Fathers,* though comparatively rarely and, mostly, in the later period." Congar, *Tradition and Traditions,* 120. And Jacques Guillet: "To treat revelation in the New Testament presents a fundamental difficulty and requires an option of method at the outset. While it is the case that, in the Christian perspective and common language of Catholicism as well as Protestantism, Revelation expresses in one word the definitive communication that God made to humanity in the person of Jesus and covers completely all the material of the New Testament and even the Old, there does not exist in the vocabulary of the New Testament a word that responds to this reality." *Supplément au Dictionnaire de la Bible,* vol. 10 (Paris: Letouzey et Ané, 1985), col. 600. And Wolfgang Wieland: "The concept of 'Revelation,' while belonging to the central concepts of theology, is nevertheless not completely articulated in the period of early Christianity. What corresponds to the various modes and manners of the announcement of God to men are different Greek and Latin terms that nevertheless are not distinguished univocally from one another." G. Scholtz, "Offenbarung," in Ritter, Gründer, Gabriel, eds., *Historische Wörterbuch der Philosophie,* vol. 6, col. 1105. Or Ulrich Dierse and Wenzel Lohff: "Contrary to what is commonly assumed, it must be firmly maintained that, from the point of view of the history of concepts, the concept of Revelation initially

had no great meaning in the Reformation. An analogous situation occurs in Catholic theology of the sixteenth and seventeenth centuries" (col. 1114). Or further, Thomas Söding: "The terminology is not unified; in the NT an explicit reflection on revelation is missing," as is also the case in "the OT [which] knows no conceptual equivalent to the abstract notion of revelation." *Lexikon für Theologie und Kirche*, vol. 7, cols. 986 and 985. But above all Joseph Ratzinger: "When about thirty years ago I tried to make a study of the way Revelation was treated in thirteenth-century theology, I collided with an unexpected fact: nobody in that period ever thought to call the Bible 'Revelation,' nor was it called 'source.' It is not that they held the Bible in less esteem than today. On the contrary, they had a less conditional respect for it, and it was clear that theology must not and could not be anything else but interpretation of Scripture. It was their idea of the harmony between Scripture and life that was different. That is why they applied the word 'Revelation,' on the one hand, only to an act which was never expressible in human words and by which God made himself known to his creature and, on the other hand, to the reception by which the divine condescendence became perceptible to man under the form of Revelation. Everything that must be fixed in words, thus Scripture itself, testifies to the Revelation without being that Revelation in the strict sense of the word." "Sources and Transmission of the Faith," trans. Thomas Langan, *Communio* 10:1 (Spring 1983): 17–34, here 27. See above, chapter 3, notes 6–9.

3. Wolfhart Pannenberg, "Das Wort 'Offenbarung' ist zu einer gängigen Scheidemünze geworden," in Wolfhart Pannenberg, ed., *Offenbarung als Geschichte*, 3rd ed. (Göttingen: Vandenhoeck & Ruprecht, 1965), 7. English translation (which removes all color from the word "Scheidemünze"): "Today, the term 'revelation' has lost its value in theological usage." Wolfhart Pannenberg, ed., *Revelation as History*, trans. David Granskou (London: Macmillan, 1968), 3.

4. Paul Althaus, "Die Inflation des Begriffs der Offenbarung in der gegenwärtigen Theologie," *Zeitschrift für systematische Theologie* 18 (1941): 134–49. See Avery Dulles denouncing those who "inordinately intellectualized the notion of revelation" (*Revelation Theology*, 51). And Henri Bouillard: "It is worth asking whether it would not be opportune to reduce the usage of the words 'revelation' or 'revealed religion' and instead replace them with 'Gospel' or 'Christian message.'" Geffré et al., eds., *Révélation de Dieu et langage des hommes*, 38.

5. F. G. Downing, *Has Christianity a Revelation?* (London: SCM Press, 1964)—a discussion that is pursued within the current of "narrative theology" by George W. Stroup, *The Promise of Narrative Theology: Recovering the Gospel in the Church* (Eugene: Wipf and Stock, 1997), particularly in chapter 2, "Revelation Under Siege"; and Basil Mitchell and Maurice Wiles, "Does Christianity Need a Revelation? A Discussion," *Theology* 83 (1980): 103–14.

6. See François Nault, "Révélation sans théologie. Théologie sans révélation," in Philippe Bordeyne and Laurent Vuillemin, eds., *Vatican II et la théologie.*

Perspectives pour le XXIième siècle (Paris: Cerf, 2006), 127–49. While he reduces my own efforts to the production of a "revelation without theology, a revelation without hermeneutics" (142), and I am trying here to show that he is wrong, this author is worthy of more attention than the conventional declaration of Marcel Gauchet, "Tradition, revelation: none of these categories is acceptable any more today in civil society [*sic*]." *Projet* 255 (1991): 43. The syntax here is just as vague as the thinking.

7. Karl Barth, *Kirchliche Dogmatik*, I/1, 312; English translation: *Church Dogmatics*, I.1, 296.

8. [Translators' note: French uses *la Parole* to denote the biblical Word, and *le Verbe* to denote the Word or Logos, second person of the Trinity, incarnated in Jesus Christ.]

9. Barth, *Kirchliche Dogmatik*, I/1, 194; *Church Dogmatics*, I.1, 186.

10. Augustine, *Confessions* VIII.12.29, quoting Romans 13:13–14. See Marion, *In the Self's Place*, §3, in particular 25–27.

11. On all these points, see the classic developments in Barth's *Kirchliche Dogmatik*, I/1, 128–94; *Church Dogmatics*, I.1, 125–86. One thus sees that the distinction, made by both Luther and Calvin, between what God reveals for salvation and his absolutely concealed and incomprehensible decree on the predestination of the elect could have no real object. For the secret of God is found entirely manifested in Revelation, without any reserve. "In giving us, as He did, His Son, which is His Word—and He has no other—[God] spake and revealed to us all together, once and for all, in this single Word, and He has no occasion to speak further." Saint John of the Cross, *The Ascent of Mount Carmel* II.22.3, in *Vida y Obras de San Juan de la Cruz* (Madrid: BAC, 1974), 535; English translation: *The Complete Works of St. John of the Cross*, vol. 1, trans. P. Silverio de Santa Teresa, C.D., ed. E. Allison Peers (Westminster, MD: Newman Press, 1949), 173, modified. As a consequence, the only reserve limiting Revelation results not from the secret of God, but lies instead in the deficiency of the finite responses of those who find themselves called by it. God keeps nothing secret; the closing of our hearts alone is enough to explain our darkness.

12. Rudolf Bultmann, "Der Begriff der Offenbarung im Neuen Testament" [1929], collected in *Glauben und Verstehen*, vol. 3 (Tübingen: JBC Mohr Siebeck Verlag, 1960, 1965), 9–10; English translation: *Existence and Faith: Shorter Writings of Rudolf Bultmann*, trans. Schubert M. Ogden (New York: Meridian, 1960), 60, translation modified. Revelation does not consist in set statements, informing us about God in the way a museum exhibition (such a strange comparison!) would inform us about "old locomotives" (ibid.). On this text, I point the reader toward an old article of mine: "Remarques sur le concept de Révélation chez Rudolf Bultmann," *Résurrection* 27 (1968): 29–42.

13. Bultmann, "Der Begriff der Offenbarung," 6; *Existence and Faith*, 62. See "We know about revelation because it belongs to our life" (62).

14. Bultmann, "Der Begriff der Offenbarung," 7 (see other occurrences of *Anrede*, 22, 30, 31); *Existence and Faith*, 64.

15. Bultmann, "Der Begriff der Offenbarung," 15; *Existence and Faith*, 72, quite rightly citing Matthew 7:14, Mark 9:43ff, 1 John 1:1–2, and Acts 5:20, etc. But with a further point: "Revelation is an *event* that abolishes death, not a theory [teaching] that death does not exist" (72, modified).

16. Bultmann, "Der Begriff der Offenbarung," 18; *Existence and Faith*, 75, modified, relying correctly on 1 John 1:2; 3:2 and 3:8; 4:9; 1 Peter 1:20; Hebrews 9:26, etc.

17. Bultmann, "Der Begriff der Offenbarung," 18; *Existence and Faith*, 75, by opposition to the world: "*nicht als ein Weltfaktum*," "*nicht als eine Weltanschauung*" ("Der Begriff," 31, 30).

18. Bultmann, "Der Begriff der Offenbarung," 21 and 22; *Existence and Faith*, 78. See "*Verkündigung, im Wort*," "*Verkündigung auch als die Offenbarung*" ("Der Begriff," 19).

19. Bultmann, "Der Begriff der Offenbarung," 23; *Existence and Faith*, 79.

20. Bultmann, "Was ist also offenbart worden? Gar *nichts*, sofern die Frage nach Offenbarung nach Lehren fragt." "Der Begriff der Offenbarung," 29; *Existence and Faith*, 85, emphasis added. See "Der Begriff," 31, 33, and 34; *Existence and Faith*, 87, 89, 90–91.

21. Karl Rahner, in his contribution to Karl Rahner and Joseph Ratzinger, *Offenbarung und Überlieferung*, 16; *Revelation and Tradition*, 13. See also: "If what has been said is correct, then transcendental and predicamental [categorical] revelation and the history of revelation are co-extensive with the *spiritual history of mankind as such*" (*Revelation and Tradition*, 16, emphasis added). Or what elsewhere Rahner calls a "supernatural existential," which *in principle* would allow one to understand "the relationship between the history of universal, transcendental revelation and special, categorical revelation." Karl Rahner, *Grundkurs des Glaubens. Einführung in den Begriff des Christentums* (Freiburg: Herder, 1976), 146, 157; English translation: Karl Rahner, *Foundations of Christian Faith: An Introduction to the Idea of Christianity*, trans. William V. Dych (New York: Crossroad, 1978, 1984), 141, 153.

22. Paul Tillich, *Systematic Theology*, vol. 1 (Chicago: University of Chicago Press, 1951), 60. Or later: the "correlative character of revelation" (126).

23. Tillich: "If the concept of revelation contains a reality, a reality that also happens to us, indeed perhaps the only reality that happens to us unconditionally (*unbedingt*), then it could not be the reality of an object that fits reality, but only the reality of an idea"; and he comments: "Revelation is a word and, as a word, a concept and, as a concept, the object of a conceptual elaboration; but the content of the concept is an idea, not an object" ("Die Idee der Offenbarung," 403). And: "It [Revelation] is the appearing of the unconditioned (*Unbedingte*), hidden in our conditioned-condition (*Bedingtheit*)" (412). Or: "This is not the occult—the relatively hidden—but the unconditionally hidden (*unbedingt Verborgene*) that reveals itself" (407).

24. Tillich, "Whatever is essentially mysterious cannot lose its mysteriousness even when it is revealed." *Systematic Theology*, vol. 1, 109; see 127, 129. Or: "that [what is hidden] does not cease, once it is revealed, to be hidden; for being hidden belongs to its essence (*seine Verborgenheit gehört zu seinem Wesen*). And, when that which is hidden reveals itself, the fact that it is hidden is also revealed." "Die Idee der Offenbarung," 406.

25. Tillich, *Systematic Theology*, vol. 1, 61 (and 59–64).

26. Tillich, *Systematic Theology*, vol. 1, 110 (which echoes Bultmann). See: "There is no revelation if there is no one who receives it as his ultimate concern" (111).

27. Tillich, *Systematic Theology*, vol. 1, 117 (see 129, emphasis added). The same ambiguity is found regarding the status of "reason," sometimes divided into finite or ecstatic (53 and 57), into "controlling and receiving knowledge" (109), and sometimes remaining, even in the case of a miracle, "the rational structure of reality" (117); it is not enough to denounce (rightly) "irrationalist rationalism" (115) to dispel this indecisiveness.

28. Tillich, *Systematic Theology*, vol. 1, 156, emphasis added (on "the ground of being," see 24, 35, 50, 53).

29. Rahner, *Foundations of Christian Faith*, 121–22 (emphasis added). At issue is a radical thesis: "Because there is self-transcendence on man's part through God's ontological and revelatory self-communication, the history of revelation takes place wherever this transcendental history has its history, and hence in the whole history of man" (153). In this way, are we not approaching an updating of the theology of "pure nature," where the ontico-ontological postulation ("absolute being and the mystery of God," 121) would be doubled by the postulate of absolute historicization so as to find man *in puris naturalibus*, in being and history? This objection has been made, as we know (see chapter 15).

30. Pannenberg, ed., *Offenbarung als Geschichte*, 12; see 13, as well. English translation: Pannenberg, ed., *Revelation as History*, 9, modified.

31. Pannenberg, "Dogmatische Thesen zur Lehre von der Offenbarung," his own contribution to the collection *Offenbarung als Geschichte*, 91; English translation: "Dogmatic Theses on the Doctrine of Revelation," in *Revelation as History*, 125. Let us once again underline that this indirect character in no way implies a diminution of the direct Revelation, but specifies its mode of accomplishment: "Indirect communication is on a higher level: it always has direct communication as its basis, but takes this into a new perspective. . . . Indirect Revelation is distinguished by not having God as the content in any direct manner." *Offenbarung als Geschichte*, 16–17; *Revelation as History*, 13, 14, modified.

32. Pannenberg, "Dogmatische Thesen zur Lehre von der Offenbarung," respectively thesis 2 (95), thesis 3 (99 and 100); "Dogmatic Theses on the Doctrine of Revelation," 131, 135, and 136.

33. Pannenberg, "Dogmatische Thesen zur Lehre von der Offenbarung," thesis 6 (109); "Dogmatic Theses on the Doctrine of Revelation," 149.

34. See Karl Rahner: "The historicity of the history of salvation on God's part and not only on man's part, a history which really is the one true history of God himself." *Foundations of Christian Faith*, 141–42. And Pannenberg: "History is the most comprehensive horizon (*umfassendste Horizont*) of Christian theology." *Grundfragen systematischer Theologie* (Göttingen: Vandenhoeck & Ruprecht, 1967), 22; English translation: *Basic Questions in Theology*, vol. 1 (London: SCM, 1970), 25.

35. Pannenberg, "Dogmatischen Thesen zur Lehre der Offenbarung," thesis 3, respectively 100, 99, 101; "Dogmatic Theses on the Doctrine of Revelation," 137, 136, 138.

36. Quoted in Barth, *Kirchliche Dogmatik*, I/1, 132; *Church Dogmatics*, I.1, 129.

37. Barth, *Kirchliche Dogmatik*, I/1, 123, *Church Dogmatics*, I.1, 120, responding to Friedrich Gogarten, "Karl Barths Dogmatik," *Theologische Rundschau*, 1929 (discussed in *Kirchliche Dogmatik*, I/1, 128–36; *Church Dogmatics*, I.1, 125–31). Or: "It [revelation] does not stand, therefore, under any condition (*Bedingung*)—one can say this only of our knowledge of revelation—but is itself the condition"; or: "revelation denotes the Word of God itself in the act of its being spoken in time. Above this act there is nothing other or higher on which it might be based (*begründen*) or from which it might be derived. . . . It is the condition which conditions all things without itself being conditioned (*daß er wohl die Bedingung ist, die alles bedingt, ohne doch selber bedingt zu sein*). This is what we are saying when we call it revelation." *Kirchliche Dogmatik*, I/1, 121 and 122, respectively; *Church Dogmatics*, I.1, 118.

38. Hans Urs von Balthasar, *Glaubhaft ist nur Liebe* (Einsiedeln: Johannes Verlag, 1966), 36; English translation: *Love Alone Is Credible*, trans. D. C. Schindler (San Francisco: Ignatius Press, 2004), 56.

39. Balthasar, *Glaubhaft ist nur Liebe*, 76; *Love Alone Is Credible*, 113. Thus "love is known only through love," because "love desires no recompense other than to be loved in return." Ibid., 75 (=107).

40. On the inversion of the impossible *for us* (thus the impossible) into the possible *for God* (for whom "nothing is impossible"), see my indications in Marion, *Negative Certainties*, 51–82.

41. Bernard of Clairvaux, *Sermons sur le Cantique des Cantiques* VIII.3, SC 414, 180 (see above, chapter 2).

42. Hans Urs von Balthasar, *Herrlichkeit*, I: 462 and 448; *The Glory of the Lord*, I: 480 (modified), 465, 466. [Translators' note: There is an important difference in terminology here: Balthasar's key term *Gestalt* is usually translated into English as "form," but in keeping with the French text, we translate it here as "figure."]

43. On this formula see my outline: "Le 'phénomène du Christ' selon Hans Urs von Balthasar," *Revue catholique international Communio* 30, no. 2 (March–April 2005): 77–82.

44. Balthasar, *Glaubhaft ist nur Liebe*, 84; *Love Alone Is Credible*, 128.

45. Balthasar, *Glaubhaft ist nur Liebe*, 86; *Love Alone Is Credible*, 130; or put another way, in the "kenotic figure of revelation" 191 (=148).

46. Balthasar, *Glaubhaft ist nur Liebe*, 37 and 39; *Love Alone Is Credible*, 58 and 60.

47. Balthasar, *Herrlichkeit*, I: 416; *The Glory of the Lord*, I: 432.

48. Balthasar: "Christus aber ist die Form, weil er der Inhalt ist," *Herrlichkeit*, I: 445; English translation: "Christ, by contrast, is the form because he is the content." *The Glory of the Lord*, I: 463.

49. Balthasar, *Glaubhaft ist nur Liebe*, 58; *Love Alone Is Credible*, 87–88. See Jean-Yves Lacoste, "Du phénomène à la figure: pour réintroduire à *La Gloire et la Croix*," *Revue Thomiste* 86, n o. 1 (1986): 606–16.

50. Dionysius the Areopagite, *Divine Names* IV.14, PG 3, 712c, ed. Ysabel de Andia, SC 578 (Paris: Cerf, 2016), 478; *Complete Works*, 82.

Chapter Eight

1. Hans Urs von Balthasar, *Glaubhaft ist nur Liebe*, 83; *Love Alone Is Credible*, 125.

2. Balthasar, *Glaubhaft ist nur Liebe*, 87: "vollendende Form aller Vorformen"; *Love Alone Is Credible*, 131.

3. Balthasar, *Glaubhaft ist nur Liebe*, 91; *Love Alone Is Credible*, 135–36.

4. Balthasar, *Glaubhaft ist nur Liebe*, 94; *Love Alone Is Credible*, 142, translation modified.

5. Balthasar, *Glaubhaft ist nur Liebe*, 94; *Love Alone Is Credible*, 143, modified by reestablishing *lieber*.

6. Martin Heidegger, "Was ist Metaphysik (1929)?" *Wegmarken*, GA 9 (Frankfurt: V. Klostermann, 1976), 382; English translation in *Pathmarks*, ed. William McNeill (Cambridge: Cambridge University Press, 2007), 290, modified.

7. On this passage, see Marion, *The Erotic Phenomenon*, §§2–3, 16–26.

8. Friedrich Schleiermacher, *Über die Religion. Reden an die Gebildeten unter ihren Verächtern*, II, ed. Hans-Joachim Rothert (Hamburg: Meiner, 1958, 1970), 37; *On Religion: Speeches*, 28.

9. Ludwig Wittgenstein, *Culture and Value*, ed. G. H. von Wright and Heikki Nyman, rev. ed. Alois Pichler, trans. Peter Winch (Oxford: Blackwell, 1998), 89–89e.

10. F. W. J. Schelling, "Auch bei dem Christenthum soll man nicht fragen, wie habe ich es zu deuten, um es mit irgend einer Philosophie in Uebereinstimmung zu setzen, sondern umgekehrt, von welcher Art muß die Philosophie sehn, um auch das Christenthum in sich aufnehmen und begreifen zu können." *Philosophie der Offenbarung*, Lecture XXV, in Schröter, ed. *Werke*, Erg. Bd. VI, 34.

11. On this analysis (and on the reserve that strains this quasi-dematerialization), see Jean-Luc Marion, *Sur l'ontologie grise de Descartes. Science cartésienne et savoir aristotélicien* (Paris: Vrin, [1975], 2017), §§4, 5, and 22; Marion, *Negative Certainties*, chapter 5; and "Le réalisme réel: l'objet ou la chose," in Emmanuel Alloa and Elie During, eds., *Choses en soi* (Paris: PUF, 2017). It could be that the dematerialization

of the world (material nature) answers, at the other extreme of the spectrum, the critique of Revelation through the unique enterprise of conceptualization deployed by metaphysics.

12. Descartes, *Regulæ ad directionem ingenii* XII, AT X, 418; CSM 1, 44, modified. It is in a literal sense a question of what Kant will name "the distinction between things as objects of experience (*als Gegenstände der Erfahrung*) and the very same things as things in themselves (*von ebendenselben, als Dingen in sich*), which our critique has made necessary." *Kritik der reinen Vernunft*, B XXVII, *Critique of Pure Reason*, 115.

13. See Jean-François Courtine, *Suarez et le système de la métaphysique* (especially II, chapters 4 and 5, and IV, chapters 2 and 3), and Michäel Devaux and Marco Lamanna, "The Rise and Early History of the Term Ontology (1606–1730)", in C. Esposito, ed., *Quæstio* 9, "Origini e sviluppi dell' ontologia secoli XVI-XXI" (Turnhout/Bari: Brepols/Pagina, 2009), 173–208, here 173ff.

14. Kant, *Critique of Pure Reason*, B131–32 (see also A123 and A382). On the partial legitimacy of the reformulation of Descartes's *cogito* by Heidegger, see the clarification in Jean-Luc Marion, *Cartesian Questions: Method and Metaphysics* (Chicago: University of Chicago Press, 1999), §1, and *On the Ego and on God: Further Cartesian Questions,* trans. Christina M. Gschwandtner (New York: Fordham University Press, 2007), §3.

15. G. W. Leibniz, *Les principes de la Philosophie, ou monadologie*, §§31–32; English translation: *G. W. Leibniz's Monadology: An Edition for Students*, trans. Nicholas Rescher (Pittsburgh: University of Pittsburgh Press, 1991), 21; original French is found on 113 and 116.

16. Besides the variation of his different approaches to *alētheia*, since before *Sein und Zeit* until *Zeit und Sein*, and besides the complexity of the status successively assigned to "forgetting (λήθη)," the primary difficulty for relying on Heidegger here is found, no doubt, in the brutality of the denial of every theological and Christian equivalent of "truth" itself. Hence his commentary on John 14:6, where the formula "Ἐγώ εἰμι ἡ ὁδὸς καὶ ἡ ἀλήθεια καὶ ἡ ζωή, I am the way, the truth, and the life" is disqualified without discussion, at first as "only verbally Greek" but then, worse still, as belonging to the Latin *veritas,* itself "an un-German word, *ein undeutsches Wort*." *Parmenides* (1942–43), GA 54 (Frankfurt: V. Klostermann, 1982), 68ff; English translation by André Schuwer and Richard Rojcewicz (Bloomington: Indiana University Press, 1998), 46 and 47, modified. On these points, see Didier Frank, *Le Nom et la chose. Langue et vérité chez Heidegger* (Paris: Vrin, 2017), especially I, chapter 1.

17. Jerome, continuing a few lines later: "when something is shown covered and veiled, they expressed it by removing the cover from the top and bringing it out into the light.—Verbum quoque ipsum ἀποκαλύψεος, id est *revelationis* proprie Scripturarum est et a nullo sapientium sæculi apud Græcos usurpatum.... sonare,

cum quid tectum et velatum, ablato desuper operimento, ostenditur et profertur in lucem." *In epistulam ad Galatas* 1.12, PL 26, 323a; translated by Thomas P. Scheck in *St. Jerome's Commentaries on Galatians, Titus, and Philemon* (Notre Dame, IN: University of Notre Dame Press, 2010), 71–72. I owe this enlightening distinction to Jean Vioulac, *Apocalypse of the Truth*, trans. Matthew J. Peterson (Chicago: University of Chicago Press, 2021), in particular, chapter 4, "Apocalypse and Truth," 53–62. This attempt, remarkable in every respect, does not, however, remove certain ambiguities that I will not attempt to resolve *here*: Does this model of *alētheia* equally cover Greek philosophy, modern *metaphysics*, and its (partial) retrieval by Heidegger? Conversely, does the term *apokalypsis* and its biblical usages allow us to use it immediately in support of a properly *theo*-logical concept of Revelation?

18. Nicholas of Cusa, *De visione Dei* XVII.79; *Selected Spiritual Writings*, 270.

19. Descartes, *Meditatio III*, AT VII, 59; CSM 2, 41, modified. There is no need to object that we are dealing here with a very particular determination of the truth, in that it submits the true proposition to the approval of the will, while we can support the self-affirmation of evidence without falling into this "voluntarism" (the objections of Spinoza and Leibniz, among others). Such objections do not hold, first because founding the truth directly on evidence only radicalizes the bringing to evidence of what is thus unconcealed, even more than the recourse to the approval of the will. And further, because contemporary debates on belief (articulated by propositions and then founded in reasons and arguments) would confirm instead the Cartesian approach.

20. William of Saint-Thierry, *Speculum fidei*, §25, in *Deux traités sur la foi*, 46; English translation: *The Mirror of Faith*, trans. Thomas X. Davis (Kalamazoo, MI: Cistercian, 1979), 33, modified. Gregory the Great describes this quite precisely: "But among these things, it is necessary to know that often *love puts lazy souls to work*, and fear holds restless souls back from the exercise of contemplation. . . . Hence it is necessary, for whoever is eager to study contemplation, to *first* question himself with care *to what degree he loves*. *The soul is an engine operated by the force of love*, and as long as it tears itself away from the world, it will rise to the heights. Let him then *first* discuss *whether he loves to seek higher things by loving them*, of if he knows how to understand unknown things by loving them. For in contemplation, *if love does not stimulate the mind*, the dullness of its tepidity darkens it.—Sed inter haec, sciendum est quia saepe et pigras mentes amor ad opus excitat, et inquietas in contemplatione timor refrenat. . . . Unde necesse est ut quisquis ad contemplationis studia properat, semetipsum prius subtiliter interroget quantum amat. Machina quippe mentis est vis amoris, quae hanc dum a mundo extrahit, in alta sustollit. Prius ergo discutiat, si summa inquirens diligit, si diligens timet, si novit incognita aut amando comprehendere, aut non comprehensa timendo venerari. In contemplatione etenim mentem si amor non excitat, teporis sui torpor obscurat." *Moralia in Job* VI.37, PL 75, 762–63, emphasis added; English translation in *Morals on the*

Book of Job, trans. Charles Marriot and James Bliss (Oxford: John Henry Parker, London: J. G. F. and J. Rivington, 1844), vol. 1, 358, modified.

21. Blaise Pascal, *De l'art de persuader*, in *Œuvres complètes*, ed. Louis Lafuma (Paris: Seuil, 1963), 355: "Et de là vient qu'au lieu qu'en parlant des choses humaines, on dit qu'il faut les connaître avant que de les aimer, ce qui a passé en proverbe, les saints au contraire disent en parlant des choses divines qu'il faut les aimer pour les connaître et qu'on n'entre dans la vérité que par la charité, dont ils ont fait une de leurs plus utiles sentences"; English translation: *Pensées and Other Writings*, trans. Anthony Levi (Oxford: Oxford World's Classics, 1999), 193, modified. I have commented on this thesis in *On Descartes' Metaphysical Prism*, §25, 333ff, and *In the Self's Place*, §21, 128ff, to which I refer for the whole Augustinian horizon of this reversal. This key text is also cited by Heidegger, *Being and Time*, §29, 135, and only commented on by a later remark: "Scheler first made it clear, especially in the essay 'Liebe und Erkenntnis,' that intentional relations are quite diverse, and that even, for example, love and hatred ground knowing. Here Scheler picks up a theme of Pascal and Augustine." Heidegger, *Metaphysische Anfangsgründe der Logik*, 9, GA 26 (Frankfurt: V. Klostermann, 1978), 169; English translation: *The Metaphysical Foundations of Logic*, trans. Michael Heim (Bloomington: Indiana University Press, 1984), 134. We can also return to Scheler's neat formula: "love is nevertheless the essence of the 'intentional,' of being reaching beyond itself." "Liebe," *Schriften aus dem Nachlaß*, II, *Gesammelte Werke*, 11 (Berne and Munich: Francke Verlag, 1979), 243. For a commentary on Heidegger's reference to Pascal, see Jean-Yves Lacoste, "Existence and the Love of God: Remarks on a Note in *Being and Time*," in *The Appearing of God*, trans. Oliver O'Donovan (Oxford: Oxford University Press, 2018), 91–111.

22. Augustine, *Contra Faustum* XXXII.18, PL 42, 507; English translation: Philip Schaff, ed., *St. Augustine: The Writings Against the Manichaeans and Against the Donatists* (1887; repr. Grand Rapids, MI: Eerdmans, 1979), 338, modified: "He [the Holy Spirit] leads into all truth, for the only way to truth is by love, and 'the love of God,' says the apostle, 'has been poured out into our hearts through the Holy Spirit who has been given to us.'" Observe that Saint Augustine's use of *inducere* here is found in the "*entrer*" of Pascal and the "*trahere*" of William of Saint-Thierry.

23. According to the argument of Descartes: "priorem quodammodo in me esse perceptionem infiniti quam finiti, hoc est Dei quam mei ipsius—in a certain way the perception of the infinite in me is prior to that of the finite, that is, the perception of God precedes my own." *Meditatio III*, AT VII, 45; CSM 2, 31, modified.

24. According to another argument of Descartes: "Sola est voluntas, sive arbitrii libertas, quam tantam in me experior, ut nullius majoris ideam apprehendam; adeo ut illa praecipue sit, ratione cujus imaginem quandam et similitudinem Dei me referre intelligo—It is only the will, or freedom of choice, which I experience as so great within me that I cannot apprehend the idea of anything greater; so that

I understand that it is principally by it that I bear a certain image and likeness of God." *Meditatio IV*, AT VII, 57; CSM 2, 31, modified.

25. Augustine, *Enarrationes in Psalmos* CXVIII.18.3, PL 37, 1552; English translation: *Exposition of the Psalms*, vol. 5, *Psalms 99–120*, trans. Maria Boulding, O.S.B. (Hyde Park, NY: New City Press, 2003), 426.

26. Augustine, *De diversis quaestionibus LXXXIII*, q.48, BA 10, ed. G. Bardy, et al. (Paris: Desclée de Brouwer, 1952), 128–30; cf. *Saint Augustine: Eighty-Three Different Questions*, trans. David L. Mosher (Washington, DC: Catholic University of America Press, 1982), 83.

27. Gilbert of Poitiers: "In caeteris facultatibus, in quibus semper consuetudini regulae generalitas atque necessitas accommodatur, non ratio fidem, sed fides sequitur rationem. . . . In theologicis autem, ubi est veri nominis atque absoluta necessitas, non ratio fidem, sed fides praevenit rationem. In his enim non cognoscentes credimus, sed credentes cognoscimus. Nam absque rationum principiis fides concipit non modo illa, quibus intelligendis humanae rationes suppeditare non possunt, verum etiam illa quibus ipsae possunt esse principia." *Boethii de praedicatione trium personarum*, II.1.9, PL 64, 1303; reprinted in *The Commentaries on Boethius by Gilbertus of Poitiers*, ed. N. Häring (Toronto: Pontifical Institute of Medieval Studies, 1966), 164.

28. Simon de Tournai, *Expositio in Symbolum "Quicumque,"* BN 14886, fol. 73a, cited by M.-D. Chenu, *La Théologie comme science au XIIIe siècle*, 35n3.

29. Respectively, William of Saint-Thierry, *Ænigma fidei*, §41, in *Deux traités sur la foi*, 128, translation modified. [Translators' note: We follow here the French translation of the Latin, with some reference to the English translation, *The Enigma of Faith*, 69]; and Alexander of Hales: "eleganter quidam respondendo dixerunt quod aliter se habet ratio in logicis ad fidem, aliter in theologicis. In logicis enim ratio causat fidem: unde argumentum est ratio rei dubiæ faciens fidem. In theologicis vero est e converso, quia fides causat rationem: unde fides est argumentum faciens rationem; fides enim qua creditur sat lumen animarum, quo quanto quis magis illustratur, tanto magis est perspicax ad inveniendas rationes quibus probentur credenda." *Summa Theologica*, L. I, tract. introd., q.2, membrum 3, c.4, ed. B. Klumper (Rome: Quaracchi, 1924), 35n23.

30. William of Saint-Thierry, *Ænigma fidei*, §47, in *Deux traités sur la foi*, 132 (cf. *The Enigma of Faith*, 73–74).

31. William of Saint-Thierry, *Supra Cantica Canticorum*, §64, ed. J.-M. Déchanet, SC 82 (Paris: Cerf, 1962), 162. [Translators' note: We follow here the French translation of the Latin, using as a loose reference the English translation in *Exposition on the Song of Songs. Monastic Studies* 16, trans. Columba Hart, OSB (Kalamazoo, MI: Cistercian, 1968), 52.]

32. William of Saint-Thierry, *Speculum fidei*, §16, in *Deux traités sur la foi*, 40. It should be noted that this citation of Isaiah reproduces the old translation of the

Septuagint by Saint Augustine. See for example: "For he sees and understands the one to whom he offers [the sacrifice of his prayer] as much as he is in a state of affection for him, and love is his very understanding (*et ei amor ipse intellectus est*)." *Epistula ad Fratres de Monte-Dei,* §173, ed. M.-M. Davy, *Un Traité de la vie solitaire. Epistula ad Fratres de Monte-Dei* (Paris, Vrin, 1940), 121. This final formula could have come from Gregory the Great: "Dum enim audita supercoelestia amamus, amata jam novimus, quia amor ipse notitia est." *Commentaire du psaume 138,* 17, PL 76, 1207. See the discussion of texts and interpretations of J.-M. Déchanet and P. Rousselot by M.-M. Davy, *Théologie et mystique de Guillaume de Saint-Thierry, I. La connaissance de Dieu* (Paris: Vrin, 1954), 204 ff.

33. William of Saint-Thierry, *Supra Cantica Canticorum,* §136, Déchanet, 290 [cf. *Exposition on the Song of Songs,* 109, modified]. Also: "Cum vero illustrantur a gratia, multum se adjuvant ad invicem, quia et amor vivificat rationem, et ratio clarificat amorem, fitque columbinus intuitus, simplex ad contemplandum, prudens ad cavendum—Because they are illumined by grace, they [i.e., the two eyes] are of great mutual assistance, because love gives life to reason and reason gives light to love; thus their gaze becomes like that of a dove, simple in contemplation, prudent in vigilance." §92, Déchanet, 212 (cf. *Exposition on the Song of Songs,* 74, modified).

34. William of Saint-Thierry, *Supra Cantica Canticorum,* §76, Déchanet, 188 (cf. *Exposition on the Song of Songs,* 64). See "Cognitio vero Sponsae ad Sponsum et amor idem est, quoniam in hac re amor ipse intellectus est—The Bride's knowledge of the Bridegroom and her love are the *same;* because in this thing love itself is understanding *itself"* (§57); Déchanet, 152, emphasis mine (cf. *Exposition on the Song of Songs,* 46). And again: "Cum retroacta ratione, amor pius ipse efficietur intellectus suus—with a retroactive reason, devout love itself will become its own understanding." Déchanet, §144, 304, modifying the French translation of "la raison mise de côté—reason set aside," [or "reasoning draws back," in the English] which is a mistranslation [cf. *Exposition on the Song of Songs,* 115, modified].

35. William of Saint-Thierry thus speaks of "coalescence" and "transition," for example, in *Supra Cantica Canticorum,* §§82 and 122, Déchanet 210 and 264 (cf. *Exposition on the Song of Songs,* 82 and 98).

36. William of Saint-Thierry, *Speculum fidei,* §73, in *Deux traités sur la foi,* 84. I modify here the punctuation of the text and thus the translation proposed by M.-M. Davy ("God is, he is always the same, *il est toujours le même*"), which adds a temporal adverb, absent from the text (85), to take account of the term *idipsum,* a quasi-invention of Saint Augustine that is often poorly understood (on this debate, see *In the Self's Place,* §§44–48, 289–306). *Idipsum* means not only a similarity ("the same thing, *la même chose*") but ipseity of the thing itself ("the very thing, the thing itself, *cela même*"). Here, God is the very thing, loving and thinking are conflated in this very thing. Another possible reading, deleting the second *est,* reads, "Nimirum Deus est idipsum, quod cogitare et amare idipsum est."

Chapter Nine

1. Gregory of Nazianzus, quoting Plato (*Timaeus* 28c), does not hesitate to coin a rarely used superlative, in his *Theological Oration* XXVIII.4, ed. Paul Gallay, SC 250 (Paris: Cerf, 1978), 108; English translation: *On God and Christ: The Five Theological Orations and the Two Letters to Cledonius*, trans. Frederick Williams and Lionel Wickham (Crestwood, NY: Saint Vladimir's Seminary Press, 2002), 39, modified.

2. Immanuel Kant: "Das Begehrungsvermögen ist das Vermögen desselben, durch *seine Vorstellungen Ursache von der Wirklichkeit der Gegenstände dieser Vorstellungen zu sein.*" *Kritik der praktischen Vernunft*, Ak. A. V, 8; English translation, *Practical Philosophy*, trans. Mary J. Gregor (Cambridge: Cambridge University Press, 1996), 144, modified. A definition that is later maintained and defended: "I have been reproached for . . . defining the power of desire as the *power of being the cause, through one's representations, of the reality of the objects of these representations.* The criticism was that, after all, mere wishes are desires too, and yet we all know that they alone do not enable us to produce their object. That, however, proves nothing more than that some of man's desires involve him in self-contradiction, inasmuch as he uses the representation by itself to strive to produce the object, while yet he cannot expect success from it. Such is the case because he is aware that his mechanical forces . . . are either insufficient, or perhaps even directed to something impossible. . . . In such fanciful desires we are indeed aware that our representations are insufficient (or even unfit) to be the *cause* of their objects. Still their causal relation, and hence the thought of their *causality*, is contained in every *wish.*" *Kritik der Urteilskraft*, Introduction III, footnote to the second edition, Ak.A. V, 177; English translation: *Critique of Judgment*, trans. Werner S. Pluhar (Indianapolis and Cambridge: Hackett, 1987), 16–17, modified.

3. Yet one could discuss further the pertinence of such an autonomy: Doesn't the moral law still come from *elsewhere*? If not, how would we explain its imposing of "respect," or that it constrains, or even "humiliates" the moral conscience? In fact, the opposition between autonomy and heteronomy remains imprecise and ungrounded, all the more in that even Heidegger had to give up on it, and Levinas inverted it.

4. William of Saint-Thierry, *Speculum fidei*, §73, in *Deux traités sur la foi*, ed., 84; *The Mirror of Faith*, 81.

5. "No more than the other Fathers did St. Augustine deal *ex professo* with the idea of revelation," notes René Latourelle (*Théologie de la Révélation*, 151). But how, then, are we to understand that "[i]ncontestably, the theme of revelation is in the forefront of the Christian consciousness of the first three centuries" (152)? Would the *idea* be lacking when the "consciousness" of it was "incontestable"? Unless what is retrospectively called the (modern) "idea" of revelation has but little in common

with that of which the Fathers had an "incontestably" clear "consciousness"; it would be fitting, then, to reform our idea of revelation on the basis of this consciousness. See, nevertheless, Albert C. de Veer, "*'Revelare-revelatio*': Éléments d'une étude sur l'emploi du mot et ses applications chez saint Augustin," in Maurice Nédoncelle et al., eds., *Recherches augustiniennes*, II, *Hommage au R. P. Fulbert Cayré* (Paris: Études augustiniennes, 1962), 331–57.

6. Augustine, *Tractatus in Iohannis Evangelium* XXVI.5, PL 35, 1609. Joseph de Ghellinck quotes another formulation of the same thesis: "Et si ab hominibus audiunt, tamen quod intellegunt intus datur, intus coruscat, intus revelatur. Quid faciunt homines forinsecus annuntiantes? Quid facio ego modo cum loquor? Strepitum verborum ingero auribus vestris. Nisi ergo revelet ille qui intus est, quid dico aut quid loquor?—And if they hear from men, still what they understand is given within, it gleams within, it *is uncovered* within. What do men who proclaim from without do? What am I now doing when I speak? I bring the noise of words to your ears. Unless he who is within should *uncover*, what do I say, or what do I speak?" *Tractatus in Iohannis Evangelium* XXVI.7, PL 35, 1609–1610, emphasis added; English translation: *Tractates on the Gospel of John, 11–27*, trans. John W. Rettig (Washington, DC: Catholic University of American Press, 1988), 265, modified. De Ghellinck comments, "his theory of intellectual knowledge is in a way symmetrical with his doctrine of supernatural grace; the role of divine illumination in purely natural knowledge resembles that of grace in the supernatural order." "Pour l'histoire du mot 'revelare,'" *Recherches de sciences religieuses*, no. 6 (1916): 149–57, at 156. But by introducing a non-Augustinian dichotomy (natural/supernatural), the stake of the thesis is masked, because here, manifestly, *revelare intus* indicates that knowledge, even inner knowledge, proceeds from *elsewhere*, from a deeper source than itself, in the sense of the *interior intimo meo*, as in *Confessions* III.6.11, BA 14 (Paris: Desclée de Brouwer, 1992), 382—is it not then more exclusively "natural" that grace is not limited exclusively to the sole "supernatural order"? The challenge consists in conceiving of a rational knowledge, one that is therefore "natural," by other means ("supernatural," if you like). On the evolution of Augustine's interpretation of John 6:44, see M.-F. Berrouard's detailed note in BA 72, 804–9.

7. *Tractatus in Iohannis Evangelium* XXVI.2, PL 35, 1607; *Tractates on the Gospel of John, 11–27*, 261 (modified).

8. Ibid.

9. *Tractatus in Iohannis Evangelium* XXVI.4, PL 35, 1608; *Tractates on the Gospel of John*, 262 (modified).

10. Ibid. See "Tu refulges et places et amaris et desideraris, ut erubescam de me et abiciam me atque eligam te et nec tibi nec mihi placeam nisi de te" (*Confessions* X.2.2, BA 14, 142); and: "Uocasti et clamasti et rupisti surditatem meam, coruscasti, splenduisti et fugasti caecitatem meam, fragrasti, et duxi spiritum et anhelo

tibi, gustaui et esurio et sitio, tetigisti me, et exarsi in pacem tuam" (X.27.38, BA 14, 208); or: "O Domine, perfice me et reuela mihi eas [namely, the obscure and secret pages of the Scriptures]. Ecce uox tua gaudium meum, uox tua super afluentiam uoluptatum. Da quod amo: amo enim" (XI.2.3, BA 14, 274); and finally, "Exarsit animus meus nosse istuc inplicatissimum aenigma. Noli claudere, Domine Deus meus, bone Pater, per Christum obsecro, noli claudere desiderio meo ista et usitata abdita.... Da quod amo: amo enim et hoc tu me dedisti" (XI.22.28, BA 14, 314–16). On this desire and the access to the truth as beauty, which seduces and draws its willing lover, see some indications in my book *In the Self's Place*, §22, 138–44.

11. *Tractatus in Iohannis Evangelium* XXVI.5, PL 35, 1609, quoting Virgil, *Eclogues* 2.65; *Tractates on the Gospel of John, 11–27*, 262. Regarding the record of Augustine's quotations of pagan authors, see Harald Hagendahl, *Augustine and the Latin Classics* (Göteborg: Institute of Classical Studies of the University of Göteborg, 1967).

12. *Tractatus in Iohannis Evangelium* XXVI.4, PL 35, 1608; *Tractates on the Gospel of John, 11–27*, 262. See "nos dicere debemus trahi hominem ad Christum, qui delectatur veritate, delectatur beatitudine, delectatur justicia, delectatur sempiterna vita, quod totum Christus est—we ought to say that a man is drawn to Christ who delights in truth, delights in happiness, delights in justice, delights in eternal life—and all this is Christ" (PL 35, 1608 =262).

13. *Tractatus in Iohannis Evangelium* XXVI.5, PL 35, 1609; *Tractates on the Gospel of John, 11–27*, 263 and 264 (modified).

14. *Tractatus in Iohannis Evangelium* XXVI.7, PL 35, 1610.

15. *Tractatus in Iohannis Evangelium* XXVI.5, PL 35, 1609; *Tractates on the Gospel of John*, 264 (modified).

16. *Tractatus in Iohannis Evangelium* XXVI.5, PL 35, 1609; *Tractates on the Gospel of John*, 263.

17. *Tractatus in Iohannis Evangelium* XXVI.5, PL 35, 1609; *Tractates on the Gospel of John*, 264. See also "Revelare se voluit quid esset" (XXVI.10, PL 35, 1610).

18. "*Violentia cordi fit*," "*dulcis est, suauis est*," *Sermo* 131.2.2, PL 38, 730. See "Habet enim potestatem adducendi et trahendi—He has the power to lead and to draw." *Contra Juliam* V.14, PL 44, 793; English translation in *Answer to the Pelagians, II*, trans. Roland J. Teske, SJ (Hyde Park, NY: New City Press, 1998), 443.

19. "Ille quippe trahitur ad Christum, cui datur ut credat in Christum.... Quae potestas nisi detur a Deo, nulla esse potest ex libero arbitrio: quia nec liberum in bono erit, quod liberator non liberavit." *Contra duas epistulas Pelagianorum* III.6, PL 44, 553; English translation: *Answer to the Pelagians, II*, 119. See: "Nemo igitur habere voluntatem justam, nisi nullis praecedentibus meritis acceperit veram, hoc est, gratuitam desuper gratiam—None, then, can have a righteous will unless they have received true grace without any preceding merits, that is, grace which has been gratuitously given from on high." Ibid., III.7, PL 44, 554; English translation: 119.

20. *Tractatus in Iohannis Evangelium* XXVI.7, PL 35, 1609–10; *Tractates on the Gospel of John*, 265.

21. Clement of Alexandria, *Stromates* V.1.1, ed. Alain Le Boulluec, SC 278 (Paris: Cerf, 1981), 24. English translation: *The Writings of Clement of Alexandria, Ante-Nicene Christian Library: Translations of the Writings of the Fathers of the Church*, vol. 12, *Clement of Alexandria II*, trans. William Wilson (Edinburgh: T&T Clark, 1867), 220, modified.

22. This is what is confirmed indirectly by the use of the word *revelare* in the discussion about the error committed by Saint Cyprian regarding the possibility of rebaptizing heretics: the lack of Revelation that impacts him gives him an opportunity for humility and conversion, and thus confirms its charity: "And that is why oftentimes something is not *revealed* to those who are more learned, so that their patient and humble charity, in which there is a greater fruit, may be tested, . . . or in regard to how they would accept the truth once they realize that what has been proclaimed [as such] contradicts what they think—Et ideo plerumque doctioribus minus aliquid revelatur, ut eorum patiens et humilis charitas, in qua fructus major est, comprobetur, . . . vel quomodo accipiant veritatem, cum contra id quod sentiebant, declaratam esse cognoscunt." Saint Augustine, *De Baptismo contra Donatistas* II.V.6, PL 43, 129, emphasis added; English translation in *The Donatist Controversy I*, trans. Maureen Tilley and Boniface Ramsey (Hyde Park, NY: New City Press, 2019), 425. The argument is all the more significant in that Saint Cyprian himself used it to explain how Paul was right against the initial position of Peter regarding the baptism of pagans. Saint Cyprian, *Epistolae LXXI*, PL 4, 410–11. Whence the possibility, indeed the necessity, of knowing to submit oneself sometimes to the *revelatio* of someone else (thus from elsewhere), in conformity with Paul's recommendation (1 Corinthians 14:30).

23. Isaiah 7:9, LXX: καὶ ἐὰν μὴ πιστεύσητε, οὐδὲ μὴ συνῆτε.

24. William of Saint-Thierry, *Speculum fidei*, §64, in *Deux traités sur la foi*, 76; English translation: *The Mirror of Faith*, 71, modified. See: "fides voluntarius est assensus mentis in eis que fidei sunt; credere vero [sc. est] cum assensu de eis cogitare—faith is a voluntary assent of the mind to matters of faith, but to believe is to deliberate on, while assenting to them." Ibid., §23, 44 (=31).

25. "Scientia vero haec modus quidam est vel habitus mentis, ad suscipienda ea, que proprie fidei sunt." *Speculum fidei*, §50, *Deux traités sur la foi*, 66; *The Mirror of Faith*, 58, modified.

26. "Quis cogitat, et non amat? Nimirum Deus est idipsum est, quod cogitare et amare idipsum est. *Ipsum dico, non de ipso*. De ipso enim multi cogitant, qui non amant, ipsum autem nemo cogitat, et non amat." *Speculum fidei*, §73, 84, emphasis added; *The Mirror of Faith*, 81, modified. This rule is so important that William does not hesitate to correct a verse from John 2:23: "quia credebant [sc. certain

hearers] in eum quem non diligebant" (in fact an unfounded amalgam of two verses from the Vulgate: v. 23, "multi crediderunt," and v. 24, "Ipse autem Iesus non credebat semetipsum eis," where it is not the listeners who believe without loving, but Jesus who refuses his trust in those who *say* they believe and nothing more). William comments, "Abusive quippe dictum de illis est, quia credebant in eum, quem non diligebant. Credere enim in eum, amando in eum ire est—It has been said of them [those of whom it is said in the gospels that they believed in Jesus but he did not believe in them], incorrectly, that they believe in him whom they did not love. But to believe in him is to go to him by loving him." *Speculum fidei*, §43,60; *The Mirror of Faith*, 50–51.

27. *Speculum fidei*, §2, 26. In other words, "Non credis quia non diligis; non diligis, quia non credis—You do not believe because you do not love; you do not love because you do not believe." *Speculum fidei*, §12, 36; *The Mirror of Faith*, 18.

28. "Equidem si non vis credere, non credis; credis autem, si vis: sed non vis, nisi a gratia preveniaris: quia 'nemo venit ad Filium, nisi Pater traxerit eum.' . . . Si vis credis, sed non vis, nisi a Patre traharis; et si vis, ideo utique vis, quia a Patre traheris." *Speculum fidei*, §12, 34–36; *The Mirror of Faith*, 17–18, modified.

29. *Speculum fidei*, §12, 36; *The Mirror of Faith*, 18 (modified).

30. *Speculum fidei*, §12, 36; *The Mirror of Faith*, 18. Saint Augustine said: "voluntatem nostrum, vel amorem seu dilectionem quae valentior est voluntas—our will, or love or dilection, which is only a stronger will." *De Trinitate* XV.21.41, BA 16, 532; *The Trinity*, 427, modified. Or "si tam violentia est [sc. voluntas], ut possit vocari amor, aut cupiditas, aut libido—if it [the will] is violent enough that one can name it a love, a desire, or a concupiscence." Ibid., XI.2.5, BA 16, 172; *The Trinity*, 307, modified. Complementary material to this doctrine can be found in Marion, *In the Self's Place*, 181–2, and see above, chapter 8. In this sense, one can rightly say that "Amor quippe illuminatus caritas est—Love enlightened is charity." William of Saint-Thierry, *De Natura et dignitate amoris*, §15, PL 184, 387, and in *Deux traités de l'amour de Dieu*, 88; *The Nature and Dignity of Love*, 67. Referring to Saint Augustine, Max Scheler saw that the issue here was not only, or perhaps primarily that of the primacy of the will over the understanding, but rather that of the primacy of love over the understanding *and* over the will. *Liebe und Erkenntnis* (1915), in *Gesammelte Werke*, vol. 6, *Schriften zur Soziologie und Weltanschauungslehre* (Berne and Munich: Francke Verlag, 1963), 77–98, at 93–96. Also, that, in this scheme, love provokes "a veritable *self-revealing (ein wahrhaftiges Sichoffenbaren)* of the object" (97); English translation: "Love and Knowledge," in Max Scheler, *On Feeling, Knowing, and Valuing: Selected Writings*, ed. Harold J. Bershady (Chicago: University of Chicago Press, 1992), 147–65, at 164 (modified).

31. *De contemplando Deo*, §18: *Deux traités de l'amour de Dieu*, 54, 52. See "vehementer velle, quod est amare." §21, *Deux traités de l'amour de Dieu*, 56.

32. *De Natura et dignitate amoris*, §25, 102; *The Nature and Dignity of Love*, 78. See "Voluntas crescit in amorem, amor in caritatem, caritas in sapientiam—The will ... grows into love, love into charity and charity into wisdom." §4, 74; *The Nature and Dignity of Love*, 53.

33. *Speculum fidei*, §36, 54; *The Mirror of Faith*, 42, modified.

34. Respectively, Athenagoras of Athens *Legatio* VII.2, ed. W. R. Schoedel (Oxford: Clarendon Press, 1972), 14–15 (Greek with English translation); and Irenaeus of Lyon, *Adversus Haereses* IV.6.4, ed. Adelin Rousseau, SC 100/2 (Paris: Cerf, 1965), 446. See also Clement of Alexandria: "it is only through divine grace, and through the Logos alone, which is with Him, that one knows the unknown—μόνῳ τῷ παρ' αὐτοῦ λόγῳ τὸ ἄγνωστον νοεῖν." *Stromates* V.12.82.4, 160; *The Writings of Clement of Alexandria*, vol. 2, 270, modified. Gregory the Great: "When we love the supercelestial things we have heard about, we already know the things we love, *because love itself is knowledge*—Dum enim audita supercoelestia amamus, amata jam novimus, quia *amor ipse notitia est.*" *Homilia in evangelia* II.27.4, PL 76, 1207, emphasis added; English translation: Gregory the Great, *Forty Gospel Homilies*, trans. Dom David Hurst (Kalamazoo, MI: Cistercian, 1990), 215, emphasis added. John of Damascus: "No one can know God unless God instructs him; that is, God is not known without God—ἄνευ θεοῦ μὴ γινώσκεσθαι τὸν θεόν." *Illustrium Ecclesiae Orientalis scriptorum secundi saeculi vitae et documenta*, vol. 2, ed. Pierre Halloix (Douai: Bogard, 1636), 483, quoted by Adelin Rousseau, in Irenaeus, *Adversus Haereses*, SC 100/2, 446; see also SC 100/1, 54ff. And of course, see Blaise Pascal: "God can well speak of God." *Pensées*, L 303, trans. Krailsheimer, 95.

35. Gregory of Nazianzus, *Theological Oration* XXVII.5 in SC 250, 82; *On God and Christ*, 29, modified.

36. Here I depend on the exegetical synthesis of this text compiled by Francis J. Moloney, S.D.B., *The Gospel of John*, Sacra Pagina Series, vol. 4, ed. Daniel J. Harrington, SJ (Collegeville, MN: Liturgical Press, 1998), 114–50. In a different context, see also Jean-Luc Marion, "La reconnaissance du don," *Revue catholique internationale Communio* 195 (2008): 169–82, collected in Marion, *Believing in Order to See*, 125–35.

37. *Dōrea* (gift) is a *hapax* in John; thus its importance, since the term does not appear in the synoptic gospels. The almost Socratic irony of Jesus has been rightly noticed by P. D. Duke in *Irony in the Fourth Gospel*, and especially, in a different style, by Jean Grosjean, *L'Ironie christique. Commentaire de l'Évangile selon Jean* (Paris: Gallimard, 1991). The living water (τὸ ὕδωρ τὸ ζῶν) can be understood as spring water ("welling up, ἁλλομένου," verse 14), which, unlike well water, does not stagnate. The Samaritan woman thus understands that perhaps he is talking about a fresher and cleaner source of water. But Jesus means the water that brings life, the life of God. We find a similar discrepancy in the encounter with Nicodemus,

who asks, "How can a man be born when he is old? Can he enter a second time into his mother's womb and be born again?" (John 3:4), and receives the response, "If I have told you earthly things and you do not believe, how can you believe if I tell you heavenly things?" (John 3:12) We also note that Pascal justifies Christ's irony "when he wanted to humiliate Nicodemus, who thought himself clever in his knowledge of the law." Pascal, *XIe Provinciale, Œuvres complètes*, 420. But the parallel between the dialogues of Jesus and those of Socrates shows their difference: Socrates intentionally puts his interlocutors on the spot, while in front of Jesus they spontaneously put themselves into self-contradiction, opening the double possibility of either challenging Christ by refusing to take up his point of view, or of following him by adapting themselves to his word. Socrates triumphs and judges; Jesus, in contrast, leaves each one to judge himself in relation to him.

38. This is the double function of the truth according to Saint Augustine, *Confessions* X.23.34, BA 14, 202; see my *In the Self's Place*, §17, 108–13. See André Scrima: "'If you knew': this means that the revelation comes from God and that it requires the Samaritan woman's faith in the one who is speaking with her: 'you would have asked him and he would have given you living water.'" *L'Évangile de Jean. Un commentaire* (Paris: Cerf, 2017), 73. We can compare the Samaritan woman's error (Christ must want to drink physical water, or give her water that definitively quenches physical thirst) to that of the disciples (who insist on proposing physical nourishment to Jesus, verses 31, 33). The Samaritan woman is unaware that Christ alone has "living water" at his disposal, just as the disciples are unaware that he has no physical food at his disposal only because he is nourished solely by doing the will of his Father (verse 34).

39. On this point we can reread François Roustang, "Les moments de l'acte de foi et ses conditions de possibilité. Essai d'interprétation du dialogue avec la Samaritaine," *Recherches de sciences religieuses* 46, no. 3 (1958): 344–78, who clearly distinguished the moments of uncovering: the stated appearance (material water, Jesus's thirst), the denied appearance (the Samaritan woman's desire to no longer be thirsty, a desire for unreality), the exclusion of the appearance (exiting the denial, recognizing reality, not having a husband in reality signifies having had five), and finally, a position of truth. Which then opens to the disciples the definition of mission through the distinction between sowing (manifesting) and reaping (accepting the manifestation) (verses 34–38), or, in other words, the two phases of uncovering.

40. See above, chapter 2, n21, 384–85. William James, *Varieties of Religious Experience*, Lecture XVII (Gifford Lectures, 1902), in *Writings 1902–1910*, 399. See: "The pragmatic method . . . is to try to interpret each notion by tracing its respective practical consequences. What difference would it practically make to anyone, if that notion were true?" William James, *Pragmatism*, Lecture II (1907), in *Writings 1902–1910*, 506. And see: "*The true is the name of whatever proves itself to be good in the way of belief, and good, too, for definitive, assignable reasons.*" Ibid., 520, emphasis in the original.

41. James, *Pragmatism*, 509, 519, 523, 525, etc. "They *pay*" (581), at least those that "work best" (619; and 522, 588, etc.), being thus "true *instrumentally*" (512), ending up at truth as "a credit system" (Lecture VI, 576). At no moment does James seem to take stock of the strangeness and even the absurdity of the whole modern project of metaphysics. The most unconscious nihilism is the most triumphant.

42. James, *Varieties of Religious Experience*, Lecture XVII, 402. According to James, dogmatic theology is as "worthless" as what "metaphysics" (which?) claims to know of the divine attributes (401, see *Pragmatism*, Lecture III, 539–40). And of course, the Eucharist furnishes the 'usual suspect' (see *Pragmatism*, Lecture III, 524). The critique is indistinguishable from triviality.

43. James, *Pragmatism*, Lecture II, 518–19.

44. James, *Varieties of Religious Experience*, Lecture XX, 461. See: "God, if you will, produced immediate effects within the natural world" (Postscript, 467).

45. James, *Varieties of Religious Experience*, Lecture XX, 453. See: "[Universal conceptions] have, indeed, no meaning and no reality if they have no use." *Pragmatism*, Lecture VIII, 606. Here "to use" means not only, we hope, "to make use of," but also "to frequent," "to put into operation," and thus perhaps "to get used to," "to enter into"; it would then be instructive to take seriously this use of "to use," to the point, probably excessive, of leading it back to the Augustinian pair *uti/frui*.

46. William of Saint-Thierry, *De contemplando Deo*, §16, in *Deux traités de l'amour*, 50.

47. William of Saint-Thierry, ibid., §25, 60.

Chapter Ten

1. Gregory of Nyssa, *In Canticum Canticorum* I, PG 44, 765d; ed. H. Langerbeck, in W. Jaeger, ed., *Gregorii Nysseni Opera*, vol. 6 (Leiden: Brill, 1960), 17.

2. Respectively, Athenagoras of Athens, *Legatio* VII.2.14–15, and Ireneus, *Adversus Haereses*, IV.6.4, SC 100/2, 446; English translation in *Apostolic Fathers, with Justin Martyr and Irenaeus*, trans. Alexander Roberts and William H. Rambaut (Edinburgh: T&T Clark, 1868) 468. It is here that Duns Scotus proves his greatest relevance: "Theologia est de illo tanquam de subjecto quod soli Deo est notum naturaliter—Theology is about that which as a subject is naturally known by God alone." *Lectura*, Prologus, p. 1, q.2, n.73, *Opera omnia*, éd. C. Balic, v. 17, Civitas Vaticana, 1960, p. 28, and: "Theologia est de his quæ soli intellectui divino sunt naturaliter nota, igitur est de objecto soli Deo naturaliter noto : sed solus Deus est sibi soli naturaliter notus—Theology is about those things that are naturally understood by the divine intellect alone, therefore it is about an object known naturally to God alone" (*Ordinatio*, Prologus, p. 3, q.1, n.152, ibid., 1950, v. 1, p. 102).

3. Jean Vioulac rightly remarks that this "foolishness" (folly, *mōria*) must be distinguished from *mania*, delirium or dementia, which supposedly at times made one hear the voices of the gods, for the former is the "stupor, stupidity, folly" (*Apocalypse of Truth*, 58) of someone who, struck by stupor and powerlessness, "is dulled" or

"becomes insipid" (in the same way as salt goes flat, μωρανθῇ, loses taste, Matthew 5:13, Luke 14:34, if we accept the majority of manuscripts). God upsets the wisdom of the world by making it dull: "All wisdom of this world becomes dull before God" (1 Corinthians 3:19). A logic so dulled before another more powerful logic thus sees in it only paradoxes which it would like to dispel. And this is what modern *metaphysica* has ceaselessly attempted to do.

4. Aristotle, *Metaphysics* Z.1.1, 1028b3; trans. Richard Hope (Ann Arbor: University of Michigan Press, 1960), 131, modified. See my "La science toujours recherchée et toujours manquante," in Jean-Marc Narbonne and Luc Langlois, *La Métaphysique. Son histoire, sa critique, ses enjeux* (Paris and Quebec City: Presses de l'Université Laval, 1999).

5. *Kritik der reinen Vernunft,* or *Critique of Pure Reason,* AIII, 234, emphasis mine. For the interpretation of the phenomenon as an object (Kantian and otherwise), see Marion, *Negative Certainties,* V, §26, 162–73.

6. "In giving he is revealed; in revealing he gives." Bernard of Clairvaux, *Sermons sur le Cantique des Cantiques* VIII.5, SC 414, 180; English translation: *Works,* vol. 2: *Song of Songs I,* 48, modified (see chapter 2, above).

7. Jerome, *In epistulam ad Ephesios* II.4.21; PL 26, 507a; translation by Ronald E. Heine in *The Commentaries of Origen and Jerome on St. Paul's Epistle to the Ephesians* (Oxford: Oxford University Press, 2002), 188. Or Irenaeus: "*Veritas* ergo Dominus noster existens—Our Lord, therefore, being the *truth.*" *Adversus Haereses* III.5.1, ed. F. Sagnard, SC 34 [Paris/Lyon: Cerf/Vitte, 1952], 122 = PG 7, 858a; English translation in *Apostolic Fathers with Justin Martyr and Irenaeus,* 417.

8. Thomas Aquinas, *De Veritate,* q.1, a.1, *resp., Questiones disputatae* (Turin: Marietti, 1914), vol. 3, 3. See Kant, "*nämlich die Übereinstimmung der Erkenntnis mit ihrem Gegenstand*—namely that it is the agreement of cognition with its object," *Kritik der reinen Vernunft,* A58/B82, *Critique of Pure Reason,* 197; Husserl: "If we at first keep to the notion of truth just suggested, truth . . . is an identity: *the full correspondence of what is meant and what is given as such* (*die volle Übereinstimmung zwischen Gemeintem und Gegebenem als solchem*)." Investigation VI, §39, *Logische Untersuchungen II, 2* (Tübingen: Niemeyer, 1968), 123; in *Logical Investigations,* vol 2., trans. J. N. Findlay (London and New York: Routledge, 2001), 263, modified; and the discussion by Heidegger, *Being and Time,* §44, 197–211.

9. The objection that there must be a third term to sanction the *adaequatio* between thing and mind does not have the weight that is attributed to it. Spinoza is right in this case: the *adaequatio* is felt and imposes itself from itself, directly, as evidence. The *idea vera* does indeed appear as the *index sui et falsi,* it weighs down its own glory—all the more as it saturates the inevitable finitude of the mind that receives it.

10. Descartes, *Meditationes, Vae Responsiones,* AT VII, 368, 3–5; CSM 2, 253: "the impossibility of being grasped is contained in the formal idea of the infinite."

11. "Qui autem ad singulas ejus [Dei] perfectiones attendere, illasque non tam capere quam ab ipsis capi," *Meditationes, Iae Responsiones,* AT VII, 114, 5–11; see also 106, 23: "those who try to attain to God's individual perfections, not so much to take hold of them as to surrender to them." CSM 2, 82, modified; see also 77.

12. The objection according to which I could have voluntarily provoked error, misinterpretation, obscurity, etc., and that I am therefore responsible for withdrawal and non-manifestation does not hold; for, in this case, *I wanted* to provoke the withdrawal, and this move is all the more rational as it succeeds in fooling someone else; thus, at the second level, there is no withdrawal *for me*. If I fool another by concealing the thing (and withdrawal) from him, I am not fooling *myself*, I remain outside of the (non-)manifestation. I am fooling the other, but not myself: I remain unaffected.

13. This sheds light on the parable of the feast that the guests refused to attend: not only were they "busy" (Matthew 22:5) in their fields or their work, and "all excused themselves" (Luke 14:18); but they were able to go as far as "mistreating and killing" those who invited them (Matthew 22:6). Even discovering a treasure in a field could become an ordeal, as in order to buy the field and receive the treasure, it is necessary to sell everything. Few do, still fewer "in a burst of joy, ἀπὸ τῆς χαρᾶς, *prae gaudio*" (Matthew 13:44). One must never underestimate the risk and the danger there is in receiving, often greater than the difficulty of giving.

14. See Heidegger, *Zeit und Sein* (1962) (*Zur Sache des Denkens*, Tübingen: Klostermann, 1969, reprinted in GA 14); English translation, *On Time and Being* (New York: Harper & Row, 1972). See also *Die onto-theologische Verfassung der Metaphysik* (1957) (*Identität und Differenz*, reprinted in GA 11); English translation, "The Onto-theo-logical Constitution of Metaphysics," in *Identity and Difference,* 42–74, trans. Joan Stambaugh (New York: Harper & Row, 1969). On the emergence of this question, see my study, Jean-Luc Marion, "Remarques sur le rôle de la donation (*Gegebenheit*) dans la première pensée de Heidegger," in *Figures de phénoménologie,* 45–58. On the theme of the withdrawal of the *es gibt* in general, see Marion, *Being Given,* §3 [27ff], and *Negative Certainties,* §20 [120ff].

15. [Translators' note: These two uses of "there is" were originally in English.]

16. That is, to knot, intertwine, scramble, clutter, ensnare, confound, and finally (in the logical sense) to contradict itself, to fall into contradiction. *Implicare* here most closely means "to complicate."

17. Augustine: "Quid ergo dicamus, fratres, de Deo? Si enim quod vis dicere, si cepisti, non est Deus: si comprehendere potuisti, aliud pro Deo comprehendisti. Si quasi comprehendere potuisti, cogitatione tua te decepisti. Hoc ergo non est, si comprehendisti: si autem hoc est, non comprehendisti.—So, brothers, what can we say about God? For if you have grasped what you want to say, it is not God. If you have been able to comprehend it, you have comprehended something else instead of God. If it seems you have been able to comprehend it, you have deceived yourself

through your thoughts. So he is not this, if you have comprehended it; but if he is this, you have not comprehended it." Sermon 52, PL 38, 360; translation by Mark DelCogliano, in *The Cambridge Edition of Early Christian Writings*, ed. Andrew Radde-Gallwitz (Cambridge: Cambridge University Press, 2017), 1: 309–10. See *In the Self's Place*, §44, 289ff. Let us note that it is not a question of (not) knowing God, but only of (not) comprehending (*comprehendere, comprehensibilis*) him; and comprehending implies reaching the adequate concept of an object. This essential distinction is found explicitly in Descartes and Kant, but many contemporary discussions are unaware of this.

18. See below, chapters 13–14.

19. See again *Confessions* X.23.34, BA 14, 202, and *In the Self's Place*, §§17–20, 108ff.

20. See chapter 2 above, and Marion, *Being Given*, IV, §§21–23, 199ff, which completes and corrects "The Saturated Phenomenon," which was first published in *Phénoménologie et théologie,* ed. Jean-François Courtine (Paris: Critérion, 1992) and reprinted in *The Theological Turn*, then reproduced in *The Visible and the Revealed*, 18–48.

21. I am extending here the indications sketched out in Marion, *Being Given*, IV, §24, 234, and in Marion, *In Excess*, I §5, 23ff.

22. See Mark 7:7. More than the storm itself, the fishermen were afraid of the miracle that ended it (Mark 4:39–41); the women who came to the tomb were afraid of the Resurrection (Mark 16:8). Likewise, during the arrest in Gethsemane, the guards "fell to the ground" when Jesus responded to them, "I am, ἐγώ εἰμι," which is to say that he was manifest as such.

23. Thus a theological difficulty recalls, confirms, and intensifies the philosophical difficulty of fixing a signification to proper names in general, and to "essentially occasional expressions." See Edmund Husserl, Investigation I, §26, in *Logical Investigations,* vol. 1, trans. J. N. Findlay (New York: Routledge, 2001), 217–21.

24. On this episode, see a more complete commentary in "They Recognized Him and He Became Invisible to Them," in *Believing in Order to See*, 136–43.

25. John 20:14, 16. We can remark that Mary Magdalene "turns" two times. The first time (ἐστράφη) in v. 14, when, after having said to the angels that she "does not know, οὐκ οἶδα" where the body of Jesus is found, she turns to see (θεωρεῖ) the one who is standing behind her, but again without "knowing, οὐκ ᾔδει, that it was Jesus": thus an intuition without signification. The second time, after hearing Jesus name her by *her* name ("Mary!" v. 16), she understands who it is and returns to him the corresponding signification: "Rabboni, my good master!" Why say again here that she "turned, στραφεῖσα" (v. 16)? Perhaps to mark that, this time, it is her mind that changes and returns, in short, that is converted to the signification coming from *elsewhere*. So she understands what she sees after receiving the correct signification and believing it. See also Jean Grosjean, *L'Ironie christique,* 257ff.

26. See below, chapter 13, relating Matthew 10:26, Mark 4:22, Luke 8:17.

27. This *anthrakia* is without doubt related to the other brazier, set up in the court of the house of Caiaphas, where "the disciple" had entered with Peter (John 18:18, the only other occurrence of the term in the New Testament). Peter finds himself thus confronted with his betrayal, facing the Resurrected One, whom he had denied in front of a similar fire; we can better understand the dialogue that will follow (John 21:15–17). Thus it may be that the "I am not, Οὐκ εἰμί," of denial is turned back in the "It is the Lord!" (John 18:18 and 21:7)

28. I refer here to Marion, *Being Given*, V, §22, "The Paradox and the Witness," 216, and to chapter 2 above.

29. Karl Barth, *Kirchliche Dogmatik*, I/1, 115; English translation: *Church Dogmatics*, I.1, 112.

30. To transform a (seemingly) saturated phenomenon into a common law phenomenon is the method of every detective, above all of Sherlock Holmes: "This process," he says in laying out his method, "starts upon the supposition that, when you have eliminated all which is impossible, then whatever remains, however improbable, must be truth. It may well be that several explanations remain, in which case one tries test after test until one or other of them has a convincing amount of support." Sir Arthur Conan Doyle, *The Adventure of the Blanched Soldier*, in *The Complete Novels and Stories* (New York: Bantam Classics, 2003), vol. 2, 556. Clearly, Sherlock Holmes runs up against the same difficulty as Hume: how to distinguish between the impossible and the improbable, and even how to define the impossible? A good *Christian* exegete should thus define himself as an anti–Sherlock Holmes, as one who knows how to recognize the impossible in the improbable, at least when he *sees* the signification of this impossible. Like Chesterton's Father Brown.

31. Matthew 27:54: ἰδόντες; Mark 15:40 and Luke 23:47: ἰδών. And it is obviously not by chance that the death of Christ, a saturated phenomenon visible only to the witnesses who receive it without pretending to understand it, leads Luke to the only use of *theōria* in the entire New Testament: "and the group of those who were gathered to see this sight (θεωρίαν), seeing (θεωρήσαντες) these events (γενόμενα), returned home beating their breasts." (Luke 23:48).

32. Matthew 26:64; Mark 14:62; Luke 22:69–70, all citing Psalms 110:1 and Deuteronomy 7:13.

33. Sören Kierkegaard, *Philosophical Fragments*, in *Samlede Værker*, 2nd ed. (Copenhagen: Gyldendal, 1920–36), vol. 4, 230; English translation: *Philosophical Fragments and Johannes Climacus*, in *Kierkegaard's Writings*, vol. 7, trans. Howard V. Hong and Edna Hong (Princeton, NJ: Princeton University Press, 1985), 37. Similarly, see Jocelyn Benoist: "The fault [i.e., of the gratuitous paradox] thus lies in the gratuity and not in the paradox. There are real paradoxes, or in any case paradoxes that *reveal* the real. The paradox could even eminently take on this function. Still, it must be motivated, and there is nothing to gain in cultivating it for its own

sake." "Après l'infinitude," in Emmanuel Alloa and Élie During, eds., *Choses en soi. Métaphysique du réalisme*, 57, emphasis added.

34. "Nihil est tam incredibile, quod non dicendo fiat probabile; nihil tam horridum, tam incultum, quod non splendescat oratione et tanquam excolatur. . . . Quae, quia sunt admirabilia contraque opinionem omnium, ab ipsis etiam paradoxa appellantur, tentare volui, possentne proferri in lucem, ... et ita dici ut probarentur, an alia quædam esset erudita, alia popularis oratio." Cicero, *Paradoxa ad Brutum*, 3 and 4, *Opera omnia*, ed. C. F. A. Nobbe (Leipzig and London: Tachnitti, 1850), 1278.

35. See Elena Esposito, "Paradoxien als Unterscheidungen von Unterscheidungen," in Hans Ulrich Grumbrecht and K. Ludwig Pfeiffer, eds., *Paradoxien, Dissonanzen, Zusammenbrüche. Situationen offener Epistemologie* (Frankfurt: Suhrkamp, 1999), 35–57.

36. Wittgenstein, *Tractatus Logico-Philosophicus*, 6.123, in *Schriften* I:31; rev. ed., trans. David Pears and Brian McGuinness, 75. Wittgenstein continues, "There is not, as Russell thought, a special law of contradiction for each 'type'; one law is enough, since it is not applied to itself." This concerns the solution of Russell, *On Denoting* (1905), reprinted in *Logic and Knowledge: Essays 1901–1950*, ed. R. C. Marsh (London: Allen & Unwin, 1956), or of Quine, *The Ways of Paradox and Other Essays* (New York, Random House, 1966): in all these cases, the paradox is dissolved, by a logical distinction (for example that of classes), to relate it back to common rationality.

37. Useful indications are found in Fritz. B. Simon, "Paradoxien in der Psychologie," in Paul Geyer and Roland Hagenbüchel, eds., *Das Paradox*, 71–88.

38. Wittgenstein, *Philosophische Untersuchungen*, §95, 339; *Philosophical Investigations*, trans. G. E. M. Anscombe, P. M. S. Hacker, and Joachim Schulte, 4th ed. (Oxford: Blackwell, 2009), 49.

39. Henri de Lubac, *Paradoxes, Œuvres Complètes*, vol. 31 (Paris: Cerf, 1999), 13 and 72, respectively (reprinted in *Nouveaux paradoxes*, Paris, 1959); English translation in *Paradoxes of Faith*, trans. Ernest Beaumont (San Francisco: Ignatius Press, 1987), 11 and 10. See Simone Weil: "The contradictions the mind comes up against—these are the only realities: they are the criterion of the real," in *Gravity and Grace*, trans. Arthur Wills (New York: Van Rees Press, 1952), 151. See W. Joest, "Zur Frage des Paradoxon in der Theologie," in W. Joest and W. Pannenberg, eds., *Dogma und Denkstrukturen* (Göttingen: Vandenhoeck & Ruprecht, 1963), 16–51.

40. See, among others, *Brief über den "Humanismus,"* GA 9 (Frankfurt: V. Klostermann, 1976), 338–39 and 351ff, English translation: *Basic Writings*, rev. ed., David Farrell Krell (San Francisco: HarperCollins, 1993), 242, 253–54. See the parallels and a diagnostic in Marion, *God Without Being* (Chicago: University of Chicago Press, 2012), 108–56. Karl Barth's refutation of the claim issued by Friedrich Gogarten ("Karl Barths dogmatik," *Theologische Runschau*, 1929) of preparing the

knowledge of God by "*eine existenzial-philosophische Begründung der Theologie*—a grounding of theology in existentialist philosophy" (*Kirchliche Dogmatik*, I/1, 129–36; *Church Dogmatics*, I.1, 125–31) can be also applied against Heidegger.

41. Barth, *Kirchliche Dogmatik*, I/1, 121–22; *Church Dogmatics*, I.1, 118. See also: "Offenbarung wird von keinem Anderen her wirklich und wahr, weder in sich noch für uns. Sie ist es in sich und für uns durch sich selber—Revelation is not made real and true by anything else, whether in itself or for us. Both in itself and for us it is real and true through itself," 322 (= 305). Or: "*Gott* offenbart sich. Er offenbart sich *durch sich selbst*. Er offenbart *sich selbst*—God reveals Himself. He reveals Himself through Himself. He reveals Himself," 312 (= 296).

42. On the distinction between the phenomenon (or phenomena) of *revelation* and *Revelation* as a phenomenon, see Marion, *Being Given*, IV, §24, p. 234ff.

43. Thus the marginal and commendable attempt of Louis Charlier to think of revelation in terms of a "given" ("The revealed is above all a given reality," *Essai sur le problème théologique* [Thuillies: Ramgal, 1938], 50), would have accomplished a genuine breakthrough had this "given" itself only been questioned and defined, instead of being immediately reduced to the brute factuality of a given problem or given consciousness, or even a given sensation. But, as givenness is not seriously considered here as such, one quickly falls into a false alternative of "given-revealed-knowledge" and of "given-revealed-reality," where each term derives from the most common and the most fragile metaphysics. What does "reality" mean? What does "knowledge" mean? And what relation do they have with "revealed," a term itself left completely undetermined, except by its epistemological interpretation and its modern philosophical origin?

Chapter Eleven

1. *The Odyssey*, XVI.161, trans. Rodney Merrill (Ann Arbor: University of Michigan Press, 2002), 294, modified.

2. *The Iliad of Homer*, trans. Richmond Lattimore (Chicago: University of Chicago Press, 1961), 140 and 144.

3. *The Iliad*, XX.79ff, Lattimore, 406.

4. *The Odyssey*, VI.322–31, Merrill, 165.

5. *The Odyssey*, VIII.18–20, 14, Merrill, 175, modified. In the same way, Athena makes Odysseus "much more handsome, κάλλος πολύ," before Penelope, who is still reluctant to recognize him (XXIII.156; Merrill, 630, modified). The same is true of Laertus (XXIV.367–74). In general, the gods confer a divine radiance on their protégés (XVI.211ff, Merrill, 295.), "ὀλβιόδαιμον, blessed by god," *The Iliad*, III.182, Lattimore, 105.

6. *The Odyssey*, VIII.7ff, Merrill, 175.

7. *The Odyssey*, VIII.193–94, Merrill, 180. Athena, "closely resembling the daughter of Dymas (εἰδομένη κούρῃ ναυσικλειτοῖο Δύμαντος), renowned for his galleys," had already awoken Nausicaa (VI.22, Merrill, 157).

8. *The Odyssey*, XXII.256, 273, and 297, Merrill, 375–76; and XXIV.540–48, Merrill, 405.

9. *The Odyssey*, XXII.204–10, Merrill, 374; we find the same borrowed identity in XXIV.502–5 and 546ff, Merrill, 404–5. Unlike Odysseus, who "recognizes her, ὀϊόμενος" (XXII.210, Merrill, 374), the suitors only see Mentor. See Jenny Clay, "*Demas* and *Aude:* The Nature of Divine Transformation in Homer," *Hermes* 102, no. 2 (1974): 129–36.

10. *The Odyssey*, XXII.239, Merrill, 375.

11. *The Odyssey*, VII.200–206, Merrill, 171 modified.

12. Longinus, *On the Sublime* IX.7, ed. D. A. Russell (Oxford: Clarendon Press, 1964), 10.

13. W. E. Otto, *Die Götter Griechenlands. Das Bild des Göttlichen im Spiegel des griechischen Geistes* (Frankfurt: Verlag G. Schutte-Bulmke, 1929); translated by Moses Hadas as *The Homeric Gods: The Spiritual Significance of Greek Religion* (London: Thames & Hudson, 1954), 189 and 200. Hans Urs von Balthasar follows this line himself when he cites the response of Alkínoös without taking account of Odysseus's reply. *The Glory of the Lord: A Theological Aesthetics*, vol. 4, *The Realm of Metaphysics in Antiquity,* trans. Brian McNeil, C.R.V., Andrew Louth, John Saward, Rowan Williams, and Oliver Davies (San Francisco: Ignatius Press, 1989), 75.

14. *The Odyssey*, VII.207–9, Merrill, 171.

15. *The Odyssey*, XIII.312–13, Merrill, 257.

16. Emily Kearns concludes without hesitation that, "when they do appear to humans the Gods very often put on a human disguise." "The Gods in the Homeric Epic," in Robert Fowler, ed., *The Cambridge Companion to Homer* (Cambridge: Cambridge University Press, 2004), 59–73; here 65.

17. Ovid, *Metamorphoses*, translation in two volumes by Frank Justus Miller, revised by G. P. Goold. Loeb Classical Library 42–43 (Cambridge, MA: Harvard University Press, 1916); *Metamorphoses* VIII.626, in vol. 1, 448–49; II.425, in vol. 1, 90–91; "*Protinus induitur faciem cultumque Dianæ*—he put on the features and dress of Diana" (and "laughed to hear [Callisto], rejoicing to be prized more highly than himself—*Ridit et audit / Et sibi præferri gaudet*," v. 429–30); II.848–50, vol. 1, 118–19: "Ille pater rectorque deum, cui dextra trisulcis / Ignibus armata est, qui nutu concutit orbem / Induitur faciem tauri—And so the father and ruler of the gods, who wields in his right hand the three-forked lightning, whose nod shakes the world, laid aside his royal majesty along with his sceptre, and took upon him the form of a bull." Ovid seems to me a good guide, for with the divergence from Greek to Latin, from myth to mythology, from trust to distance, he does not contradict Homer, nor reject him, but, in a certain way, reassesses him by marking out the implicit rules, while Virgil remains undecided between the two.

18. *Metamorphoses*, XV.680, vol. 2, 412–13: "Quisquis adest, visum veneratur numen—All in the divine presence worshipped the god as they were bid."

19. *Metamorphoses* XV.743, vol. 2, 416–17.

20. *Metamorphoses* XV.844, vol. 2, 424–25, translation modified.

21. Léon Brunschvicg, "Mathématique et métaphysique chez Descartes," *Revue de métaphysique et de morale* 34 (1927): 277–324, here at 323, was the inventor of this misappropriation of Descartes's formula, "Ut comœdi moniti, ne in fronte appareat pudor, personam induunt; sic ego, hoc mundi theatrum conscensurus, in quo hactenus spectator existiti, larvatus prodeo" (AT X, 213). For the real meaning of this text, see Vincent Carraud and Gilles Olivo, eds., *Descartes. Études du bon sens. La Recherche de la Vérité. Et autres textes de jeunesse (1616–1631)* (Paris: PUF, 2013), 64–65 and 81ff. The gods too venture out onto the stage of our world by concealing their face with a mask, but a face that, without a doubt, *they do not have*.

22. *Metamorphoses* III.275, 277, 281ff, respectively ("Multi / Nomine divorum thalamos iniere pudicos"), III.283ff ("Det pignus amoris,/ Si modo verus is est"), III.293ff ("Qualem Saturnia, dixit, / Te solet amplecti, Veneris cum fœdus initis / Da mihi te talem"), and III.308ff; translations in vol. 1, 144–47, modified. (Note that the god, foreseeing disaster, tries to restrain his lightning to a *levius fulmen*, "lighter bolt," what the other gods call his *tela seconda*, "secondary armory," thunderbolts nonlethal to them, but still too violent for a mortal, III.305–6.) Jean-Pierre Vernant perfectly underlines this unbearable excess of the presence of the god when it immediately bursts forth: "The body of the god burns with a radiance so intense that no human eye can bear it. Its splendor is blinding.... The paradox of the divine body is that, in order to appear to mortals, it must cease to be itself, and clothe itself in mist. "Corps obscur, corps éclatant," in Charles Malamoud and Jean-Pierre Vernant, eds., *Le Temps de la réflexion*, VII, *Corps des dieux* (Paris: Gallimard, 1986), 19–58, here 39, to be complemented by Christoph Markschies, *Gottes Körper. Jüdische, christliche und pagane Gottesvorstellungen in der Antike* (Munich: C. H. Beck, 2016).

23. See Aeschylus, *The Eumenides*. This is what Charles Picard has shown in a seminal article that opened the question of the *apparent* visibility of Greek gods, "θεοὶ ἐπιφανεῖς. Note sur les apparitions des dieux," in S. P. Lampros, *Xenia. Hommage international à l'Université nationale de Grèce à l'occasion du soixante-quinzième anniversaire de sa fondation (1837–1912)* (Athens: Hestia, 1912), 67–84. And he insisted on the fact that, if Greece tried to attain the god(s) as such, it ultimately confirmed the impossibility of doing so, by an "equivalence, which recalled the old religions of Egypt and Israel" (84; see also 36 and 72 n3.).

24. Even though Jean-Pierre Vernant attributed to them a "super-body," an "immortal body, unaware of hunger," and whose blood "is not really blood," in his "Corps obscur" (35 and 27), in contrast to the obscure body of mortals, he still

cannot help asking, before the gaping equivocity of the term: "why do we speak of the body of gods?" (41) His response—which is perfectly correct—amounts to their maintaining a hypothetical body because they at least keep a name; but it is precisely this name that *gives* them nothing more than their "super-body." And besides, do they really have a name that would allow them to say "I"?

25. Hans Urs von Balthasar, *Glory of the Lord,* vol. 4, 75. The same expression is found in Jean-Pierre Vernant, speaking of "an incognito of two kinds": first, because the god conceals his appearance among men under a mist; second, because he wants only "to make himself visible under the figure of *a* body, rather than of *his* body." "Corps obscur," 37. See B. C. Dietrich's insistence on the gods manifesting themselves "anonymously, that is without specific identity," "visible only in temporal identity," "generally anonymous and unidentified in their interventions," "which did not involve any actual *parousia* or presence." He concludes: "The idea of divine epiphany as a means of religious revelation was out of the ordinary for Homer and consequently less familiar to the mainstream official Greek religion." Dietrich, "Divine Epiphanies in Homer," *Numen: International Review for the History of Religion* 30, no. 1 (1983): 53–79, citing 60, 66, 59, 62, and 67, respectively.

26. I can only approve of Renée Piettre's analysis here: "Unless we choose to take the frequently-stated resemblance of the gods with men at its word (and then it is a question of *eidos* and *demas*), but in that case, which is the model for the other? When is there disguise, and when does the god show himself? And what about birds and meteors? The body of the gods is communicated to men as a *non-body, a body that has always vanished, or the body of another*." *Le Corps des dieux dans les épiphanies divines en Grèce ancienne* (Lille: ANRT, 1996), 153, emphasis added.

27. For the definition of the idol, see Marion, *God Without Being,* chap. 1, §§1–7, and Marion, *Being Given,* §23. Here an incidental remark of Marcel Détienne takes on all its importance: "the monuments of Greek art are *tautegorical* of religious thought." Preface to the French translation of Walter F. Otto, *Die Götter Griechenlands,* by Claude-Nicolas Grimbert and Armel Morgant, *Les Dieux de la Grèce. La figure du divin au miroir de l'esprit grec* (Paris: Payot 1981), 7–19, here 16. Jean-Pierre Vernant perfectly explains this concealment by appearing itself: "The invisible body in its radiance, the face which shirks the face-to-face: even more than revealing the being of the god, the apparition conceals it under the disguises of a 'seeming' that is adapted to the weak vision of humans." "Corps obscur," 40. Hence Piettre's conclusion: "These images communicate to us simultaneously the greatness of the god and the prohibition, the impossibility of the face-to-face encounter. . . . And so it must be said that the Greeks never, or almost never, see their gods." Thus the Greek religion "has little to do with a face-to-face encounter with the gods." *Le Corps des dieux,* 625 and 631.

28. Ovid, *Metamorphoses* III, respectively: v. 416–18, vol. 1, 152–53; v. 424ff and v. 433–34, vol. 1, 154–55; v. 461 and v. 466, vol. 1, 156–57, all translations modified.

The aporia of Narcissus in the visible order corresponds exactly to the aporia of Echo in the order of speech. For according to Ovid, as a result of Juno's vengeance, Echo could no longer either speak first or refrain from responding; she had only the ability to repeat ("nec reticere loquenti, / Nec prior ipsa loqui didicit," *Metamorphoses*, III.357ff), and to repeat only the last words of a sentence spoken by someone else ("Reddere de multis ut verba novissima posset," v. 361), at the risk of never being able to speak her exact feelings. And so, just as the visible left to Narcissus shows nothing and reflects his empty image, the speech left to Echo is empty resonation; she re-sounds, the resounding Echo ("resonabilis Echo," v. 358).

29. Gerhard von Rad, *Theologie des Alten Testaments* (Munich: C. Kaiser, 1957); translated by D. M. G. Stalker as *Old Testament Theology*, vol. 1, *The Theology of Israel's Historical Traditions* (New York: Harper & Row, 1962), 214. This does not rule out the fact that other religions had also realized the invisibility in principle of a supreme God. See Hubert Schrade, *Der verborgene Gott. Gottesbild und Gottesvorstellung in Israël und im alten Orient* (Stuttgart: W. Kohlhammer Verlag, 1949), especially "Des Gottes verborgene Gestalt" (128ff). Certainly we could recognize not only Yahweh, but indeed Amon, as "both a form and without a form, possible to look at and impossible to look at" (129). Yet there remain essential differences from Exodus: first of all Moses is able to serve as an exception to the prohibition and impossibility; and above all Yahweh speaks and "his voice creates a face-to-face meeting (*die Stimme schafft ein Gegenüber*)," (135). The prohibition (known by Homer and the Egyptians alike) is thus inverted into the opening of a face-to-face meeting, and thus a possibility for a face-to-face encounter *by the translation of* the invisibility that has become manifest.

30. Confirmed by the fact that "[Aaron] should not come at any time into the Holy place before the veil of the mercy seat, which is on the ark: he might die, for I appear in the cloud above the mercy seat" (Leviticus 16:2). "But they shall not go in to look when the holy things are covered: they will die" (Numbers 4:20). This also defines the New Testament's point of departure: "God, no one has ever seen" (John 1:18); see also, "You have never heard his voice, nor seen his form, *eidos*, nor do you have his *logos* abiding within you" (John 5:37–38).

31. The majority of modern translations, by an understandable simplification, omit the original "saw"; however, the Greek maintains it: "And all the people saw (ἑώρα) the voice, the lightning, the voice of the trumpet and the mountain smoking" (LXX, Exodus 20:18). We must preserve the welcome approximation of a vision of sounds and light, which are certainly not seen in the literal sense, but which *make seen*, so to speak, the invisibility of God who manifests himself by the word, by the dictum of the Ten Words (34:10–27), and thus gives the Covenant. We can also think of a formula by Paul Claudel: "what I will call a *voice that sees*, a voice that does not cease testifying, knowing, and praying with the very words that God has imbued in our hearts and mouths," from "Discours de réception à l'Académie

française," in *Œuvres en prose,* ed. Jacques Petit and Charles Galpérine (Paris: Gallimard, Pléiade, 1965), 636. Not only does the eye listen, but the voice that speaks (and hears) in turn sees in its own way. And so the distinction between partial epiphanies (by the intermediary of natural phenomena) and total epiphanies (in a body) introduced by Elpidius Pax, O. F. M., *Epiphaneia. Ein religiongeschichtlicher Beitrag zur biblischen Theologie* (Munich: Karl Zinc, 1955), loses much of its pertinence.

32. See Alfons Deißler, who emphasizes that it is first an "experience of hearing (*Hörerfahrung*)." "Gottes Selbstoffenbarung im Alten Testament," in Johannes von Feiner and Magnus Löhrer, eds., *Mysterium Salutis. Grundriß Hilsgeschichtlicher Dogmatik* (Zürich and Bern: Benzinger Verlag, 1967), especially 227ff.

33. The LXX translates it σεαυτόν/αὐτὸς, the Vulgate *te/tu ipse,* and the *Bible de Jérusalem* translates it "moi-même, toi-même." The *Bibel* of Luther transcribes it with the literal term: "face": "Er sprach: Mein *Angesicht* soll vorangehen; damit will ich dich leiten" (leaving an ambiguity concerning this self without a visible face). The King James sees the paradox: "My presence shall go *with thee*" and "thy presence," while Lemaître de Sacy successively uses both possibilities: "Si j'ai trouvé grâce devant vous, faites voir votre *visage*" (Exodus 33:13), then "Si vous marchez *vous-même* devant nous" (Exodus 33:15).

34. Here, "without drinking or eating," while Moses, Aaron, Nadab, Abihu, and the seventy elders who went up the mountain "were able to contemplate God. . . . They ate and drank" (Exodus 24:11)?

35. Hans Urs von Balthasar, *The Glory of the Lord,* vol. 6, *Theology: The Old Covenant,* trans. Brian McNeil and Erasmo Leiva-Merikakis (San Francisco: Ignatius Press, 1991), 47.

36. According to Franz Dirlmeier, this is a striking contrast from the pagan gods, for whom "there is a friendly attitude towards humans—but no love (*Liebe*) of the god towards human beings, nor any love (*Liebe*) of human beings for the god." "Theophilia-philotheia," *Philologus: Zeitschrift für das klassische Altertum* 90, no. 1–2 (1935): 57–77, 176–93; here 191. He attributes the construction of *theophilia* instead to Cyril of Alexandria.

37. This explains why the people who "do not believe" Moses, nor listen to his word, take exactly as their argument "the Lord did not appear to you (לא נראה אליך), οὐκ ὦπταί" (Exodus 4:1). Hence the divine response: signs that are perfectly obvious and visible (the serpent/staff, the leprous or healthy hand, Aaron's eloquence), but which, once again, are only able to convince those who listen to what they see. The manifestation is strictly not enough to accomplish the uncovering of revelation. What manifests this revelation is precisely the uncovering of God's very invisibility.

38. Cf. Franz Rosenzweig, *The Star of Redemption,* 178.

39. Paul Beauchamp, *L'Un et l'autre Testament,* vol. 2, *Accomplir les Écritures* (Paris: Seuil, 1990), 46. Indeed, the whole history of Isaac (given freely by Yahweh to Abraham, unjustly claimed by Abraham as his own, rightly reclaimed by Yahweh,

finally given back to Yahweh by Abraham, then given back infinitely by Yahweh to Abraham's faith in the vast number of descendants) can be read as a definitive passage from vision to promise. On the nonsacrifice of Isaac, see my suggestions in Marion, *Negative Certainties*, §21.

40. Walther Zimmerli insists on this fact: "Ein bisher Unbennanter tritt aus seiner Unbekanntheit heraus, indem er sich in seinem Eigennamen erkennbar und nennbar macht—A hitherto unnamed person emerges from his anonymity, in that he makes himself knowable and nameable in his own name." "Ich bin Yahve," in W. Foxwell Albright et al., eds., *Geschichte und Altes Testament. Festschrift Albrecht Alt zum 70, Beiträge zur historischen Theologie*, vol. 16 (Tübingen: J. B. Mohr Siebeck, 1953), 33; as does Dießler, "Gottes Selbstoffenbarung im Alten Testament," 243ff. The name makes itself known precisely as always unknown and all the more unknowable in itself.

41. For example, Exodus 8:6, 9:14, 20:5; Isaiah 41:4, 43:10, 46:5, 48:12, 51:12; 54:5.

42. Rosenzweig, *Star of Redemption*, 178. See Paul Beauchamp: "It is enough to say that God himself names himself as subject. He does not say, 'I am God,' but 'I am.' He has 'I' as his proper name. Hosea indicates how clearly this value is perceived. 'You will be called "Not-my-people" says Yahweh, for you are not a people and for you 'I-am-not.'" *L'Un et l'autre Testament* 1: 284; see also Deißler, "Gottes Selbstoffenbarung im Alten Testament," 247.

Chapter Twelve

1. In this lesson of biblical hermeneutics, it must be understood that Jesus was not choosing from *among* the Scriptures the passages that concern him, but that he was explaining *all of them as* referring to him. For "these are the ones which bear witness about me (περὶ ἐμοῦ)" (John 5:39). One must not, however, imagine that the Scriptures in themselves proclaimed their accomplishment by Jesus, as if, in the explicit text, a subtext was already saying something other than the literal sense. In fact, the Scriptures say what they say and do not predict anything by themselves; but, after they are fulfilled by Christ, they uncover to the one who rereads them that they have said more than they said. They then deliver, suddenly and retrospectively, a meaning that could not be conceived before their performance by Christ. "The story told here is no mere illustration of the ancient words: it is the reality to which they were referring. In those words alone [the reality] could not be recognized, but they now attain their full meaning through the event in which they become reality"; it is because of "some passages that are still, as it were, 'stray'" that we can, with Christ, "provide these 'waiting' words with their 'owner.'" Joseph Ratzinger, *Jesus of Nazareth: The Infancy Narratives,* trans. Philip J. Whitmore (New York: Image, 2012), 15 and 17, modified. See the excellent analyses in Marius Reiser, *Bibelkritik und Auslegung der Heiligen Schrift: Beiträge zur Geschichte der biblischen Exegese und Hermeneutik* (Tübingen: J. C. B. Mohr

Siebeck, 2007), 328; in Richard Swinburne, *Revelation*, esp. 161ff and 188ff; and in John Barton: "The question is not 'How is the New Testament related to the Old as a piece of literature?', but 'Does Jesus fulfil the hopes of Israel (for which the Old Testament is simply *evidence*),' not 'Is the meaning of a *piece of writing* capable of reacting on the meaning of both earlier and later pieces?', but 'How is the meaning of a *man* (Jesus) related to his cultural and religious background and the history of his people? Who is Jesus; in what context are we to understand him, does he create his own context?'" "Judaism and Christianity: Promise and Fulfilment," *Theology* 79, no. 671 (1976): 260–66, here 263. Irenaeus already said it perfectly: "Omnis enim prophetia, priusquam habeat effectum, ænigmata et ambiguitates sunt hominibus; cum autem venerit tempus et evenerit quod prophetatum est, tunc prophetiæ habent liquidam et certam expositionem—For every prophecy, before its fulfilment, is to men [full of] enigmas and ambiguities. But when the time has arrived, and the prediction has come to pass, then the prophecies have a clear and certain exposition." *Adversus Hæreses* IV.26.1, PG 7, 1052–53; English translation in *Apostolic Fathers*, Schaff, ed., 496. Or Origen: "It must also be said that the inspiration of the prophetic words and the spiritual character of the Law of Moses shone forth with the coming of Jesus (ἐπιδημήσατος Ἰησοῦ). For it was not at all possible (οὐ πάνυ δυνατὸν) to bring forward clear arguments concerning the inspiration of the ancient Scriptures before the coming of Christ (πρὸ τῆς ἐπιδημίας τοῦ Χριστοῦ); but the coming of Jesus (Ἰησοῦ ἐπιδημία) led those who might have suspected the Law and the Prophets not to be divine to the clear conviction that they were composed by heavenly grace.... And the light contained by the Law of Moses, formerly hidden (ἐναποκεκρυμμένον) under the veil, has shone with the coming of Jesus who has parted the veil." *Traité des Principes,* IV.1.6, ed. H. Crouzel and M. Simonetti, SC 268 (Paris: Cerf, 1980), 280–84; English translation *Origen: On First Principles. A Reader's Edition*, trans. John Behr (Oxford: Oxford University Press, 2019), 241–42, modified. And again, "One might reply to this, however, that before the coming of Christ, the Law and the prophets did not contain the proclamation which belongs to the definition of the gospel since he who explained the mysteries in them had not yet come (μηδέπω ἐληλυθότος). But since the Savior has come, and has accomplished (ἐπιδημήσας καὶ ... ποιήσας) the incarnation of the gospel, he has, by the Gospel, made all things like a gospel (πάντα ὡσεὶ εὐαγγέλιον πεποίηκεν)." *Commentaire sur saint Jean,* I.33, ed. C. Blanc, SC 120 (Paris: Cerf, 1966), 76–78; English translation *Origen: Commentary on the Gospel of John, Books 1–10,* trans. Ronald E. Heine (Washington, DC: Catholic University of America Press, 1989), 40, modified. It is thus not the prophecies that show the figure of Christ in advance, it is the figure in action of Christ in person who retrospectively confers on the texts a meaning more radical than the one that, of themselves and up until then, they set forth. Péguy explains this perfectly: "In a word, the passage from the prophecies to the Gospels is in the order of the human and of the event, not in the order of the logical, mathematical, physical, supposedly scientific deduction, not in the order of modern determinism. In a word, *the Gospels are not the prophecies put into the past tense*, transferred just as they are, transferred in whole, transferred in bulk from the future into the past through the ministration of the present. It was not only necessary, it was not enough that Jesus made them pass, transferred them, in time, made them past. It was also necessary that he realized them, that he accomplished them." *Note conjointe sur M. Descartes et la philosophie cartésienne, Œuvres en prose complétes,* 3: 1403, Péguy's emphasis; English translation: *Notes on Bergson and Descartes: Philosophy, Christianity, and Modernity in Contestation*, trans. Bruce K. Ward (Eugene, OR: Cascade Books, 2019), 168. It is only here that the discussion with contemporary Judaism can have meaning and find a place. For we can also say, like Emmanuel Levinas, "The Old Testament does not prefigure the New: it receives its interpretation from the Talmud." *Difficult Freedom: Essays on Judaism,* trans. Seán Hand (Baltimore: John Hopkins University Press, 1997), 161. The question consists in deciding if the biblical text is interpreted from a subtext that we decipher in it, or through an event outside the text that is added to it and that comes to it from elsewhere. Either the *verba* produce their final word [*verbe*], or the Word [*Verbe*] makes the *verba* finally legible. And the New Testament re-figures the Old starting from Christ, because Christ, as charity in act, does not figure anything further, but accomplishes in person what is outlined in figures. "Everything which does not lead to charity is figurative." Blaise Pascal, *Pensées,* L 270, trans. Krailsheimer, 83.

2. Irenaeus, *Adversus Hæreses,* IV.34.1, PG 7, 1083; translation *Apostolic Fathers,* 511, modified. And Augustine: "Quid est ergo Deus meus? . . . numquam novus, numquam vetus, innovans omnia—Who then are you, my God? . . . never new, never old, making everything new." *Confessiones* I. 4.4, BA 13, 278; English translation Henry Chadwick (Oxford: Oxford University Press, 1991), 4, 5. See Joseph Ratzinger: Jesus did not bring anything that was not already stated about God in the Scriptures, for "He brought God" himself. Joseph Ratzinger, *Jesus of Nazareth: From the Baptism in the Jordan to the Transfiguration*, trans. Adrian J. Walker (New York: Doubleday, 2007), 115 modified, see also 121. And we find this already in Yves Congar: "Jesus Christ himself left nothing in writing, but he bequeathed to us Christianity" and "Scripture is (only) a sign of the active presence of the uncreated word, a demand for his coming, a kind of institutionalized Word that calls for the Event." Yves Congar, *Tradition and Traditions*, 350 and 405–6.

3. On these points, I follow Louis Bouyer, *Musterion. Du mystère à la mystique* (Paris: O.E.I.L., 1986).

4. Certainly, all *are able to not* receive—which, because we have tended to gloss over the problem at least since the Reformation, is different from saying that all *are*

not able to receive it, as if the un-covering were refused to all and reserved for only some. But God does not hold any of his gifts in reserve and gives to everyone; it is precisely for this reason, the excess of the gift, that everyone is *able to not want* to receive what is nevertheless given without reserve to everyone.

5. Wittgenstein: "The Old Testament seen as the body without its head; the New T.: the head; the Epistles of Paul: the crown . . . but I do not necessarily think of a head as having a *crown*." *Culture and Value*, 40–40e, modified.

6. See also 1 Corinthians 1:19, which cites Isaiah 29:14, LXX: "I will destroy the wisdom of the wise and I will close (conceal, κρύψω) the knowledge of those who know."

7. Athenagoras of Athens, *Legatio* VII.2, ed. W. R. Schoedel, 14.

8. Already we find: "The depth of the riches and the wisdom and the knowledge of God" (Romans 11:33).

9. We have seen that "to you it has been given to know the *mystēria* of the Kingdom of God" (Matthew 13:11 and Luke 8:10).

10. See Romans 8:4–9; and: "For you did not receive the spirit of slavery to fall back into fear, but you have received the spirit of sonship (πνεῦμα υἱοθεσίας). When we cry, 'Abba! Father!' it is the Spirit himself bearing witness with our spirit that we are sons of God, and if sons, then heirs, heirs of God and co-heirs with Christ, provided we suffer with him in order that we may also be glorified with him" (8:15–17).

11. See Marion, *Being Given*, III, §13, 123–25. Edgar Haulotte speaks, in passing but rightly, of a "broad and undecided use" of Revelation. "Le 'texte' du Testament Nouveau: écriture et lecture d'une 'Révélation,'" in D. Coppieters de Gibson, *La Révélation* (Brussels: Facultés universitaires Saint-Louis, 1977), 132.

12. Aristotle, *Metaphysics* Z.1, 1028b 2–4; cf. trans. Richard Hope, 131, modified. H. Greeven remarks that what is involved here is a "technical term for philosophical investigation," which "characterizes the human philosophical quest or inquiry in general." "ζητέω," in *Theologisches Wörterbuch zum Neuen Testament,* ed. G. Kittel, vol. 2 (Stuttgart: Kohlhammer, 1935), s.v., 894.

13. In this way it is possible to relate this "stupidity" to the "stubborn and rebellious son who does not obey his father and mother and will not listen to them when they discipline him" (Deuteronomy 21:18), or to the "foolish (נבל) people and without wisdom (32:28) "(חכם לא). See Walter Bauer and Frederick William Danker, *A Greek-English Lexicon of the New Testament and Other Early Christian Literature* (Chicago: University of Chicago Press, 2000), 663.

14. Parmenides, *Fragment 6*, in Hermann Diels and Walter Kranz, eds., *Die Fragmente der Vorsokratiker* (Zurich and Berlin: Weidmann, 1966), vol. 1, 232. I follow here the translation of Jean Beaufret, *Parménide. Le Poème* (Paris: PUF, 1984), 80; see also the translation and commentary by Marcel Conche, *Parménide. Le Poème: Fragments* (Paris: PUF, 1986), 100–114.

15. Aristotle: "it is true to affirm that no *ousia* is relative (τῶν πρὸς τι)." *Categories* VII, 8b21, in *Categories: On Interpretation: Prior Analytics,* trans. H. P. Cooke and Hugh Tredennick, Loeb Classical Library 325 (Cambridge, MA: Harvard University Press, 1938), 63.

16. This is confirmed by the *hapax* of *ousia* in Luke 15:13 (see my commentary in Marion, *God Without Being,* 98, and for all these texts, chap. 3, §4, 83–102.).

17. These four dimensions of hyperbolic charity therefore define a cross: for the one who enters into "hyperbolic charity" finds himself attached to the crossing of the four, in their midst, as on a cross. Like the Jesuit in the opening scene of *The Satin Slipper*: "True, also, I am fastened to the cross, but my cross is no longer fast to anything. 'Tis flooding in the sea, / the free sea, away to the point where the limit [*horos*] of the known sky melts / and is equally distant from this old world, which I have left / and from the other world the new." Paul Claudel, *The Satin Slipper, or The Worst Is Not the Surest,* trans. Rev. John O'Connor (New York: Sheed & Ward, 1945), 2.

18. Here I follow the Nestle-Aland *Novum Testamentum Graece,* 25th ed. (Stuttgart: Deutsches Bibelgesellschaft, 1963), *ad. loc.,* critical apparatus, 511. This reading finds confirmation in "the manifestation (ἐπιφάνειαν) of the glory of our great God and savior, Jesus Christ" (Titus 2:13).

19. See Hebrews 9:28. See also Romans 8:3; 2 Corinthians 5:21; and John 8:46 and 7:26.

20. See also "ἀποκαλύψει Ἰησοῦ Χριστοῦ" (1 Peter 1:7, and 4:13).

21. Following Eduard Norden (*Agnostos Theos. Untersuchungen zur Formgeschichte religiöser Rede* [Leipzig: Teubner, 1913], 37–55) and, among others, Hans Conzelmann ("The Address of Paul on the Areopagus," in Leander E. Keck and J. Louis Martyn, eds., *Studies in Luke—Acts* [London: SPCK, 1968]). The speech in Acts 17 has for a long time been considered as a pure literary reconstruction by Luke, modeled after the speeches of Thucydides, not on any historical grounds but only on its probability as presumed by the author. This reading goes so far as to see in it, as Martin Dibelius writes, "a *hellenistic* speech about the true knowledge of God," "Stoic rather than Christian," not only in contradiction with the authentic teaching of Paul, but even forming a corpus "foreign to the entire New Testament." "Paulus auf dem Aeropag" (1929), translation in *Studies in the Acts of the Apostles,* trans. Mary Ling, ed. Heinrich Green (London: SCM Press, 1956), 57, 63, 71. However, the evolution of studies, remarkably synthesized by Daniel Marguerat in *Les Actes des Apôtres (13–28)* (Geneva: Labor & Fides, 2015), 148–67, reaches an entirely different conclusion today: Luke deliberately uses a "procedure of systematic ambivalence" (153) to attain "maximal inculturation" (159), allowing for the presentation of the evangelical call in terms that are intelligible to the culture of pagans; but this "remarkable exercise in semantic ambivalence" (163) remains in agreement

446 Notes to Chapter Twelve

with Paul's other discourses (in particular Romans 1:18–32). And it is in the open space of inculturation that the journey of anamorphosis that I wish to identify plays out.

22. The only difference from Romans 1, where men know God without recognizing him (and without giving thanks, v. 19–21), is that here the Greeks honor (Acts 17:22) without knowing (v. 23 and 30); but in both cases, they are exposed to the same judgment (Romans 2:1 and Acts 17:31).

23. The ambiguity of the terms *metanoein, pistis,* and *ex enos,* which can be understood both in a Greek and a Jewish way, is extended in the use of *kosmos* (rather than "earth and heaven") and of *chronos* (rather than *kairos*). This deliberate ambiguity of Luke could result in a possible misinterpretation by listeners who may have included in the number of "foreign gods" *anastasis* itself, taken as the proper name of a goddess ("he was proclaiming Jesus and *anastasis,*"17:18).

24. Saint Jerome had already remarked, "Now the inscription of the altar was not precisely as Paul claimed: 'to an unknown God,' but 'to the gods of Asia and of Europe and of Africa, to the unknown and foreign gods.' But because Paul did not require several unknown gods but only one unknown God, he used the word in the singular, in order to teach that God is his own, whom the Athenians had designated on the inscription of the altar; and that by knowing him in the right way, they ought to worship him whom they were venerating in ignorance and whom they were unable not to know." *In epistulam ad Titum* 1.12, PL 26, 572–74; translated by Thomas P. Scheck in *St. Jerome's Commentaries on Galatians, Titus, and Philemon* (Notre Dame, IN: University of Notre Dame Press, 2010), 305–6. See Marguerat, *Les Actes des Apôtres,* 161.

25. [Translators' note: "God is near you, he is with you, he is within you." Seneca, *Ad Lucilium Epistulae Morales* XLI.1, translated by Richard M. Gummere in *Epistles,* vol. 1, Loeb Classical Library 75 (Cambridge, MA: Harvard University Press, 1917), 272–73.] Cicero relates the two: "modo enim menti tribuit omnem divinitatem, modo mundum ipsum deum dicit esse [sc. Aristotle], modo alium quendam præficit mundo—At one moment he [Aristotle] assigns divinity exclusively to the intellect, at another he says that the world itself is a god, then again he puts some other being over the world." *De Natura deorum* I.12, 33; translated by H. Rackham in *On the Nature of the Gods. Academics,* Loeb Classical Library 268 (Cambridge, MA: Harvard University Press, 1933), 34–35. Or "sic hominem ad duas res, ut ait Aristoteles, ad intelligendum et ad agendum esse natum quasi mortalem deum—so man, as Aristotle observes, is born for two purposes, thought and action: he is as it were a mortal God." *De finibus* II.13, 40; translated by H. Rackham in *On Ends,* Loeb Classical Library 40 (Cambridge, MA: Harvard University Press, 1914), 126–27. Iamblichus attributes to him the same thesis: "ὁ νοῦς γὰρ ἡμῶν ὁ θεός." *Protreptikus* 8, cited in W. D. Ross, ed., *Aristotelis Fragmenta Selecta* (Oxford: Oxford

University Press, 1987), 42. But Aristotle himself explicitly supports it: "If the intellect, then, is something divine (εἰ δὴ θεῖον ὁ νοῦς) compared with the human being, the life in accordance with it will also be divine compared with human life." *Nicomachean Ethics* X.7, 1177b30; trans. Roger Crisp (Cambridge: Cambridge University Press, 2000), 194.

26. The hypothesis (coming from Theodore of Mopsuestia) that the formula of Acts 17:28a quotes Epimenides the Cretan has been abandoned today (see Marguerat, *Les Actes des Apôtres*, 161, despite its mention in Titus 1:12, and Pierre Courcelle, "Un vers d'Épiménide dans le 'discours sur l'Aréopage,'" *Revue des études grecques*, no. 76 [1963]: 404–13), if only because it is a reconstitution from Syriac. See Marc Delage, "Résonances grecques dans le discours de saint Paul à Athènes," *Bulletin de l'Association Guillaume Budé*, no. 3 (1956): 49–69. On the other hand, Acts 17:28b does cite a verse of Aratus, *Phaenomena*: "Let Zeus be foremost. . . . By Zeus alone we live, / born as his children too" *Phaenomena*, trans. Aaron Poochigian (Baltimore: Johns Hopkins University Press, 2010), v. 1–51, taken up widely by Cicero, Caesar, Cleanthe, Aristobulus, etc. See Marguerat, *Les Actes des apôtres*, 161; and Lucien Legrand, "Aratos est-il aussi parmi les prophètes?," in *La Vie et la parole. De l'Ancien et du Nouveau Testament. Études d'exégèse et d'herméneutique bibliques offerts à Pierre Grelot* (Paris: Desclée, 1987).

27. Augustine describes this alternative as a reversal—God is not in me because, more originarily, I am in him: "Then, since I, too, am, why do I ask for you to come to me, when I would have no being at all unless you were within me. . . I would therefore not be at all, if you were not in me. Or rather, I would not be, if I were not in you—Quoniam itaque et ego sum, quid peto, ut venias in me, qui non essem, nisi esses in me? . . . non ergo essem, nisi esses in me, an potius non essem, nisi essem in te." *Confessiones* I.2.2, BA 13, 274–76; English translation Chadwick, 4, modified.

28. The universality that the "gospel" of Paul provokes (Romans 2:16) therefore cannot be abstracted from the judgment that it provokes, separating those who accomplish anamorphosis from those who refuse it. This division is accomplished for exactly the same reasons that the difference disappears between Jews and Greeks, free men and slaves, male and female, etc. Nothing makes a difference anymore except the reference to Christ. Troels Engberg-Pedersen emphasizes this perfectly: "Badiou can see Paul's religious stance as universalist, because he fails to consider its content and sees it only in formal terms, as the articulation of a relationship between an event and a subjective stance toward that event. This is the position of the militant truth claim." "Paul and Universalism," in Ward Blanton and Hent de Vries, *Paul and the Philosophers* (New York: Fordham University Press, 2013), 87–104, here 102.

Chapter Thirteen

1. But in different contexts: if Mark 4:22 and Luke 8:17 state this principle in connection with the parable of the lamp, Matthew 10:26 mentions it in the middle of a variety of scattered passages, without precise attribution and with a general scope. Thus Joachim Jeremias was not wrong to see that these "generalizing conclusions" are not "in any way calling in question the authenticity of these logia themselves" but only suggesting "that they were not originally uttered as the conclusion of a parable." *The Parables of Jesus*, trans. S. H. Hooke (London: SCM Press, 1963), 110. Hermann Dieckmann, speaking here of a "terminus technicus" (*De Revelatione Christiana*, §195, 135), arrives at the same abstraction, which also does not recognize the reasons why "the saying stresses that concealment is temporary and that its ultimate purpose is disclosure." John R. Donahue and Daniel J. Harrington, *The Gospel of Mark* (Collegeville, MN: Liturgical Press, 2002), 150.

2. Other texts confirm these three formulas: "Nothing covered up (συγκεκαλυμμένον) will not be uncovered (ἀποκαλυφθήσεται), nor hidden (κρυπτὸν) that will be known. Therefore, whatever you have said in the dark will be heard in the light, and whatever you have whispered behind closed doors will be proclaimed from the housetops" (Luke 12:2–3), here again without any specific editorial context (except perhaps the denunciation of the hypocrisy of the Pharisees). But "the sign that contradicts the *logos* (σημεῖον ἀντιλεγόμενον)" is given "so that the thoughts of many hearts may be uncovered (ἀποκαλυφθῶσιν)" (Luke 2:34–35). In the same way, "The work of each will become manifest (φανερὸν). The Day of [the Lord] will bring it to light (δηλώσει) because it will be uncovered (ἀποκαλύπτεται) in the fire and the fire will test the quality of each person's work" (1 Corinthians 3:13, see also 4:5); and again, "And now you know what is held back (τὸ κατέχον), so that he is only uncovered (ἀποκαλυφθῆναι) in his time. For already the *mystērion* of lawlessness (μυστήριον τῆς ἀνομίας) is at work. Let only the one who holds [him] back make way. And then the Lawless one (ὁ ἄνομος) will be revealed, whom the Lord Jesus 'will destroy with the breath of his mouth' (Isaiah 11:15) and overcome by the manifestation of his presence (ἐπιφανείᾳ τῆς παρουσίας)" (2 Thessalonians 2:6–8). Despite appearances, John 7:4 develops an inverse problematic (see below, chapter 14).

3. Edmund Husserl, *Ideas I*, §24, 43, modified.

4. Martin Heidegger, *Being and Time*, §7, 32.

5. See Matthew 26:55; see John 7:26 (παρρησίᾳ λαλεῖ, *palam loquitur*), Luke 19:47–48, or Acts 26:26 ("for this was not done in a little corner, οὐ γάρ ἐστιν ἐν γωνίᾳ"). See Jean-Luc Marion, "Remarques sur quelques remarques," *Recherches de Science Religieuse* 99 (2011): 489–98.

6. Like the irony of Socrates, which is staged at will in the public square, the very same irony is applied by "his brothers" to Christ: "His brothers said to him, 'Leave here and go to Judea, that your disciples may see the works that you are doing; for

no one acts in secret (ἐν κρυπτῷ), if he wants to be made known (ζητεῖ αὐτὸς ἐν παρρησίᾳ εἶναι). Since you are doing these things, make yourself manifest to the public (φανέρωσον σεαυτὸν τῷ κόσμῳ).' For even his brothers did not believe in him. Jesus said to them, 'My time is not yet here, but your time is always ripe'" (John 7:3–6).

7. Joachim Jeremias, *New Testament Theology: The Proclamation of Jesus*, trans. John Bowen (New York: Charles Scribner's Sons, 1971), 36. The introductory *amen, amen* belongs to Christ alone, and especially in John (1:51; 3:3, 5, and 11; 5:19, 24–25; 6:26, 32, 47, 53; 8:34, 51, 58; 10:1, 7; 12:24; 13:16, 20, 21, 38; 14:12; 16:20, 23; 21:18). The responsive *amen*, by contrast, belongs to the faithful. See Romans 1:25, 11:36; 15:33, 16:27; Galatians 1:5, 6:18; Ephesians 3:21, Philippians 4:20, etc.

8. Jeremais, *New Testament Theology*, respectively 20 and 30, modified. Similarly: "For Mark, speech in parables is the required form of preaching." Élian Cuvellier, *Le concept de παραβολή dans le second évangile. Son arrière-plan littéraire, sa signification dans le cadre de la rédaction marcienne, son utilisation dans la tradition de Jésus* (Paris: Gabalda, 1993), 205 and 119, respectively, referring to Daniel Marguerat, "La parabole, de Jésus aux évangiles," in Jean Delorme, ed., *Les Paraboles évangéliques. Perspectives nouvelles* (Paris: Cerf, 1988), 61–88.

9. Jeremias, *Theology of the New Testament*, 29, to the point of being able "to hear [in it] again his authentic voice"—his "*ipsissima vox*." Jeremais, *Parables of Jesus*, 17, see also 103, in agreement for once with Adolph Jülicher, "Parables," in T. K. Cheyne and J. Sutherland Black, eds., *Encyclopædia Biblica*, vol. 3 (London: Macmillan, 1902), 3563–67, reprinted in Wolfgang Harnisch, ed., *Gleichnisse Jesu. Positionen der Auslegung von Jülicher bis zur Formgeschichte* (Darmstadt: Wissenschaftliche Buchgesellschaft, 1982), 1–10. This literary form is not found in the Greek or Latin classics, as Cuvellier's very detailed analysis confirms (Cuvellier, chap. 1–4), which also highlights, among other things, that the Hebrew משל, *mashal,* covers a much wider and more equivocal field than that of the parable (fable, proverb, maxim, sentence, pamphlet, song, poem, etc.), and that, in most cases, the Septuagint does not translate the one by the other (see Cuvellier, 50 ff).

10. On the relationship between the first and last parables, see Ivan Almeida, "La structure conversationnelle de la parabole," in Jean Delorme, ed., *Parole, figure, parabole* (Lyon: Presses universitaires de Lyon, 1987), 61–84, 78 ff.

11. We can consider that the final parables of Matthew (the thief in the night, 23:43–44; the faithful watchman, 24:45–51; and the wise and foolish virgins, 25:1–13; and even that of the talents, 25:14–29) do nothing but insist on the unique problematic of that initial parable of the sower. Likewise, other parables in Matthew (of the weeds, 13:24–30; the mustard seed, 13:31–32; the leaven, 13:33) can be seen as variations on this initial parable of the sower. In any case, Jeremias is right: "In the sayings of Jesus which deal with the *basileia*, a great many phrases appear which

have *no parallels* (not even secular ones) in the language of Jesus' contemporaries." *New Testament Theology*, 32.

12. Jeremias discusses these possible translations and prefers "unless" for μήποτε, starting from the Aramaic *dilema* (*Parables of Jesus*, 17).

13. Recorded in the *Gospel of Thomas*, §82; ed. Simon Gathercole (Leiden: Brill, 2014), 508; Origen, *Homily on Jeremiah* XXVII.3, PG 13; translation by John Clark Smith in *Homilies on Jeremiah, Homily on 1 Kings 28* (Washington, DC: Catholic University of America Press, 1998), 254–55; and Didymus, *In Ps. 88*, 8, PG 39, 1498d, cited by Joachim Jeremias, *Unknown Sayings of Jesus*, trans. Reginald H. Fuller (New York: Macmillan, 1957), 54, with the comment, "It is dangerous to be near Jesus" (56).

14. Aristotle, *Rhetoric* II.20, 1393b3–7. The parable thus belongs under the relation of similitude, in the same register as *metaphora*. *Rhetoric* III.4, 1406b20–23.

15. Here Adolph Jülicher's demonstration of the difference between the original parables of Jesus and their redactional interpretations by the Synoptics as allegories takes on its full importance. *Die Gleichnisreden Jesu*, 2 vols. (1888–89). See his article "Parables" in *Encyclopædia Biblica*, 2–10. The weakness of this achievement lay in the impoverishment of their meaning to the level of moral evidence that liberal Protestant theology could accept. But Jeremias confirms the primary result. *Parables of Jesus*, 66–89.

16. Against the paraenetic interpretation of the parable of the sower (according to which God in his foolish generosity would sow precisely where nothing can grow, in the brambles, among the rocks, and on the path), the most striking example comes from the reconstitution of the Palestinian method of sowing (according to Jeremias): one first sows, then tills the soil, because the brambles and the path will disappear, and the rocks will only appear once the earth is broken. In fact, the sower sows as he should.

17. I follow Cuvellier's analysis (*Le Concept de παραβολη dans le second évangile*, 46). It is only in the late eschatological and intertestamental literature that "the illustrative discourse that designates *parable* gradually becomes an enigmatic discourse, then a downright obscure and mysterious one, conveying divine secrets concerning the end of time" (79). Thus the parable is already similar to the enigma (Sirach 1:25 and 47:15; Proverbs 1:6; even Daniel 12:8). In this sense, in the way Jesus uses them, "[t]his sense of the divineness of the natural order is the major premiss of all the parables." C. H. Dodd, *The Parables of the Kingdom* (London and New York: Charles Scribner's Sons, 1961), 10, by which it is distinguished from the Jewish apocalypse, which is itself strongly allegorical (80).

18. Aristotle, *Rhetoric* III.19. Polybius distinguishes, in the same account of a naval combat, "*ex hypobolēs*, to appear suddenly," "*parabalein*, to board," and "*ek parabolēs . . . promachomenoi*, deck-to-deck combat." *The Histories*, vol 4, *Books*

9–15, trans. W. R. Paton, rev. F. W. Walbank, Christian Habicht. Loeb Classical Library 159 (Cambridge, MA: Harvard University Press, 2011), 522–23. The adjective *parabolos,* usually rendered "bold" or "combative," means literally "the one who makes contact with the enemy," "who engages as closely as possible."

19. We must also not grant too much importance to the question of titles claimed *or not* by Jesus (Son of Man, Messiah, Son of God, Son of David, Elijah, etc.). First, because his listeners and his public no doubt lacked a clear or univocal understanding of them. Next, and above all, because in any case Jesus did not understand them in the same way as the crowds. We can observe as well that the explanations of the parable reserved for those nearby (for example Mark 4:13–20), not only do not explain everything (i.e., who is the sower, what does the Word say?), but also do not suffice to deliver the disciples from the misunderstanding of the crowd *exō* (outside). The prohibition made to the disciples and to the beneficiaries of healing (incidentally, in vain) against publicly sharing what they had seen and received is explained by this: they could not yet know what they were saying, because they were still reasoning according to the old and outdated significations; only the cross and the Resurrection, interpreted according to the Spirit, will *later* permit them to say what they have seen and heard according to an adequate signification. See Cuvellier, "La rift permet de déchiffrer les paraboles," *Le Concept de παραβολή dans le second évangile,* 267. If the Synoptics thus simultaneously report the parables and their explanations, it is not in order to abolish the former by the latter (by allegorical interpretation), but to *reinforce* the *mystērion* of the former by the detail of the latter: the parable always requires one to make a choice in the face of the *possibility* (or impossibility) of a signification that is as yet incomprehensible.

20. [Translators' note: Where *écouter* means to listen and *comprendre* means to understand or grasp, *entendre* is used both for hearing and understanding. The author here is deliberately playing on both meanings.]

21. Cuvellier: "In Mark [the concept of the *parabolē*] designates a means of communication that leaves a *space* for the human responsibility of listening." *Le Concept de παραβολή dans le second évangile,* 223, emphasis added. Indeed, the parable gives a certain access to the signification, but not possession of it: "through the discourse in parables, man can understand [*entendre*] the Word (Mark 4:33), but he does not possess an *objective* knowledge. This word requires an explanation that will be called into question: it will make man understand that the Word runs counter to his deepest desires" (121, emphasis added). See C. H. Dodd, who emphasizes that this parable develops an "argument, in that it entitles the hearer to a judgment," since "the way to an interpretation lies through a judgment on the imagined situation, and not through the decoding of the various elements in the story." Dodd, *The Parables of the Kingdom,* 11, 12.

22. Daniel Marguerat aptly speaks of an "extravagance of the parable." "Jésus le poète, maître de sagesse. Une rhétorique de l'excès," in Andreas Dettwiller, ed., *Jésus de Nazareth. Études contemporaines* (Geneva: Labor & Fides, 2017), 147–72, here 152.

23. Here we must follow the decisive analysis of Jean-Louis Chrétien: "The word, whose end is to manifest, will, as a parable, be veiled, encrypted, covered, manifesting only under and through the secret. But what this encrypted word begins to say is its own cipher and its own destiny. . . . The frontier between within and without does not separate the initiated from the profane; it crosses, in and through the event of a crisis, the heart of each person facing Jesus. . . . The word of God advances into a space of deafness and of muteness, and not into a space that is all hearing. By his incarnation, he breaks a double silence, the human silence of sin and the divine silence of anger. In this first sense, revelation must by definition allow for blindness, this blindness which is directly contrary to it and which constitutes at the same time that which requires it. But it must allow for it in another sense as well: to the violence of this blindness that attacks it head-on and seeks to forbid it, it does not wish to respond by another violence, nor should it do so. It cannot be imposed on man, only proposed to him. . . . Revelation illuminates man in such a way that he can be blinded to this clarity." Jean-Louis Chrétien, *Lueur du secret* (Paris: L'Herne, 1985), 51, 53, 55, and 56, respectively.

24. See François Bovon: "When proper language is blocked, the parable is an indirect way"; for, in itself, the "figure of the suffering Son of Man is an incomprehensible and scandalous paradox, it can only be conveyed in an indirect and paradoxical fashion." "Parole d'Évangile, parabole du royaume," *Revue de Théologie et de Philosophie,* 122 (1990): 33–41; 122 and 239, respectively. This recourse to an "indirect discourse" exegetically reinforces the legitimacy of the "indirect Revelation" advanced by Pannenberg in dogmatics (see chapter 7 above).

25. Every parable provokes a crisis, and C. H. Dodd defines it as "a metaphor or a simile drawn from nature or common life, arresting the hearer by its vividness or strangeness, and leaving the mind in sufficient doubt about its precise application to tease it into active thought." Dodd, *The Parables of the Kingdom*, 5.

26. See the analysis of Michel Le Guern, which summarizes the decisive points: first the parable "serves to say the unsayable, that is, what escapes the intellect" (the missing signification); then, what it recounts, "the similar, is not of the order of the object, but of the event" and is not "presented as being, but as happening"; finally, it remains "totally paradoxical. But perhaps it is important to explain that we cannot really explain it." "Parabole, allégorie et métaphore," in Delorme, *Parole, figure, parabole,* 23–35; 31, 34, and 35, respectively.

27. Eberhart Jüngel, in the conclusion of his excellent synthesis on the evolution of the interpretation of parables in *Paulus und Jesus. Eine Untersuchung zur*

Präzisierung der Frage nach dem Ursprung der Christologie. Hermeneutische Untersuchungen zur Theologie 2 (Tübingen: J. C. B. Mohr, 1979), 87–139, cited following Harnisch, ed., *Gleichnisse Jesu*, 338.

28. I am preserving the literal translation of *blepete* as "look" (*regardez*), and not as "take care" (*prenez garde*), if only to respect the obvious reference to the verb *blepein* in Isaiah 6:9, LXX, cited in Mark 4:10 and Luke 9:2. Why weaken this significant allusion?

29. See above, chapter 11, n31, 439–40. In both cases, the senses are crossed and their difference rescinded before the phenomenon that saturates intuition in such a way that incomprehension, the deficit of signification, is imposed.

30. See the *ekstasis* and fear before the physical and spiritual healing of the paralytic, 5:26, or the daughter of Jairus, 8:56. The Transfiguration of course inspires the same fear (φοβεῖν, Matthew 17:7, Mark 9:6).

31. See also "the wise and the fools (ἀνοήτοις), both Greeks and barbarians" (Romans 1:14); "You senseless (ἀνόητοι) Galatians!" (Galatians 3:1).

32. Contrary to Mark 4:22: "Nothing, indeed, is hidden (κρυπτὸν) if not to be manifested (ἐὰν μὴ ἵνα φανερωθῇ), nothing secret (ἀπόκρυφον) that will not come to light (ἔλθη εἰς φανερόν)"; here it concerns the kingdom of God (4:11). The same for Luke 8:17: "There is nothing hidden (κρυπτὸν) that will not become manifest (φανερὸν), nor anything secret (ἀπόκρυφον) that will not become known and come to light (εἰς φανερὸν ἔλθη)"; it is clearly a question of "listening" (8:18). It is not by chance, therefore, if Matthew is also the only one to formulate the fullest version of the confession of Peter, which must be understood as the first instance of un-covering accomplished by one of the men to whom Jesus announced the coming of the Kingdom of God.

33. [Translators' note: A reference to Mallarmé's poem "Une dentelle s'abolit."]

34. See the analysis in Gérard Claudel, *La Confession de Pierre. Trajectoire d'une périscope évangélique* (Paris: Gabalda, 1988), 382, 386, and 387, which I will follow despite or because of its dry, laborious, and minimally theological approach.

35. "The great jubilation of Mt 11:27/Lk 10:22," Claudel, *La Confession de Pierre*, 330.

36. See Luke 10:22, which follows from the fact that "the Father and I, we are one" (John 10:30). By consequence, "all the things the Father has are mine (πάντα ὅσα ἔχει ὁ πατὴρ ἐμά ἐστιν)" (John 16:15); "All the things which are mine are yours, and all that are yours are mine (τὰ ἐμὰ πάντα σά ἐστιν καὶ τὰ σὰ ἐμά)" (John 17:10; literally also in Luke 15:31). The supposed incommunicability between the Synoptics and John, to whatever extent it still remains dogma for some, on these points appears fragile.

37. As Luke 6:20 confirms: "Happy are you poor, for the Kingdom of God is (ἐστὶν) yours (ὑμετέρα)" (in the present tense).

38. The name or nickname is already mentioned in 10:2: "Simon, called Peter." The family name *Bar Jonah* does not seem actually to go back to the prophet Jonah, but to Yohanan, John. English does not reflect the wordplay of Peter/rock, but it works as well in French (*pierre*) as in Greek (*petra*) and Aramaian (*kepha*), and can serve as a popular nickname, "*tête de pierre*, rocky." But henceforth it is the cornerstone evoked by Isaiah 51:1ff and by Psalm 118:12, applicable first to Christ (1 Corinthians 3:11), then, based on the "cornerstone" of Christ, to the "foundation of the Apostles and Prophets" (Ephesians 2:20), and therefore to the "foundation of my church in heaven" (16:19). This "foundation (θεμέλιον)" recalls the rock on which the *practicing* disciple builds his house (Luke 6:48). As for the debate about whether the power of the keys and the promise of indestructibility of the "church" (16:18) is attached to the function of Peter or to his individual person, it has no meaning unless we distinguish one from the other, which remains questionable.

39. Paradoxically, this is what even the most critical exegesis must concede, even reluctantly, before the Matthean confession of Peter: "there is without any doubt an authentic word underlying Matthew 16:18" (Claudel, 373).

Chapter Fourteen

1. To understand Jesus's reserve toward the effect of his own signs, there is no need to follow Bultmann in imagining a laborious and arbitrary reconstruction of John from a supposed "sign-source," subsequently corrected by a proto-Gnostic collection of apocalyptic discourses. The point here is that the signs themselves do not yet—if they ever will—allow un-covering (*apokalypsis*), even and especially if they clearly mark that the moment of un-covering (or its denial) has come, that the hour of the crisis is at hand.

2. See "truly" added to the titles applied to Jesus in Matthew (14:33, 27:54) and Mark (15:39), which confirm the use in John (4:42, 6:14, 7:26). But the real "truly, *alēthōs*" only occurs when Christ in person acknowledges it to the apostles: "For these words you gave me I have given them also, and they have received them, and they truly, *alēthōs*, knew that I came from you; and they have believed that you sent me" (John 17:8).

3. I rely here on Ignace de la Potterie, among others, who shifts the dialogue from its late sacramental interpretation toward the question of the Spirit; "'Naître de l'eau et de l'esprit.' Le texte baptismal de *Jn* 3,5," *Sciences ecclésiastiques* 14 (1962): 417–43, reprinted in Stanislas Lyonnet and Ignace de la Potterie, eds., *La vie selon l'Esprit. Condition du chrétien* (Paris, Cerf: 1965); see also Marinus de Jonge, "Nicodemus and Jesus: Some Observations on Misunderstanding and Understanding in the Fourth Gospel," *Bulletin of the John Rylands Library* 53, no. 2 (1971): 337–59, which describes precisely the gap between the stated significations and their misunderstanding: "Misunderstanding is not a matter of understanding incompletely or inaccurately, it reveals a fundamental lack of understanding" (359).

4. When Joseph of Arimathea arranges with Pilate to bury the body of Jesus, he is described as "a disciple of Jesus in secret for fear of the Jews" (John 19:38). Does this apply to Nicodemus, mentioned just afterward as "he who first came to him [Jesus] by night?" (19:39)?

5. Of course we find this temporal understanding in Galatians 4:9 (πάλιν ἄνωθεν, *iterum*); but it relates to "falling back into the slavery" of sin, and not to the nature of the Spirit. In John 19:11, Pilate's power comes to him "from above, ἄνωθεν" and clearly not "again." See de Jonge, "Nicodemus and Jesus," 347ff, and Herbert Leroy, *Rätsel und Mißverständnis: ein Beitrag zur Formgeschichte des Johannesevangeliums* (Bonn: Hanstein, 1968), 124–36. Marc Michel, "Nicodème ou le non-lieu de la vérité," *Revue des sciences religieuses* 55, no. 4 (1981), 227–36, flawlessly demonstrates that the "person and the work of Jesus surpass the theoretical knowledge of Nicodemus: to perceive them one must be situated *elsewhere*, this *other place* where knowledge proceeds from a seeing and a belonging. The error of Nicodemus was in not being *there where* one could see, and as a result, know; the place of the truth turns out to be a non-place" (232, emphasis added).

6. [Translators' note: This phrase originally in English.] This is how the Vulgate translates it ("*denuo*," in 3:3 and 7; "*iterato*" in 3:4), an unfortunate choice followed by Luther ("*vom neuen*" in 3:3 and 7; "*wiederum*" in 3:4) and the King James Version ("again" in 3:3 and 7; "the second time" in 3:4).

7. The Vulgate translates this literally: "Vado et venio ad vos (I go and I come to you)," as do Segond ("Je m'en vais et je viens à vous"), Osty ("et je viens vers vous"), Grosjean (*La Bible. Le Nouveau Testament* [Paris: Gallimard, Pléiade, 1971], 322), and Chouraqui ("je viens vers vous"). This is better than the quasi-contradiction of Luther ("Ich gehe hin und komme *wieder*"), the King James ("I go away and come *again* to you"), Lemaître de Sacy ("Je m'en vais et je *re*viens à vous"), *La Bible de Jérusalem* ("Je m'en vais et je *re*viendrai vers vous"), or La Bible ("Je pars et je vous reviens" [Paris: Bayard, 2001], 2042).

8. See Matthew 19:10 and 25; Mark 10:26; Luke 18:26–27. In this bewilderment, one can observe "Christian hermeneutics in its clash with Jewish hermeneutics." Michel, "Nicodème ou le non-lieu de la vérité," 231.

9. Jean Grosjean sees this perfectly (better than he formulates it): "This verse (3:12) which legitimates the indispensability of the Synoptics is at the same time the threshold that separates them from the Johannine text. The Synoptics reported above all the most urgent and perhaps the most accessible earthly side of the Christian life; but John is afraid that we will end up getting bogged down, and always evokes the heavenly source of this life. He thinks that the captivating relation between the Father and the Son will draw us bit by bit into the abyss above." Grosjean, *L'Ironie christique*, 65.

10. This allusion is confirmed by the phrase, "whoever believes in me will never thirst" (6:35).

11. Matthew 16:22. I have intentionally overtranslated "Ἴλεώς σοι," literally "that it be favorable to you," as if it were the developed formula: Ἴλεώς σοι ἔστω ὁ θεός. Bringing to light the pagan background gives Peter's reaction a blasphemous tone.

12. We find the same dilemma in Matthew 16:17. There is no reason to be surprised that the "flesh" of Christ is to be "eaten," but rather that "the flesh" of men nevertheless does not understand him. The former constitutes "life" (John 6:51ff) and, when the Word comes (1:14), he does not come from men ("what is born from the flesh is flesh"), nor from his will, but from the Spirit (". . . and what is born of the Spirit is spirit," 3:6). Once again, everything depends on the origin, on *from where* (*pothen*) the flesh comes. In a perfect confession, the un-covering (*apokalyptein*) results from the irruption of the Spirit into the "flesh" of men (Luke 10:21).

13. Ignatius of Antioch, *Letter to the Romans* II.3, translation following Pierre-Thomas Camelot in SC 10 (Paris: Cerf, 2007), 110.

14. The positive thesis, "Just as the Father knows me, I also know the Father" (John 10:15), is confirmed by contrast: "The one who hates me, also hates my Father. If I have not done among them works that no one else has done, they would not have sinned, but now (νῦν) they have [really] seen them and they have hated both me and my Father. . . ." (John 15:23–24, see 9:41 and Romans 1:20). And: "they will do this to you, because they have known neither the Father, nor me" (John 16:3).

15. Here again, we observe the striking similarity of this verse to Luke 15:31: "All that is mine is yours." The nearly word-for-word identity of these expressions does not, however, result in their equivalence: in Luke, the parable suggests what the anonymous "father" promises to the older "son" and hopes of him, while the latter does not understand it; in John, the known Son expresses what he understands perfectly, because he himself carries it out as perfectly as the recognized Father. The imagined directive is transformed into proven performance.

16. The same claim, of identifying oneself as the only one with no part in sin, is found in the negative in his response to the accusers of the adulterous woman: "Let the one without sin (ἀναμάρτητος) be the first to throw a stone at her" (John 8:7). As no one was without sin, no one cast the first stone.

17. Despite the opinion, in itself quite right, of Péguy: "For at forty one has known for five years who one is." *Note conjointe sur Descartes et la philosophie cartésienne, Œuvres en prose complètes*, 3:1284; *Notes on Bergson and Descartes*, 62. In fact, he knows what he is not and will never be (in terms of career, various achievements, etc.) but not yet who he is and will be in the end. Nevertheless, it is probably not by accident that Péguy's calculation almost corresponds to the age traditionally assigned to the death of Jesus.

18. The cry, Mark 15:34 and Luke 23:46; the blood, Luke 22:44; the prayers, Mark 13:45 and 39; and the supplications, Matthew 26:39 and 41.

19. This is how it was understood by Adolf Von Harnack, who here introduced a negation, as philologically arbitrary as it was theologically aberrant since it runs contrary to all the manuscripts: "He was *not* (οὐκ) heard." Nestle-Aland, *Novum*

Testamentum græce et latine. That God can do everything (Mark 14:26 and Luke 1:37) can certainly be understood as the possibility of dispensing with death (but in this case that amounts to privileging human will); but also as the power to freely give his life (John 10:17–18) in order to do, even here (in sin), the will of the Father.

20. Wolfhart Pannenberg, who privileges this verse, has quite rightly insisted on the paradox that Jesus's obedience to God (his submission to the will of the Father, his ignorance of the hour, his powerlessness to do anything on his own, etc.) constitutes precisely his qualification as Son, and thus his true divinity: "The distinction Jesus maintained between himself and the Father also belongs to the Divinity of God." *Grundzüge der Christologie* (Munich: Gütersloher Verlagshaus Gerd Mohn, 1964), translated by Lewis L. Wilkins and Duane A. Priebe as *Jesus: God and Man* (Philadelphia: Westminster Press, 1974), 159. In the same way, regarding Matthew 24:36 ("Concerning that day and hour no one knows, not even the angels of heaven, nor the Son, but the Father only") see Acts 1:7, "It is not for you to know times or seasons that the Father has fixed by his own authority," and concerning 1 Thessalonians 5:1, he adds that, "Precisely this fact of Jesus' perfection in dedication to God of the eschatological future reaches its consummation. This lack of knowledge is actually the condition of Jesus' unity with this God" (333–34). "Precisely *in* his particular humanity Jesus is the Son of God" (342).

21. Parallel to this, we must add at least the "voice" at the baptism that Christ received from John, which consecrates him as "my beloved Son, in whom I am well pleased" (Matthew 3:16, Mark 1:11, Luke 3:22). If, on the other hand, John 1:32–34 does not recount Jesus's baptism as such, it substitutes for it a teaching given directly to the Baptist, for "the Spirit came down like a dove," which recognizes Jesus as "the one who baptizes in the Holy Spirit" and thus indeed "the Son of God." Here the Trinitarian investiture occurs all at once as such (as everywhere in John), without the intermediary of the baptism with water.

22. See ἐξομολογοῦμαί in Matthew 11:25 and Luke 10:21.

23. The "now (νῦν)" anticipated in John 4:23 and 5:25 ("Amen, amen, I say to you, the hour is coming and is now here") is also realized *nyn* in John 13:31; 16:5; 17:7 and 13.

24. In contrast to its use in Romans 8:29: "those whom he [i.e., God] foreknew and identified to be in conformity with the icon of his Son, in order that he become the firstborn among many brothers." Or in Hebrews 10:1, "The shadow of the good things, σκιὰν τῶν μελλόντων ἀγαθῶ," is in opposition to "the true form (or image) of these realities, τὴν εἰκόνα τῶν πραγμάτων." In these two cases, we can speak of one *image*, because the two terms of the likeness offer one visibility.

25. The occurrences of the "icon of the Beast" (Revelation 13:14, 15:2, and 16:2) are related to the case of the coin, since it is the sign (χάραγμα) inscribed on the forehead or on the hand, without which "no one can buy or sell" (13:17). This character, in fact the number of the Devil, anticipates the bar code and bank card code, information that allows trade, but does not show anything, and certainly not a face, whether of man or God.

Chapter Fifteen

1. Barth, *Kirchliche Dogmatik*, I/1, 312; *Church Dogmatics* I.1, 296; see above, chapter 7.

2. *Kirchliche Dogmatik*, I/1, 313; *Church Dogmatics* I.1, 297. Thus, "the Bible answers in such a way that we have to reflect on the triunity of God." *Kirchliche Dogmatik*, I/1, 310; *Church Dogmatics*, 303.

3. *Kirchliche Dogmatik*, I/1, 329; *Church Dogmatics*, 312. See also: "our rule that material dogmatic statements about the immanent Trinity can and must be taken from definitions of the modes of being of God in revelation," ibid., 509; *Church Dogmatics*, 485.

4. *Kirchliche Dogmatik*, I/1, 318; *Church Dogmatics*, 301.

5. *Kirchliche Dogmatik*, I/1, 312; *Church Dogmatics*, 296.

6. Athanasius, *De Decretis Niceae Synodi* 26, PG 25, 465a, quoting Denys of Rome; translated by John Henry Newman and Archibald Robertson in *Athanasius: Select Writings and Letters*, ed. Philip Schaff and Henry Wallace (Grand Rapids, MI: Eerdmans, 1891), 168.

7. Erik Peterson, *Der Monotheismus als politisches Problem* (Leipzig: Jakob Hegner, 1935), and translated by Michael J. Hollerich as "Monotheism as a Political Problem: A Contribution to the History of Political Theology in the Roman Empire," in *Theological Tractates* (Stanford, CA: Stanford University Press, 2011), 68–105. This was indisputably the case in Western history during the Christian era, except that this shift came from the incorrect interpretation of the Trinity as the subordination of the Son to the Father, reducing the dignity of Christ to the level of a creature and allowing him to be identified with the sovereign. Arianism and all its modern substitutes (including the claim of the kings' *imperium* against pontifical authority, then of states against the Church) prove Peterson right, but confirm by contrast that the Trinity in the orthodox sense (precisely not the same as in the supposed "Greek theology") has always resisted this idolatrous drift.

8. See Marion *The Idol and Distance*, §11, and *God Without Being*, §§4–5; Didier Franck, *Nietzsche et l'ombre de Dieu* (Paris: PUF, 1998), chap. 6, and *Le nom et la chose. Langue et vérité chez Heidegger* (Paris: Vrin, 2018), XIX, §1, XX, §1; see also Christian Sommer, *Mythologie de l'événement. Heidegger avec Hölderlin* (Paris: PUF, 2017), chap. 3, 5–6.

9. Gregory Nazianzen makes use of these terms to turn Arian and Pneumatological objections against their authors within the Trinitarian discussion itself. *Theological Oration* XXXI.13; *On God and Christ*, 126–27.

10. On this point, I follow Rémi Brague, notably *Du Dieu des chrétiens et d'un ou deux autres* (Paris: Flammarion, 2008), translated by Paul Seaton as *On the God of the Christians (and on One or Two Others)* (South Bend, IN: St. Augustine's Press, 2013) and *Sur la religion* (Paris: Flammarion, 2018).

11. See Basil's correction of Aetius in *Contra Eunomium* I, 4: "We believe that the unbegotten (ἀγεννηγσία) is the essence (οὐσία) of the God of the universe" (PG 29, 512b); trans. Mark Delcogliano and Andrew Radde-Gallwitz, *St. Basil of Caesarea Against Eunomius* (Washington, DC: Catholic University of America Press, 2011), 89, modified; cf. Aetius's treatise, reproduced in *Panarion* II, PG 42, 536b-545a; translated by Frank Williams in *The Panarion of Epiphanius of Salamis Books II and III. De Fide* (Leiden: Brill, 2013), 522–27. See also Eunomius: "By saying 'Unbegotten' (ἀγέννητος), we do not imagine that we ought to honor God only in name, in conformity with human conceptuality (ἐπίνοια); rather we think we are truly repaying the most necessary debt of all by confessing that he is what he is (τοῦ εἶναι ὅ ἐστιν). . . . But God . . . both was and is Unbegotten (ἀγέννητος)." *Apologia,* §8, PG 30, 841c, and *Eunomius: The Extant Works*, trans. Richard Paul Vaggione (Oxford: Clarendon Press, 1987), 41–43, which lays out perfectly the metaphysical and idolatrous claim of the most significant Arianism.

12. See above, chapter 7, n11, page 412, on Calvin.

13. Aristotle, *Metaphysics* I.2, 1054a16 and following, translation by Hope, 205, modified; see also 1053b25, 204.

14. "Aus der Dreieinigkeitslehre, nach dem Buchstaben genommen, läßt sich schlechterdings nichts fürs Praktische machen, wenn man sie gleich zu verstehen glaubte, noch weniger aber wenn man inne wird, daß sie gar alle unsere Begriffe übersteigt.—Ob wir in der Gottheit drei oder zehn Personen zu verehren haben, wird der Lehrling mit gleicher Leichtigkeit aufs Wort annehmen, weil er von einem Gott in mehreren Personen (Hypostasen) gar keinen Begriff hat, noch mehr aber weil er aus dieser Verschiedenheit für seinen Lebenswandel gar keine verschiedene Regeln ziehen kann." Kant, *Streit der Fakultäten*, I, 1, appendix II, 1, Ak. A. VII, 38–39; English translation in *Religion and Rational Theology,* 264. See Ingeborg Schüßler, "Religion rationelle et philosophie révélée. L'interprétation pratico-morale de la Trinité chez Kant (avec un aperçu sur son dépassement chez Hegel et Schelling)," *Revue de théologie et de philosophie* 144 (2012): 47–72. Friedrich Schleiermacher remains in the same vein: "They [more poetic minds] show me the revelations through which they know such a God—one or more revelations, for I despise nothing in religion as much as numbers (*einen oder mehrere, ich verachte in der Religion nichts so sehr als die Zahl*)." *Über die Religion*, 70; *On Religion*, 135. See above, chapter 6, n25, page 405.

15. Paul Tillich corrects the misinterpretation well: "Trinitarian monotheism is not a matter of the number three. . . . The number three has no specific significance in itself. . . . The trinitarian problem has nothing to do with the trick question how one can be three and three be one. The answer to this question is given in every life-process. The trinitarian problem is the problem of the unity between ultimacy and concreteness in the living God." *Systematic Theology,* vol. 1, 228. In fact, he is only taking up the development of Thomas Aquinas: "Therefore numerical terms

in God signify the things of which they are said, and beyond this they add only negation, *nihil addunt, nisi negationem*"; in effect, the quantity and the quality are properly said of material things alone, and only *metaphorice* of God. *Summa Theologiae* Ia, q. 30, a. 3, *resp.*; English translation Pegis, 304.

16. *Das älteste Systemprogramm des deutschen Idealismus*, in Hegel, *Werke*, vol. 1 (Frankfurt: Suhrkamp, 1979), 235–36. See Goethe: "Wir sind naturforschend Pantheisten, dichtend Polytheisten, sittlich Monotheisten—We are pantheists when we study nature, polytheists when we write poetry, monotheists in our morality." *Maximen und Reflexionen*, § 807.

17. F. W. J. Schelling, *Philosophie der Offenbarung*, II, 1, Lecture XIII: "auf den Begriff des *Monotheismus* geführt, d.h. auf denjenigen Begriff, der der höchste aller wahren Religion ist—eben deshalb auch der, von welchem eine (objektive) Erklärung der falschen Religion auszugehen hat.... Wir unterschieden damals den Monotheismus im Begriff vom Monotheismus als Dogma oder dem wirklichen Monotheismus. Letzterer ist da, wo die Potenzen sich gegenseitig ausschließen, also eine wirkliche Mehrheit in Gott gesetzt ist. Denn vor der Spannung ist viele Mehrheit in Gott nur potentiell, und dies nannten wir den Monotheismus im Begriff. Diesem selbst aber liegt als letzter Gedanke zu Grund, daß Gott nicht (wie im bloßen Theismus) der schlechthin Einzige, sondern der *als* Gott einzige ist, oder daß die Behauptung der Einzigkeit in Gott nicht eine bloß negative, daß sie nur eine positive, d.h. affirmative sein könnte." In Schröter, ed., *Werke*, Ergänzungsband VI, 281ff. See also: "If God is *one* according to his *essence*, nevertheless *in his forms of existence* he is *many*. Thus polytheism contains the forms of existence, and the monotheism which follows from the surpassing of polytheism is the unity *known* as the result. True monotheism is a *free* relation of man to God [understood] as an absolutely free spirit—Ist Gott seinem Wesen nach Einer, in seinen Existenzformen aber Mehrere, so enthält Polytheismus die Existenzformen, und der darauf folgende aus der Überwindung des Polytheismus hervorgehende Monotheismus ist die gewußte Einheit als Resultat. Der wahre Monotheismus ist ein freies Verhältnis des Menschen zu Gott als absolut freiem Geist." *Philosophie der Offenbarung*, notes taken by Julius Frauenstädt, WS 1841/42, ed. Manfred Frank (Frankfurt: Suhrkamp, 1977), 381.

18. "Virtus autem creativa Dei communis est toti Trinitati; unde pertinet ad unitatem essentiae, non ad distinctionem personarum. Per rationem igitur naturalem cognosci possunt de Deo ea quae pertinent ad unitatem essentiae, non autem ea quae pertinent ad distinctionem personarum." *Summa Theologiae* Ia, q.32, a.1, *resp.* 163; English translation Pegis, *Basic Writings I*, 316. Karl Rahner remarks: "One might almost dare to affirm that if the doctrine of the Trinity were to be erased as false, most religious literature could be preserved almost unchanged throughout the process.... One could suspect that as regards the catechism of the head and the heart, in contrast to the catechism in books, the Christian idea of the Incarnation

would not have to change at all, if there were no Trinity." "Remarks on the Dogmatic Treatise 'de Trinitate,'" in *Theological Investigations,* vol. 4, *More Recent Writings,* trans. Kevin Smyth (New York: Seabury Press, 1974), 79. Or again Louis Bouyer: "This was even true of our view of God and of the Trinity. The relationship to Christ was so tenuous that one could write a complete treatise on *De Deo uno et trino* without mentioning the Incarnation even in passing." *The Eternal Son: A Theology of the Word of God and of Christology,* trans. Simone Inkel, S. L. and John F. Laughlin (Huntington, IN: Our Sunday Visitor, 1978), 15.

19. Suárez: "Dicemus igitur in hoc opere de Deo, ut unus est, et ut trinus, et ita duas habebit partes principales, prior de Dei Unitate dici potest, altera de Trinitate." *Tractatus de divina substantia,* Proœmium, *Opera omnia,* vol. 1, p. XXIII.

20. "Contraria sententia mihi semper placuit, juxta quam assero, relationes, seu personalitates, vel personas divinas non esse de essentia Divinitatis, nec Dei, ut Deus est." Ibid., IV.5.2, 628, emphasis added. Karl Rahner clarifies: "This division [of the treatise *De Deo uno* and *De Deo trino*] is only done by St. Thomas, for reasons which have not yet been clearly explained." *Theological Investigations IV,* 83. But this observation holds not only for the readers of the catechism, but also and above all for the theologians themselves. On the history of this separation, see Alberto Frigo, "La Trinité indifférente. L'évolution moderne des traités *De Deo uno* et *De Deo trino,*" *Revue catholique internationale Communio* 45, no. 3–4 (2020): 117–32.

21. Boethius: "Ita igitur substantia continet unitatem, relatio multiplicat trinitatem." *Quomodo Trinitas unus Deus ac non tres dii,* chap. VI, PL 64, 1255a; translation *On the Trinity* in *Theological Tractates. The Consolation of Philosophy,* trans. H. F. Stewart and E. K. Rand, Loeb Classical Library 74 (Cambridge, MA: Harvard University Press, 1973), 29, modified.

22. See Barbara Cassin, ed., *Vocabulaire européen des philosophies. Dictionnaire des intraduisibles* (Paris, Seuil/Le Robert, 2004); English edition, *Dictionary of Untranslatables: A Philosophical Lexicon,* ed. Barbara Cassin, Emily Apter, Jacques Lezra, and Michael Wood (Princeton, NJ: Princeton University Press, 2014). See a good diagnostic of these difficulties in Jean-Yves Lacoste, "*Homoousios et homoousios.* La substance entre théologie et philosophie," in *L'Intuition sacramentelle et autres essais* (Paris: Ad Solem, 2015), 211–33, first published in *Recherches de science religieuse* 98, no. 1 (2010): 85–100.

23. We need only to consult Endre von Ivánka, *Plato Christianus. Übernahme und Umgestaltung des Platonismus durch die Väter* (Einsiedeln: Johannes Verlag, 1964), and all the work that has arisen from it.

24. Boethius, *Quomodo Trinitas unus Deus ac non tres dii* VI, PL 64, 1255a; *On the Trinity,* in *The Theological Tractates,* 29, modified.

25. Saint Augustine, *De Trinitate* VII.5.10, BA 15, 538; *The Trinity,* 228, modified. See: "*substantia, vel, si melius dicitur, essentia Dei*—the substance, or to say it better, the essence of God." *De Trinitate* III.11.21, BA 15, 328; *The Trinity,* 140,

modified. See my remarks in *"Substantia*. Note sur l'usage de *substantia* par saint Augustin et sur son appartenance à l'histoire de la métaphysique," in I. Atucha, D. Calma, C. König-Paralong, and I. Zavarrero, eds., *Mots médiévaux offerts à Ruedi Imbach* (Turnhout: Brepols, 2011), 691–701, and those of Axel Tisserand, in Boèce, *Traités théologiques*, Bilingual Latin-French edition, ed. and trans. Axel Tisserand (Paris: Flammarion, 2000), 53. The question can be reaffirmed: Can *essentia* itself be understood univocally and properly of God (as we know that Saint Thomas will debate)?

26. When it comes to the Trinity, the Greek Fathers do not often use the category of *pros ti* (in relation to) that Aristotle considered last and from which he exempted *ousia* ("no *ousia* is among the *pros ti*," *Categories* VII, 8a14 and 8b21; English trans., 59, 63, modified), but precisely make use of the term *schesis* (relation, manner of relating). See Gregory of Nazianzus: "I should have felt some awe myself at your dilemma [between the name of *ousia* and the name of *energeia*], had it been necessary to accept one of the alternatives and impossible to avoid them by stating a third, and truer possibility. My expert friends, it is this: 'Father' designates neither the *ousia* nor the *energeia*, but the relationship (*schesis*), a word indicating how (*pōs*) the Father is towards (*pros*) the Son and the Son is towards the Father." *Theological Oration* XXIX.16, in SC 250, 210; *The Five Theological Orations*, 84, modified. Difficult to translate, the gap between the relation (*pros ti*), the last and the least of the Aristotelian categories of being, and the Trinitarian *schesis* plays an essential role: God is not an *ousia* in the sense of that which would receive accidents, nor is he refractory to the relation that, now named *schesis*, becomes essential, against the ontic thematic.

27. Augustin, *De Trinitate* V.9.10, BA 15, 448; *The Trinity*, 196. See Anselm: "Behold! Clearly it is beneficial for every human being to believe in an ineffable threefold Unity and unified Trinity (*in quandam ineffabilem trinam unitatem et unam trinitatem*). They are indeed one and a Unity in virtue of one essence, but I do not know what it is in virtue of which they are a three and a trinity (*trinam vero et trinitatem propter tres nescio quid*). For although I can say 'Trinity' because of the Father, the Son, and the Spirit of both, who are three, I cannot express by any one word what it is in virtue of which they are three (*non tamen possum proferre uno nomine propter quid tres*), as if I were to say [they are a Trinity] by virtue of being three persons in the same way that I would say they are a Unity in virtue of being one substance. For they are not to be thought of as three persons, since whenever there are two or more persons, the persons subsist separately from each other in such a way that there must be as many substances as there are persons. This is known to be true in the case of human beings, who are as many individual substances as they are persons." *Monologion* LXXIX (Paris: Cerf, 1986), 200; *Anselm: Basic Writings*, trans. Thomas Williams (Indianapolis, IN: Hackett, 2007), 72.

28. Augustine, *De Trinitate* VII.4.7: "Et, dum intelligatur saltem in ænigmate quod dicitur, placuit ita dici, ut diceretur aliquid cum quæreretur quid tria sint, quæ tria esse fides vera pronuntiat, cum et Patrem non dicit esse Filium et Spiritum sanctum quod est donum Dei, nec Patrem dicit esse nec Filum. Cum ergo quæritur quid tria, vel quid tres, conferimus nos ad inveniendum aliquod speciale vel generale nomen, quo complectamur hæc tria, neque occurrit animo, quia excedit supereminentia divinitatis usitati eloquii facultatem. Verius enim cogitatur Deus quam dicitur, et verius est quam cogitatur." BA 15, 526; *The Trinity*, 224, modified.

29. Boethius, *Contra Eutychen* III, in *Theological Tractates*, 84; taken up magisterially by Thomas Aquinas, *Summa Theologiae*, Ia, q. 29, a.1. On the difficulties of this definition, see Maurice Nédoncelle, who distinguished at least six variations of *persona*, and saw by this "a metaphysician invaded and inhibited, though not eradicated, by logic," in "Les variations de Boèce sur la personne," *Revue des sciences religieuses* 29, no. 3 (1955): 209-2-38; and Emmanuel Housset, *La Vocation de la personne. L'histoire du concept de personne, de sa naissance augustinienne à sa redécouverte phénoménologique* (Paris: PUF, 2007), especially chaps. III and IV.

30. Thomas Aquinas, *Summa Theologiae* Ia, q.29, a.3. Already Jerome was hesitant to use *hypostasis*, "because some bane I don't know lies hidden in its syllables—*nescio quid veneni in syllabis latet*." Letter XV.3 to Pope Damasus, in *Lettres de saint Jérôme*, vol. 1, ed. J. Labourt (Paris: Belles Lettres, 1947), 47; *The Letters of St. Jerome*, vol. 1, *Letters 1–22*, trans. Charles Christopher Mierow (New York: Newman Press, 1963), 71, modified. Karl Barth clearly lays out the reservations against a systematic usage of *persona*, preferring to say strictly that "God. . . is One in three distinctive modes of being." *Kirchliche Dogmatik*, I/1, 368–88; *Church Dogmatics*, 348–353.

31. Louis Bouyer, *The Invisible Father: Approaches to the Mystery of the Divinity*, trans. Hugh Gilbert, OSB (Petersham, MA: St. Bede's, 1999), 229.

32. As both traditional and heterodox Thomists do not hesitate to conclude without ever calling it into question: "The doctrine of the Trinity should be brought back to unity. Unity is the primary truth *for us*, the Trinity is the secondary truth." B. Bartmann, *Lehrbuch der Dogmatik* (Freiburg: Herder, 1932), cited by Joseph Wolinski in Jean-Yves Lacoste, ed., *Dictionnaire critique de théologie*, 1431; English translation *Encyclopedia of Christian Theology* (New York: Routledge, 2004), 611.

Chapter Sixteen

1. Karl Rahner, "Bemerkungen zum Dogmatischen Traktat 'De Trinitate,'" *Schriften zur Theologie*, vol. 4, 115; English translation: *Theological Investigations*, vol. 4, trans. Kevin Smyth, 87. See also "We are starting out from the proposition that the economic Trinity *is* the immanent Trinity and vice versa." "Einzigkeit und

Dreifaltigkeit Gottes im Gespräch mit dem Islam," in *Schriften zur Theologie*, vol. 13 (Einsiedeln: Benziger, 1978), 139; English translation: *Theological Investigations*, vol. 18, trans. Edward Quinn (New York: Crossroad, 1983), 114.

2. Karl Barth, *Kirkliche Dogmatik*, I/1, 503; *Church Dogmatics*, I.1, 479. See his convincing remarks: "Our concepts of unimpaired unity and unimpaired distinction, the concept of the one essence of God and of the three persons or modes of being (*Seinsweisen*) to be distinguished in this essence, and finally the polemical assertion, which we touched on only briefly, that God's triunity is to be found not merely in His revelation but, because in His revelation, in God Himself and in Himself too, so that the Trinity is to be understood as 'immanent' and not just 'economic'—none of this is directly biblical, i.e., explicitly stated in the Bible; it is Church doctrine. We have established no more than that the biblical doctrine of revelation is implicitly, and in some passages explicitly, a pointer to the doctrine of the Trinity. In its basic outline it must be interpreted as also an outline of the doctrine of the Trinity. If the doctrine of the Trinity can be established and developed as such, we have to say that in respect of revelation there is a genuine and necessary connexion with the doctrine of the Trinity." Ibid., I.1, 333.

3. Karl Rahner, "Der dreifaltige Gott als transzendenter Urgrund der Heilsgeschichte," chap. 5 in K. Rahner, *Mysterium Salutis. Grunriß Heilsgeschichtlicher Dogmatik*, ed. Johannes Feiner and Magnus Löhrer, vol. 2, *Die Heilsgeschichte vor Christus* (Einsiedeln: Benziger Verlag, 1967), 336, 329, 337, 346, and 328, respectively; English translation: *The Trinity*, trans. Joseph Donceel (New York: Herder & Herder, 1970), 34, 24, 35, 47 (modified), 22 (modified), respectively.

4. Rahner, "Der dreifaltige Gott," 335; *The Trinity*, 32, 33.

5. This is what Hans Urs von Balthasar very rightly condemns: "while, according to Christian faith, the economic Trinity assuredly appears as the *rendering explicit* (*Auslegung*) of the immanent Trinity, it may not be identified with it, for the latter grounds and supports the former. Otherwise the immanent, eternal Trinity would threaten to dissolve (*auszugehen*) into the economic; in other words, God would be swallowed up in the world process, and could not return to himself except through it." Hans Urs von Balthasar, *Theodramatik*, II/2 (Einsiedeln: Johannes Verlag, 1978), 466; English translation: *Theo-Drama: Theological Dramatic Theory*, vol. 3, *The Dramatis Personae: The Person in Christ*, trans. Graham Harrison (San Francisco: Ignatius Press, 1992), 508, modified. The same discussion of the reciprocity of the terms (*"umgekehrt"*) is found in Ghislain Lafont, *Peut-on connaître Dieu en Jésus-Christ?* (Paris: Cerf, 1969), 190ff. At stake is conceiving the very economy of the immanent Trinity as giving place to an *interpretation* that is not summed up by the chronological course of the history of the world.

6. G. W. F. Hegel, *Enzyklopädie der philosophischen Wissenschaften im Grundriße* (1827), ed. Wolfgang Bonsiepen and Hans-Christian Lucas, *Gesammelte*

Werke, vol. 19 (Meiner: Hamburg, 1989); English translation: *Philosophy of Mind: Being Part Three of the Encyclopaedia of the Philosophical Sciences* (1830), trans. William Wallace (Oxford: Clarendon Press, 1971), §564.

7. G. W. F. Hegel, *Phänomenologie des Geistes*, ed. Wolfgang Bonsiepen and Reinhard Heede, *Gesammelte Werke*, vol. 9 (Hamburg: Meiner Verlag, 1980), 18; English translation: *Phenomenology of Spirit*, trans. Terry Pinkard (Cambridge: Cambridge University Press, 2018), 12, modified.

8. Hegel, *Enzyklopädie* (1827); *Philosophy of Mind*, §564, modified.

9. See the texts quoted and cited above, in chapter 6, notes 55, 56, 57, 411–12.

10. Hegel, *Enzyklopädie* (1827); *Philosophy of Mind*, modified.

11. Ibid.

12. Ibid.

13. Ibid., §564, translation modified, emphasis added. According to the edition of Friedhelm Nicolin and Otto Pöggeler (*Enzyklopädie der philosophischen Wissenschaften im Grundriße* [1830], 6th ed. [Hamburg: Meiner, 1959], 446), and confirmed by Bernard Bourgeois's note in the French translation (*Encyclopédie des sciences philosophiques*, II, *Philosophie de l'esprit* [Paris: Vrin, 1988], 354–55), Hegel ended §564 (in 1830) with a reference to Carl Friedrich Göschel, who, in fact, took up Hegel's thesis (of 1827) without any reservations: "The being of God and the knowledge of God is all one (*Eins*), which is to say that God is actual only so far as he knows himself: his existence (*Dasein*) comes about and disappears with his consciousness.... Just as the knowledge of God in himself and the being of God in himself are all one (*eins*), the knowledge and the being of God are also all one in me, that is, God is actual in me only so far as he actually comes to me in consciousness.... The being and the knowledge of God in me thus contains not only the knowledge that God has of me, but also the knowledge that I have of him." *Aphorismen über Nichtwissen und absolutes Wissen im Verhältnisse zur christlichen Glaubenserkenntniss. Ein Beytrag zum Verständnisse der Philosophie unserer Zeit* (Berlin: Franklin Verlag, 1829), 65.

14. G. W. F. Hegel, *Wissenschaft der Logik*, ed. Georg Lasson, vol. 1 (Hamburg: Meiner, 1967), 31. English translation, *The Science of Logic*, translated and edited by George di Giovanni (Cambridge: Cambridge University Press, 2010), 29. Hegel argues (in the *Encyclopaedia* §564) that God manifests himself in himself to man in the same knowledge of man that man has of himself because God is not an "envious (*aphthonos*)" god. But the argument refutes itself if what God reveals in this way remains, at best, a God *for* us (*quoad nos*), who manifests only what we make manifest to ourselves, and thus who jealously keeps his secret to himself.

15. Hegel, *Enzyklopädie* (1827); *Philosophy of Mind*, 299 and 301 (modified).

16. Ibid., 301.

17. This conclusion is all the more necessary because Hegel takes these three "moments" from Kant's table of judgments. *Kritik der reinen Vernunft*, A70/B85, 826.

18. Michel Henry, "The Bringing to Light of the Original Essence of Revelation in Opposition to the Hegelian Concept of Manifestation (*Erscheinung*)," in *The Essence of Manifestation*, trans. Girard Etzkorn (The Hague: Martinus Nijhoff, 1973), respectively 694, 697, 717 (and 705, 733).

19. Henry, *The Essence of Manifestation*, 698, 697. See also "In Hegel, there is no ontology of subjectivity" (702), and "Subjectivity is objectivity as such" (704). This critique of Hegel by Henry was taken seriously by Jean-François Courtine: see "Temporalité et révélation," in Jean-François Courtine and Jean-François Marquet, eds., *Le Dernier Schelling. Raison et positivité* (Paris: Vrin, 1994), which likewise shows perfectly the overturning of Hegel's thesis on Revelation.

20. Hegel, *Phänomenologie des Geistes*, 18; *Phenomenology of Spirit*, 13. And also: "What is distinguished is defined in such a way that the distinction immediately disappears, and we have a relationship of God, of the idea, merely to himself. The act of differentiation is only a movement, a play of love with itself (*ein Spiel der Liebe mit sich selbst*), which does not arrive at the seriousness of other-being (*nicht zur Ernsthaftigkeit des Andersstehens kommt*), of separation and rupture. The other is to this extent defined as 'Son'; in terms of sensibility, what-has-being-in-and-for-itself is defined as love (*Liebe*), while in a higher mode of determinacy, it is defined as spirit that is present to itself and free. In the idea as thus specified, the determination of the distinction is not yet complete, since it is only abstract distinction in general. We have not yet arrived at distinction in its own proper form; [here] it is just one determinate characteristic." *Vorlesungen über die Philosophie der Religion*, III, 2, 1, ed. Walter Jaescke, vol. 3, *Die vollendete Religion*, 216–17; *Lectures on the Philosophy of Religion, One Volume Edition: The Lectures of 1827*, ed. Peter C. Hodgson, trans. R. F. Brown, P. C. Hodgson, and J. M. Stewart (Berkeley: University of California Press, 1988), 433–34. Schelling, however, condemned this text, writing: "All this is just as theosophical as anything in J. Böhme could be." *Philosophie der Offenbarung*, Lecture VII; *The Grounding of Positive Philosophy*, 176.

21. In the sense that love says and does nothing: "Farewell, I have absolutely nothing to say to you, other than that I love you." Gustave Flaubert, letter to Louis Bouilhet, August 2, 1855, in Gustave Flaubert, *Œuvres complètes*, vol. 16/3, *Correspondance, Troisième série (1854–1869)* (Paris: Louis Conard, 1910), 39.

22. Friedrich Nietzsche, *Nachgelassene Fragmente* I [216], in *Nietzsche Werke* ed. Giorgio Colli and Mazzino Montinari (Berlin: De Gruyter, 1974), vol. VIII/1, p. 54. On this point, see Jean-Luc Marion, "D'un phénomène érotique," *Alter: Revue de phénoménologie* 20 (2012): 129–42.

23. Jean-François Marquet claims that "one can even say that we have here the last great systematic summa of the West . . ., a grandiose legend of the ages, the editing of which, constantly restarted, occupied Schelling for more than forty years, ending up in a sort of 'unknown masterpiece' that, in its posthumous publication,

fell into a world that had become irremediably foreign." "Présentation" to Schelling, *Philosophie de la Révélation*, ed. and trans. Jean-François Courtine, Jean-François Marquet, et al. (Paris: PUF, 1989), vol. 1, 6.

24. See above, chapter 8, n10, page 416.

25. Schelling, *Philosophie der Offenbarung*, Lecture III, in Schröter, ed. *Werke*, Erg. Bd. VI, 41; *Grounding of Positive Philosophy*, 118, modified.

26. Schelling, *Philosophie der Offenbarung*, 48; *Grounding of Positive Philosophy*, 122.

27. Schelling, *Philosophie der Offenbarung*, 46; *Grounding of Positive Philosophy*, 121, modified.

28. Schelling, *Philosophie der Offenbarung*, Lecture IV, 70; *Grounding of Positive Philosophy*, 137. See also in Lecture IV: "Kant had determined God as the final concept *necessary* for the consummation of human knowledge. . . . In this philosophy, every consequence was justified by what had preceded it, but it was justified only as a mere *concept*. It was from beginning to end and *immanent* philosophy, that is, it progressed in mere thought and was by no means a *transcendent* philosophy. In the end therefore, whereas it had only demonstrated God as a necessary idea of reason, which of course was already *secured* (*versichert*) by Kant, the necessary consequence of it laying claim to a knowledge of God was to rob God of all transcendence and draw him into this logical thinking, into merely logical concept, into an *idea itself*." *Philosophie der Offenbarung*, 72–73; *Grounding of Positive Philosophy*, 138.

29. Schelling, *Philosophie der Offenbarung*, Lecture VIII, 162, 163; *Grounding of Positive Philosophy*, 203.

30. Schelling, *Philosophie der Offenbarung*, Lecture VII, 128; *Grounding of Positive Philosophy*, 179.

31. Schelling, *Philosophie der Offenbarung*, Lecture VII, 128; *Grounding of Positive Philosophy*, 179, modified.

32. Schelling, *Philosophie der Offenbarung*, Lecture V, 89; *Grounding of Positive Philosophy*, 151. See Lecture VI: "This is easy to realize: only resolve and action can *ground* an actual experience. If in geometry experience has no place this is precisely because in this case everything can be accomplished through pure thought, because in this case there is no *happening* (*kein Geschehen*) to be presupposed." For a "free action is something more than what allows itself to be discerned in mere *thought*" and it is "an *actual event*, that is resolve and action, and that extends beyond the sensible world." *Philosophie der Offenbarung*, 114; *Grounding of Positive Philosophy*, 169, 168, 169 modified.

33. Schelling, *Philosophie der Offenbarung*, Lecture VII, 126–27; *Grounding of Positive Philosophy*, 178, 179.

34. Schelling, *Philosophie der Offenbarung*, Lecture VII, 127; *Grounding of Positive Philosophy*, 179.

35. Schelling, *Philosophie der Offenbarung*, Lecture VII, 129; *Grounding of Positive Philosophy*, 180.

36. Schelling, *Philosophie der Offenbarung*, Lecture VII, 145; *Grounding of Positive Philosophy*, 191.

37. Schelling, *Philosophie der Offenbarung*, Lecture VIII, 158; *Grounding of Positive Philosophy*, 200. See also: "The most supreme being, *if it exists*, can only a priori be that which is, thus, it must be that which necessarily exists, it must be that which *is* before (*voraus seyende*) its concept, and, thus, before every concept" (168 = 208]); "start from being, devoid of the concept.... But in God it is precisely... that before which reason stands motionless" (Lecture VIII, 164 [= 205]); "[the positive philosophy] lets go of the concept, *den Begriff fallen läßt*" (161 [= 202]); "a still nonconceptual *prius*" (167 [= 207]); "that which is opposed to all concepts (*das allem Begriff Entgegengesetzte*)" (170 [= 209]). Reason "posits nonconceptual being in order to reach from it to the concept" (170 [= 209]).

38. See also: "*die Nothwendigkeit seines unvordenklichen Seyns*" (*Philosophie der Offenbarung*, Lecture XIII, 268). And: "*Hence the beginning of the positive philosophy is being that has never been* potentia; *it has always been* actu. One should say that what precedes all potency, also precedes all activity of thought! We must also, however, name being that precedes all potency *unprethinkable* being (*unvordenkliche Seyn*), that which *precedes (vorausgehend) all activity of thought.*" *Philosophie der Offenbarung 1841–1842*, ed. Manfred Frank (Frankfurt: Suhrkamp, 1977), 161; English translation: *Philosophy of Revelation (1841–42)*, trans. Klaus Ottmann (Thompson, CT: Spring, 2020), 124–25, modified. And further: "Unprethinkable being is the real First" (*Offenbarung*, 164 [English 127, modified]); or the "lord of unprethinkable being (*Herr des unvordenklichen Seyns*)" (*Offenbarung*, 164 [English 129, modified]). However rough it may sound, this translation of *unvordenklich* as "un-pre-thinkable" remains the only one possible for transposing the immemorial, "a past that is not a former present." Xavier Tilliette, *Schelling. Une philosophie en devenir*, vol. 1 (Paris: Vrin, 1970), 509, a past in which "there is no *before self*, but only an *after self*; that is to say, there is no past but only a future." Luigi Pareyson, "La stupeur de la raison selon Schelling," in Jean-François Courtine and Gérard Bensussan, eds., *Schelling* (Paris: Cerf, 2010), 506.

39. Schelling, *Philosophie der Offenbarung 1841–1842*, 164; *Philosophy of Revelation (1841–42)*, 128. Regarding the context of this capital question, see Marion, *In Excess: Studies*, chap. 4, "In the Name: How to Avoid Speaking of It," 128–62. I can only express approval of Jean-François Courtine's remark: "Positive philosophy is not a sublime foundation of the existing being as a whole, but rather the very contrary of a foundation, the attempt at a phenomenological thinking of... the divine!" Jean-François Courtine, *Extase de la raison. Essais sur Schelling* (Paris: Galilée, 1990), 166.

40. Schelling, *Philosophie der Offenbarung*, Lecture VIII, 174; *Grounding of Positive Philosophy*, 212, modified. This is contrary to Hegel: "For this reason, it would, for example, be expedient to avoid the name, '*God*,' because this word is not immediately the concept but is rather at the same time the genuine name, the fixed point of the rest of the underlying subject, whereas in contrast, e.g. 'being,' or 'the one,' 'individuality,' 'the subject,' etc., themselves immediately point to concepts." *Phänomenologie des Geistes*, 46; *The Phenomenology of Spirit*, §66, 41. But Schelling suggests (before Marx) that Hegel has it upside down: "To begin philosophy with being is to turn it squarely on its head." *Philosophie der Mythologie*, II, 2, ed. Cotta (1857), (Darmstadt, 1990), 34.

41. Schelling, *Philosophie der Offenbarung*, Lecture V, 75–76; *Grounding of Positive Philosophy*, 142.

42. Schelling, *Philosophie der Offenbarung*, Lecture V, 79; *Grounding of Positive Philosophy*, 144.

43. Schelling, *Philosophie der Offenbarung*, Lecture VII, 132; *Grounding of Positive Philosophy*, 182.

44. Schelling, *Philosophie der Offenbarung*, Lecture XV, 316, 317.

45. In what follows we refer to Schelling, *Philosophie der Offenbarung*, Lecture XII, 250–56.

46. See Xavier Tilliette, *Schelling. Une philosophie en devenir*, vol. 2, part 4, chap. 3, 435–88. See also Tilliette, *La Christologie idéaliste* (Paris: Cerf, 1990) and *La Semaine sainte des philosophes* (Paris: Cerf, 1992); Jean-François Marquet, *Liberté et existence. Étude sur la formation de la philosophie de Schelling* (Paris: Gallimard, 1973); Thomas F. O'Meara, "Christ in Schelling's *Philosophy of Revelation*," *Heythrop Journal* 27 (1986): 275–87; Marc Maesschalk, *Philosophie et révélation dans l'itinéraire de Schelling* (Paris and Leuven: Vrin/Peeters, 1989); and the synthesis of Jean Greisch, *Le Buisson ardent et la lumière de la raison. L'invention de la philosophie de la religion*, vol. 1, *Héritages et héritiers du XIXième siècle*, I, chap. 3 (Paris: Cerf, 2002), 175–205.

47. Schelling, *Philosophie der Offenbarung*, 2nd part, vol. 3, *Werke*, ed. Schröter, Hauptband VI (Munich: Beck, 1979), Lecture XXV, 431–37 (= ed. Cotta, vol. 14, 40 and following). The arguments are as follows: *morphē* and *hyparchōn* indicate a provisional and contingent situation, and thus an incomplete divinity; *kenoō* (*ekenōsen*) equals *entäussern*, to alienate. Exegetically this barely holds together.

48. Schelling, *Philosophie der Offenbarung*, 2nd part, vol. 3, Lecture XXV, 432 (= ed. Cotta, vol. 14, 40). See also: "an intermediate state, in which he was independent of the Father, Lord of the being alienated (*entfremdeter*) from God and from the Father" (433 [=41]); "the intermediate state of an independent sovereignty of the Father that the Son possessed before his manifestation as Christ" (433 [=42]);

"an exterior existence completely independent of the Father ... an extra-divine existence (*außergöttliche Existenz*)" (Lecture XXVI, 442 [=50]).

49. Schelling, *Philosophie der Offenbarung*, 2nd part, vol. 3, Lecture XXV, 431 [= ed. Cotta, 39]. See: "I repeat, the whole New Testament is incomprehensible if one does not attribute to the Son, and clearly since the beginning of the world (for once the world is, the fall occurs), an existence outside of the Father (*extra Patrem*) and independent of the Father" (ibid., 440 [=48]). Here one finds the grouping together, constant in Hegel, of the generation of the Son, creation, and evil; and for the same and sole reason: there is only one principle of differentiation, the logical division (the negative, in-itself/for-itself, freedom, etc.), *agapē* remaining unknown as distinction within communion (distance); thus the only remaining way to conceive the Trinity is to render it worldly and historicize it.

50. Schelling, *Philosophie der Offenbarung*, 2nd part, vol. 3, Lecture XXV, 430 [= ed. Cotta, vol. 14, 38]. See: "Such is the mystery of eternal love that what could be absolutely for-itself has nevertheless not considered as a prize [to possess, *Raub*, therefore *harpagmon*] to be for-itself, but to be only in and with the other. If each one was not a whole, but only a part of the whole, there would be no love; but there is love, because each is a whole, and nothing is nor can be without the other." *Aphorismen zur Einleitung in die Naturphilosophie*, Würzburg Lectures, 1806, §163 [ed. Cotta, vol. 7, 174].

51. Schelling, *Philosophie der Offenbarung*, 2nd part, vol. 3, Lecture XXXI, 589 [= ed. Cotta, vol. 14, 197].

52. Schelling, *Philosophie der Offenbarung*, 2nd part, vol. 3, Lecture XXV, 428–29 [= ed. Cotta, vol. 14, 36–37] (Schelling's emphases).

53. Schelling, *Philosophie der Offenbarung*, 2nd part, vol. 3, Lecture XXV, respectively 431 [= ed. Cotta, vol. 14, 39]; 433 [=41]; Lecture XXX, 552 [=160]; and Lecture XXXI, 579 [=187]. See Tilliette, *Schelling*, vol. 2, 456.

54. Schelling, *Philosophie der Offenbarung*, Lecture XXV, in Schröter, ed., *Werke*, Erg. Bd. VI, 429 [= ed. Cotta, vol. 14, 37].

55. Schelling, *Philosophie der Offenbarung*, Lecture XII, 252–53.

56. Schelling, *Philosophie der Offenbarung*, Lecture XII, 336 (emphasis added). But sometimes, interpreting John 5:26 ("For just as the Father has life in himself, so has he likewise given to the Son to have it in himself"), Schelling immediately crosses out the gift by specifying first that "the Father has this life as something that is not given," but that he possesses originarily through the "paternal potency"; and "that it is necessary that the power, the potency be first given to the Son." *Philosophie der Offenbarung*, Lecture XII, 325. Must the gift be understood starting from the potency, or the other way around? Xavier Tilliette speaks of a "semi-failure," "because Schelling was, so to speak, blocked by his initial analysis." Tilliette, *Schelling*, vol. 2, 483 and 482.

57. Schelling, *Philosophie der Offenbarung*, Lecture XXV: "The content of Revelation is nothing other than a higher history that goes back to the beginning of things and extends as far as their end. The philosophy of Revelation has no other goal than to explain this higher history." Schröter, ed. Hauptb. VI, 422 [= ed. Cotta, vol. 14, 30]. Such a higher history would not be higher than common history, and it would only be so if it were no longer written according to the logic of the concept, but instead *from elsewhere* (see below, chapter 19).

58. Schelling, *Philosophie der Offenbarung 1841–42*, Lecture XXV, 322; *Philosophy of Revelation (1841–42)*, 324.

59. Gregory of Nazianzus, *Theological Oration* XXXI.26, in PG 36, 161c; *On God and Christ*, 137.

Chapter Seventeen

1. Thomas Aquinas, *De Potentia* q. 7, a. 2, *ad* 1m. See other texts in Marion, *God Without Being*, chap. 8.

2. Basil of Caesarea, *On the Holy Spirit* XVIII.44, PG 32, 148a; *Sur le Saint-Esprit*, ed. Benoît Pruche, SC 17 (Paris: Cerf, 1968), 404; English translation, Saint Basil the Great, *On the Holy Spirit*, ed. and trans. Stephen Hildebrand (Yonkers, NY: Saint Vladimir's Seminary Press, 2011), 80, modified. [Translators' note: Marion cites the Greek-French edition of this text from *Sources chrétiennes*, but he heavily modifies Benoît Pruche's translations throughout. We will render Marion's retranslations as faithfully as possible, while using Stephen Hildebrand's English translation as a reference.]

3. See Ephesians 1:13–14, "you have been marked by a seal by the Spirit of the Promise, this Holy Spirit who is the deposit of our inheritance and prepares the redemption of the People that God has acquired for the praise of his glory." See 2 Corinthians 1:22: "He [Christ] who has marked us by his seal and placed in our hearts the deposit of the Spirit." The Spirit does not promise, he gives advances on the promised heritage. See Vincent Carraud, "La foi n'est pas une croyance dans la Lettre aux Hébreux," in *Ce que sait la foi* (Paris: Parole et silence, 2020), 15–38.

4. A patent difficulty remains: to conceive how the discontinuity of the *elsewhere*, which ends in the suddenness (*exaiphnēs*) of what is uncovered "once for all," can be produced in an anamorphosis that, for its part, must "now (*nyni*)" still believe and hope, that is, progress. The connection of the temporized economy of the Trinity with its timeless immanence will thus be addressed, if not exposed, in the conclusion (chapter 20, below).

5. *On the Holy Spirit* XVIII.18.45; PG 32, 149b-c; Pruche, 404; Hildebrand, 80, modified.

6. *On the Holy Spirit* XVIII.18, 45; PG 32, 149c; Pruche, 404; Hildebrand, 81, modified. This text is found in the canon of Nicaea II in 787 (Denzinger, ed.

Enchiridion, no. 601), which comments: "and whoever venerates [the icon] venerates in it the hypostasis of the one who is painted there."

7. *On the Holy Spirit* XVIII.18, 45; PG 32, 149c; Pruche, 404; Hildebrand, 80.

8. Pruche's translation, 406, upholds this lesson, attested by the principal manuscripts, against *enizomenēn* (reduced to unity), chosen by C. F. H. Johnston in his 1892 Oxford Clarendon edition.

9. G. W. H. Lampe's *Greek Patristic Lexicon* (Oxford: Oxford University Press, 1961) devotes no entry to *eneikonizō*, and Anatole Bailly's *Dictionnaire Grec-Français*, 4th ed. (Paris: Hachette, 1903), which includes it (675), only mentions two occurrences, including Stobaeus: "The idea subsisting by itself iconifies (*eneikonizousa*) formless matter." *Eclogarum physicarum et ethicarum libri II*, 13th ed., A. H. L. Heeren (Göttingen: Vandenhoeck & Ruprecht, 1792), vol. 1, 326. More circumspect, Anca Vasiliu takes it for an "ancient and specialized word in Neo-Platonic language... not used before the second century, before Plutarch, Maximus of Jerusalem and Methodius of Olympus." *Images de soi dans l'antiquité tardive* (Paris: Vrin, 2012), 241. Not to mention Proclus, *Elements of Theology*, §152, ed. E. R. Dodds (Oxford: Clarendon Press, 1963), 134. Following Jean Trouillard's French version, "every principle... infuses the terms which follow it with the power of the fruitful processions and reflects (*eneikonizetai*) in them the infinite." *Proclos. Éléments de théologie* (Paris: Aubier-Montaigne, 1965), 152.

10. And so Pruche translates it by "une seule forme *se réfléchissant* comme en un miroir—a single form *reflecting itself* as in a mirror" (407), a solution that confirms with stronger theoretical arguments the claim made by Anca Vasiliu: "Basil describes the relation between the Father and the Son with the help of the verb *eneikonizomai* (*eneikonizein*): they reciprocally reflect each other in the intimacy of their iconic relation (XVIII.45)." *Penser Dieu. Noétique et métaphysique dans l'antiquité tardive* (Paris: Vrin, 2018), 282. Or, we can say that it is a "common act, that of being reflected reciprocally without being separated" (134), of a "reflexive condition" (137). But can we go so far as to comment on §45 by claiming that "the three inter-reflect (*eneikonizō*) each other perfectly" (*Images de soi*, 132), when no Greek term indicates the least reflection, and only two and not three hypostases appear here?

11. *On the Holy Spirit* VIII.20, PG 32, 104c; Pruche, 316; Hildebrand, 50, trans. modified. See "the goodness of will" (VIII.21, PG 32, 105a), or "unity of will" (105c); Pruche, 316; Hildebrand 50, modified.

12. According to another, much more convincing formulation by Anca Vasiliu in *Penser Dieu*, 134. See other formulas in Anca Vasiliu, *Eikôn. L'image dans le discours des trois Cappadociens* (Paris: PUF, 2010), 194–202.

13. John Damascene, *On the Orthodox Faith* IV.16, in ed. P. Ledrux, SC 540 (Paris: Cerf, 2011), 236; see also the commentary of Basil in *Contre Eunome* II.16, ed. Bernard Sesboüé, SC 305 (Paris: Cerf: 1983), 64; English translation: *St. Basil of Caesarea Against Eunomius*, 152.

14. Irenaeus, *Adversus Hæreses* IV.6.6 and IV.6.3, in SC 100/2, respectively, 450 and 442. This sheds light on another formula: "Agnitio enim Patris Filius, agnitio autem Filii in Patre et per Filium revelaverit—For the Son is the knowledge of the Father; but the knowledge of the Son is in the Father, and has been revealed through the Son." Ibid., IV.6.7, 452ff; English translation: *The Apostolic Fathers*, 469. It also is close to Nicholas of Cusa: "Es, Ihesu, revelatio Patris. Nam Pater est omnibus hominibus invisibilis et tibi filio ejus solum visibilis—O Jesus, you are the revelation of the Father. For the Father is invisible to all humans and visible only to you, his Son." *De visione Dei* XXI, § 93, *Opera omnia* vol. 6, 73; English translation in *Selected Spiritual Writings*, 278.

15. Augustine, *De Trinitate* II.10.18; BA 15, 228; *The Trinity*, 110, modified. This must be further clarified by saying that "the invisible Father, together with the jointly invisible Son, is said to have sent this Son by making him visible... plainly, the Father and Son, who do not appear, have made him appear in the Son; that is, the very visible Son sent by the invisible Father together with the invisible Son is the same Son (*idem ipse Filus visibilis mittetur*)." II.5.9; BA 15, 204; *The Trinity*, 103, modified.

16. *De Trinitate* II.5.10; BA 15, 208; *The Trinity*, 104.

17. Origen, *De Principiis* I.3.4; SC 252, 150, who continues, "And one must understand therefore that as the Son, who alone knows the Father, reveals him to whom he will (*revelat cui vult*), so the Holy Spirit, who alone searches even the deep things of God, reveals God to whom he will (*revelat Deum cui vult*)." English translation *Origen: On First Principles*, 36–37.

18. Basil, *On the Holy Spirit* XVI.37; PG 32, 133d; Pruche, 376; Hildebrand, 70, modified.

19. Basil, *On the Holy Spirit* XVI.38; PG 32, 136b; Pruche, 378; Hildebrand, 71, modified.

20. Basil, *On the Holy Spirit* XVI.38; PG 32, 137c; Pruche, 382; Hildebrand, 72, modified.

21. Basil, *On the Holy Spirit* XVIII.46; PG 32, 152ab; Pruche, 410; Hildebrand, 81–82, modified.

22. Basil, *On the Holy Spirit* XVIII.47; PG 32, 153ab; Pruche, 412; Hildebrand, 82–83, modified: not *power to see the icon,* but optical power [of making seen] *of the icon.* See in comparable terms IX.23: "And, just like the sun captured by a purified eye, he will show you in himself (ἐν ἑαυτῷ) the icon of the invisible, and in the blessed vision of the icon you will see the unspeakable (ἄρρητον) beauty of the archetype." PG 32, 109b; Pruche, 328; Hildebrand, 54, modified.

23. Basil of Caesarea, Letter 226, PG 32, 849a, translated by Roy J. Deferrari in *Saint Basil: The Letters,* vol. 3 (Cambridge, MA: Harvard University Press, 1953), 339, modified; quoted by Louis Bouyer as the summit of Basil's reflection in *Le Consolateur. Esprit saint et vie de grâce* (Paris: Cerf, 1980), 181.

24. Basil, *On the Holy Spirit* XVIII.46; PG 32, 152b; Pruche, 410; Hildebrand, 82, modified.

25. Basil, *On the Holy Spirit* XXVI.64; PG 32, 185bc; Pruche, 476; Hildebrand, 103, modified.

26. Basil, *On the Holy Spirit* XIX.48; PG 32, 156a; Pruche, 416; Hildebrand, 86, modified. See also: "For nothing is made holy, except by the presence of the Spirit," *Homilies on the Psalms* XXXII.4, PG 60, 333c; translated by Agnes Claire Way, CDP, in *Saint Basil: Exegetic Homilies* (Washington, DC: Catholic University of America Press, 1963), 235.

27. Gregory of Nazianzus, *Theological Oration* XXV.16, ed. Justin Mossay, SC 284, 196, modified. The common origin is more likely found in Athanasius: "If the Holy Spirit were a creature, we should have in him no participation of essence (μετουσία) with God, but we should be joined to creation and made strangers to the divine nature inasmuch as we would not partake therein. But, as it is, the fact of our being called partakers of Christ and partakers of God (μέτοχοι Χριστοῦ καῖ μέτοχοι θεοῦ) shows that the unction and the seal that is in us belongs, not to the nature of created things, but to the nature of the Son who joins us to the Father through the Spirit who is in him. . . For it is on this account that those in whom he is are divinized. If he divinizes, it is not to be doubted that his nature is that of God." *Letters to Serapion* I.24, PG 26, 585b-c, translated in *The Letters of Saint Athanasius Concerning the Holy Spirit*, trans. C. R. B. Shapland (London: Epworth Press, 1951), 126–27, modified.

28. Irenaeus, *Démonstration de la prédication apostolique* VII, ed. J. Massay and G. Lafontaine, SC 284 (Paris: Cerf, 1981), 92; English translation: *Proof of the Apostolic Preaching*, trans. Joseph P. Smith, SJ (Westminster, MD: Newman Press, 1952), 51–52, modified.

29. John Chrysostom, *Commentary on the Epistle to the Romans* XIII.8; PG 60, 519b; English translation: *St. John Chrysostom: Homilies on the Acts of the Apostles and the Epistle to the Romans*, trans. J. B. Morris and W. H. Simcox (Grand Rapids, MI: Eerdmans, 1889), 436, modified.

30. Respectively, Pruche's "Introduction" to *Sur le Saint-Esprit*, 188, and Anca Vasiliu, *Penser Dieu*, 282, and 274. He needed to "avoid *ousia* at all costs" (273), contrary to Marius Victorinus (286), in order to present "a Trinity determined exclusively by relation" (280; see 276). Keeping in mind that relation here is not among the ontic categories of Aristotle (*pros ti*), but is determined as *schesis* (274).

31. Basil, *On the Holy Spirit* XXVI.62; PG 32, 181c-d; Pruche, 470 and 472; Hildebrand, 101, modified.

32. Basil, *On the Holy Spirit* XVIII.46; PG 32, 152c; Pruche, 410; Hildebrand, 82, modified.

33. Basil, *On the Holy Spirit* XII.28; PG 32, 117b; Pruche, 346; Hildebrand, 59, modified. See also, "And the proof of this true conviction is not to separate him from the Father and the Son (for we must be baptized as we have received him, and

we must believe as we are baptized, and we must give glory as we have believed to the Father, the Son, and the Holy Spirit)." Saint Basil, Letter 125, PG 32, 549b; *Saint Basil: The Letters,* vol. 2, 267–69, modified. The same argument is made by Gregory of Nazianzus: "Were the spirit not to be worshipped (οὐ προσκυνητόν), how could he deify me through baptism (πῶς ἐμὲ θεοῖ διὰ τοῦ βαπτίσματος)? If he is to be worshipped, why is he not venerable (σεπτόν)? And if venerable, how can he fail to be God?" Gregory of Nazianzus *Theological Oration* XXXI.28, SC 250, 332; *On God and Christ,* 139, modified.

34. Basil, *On the Holy Spirit* XXVII.68; PG 32, 193c; Pruche, 490; Hildebrand, 107, modified.

Chapter Eighteen

1. Gregory of Nazianzus, "The First Letter to Cledonius the Presbyter" (Letter 101), PG 37, 181c; *On God and Christ,* 158.

2. Ambrose of Milan, *De Pœnitentia* II.2.12, PL 16, 499c; English translation: *Concerning Repentance,* in P. Schaff and H. Wace, eds., trans. H. de Romestin, E. de Romestin, and H. T. F. Duckworth (Buffalo, NY: Christian Literature Publishing, 1896), 346, modified.

3. Basil of Caesarea, *On the Holy Spirit* XXIV.55; PG 32, 172b; Pruche, 450; Hildebrand, 94, modified.

4. Augustine quotes Basil in *Contra Julianum* I.5.15–18, PL 44, 647–52. See Sévérien Salaville, "La connaissance du grec chez saint Augustin," *Revue des études byzantines* 21, no. 127–28 (1922): 387–93; as well as Berthold Altaner, "Augustinus und die griechische Patristik," *Revue bénédictine* 62 (1952): 201–15. Benoît Pruche concludes that "whether through Ambrose—whose *De Spiritu Sancto,* fed by the Greek sap, brought to Hippo, without saying so, the ideas of the last master of the Didascalia [*sc.* Didymus the Blind] and those of Basil on the Holy Spirit—or directly, through the faithful if not always literal translation of Saint Jerome, Greek theology of the Holy Spirit reached the monastery of Hippo." Basil of Caesarea, *Traité sur le Saint-Esprit,* Pruche, 222.

5. Saint Augustine, *De Trinitate* I.9.18, BA 15, 138; *The Trinity,* 79, emphasis added.

6. *De Trinitate* II.10.18; BA 15, 229; *The Trinity,* 110, modified.

7. *De Trinitate* XIV.18.24; BA 16, 412; *The Trinity,* 390.

8. *De Trinitate* II.5.9: "Quapropter Pater *invisibilis,* una cum Filio secum *invisibili, eundem Filium visibilem* faciendo misisse eum dictus est. . . . Cum vero sic accepta est 'forma servi' ut maneret incommutabilis 'forma Dei,' manifestum est quod a Patre et Filio *non apparentibus* factum sit quod *appareret* in Filio, id est, *ab invisibili Patre cum invisibili Filio, idem ipse Filius visibilis* mitteretur." BA 15, 204; *The Trinity,* 103, emphasis added.

9. *De Trinitate* II.1.3: "inseparabilis est operatio Patris et Filii, sed tamen ita operari Filio de illo est, de quo ipse est, id est de Patre; et ita *videt* Filius Patrem, ut quo eum *videt*, hoc ipso sit Filius. Non enim aliud illi est esse de Patre, id est nasci de Patre, quam *videre* Patrem; aut aliud *videre* operantem, quam pariter operari," BA 15, 188; *The Trinity*, 99, emphasis added.

10. *De Trinitate* II.5.10: "Haec operatio *visibiliter expressa*, et oculis oblata mortalibus, missio Spiritus sancti dicta est; *non ut appareret ejus ipsa substantia*, qua et ipse *invisibilis* et incommutabilis est, sicut Pater et Filius; sed ut exterioribus visis hominum corda commota, *a temporali manifestatione venientis ad occultam aeternitatem semper praesentis* converterentur" BA 15, 206; *The Trinity*, 104, modified, emphases added. Thomas Aquinas in his own manner also emphasizes that "the Holy Spirit did not assume the visible creature, in which He appeared," and manifests himself in creatures only as "the one signified in the sign," indirectly. *Summa Theologiae* Ia, q.43, a.7, *ad* 1 and *ad* 5; English translation Pegis, *Basic Writings* 1, 422, 423.

11. *De Trinitate* V.11.12, BA 15, 452; *The Trinity*, 197. Thomas Aquinas observes that the procession of the Holy Spirit "has remained without a special name (*sine speciali nomine*)." *Summa Theologiae* Ia, q.27, a.4, *ad* 3; Pegis, *Basic Writings 1*, 280. Just like the procession of love (q.28, a. 4, *resp*. and q. 36, a. 1, *resp*.), but he sees in this only the "poverty of our vocabulary (*vocabulorum inopiam*)" (q.37, a.1, *resp*.; Pegis, *Basic Writings 1*, 354).

12. Bernard of Clairvaux, *Sermons sur le Cantique des Cantiques* VIII.5, SC 414, 180; English translation in *Works, Song of Songs I*, 48, modified.

13. Augustine, *De Trinitate* V.11.12, BA 15, 452; *The Trinity*, 197.

14. But Augustine is also aware that he must extend and deepen the determination of the Holy Spirit as gift: "Those learned and eminent exponents of sacred scripture have not so far, in any extensive or detailed way, argued (*disputam*) the subject of the Holy Spirit. This would help us to understand what property is unique to him, what constitutes him properly as he is (*proprium, quo proprio fit*), so that we are able to state that he is neither the Father nor the Son but the Holy Spirit only. What they do postulate about him is that he is the gift of God (*eum donum Dei prædicant*), enabling us to believe that the gift God gives in no way ranks inferior to himself." Saint Augustine, *De Fide et Symbolo* IX.19, ed. Jean Rivière, BA 9 (Paris: Desclée de Brouwer, 1947), 45; English translation: *On Christian Belief, Part I: Books*, vol. 8, ed. Boniface Ramsey, trans. Michael G. Campbell, OSA (Hyde Park, NY: New City Press, 2005), 168, modified. The point is not simply to define the Holy Spirit as gift but to define what the gift means, in itself and *properly*, with regard to the Holy Spirit.

15. Basil of Caesarea, *On the Holy Spirit* XVI.37; PG 32, 133d; Pruche, 376; Hildebrand, 70, modified. Whence comes the objection of the Pneumatomachi: "the

gift [the Spirit] is not exalted by the same honors as the giver [the Father]." Ibid., XXIV.57; PG 32, 173a; Pruche, 452; Hildebrand, 95.

16. Augustine, *In Epistolam Primam Iohannis Tractatus* II.11, in PL 35, 1995; English translation in *St. Augustine, Tractates on the Gospel of John, 112–24, Tractates on the First Epistle of John*, trans. John W. Rettig (Washington, DC: Catholic University of America Press, 1995), 154. See my analysis in Marion, *Negative Certainties*, §20, 123–24.

17. *De Trinitate* VI.5.7, BA 15, 482–84; *The Trinity*, 209.

18. *De Trinitate* V.11.12, and VI.5.7, BA 15, 452 and 484; *The Trinity*, 197, 209.

19. *De Trinitate* VII.6.12, BA 15, 548; *The Trinity*, 231. See: "nec Donum Dei nisi Spiritus sanctus" (XV.17.29, BA 16, 504). And: "rectissime Spiritus sanctus, cum sit Deus, vocatur etiam Donum Dei" (XV.18.32, BA 16, 512). And again: "donum, quod est Spiritus sanctus" (XV.19.34, BA16, 516). Or: "Donum Dei esse Spiritum sanctum, in quantum datur eis qui per eum diligunt Deum" (XV.19.35, BA 16, 52).

20. *De Trinitate* V.11.12, BA 15, 452; *The Trinity*, 197, modified. Perhaps the judgment of Louis Bouyer needs to be modified: "Doubtless one can glean in the earlier Fathers many expressions of the fact that the Spirit is the unmatchable gift that God gives us. But Augustine indeed seems to be the first to have considered the Spirit as the gift in itself, and this seems to have come to him directly from the doctrine of Marius Victorinus on the Spirit as bond between the Father and the Son." Bouyer, *Le consolateur: Esprit-Saint et vie de Grâce*, 219. Nevertheless, if this "intuition [is] incontestably brilliant" (ibid.), if it is also found to be exonerated of its critique by Anders Nygren (227–28, see too my discussion in Marion, *In the Self's Place*, §42, 272–75), then it is also probably necessary to stop holding it responsible for the "most inextricable controversies between the East and the West" on the *Filioque* (Bouyer, *Le consolateur*, 219), consequences that are attributed to it too quickly and exclusively. See other approaches in George E. Demacopoulos and Aristotle Papanikolaou, eds., *Orthodox Readings of Augustine* (New York: Fordham University Press, 2008).

21. On givability as a characteristic of the gift reduced to givenness (that is, of the gift given, but which nevertheless *is* neither a thing nor an object), see Marion, *Being Given*, §11, 106–8.

22. *De Trinitate* V.15.16, BA 15, 460–62; *The Trinity*, 200, modified, emphasis added. Thomas Aquinas explains this quite well: "The gift is not so called from being actually given (*actuale datur*), but from its aptitude to be given (*aptitudinem ut possit dari*). Hence the divine person is called Gift from eternity, although He is given in time (*licet ex tempore datur*)." *Summa Theologiae* Ia, q. 38, a. 1, *ad* 4; Pegis, *Basic Writings 1*, 360; see Karl Barth's commentary, *Kirchliche Dogmatik*, I/1, 494; *Church Dogmatics* I.1, 471. What is more, the Spirit is gift insofar as givable before giving (itself) in the economy as the Son is Son before appearing in the economy of

the world. "Non ergo eo ipso quod de Patre natus est, missus dicitur Filius, sed vel eo quod *apparuit* huic mundo Verbum caro factum. . .; vel ex eo quod ex tempore *cujusquam mente percipitur.*—So the Son of God is not said to be sent in the very fact that he is born of the Father, but either in the fact that the Word made flesh *showed* himself to this world . . . or else he is sent in the fact that he is *perceived* in time *by someone's mind.*" Saint Augustine, *De Trinitate* IV.20.28, BA 15, 410, emphasis added; *The Trinity*, 173, modified.

23. *De Trinitate* XV.19.36, BA 16, 522; *The Trinity*, 424, modified. Thomas Aquinas takes up these two distinctions. First, in the text already cited in the previous foonote: "The gift is not so called from being actually given, but from its aptitude to be given (*aptitudinem ut possit dari*). Hence the divine person is called Gift from eternity, although He is given in time." *Summa Theologiae* Ia, q. 38, a. 1, *ad* 4; Pegis, *Basic Writings 1*, 360. Then, against the objection that the gift "implies a subjection both as regards him to whom it is given, and as regards him by whom it is given (*quandam subjectionem et ad eum cui datur, et ad eum a quo datur*)," he replies that "in divine matters, gift does not imply subjection, but only origin, as regards the giver (*in comparatione ad dantem*)." Ibid., q. 38, a. 1, *obj.* 3 and *ad* 3; Pegis, *Basic Writings 1*, 359 and 360, modified.

24. See in particular Marion, *Being Given*, II, §10 and Marion, *Negative Certainties*, IV, §§19–24. Also, see above, §10.

25. Saint Augustine, *De Trinitate* XV.19.35, BA 16, 520; *The Trinity*, 424.

26. Hilary of Poitiers, *De Trinitate* II.29, ed. G. Pellan et al., SC 443 (Paris: Cerf, 1999), 322; English translation: *The Trinity*, 57–58, modified.

27. Hilary of Poitiers, *De Trinitate* XII.56, SC 443, 468; *The Trinity*, 543, modified.

28. Hilary of Poitiers, *De Trinitate* XII.55, SC 443, 466; *The Trinity*, 541, modified.

29. Thomas Aquinas, *Summa Theologiae* Ia, q. 38, a. 2, *resp.*; Pegis, *Basic Writings 1*, 361. Curiously the passage relies on an interpolation from Aristotle defining what is proper to the gift (δωρεά) as δόσις ἀναπόδοτος. *Topics* IV.4, 125a18, in *Topica et Sophistici Elenchi*, ed. W.D. Ross (Oxford: Clarendon Press, 1958, 1979), 73. On this question it is worth consulting Louis-Marie Rineau, *"Celui qui donne": Le don d'après saint Thomas d'Aquin* (Paris: Vrin, 2019).

30. See Marion, *Negative Certainties*, chap. 4, §§19–24, 115–54.

31. Richard of Saint-Victor: "in Patre est plenitudo amoris gratuiti, in Spiritu sancto, plenitudo amoris debiti, in Filio plenitudo amoris debiti simul et gratuiti." *De Trinitate* VI.14, PL 196, 978c.

32. See Marion, *Being Given*, II, §11, 102–13.

33. Basil of Caesarea, *On the Holy Spirit* XXIV.55; PG 32, 172b; Pruche, 450; Hildebrand, 94, modified.

34. Basil of Caesarea, *On the Holy Spirit* XVIII.47; PG 32, 153b; Pruche, 412; Hildebrand, 83.

35. Basil of Caesarea, *On the Holy Spirit* XXVI.63; PG 32, 184c; Pruche, 474; Hildebrand, 102, modified.

Chapter Nineteen

1. See Marion, *Being Given*, §1, 7–19.

2. Regarding the present state of the possible understanding of *Ereignis*, no one has advanced as far as Didier Franck, especially in his *Le Nom et la chose. Langue et vérité chez Heidegger* (Paris: Vrin, 2017). I follow him here, in my own way.

3. For this examination I have relied on Kurt Aland et al., *Vollständige Konkordanz zum griechischen Neuen Testament* (Berlin and New York: De Gruyter, 1983). Unfortunately, one can hardly rely on what nevertheless remains one of the few attempts to study εἶναι in this context, that of Lane McGaughy, *Toward a Descriptive Analysis of εἶναι as a Linking Verb in New Testament Greek* (Missoula: University of Montana Press, 1972). As the title indicates, the subject is merely the usage of the verb as copula, while the occurrence in Philippians 2:6, τὸ εἶναι ἴσα θεῷ, indicates the absolute position, in the "existential" and verbal sense, confirmed by an expression with an adverbial value, τὸ εἶναι ἴσα θεῷ.

4. See Romans 4:11; 4:16; 8:29: εἶναι αὐτὸν πρωτότοκον; 15:16: τὸ εἶναί με λειτουργὸν Χριστοῦ; see 1 Corinthians 10:6; Ephesians 1:12; Philippians 1:23, etc.

5. See 1 Corinthians 15:12: "There is no (οὐκ ἔστιν) resurrection" (but note the absolute position, ἀνάστασιν μὴ εἶναι in Mark 12:18; Matthew 22:23; and Acts 28:8). And, of course, the opposite: "He is, ἔστιν" (Hebrews 11:6), and "ὁ ὢν ἐπὶ πάντων θεός" (Romans 9:5), or "ὁ ὤν" (Revelation 1:4; 1:8; 11:17; and 16:5).

6. Homer: "The Achaeans shall honor you as they would a god, ἶσον γάρ σε θεῷ." *Iliad* IX.603, trans. Lattimore, 214, modified; the same is said of Castor and Pollux, "the honor they are allotted is equal of the gods', ἶσα θεοῖσι." *The Odyssey* XI.304, trans. Merrill, 227, modified; or of Eurymachus, "these days the Ithacan people regard him much like a god, ἶσα θεῷ." *The Odyssey* XV.520, Merrill, 288, modified. But Philo denounces the one who, "loving himself and atheistic, thinks himself, ἴσος εἶναι θεῷ." *Legum allegoriæ* I.49, ed. Claude Mondésert (Paris: Cerf, 1962) p. 64, translation mine. See Wayne A. Meeks, "Equal to God," in R. T. Forton and B. R. Gaventa, eds., *The Conversation Continues: Studies in Paul and John. In Honor of J. Louis Martyn* (Nashville, TN: Abingdon Press, 1990), quoting among others Thucydides, *The Peloponnesian War* III.14.

7. This incomprehension is found in an even clearer sense among the disciples. For they think as all men think: if Jesus is the Christ, the Holy One of God, and if they are his disciples, the question is posed right away of what they will possess, which they only know how to see as an appropriation to lay claim to, a privilege to possess.

Whence arises the haunting question, perhaps first launched by a possessive mother who wanted to promote her sons' careers (Matthew 20:20–21), but then taken up several times in "an argument, διλογισμός," indeed in "dispute, φιλονεικία" (Luke 9:46 and 22:24), among them all: "At that time the disciples came to Jesus, saying, 'Who is the greatest in the kingdom of heaven?'" (Matthew 18:1). Or again: "When he was in the house he asked them, 'What were you discussing on the way?' But they were silent; for on the way they had discussed with one another who was the greatest" (Mark 9:33–34). The disciples spontaneously conceive of themselves as "kings of the Gentiles," who "exercise lordship" and "have the power (ἐξουσιάζοντες) to make themselves called benefactors" (Luke 22:25). They too want power to possess.

8. Respectively these are the translations of Lemaître de Sacy, Vigouroux, and the Traduction œcuménique de la Bible; *La Bible*, new translation, Paris: Bayard; and *La Bible de Jérusalem*. See the article on ἁρπαγμὸν by W. Bauer and F. W. Danker, *A Greek-English Lexicon of the New Testament and Other Early Christian Literature*, 133–34.

9. Matthew 16:24–25; see 10:38, Mark 8:34–35, and Luke 9:24. We note here too the same *imitatio Christi* as found in Philippians 2:5; and that "to deny oneself, ἀπαρνησάσθω ἑαυτὸν" corresponds to "emptying oneself, ἀπαρνησάσθω ἑαυτὸν" (Philippians 2:7) or to "humbling oneself, ἐταπείνωσεν ἑαυτὸν" (Philippians 2:8).

10. To dare to correct this verse by adding a negation (οὐκ), one must, like Harnack, assume that the obedience *was not* answered. Here exegetical science obeyed the logic of metaphysics. In contrast Paul perfectly conceives obedience as a principle of interpretation (Romans 5:19; 2 Corinthians 2:9 and 7:15) that overturns the modes of being: "We destroy arguments (λογισμοὺς) and every proud obstacle (ὕψωμα) raised up against the knowledge of God, and we take every thought (πᾶν νόημα) captive to [bring it into] the obedience (εἰς τὴν ὑπακοὴν) to Christ" (2 Corinthians 10:4–5).

11. Pascal, *Pensées*, L 597, trans. Krailsheimer, 229: "The self is hateful."

12. Gregory of Nyssa, *Oratio Catechetica Magna* XXIV, PG 45, 65; English translation: *Catechetical Discourse: A Handbook for Catechists*, trans. Ignatius Green (Yonkers, NY: Saint Vladimir's Seminary Press, 2019), 115, modified.

13. On this point, see examples of other analyses in Jean-Luc Marion, "Dieu et l'ambivalence de l'être," *Transversalités: Revue de l'Institut catholique de Paris* 125 (January–March 2013): 149–73.

14. Schelling, *Philosophie der Offenbarung*, Lecture VII, *Werke*. Ergänzungsband VI, 125; *The Grounding of Positive Philosophy*, 177–78.

15. Schelling, *Philosophie der Offenbarung*, Lecture XXX, 568.

16. Schelling, *Philosophie der Offenbarung*, Lecture XXX, 563.

17. Schelling, *Philosophie der Offenbarung*, Lecture XXXI, 577. The limit of Schelling's appropriate and powerful enterprise to fracture the Hegelian totality

lies essentially in his desire to maintain within the orb of being (a being of course that is assumed as superior, divine or free) that which would seemingly pass beyond being as understood by the "negative philosophy," which is to say by *metaphysica*. He does not cross the frontier: that which passes beyond being as we understand it and experience it is not called an *other* being, but *otherwise* than being.

18. See Marion, *God Without Being*, III, §4, 95–102, and *Negative Certainties*, IV, §24, 147–54.

19. Other closely related terms would confirm this disqualification of the persistent presence of a being in its being. For example, the *epiousion* bread (Matthew 6:11, Luke 11:3), at once both daily and given day by day such that one cannot make it last, nor keep possession of it, *superessentialis* if one prefers, but in the sense of that which surpasses the essence. Likewise, the *exousia* that "comes only from God," for all the *exousias* as "*existing* (οὖσαι) have been instituted by God (ὑπὸ θεοῦ τεταγμέναι εἰσίν)" (Romans 13:1); they are and their being is found under God.

20. Nietzsche, *Nachgelassene Fragmente*, 2 [84], *Werke* VIII/1, 101–2; English translation: *Writings from the Late Notebooks*, ed. Rüdiger Bittner, trans. Kate Sturge (Cambridge: Cambridge University Press, 2003), 75–76. See my commentary in Marion, *Negative Certainties*, V, §27, 176–77.

21. On this point, once again, see Johannes Clauberg, *Metaphysica de ente, quæ rectius ontosophia*, I, II, §6: "Ens est quicquid quovis modo est, cogitari ac dici potest—A being is anything that exists in any way, that can be thought and said"; and §10: "Nam eo ipso quo quid apprehendimus, jam est intelligibile, et per consequens Ens in prima significatione—For by the very thing by which we apprehend something, it is already intelligible, and consequently Being in its first meaning." *Opera philosophica omnia*, 285.

22. Nietzsche, *Nachgelassene Fragmente*, 9 [89], in *Nietzsche Werke* VIII/2, 468.

23. Nietzsche, *Götzen-Dämmerung, oder Wie man mit dem Hammer philosophirt*, "Die 'Vernunft' in der Philosophie," §4, *Nietzsche Werke* VI/3; English translation: *Twilight of the Idols, or How to Philosophize with a Hammer*, trans. Duncan Large (Oxford: Oxford University Press, 1998), 17. This diagnosis of the (metaphysical) concept of "being" is found literally at the beginning of Heidegger's *Sein und Zeit*.

24. Nietzsche, *Nachgelassene Fragmente*, 11 [330], in *Nietzsche Werke* V/2, 468.

25. To this one could add: "If it seems to someone [to be able] to know something, he does not yet know as he ought to know" (1 Corinthians 8:2).

26. See Heinrich August Wilhem Meyers, *Kritischer exegetischer Kommentar über das Neue Testament*, II/4 (Göttingen: Vandenhoeck & Ruprecht, 1836), 102ff., who emphasizes that it is "a constant characteristic of God" to consider, through his word, that which does not exist as if it existed, quoting Deuteronomy 32:39: "It is I who kill and it is I who make live"; 1 Samuel 2:6: "Yahweh puts to death and makes live, casts down to Sheol and brings up again"; Wisdom 16:13 (and see Tobit 13:2): "For thou hast power over life and death"; and above all John 5:21: "For as the Father

raises (ἐγείρει) the dead and makes them live (ζωοποιεῖ), so also the Son makes live those he wills."

27. Parmenides, *Fragment* 6, H. Diels and W. Kranz, *Die Fragmente der Vorsokratiker* (Zurich and Berlin: Weidmann, 1966), vol. 1, 232; English translation: Leonardo Tarán, *Parmenides: A Text with Translation, Commentary, and Critical Essays* (Princeton, NJ: Princeton University Press, 1965), 54, modified.

Chapter Twenty

1. *Confessions* XI.15.20; BA 14, 304. See *In the Self's Place*, §§31–32.

2. Mallarme, "Grands faits divers," *Divagations sur un sujet*, in *Œuvres complètes*, vol. 2, 256; English translation: *Divagations*, 270, modified. That is, "there's no such thing as a Present, no—a present doesn't exist. . ." "Quant au livre," ibid., 217; "About the Book," *Divagations*, 218. This is the initial diagnosis of Jean-Yves Lacoste: "Presence is not the parousia. This is perhaps the drama of philosophy." *Note sur le temps. Essai sur les raisons de la mémoire et de l'espérance* (Paris: PUF, 1990), 156. I intersect with his analyses here on several points.

3. See, of course, Heidegger, *Sein und Zeit* §§46–53.

4. See my sketch "La vie comme survie: le don," in Danielle Cohen-Levinas and Perrine Simon-Nahum, eds., *Survivre. Résister, se transformer, s'ouvrir*, (Paris: Hermann, 2019), 211–20. Or, see as well from the same book the conclusion of Dan Arbib on "the profoundly a-historical character of eschatology." "Le Juif: la vie comme survie," 195–209, here 207.

5. For a critical engagement with anticipatory resolution, see Marion, *The Erotic Phenomenon*, §§36–37, 184–95.

6. In this sense, Heidegger retreats from Husserl, for whom the point of the originary impression of time comes to me before my consciousness of time and gives rise to it, because, far from my being able to anticipate it, it precedes me in "the self-appearance of the flow (*Selbsterscheinung des Flußes*) . . . [which] is constituted in itself (*konstituiert er sich in sich selbst*)." Husserl, *Zur Phänomenologie des inneren Zeitbewußtseins*, §39, ed. Rudolf Boehm, Hua X (The Hague: Nijhoff, 1966), 83; English translation: *The Phenomenology of Internal Time-Consciousness*, translated by James Churchill (Bloomington: Indiana University Press, 1964), 109, modified. Could we understand the "before, previously, *vorher*," where the flow comes from (ibid., §36, 75; English, 100), as an elsewhere, an *ailleurs*?

7. *Epiousios* (Matthew 6:11 and Luke 11:3) is translated by *superessentialis* (Vulgate), but first of all by *quotidianus* (Itala). Origen also mentioned a temporal meaning: "Some will say that the term *epiousios* is formed from the verb *epienai* ("to happen, to come") . . . such that we are bidden to ask for the bread that properly belongs to the age that is to come, in order that God gives it to us now by anticipation, and in this way we are given today what should be given to us as it were tomorrow." *De Oratione* XXVII.13; PG 11, 517a; English translation: *Prayer, Exhortation to*

Martyrdom, trans. John J. O'Meara, Ancient Christian Writers, vol. 19 (Westminster, MD: Newman Press, 1954), 102, modified.

8. Rabelais: "I am going to seek the great perhaps; draw the curtain, the farce is played." In P.-A. Motteux, *Life of Rabelais*, supplement to his translation, *The Works of Mr. Francis Rabelais Doctor in Physick Containing Five Books of the Lives, Heroick Deeds & Sayings of Gargantua & His Sonne Pantagruel* (London, 1694). Doubtless Stendhal remembered this when he put these words in Julien's mouth: "Well! In three days, I'll have the answer, and know all about *the great perhaps*." Stendhal, *Red and Black*, II, chap. 41, trans. Raymond N. MacKenzie (Minneapolis: University of Minnesota Press, 2022).

9. Among the parallel passages, Mark 14:35–36, to be sure, does not place the scene under the rule of this *nyn*, but it refers to "this hour" (14:35, clarifying also 14:37 and Matthew 26:40: "Watch for an hour"). On the other hand, John 17 consists of an entire intra-Trinitarian dialogue on earth (as also John 18:9): "Of those whom you gave me, I have lost none." On this ahistorical and Trinitarian dialogue, see my remarks in *Givenness and Revelation*, 87ff.

10. This would perhaps allow a clarification of the difficult verse 8:25: "Jesus said to them, 'Τὴν ἀρχὴν ὅτι καὶ λαλῶ ὑμῖν.'" Certainly, at a minimum, we can understand it as simply "I am what I told you since the beginning"; but we can also follow the Vulgate ("*Principium, qui et loquor vobis*") in the sense of "The principle, as I say to you," the *egō eimi* as received from the Father, "I am, from above . . . I am not of this world" (John 8:23). The *egō eimi* does not come to Christ from the world (John 18:36), even if it comes into the world through him.

11. See Ephesians 3:5 and 5:8; Colossians 1:26.

12. On this point, as on many others dependent on or related to it, the best introduction and discussion is found in Joseph Ratzinger, *Eschatology: Death and Eternal Life* (Washington, DC: Catholic University of America Press, 2007), the English translation of *Eschatologie—Tod und ewiges Leben* (Regensburg: Friedrich Putset Verlag, 1977).

13. "There is nothing easier than to believe that historical reality 'means' something and nothing easier than to piously believe that the Absolute wants to say something to us. The theme of a divine manifestation coextensive to universal history is a banal theme of our theological *koine*." Lacoste, *Note sur le temps*, §66, 145, which of course refers to the thesis of Karl Rahner: "We are beginning with the proposition, therefore, that transcendence itself has a history, and that history itself is always the event of this transcendence." *Foundations of Christian Faith*, 140.

14. Hans Urs von Balthasar, "Umrisse der Eschatologie," in *Verbum Caro. Skizzen zur Theologie I* (Einsiedeln: Johannes Verlag 1960), 287; "Some Points of Eschatology," in *Explorations in Theology. I: The Word Made Flesh*, trans. A. V. Littledale and Alexander Dru (San Francisco: Ignatius Press, 1989), 265, citing Augustine: "May [God], who sees us in the place of our life, be our place after this life."

Enarratio in Psalmos XXX/2.3.8; PL 36, 252; trans. Maria Boulding in *Exposition of the Psalms,* vol 1, *Psalms 1–32* (Hyde Park, NY: New City Press, 2000), 353, modified; and, "Behold, God himself has become your place of refuge (*ecce ipse Deus factus est locus refugii*); he who was at first the terror from which you fled." *Enarratio in Psalmos* LXX.1.8, PL 36, 878; trans. Boulding, in *Exposition of the Psalms,* vol. 3, *Psalms 33–50,* (Hyde Park, NY: New City Press, 2001), 417–18, modified. Balthasar concludes from this, "The *eschata* must be interpreted throughout christologically, which means, at the deepest level, in trinitarian terms. . . . Only then will eschatology be sufficiently decosmologized (*entkosmologisiert*), freed of the remnants of sub-Christian philosophy, and become, in its object, an integral part of personal obedience in faith to Jesus Christ." "Umrisse der Eschatologie," 292; "Some Points of Eschatology," 270.

15. Karl Rahner has lucidly shown the theological fragility of such a temporal interval between judgments. "Über dem 'Zwischenstand,'" *Schriften zur Theologie*, vol. 12 (Einsiedeln: Benziger, 1975), 455–66. Yet he only attempts to move beyond this by modifying the soul/body relation (in a very Thomist style: see *Contra Gentes*, IV, 79 or *Summa Theologiae*), by redefining the relation of the individual to the community, by distinguishing the time of decision and a time after decision, by rethinking the assumption of Mary, etc.; all very illuminating analyses, but which lack what seems nevertheless essential: it is not even possible to speak of two judgments, "*gleichzeitig*, contemporaneous" (455), since the death of the individual (thus individual judgment) cancels out the temporality of the world, and in this way the eternal *ephapax* of God resumes control. There is no longer any possible (temporal) gap, which would compel us to *wait for* the eschatological accomplishment, with any kind of delay—since everything is *already* accomplished. Some good remarks by Hans Kessler: "This conception of a transitory state (*Zwischenzustand*) of the lifeless soul is an unfortunate (*unglücklich*) model of representation," since God remains "the supporting foundation always already present (*schon immer allpräsente tragende Grund*), which remains immediately present (*unmittelbar gegenwärtig*) to the person, even in his striving and death." "Personale Identität und leibliche Auferstehung: Systematisch-theologische Überlegungen," in Georg Gasser, Ludwig Jaskulla, and Thomas Schärtl, eds., *Handbuch für analytische Theologie* (Münster: Aschendorff Verlag, 2017), 658 and 660.

16. Nicholas of Cusa, *De docta ignorantia* III.9, *Opera omnia*, vol. 1, 482; *On Learned Ignorance*, trans. Jasper Hopkins (Minneapolis, MN: Arthur J. Banning Press, 1981), 136, modified.

17. It is not clear that the so-called "existential" eschatology of Barth and especially Bultmann has escaped this danger. Jean-Yves Lacoste suggests instead that we think of the time of the Church as "pre-eschatological." *Note sur le temps*, 176ff and 185.

18. Joseph Ratzinger, *Eschatology*, 61. Here, too, we may ask if eschatology "which is realized" in a theology of hope, despite all its validity and strength, does not fall back into more ancient aporias.

19. See also: "He loved them to the end, εἰς τέλος ἠγάπησεν αὐτούς" (John 13:1), and "what was written must find its end in me, περὶ ἐμοῦ τέλος ἔχει" (Luke 22:37). The question of the Messiah's coming, or not, and thus also its extrapolation (messianism without Messiah, according to Levinas, Derrida, and so many others), can only occur on the ground of the hypothesis about *our* history, itself conceived as a succession of heterogeneous moments, without meaning or *telos*.

20. We find here, of course, the central thesis of Hans Urs von Balthasar, "Umrisse der Eschatologie" (note 14), and the entire conclusion of *Theodrama* IV, in particular section 2. See the concise but accurate presentation by Geoffrey Wainwright, "Eschatology," in Edwards T. Oakes, SJ, and David Moss, eds., *The Cambridge Companion to Hans Urs von Balthasar* (Cambridge: Cambridge University Press, 2004), 113–27.

21. [Translators' note: Italicized words originally in English.]

22. In the interests of clarification, we could from now on distinguish the instant (restricted, without a stable presence, thus absent) from the moment (which exerts a *momentum*, weighs on time, and remains in it).

23. This relies on the text of Haggai 2:6 ("Once more in a little while, I will shake the sky and the earth, the sea and the dry land," translation from the Bible of Jerusalem), where the Greek LXX term *eti hapax* (for the Hebrew *'alhat*) can be translated either by "once again" or emphatically by "only once"; but the author of the epistle nevertheless modifies it: "Yet again, I will shake" not only the "earth" but also "heaven." I follow the indications of Michel Casevitz, Cécile Dogniez, and Marguerite Harl, in their remarkable edition of the *Bible d'Alexandrie LXX, Les douze prophètes*, vol. 23, 10–11 (Paris: Cerf, 2007), 54ff, 81ff. From the perspective of the New Testament, the author also insists on a definitive, and thus unique, transposition (*metathesis*) of the world taken up from *elsewhere*. For the whole argument rests on the opposition between the great priest who repeats his sacrifice "each year," and thus enters the sanctuary in vain, and Christ, who "is manifested once [for all] at the end of ages to abolish sin by his sacrifice" (Hebrews 9:25–27; 10:2). This sense can also shed light on the irreversibility of the apostasy of the baptized (Hebrews 6:4–6).

24. The adverb in fact relates to both verbs. See Hebrews 9:12: "He entered once into the Holy place."

25. Literally, the texts repeats itself: "waiting awaits." For it is all of creation that awaits: "We know that every creature moans in the pains of childbirth until the moment (ἄχρι τοῦ νῦν)" (8:22).

26. Hans Urs von Balthasar: "when the Son has been resurrected and the economic form of the Trinity is suspended and absorbed into the immanent, there is no reversion to former conditions; nothing needs to be 'inverted' once again. What happens is that the temporal and vertical form is lifted up into the eternal and horizontal dimension." *Theodramatik*, II/2, 478; *Theo-Drama* 3, 522–23. The same unique Trinity pivots, so to speak, from the verticality according to which it immerses itself in our temporality, and rises to the horizontal of its eternal communion. The pivot, at all times, remains the Father.

27. Louis Bouyer, *Dictionnaire théologique* (Paris: Desclée, 1990), 125.

28. See the related formulation of Jean-Yves Lacoste: "The present has then been constructed as the memory of a future." *Note sur le temps*, 187. In other words, the present regains presence if it lets itself be taken up by the *elsewhere* (filiation in the Trinitarian play) as it comes to it from the unforgettable *ephapax* of Christ. Hence the definition of faith as the *hypostasis of things hoped for*, that is, as their anticipated possession, possession that is real *because anticipated*, like the payment of an inheritance, like the first withdrawal of a credit already granted, of a deposit already placed.

Index

Abelard, Peter, 55, 387n7
Aeschylus, 437n23
Aetius, 459n11
Aland, Kurt, 445n18, 456–57n19, 479n3
Alexander of Hales, 420n29
Almeida, Ivan, 449n10
Alquié, Ferdinand, 407n38
Altaner, Berthold, 475n4
Althaus, Paul, 411n4
Ambrose of Milan, 316, 475n2, 475n4
Anselm of Canterbury, 61, 462n27
Arbib, Dan, 482n4
Aristotle, 41, 45, 51, 69, 74, 83, 119–20, 138, 189, 192, 193, 195, 203, 211, 284, 351, 358, 390–91n23, 396n29, 406n36, 430n4, 444n12, 445n15, 446–47n25, 450–51n18, 450n14, 459n13, 462n26, 474n30, 477n20, 478n29
Athenagoras of Athens, 427n34, 429n2, 444n7
Augustine of Hippo, xxv, 54, 60, 72, 97, 117–19, 120, 122, 126, 129–30, 132, 149, 270, 271, 316–18, 321, 322, 358, 387n7, 389n20, 397n34, 403–4n8, 419n21, 419n22, 420–21n32, 420n25, 420n26, 421n36m 422n5, 423n6, 424n11, 425n22, 426n30, 428n38, 431–32n17, 443n2, 447n27, 461–62n25, 463n28, 473n15, 475n4, 475n5, 476n13, 476n14, 477–78n22, 477n16, 477n20, 478n25, 483–84n14

Badiou, Alain, 447n28
Bailly, Anatole, 472n9
Bakunin, Mikhail, 283
Balthasar, Hans Urs von, 105, 107, 109, 111, 276, 311, 382n5, 383n12, 391n31, 400n8, 415n38, 415n39, 415n42, 415n43, 415n44, 415n45, 416n1, 416n2, 416n3, 416n4, 416n5, 416n47, 416n48, 416n49, 436n13, 438n25, 440n35, 464n5, 483–84n14, 485n19, 486n16
Bardout, Jean-Christophe, 396–97n31, 396n30

Barth, Karl, xxxi, 65, 95, 96, 98–100, 102–5, 154–55, 159–60, 258, 259, 273, 298, 379n2, 400n8, 412n7, 412n9, 412n11, 415n36, 415n37, 433n29, 434–35n40, 435n41, 458n1, 463n30, 464n2, 477–78n22, 484n17
Bartmann, Bernhard, 463n32
Barton, John, 444–43n1
Basil of Caesarea, xxiv, 298, 304–15, 321, 471n2, 473n18, 473n19, 473n20, 473n21, 473n22, 473n23, 473n24, 474–75n33, 474n25, 474n26, 474n31, 474n32, 475n3, 475n4, 475n34, 476–77n15, 478n33, 479n34, 479n35
Baudelaire, Charles, 13, 380n2
Bauer, Walter, 444n13, 480n8
Beauchamp, Paul, 440–41n39, 441n42
Beaufret, Jean, 444n14
Benedict XVI (see Ratzinger, Joseph)
Benoist, Jocelyn, 433–34n33
Bergier, Nicolas-Sylvestre, 38–39, 386n5
Bergson, Henri, 358
Bernard of Clairvaux, 386n26, 415n41, 430n6, 476n12
Berrouard, Marie-François, 423n6
Boethius, 41, 268, 270, 271, 461n21, 463n29
Bonaventure, Giovanni di F., 60
Bouillard, Henri, 398–99n2, 411n4
Boulnois, Olivier, 390–91n27
Bourgeois, Bernard, 465n13
Bouyer, Louis, 272, 377, 443n3, 460–61n18, 463n31, 473n23, 771n20, 486n27
Bovon, François, 452n24
Brague, Rémi, 458n10
Brito, Emilio, 405–6n27
Brown, Stephen F., 390–91n27, 394–95n21

Brunschvicg, Léon, 437n21
Bultmann, Rudolf, 98, 100, 102, 105, 270, 412n12, 412n13, 413n14, 413n15, 413n16, 413n17, 413n18, 413n19, 413n20, 414n26, 454n1, 484n17
Burckardt, Jacob, 28
Busa, Roberto, 391n28

Cajetan, Thomas de Vio, 46, 391n29
Calvin, John, 412n11, 459n12
Camilleri, Sylvain, 384–85n21
Carraud, Vincent, 396–97n31, 437n21, 471n3
Char, René, 384n20
Charlier, Louis, 435n43
Chenu, Marie-Dominique, 390n26, 420n28
Chesterton, G. K., 433n30
Chouraqui, André, 455n7
Chrétien, Jean-Louis, 452n23
Cicero, Marcus T., 157, 434n34, 446–47n25, 447n26
Clauberg, Johann, 404n17, 481n21
Claudel, Gérard, 453n34, 453n35, 454n39
Claudel, Paul, 439–40n31, 445n17
Clavier, Paul, 401n16
Clay, Jenny, 436n9
Clement of Alexandria, 128, 425n21, 427n34
Conan Doyle, Arthur, 433n30
Conche, Marcel, 444n14
Conzelmann, Hans, 445–46n21
Corbin, Michel, 388n19
Courcelle, Pierre, 447n26
Courtine, Jean-François, 391n29, 417n13, 432n20, 466–67n23, 466n19, 468n38, 468n39

Cuvellier, Élian, 448n9, 449n8, 450n17, 451n19, 451n21
Cyprian of Carthage, 425n22

Danker, Frederick William, 444n13, 480n8
Davy, Marie-Madeleine, 384n17, 395–96n25, 400–401n15, 420–21n32, 421n36
Déchanet, Jean-Marie, 420–21n32, 420n31, 421n31, 421n34, 421n35
Delage, Marc, 447n26
Derrida, Jacques, 485n19
Descartes, René, xi, 26–27, 59, 61, 72, 74–75, 80, 83, 85, 113, 114, 117, 118–19, 121, 132, 141, 284, 361, 396–97n31, 397n35, 402n1, 402n2, 403n5, 406n31, 417n12, 417n14, 418n19, 419n23, 419n24, 430n10, 431–32n17, 437n21
Détienne, Marcel, 438n27
Devaux, Michäel, 417n13
Dibelius, Martin, 445–46n21
Didymus the Blind, 450n13, 474n4
Dieckmann, Hermann, 50, 393n3, 393n4, 393n5, 395n22, 397n33, 448n1
Dierse, Ulrich, 410–11n2
Dießler, Alfons, 441n40
Dietrich, B.C., 438n25
Dionysius the Areopagite, 383n8, 416n50
Dirlmeier, Franz, 440n36
Dodd, C.H., 450n17, 451n21, 452n25
Donahue, John R., 448n1
Downing, F.G., 411n5
Dubarle, Dominique, xxxii
Duke, Paul D., 382n3, 427–28n37
Dulles, Avery, 39, 386–87n6, 399–400n7, 405–6n27, 411n4
Duns Scotus, John, 429n2

Engberg-Pedersen, Troels, 447n28
Esposito, Constantino, 396–97n31
Esposito, Elena, 434n35
Eunomius, 459n11

Fédier, François, 381n10
Feuerbach, Ludwig, 81, 405n24
Feuillet, André, 400–401n15
Fichte, Johann Gottlieb, 77, 80, 85–87, 89, 408n46, 408n47, 408n48, 408n49, 408n50, 408n51, 409–10n56, 409n52, 409n54, 410n58
Flaubert, Gustave, 13, 466n21
Franck, Didier, 458n8, 479n2
Fries, Heinrich, 39, 386–87n6, 398n38
Frigo, Alberto, 461n20

Gaffiot, Félix, 383–84n14
Garniron, Pierre, 409–10n56, 409n55
Garrigou-Lagrange, Réginald, 392n34, 395n23
Gauchet, Marcel, 411–12n6
Geiselmann, Josef Rupert, 398n39
Ghellinck, Jean de, 423n6
Ghent, Henry of, 390–91n27
Gilbert of Poitiers, 29, 120, 384n16, 420n27
Gilson, Étienne, 69, 390n26, 391n29, 391n30, 401n16
Godfrey of Fontaines, 390–91n27
Goethe, Johann Wolfgang, 460n16
Gogarten, Friedrich, 104, 415n37, 434–35n40
Göschel, Carl Friedrich F., 465n13
Gregory of Nazianzen, 295, 305, 313, 422n1, 427n35, 458n8, 426n26, 471n59, 474–75n33, 474n27, 475n1
Gregory of Nyssa, 137, 305, 429n1, 480n11
Gregory the Great, 418–19n20, 420–21n32, 427n34

Greisch, Jean, 469n46
Grosjean, Jean, 427–28n37, 432n25, 455n7, 455n9
Gründer, Karlfried, 409n54, 410–11n2
Guillet, Jacques, 410–11n2

Hagendahl, Harald, 424n11
Harnack, Adolf von, 456–57n19, 480n10
Harrington, Daniel J., 427n36, 448n1
Haulotte, Edgar, 444n11
Hegel, Georg Wilhelm Friedrich, xxiv, 60, 88–89, 94, 104, 111, 160, 265–66, 276–83, 289, 292, 294, 297, 354, 358, 409–10n56, 409n55, 410n57, 460n16, 464–65n6, 465n7, 465n8, 465n10, 465n14, 465n15, 465n17, 466n19, 466n20, 469n40, 470n49, 480–81n17
Heidegger, Martin, xiv, xv, 16, 28, 111, 114, 115, 144, 160, 262, 267, 270, 338, 339, 340, 361, 381n15, 395–96n26, 416n6, 417–18n17, 417n14, 417n16, 419n21, 422n3, 430n8, 431n14, 434–35n40, 448n4, 481n23, 482n3, 482n6
Henry, Michel, 278, 466n18, 466n19
Herbert of Cherbury, Edward, 75, 76, 402–3n4, 403n5
Hering, Jean, 384–85n21
Hilary of Poitiers, 1, 328, 478n26, 478n27, 478n28
Hobbes, Thomas, 76, 403–4n8, 403n6, 403n7
Hölderlin, Friedrich, 14–15, 33, 151, 261–62, 265–66, 381n11, 386n25
Homer, 165, 166, 167, 168, 436n17, 438n25, 439n29, 479n6
Housset, Emmanuel, 463n29
Hugh of Saint-Victor, 395–96n26
Hume, David, 24, 77, 78, 284, 404n11, 404n14, 404n15, 433n30

Husserl, Edmund, 15–16, 26–27, 141, 206, 381n14, 384–85n21, 430n8, 432n23, 448n3, 482n6

Iamblichus, 446–47n25
Ignatius of Antioch, 241, 456n13
Irenaeus, 427n34, 430n7, 441–43n1, 443n2, 473n14, 474n28
Ivánka, Endre von, 461n23

James, William, 135–36, 384–85n21, 428n40
Jaspers, Karl, 383–84n14
Jeremias, Joachim, 208–9, 448n9, 449–50n11, 449n7, 450n12, 450n13, 450n15, 450n16, 458n1
Jerome, 116, 417–18n17, 430n7, 446n24, 463n30, 475n4
Joachim of Fiore, 295
Joest, W., 434n39
John Chrysostom, 314
John Damascene, 308, 427n34, 472n13
John of the Cross, 412n11
John Scotus Eriugena, 60, 400–401n15
Jonge, Marinus de, 454n3, 454n5
Jülicher, Adolph, 448n9, 450n15
Justin Martyr, 269

Kant, Immanuel, xiv, xxiv, 12, 16, 26–28, 61, 71, 74, 77, 79–80, 83–86, 106, 114, 124–25, 135, 154, 196, 206, 264–66, 284, 361, 381–82n16, 405n26, 406n31, 407–8n42, 407n39, 407n40, 407n41, 408n43, 408n44, 408n45, 409–10n56, 409n54, 417n12, 417n14, 422n2, 430n5, 430n8, 431–32n17, 459n14, 465n17, 467n28
Kearns, Emily, 436n16
Kessler, Hans, 484n15

Kierkegaard, Søren, 94, 157, 280–81, 283, 433–34n33

Lacoste, Jean-Yves, 40, 387n8, 416n49, 419n21, 461n22, 463n32, 482n2, 483n13, 484n17, 486n28
Lafont, Ghislain, 464n5
Lamanna, Marco, 417n13
Lamartine, Alphonse de, 380n3
Lampe, G.W.H., 472n9
Latourelle, René, 387n9, 398–99n2, 398n1, 399–400n7, 399n3, 400n11, 422n5
Legrand, Lucien, 447n26
Le Guern, Michel, 452n26
Leibniz, Gottfried Wilhelm, 75, 111, 115, 402n3, 417n15, 418n19
Lemaitre, Christophe, 380n5
Lemaître de Sacy, Louis-Isaac, 440n33, 455n7, 480n8
Léonard, Augustin, 387n9
Leroy, Herbert, 455n5
Levering, Matthew, 399–400n7, 403–4n8, 407–8n42
Levinas, Emmanuel, xxxii, 175, 269, 380–81n8, 381–82n16, 402n19, 422n3, 441–43n1, 485n19
Lochbrunner, Manfred, 400n8
Locke, John, 57, 76, 77, 78, 284, 383n9, 396n28, 403n1, 404n9, 404n10
Lohff, Wenzel, 410–11n2
Longinus, 436n12
Lubac, Henri de, 43, 159, 389n22, 397n33, 399–400n7, 400n8, 407–8n42, 434n39
Luther, Martin, 412n11, 440n33, 455n6, 455n7

Maesschalk, Marc, 469n46
Maimonides, 390–91n23, 406n34
Malebranche, Nicolas, 38, 78, 386n1, 386n3, 396n30
Mallarmé, Stéphane, 27, 358, 383n11, 453n33, 482n2
Marguerat, Daniel, 445–46n21, 446n24, 447n26, 449n8, 452n22
Markschies, Christoph, 437n22
Marmasse, Gilles, 409n55
Marquet, Jean-François, 466–67n23, 466n19, 469n46
Marx, Karl, 469n40
Mauss, Marcel, 340
McGaughy, Lane, 479n3
Meeks, Wayne A., 479n6
Metz, Jean-Baptiste, 103
Meyer, Heinrich August Wilhelm, 481–82n26
Michel, Marc, 455n5, 455n8
Mitchell, Basil, 411n5
Moloney, Francis J., 427n36
Moltmann, Jürgen, 103
Montaigne, Michel de, 38, 386n2, 402n2
Montesquieu, Charles-Louis Secondat, Baron de, 38, 386n4
Montini, G.B. (see Paul VI)
Muncunill, Juan, 395n22

Nault, François, 411–12n6
Nédoncelle, Maurice, 422–23n5, 463n29
Nicholas of Lyre, 407–8n42
Nicholas of Cusa, xxxiv, 116, 379n6, 400–401n15, 418n18, 473n14, 484n16
Nietzsche, Friedrich, 87–88, 179, 207, 261, 267, 270, 352, 353–54, 361, 409n53, 466n22, 481n20, 481n22, 481n23, 481n24
Norden, Eduard, 445–46n21
Nygren, Anders, 477n20

Ockham, William of, 55–56, 394–95n21, 395n22, 395n23, 395n24, 395n25
Origen, 269, 309, 407–8n42, 441–43n1, 450n13, 473n17, 482–83n7
Otto, Walter F., 167, 436n13, 438n27
Ovid, P. Naso, 168, 169, 171, 436n17, 438–39n28

Pannenberg, Wolfhart, 102, 105, 411n3, 414n30, 414n31, 414n32, 414n33, 415n34, 415n35, 434n39, 452n24, 457n20
Pareyson, Luigi, 468n38
Parmenides, 355, 444n14, 482n27
Pascal, Blaise, 58, 117–23, 125, 129, 137–38, 383n7, 429n21, 429n22, 427–28n37, 427n34, 441–43n1, 480n11
Patočka, Jan, 401–2n18
Paul of Tarsus, 28, 40, 67–68, 70, 97, 118, 178, 181–203, 205, 209, 216, 218, 231, 252, 282, 291, 294, 342, 346, 352–54, 371, 425n22, 444n5, 445–46n21, 446n24, 447n28, 480n10
Paul VI (see Montini, G.B), 66, 400n11
Pax, W. Elpidius, 439–40n31
Pecina, Björn, 410n58
Péguy, Charles, 11–12, 381n9, 381n10, 441–43n1, 456n17
Peterson, Erik, 458n7
Philo of Alexandria, 344
Picard, Charles, 437n23
Pierre d'Auriole, 390–91n27
Piettre, Renée, 438n26, 438n27
Plato, 69, 119–20, 124, 422n1, 472n9
Polybius, 450–51n18
Potterie, Ignace de la, 454n3
Pouivet, Roger, 397–98n37
Pradelle, Dominique, 384–85n21
Proclus, 472n9

Pruche, Benoît, 471–72n6, 471n2, 471n5, 472n7, 472n8m 472n10, 472n11, 473n18, 473n19, 473n20, 473n21, 473n22, 473n24, 474–75n33, 474n25, 474n26, 474n30, 474n31, 474n32, 475n3, 475n4, 476–77n15, 478n33, 479n34, 479n35

Quine, Willard van Orman, 434n36

Rabelais, François, 483n8
Rad, Gerhard von, 439n29
Rahner, Karl, 100, 101, 102, 105, 106, 273, 276, 294, 386–87n6, 398n39, 413n21, 414n29, 415n34, 460–61n18, 461n20, 463–64n1, 464n3, 464n4, 483n13, 484n15
Ratzinger, Joseph, 172, 398n39, 410–11n2, 413n21, 441–43n1, 443n2, 483n13, 484n15
Reiser, Marius, 441–43n1
Renan, Ernest, 182
Rimbaud, Arthur, 6, 380n4, 381n11
Rineau, Louis-Marie, 478n29
Riquier, Camille, 398–98n37
Rivière, Jean, 387n7, 476n14
Rosenzweig, Franz, 70, 180, 402n19, 440n38, 441n42
Rousselot, Pierre, 420–21n32
Roustang, François, 428n39
Russell, Bertrand, 434n36

Salaville, Sévérien, 475n4
Sartre, Jean-Paul, 278
Scheler, Max, 419n21, 426n30
Schelling, Friedrich Wilhem Joseph, xxiv, 26, 94, 112, 265–67, 283–85, 287–95, 297, 350, 405–6n27, 416n10, 460n17, 466–67n23, 466n20, 467n25, 467n26, 467n27, 467n28, 467n29, 467n30, 467n31, 467n32,

Index   493

467n33, 467n34, 468n35, 468n36,
468n37, 468n39, 469–70n48,
469n40, 469n41, 469n42, 469n43,
469n44, 469n45, 469n47, 469n49,
470n50, 470n51, 470n52, 470n53,
470n54, 470n55, 470n56, 471n57,
471n58, 480–81n17, 480n14,
480n15, 480n16
Schleiermacher, Friedrich, 80, 81, 111,
    135, 404n18, 405–6n27, 405n19,
    405n20, 405n21, 405n22, 405n23,
    405n24, 405n25, 405n26, 416n8,
    459n14
Schröer, Henning, 383n13
Schrade, Hubert, 439n29
Schüßler, Ingeborg, 459n14
Scrima, André, 428n38
Segond, Louis, 455n7
Serban, Claudia, 384–85n21
Sesboüé, Bernard, 39, 386–87n6,
    398–99n2, 399n3, 472n13
Simon, Fritz B., 434n37
Simon, Josef, 384n13
Simon of Tournai, 420n28
Socrates, 211, 363, 383n13, 427–28n37,
    448–49n6
Söding, Thomas, 410–11n2
Sommer, Christian, 458n8
Spinoza, Baruch, 71, 82, 83, 84, 119–20,
    402n1, 406–7n37, 406n28, 406n29,
    406n30, 406n31, 406n32, 406n33,
    406n34, 406n35, 469n36, 418n19,
    430n9
Sponde, Jean de, 380n2
Stendhal, 483n8
Strauss, David, 182
Stobaeus, 475n9
Stroup, George W., 411n5
Suárez, Francisco, 49–62, 75, 78, 268,
    393n6, 393n7, 393n8, 393n9, 393n10,
    393n11, 394n12, 394n13, 394n14,

394n15, 394n16, 394n17, 394n18,
394n19, 394n20, 396n27, 396n30,
461n19
Swinburne, Richard, 397–98n37,
    441–43n1
Synave, Paul, 389–90n23

Tardivel, Émilie, 401–2n18
Teilhard de Chardin, Pierre, 369
Tertullian, 28, 383–84n14
Theobald, Christoph, 386–87n6,
    398–99n2, 399–400n7, 399n3
Theodore of Mopsuestia, 447n26
Thomas Aquinas, xxi, 37–48, 49, 50,
    54, 55, 56–58, 60, 63, 64, 68–69,
    82, 94, 268, 271, 298, 328, 387n10,
    387n11, 387n12, 388n19, 389n20,
    389n21, 389n22, 390n26, 391n29,
    391n32, 392n34, 396n29, 397–98n37,
    397n32, 401n17, 406n36, 430n8,
    459–60n15, 463n29, 463n30, 471n1,
    476n10, 476n11, 477–78n22,
    478n23, 478n29
Thucydides, 445–46n21, 479n6
Tillich, Paul, 93, 100, 105, 410n1,
    413n22, 413n23, 414n24, 414n25,
    414n26, 414n27, 414n28,
    469–60n15
Tilliette, Xavier, 405–6n27, 468n37,
    469n46, 470n53, 470n56
Tindal, Matthew, 404n9
Tisserand, Axel, 461–62n25
Toland, John, 404n9
Torrell, Jean-Pierre, 390n26,
    392n34
Trouillard, Jean, 472n9

Vasiliu, Anca, 472n9, 472n10, 472n12,
    474n30
Veer, Albert C. de, 422–23n5
Verlaine, Paul, 380n6

Vernant, Jean-Pierre, 437–38n24, 437n22, 438n25, 438n27
Vigouroux, Fulcran, 480n8
Vioulac, Jean, 417–18n17, 429–30n3

Wainwright, Geoffrey, 485n20
Weber, Dominique, 403n7
Weil, Simone, 434n39
Wieland, Wolfgang, 410–11n2
Wiles, Maurice, 411n5
William of St. Thierry, 29, 117, 120–21, 126, 129–30, 136, 137, 384n17, 395–96n26, 400–401n15, 418–19n20, 419n22, 420–21n32, 420n29, 420n30, 420n31, 421n33, 421n34, 421n35, 421n36, 422n4, 425n24, 426n30, 429n46, 429n47
Williams, Bernard, 383–84n14
Wittgenstein, Ludwig, 112, 384n19, 416n9, 434n36, 434n38, 444n5
Wolinski, Joseph, 463n32

Zaguri-Orly, Raphael, 380–81n8
Zimmerli, Walther, 441n40

Cultural Memory in the *Present*

Peter Sloterdijk, *Out of the World*
Christopher J. Wild, *Descartes' Meditative Turn: The Practice of Thought*
Eli Friedlander, *Walter Benjamin and the Idea of Natural History*
Helmut Puff, *The Antechamber: Toward a History of Waiting*
Raúl E. Zegarra, *A Revolutionary Faith: Liberation Theology
    Between Public Religion and Public Reason*
David Simpson, *Engaging Violence: Civility and the Reach of Literature*
Michael Steinberg, *The Afterlife of Moses: Exile, Democracy, Renewal*
Alain Badiou, *Badiou by Badiou*, translated by Bruno Bosteels
Eric Song, *Love against Substitution: Seventeenth-Century
    English Literature and the Meaning of Marriage*
Niklaus Largier, *Figures of Possibility: Aesthetic Experience,
    Mysticism, and the Play of the Senses*
Mihaela Mihai, *Political Memory and the Aesthetics of Care:
    The Art of Complicity and Resistance*
Ethan Kleinberg, *Emmanuel Levinas's Talmudic Turn: Philosophy and Jewish Thought*
Willemien Otten, *Thinking Nature and the Nature of Thinking: From Eriugena to Emerson*
Michael Rothberg, *The Implicated Subject: Beyond Victims and Perpetrators*
Hans Ruin, *Being with the Dead: Burial, Ancestral Politics,
    and the Roots of Historical Consciousness*
Eric Oberle, *Theodor Adorno and the Century of Negative Identity*
David Marriott, *Whither Fanon? Studies in the Blackness of Being*
Reinhart Koselleck, *Sediments of Time: On Possible Histories*, translated
    and edited by Sean Franzel and Stefan-Ludwig Hoffmann
Devin Singh, *Divine Currency: The Theological Power of Money in the West*
Stefanos Geroulanos, *Transparency in Postwar France: A Critical History of the Present*
Sari Nusseibeh, *The Story of Reason in Islam*
Olivia C. Harrison, *Transcolonial Maghreb: Imagining
    Palestine in the Era of Decolonialization*
Barbara Vinken, *Flaubert Postsecular: Modernity Crossed Out*
Aishwary Kumar, *Radical Equality: Ambedkar, Gandhi, and the Problem of Democracy*
Simona Forti, *New Demons: Rethinking Power and Evil Today*
Joseph Vogl, *The Specter of Capital*
Hans Joas, *Faith as an Option*
Michael Gubser, *The Far Reaches: Ethics, Phenomenology, and the Call
    for Social Renewal in Twentieth-Century Central Europe*

Françoise Davoine, *Mother Folly: A Tale*
Knox Peden, *Spinoza Contra Phenomenology: French Rationalism from Cavaillès to Deleuze*
Elizabeth A. Pritchard, *Locke's Political Theology: Public Religion and Sacred Rights*
Ankhi Mukherjee, *What Is a Classic? Postcolonial Rewriting and Invention of the Canon*
Jean-Pierre Dupuy, *The Mark of the Sacred*
Henri Atlan, *Fraud: The World of Ona'ah*
Niklas Luhmann, *Theory of Society, Volume 2*
Ilit Ferber, *Philosophy and Melancholy: Benjamin's Early Reflections on Theater and Language*
Alexandre Lefebvre, *Human Rights as a Way of Life: On Bergson's Political Philosophy*
Theodore W. Jennings, Jr., *Outlaw Justice: The Messianic Politics of Paul*
Alexander Etkind, *Warped Mourning: Stories of the Undead in the Land of the Unburied*
Denis Guénoun, *About Europe: Philosophical Hypotheses*
Maria Boletsi, *Barbarism and Its Discontents*
Sigrid Weigel, *Walter Benjamin: Images, the Creaturely, and the Holy*
Roberto Esposito, *Living Thought: The Origins and Actuality of Italian Philosophy*
Henri Atlan, *The Sparks of Randomness, Volume 2: The Atheism of Scripture*
Rüdiger Campe, *The Game of Probability: Literature and Calculation from Pascal to Kleist*
Niklas Luhmann, *A Systems Theory of Religion*
Jean-Luc Marion, *In the Self's Place: The Approach of Saint Augustine*
Rodolphe Gasché, *Georges Bataille: Phenomenology and Phantasmatology*
Niklas Luhmann, *Theory of Society, Volume 1*
Alessia Ricciardi, *After La Dolce Vita: A Cultural Prehistory of Berlusconi's Italy*
Daniel Innerarity, *The Future and Its Enemies: In Defense of Political Hope*
Patricia Pisters, *The Neuro-Image: A Deleuzian Film-Philosophy of Digital Screen Culture*
François-David Sebbah, *Testing the Limit: Derrida, Henry, Levinas, and the Phenomenological Tradition*
Erik Peterson, *Theological Tractates*, edited by Michael J. Hollerich
Feisal G. Mohamed, *Milton and the Post-Secular Present: Ethics, Politics, Terrorism*
Pierre Hadot, *The Present Alone Is Our Happiness, Second Edition: Conversations with Jeannie Carlier and Arnold I. Davidson*
Yasco Horsman, *Theaters of Justice: Judging, Staging, and Working Through in Arendt, Brecht, and Delbo*
Jacques Derrida, *Parages*, edited by John P. Leavey
Henri Atlan, *The Sparks of Randomness, Volume 1: Spermatic Knowledge*
Rebecca Comay, *Mourning Sickness: Hegel and the French Revolution*
Djelal Kadir, *Memos from the Besieged City: Lifelines for Cultural Sustainability*
Stanley Cavell, *Little Did I Know: Excerpts from Memory*

For a complete listing of titles in this series, visit the Stanford University Press website, www.sup.org.

The authorized representative in the EU for product safety and compliance is:
Mare Nostrum Group
B.V Doelen 72
4831 GR Breda
The Netherlands

www.ingramcontent.com/pod-product-compliance
Lightning Source LLC
Chambersburg PA
CBHW030559230426
43661CB00053B/1772